THE SOUTHERN AFRICAN ENVIRONMENT

Profiles of the SADC Countries

Sam Moyo, Phil O'Keefe and Michael Sill

EARTHSCAN

Earthscan Publications Ltd, London

First published in 1993 by
Earthscan Publications Limited
120 Pentonville Road, London N1 9JN

Copyright © The ETC Foundation, 1993

A catalogue record for this book is available from the British Library

ISBN: 1 85383 171 9

Cartography and typesetting by Professional Cartographic Services
Printed and bound in Great Britain by
Biddles Ltd, Guildford and King's Lynn

Earthscan Publications Limited is an editorially independent subsidiary of Kogan Page
Limited and publishes in association with the International Institute for Environment and
Development and the World Wide Fund for Nature.

CONTENTS

List of figures   vii
List of tables   ix
Glossary   xi
Foreword   xiii
Acknowledgements   xiv

Introduction: Sustainable development and the SADC environment   **1**
    Beyond technological analysis   1

1 Angola   **5**
    Introduction   5
    Economic structure   5
    Environmental problems   11
    The natural resource base and its legal framework   16
    Strategies and solutions for sustainable development   26
    Conclusion   31

2 Botswana   **32**
    Introduction   32
    Resource-use conflicts   35
    Principal environmental problems   40
    The natural resource base and legal underpinnings   44
    Strategies and solutions for environmental sustainability   57
    Conclusion   63

3 Lesotho   **65**
    Introduction   65
    Environmental problems   67
    The natural resource base and legal underpinnings   80
    Strategies for sustainable development   85

4 Malawi   **92**
    Introduction   92
    Environmental problems: an initial statement   94
    Environmental issues   97
    The natural resource base and legal underpinnings   100

5 Mozambique   **126**
    Introduction   126
    Economic structure   128
    Environmental problems   129
    The natural resource base and legal underpinnings   138
    Strategies and solutions for sustainable development   153
    Conclusion   157

6 Namibia   **158**
    Introduction   158
    Environmental issues   166
    Environmental problems   168
    The present resource base and legal underpinnings   174
    Strategies and solutions for environmental sustainablility   187
    Conclusion   193

7 **Swaziland**   **195**
   Introduction   195
   Economic structure   197
   Environmental issues   203
   The present resource base and legal institutions   216
   Environmental policies and legislations   222
   Strategies and solutions for environmental sustainability   225
   Conclusion   230

8 **Tanzania**   **234**
   Introduction   234
   Environmental issues   239
   Environmental problems   243
   The present resource base and legal institutions   247
   Strategies and solutions for environmental sustainability   263

9 **Zambia**   **270**
   Introduction   270
   Environmental issues   274
   Environmental problems   278
   The natural resource base and legal underpinnings   283
   Strategies and solutions for sustainable development   297
   Conclusion   301

10 **Zimbabwe**   **303**
   Introduction   303
   Environmental issues   310
   Environmental problems   316
   The natural resource base and legal underpinnings   322
   Strategies and solutions for environmental sustainability   332
   and rural transformation
   Conclusion   339

Index   341

LIST OF FIGURES

Angola
1.1 Rainfall patterns   6
1.2 Temperature and rainfall: monthly variation   9
1.3 Mineral resources   15
1.4 Geomorphology and relief   17
1.5 Vegetation zones   18
1.6 Conservation areas   21

Botswana
2.1 Rainfall and rainfall variability   41
2.2 Land tenure types   45
2.3 Vegetation types   48
2.4 National Parks and Game Reserves   51
2.5 Game migration routes   52
2.6 Controlled hunting areas   53

Lesotho
3.1 Relief, drainage and sampled catchments   66

Malawi
4.1 Physical divisions   93
4.2 Soils   103
4.3 Vegetation resources   106
4.4 Hydrology   109

Mozambique
5.1 Mining resources   137
5.2 Agro-ecological regions   139
5.3 Average annual rainfall   141
5.4 Soils   143
5.5 Accessibility under conditions of war, 1989   145
5.6 The mangrove ecosystem   147
5.7 Electricity generation   150
5.8 Nature Conservation Zones and Game Reserves   152

Namibia
6.1 Physical divisions   159
6.2 Mean annual rainfall   160
6.3 Major vegetation regions   161
6.4 Population distribution   163
6.5 Mineral resources   165
6.6 Resources of the Namibian fishing industry   171
6.7 Land tenure systems   175

Swaziland
7.1 Physical divisions   196
7.2 Administrative divisions   198
7.3 Rainfall patterns   200
7.4 Principal centres of economic activity   202
7.5 Population density, 1986   206

Tanzania

8.1 Population density by district, 1988   235
8.2 Average annual rainfall   236
8.3 Landuse resource zones   237
8.4 Cattle population, 1989   238
8.5 National Parks   246
8.6 Coal and gas resources   253
8.7 Fisheries: annual catch and potential by source   262
8.8 Industrial forestry plantations   266

Zambia

9.1 Physical divisions   271
9.2 Population distribution   272
9.3 Precipitation, evapotranspiration zones and rainfall variability   279
9.4 Soil types   284
9.5 Vegetation types   286

Zimbabwe

10.1 Principal physical features   304
10.2 Natural regions and farming areas   307
10.3 Land tenure systems   309
10.4 Population density, 1982   312

LIST OF TABLES

Angola
1.1 Principal characteristics of the population   7
1.2 Change of GDP by economic sector, 1985–1989   8
1.3 Changes to the structure of the GDP, 1970–1989   8
1.4 Indices of manufacturing, 1970–1987   10
1.5 Urban drinking water provision: per cent access   12
1.6 State of fish reserves in 1989   19
1.7 National Parks and Reserves in Angola   22
1.8 Summary of household energy consumption, 1980   23

Botswana
2.1 Population census returns, 1904–1981   35

Lesotho
3.1a Urban and rural population distribution by district, 1986   68
3.1b Total population by district, 1986   69
3.2 Absolute population densities and population densities per km² of arable land   70
3.3 Land use in Lesotho, 1988   71
3.4 Land use by district, 1988   72
3.5 Land use by agro-ecological zone, 1988   72
3.6 Rates of erosion and sedimentation, Roma Valley, Maliele Catchment   74
     and Little Caledon Catchment
3.7 Fuelwood sources   77
3.8 Potential supplies from hydropower stations   78

Malawi
4.1 Population numbers and density, 1967 and 1987   94
4.2 Population: rural and urban components, 1977 and 1987   94
4.3 Population: intercensal annual growth rates   94
4.4 Trends in landholding sizes   98
4.5 Known mineral resources   101
4.6 Coal production   101
4.7 Fish production, 1965–1985   111
4.8 Leasehold estate expansion, 1970–1989   113
4.9 Estate landuse patterns   114
4.10 Landuse patterns on tea estates   115
4.11 Estimated accessible wood production and consumption, 1984 and 1985   116

Mozambique
5.1 Distribution of the GDP by sectors   128
5.2 Economically active population by sectors   129
5.3 Environmental problems and issues characteristic of many sub-Saharan   130
     countries and their relevance to Mozambique
5.4 Two recent analyses of environmental problems   131
5.5 Outstanding environmental issues   132

Namibia
6.1 Gross output from commercial farming, 1976–1981   178
6.2 Commercial forestry output, 1983   180
6.3 Woody biomass resources: preliminary estimates   181
6.4 Major mineral resources   182
6.5 Contribution of mining to GDP, 1974–1983   182
6.6 Estimated Namibian energy demand, 1980   183
6.7 Energy balance, 1980   184
6.8 Catches of the six principal species of fish, 1966–1983   186

Swaziland
7.1 Land use by land tenure type, 1986   197
7.2 Estimated paid employment, 1981–1987   199
7.3 Employment by sector, 1985–1986   199
7.4 Swazis recruited for South African mines   201
7.5 Employment in the traditional sector by region, 1985   201
7.6 GDP at factor cost by sector of origin, 1981–1985 at constant 1980 prices (E '000)   203
7.7 Population growth, 1976–1989   204
7.8 Population projections, 1986–2006   204
7.9 Population distribution by district and land tenure type, 1986   207
7.10 Population density by land tenure and district, 1986   208
7.11 Industrial emissions in the Eastern Transvaal   214
7.12 Acidity of soils   215
7.13 National livestock population, 1985–1988   219
7.14 Man-made forests   220

Tanzania
8.1 Hydroelectricity stations   255
8.2 National demand forecast for electricity   255
8.3 Natural gas reserves   256
8.4 Coal resources   257
8.5 Crop and livestock wastes   258
8.6 National Parks   260
8.7 Game Reserves   261
8.8 Tree planting in villages, 1981/2–1985/6   267

Zambia
9.1 Population by province, 1990   272
9.2 Land utilisation classification, 1974–1975   273
9.3 Sectoral pattern of energy consumption, 1987   291
9.4 Relative use of different household energy sources, 1980   291
9.5 Per capita annual consumption levels in the household sector, 1980   292
9.6 Acceptability to local and other élites of rural development approaches   300

Zimbabwe
10.1 Characteristics of eight main soil groups   305
10.2 Age structure in rural and urban areas   311
10.3 Land tenure types   313
10.4 Distribution of land categories by natural region   313
10.5 Distribution of natural regions by land category   314
10.6 Extent of soil erosion by land tenure class   317
10.7 Total wood stocks and supplies by land tenure category   319
10.8 Environmental factors influencing agricultural potential   323
10.9 Mineral production, 1985   328
10.10 National fuelwood supply and demand   330

GLOSSARY

AAA	Angolan Environmental Association
CNU	National Commission for Unesco
CITES	Convention on International Trade in Endangered Species
CHA	Controlled hunting area
DANIDA	Danish International Development Agency
DDT	Dichloro-Diphenyl-Tetrachlorethane
EEC	European Economic Community
FAO	Food and Agriculture Organization
FINNIDA	Finnish International Development Agency
ICA	Intensive Conservation Area (Zimbabwe)
ILO	International Labour Office
ITL	Individual Tenure Land
IUCN	International Union for the Conservation of Nature
K	Kwacha (Zambian currency)
LSU	Livestock unit
MAB	Man and the Biosphere programme
MNC	Multinational corporation
NEAP	National Environmental Action Plan
NCS	National Conservation Strategy
NGO	Non governmental organisation
NORAD	Norwegian Agency for International Develoment
R	Rand (South African currency used in Namibia)
RAD	Remote area dweller
RDA	Rural development areas
SACU	South African Customs Union
SADC	Southern African Development Community
SADCC	Southern African Development Coordination Conference (former name)
SIDA	Swedish International Development Agency
SNL	Swazi National land
SWAPO	South West Africa People's Organisation (Namibia)
TGLP	Tribal Grazing Lands Policy (Botswana)
UNCED	United Nations Conference on Environment and Development
UNEP	United Nations Environment Programme
Unicef	United Nations Children's Fund
Unesco	United Nations Education, Scientific and Cultural Organization
VDC	Village development council
WCED	World Commission on Environment and Development
WCS	World Conservation Strategy
WMA	Wildlife management area
WWF	World Wildlife Fund

FOREWORD

The environment of Southern Africa is our home. It is not, however, a piece of property where we can buy and sell the freehold at cost. The environment is handed down to us, we use it and we must pass it on to our children so they can be sustained by it.

Africa's environmental debate is essentially a debate about land. The history of changing landuse practices, from open range pastoralism and slash and burn, through traditional settled agriculture and colonisation, to the fight for independence and development, is focused on land debates. Customary rights to land and communal control of land are still dominant throughout the region.

Increasingly, under these legal systems, land is under pressure, a pressure that leads to environmental degradation. Frequently, environmentalists argue that only when land is privatised, when local people no longer have access to land will environmental degradation cease. This approach significantly underestimates the real cause of environmental degradation which lies in the history of people's poverty, in a history which has seen land resources removed from local people with consequent diminishing opportunity to create wealth. Without wealth creating opportunity, land degradation will continue.

Yet, even as I write, Southern Africa is undergoing a massive transformation. Cities and towns are mushrooming across the region. Demand for permanent housing, for water, sewage and transport systems, for industrial and consumer products is increasing. Building on the real post-independence improvements in health and education provision, the people of Southern Africa are creating a new landscape much as they created the agricultural landscape of the past. Yet such a process of development brings new problems – not just of pollution and resource exhaustion but, significantly, of renewable resources. Energy requirements, wood consumption and, most importantly, water demand will be critical resource issues to address in the 21st century.

This volume of environmental profiles of the Southern African Development Community (SADC) addresses these issues at the level of each nation state. Each profile provides a pen picture of the opportunities and constraints in each member state. Of course, such an overview does not provide specific analysis of local problems at a district or village level – that is a task that will continue to be done by others as environmental considerations are built into development planning. This volume is welcome as it seeks to provide a broad environmental framework to parallel the macro-economic debates on structural changes that are ongoing throughout the region.

It is doubly welcome because of its origins. ZERO, the regional network of environment and energy experts, has drawn together expertise from the SADC region to produce this volume. It is a demonstration of what can be achieved within the region using local knowledge and builds on the continuing environmental debate that began before, and continues after, the UNCED Earth Summit in June 1992. To ZERO, and its northern partners, the ETC Foundation, I offer congratulations. But the writers of this volume would agree with me – this overview is only a start. It must be improved and such improvement requires that everyone joins the debate over Southern Africa's environmental future. It is, after all, the debate about the future of your children and your children's children.

Mr B Leleka
SADC Environment and Land Management Sector

ACKNOWLEDGEMENTS

Dr Michael Sill served as technical editor for the whole project and Gary Haley was responsible for final production and cartography of this volume. Individual contributors by country included:

Angola	Oscar Marleyn
	Phil O'Keefe
	Nazare Salvador
	Walter Viegas
Botswana	Masego Mpotokwane
	Sandra Shaw
	Richard Segodi
Lesotho	Ina Tabirih
	TAB Consult (Pty) Ltd
Malawi	Guy Mhone
	Austin Nguira
Mozambique	Jose de Cruz Francisco
	Henrique Lopes
	Maida Mussa
	Phil O'Keefe
Namibia	Admos Chimhowu
	Frances Chinemana
	Amson Sibanda
	Daniel Tevera
Swaziland	Funekile Mdluli
Tanzania	Abneri Senyagwa
Zambia	Moses Banda
	Griffin Nyirongo
Zimbabwe	Yemi Katerere
	Sam Moyo
	Peter Ngobese

INTRODUCTION:

SUSTAINABLE DEVELOPMENT AND THE SADC ENVIRONMENT

Sustainable development is now a focal concept of development practice. The term has an ecological basis, first used in fisheries management to mean an annual harvest that could be taken in perpetuity. Sustainable development builds development strategies to manage natural resources so that they provide for the needs of today while ensuring the resources of tomorrow.

BEYOND TECHNOLOGICAL ANALYSIS

The definition of sustainable development has an intergenerational dimension and, as such, means different things to different people. Within the agricultural sector, for example, one can identify at least three schools of thought concerning the meaning of sustainability.

There is the 'food-sufficiency' or 'productivity' viewpoint that regards sustainability as simply supplying enough food to meet everyone's requirements. On the other hand, the 'stewardship' school maintains that sustainability should be regarded primarily as an 'ecological phenomenon' where concern should be the maintenance of an 'average level of output over an indefinitely long period without depleting the renewable resources on which it depends'. A third and broader school of thought on sustainability, though, would be the 'community' perspective which pays attention to the effects of different production systems on the viability of agrarian life.

The 'productivity' viewpoint is simply another way of presenting food security arguments but if the 'stewardship' school, is followed within an agricultural setting, the following propositions for environmental stability could apply:

- The chemical nutrients removed by crops must be replenished.
- The physical condition of the soil must be suited to the land utilisation type, which means that the humus level in the soil must be constant or increasing.
- There should not be any build-up of weeds, pests or diseases.
- There should be no increase in soil acidity or toxic elements.
- Soil erosion must be controlled.

At a global level, then, the following would occur;

- The minimisation of dependence on non-renewable energy, mineral and chemical resources;
- A reduction of off-farm or other types of contamination of air, water and land by nutrients and toxic materials to levels at which self-cleansing is continually possible;
- The maintenance of an adequate habitat for wildlife; and
- A conservation of the genetic resources in plant and animal species needed for agriculture.

It is obvious then, that discussion of sustainable development in a 'stewardship' model is largely a technological argument. What is missing is a perspective on people or community.

Since the 1960s governments in the South have found that increasing production of raw materials was necessary to sustain the import of manufactured goods, consumption exceeded natural rates of replenishment and, in Africa, the stage was set for the succession of environmental crises in the Sahel and the Horn. In the 1970s, the nature of, and reactions to, environmental problems in the North and South underwent their widest divergence, between the problems of plenty and the problems of scarcity.

Some development agencies in the 1970s did begin to address the social concerns of disadvantaged groups, such as women, in their aid programmes. More commonly, however, aid programmes continued to reflect Northern preoccupations by rewarding political and military friends, by promoting exports and securing strategic imports.

Parallel to those developments, but born out of concern for the progressive environmental degradation evident in the South, a new development philosophy emerged in 1980, with the production of the World Conservation Strategy (WCS) by the International Union for the Conservation of Nature (IUCN), the World Wildlife Fund (WWF) and the United Nations Environment Programme (UNEP).

The objectives of conservation were defined in the World Conservation Strategy in biological terms, namely:

- the maintenance of essential ecological processes;
- the preservation of genetic diversity; and
- the sustainable utilisation of species and ecosystems.

Little acknowledgement was paid to human interactions with the biological environment. Widespread support in the North for the objectives of the World Conservation Strategy was rapidly followed by the incorporation of its principles into some bilateral and non-government aid programmes for the South, though not into major multilateral funding agency programmes. International trade was, however, immune to considerations of sustainable development. Public opinion in the North did, nevertheless, begin to question the role of some multinational corporations (MNCs), especially agro-chemical companies, in the South.

In biological terms, the three objectives of the WCS were, and remain, valid. They were widely incorporated into national conservation strategies (NCSs), but more radical suggestions such as the proposal that land suitable for arable cultivation should not be used for cattle herding were less readily adopted.

However, the realisation grew that the conservation of natural resources was unlikely to change the inequalities of access to resources between rich and poor countries, or between the rich and poor sectors of individual societies. Pleas for conservation, however impassioned, could not check environmental degradation while great inequities of access to natural resources remained. Nevertheless, public opinion in the North continued to be shaped by dramatic presentations of disasters to people and livestock in areas such as the Sahel. Generous public responses to food aid appeals and disaster funds illustrated a willingness to help.

In 1987, the World Commission on Environment and Development (WCED) was able to define sustainable development in *Our Common Future* as 'Development that meets the needs of the present without compromising the ability of future generations to meet their own needs'. The World Commission on Environment and Development went further than the biological principles of the WCS by relating 'the environment's ability to meet present and future needs' to the 'state of technology and social organisation'. It was much more focused on human needs, particularly those 'of the world's poor, to which overriding priority should be given'. The World Commission on Environment and Development usefully broadened the debate to include the roles of the international economy and of armed conflict as causes of unsustainable development.

It is unlikely that the contradictions surrounding sustainable development will be resolved in the coming decade. Ample evidence of unsustainable development practices exist with further destruction of the tropical moist forests, the loss of endangered species, and the threat of global disaster attributable to the greenhouse effect and the depletion of the ozone layer. Yet the debate after the Global Environmental Summit in Rio de Janeiro last year (1992) remains polarised. The North is increasingly 'stewardship'-focused arguing for nature; the South is 'community'-focused arguing for people.

SADC (Southern Africa Development Community) as a regional body is beginning to address these issues. The environment of SADC member countries and South Africa is undergoing substantial change. As economic development occurs, local people are moving from husbanding resources to mastering resources, a substantial change in the people-environment relationship that parallels industrialisation and urbanisation. Such change has given rise to political concern at an international, regional, national and local level, although, as yet, there has been little political action to resolve environmental problems.

Central to these concerns are the depletion of non-renewable resources such as hydrocarbons, the destruction of conditionally-renewable resources such as water and soil and the reduced capacity of the environment to act as a sink of pollution. In the SADC region, particularly if South Africa is included in wider membership, the most significant resource shortfall is the provision of water. As individual nation states share river basins there is a need for urgent negotiation over riparian rights. Future capital investment in water resource development will require rigorous environmental analysis to ensure that supply meets demand, that regional scarcity is avoided and that fossil aquifers are not substantially depleted. Such a regional approach to water resource management – which is the only way to avoid scarcity – will require careful cost analysis and the establishment of a water pricing policy that reflects the scarcity.

Significant environmental issues underlie the energy sector where the dominant mode of regional integration is likely to be the expansion of an international grid system. Such a strategy would provide electricity most cheaply to new subscribers and would offer the opportunity for least-cost investment that accommodated a level of real environmental cost. It is important that this issue is taken seriously because future international trading will probably require evidence of environmental best practice and energy inputs will be closely monitored for their international impact – carbon emission and regional pollution (acid rain) – as well as local despoliation.

Although there are significant levels of land degradation in the region, especially in the more marginal, communal land, the environmental problems cannot be adequately addressed until the inequities of land distribution are addressed. Ironically, given such an inequity, it is surprising that only a relatively small portion of land is currently devoted to agriculture. The constraints, however, on an expansion of sustainable agriculture are the ecological and climatic conditions in much of the region. Land degradation can only be addressed at local level and the purpose of addressing this issue at a regional scale is to search for models of best practice in areas with similar ecological, socio-economic and demographic characteristics. Parallel to the landuse issue in rural areas is the issue of urban poverty and pollution, particularly, but not only, in Southern Africa. This has a direct impact on peoples' health and there is need for the development of strong environmental health programmes to combat this growing problem.

Significant areas of land in the region are given over to wildlife conservation. Wildlife makes a substantial contribution to national economies through wildlife viewing, safari hunting and game cropping. Existing SADC member countries can strengthen their wildlife industries by examining South Africa's own wildlife industry as wildlife industries offer significant opportunities for foreign exchange earnings.

At present, there is significant institutional under capacity in the environment sector. Multilateral, bilateral and private funds must be sought to ensure that at a national and regional level global and regional environmental standards can be adhered to without limiting development opportunity. Such institutional development requires significant support for policy formulation, research and training, particularly as with industrial development there will be substantial opportunity for the regional provision of toxic waste facilities. Above all, it is important to accept that there has to be a level of political choice with regard to environmental resources. Increasingly, commercial considerations will have to underlie conservation initiatives. Unless conservation pays its own way, it will be a drain on the decreasing resources available to the public purse for other developments.

This volume contains detailed country case studies that explore these issues within SADC member countries. It is hoped that they will be useful in informing development practitioners of environmental constraints and environmentalists of development needs. It is but a building block to help SADC create a sustainable future for the people of Southern Africa.

1

ANGOLA

INTRODUCTION

Angola is currently experiencing a thirty-year war. The war has had a catastrophic effect on the country's economic and social infrastructure. Many Angolans have been forced into becoming refugees.

After hostilities cease it will take years for the country to re-establish its disrupted production systems and to reorganise and re-build the collapsed state health and education services. The intricate, informal social security network, through which the majority of the population were able to survive, will have to be re-created. In addition, problems in the urban areas created by the forced concentration of a large part of the population will have to be addressed.

As one can imagine, given the magnitude of problems that have to be dealt with, official institutions in Angola do not place environmental issues very high on the agenda. Environmental problems are therefore only identified by a handful of technicians, specialists and politicians. The government perceives environmental issues as being of primary concern to, and to be solved by, the rich industrialised nations. Apart from the rare occasions when new laws and regulations are announced that have some bearing on the environment, little is done. The principal aim of the Angolan government and the political parties is to achieve economic recovery. Environmental issues are of secondary importance and are still seen by many as no more than the protection of wildlife and natural habitats.

Nevertheless, what needs to be realised and accepted, is that environmental problems – such as the pollution of drinking water, sewage and waste overspill, the degradation of agricultural land in densely populated areas and the shortages of woodfuel around the cities – directly affect the lives, as well as the survival, of many Angolans.

Although Angola's future aim is to achieve economic recovery, it is crucial for the well- being of the population that all those who make and influence decisions adjust their perception of environmental matters and come to terms with the realisation that environmental issues are not just luxury items for a privileged few.

ECONOMIC STRUCTURE

Angola has an area of 1,246,700 km² making it the second-largest country in sub-Saharan Africa. The distance from north to south is 1277 km and from east to west is 1236 km. It is bordered by Zaire, the Congo People's Republic, Zambia and Namibia.

The climate is tropical but locally tempered by altitude. The coast is arid or semi-arid due to the influence of the Benguela current. The area along the Namibian border experiences very high temperatures and heavy seasonal rainfall (Figure 1.1). The interior uplands have a much more pleasant climate (Figure 1.2). Angola is a sparsely populated country with a total population of 10,020,000 in 1990 (Table 1.1). Approximately 25 per cent of the population reside in urban centres. This is mainly due to the war. The high population density in the cities has created serious economic, social and environmental problems.

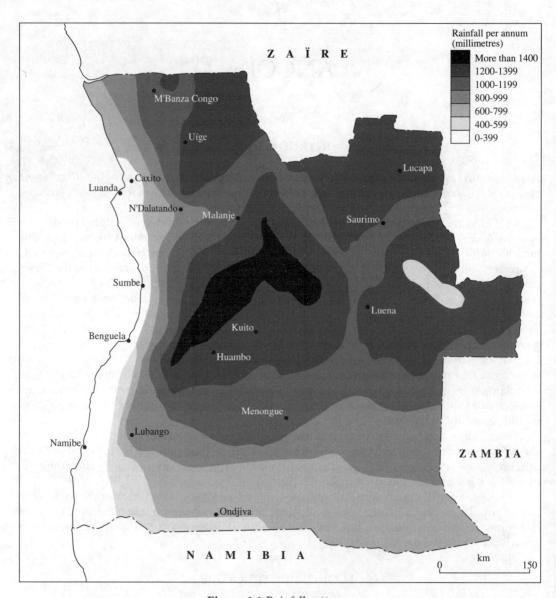

Figure 1.1 *Rainfall patterns*

According to Munslow (1992), conditions have not existed in the country to allow for the collection of any reliable population figures. Hence, all figures should be regarded as indicative only. Broadly, the population doubled from 2.7 million in 1900 to 5.6 million in 1970. In the latter part of this period, large-scale Portuguese immigration was a significant factor. However, the uprising and massacres of the early 1960s also promoted a population exodus to neighbouring countries as a countervailing tendency. On the eve of Independence there were 400,000 Portuguese settlers in the country, but during the transition to Independence, virtually all left. As they monopolised the skills, this left the country in a difficult situation. According to official estimates, by 1980 the population had reached 7.7 million.

Table 1.1 *Principal characteristics of the population (000 inhabitants)*

Population	1987	1988	1989	1990
Total	9233	9483	9739	10020
Urban	2933	3209	3448	2836
Rural	6300	6274	6291	7184
Female	4801	4931	5064	5084
Male	4432	4552	4675	4936
According to age				
0 - 14 years	4132	4243	4357	4510
15- 19 years	900	925	951	982
20- 29 years	1460	1499	1539	1583
Over 30 years	2741	2816	2892	2945
Per Province				
Luanda	1302	1379	1459	1545
Huambo	1383	1418	1460	1484
Bié	1019	1044	1069	1093
Malange	822	838	855	872
Huila	803	818	834	860
Uige	738	761	785	812
Other provinces	3167	3226	3287	3354

Population density is relatively low, 7.2 inhabitants per km², but is very unevenly distributed. The south-east quarter of the country has a population of less than one person per km², whilst the north-east quarter has a population density of between one and five persons per km². Large parts of Huambo province have a particularly dense population concentration greater than thirty persons per km², as do parts of Cuanza-Sul and Malanje provinces.

One of the most striking features is the very high rate of urban growth, in particular in the capital city of Luanda. The urban population is estimated to have grown at 7.6 per cent per annum over the 1980s, compared with a 0.8 per cent growth rate for the rural population. The war intensified rural-urban migration. Hence, the urban population increased from 23 per cent to 37 per cent of the total population between 1980 and 1990. Luanda accounted for 1.2 million of the urban population by 1986, or 44 per cent of the total urban population. By 1990, Luanda's estimated population had reached 1.5 million, some 54 per cent of the total urban population.

There are three major factors which have adversely affected economic growth since independence in 1974:

- the war effort which consumes not only a considerable part of the national budget but also a large part of the country's qualified manpower;
- the exit of thousands of Portuguese after the declaration of Independence, in some cases destroying economic property and leaving the country without qualified personnel to manage the economy and government services;
- the government's economic policy which, influenced by a state of permanent war and the lack of personnel, aimed at directing the economy by quantitative, centralised planning.

These three factors have resulted in a slow – and sometimes negative – growth of the national economy. The following table shows the rate of change of GDP for the period 1985–1989.

Table 1.2 *Change of GDP by economic sector, 1985–1989 (at 1980 prices and factor costs)*

Sector	Annual growth rate (%)
Petrol products	+19.3
Diamonds	+16.8
Electricity	+5.0
Commerce	+0.3
Services	-0.2
Transport and communications	-0.1
Agriculture, silviculture and fishing	-3.6
Construction	-5.3
Transforming industries	-6.1
Total GDP	+8.5

The following table shows that the growth of the national economy over the period 1970–1989 was almost entirely dependent on the growth of output in the petroleum and diamond sectors.

Table 1.3 *Changes to the structure of the GDP, 1970–1989*

Sector	Structure of GDP (%)		
	1970 [1]	1987 [2]	1989 [2]
Petroleum products	7.7	41.1	60.2
Services	12.1 [3]	19.1	13.4
Agriculture, silviculture and fisheries	17.1 [4]	18.5	11.5
Commerce	31.8	6.7	4.7
Construction	5.7 [5]	4.5	2.6
Transforming industries	11.1	4.3	2.6
Transport and communication	6.2	3.8	2.7
Diamonds	7.5	1.6	2.1
Electricity	0.9	0.3	0.2

Notes
1 adapted from Dilolwa (1978) and not including other extractive industries, banking, securities and transactions, housing, public administration and household work
2 at constant 1980 prices and factor costs
3 including 'non defined' activities and public services
4 including production for direct consumption in the household
5 including traditional, self-help housing

The crisis in the national economy is therefore structural. Diamond extraction and the output of petroleum products have gradually increased over the years while other sectors of the economy have been in steady decline. The economy has come to rely on petroleum earnings and therefore on the price levels of the international oil market. Oil accounted for 78 per cent of exports in 1981, but coffee and diamonds have also traditionally been important foreign exchange earners. However, coffee earnings have been depressed by the huge fall in production since Independence and, between 1979 and 1983, by low prices on the world market. The income from exports was also depressed by the dramatic slump in diamond prices in 1981–82 combined with the loss of much revenue to smugglers.

Import restrictions appear to have had a dramatic and adverse impact on the economy. The government's foreign exchange ceilings cut allocations for machinery and vehicles in the mid-eighties, while at the same time giving priority to the import of food and military equipment. This had a drastic effect upon the output capacity in industry, in agriculture and upon the transport of agricultural produce.

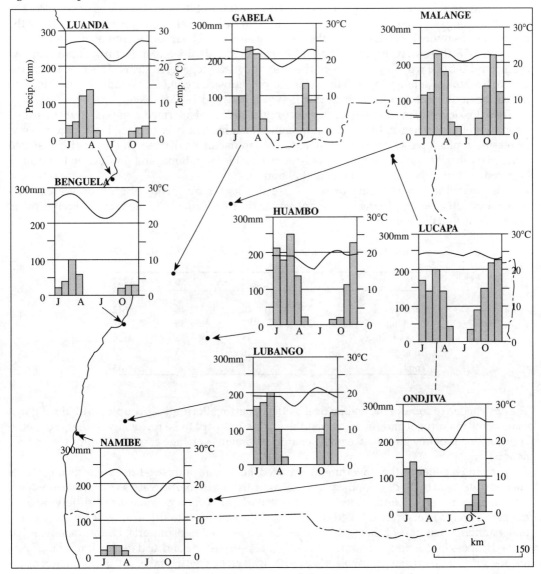

Figure 1.2 *Temperature and rainfall: monthly variation*

Agriculture, which at one time was the main activity of the majority of the population, has been particularly badly hit over the last two decades. The displacement of farmers, the lack of inputs and the disruption of trading systems have resulted in an acute shortage of agricultural produce for consumption and for industrial processing. The war has also created a large unemployed labour force, gathered in and around the major urban centres. This population is now being fed by imported food such as cereals, vegetable oils, flour and milk products.

The post independence era has been characterised by a stagnant mining industry. The mining sector, under the direct control of the government, has suffered because of a lack of investment, military incursions and a general shortage of qualified managerial personnel. With the exception of diamonds, the production of other minerals such as granite, marble, quartz, phosphates and iron ore has declined. The mining of quartz stopped completely in 1982 and that of iron ore in 1986. The mine in Cassinga was rehabilitated in 1986, but iron production has not, as yet, restarted. One of the policy options under consideration is the de-nationalisation of part of the mining industry.

In 1974–75, there were approximately 4000 registered industrial manufacturing units employing around 200,000 workers. At present there are only 1823 registered firms. This means that the country is almost totally dependent on imported industrial goods. The table below gives an indication of the decline of manufacturing between 1970 and 1987.

These low levels of production are due not only to the lack of intermediate goods, but also to low standards of maintenance. Obsolete equipment which has not been replaced will require ever-increasing capital investment in order to reverse manufacturing decline. Of the existing installed industrial capacity, excluding mining, only 60 per cent is operational and production levels have been reduced to 25 per cent of total potential output.

The government is planning to reorganise this sector by giving priority to strategically-important industries, by placing more emphasis on the role of small and medium-scale enterprises and by de-nationalisation.

Table 1.4 *Indices of manufacturing 1970–1987 (1970 = 100)*

Sector	1977	1983	1986	1987
Food	37	48	48	42
Light industry	31	87	88	61
Heavy industry	24	45	52	36
Mining	10	28	23	17
Total	28	57	56	43

The destruction of some of the fishing fleet by the departing Portuguese, coupled with the flight of some boats to Portugal and Brazil caused the fishing industry to be nationalised after Independence. Fishing is of key importance to the country's foreign exchange earnings and for feeding the population.

After Independence the government invested heavily in industrial deep-sea fishing. Little attention was paid to the development of small-scale fishing in coastal waters which, by employing thousands of fisherman and traders, was particularly important as a means of supplying local markets. Foreign fleets were granted concessions allowing them to fish in Angolan waters on the understanding that part of their catch would be landed in Angolan ports. Unfortunately, it has proved impossible for the government to control deep-sea fishing and, to date, foreign fishing fleets are operating unrestricted in Angola's territorial waters. In 1990 a total of 150,000 tonnes of deep-sea fish was landed. This represents only 30 per cent of the catch in the 1970s.

The level of unemployment is acute but difficult to measure. An enormous informal sector has sprung up in the cities. This sector is involved with everything from the sale of imported goods to the provision of the daily food ration and the delivery of services to families. Because of government restrictions on official prices and supplies, the unofficial sector has gradually taken over and has become the main source of supply for most urban dwellers. Prices in the unofficial sector are set by the market and the goods that are available for exchange. The general shortage of commodities raises prices beyond the reach of many Angolans. The return of many soldiers to civilian life can only make this situation worse.

The economic structure of the country has, over the years, been heavily distorted. The commercial balance of payments has more than doubled since 1987, reaching a net surplus of US $ 2362 million in 1990. More than 90 per cent of this revenue came from the petroleum sector. The rest of the economy, apart from diamond extraction, has virtually ground to a halt. This does not provide employment opportunities for the millions who are displaced and unemployed. The new government which was elected in 1992 will be faced with the daunting task of providing employment opportunities. The rehabilitation of the other sectors of the economy should therefore be one of the main tasks. This must be achieved through a strategy which also acknowledges that the present economy is floating on oil, the price of which is entirely dependent on the international market. It also needs to be remembered that the renewal of the civil war in 1993 has limited the government's control over much Angolan territory.

ENVIRONMENTAL PROBLEMS

One important issue affecting most Angolans is environmental health. The majority of the population has no access to a clean water supply; there is a lack of basic sanitary provision; inadequate health facilities; insufficient fuel to cook with and often an irregular supply of food. The misery caused by the massive concentration of families in the *musseques* (shanty towns) in nearly every urban centre summarises environmental problems for millions of Angolans.

The major urban environmental health issues can be summed up as follows:

- the rapid deterioration of existing housing facilities due to over-population and the lack of maintenance and appropriate building materials;
- the collapse of sewage and surface water drainage systems resulting in the spillage of sewage causing serious public health problems;
- the lack of public sanitation caused by the accumulation of household refuse in public places;
- serious deterioration of the water-supply system causing pollution and the rapid spread of water-borne diseases.

Water, sanitation, health, energy and food are the most important items on the environmental agenda against which most other issues pale into insignificance. This does not mean that issues such as the industrial pollution of water resources, the degradation of the coastal ecosystems and the protection of the productive capacity of the land can simply be ignored. Indeed, we would argue that due care and attention has to be given to these now in order to protect the resources of the future. The proper and effective management of these resources cannot be effectively dealt with by government authorities alone. Only the active participation and involvement of the population can create a system of management which is both effective and sustainable.

Urban and rural drinking water supplies

The provision of clean drinking water is a fundamental indicator of the state of the urban environment. The best available statistics demonstrate the following relative deterioration of the situation, given the high rate of urbanisation.

Table 1.5 *Urban drinking water provision: per cent access*

Population with	1985	1988
Piped water	18.4	15
Public fountains	61.4	60
Without access to satisfactory water supplies	20.2	25

Source: Angola UNCED National Report, 1992

Those fortunate in having water piped to their homes have to put up with an intermittent supply and regular cuts in provision. Given pressure problems within the system, those living either on high ground or in high-rise flats rarely obtain water through the installed system.

There is great inequality in the system, with some homes having their own pumping system, whilst others have no clean water provision at all. Those areas with no water provision whatsoever are obliged to purchase water shipped in from rivers in the adjacent countryside and sold unhygienically.

The absence of an adequate urban sanitation network is a serious problem. Only 10 per cent of the urban population has access to the drains system; 15 per cent have a household disposal system; and 75 per cent no system at all (1988 figures). Yet again, the urban growth rate means that according to figures produced for the UNCED national report, the percentage of the urban population with access to the drains system was diminishing, whilst those with no access whatsoever was increasing.

Few urban centres have a drainage system, leading to flooding of many low-lying areas, accompanied by the diseases attendant upon stagnant water. Flooding also creates hazards to buildings and the lives of the inhabitants through subsidence and landslides.

There is a serious lack of basic hygiene knowledge amongst the population and a major environmental health education initiative is required.

In terms of health provision, the health budget as a percentage of Gross Domestic Product declined from 3.3 per cent in 1985 to 1.8 per cent in 1989. The key health problems are a high level of infant mortality, low levels of immunisation, huge discrepancies in access to health facilities, very little health education or knowledge amongst the general public, a high level of transmittable diseases, and low nutritional levels. In addition, there are no controls on food quality concerning food production, storage, transformation, packaging and distribution.

In general, there is very little recycling of products in the urban areas. People's consumption habits are wasteful. There has been no mass education on the subject.

Water resources

There is no substantial pollution of land water because industrial production has been insignificant over the last decade. A certain amount of pollution in the rivers of the Luanda-Norte province occurs because of diamond mining, but the direct recipients of these waters are the tributaries of the

Kasai river in Zaïre, immediately to the north. An increase in manufacturing and mining could create higher levels of water pollution and it needs to be noted that there is no existing legislation which would control future pollution levels.

Coastal ecosystems and marine resources

At the beginning of the 1970s various independent researchers came to the conclusion that the stock of 'Cachucho' (*Dentex macrothalmus*) had been severely over-fished during the previous decades. These conclusions were based on a comparison made between the total catch and the number of fishing boats in operation along the coast. Insufficient scientific research has been undertaken in recent years to confirm these findings.

There is no control over the fishing methods used in the coastal waters and there is a considerable amount of illegal fishing. But, as already stated, there is no systematic scientific testing to prove or disprove the impact of these practices on fishing reserves. The impact of oil exploitation and the discharge of urban and industrial waste in coastal waters could have a greater impact on resources. Industrial waste, particularly from cement and oil refineries, combined with urban waste materials from Luanda are poured into Cacuaco and Luanda Bay, affecting the fish population in the immediate vicinity.

Agriculture and land resources

Agriculture remains the most important economic activity. Because of low population densities most farmers used shifting forms of agricultural systems in the past. New farming plots were opened up on a yearly basis by burning the existing vegetation. The land was then cultivated until production levels declined, at which point the land was allowed to regenerate naturally. This practice was condemned by the authorities, both during and after the colonial period, because the fires used for clearing the land often reduced large tracts of forest to ashes. The practice was denounced as 'traditional' and backward. In fact the same method was used by the colonial regime to clear large tracts of land for plantations and later also in the modern agricultural sector.

The practice continues and is used not only for clearing land for agriculture but also to open routes for trading and for hunting wild animals. There is no doubt that the method could be improved to reduce the often widespread damage that it causes but the major current agricultural problems are of a different nature.

Population concentrations due to war conditions have created enormous pressure on the land. The situation has become so critical that 'traditional' shifting agricultural practices can no longer be used. Many farmers have had to switch to sedentary farming for the first time, often without having the necessary technical skills and resources. Having moved, farmers have to adapt not only to new production techniques but to new environmental conditions as well. The newly-created urban and peri-urban communities do not have the same social structures as those in rural areas. Land use is not controlled by the community and the available land resources are in many instances being mined, causing declining fertility, soil erosion and in some cases intense degradation.

Land degradation is a serious problem in areas of large population concentration and in the high rainfall zones of the Planalto region (in the provinces of Huambo, Bié, south of Cuanza-Sul and the north of Huila). In most other areas agriculture has ceased, leaving the land underutilised.

Grazing lands have been similarly affected through the restriction of cattle herds to certain areas. Prolonged periods of drought in the southern region have caused increased cattle concentrations around water holes and in areas where water is still available. The traditional exchange of cattle for foodstuffs no longer operates. Pastoral people are now obliged to cultivate their own food, sometimes in areas unsuited for agricultural production.

Fuelwood production and environmental degradation

The concept of 'biomass' includes fuelwood, wood used in industrial production, crops, residues and all other vegetation that is now regarded as 'waste'. Nearly 50 per cent of the land area of Angola is covered by natural forests (61 million ha) and another 235,000 ha of man-made forest can be identified. The natural forests of Angola are estimated to be able to produce between 510 and 1020 million cubic metres of wood per year, of which around 50 million cubic metres is utilised for industrial purposes and the remainder for fuelwood.

It is evident that Angola's biomass potential per capita, both present and future, is enormous. The problem is that most of it is inaccessible as a source of energy. It is in the areas with a high population density that most of the damage and consequent degradation takes place. In the urban areas people generally rely on charcoal and wood for cooking. To meet the demand, charcoal is produced for sale. Because of this practice the forests around the urban areas have decreased drastically over the last decade.

A great deal of ecological damage is being inflicted on the biomass resources in the littoral and sub-littoral regions by the present methods of charcoal production. Another contributing factor to the low rate of regeneration is the lower level of rainfall. The outcome is serious deforestation and soil erosion, not only in these areas but also around the major towns in the interior and in some of the more densely populated provinces such as Huambo and Bié. Forest exploitation for woodfuel and timber has caused severe desertification around the town of Namibe in the south of the country. In the early 1980s the government started a scheme to arrest this process, but without the necessary resources its success has been limited.

Forest industries and the destruction of habitats

During the colonial period one of the main economic activities in Angola was the export of timber. Even at that time, the forest resources in certain areas such as Cabinda were heavily overexploited. Since Independence, the government has introduced a system of re-planting. Despite this the degradation continues, and has had a severe impact upon the habitats and the future survival of primates such as the gorilla (*Gorilla gorilla*) and chimpanzee (*Pan troglodytes*).

For some time now hardwood forests have been severely depleted in the south of the country for sale to South Africa. There is, however, no factual information available on the state of the forest in that region.

The impact of mining and industry

Because of reduced mining and industrial activity the impact of this sector on the environment has, up to now, been limited. However, a survey of three factories in Luanda* has shown that gases were emitted and waste, including toxic zinc residues, were dumped around the factories without any control over their toxicity or possible impact on the immediate environment.

---

* These are a factory producing vegetable oils (INDUVE), the tobacco factory (FTU) and the metal firm FATA/METANG

Diamond production around Dundo in the north-east of the country has caused a certain amount of pollution to the tributaries of the Kasai river flowing into Zaïre. Diamonds are also extracted by opening up the river beds. The damage caused by this method of working has not been evaluated but should be investigated for possible future action (Figure 1.3).

The mining of phosphates and iron in Cassinga caused considerable pollution of the rivers Calonga and Cunene during the colonial period, as did the production of cellulose in Alto Catumbela and the sisal factories in Benguela and Cuanza-Sul. However, the real extent of pollution and damage to other resources and ecosystems is not known.

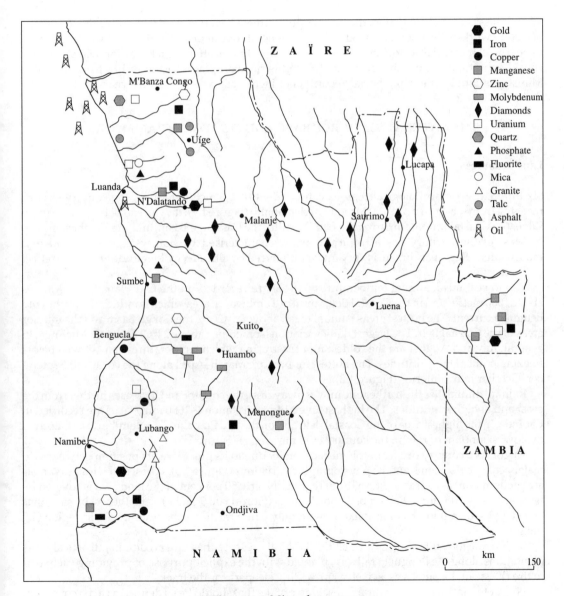

Figure 1.3 *Mineral resources*

The impact of hydro-electric schemes on ecosystems has not been analysed and is thought, probably wrongly, to be minimal. The potential for new schemes is great and their environmental impact could be significant in the future.

The dumping of toxic waste has been confined to one known case in the Quissama National Park. The origin of the dump has never been discovered, but attempts have been made by specialised European firms to use Angolan territory as a dumping ground for toxic industrial waste.

Industrial health and hygiene

With the assistance, since 1986, of the ILO, the government has attempted to improve the conditions of factory workers through the introduction of a general code of practice. This code was introduced in nearly all industrial sectors between 1988 and 1990 but its effective application will still take a considerable time. The number of accidents in industrial workplaces has, according to figures of the Ministry of Employment and Social Security, not increased over the last five years.

THE NATURAL RESOURCE BASE AND ITS LEGAL FRAMEWORK

Land resources

Six different geomorphological regions can be identified which determine the country's relief, reaching from sea-level up to a 2000 metre high planalto (Figure 1.4): the Coastal Belt, the Transition Zone, the Coastal Mountain Strip, the Old Planalto, the Cassange Basin, and the Zambesi massif.

Most of the territory has a tropical climate, characterised by hot, wet summers and dry, mild,winters. Regional climate is very much influenced by altitude, by longitude and by the effect of the coastal climate.

The lowest mean annual temperatures (-19°C) are recorded on the Old Planalto at altitudes above 1600 metres and in the Coastal Belt, south of Tombwa, an area which is influenced by the cold Benguela current. The hottest areas (annual mean above 25°C) are the Congo Basin and the interior areas of the Coastal Belt. The largest daily variation (sometimes above 24°C) occurs in Mavinga. In general, July and August are the coldest months, during which temperatures can fall well below freezing point at high altitudes. The hottest months are March–April along the coast and September–October in the interior (Figure 1.2).

Rainfall diminishes the further one moves away from the equator and increases further from the coast and at higher altitudes. The highest levels of precipitation (+1600 mm/year) are recorded in Cabinda, in the highest area of the Coastal Belt, and on the Old Planalto. The Namibe desert receives the lowest amount of rain in the country (±50 mm/year) (Figure 1.2).

Angola is a country of great ecological diversity due to its great size, its position between two major ecological systems and its physiographic variations (Figure 1.5). Forest and shrub savannas are predominant as characteristic natural regions. Nearly 50 per cent of the land area is covered by natural forests (61 million ha) – mostly *Brachystegia* (Floresta de 'Panda') – and the rest by savannas and steppes (62 million ha of grassland), with only a tiny fraction constituting an arid region (1.5 million ha).

Man-made forests take up as little as 235,000 ha at present – these are predominantly eucalyptus plantations along the Benguela railway, planted with the explicit purpose of providing fuelwood to fire the steam locomotives as well as providing sleepers for the track.

The 'potential yield' of a natural forest is an offtake that should be so defined as to be consistent

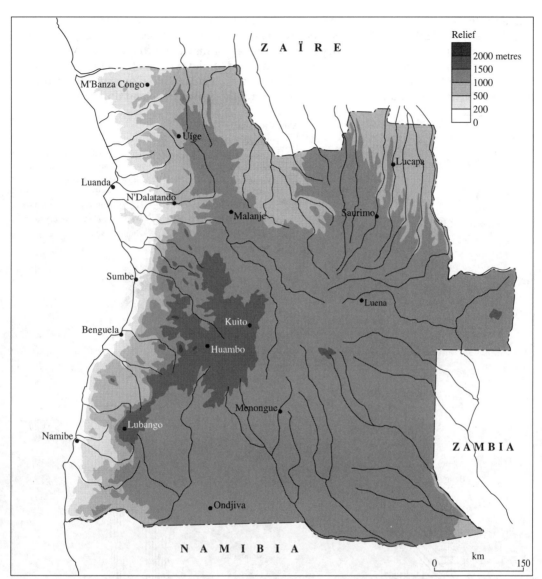

Figure 1.4 *Geomorphology and relief*

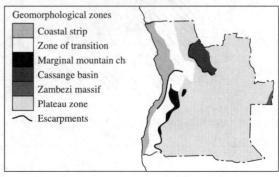

Geomorphological zones
- Coastal strip
- Zone of transition
- Marginal mountain ch
- Cassange basin
- Zambezi massif
- Plateau zone
- Escarpments

with a process of natural self-regeneration. For the tropical and sub-tropical forests as well as for woodlands, the potential yield is (theoretically) estimated by forest experts to be between 10 and 20 cubic metres per ha per year. For dry forest areas it is estimated to be half as much.

During the colonial period, forests were overexploited for the export of timber in certain areas. In 1962, a Forest Decree (nr.44531) was introduced – the 'Regulamento Florestal' – to curb these practices. The forest regulations are directed to control the timber trade and do not include

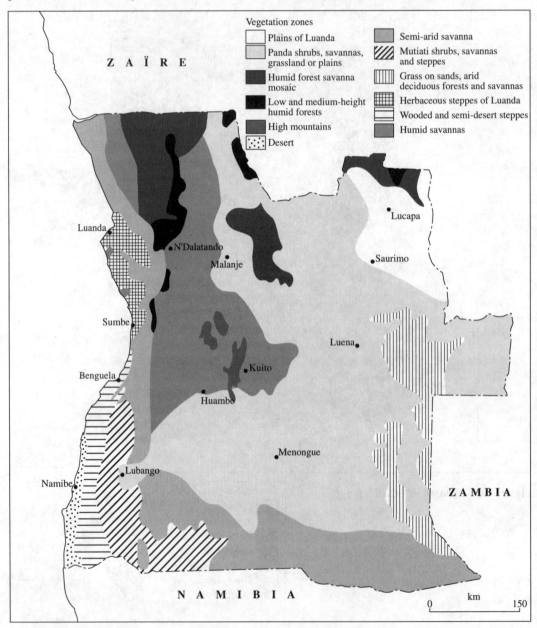

Figure 1.5 *Vegetation zones*

measures for re-afforestation or the use of forest residues from timber exploitation for energy purposes.

On the non-forested land of about 63.5 million hectares, 40 per cent has a high agricultural potential (areas with more than 850 mm of rain per annum), 45 per cent has a medium potential (rainfall between 600–850 mm per annum) and the remaining 15 per cent has a low potential (less than 600 mm of rainfall per annum).

There are three major agro-ecological regions. In the Northern region cassava, tropical oil-seed crops (peanuts, palm oil, castor oil), coffee and cotton are predominant. The Central region is suitable for crops such as maize, sisal, sunflower and wheat, while the Southern region is used mainly for grazing and the cultivation of sorghum and wheat.

Sugar cane is grown in the coastal flats near Luanda but can also be grown in many other areas. Cattle production (3.5 million head) is concentrated in the Southern region because it is tsetse free. Apart from the sugar-cane estates and on the Planalto in the Central Region, irrigation has hardly been developed.

Marine and littoral resources

During the 1950s, Angola was, after South Africa, the second most important fish-producing nation in the whole of Africa. During this period the annual catch delivered by the coastal fisheries was estimated to be 685,000 tonnes per year.

As mentioned above, there is clearly an urgent need for tighter controls over the fishing methods used by Angolan and foreign vessels. It is generally known that fish-mining is taking place on a relatively large scale. The government has recently acquired a boat for the supervision and control of fishing, but the size of the operations has proved too large for these controls to be effective.

Research needs to be undertaken on the state of the stock of certain fish species. This would assist the government in introducing legislation to limit the size of the catch of such fish types. Table 1.6 gives an indication of the size of fish reserves. It has to be admitted, however, that hardly any research has been undertaken to establish the size of the stock and the table gives no more than a very approximate set of estimates.

Table 1.6 *State of fish reserves in 1989*

Type of fish	Estimate of available stock (000 tonnes)	Comments
Dentex macrothalmus (Cachuco)	?	Heavily overfished
Mackerel (Carapau)	530	Control of the catch is necessary
Sardines	100	Reduced stock but large future potential
Anchovy (Biqueirao)	low	Stock overexploited
Whiting (Pescada)	8	Catch is too high
Prawns	40–50	Overexploited, overall quotas reduced to 5000 tonnes in 1989

Inland water resources

Angola's only large lake is situated in the province of Moxico but there is an extensive network of rivers and streams covering the whole of the country. Hardly anything is known about the quality of the water or its economic potential for generating energy or fishing. There are only six dams, which are used for producing hydroelectricity and waterflow control.

Pollution levels are generally low – with the exception of the diamond mining area in Lunda-Norte. There is no legislation which would control pollution levels in the future.

There is a large number of small inland lakes, covering a total area of 2000 km², with an unknown potential for fishing. The potential for fishing in the natural waterways is estimated at between 50,000–115,000 tonnes per year, with a present catch of 6000–8000 tonnes.

Geological resources

Geologically, the country can be divided up into three distinct areas:

- the Old Massif;
- a Continental Crust;
- the Coastal Sediment Belt.

The Old Massif includes the Pre-Cambrian Complex, the Western Congolese System and outcrops of Volcanic Rock. The Continental Crust covers nearly half of the country and includes Karroo sediments and thick aeolian sand deposits from the Kalahari. The Coastal Sediment Belt covers five different marine sediment basins (Figure 1.4).

Up to now there has been no systematic evaluation of the geological resources of the country. The updating of the geological maps stopped because of the war. The last geological research undertaken by the government took place between 1978 and 1984 but this was insufficient to update the data surveyed during the colonial period. The geological potential of the country is therefore unknown and information is reduced to optimistic observations about possible reserves.

The exploitation of diamonds in the Luanda region began in 1920 but no complete survey including estimates of future potential reserves has ever been undertaken.

Mining and geological legislation (Law No.5 of 27 April 1979) includes an indemnity clause for damage caused by mining activities. Unfortunately there are no proper regulations to ensure its practical implementation and the authorities do not have the means to enforce or control mining activity.

Wildlife and biological diversity

Although no data are available and no surveys have been undertaken for a considerable period, the official position is that no large-scale destruction of natural habitats has occurred. Even so, there are a number of animal and plant species which are in urgent need of protection. These include the sable antelope (*Hippotagus niger variani*), the hippopotamus (*Hippopotamus amphibius*), the elephant (*Loxodonta africana*), the mountain zebra (*Equus zebra hartmann*) and the desert plant welwitschia (*Welwitschia mirabilis*). Regrettably, the government services which used to monitor and control these species and their habitats are no longer operational.

The large-scale commercial exploitation of valuable timber in the tropical forests of Cabinda has had a severe impact on the habitat and the future survival of primates such as the gorilla (*Gorilla gorilla*) and the chimpanzee (*Pan troglodytes*).

National Parks and Reserves

Six National Parks, and a number of smaller Nature Reserves covering a total area of less than 6 per cent of the national territory, have been officially designated. The national parks are, from north to south, Quissama (south of Luanda), Kangandala, Kameia, Bikuar, Mupa and Iona (south of Namibe). There is also a controlled hunting area (*coutada*) in Cuando-Cubango, in the south-eastern tip of the country (Figure 1.6).

They were established in the colonial period (Table 1.7). These parks and reserves did not command a high priority in colonial government thinking, and none met international standards. The country's fauna was mainly valued for hunting purposes.

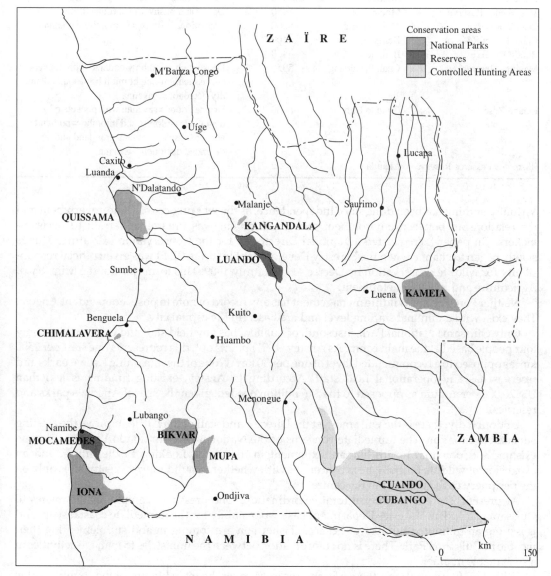

Figure 1.6 *Conservation areas*

Table 1.7 *National Parks and Reserves in Angola*

Name	Province	Area (km²)	
Quissama, N.P.	Bengo	9500	Dry coastal savanna, arid coastal thicket and dense medium-height miombo woodland
Kangandala N.P.	Malange	630	Transitional rainforest, miombo woodland
Bikuar N.P.	Huila	7900	Dense medium-height miombo woodland
Mupa N.P.	Cuene	6600	Dry deciduous woodland
Iona N.P.	Mocamedes	15150	Desert and bushy arid shrubland
Kameia N.P.	Moxico	14450	Dry deciduous woodland grassland
Mocamedes Reserve	Mocamedes	4450	Desert and bushy arid shrubland
Luando Reserve	Malange/Bié	8280	Transitional rainforest, miombo woodland
Chimalavera Reserve	Benguela	100	
Bufalo Reserve	Benguela	400	
Mavinga Reserve	Cuando Cubango	5950	Dense high miombo woodland with pockets of dense medium-height miombo woodland and dry deciduous savanna
Luiana Reserve	Cuando Cubango	8400	Dry deciduous savanna with pockets of degraded rainforest and miombo woodland and 'chanas da borracha' grassland and degraded deciduous savanna
Ilhere dos Passaros Reserve	Luanda	2	

Virtually nothing has been done since Independence, as the war preoccupied the government and the relationship between environment and development was unfamiliar terrain to decision-makers. On paper there existed a National Directorate for the Conservation of Nature. Things slowly began to change when the Forestry Development Institute (IDF) was given official responsibility for wildlife conservation by Decree 41/89 of July 1989. This forms part of the Ministry of Agriculture and Rural Development.

Neither Forestry nor Wildlife management has any record of note in post-independent Angola. They exist with a minimal staffing level and are based in the capital city.

Only Quissama National Park, just south of Luanda, has any field staff and even so this is only four people based at the main camp. As Anstey (1991) points out, this represents one staff per 2500 km² as opposed to a recommended level of one per 30 km². None of the remaining twelve parks and reserves has any operational field staff. According to Anstey, existing funding is less than US$20,000 per annum as opposed to the $16 million needed, given the size of Angola's parks and reserves.

Undoubtedly, there is the will amongst the Director and staff of the IDF to improve the existing lamentable situation. The immediate concerns of the National Director, Paulo Vicente, focus on existing and potential future human settlement in the parks. Looking to the future, and an expansion of wildlife tourism, he is concerned with whether to build tourist/visitor sites only on the periphery of the parks or in the centre.

At present, there is no intersectoral co-ordination. One pressing example of this relates to Quissama Park. The Fisheries Department has responsibility for the immediate coastal strip, and is issuing an unlimited number of licences. Fishermen are coming in and supplementing their income in Quissama Park. There is no co-ordination between the ministries to manage activities in a sustainable manner.

With very few exceptions, the parks and reserves cover the main biomes of the country. Table

1.7 provides a summary of the protected areas of the country, their location, area and biomass classification according to the SADC Biomass Assessment exercise. Angola is still without a park or reserve in the tropical forest/tropical savanna zone in the north of Angola, in the lowland tropical forest of Cabinda, and in the rare escarpment and montain forests of west-central Angola. It is a measure of the lack of a clear understanding of the environmental situation in the country that in the far south-east of Angola there is a clear discrepancy between the huge territory marked as a 'controlled hunting area' in the Angolan National Report to the 1992 UNCED Conference, and the area delineated as a 'national reserve' in the Anstey report. Furthermore, the UNCED report claims only 4 per cent of the national territory as parks and reserves, whereas Anstey gives a figure of 6 per cent. The Angolan UNCED report is brutally frank in its admission that all of these zones are completely abandoned by the Angolan government, with absolutely no control being exercised over the hunting of animals, the burning of forests, and human settlements in prohibited areas.

Here indeed is the crux of the problem. In the current free-for-all, unless some proper mechanisms are rapidly established, the recuperation of the parks and reserves will prove most difficult.

Energy resources

Apart from oil resources considerable potential for generating hydroelectric power exists. The coal reserves stretching along the whole length of the coast could be another rich source of energy. Again, very little has been done to determine the real economic potential of resources outside the oil sector.

Electricity production has increased slightly over the past decade – up to 886,000 Mwh in 1989 – a considerable amount of it being used for household purposes.

Table 1.8 *Summary of household energy consumption, 1980*

Form of Energy	Units	1980 actual household consumption	
		Urban	Rural
Electricity	GWh	120	None
LPG	Tonnes	13730	None
Kerosene	Cubic Metres	8560	17160
Charcoal	Tonnes	154400	neg.
Fuelwood	Tonnes	neg.	3 100 000

The institutional context for resource management

An institutional framework for effective environmental and resource management still has to be developed in Angola. Before and since Independence, the issues of environmental management remained the sole responsibility of government although a few individuals belonging to these departments have participated in different international conferences on environmental management.

Within the framework of the National Commission for Unesco (CNU) an environmental working group for the programme (MAB) 'Man and the Biosphere', has been started. Its recommendations, combined in a project proposal for environmental regulations, have been submitted to the head of the National Commission.

The CNU has the task of co-ordinating the implementation of the scientific research which should form the basis for establishing effective methods of environmental management. The CNU is officially also in charge of preparing the necessary information and keeping government bodies informed on environmental issues.

Within the government, the National Directorate of New and Renewable Resources (DNRFE) within the previous Ministry of Energy and Petroleum and the National Directorate for the Conservation of Nature (DNACO) linked to the Ministry of Agriculture, have been most active during the last decade in promoting environmental issues, the use of alternative energy sources in urban areas and investigating possible alternative forms of environmental management.

These departments collaborated quite extensively on projects such as the testing of photovoltaic waterpumps for urban areas, anti-desertification measures around the town of Namibe, improved stoves and tree planting days. Most of these small projects did little to alleviate the tremendous pressure on natural resources but they showed the eagerness of a few dedicated professionals to try to influence the thinking on environmental issues within government circles. On 31 January 1987, Angola celebrated its first 'Day of the Environment'.

The laws and regulations passed by the colonial government had as a principal aim the provision of a legal basis for protection, supervision and control. Their implementation, even after Independence, has been very much in line with colonial practices of the control and policing of state and privately-owned resources. The protection of the environment was undertaken by guards trained to implement the existing regulations. The methods utilised were very much top-down and did not seek either popular participation or community involvement. Attempts by the population to gain access to these resources are still very much considered as a nuisance by the authorities. Not surprisingly, the results of this form of management have often been very disappointing.

Non-governmental organisations are still in their infancy but are likely to expand within the context of the increased democratisation currently being promoted by western aid donors. Church organisations are likely to play an important role in this, but others, such as ADRA (Acçao par o Desenvolvimento Rural e Meio Ambiente), have been set up to deal explicitly with environmental issues.

Within the educational system, environment-related subjects are taught at university level only. The educational system as a whole faces serious problems and hardly any educational materials are available to teach the subject in primary and secondary schools. Research and environment-related projects have been undertaken by a number of government institutions:

- The Centre for Scientific Investigation (CNIC) and faculties of the Agostinho Neto University have done research on the quantity of toxic metals in water (CNIC/Faculty of Sciences), the quality and pollution of watercourses (CNIC), the toxicity of pesticides used in Angola (CNIC), studies on the country's flora (CNIC), the protection of marine tortoises (Faculty of Science), public health issues in Luanda (CNIC/Faculty of Medicine) and infectious diseases in some schools in Luanda (Faculty of Medicine). The CNIC has also continued the work of the Colonial Institute for Scientific Research, by continuing its work on the possibilities of the protection of some endangered animal and plant species;
- The Institute of Forest Development in continuing the work of the National Directorate for the Conservation of Nature (DNACO) is oriented towards project and experimental work to halt desertification and deforestation, the rehabilitation of the Quissama National Park, aqua-culture, seed production, apiculture, the production of woodfuel and the promotion of fishing in inland waters;

- The National Institute for Marine Research has a number of departments undertaking research in marine biology. Assisted by FAO, the Norwegian Government (NORAD) and the Swedish government (SIDA), the institute has made studies on the commercial potential of certain marine species, the refurbishing of laboratories and has undertaken oceanographic data collection;
- The National Institute of Geology is preparing a new geology map of Angola (1:1,000,000) and its mineral resources.

Recently, two NGOs have been formed: the Angolan Environment Association (AAA) and Angolan Ecological Youth. The latter is very interesting and has already had a visible impact on certain parts of the capital city, Luanda, being actively involved in tree planting along the streets of the city and along narrow central reservations. There is also an Angolan Political Ecology Party. It is still early days to assess the educative effects of these groups, but close attention should be paid to their future development.

The consensus is that a very high priority is to strengthen environmental education at the formal and at the informal levels. There exists a FINNIDA-funded SADC project (6.09), to establish a forestry training institute in Angola. It will be based in Dalatando in Cuanza Norte province, as some infrastructure already exists there. Unesco will participate in a project to begin strengthening environmental education. There is no doubt that environmental education should be a top priority and donor support will be required to this end.

The National Physical Planning Institute is directly concerned with improving the quality of urban life, especially housing, community services, infrastructure networks, as well as being responsible for town planning (Angola UNCED Report, 1992).

With UN help, studies are being made to restructure peripheral township areas and create new housing areas to move people from damaged and deteriorated buildings in the town centre so that these can be refurbished. In Luanda, 1432 low-cost homes are to be built, in an area that can later be expanded for up to 4000 houses. The area will be developed in phases and will allow people to self-build their own homes if they so wish. Town planning and construction will provide basic land clearing, landscaping and paved roads as well as drainage channels, stand-pipe drinking water, and street lighting.

The Department of New and Renewable Energy Sources in the former Ministry of Energy and Oil, has carried out a few projects to set up associations of charcoal producers to make the best possible use of their energy resources. It has also installed some alternative energy equipment to drive water pumps.

Other institutions concerned with environmental matters are the Agricultural Research Institute, the Veterinary Research Institute, both dating from colonial times, the National Public Health Institute and the National Institute of Hydrometeorology and Geophysics, set up in 1979.

A number of construction activities have been carried out by technical commissions directly linked to environmental problems. After a period of very heavy rainfall in 1984, an inspection team was set up to make a detailed study of short- and medium-term measures to deal with the quantities of sand and soil washed into Luanda's drainage system. The group presented a plan for future action in Luanda. In 1985 a technical committee was set up with Luanda City Council, including representatives from different building departments, to act as a consultative body for basic sanitation programmes in Luanda. Several environmental programmes were prepared, including:

- 7 projects to provide basic water and waste drainage for the city;
- a project for a third water-supply network for Luanda, approved in 1986;
- an overall waste-disposal plan for Luanda, in the form of a phased programme to deal with this serious pollution hazard.

Building departments were responsible for a number of activities in different provinces to provide people with a water supply. Several projects were prepared in provincial capitals. With the help of Unicef a number of water wells were drilled in rural areas.

Studies were made in Luanda to prevent soil erosion of the principal sandy hills on which the city is built. Others were made of coastal erosion resulting from building projects done without any previous environmental studies. Engineering works were carried out by the Hidroportos company, in association with a Dutch firm, to protect the ports of Luanda, Lobito and Namibe.

STRATEGIES AND SOLUTIONS FOR SUSTAINABLE DEVELOPMENT

Sustainable development has become a key concept in recent years. Its use has been adapted to suit the different perceptions of development agencies and national governments. The goals of sustainable development have therefore been defined in accordance with the constraints imposed by war.

A sustainable form of development will have to consider three important issues:

- The form and content of economic development should be adjusted in accordance with social needs and ecological capacity. It is clear that the resulting affluence or poverty, and the form of economic development have an impact on the quality and continuity, degradation or renovation, of the natural resources. Under a new political ideology, the economy will be liberalised. With the de-nationalisation of the economy the future beneficiaries of economic activity are to be found on four different levels: international, national, individual (smaller private enterprises) and the local (community) level. The role of managing the economy at the macro-level will be to balance the interests of these beneficiaries against the social needs of the majority of the population while avoiding the degradation of the natural resources to which all want to gain access. Differential access and the degradation of these natural assets can often result in (violent) conflicts within and between the different interest groups.
- The need to differentiate between social and ecological sustainability. In Angola, the preoccupation with economic and political survival has shifted the economy towards the exploitation of oil without much consideration for the management of other resources. The distribution of the results of production throughout society, the need to maintain the war effort and the results of this war have moved many thousands of people towards the brink of survival. Because of this, they are forced to make short-term decisions which affect their immediate environment and the quality of the resources available to them in the long term.
- To ensure that the available natural resources are managed in an effective and appropriate way. With the development of the nation state, the tendency has been to shift resource management away from the local community towards centralised bureaucracy. This was done because the results of the exploitation of these natural assets accrued to a higher level; either to private enterprise, directly to government, or to multinationals. Resource management can only be effective, and development can only be sustainable, if it involves those who will receive the benefit of their long-term maintenance and renewal. Resource management should therefore also involve those at the community level whose formal or informal institutions have gradually been further divorced from the maintenance of the assets on which their survival depends.

The institutional challenge for environmental management

The above three issues – the form of economic development, social versus ecological sustainability, and the form of resource management – pose a tremendous institutional challenge to the country.

In the long term, the following institutions should form the foundation for the protection of the environment and for the rational use of natural resources (Angola, UNCED Report, 1992):

- a technical institute specialising in environmental matters, concerned with basic and applied research on the environment and the exploitation of natural resources;
- a government institution responsible for defining environmental policy and co-ordinating the work of all organisations concerned with the protection of the environment and rational use of natural resources for sustainable development.
- there should be specialised environment departments in all ministries and companies whose activities would have a great effect on the state of the environment;
- citizens' associations and non-government organisations concerned with the environment which could guarantee active participation by ordinary people in defining and carrying out environmental policies and education; and
- an administration for national parks, reserves and protected areas, and for the enforcement of environmental legislation.

Considering the interdisciplinary and all-embracing nature of environmental matters and the need to include people from all walks of life, government departments, non-governmental bodies, company unions, etc., a National Environment Council should be set up, amongst other things, to periodically prepare reports on the state of the environment for international institutions. This Council could be set up from the Interministerial Technical Commission that prepared the Angolan UNCED report.

Taking into account real conditions and immediate priorities, the institutions proposed above can only be put into practice slowly. So, in the short term, the Angolan government should begin by:

- setting up a national organisation to co-ordinate the rational use of natural resources and the protection of the environment. In different ministerial areas there should be control of, and research into activities that interfere with the balance of nature;
- the urgent promotion of an environment education campaign, both formal and informal, that should be continued over an indefinite period of time;
- publishing laws and regulations concerning economic and social activities that have repercussions on the balance of nature; and
- organising and promoting professional courses for appropriate personnel needed to protect and control the exploitation of natural resources.

To implement these proposals it is suggested that:

1. A high-level government department should be set up (perhaps to be the national department for the environment and natural resources) with the following general functions:

   - to study and comment on all economic and social activities that have implications for the balance of nature and the use of natural resources;

- to study and propose appropriate legislation for the protection of the environment and natural resources; and
- to be responsible for the management of specially protected areas, nature reserves and national parks.

A Preparatory Commission should be set up immediately to oversee the creation of this government department, to prepare the conditions essential for its functioning, and carefully study which institutional structures will be required in the long term to define and carry out environmental policies.

The Preparatory Commission, as well as the future government department, should work at first within the Ministry of Planning and be directly responsible to the Minister. However, in view of government restructuring, consideration should also be given to the idea of the commission becoming a relatively autonomous body, directly responsible to the head of state.

2. Environment offices should be set up in all ministries, state secretariats and private companies whose activities have implications for the environment and/or who exploit natural resources. All these offices should be functionally linked to the national environment and natural resources commission.

3. Scientific projects begun by the National MAB Committee should be reinforced. A section of the Institute for Research and Development in Education (INIDE) could be set up to prepare programmes, text, atlases, films and other materials on environmental matters.

4. An education campaign on the environment should be promoted using all available resources in the country, ministries, private companies, NGOs, schools and mass media. It should be coordinated by a national commission with the support of a secretariat provided by the Ministry of Education.

5. The new environmental laws and regulations to be published should be based on those used in countries more advanced in environmental matters, but not forgetting that Angola is a tropical country with its own social and ecological characteristics.

International help will be needed to implement the proposals made in points 1 and 2, especially for the following:

- Large-scale investment in university education to train graduate personnel to carry out scientific research activities, to teach and work in the different areas of sustainable development.
- Technical, scientific and financial help will be needed to set up research programmes at different levels, so as to find out the country's true environmental and natural reserve potential. This is essential for viable planning and use of the country's reserves.
- Immediate support from the government in preparing legislation to protect the environment and the country's natural reserves for sustainable development.
- Technical and financial assistance to set up an efficient and objective environment education programme, that should start with a refresher course for teachers from primary to university level.
- Promotion of seminars, workshops, talks, and short courses for professionals, young people and the general public on general and specific subjects related to the environment. These activities could be integrated into an environment education campaign, but they do not have to wait for this to be organised, as it will require the preparation of a curriculum, the training of staff and the integration in the country's education system.

- Translations into Portuguese of all the documents published by the UN on environmental and related issues. Language has been a serious barrier to Angola joining the world movement for the conservation and protection of nature.
- Technical assistance in preparing lists of suitable areas for nature reserves and national parks, in the framework of the Heritage Fund for Unesco member states.

So far as the matters raised in this section are concerned, the following recommendations are proposed for immediate action:

1. The recently set up State Secretariat for Geology and Mines should vigorously pursue its functions in controlling mining activities. It should revise the Law on Geological and Mining Activities and prepare such regulations and measures as may be necessary to force national and foreign mining companies to minimise damage caused by the exploitation of mineral resources.

2. The Geological Survey of Angola (ex-National Institute of Geology) and the National Mines Department (both part of the new State Secretariat for Geology and Mines) should have qualified staff to deal with matters relating to the protection of the environment, so that they can ensure that companies abide by the laws and regulations in this area.

3. Former transhumance corridors should be re-opened, watering places repaired and land-mines cleared, so that cattle farmers from the south and agricultural farmers from central Angola can avoid the over-utilisation of traditional pasture land for cereal and vegetable farming.

4. Large areas of forest should be planted as soon as possible to meet the local demand for wood and charcoal, and save the natural forests. (At the moment it is impossible to avoid the use of this type of fuel.)

5. Data should be collected on coastal fishing reserves so that a development strategy can be prepared for this area, including restrictions on industrial fishing, research programmes, training, extension and various forms of credit. More efficient research is needed, based on the use of production models and more exact analytical models, using detailed descriptions of stock. Greater co-operation between SADC countries such as Angola and Namibia, would be useful to improve the management of common reserves.

6. Efforts should be made to begin the inspection and control of fishing activities, including the use of land, sea and air control. Subsystems should be integrated and linked with the fishing information. This project is awaiting approval for EEC support.

7. Small-scale fishing should be promoted rather than industrial fishing, as it requires less investment, lower technological levels and interferes less with the environmental balance. It thus guarantees long-term fishing, without detriment to future organisations.

8. Angola, having signed the Rights of the Sea Convention, should review its position in relation to the Convention, because in the event of an oil catastrophe along the coast, both fishing and any future tourism would be badly affected. Fishing laws should be revised and adapted to the country's present reality, so as to preserve fishing reserves. Angola must organise and control its own Exclusive Economic Zone, or it will lose its fishing resources and have to import fish.

9. Concerning deep-sea, as well as other oil wells, a serious study should be made of marine environmental effects before any activity is undertaken.

10. The University should forge closer links between teaching and research on the protection of the environment and the management of natural resources. The Medical Faculty should concern itself more with the promotion of the quality of life, and public health

should play a central role in the redefinition of the institutional and educational objectives of the Faculty. There should be a greater development of areas such as epidemiology, microbiology, ecology and town planning. In the Science Faculty the Departments of Geology, Geophysics and Cartography should introduce modern techniques of long distance control, meterological analysis and satellite communication. The Chemistry course should find appropriate techniques to analyse toxic substances. As a whole, the University should begin to look at the possibility of multidisciplinary teaching and research on the environment.

11.   Specialised training, linked to research of the most important environmental problems, such as the protection of rural areas, and the management of natural, agricultural and water resources, are all needed. Graduates' scientific level must be raised, because only with sound training will they be able to overcome the many difficulties they will face.

12.   Work should begin on preparing a national map of areas at risk from erosion so that an evaluation can be made of this serious environmental problem.

13.   Pollution problems that should be considered as a priority are: the emission of carbon dioxide from oil rigs from the burning of gas or oil; carbon dioxide emissions from vehicles; industrial smoke; the dumping of chemicals in the sea and in rivers; the noise from aeroplanes, generators, trains, vehicles and domestic motors. The objective is to introduce the principle of pollution fines, encouraging a reduction in pollution and providing permanent funds to help solve environmental problems, pay for research, surveys, training, information and management of natural resources and the protection of the environment.

14.   Areas subject to special protection (nature reserves and national parks) should be enlarged, and a detailed study made of areas and regions to be conserved. This work should be complemented with inventories and studies of natural resources of flora and fauna.

15.   Hunting should be reorganised; laws should be published and regulations brought up to date. A competent staff should be trained and a network of game wardens set up.

These recommendations, that should be acted upon immediately, do not include all the measures that should be taken to avoid serious environmental problems. But they are the ones that stand out amongst a host of problems that have appeared and it is necessary to act selectively and decide on the country's priorities carefully.

In relation to mining and other industrial activities attention should be focused on:

- investigating the impact of industrial production and mining, especially diamond mining, on coastal and inland water resources. Draft legislation and control measures to reduce and minimise their impact in the future need to be considered;
- giving attention to the impact of oil exploitation and refining on marine resources and the coastal environment;
- introducing measures to avoid the illegal dumping of toxic waste on Angolan territory;
- giving special attention to the protection and maintenance of areas of sub- tropical forests which have been heavily exploited over the last decades. This should include a more effective management of specific and vulnerable ecosystems.

To maintain the country's *biological diversity* and potential *tourism* resources:

- a survey should be undertaken to establish the state of the country's national parks and areas of special scientific interest. The survey should be used as a basis for drawing up a new management plan specifying the management, the use and the development potential of these resources.

CONCLUSION

There are very few studies or reports on the state of the environment in Angola. Those that exist concentrate on the state of environmental health in the urban areas because these issues are best known to the authorities.

On the whole the environment is not showing severe signs of degradation except in specific areas. One can talk of localised environmental problems. These include areas with a high population density, areas affected by oil and diamond exploitation and possibly the damage done to some of the marine resources through over-exploitation.

The concentration of the population in 'safer' areas has primarily been caused by the war but is not likely to disappear with the cessation of hostilities. It is very unlikely that a large-scale voluntary resettlement in the rural areas is going to take place. The impact of population pressure on urban and peri-urban areas will therefore have to be tackled with some urgency. As a result of the war, large areas of the rural hinterland are recuperating because of the collapse of the economy. However, the uncontrolled cutting of precious hardwoods and illegal hunting might have depleted some forest and animal species.

The impact of industrial production and mining on the environment is localised. Data on resource management are extremely scarce and mostly collected during the colonial period. Not surprisingly, Angolan institutions are weak and lack the capacity to design and implement environmental programmes. Environmental management is still very much practised as during the colonial period. The policing of, and the restriction of access to, resources is the main policy thrust. The government, and the statutory bodies implementing these measures, are therefore in continuous conflict with the local population. The biggest challenge is therefore institutional. The knowledge of the state of Angola's resources has to be updated. Management needs have to be prioritised, and the capacity to design and implement effective management systems developed.

These tasks should not be seen as purely a matter for the government. It will also be necessary to draw in available knowledge and experience from different organisations in civil society, and, wherever possible, engage enterprises and producers directly in environmental management.

REFERENCES

Angola *UNCED National Report*, (1992)
Anstey, S G (1991) *Elephant Conservation Plan, Angola* Instituto de Desenvolvimento Florestal, Luanda and AECCG, Oxford, UK
Munslow, B (1992) *Angola Environmental Profile* Desk Study for IUCN-Angola Programming Mission, The World Conservation Union, Regional Office for Southern Africa

2

BOTSWANA

INTRODUCTION

Botswana is a land-locked country with an area of some 576,000 km² and a mean altitude of 1000m, in the centre of southern Africa. One-third of the country in the east comprises an undulating plain with upstanding hill massifs developed on ancient precambrian rocks, commonly termed the hardveld, whilst the remaining two-thirds is covered by sediments of the Kalahari Group, mostly Kalahari Sand. This area is termed the sandveld.

The climate of the country is semi-arid, with a summer rainfall regime (October–March) varying in amount from 250 mm per annum in the south-west, to in excess of 600 mm per annum in the north (Figure 2.1) There is high temporal and spatial variability both between wet seasons, and within the summer rainfall months themselves. This variability is of critical importance to human use of the environment, a factor recognised in the national motto: 'pula' (rain). Drought is endemic. Temperatures are typical of a continental climate with high diurnal and seasonal ranges. Temperatures drop below freezing in southern and central parts of the country in June and July, but may exceed 40°C during the summer months. There may be in excess of 3250 hours of sunshine annually, with up to 6 KWh/m² of solar insolation received daily. Evapotranspiration may reach 2000 mm per annum, exceeding precipitation by a factor of four or more. This factor is critical to the maintenance of natural and agricultural vegetation systems.

Surfacewater resources are limited. Perennial rivers occur only in the north of the country, and include the Okavango, Kwando/Linyanti/Chobe, and a small frontage on the Zambezi. Only the Okavango Delta lies wholly within Botswana's territory. In the hardveld, drainage consists of a number of large ephemeral sand rivers draining to the Limpopo, itself a seasonal stream. Despite their erratic flow the sand rivers have important reserves of groundwater stored within their beds. Over most of the sandveld surface drainage is limited to pans and dry valleys (*mekgacha*). Groundwater is an important component in development, and it is estimated that approximately 80 per cent of the human and animal populations are dependent on this source. Groundwater is variable in depth, quality and yield throughout the country, but the main aquifers utilised are those in sand rivers, limestone outcrops and, on a larger scale, the Karoo strata underlying the Kalahari Group sediments.

Soils are poor throughout the country. In the sandveld they are mostly arenosols of poor water retention capacity developed from the Kalahari Sand, although some areas of clay-rich lacustrine soil exist. In the hardveld, highly-leached ferruginous tropical soils are developed mostly from granitic rocks. Again, fertility is low, but the soils at least are workable. Land with arable potential has limited distribution, and is prone to erosion under present climatic conditions.

Vegetation is dominated by deciduous shrub savanna, mostly *Acacia* spp., with scattered trees and perennial grasses. This grades into mopane (*Colophospermum mopane*) in the north, and mixed woodland in the north-east. Other important vegetation groups include the wetlands and riparian woodlands of the Okavango and Chobe Rivers, and the grasslands of the Makgadikgadi and Mababe fossil lake beds.

Wildlife forms an important resource in the central, western and northern parts of the country, both for tourism and hunting. Habitats were much reduced by hunting in the nineteenth century, and most large concentrations of game now occur in national parks and game reserves. Ten per cent of Africa's elephants are now found in Chobe National Park.

The population of Botswana now stands at approximately 1.3 million (Central Statistical Office, 1989), giving the country the third-lowest population density in the world of 2.3 per km². The population is unevenly distributed, with the bulk occurring in the hardveld, particularly in settlements close to the Francistown–Gaborone rail line. Areas of uninhabited land still exist in the sandveld where water resources are not available. However, the population is increasing rapidly at a rate of 3.3 per cent per annum and, although 75 per cent are still living in rural areas, it is becoming increasingly urbanised. The provision of education and employment for the burgeoning population, 50 per cent of which is under the age of 16, places considerable strain on the infrastructure of the country.

The country has a long history of settlement extending back into the Palaeolithic Age (with the development of a cattle-based economy as far back as 200 AD). However, the majority group, the Batswana, arrived in the region in a series of migrations between the seventeenth and early nineteenth centuries, pushing earlier inhabitants, such as the Basarwa and Bakgalagadi, westwards into the sandveld. This colonisation of essentially marginal land was cemented in the late nineteenth century by the development of strong political structures. Despite the presence of minority groups the population is relatively homogeneous, a factor adding to political stability.

Most of the population is engaged in pastoralism and agriculture. Arable agriculture depends on extensive rain-fed cultivation of sorghum, millet and pulses, although some natural irrigation (*molapo* farming) is practised on flood plains in the north. Yields are low, highly variable from year to year, and rainfall dependent. Commercial intensive agriculture is practised in eastern Botswana, but has limited potential.

The grazing of cattle and, to a lesser extent, sheep and goats, is a major occupation, with the cattle population now numbering some 2.5 million. Cattle numbers have increased rapidly since the beginning of the century with the provision of boreholes and watering points in hitherto inaccessible areas, particularly in the sandveld. Recent incentives, such as the provision of assured markets and veterinary services have encouraged this trend. Serious environmental degradation in the rangelands has been noted in the past two decades, particularly in times of drought, and continues to be a matter of concern for the government.

Rapid economic growth has been experienced since Independence; recent annual figures are 10.6 per cent (1987), 8.1 per cent (1988), 13.1 per cent (1989) and 8.7 per cent for 1990. In 1989 the trade surplus reached US$813 million, and foreign exchange reserves in excess of US$5 billion. This growth is based upon the exploitation of mineral resources. Diamonds were discovered in 1967, and accounted for 80 per cent of total mineral value in 1989. In that year Botswana produced 15.2 million carats from three open-cast mines, some 21 per cent of world output. Other minerals exploited include coal at Morupule and copper-nickel at Selebi-Phikwe. A soda ash plant has been constructed at Sua Pan. The plant aims to produce 300,000 tonnes of soda ash (sodium carbonate) and 650,000 tones of table salt (sodium chloride) per year, sufficient to meet the southern African demand, from a resource which is estimated to be unlimited. Smaller sectors of the economy which are expanding rapidly, include tourism and manufacturing industry.

Although rapid economic growth has brought higher per capita incomes, wealth is concentrated in few hands, and demographic growth exceeds the rate of job creation. The greater part of the population is still dependent on the land for sustenance. Increasing pressure on these resources is being experienced, and deterioration of the resource base occurs, particularly in times of drought. The traditional beliefs in the value of large families, large herds of cattle and unlimited availability of land still dominate in both rural and urban areas.

Despite the incorporation of sustainable development into the nation's objectives, initial post-independence emphasis was placed on the rapid development of available resources to provide capital. In particular, growth was based on newly-found mineral resources and the cattle industry. The latter was based on many of the perceptions developed during the decades of Protectorate status, particularly the idea that the country was an inexhaustible reservoir of good grazing land, to be utilised by the provision of watering points and improved veterinary services, and the eradication of pests and diseases such as tsetse fly and foot and mouth disease. The impetus developed during the colonial era, which in retrospect appeared to be mostly aimed at balancing the books of the impoverished Protectorate, was maintained after Independence by investment from the European Economic Community.

With the drought of the 1960s came the increasing realisation that land degradation resulting from overgrazing was widespread. The government took a number of steps to obtain better data on both farming and livestock raising, and implemented schemes to improve these sectors, including the Livestock Development Policy (LDP1&2) the Tribal Grazing Lands Policy (TGLP), the Arable Lands Development Programme (ALDEP), and the Accelerated Rainfed Agriculture Programme (ARSAP). The livestock projects were unsuccessful, largely because cattle owners were reluctant to adopt modern ranching methods and the new 'empty' lands (i.e. those without any occupation or land use whatsoever) in the sandveld were not as empty as previously supposed. Furthermore, the implementation of the agricultural projects coincided with the onset of a further major drought in the 1980s. At least the government did become aware that environmental problems existed, and that conflicts in land use, particularly between the cattle industry and wildlife resources were becoming acute. These issues were publicly debated at the Botswana Society's 'Symposium on Drought' in 1978, one of many such symposia which discussed key environmental issues.

The report of the United Nations Environment Programme (UNEP) Clearing-House Technical Mission to Botswana in 1983 led to further government-sponsored public debate on the management of Botswana's environment (Botswana Society 1984, 1986), and the first steps towards the formulation of a National Conservation Strategy (NCS). This important document was seven years in gestation, and was presented to Cabinet in 1990. In the meantime, the commitment of the Government to sustainable development through environmental conservation was summarised in the 1989 Budget Speech, by the Vice-President of Botswana, the Hon.P.S. Mmusi:

> Concerning the environment, it is vital that our development be sustainable. Botswana has only a finite quantity of groundwater, grazing land and forests. If we use up these resources faster than nature can replenish them, production that relies on them will be lower in future years, lowering the standard of living of our sons and daughters.

Botswana has many advantages in trying to implement policies of sustainable development. The rate of economic growth is high, and will continue to remain so for the foreseeable future. The population is relatively small, and the commitment of the Government to democratic principles and free speech makes it the envy of many developing and developed countries. Although environmental damage is occurring, it is not yet irreparable, nor are the pressures on resources uncontainable.

However, there are a number of warning signs. The population growth rate is extremely high, and is not being matched by job creation despite the rapid diversification of the economy. In short, economic development has done little to benefit the rural poor, who are increasing in numbers and placing increasing stress on a fragile environment. An example of this is the availability of arable land, which dropped from 0.6 ha/person in 1940 to 0.3 ha/person in 1981, and was almost non-existent during the drought of the mid-1980s (Arntzen and Veenendaal, 1986).

Meanwhile, the ownership and management of cattle, together with their impact on the environment and alternative land uses, continue to be the most contentious issue. Although pastoralism is a traditional pursuit, an increasing proportion of the national herd is owned by a decreasing proportion of the population. It is currently estimated that 45 per cent of rural households in Botswana own no cattle (Arntzen and Veenendaal, 1986) and that 60 per cent of all cattle are owned by 5 per cent of the population (Yeager, 1989). Yeager also points out that democratically-elected politicians tend to serve the interests of those with power, a major obstacle to change within the cattle industry. There are indications that the National Conservation Strategy has not fully addressed the problems of environmental management arising from the inequitable distribution of the national herd.

We suggest the main priorities in sustainable development must be directed towards this end, and may be summarised as:

- Reduction in population growth rates and the drift to urban centres;
- Diversification and improvement of agriculture;
- Attaining sustainability and equitability within the cattle industry;
- Provision of rural employment through the utilisation of other resources, such as wildlife;
- Expansion of the industrial base together with the implementation of strict pollution legislation;
- The raising of levels of environmental awareness through education;
- Regional co-operation in the utilisation of common resources, such as water.

RESOURCE-USE CONFLICTS

This section examines the dynamics of Botswana's population increase, and considers some of the resource-use conflicts that arise from it.

In Botswana the history of census-taking dates back to 1904. However, the reliability of census results prior to 1964 is seriously in doubt, owing to inadequate coverage and delays in publication. Since then, enumeration has been carried out on a house to house basis. The census results are shown in Table 2.1.

Table 2.1 *Population census returns 1904–1981*

Census year	Population
1904	120 776
1911	124 350
1921	152 982
1936	265 756
1946	296 310
1956	309 175
1964	549 510
1971	596 994
1981	941 027

Adapted from CSO, 1983:10

Based on the average intercensal growth between 1971 and 1981, of 4.7 per cent per annum, it is clear that Botswana's population growth rate is very high. Recent estimates (CSO, 1989) place the present population at 1.3 million.

A number of demographic issues may be highlighted which will affect resource use. Firstly, Botswana has a very youthful population structure. In 1981, some 47 per cent of the population was under 16 years of age. The provision of health care, education and job opportunities for this non-productive sector places a heavy burden on the resources of the state. On reaching adulthood this age cohort will have expectations of owning a household, cattle, a borehole and land, which will increase resource pressures further.

Secondly, with increased demand for resources, conflicts over use will arise. For example, attractive areas for livestock rearing which are designated for other uses may be illegally occupied, a process which has already started. Conflicts will also arise over usufructuary rights in communal areas.

Thirdly, owing to the disparity in the sizes of the Districts, different levels of pressure are experienced. The use of resources such as grazing and dryland farming require the presence of large tracts of land. Smaller districts with large populations, such as the South East and North East Districts have been overstocked for as long as records have been kept (Arntzen and Veenendaal 1986).

Fourthly, as 75 per cent of the country's population lives in rural areas, there is an increasing demand for social services and facilities such as schools, clinics and post offices. Beyond the main rural centres there has been a recent proliferation of small settlements, i.e. those with less than 5000 people. Between 1971 and 1981 the number of these settlements increased from 45 to 206. As such settlements are difficult to provide with services there has been increased urban drift. This has caused a depletion of the agricultural labour force. As a consequence of this, and drought, agricultural production is in decline.

Factors involved in the net population increase are primarily those of persistently high birth rates coupled with reduced mortality levels as a consequence of improved health facilities. The pattern is reinforced by social factors; the long tradition of labour migrating to the mines of South Africa leaves a disproportionate number of females (sex ratio = 100 females:89 males) and female-headed households, together with a belief in the desirability of large families. These social conditions are typical of the 'early expanding' phase of the Demographic Transition Model. Larson (1988) estimated that 17 years after the government introduced a birth control programme only 26 per cent of women in the reproductive age group practised any form of contraception. This finding is corroborated by the studies of Manyeneng *et al.* (1985).

Population predictions are amended frequently in Botswana; recent estimates (Tumkaya, 1987) suggest that the population may reach 3.1 million by the year 2011. The greatest growth will take place in urban areas – the estimate for Gaborone is a population of 250,000 by the year 2000 – but rural increase will also take place, albeit at a slower pace. The projected population densities for some of the eastern districts, such as Kweneng and Kgatleng, suggest rural densities of some 30 persons per km^2 in twenty years time, a figure far beyond the carrying capacity of the land under present practices.

Conflicts over resource use in rural areas are of two types:

- those due to encroachment of one activity into an undesignated zone;
- those due to a scarcity of resources.

Encroachment of land use

The problem of landuse encroachment into undesignated areas has been documented from historical times (Schapera, 1943). Many of the traditional methods used to control this, such as the use of overseers on tribal lands, have now been abandoned.

Most encroachment arises from an expansion of the concentric patterns of arable and pastoral lands around many villages. Mpotokwane (1986) recorded the encroachment of arable lands into grazing areas in the Kgatleng district from sequential aerial photography between 1950 and 1982. He found that there was a 70 per cent increase in arable lands in the first decade, followed by a 400 per cent increase in the subsequent two decades. Overall, an eightfold increase in arable land was recorded in the 32 years, of which 58 per cent was encroachment into grazing land. The result of this process is mixed farming land use where cattle and fields are spatially integrated. This results in overgrazing owing to a reduction in the available grazing area and an increase in livestock damage to crops.

A recent study by the Ministry of Local Government and Lands (MLGL, 1989) of the Makgadikgadi area has highlighted other encroachment problems:

> Cattle crushes have been located in areas of stateland such as national parks, game reserves and forest reserves. It is not clear who authorised their construction and for what reason. The provision of the crushes certainly acknowledges the presence of livestock on stateland, and probably encourages it as well. Arable farming has encroached into the state land, and in one case fields had been officially allocated. This suggests a lack of awareness of designated landuses, or perhaps deliberate flouting of the policy.
>
> Wildlife from the stateland and game reserve moved into the village, destroying crops and killing domestic animals.
>
> The boundary of the game reserve followed the Boteti River. Farmers were utilising the flood plain on the game reserve bank for irrigation (molapo) farming.
>
> Greatest pressure is encountered along the river frontage, where conflict arises between molapo farmers and livestock owners. Livestock tends to destroy crops along the river frontage. Increases in brushwood fencing led to a decrease in river access.

The activities of remote area dwellers (RADs) also create conflicts over land use. The Central Kalahari Game Reserve (CKGR) was set up in 1961 to conserve wildlife and to provide for the hunter-gatherer lifestyle of the Basarwa. Unfortunately, such foraging lifestyles only persist in the absence of other opportunities. In the case of the Central Kalahari Game Reserve, the provision of permanent water from boreholes rapidly led to permanent settlement by remote area dwellers who kept livestock and supplemented their incomes by poaching game by 'non- traditional' methods. One such settlement, at Cade, now supports over 2000 people. This obvious conflict led to a questioning of the role of the status of the Central Kalahari Game Reserve in 1984, a debate which is still continuing despite the publication of a management plan for the reserve. Similar problems with some 5000 squatters in the Ghanzi and Xanagas farms have also been recorded.

Scarcity of natural resources

A scarcity of resources, particularly grazing, is due to excess demand, low primary productivity and fluctuating levels of availability of the resource. The last-named is particularly acute during times of drought.

An issue of great concern throughout the country has been the question of dual grazing rights. This arises from the Tribal Grazing Lands Policy (TGLP) and refers to the situation where a cattle owner has access to communal grazing as a tribesman, as well as to leasehold ranch land. Large cattle owners tend to graze communal land to the point of depletion, to the disadvantage of poor herders, before retreating to the farms, where they have exclusive rights. Whereas Tribal Grazing Land Policy was intended to alleviate overgrazing in communal lands, it has allowed greater freedom of access to grazing resources for those with leasehold land, and an increase in the cattle population.

An environmental management document (Botswana Society, 1984) and a government white paper on land tenure (1985) have recommended that dual rights be abolished. Two problems face the implementation of this decision. Firstly, the intricate social networks of the Batswana, especially the Mafisa system, of cattle loans to relations, allow the transfer of cattle ownership or usufructuary right to beat any proposed controls. Secondly, there is quite simply a lack of political will to implement such a policy, as many politicians are themselves large cattle owners (Yeager, 1989).

The abolition of dual rights would help to reduce the depletion of grazing land by reducing the number of cattle on communal land. It would also encourage commercial ranches to adopt a more responsible attitude towards their farms if substitute grazing were not available elsewhere.

Some of the livestock husbandry methods employed in Botswana have raised conflicts with other resources. The best known is the impact of veterinary cordon fences. Patterson (1987) outlines the historical development of these fences from 1952 to contain future outbreaks of diseases by preventing the movement of cattle. An international outcry against the fences followed the massive decline of wildlife during the 1960s droughts (Owens and Owens, 1980; Williamson and Williamson, 1981). The Sixth National Development Plan acknowledges the inhibiting effect which cordon fences have had on wildlife migratory patterns, alongside factors such as droughts and shortages of water. Yet the same plan envisages an expansion of 'the existing cordon fence system... to provide strict control of movements of cattle and animal products...'.

This contradiction underlines the ambivalence of the government to wildlife resources. Patterson (1987) suggests that in some cases cordon fences have been beneficial (such as the special case of the 'Buffalo Fence' in the Okavango) but that they have mostly had a negative impact. The Wildlife Conservation Policy (1986) envisages the possibility of adjusting sections of fence to reduce these impacts. All that has happened so far is the construction of a new set of fences in the Makgadikgadi Basin.

The poaching of valuable species, such as elephant, rhinoceros and large cats is a serious problem. It is largely carried out by organised gangs operating on an international basis, and has been reported from northern Botswana. Local subsistence poachers concentrate on smaller game for biltong. No statistics are available to measure the scale of the problem.

At present fuelwood nationally accounts for 48 per cent of total energy consumption: in rural areas however, it supplies almost 100 per cent of demand. Demand is increasing rapidly and the present patterns of fuelwood exploitation have two consequences: first, increased harvesting distances, accompanied by higher commodity prices and/or increased time for collection; second, the cutting down of less desired species, accompanied by land degradation. Concentric zones of 'stumpveld' are now found around all major villages.

Fuelwood substitution has not been explored fully, but it is likely to be adopted by more affluent groups. With the exception of the Barolong Farms, the use of cow dung as fuel has not been observed, and would, in any case, be environmentally debatable on the grounds that the cow dung would be better used as manure. Advertising campaigns have promoted the use of Botswana's plentiful coal reserves, but coal is not popular as it cannot be used for cooking. The Rural Industries Innovation Centre, The Botswana Technology Centre and other NGOs have tried to promote alternative sources of energy, such as solar power, wind power, methane gas and fuel-efficient stoves, but their use is not widespread. In the future, the electricity network will be expanded to more villages, but there will still be extensive remote areas of the country where power transmission will be uneconomical.

Water resources for grazing remain a source of conflict. Farmers tend to adopt a flexible attitude towards cattle watering, based on the criteria of reliability, convenience and cost (Arntzen and Veenendaal, 1986). In the summer months free water sources such as pans and rivers are utilised, but in the dry season cattle converge on boreholes, which are utilised not only by the borehole owners, but also by those who buy water from them. Thus, the 8 km radius grazing range controlled by each borehole becomes heavily overstocked and a shortage of pasture becomes the critical factor in maintaining the herd. Many cattle owners see as the solution to the borehole overgrazing problem a reduction in the spacing of boreholes and a greater density of water point provision. A reduction in the number of livestock is not considered an attractive solution.

Turning to resource-use conflicts in urban areas, it needs to be underlined that towns in Botswana have experienced very rapid growth rates. At Independence only Francistown and Lobatse warranted urban status. The new capital at Gaborone, on which construction began before Independence, was initially designed to house a population of 20,000, but now has a population exceeding 120,000, excluding satellite settlements. In addition, towns were constructed at the mining centres of Orapa (1971), Selebi-Phikwe (1973) and Jwaneng (1982). Of these, Orapa, a 'closed' settlement with controlled access, remains tied to the mine, whilst the others have attracted other forms of employment. There was an overall increase in urban population of 10.7 per annum between 1971 and 1981, a rate which continued during the 1980s.

Although there is very little literature available on urban landuse conflicts, it is apparent that many arise from the rate of urban growth, and the population drift from rural areas. Although landuse zoning is carried out by the Department of Town and Regional Planning (DTRP), and an urgent programme of house construction is being carried out by the Botswana Housing Corporation (BHC), there is an acute shortage of housing, particularly in Gaborone.

At the lower end of the economic scale this has led to an influx of squatters to urban centres, where they occupy land designated for other uses, as in the Naledi section of Gaborone. Such land is unserviced, lacking roads, piped water and sewage facilities. Many of the occupants do not have formal employment, and may subsist on an informal street economy, or resort to petty crime (Letsholo, 1987). Such squalid conditions are a characteristic feature of Gaborone, Francistown and Selebi-Phikwe, and threaten to spread to other settlements such as the proposed Sua township.

The government has decided to upgrade, instead of remove, squatter settlements. In addition, the Self Help Housing Agency (SHHA) was created to provide loans for Certificate of Right (COR) holders in low-cost housing areas to improve their dwellings, particularly by the provision of pit latrines. The SHHA scheme was designed to operate at a level of cost recovery which has been found to be above income level in low cost areas. As a result, default of payment on loans is widespread (Letsholo, 1987).

A shortage of serviced land in urban areas and the associated rising costs have created pressures in adjacent rural areas. Villages within 10 km of Gaborone, such as Mogoditshane, Tlokweng and Odi, are under pressure to accommodate homeless Gaborone residents and are turning into dormitory settlements. To counter this pressure, communal land is restricted to members of the *in situ* tribal group, contradicting the spirit of the Tribal Land Act through which any citizen is entitled to land wherever he settles. It is probable that the dormitory problem is being encountered in the other large villages of the south-east, such as Molepolole, Mochudi and Ramotswa, which are themselves becoming part of a Gaborone conurbation.

The expansion of Gaborone, and, to a certain extent, Francistown, has been accommodated by the compulsory purchase of freehold farms. However, projects of national importance such as the Sir Seretse Khama Airport in Gaborone, have of necessity been constructed on tribal land. This loss of land, frequently used for arable farming, tends to affect the smaller tribal territories which can least afford to lose it. As further urban growth occurs, this loss of land will increase.

The siting and supervision of waste dumps in urban areas are issues of major concern. Uncontrolled dumping of industrial and domestic waste is common, in and on the periphery of urban land, whilst land-fill sites themselves are poorly planned and inadequately surveyed. The imminent dangers posed are those of groundwater pollution, the pollution of surfacewater supplies (such as the Gaborone Dam), and the spread of airborne pollutants during temperature inversions in the winter. A study of waste disposal in Gaborone (Segosebe and Van der Post, 1990) shows that both the quantity and diversity of waste is increasing, with the conclusion that waste disposal sites will become more hazardous.

Takirambudde (1990) has pointed out that the Public Health Act and the Town and Country Planning Act do not adequately address the management of waste. The most attractive option is to adopt the 'polluter pays' principle, whereby those industries wishing to dispose of hazardous waste will have to shoulder the financial responsibility for its disposal by a competent authority. This strategy would relieve local or central government of the financial responsibility for the offending industries, and would exercise control over the safe disposal of waste. The present *laissez-faire* attitude to waste disposal, coupled with the lack of experience of local authorities in waste disposal management, deserves urgent attention.

The impact of mining towns on the environment has been relatively small. Air and groundwater pollution from the copper-nickel smelting plant at Selebi-Phikwe is present and is being monitored. Provision is being made at Sua township for the minimisation of pollution from the soda ash plant, specifically from the coal-fired power station associated with it. Of greater concern at Sua is the potential impact of the town on the sensitive and unique ecosystem of the salt pan beyond the mining lease, for which no land use has yet been gazetted.

PRINCIPAL ENVIRONMENTAL PROBLEMS

Drought is a factor which lies beyond man's control, but it underlies many of the problems encountered in the utilisation of land-based resources within Botswana. It arises from the uneven distribution of rainfall in time and space, a function of rainfall variability (Figure 2.1). Although the common perception of drought is a prolonged, nation-wide absence of rainfall, drought conditions are probable every year in some part of the country, and even in years of above average rainfall, a break in precipitation of as little as three weeks is sufficient to drastically diminish crop production. Imposed on these annual conditions are the prolonged periods of drought which occur on a quasi-twenty-year cycle. Droughts of this type occurred in the 1960s, between 1982–87 and again in the early 1990s.

In response to the drought hazard, traditional systems of land tenure and agriculture were opportunistic, with risk spread by transhumance of livestock, utilisation of different soil types and crops, and planting at different times in the wet season. Inevitably, production of both cereals and livestock varied widely, but were sufficient to carry the population through lean times.

This pattern is no longer possible, not only because the growing numbers of people and animals have reduced the flexibility of land use but because agriculture is becoming increasingly geared to commercial production and to fixed quotas. Inevitably these cannot be met in most years because the physical constraints remain. It follows that the only safe conditions for land use are those that pertain during droughts. Any attempt to raise stock levels above the carrying capacity of the land during drought years will result in land degradation. This is precisely what has happened since the mid-1960s.

Land degradation is the inevitable result of the misuse of the land and vegetation resources by overgrazing and the adoption of inappropriate agricultural practices. It consists of a number of interlinked processes, including a reduction of soil fertility, erosion of the soil, depletion of the

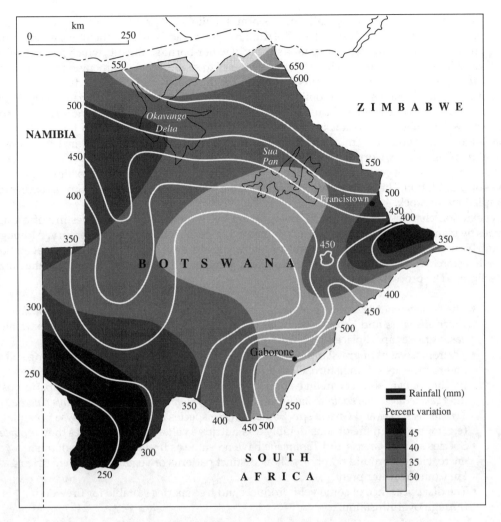

Figure 2.1 *Rainfall and rainfall variability*

vegetation biomass and the introduction of less palatable species, including bush encroachment. The end product is desertification, a situation in which widespread disappearance of vegetation cover occurs, with commensurate difficulty in vegetation rehabilitation.

Using the standard methods for assessing erosion employed in SADC countries (Stocking, 1987) it would appear that little erosion occurs in Botswana. This is because slope gradients are low, the parent material of most of the soils is highly porous, and soil fertility levels are also low. A cynic might remark that it is impossible to have soil erosion in the sandveld, as the parent Kalahari Sand does not, in itself, constitute a soil. A consequence of this perception, and a reflection of the difficulty in collecting data, is a paucity of soil erosion studies.

However, Arntzen and Veenendaal (1986) point out that soil erosion is a serious problem in the country, exacerbated by periods of drought and intense rainfall. Several types of erosion occur. For example, sheetwash, rill erosion and gully erosion have been identified in the hardveld, particularly in areas of steeper slopes, vegetation removal and shallow soil profiles. Gullying is acute along roads and livestock tracks and on the banks of sand rivers. This adds to the difficulty of maintaining adequate roads in rural areas, and creates a supply of water-borne sediments which collect behind bunds and in small cattle dams. There is some evidence to suggest that sediment mobility in sand rivers during high flow events may pose problems for the construction of large dams.

Wind activity includes dune mobility on devegetated dunes in the Kgalagadi District, the widespread presence of sand and dust storms, especially in the early summer months when soil moisture is low, and the erosion of clay soils. In the Nokaneng Flats area to the west of the Okavango, a deflation of 7 cm of silt soils was noted in a four-month period in 1986 (Snowy Mountains Engineering Corporation, 1987).

Erosion processes increase in the vicinity of boreholes and water points which exhibit concentric zones of degradation. The areas within 200 metres of the water point frequently comprise bare earth trampled by livestock.

Vegetation changes are induced by overgrazing by livestock and overharvesting of certain species by man. Such changes have been documented since the mid-nineteenth century. Although overall biomass is affected by seasonal and long-term moisture availability, with strong vegetation growth restored during good rains, there is evidence to suggest that the overall quality of the range is declining. The processes involved are:

- The replacement of 'sweet' perennial grasses, such as *Chloris gayana*, *Cyrodon dacylon*, *Eragrostis pilosa* and *Urochloa trichopus* by annuals such as *Aristida congesta*. In extreme cases grasses are replaced by poisonous weeds such as *Trilobus* spp.
- The replacement of grassland by a shrub cover, which shades out the underlying soil and reduces its soil moisture. Grasses eventually disappear, leaving thickets and patches of bare soil. The main colonisers in bush encroachment are *Acacia* spp. (*tortilis*, *hebeclada*, *erubescens*, *erioloba*, *mellifera*), *Colophospermum mopane*, *Dichrostachys cinerea*, *Terminalia sericia* and *Grewia* spp. Some of these species have limited browse potential, (e.g. mopane) but are of considerably less nutritive value than the grasses they replace.
- Species such as *Grewia* and *Terminalia* have no value as firewood. Studies of bush encroachment around boreholes show distinct patterns of vegetation change up to 4 km from the water point.
- The disappearance of some veld products and tree species suitable for firewood through overutilisation.

Land degradation varies with pressure of use and climatic parameters at a given time. Vegetation resources are heavily stressed during times of drought, but may recover in terms of biomass (but not species composition) during periods of adequate rainfall. Areas exposed to prolonged abuse, such as zones around villages and boreholes may suffer long-term irreversible desertification.

A study from satellite imagery in 1984 (Arntzen and Veenendaal, 1986) indicated that devegetated areas in that mid-drought year totalled some 20–25 per cent of the land area and were spread throughout the country. Desertification was present in the Okavango periphery, the Boteti villages (Rakops and Mopipi), the Tshane area and in parts of the Kweneng District. The geographically limited studies so far published indicate a long-term decrease in vegetation and soil resources (Arntzen and Veenendaal, 1986).

With reference to pests and diseases, Botswana is inhabited by a variety of organisms which influence resource use and require controlling measures. The distribution and impact of these organisms is obviously of great concern.

For example, the tsetse fly spreads disease amongst humans (sleeping sickness) and cattle (nagana). In the nineteenth century it was found throughout northern Botswana and was a major factor in preventing the elimination of wildlife in many areas. It declined in range after the rinderpest epidemic of the 1890s, but spread again in the early twentieth century. Elimination procedures began in the 1930s, and the fly is now restricted to a few areas in the Okavango by aerial spraying with endosulfan and endosulfan/pyrethroid mixtures.

Surprisingly, the restriction of the tsetse fly has had two negative environmental impacts, both strongly debated by conservationists. Firstly, it has increased the potential range of cattle in the Okavango, so that the presence of a cordon fence on the southern and western sides (the buffalo fence) is essential to maintain the integrity of the delta's ecosystem. Secondly, although endosulfan appears to have little impact on the food chain (although studies of economically-important fish species such as *Tilapia* are still in progress), the earlier use of dieldrin at higher concentrations may have had some negative effects on the food chain. Complete elimination of the tsetse fly is seen as desirable by the government, but it may not be in the best interests of the integrity of the game reserves, nor may it be a realistic aim, given incursions of the fly from the Caprivi Strip.

Diseases such as schistosomiasis (bilharzia) and malaria that are related to water-borne vectors have had limited impact in the past, but are now on the increase. Malaria, restricted to the Zambezi frontage a few years ago, spread as far south as Nata and Francistown in 1988, with 2000 cases in Maun alone. Bilharzia is now widespread in Maun and other high-density settlements on the fringes of the Okavango.

Pests that affect crop production, such as locusts, rodents and *Quelea* birds, reach epidemic proportions in some years, particularly during, and after, drought. The government is presently reviewing legislation for pesticide use in the light of these outbreaks.

Aquatic weeds remain a problem in reservoirs and perennial rivers. In particular, recent infestations of *Salvinia molesta* in the Okavango introduced by the illegal or unregulated movement of boats from the adjacent Chobe River system, pose a threat to the integrity of the Okavango ecosystem.

When considering the environmental impacts of industrialisation, as Botswana has only begun to industrialise over the last few years, pollution is a relatively recent phenomenon. However, three forms of pollution can be identified:

- The emission of effluents and aerosols from industrial plants has, so far, been limited. Complaints of discharges of tannery waste from the Botswana Meat Corporation abattoir in Lobatse were lodged in the early 1980s but have now stopped. The copper-nickel smelter at Selebi-Phikwe emits some 1135 tonnes of sulphur dioxide and eight tonnes of particulate matter per day, despite the fitting of filters. These have a toxic effect on vegetation on the downwind side of the plant, but no conclusive causal relationship has yet been established between air pollution and respiratory ailments in the town. The mine has also been discharging heavy-metal waste into the Motloutse River, and studies are underway to establish the consequences on downstream water supplies at Tobane.
- The dumping of industrial and toxic waste is increasingly becoming a problem due to lack of suitable sites and inadequate disposal legislation. The flytipping of waste on open spaces around towns is a common sight. Associated with this, litter is an increasing problem, making Botswana's towns some of the most unsightly in the sub-continent. The worst offender in this respect is the Kgalagadi breweries, which have a monopoly on the manufacture of beer and soft drinks, and is, in part, owned by the parastatal Botswana Development Corporation. Although several useful suggestions have been put forward to reduce the number of drink cans discarded throughout the

country, by recycling, or by introducing returnable containers, the company, as yet, has not responded positively. This problem could be tackled simply by legislation and education.

• Water supplies, both surface and groundwater, are becoming increasingly prone to contamination from sewage, industrial and agricultural waste. The problem is most acute in the south-east, where aquifers in Ramotswa and Mochudi have been reported as contaminated with faecal colliforms (Swedeplan, 1989), and in the heavily populated lower Okavango and Boteti Rivers. The implementation of the Southern Okavango Integrated Water Development Project, is largely concerned with the provision of a clean water supply to Maun and Boteti, whilst throughout rural areas a programme of pit latrine construction and piped water supplies aims to reduce this problem. In 1985 some 53 per cent of the population had access to safe drinking water, and 40 per cent to adequate sanitation facilities figures which should increase in future (International Institute for Environment and Development, 1989).

THE NATURAL RESOURCE BASE AND LEGAL UNDERPINNINGS

The idea that land is a finite resource is not accepted by many Batswana; even government policies such as the Tribal Lands Grazing Policy (TGLP) were based on the premise that free land was still available. Although population densities are low, the extent of poor soils and the unreliability of the water supply limit land potential. Less than 1 per cent of the land area is cultivated annually, yet land pressure exists in areas where cultivation is practised.

Land in Botswana is divided into three main tenure systems: Tribal Land, State Land and Freehold Land. These cover 71 per cent, 23 per cent and 6 per cent respectively of the land (Figure 2.2).

Tribal Land consists of tribal territory owned by the community as a whole. It is frequently referred to as communal land and is allocated free of charge to all tribesmen (citizens) for grazing, arable and residential use. The tenure system follows the traditional pattern where individual households own a demarcated plot for residence, but arable and grazing land are communal. Originally allocated by chiefs, authority over land is now invested in the Tribal Land Boards. The majority of rural communities reside on tribal land.

State Lands are mostly pre-independence Crown Lands, now used as national parks, game reserves and forest reserves, though some small parcels are used for other purposes. The state lands support low population densities, including communities of Basarwa ('bushmen') and Bakgalagadi hunter-gatherers.

Freehold Land is of two types. The first consists of blocks of land granted in the Protectorate era to expatriate mostly white immigrants for commercial farming. These grants occupy some of the best agricultural and grazing land in the country, including the Tuli Block, Ghanzi Block, North East and Lobatse Blocks (Figure 2.2). The second group consists of small plots in urban areas.

In response to rapid urban growth, the government has instituted other forms of tenure for townships. The Fixed Period State Grant (FPSG) provides security for urban dwellers by providing a capitalised lease under which rental is paid at the beginning of the lease instead of throughout its life. The FPSG is registerable under the Deeds Registry Act and is freely transferable, but reverts back to the government after the agreed period has elapsed. The Certificate of Rights (COR) was developed in the early 1970s as a means of providing secure tenure for urban squatters and new plot holders in the low income groups. Under the COR the plot holder has usufructual use of the plot, while the State retains ownership. The COR is inheritable and may be pledged, assigned or transferred with the permission of the local authority. It is also convertible to a 99 year Fixed Period State Grant.

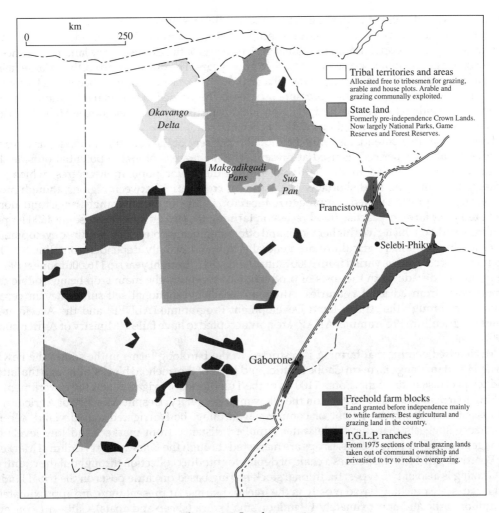

Figure 2.2 *Land tenure types*

Land use

Land use outside urban areas is influenced by land quality, the availability of water, population pressure and the policies of both local and national government. The transfer of responsibility for land management from chiefs to the Land Boards has not been effective in monitoring land use. Development in the more densely populated rural areas has tended to evolve in a haphazard way from earlier systems of centralised land use.

The dominant landuse types can be classified as;

- agricultural;
- grazing, including both traditional and commercial ranch systems;
- national parks and game reserves;
- forest reserves.

The reserves are discussed under vegetation and wildlife resources.

Arable agriculture is the second-largest sector of the economy, and is pursued, at least in part, by two-thirds of the population. Traditional agriculture is of the extensive dry land type, concentrating on sorghum, millet, pulses and maize in good years. The practice is to cultivate large fields known as 'lands' within the vicinity of the village, though in practice these are becoming located at increasing distances as population pressure increases. This has led to seasonal migration from the village to the lands at the start of the dry season and during the harvest. Fields are left fallow during the dry season and when drought conditions prevail.

Land with arable potential is limited to about 6 per cent of the country, although, as already noted, only about 1 per cent is used at present. The main areas of arable potential outside the freehold farms are found in the hardveld around the major population centres, which are consequently suffering land shortage. The choice of crop varies between regions, though most farmers tend to practise mixed cropping to reduce crop failure. In the Ovakango fringes and along the Boteti river farmers practise flood recession farming (*molapo* farming) over some 4600 ha per annum, a method which gives higher yields and offers significant potential for future development.

Yields in traditional agriculture are generally low and heavily dependent on climate. The production of cereals has varied from 9000 tonnes (1983/84 – drought year) to 116,000 tonnes (1987/88) in the last decade, with the costs of production of sorghum, the main crop being double the import costs from adjacent countries. Attempts to achieve national self-sufficiency in cereal production through the Arable Land Development Programme (ALDEP) and the Accelerated Rainfed Agriculture Programme (ARAP) are now accepted to have failed (Ministry of Agriculture, 1990).

Mechanised commercial farming is restricted to the Barolong farms in the south, the newly opened Pandamatenga farms in Chobe District, and parts of the freehold blocks, although the latter tend to specialise in ranching. Some 1100 ha of the Tuli Block are irrigated, and the government is seeking to irrigate a further 1200 ha on the Okavango periphery. Despite Ministry of Agriculture enthusiasm for the development of commercial farming, both irrigated and dryland, recent experience suggests that unreliable water supplies, distance from markets and low levels of management are limiting factors. Crops are marketed through the Botswana Agricultural Marketing Board (BAMB) which operates a chain of depots for product collection throughout the country.

Grazing is also of two types; traditional stock rearing based on cattle posts on the tribal lands, and large- scale ranching based mostly in the freehold farms. At present there are approximately 2.5 million cattle and approximately 1.9 million small stock (sheep and goats). Cattle are concentrated in eastern Botswana, but have spread into the sandveld as water supplies have been exploited. Small stock are encountered more in the drier western areas.

Livestock are dependent on the availability of water and grazing. In communal areas there is a preference for using grazing and water points which are close to the tribal lands, with some transhumance to more distant areas during the summer months. Ownership of boreholes gives *de facto* rights to the surrounding grazing lands. It is therefore not surprising that large cattle owners control water points through access to capital.

Cattle play a major role in the lives of the Botswana people and cattle ownership is regarded as the ideal form of wealth. As already noted, there is considerable inequality in cattle ownership and the traditional system of cattle loans (*mafisa*) to relatives strengthens the current pattern. Cattle are valued, not only as bank accounts, but for food, draught power, the provision of employment for the poor and as a renewable resource. Unfortunately, the present stocking rates, sometimes exceeding four livestock units (LSU)/ha far exceed the carrying capacity of the rangeland, a situation that has existed in parts of eastern Botswana since the 1930s and is now universal, resulting in widespread overgrazing. Mortality, which averaged 22 per cent during the 1980s drought (and exceeded 50 per cent in some areas), far exceeds the level of offtake which now stands at 9 per cent and has resulted in ranching inefficiency. These problems are exacerbated by a failure to rotate grazing, the over-exploitation of water points and poor breeding and management methods. In the long term, livestock numbers have increased throughout this century except during periods of drought and disease, with a peak cattle population of three million in 1982. In the past, small stock numbers have fluctuated in inverse relation to cattle during periods of drought as they are more resistant but of lower value. At present both cattle and small stock are increasing in number.

The Government has established an extensive marketing system for beef through local outlets and agents and the Botswana Meat Commission (BMC), which operates three abattoirs at Lobatse (capacity 20,000 head per annum) Maun and Francistown, for the export market. The export market is controlled largely by preferential agreement with the EEC, which takes 55 per cent of the BMC's production, paying prices up to 32 per cent above world market levels. In turn, the strict controls on foot and mouth disease demanded by the EEC have led to the erection of a network of cordon fences since the 1960s, which have achieved notoriety in conservation circles for their detrimental effects on wildlife (Patterson, 1987). Small stock are usually consumed locally, but an increasing proportion is being slaughtered by the BMC.

Legal instruments in land control

The Tribal Land Act (1970) provided for the establishment of the Land Boards to ensure the fair distribution and allocation of land. The Act also permits expatriate business communities to set up in tribal lands subject to allocation. Customary land grants provided under the Tribal Land Act are perpetual and inheritable. In addition there are subsidiary instruments which may affect the use of land in tribal areas, including the Fencing Act, the Forest Act and the Borehole Act.

In the state lands, access to land is regulated through a licensing system as well as specific acts controlling certain resources, such as the Forest Act, National Parks Act and the Town and Country Planning Act. The Stateland Act, as such, exists only to define the disposal of such lands by the state. Owners of freehold land have access to all resources with the exception of wildlife.

Sections of the Livestock Development Project (LDP) and the Tribal Grazing Lands Policies (TGLP) are also pertinent to land use. The LDP and the TGLP both sought to relieve grazing pressure on communal lands by the setting up of leasehold ranches and communal grazing units. This policy involved the assumption that 'empty' land was available for the setting up of these ranches, which were taken up by the large cattle owners. Although some of the ranches have been demarcated, some 28 per cent of the land had to be subsequently dezoned as it was already occupied whilst problems were encountered with the remainder such as access, securing water supplies (no survey of groundwater resources had taken place prior to zoning), and ultimately, overgrazing. The policy effectively allowed dual grazing rights on both communal and leasehold land for large cattle owners, an abuse of the system which has still not been addressed.

Vegetation

Although the soils of Botswana are generally of low nutrient status and water-holding capacity, they support a good floristic diversity, over 3000 species having been recorded, and a range of resource potential. However, the botanical ecosystem is very sensitive and rapidly degenerates under pressure. Although most of Botswana is still covered by natural vegetation, its composition is being altered, particularly through the replacement of 'sweet' grasses by less palatable species.

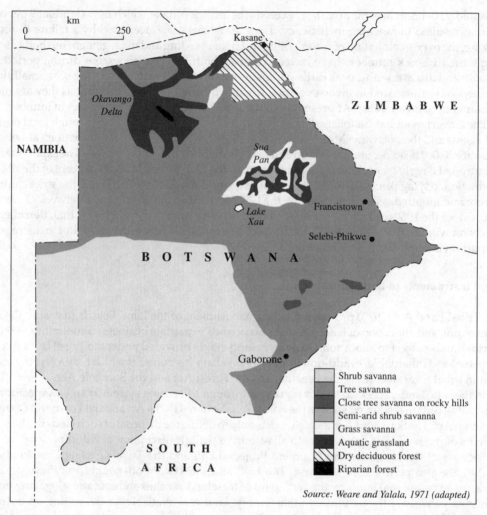

km
0   250

Kasane

Okavango
Delta

ZIMBABWE

NAMIBIA

Sua
Pan

Francistown

Lake
Xau

Selebi-Phikwe

B O T S W A N A

Gaborone

Shrub savanna
Tree savanna
Close tree savanna on rocky hills
Semi-arid shrub savanna
Grass savanna
Aquatic grassland
Dry deciduous forest
Riparian forest

SOUTH
AFRICA

Source: Weare and Yalala, 1971 (adapted)

Figure 2.3 *Vegetation types*

Vegetation classification has been undertaken by Weare and Yalala (1971) (Figure 2.3), but detailed studies are lacking for many areas. For the most part, vegetation is savanna-grassland with a variable degree of shrub and tree canopy. The density of woody species is in part determined by rainfall (Figure 2.1), with tree density lowest in the south-west and appreciable hardwood forests, including commercially-viable species such as *Baikiaea plurijunga* (*Mokus/Rhodesian Teak*) and *Pterocarpus angolensis* (*Morotomadi*), found in the north-east of the country.

Significant variation occurs within the sandveld, dependent on landform, with pans and fossil valleys providing suitable conditions for deep-rooting trees such as *Acacia erioloba* (*Mogotho*). In northern Botswana the Okavango Delta and Chobe floodplain provide unique swamp and riverine habitats with considerable floristic diversity, whilst the Makgadkgadi Basin is occupied by halotrophic vegetation.

The area of Botswana presently grazed by livestock can be conservatively estimated at about 60 per cent of the land, excluding national parks and game reserves (though there have been many cattle incursions), the Okavango Delta, areas subject to tsetse fly, and parts of the Kalahari, where water supplies have not been secured.

Veld products are increasingly used, both for subsistence, and commercial purposes. The former arises through increasing pressure, the latter through the opening-up of markets. The most important products at present include the following: the Mopane worm (*Goninbrosia melima*), a silkworm caterpillar found on the Mopane tree in northern and north-eastern Botswana; the Mokola palm (*Hyphaene ventricosa*), found in the Okavango and Makgaikgadi areas, used for both the making of beverages and for basketry; the Grapple plant (*Harpagophytum procumbens*), harvested in the Kgalagadi District for medicinal purposes; the fruits of the tree species *Sclerocarya* spp. (*Morula*) and *Grewia* spp. (*Moretlwa*); the Morama bean (*Tylosema esculentus*); melons and curcurbits, used as a water source in the western sandveld; and a variety of grasses and reeds utilised for thatching and fencing.

There is some concern about the increasing scarcity of thatching materials, particularly in eastern Botswana. The scarcity is caused by demand and by overgrazing. There is a potential market for a number of other veld products which has not yet been explored, for there are at least 150 edible wild plants available in the country.

Forest and woodland resources are important for the provision of energy, and as material for fencing, construction, commercial timber and crafts. Wood is traditionally perceived to be a free resource, to be collected as required. Commercial timber production, largely *Baiikea plurijunga* and *Pterocarpus angolensi*, is restricted to the forest reserves of north-east Botswana. The species are slow growing and widely dispersed in the forest, which makes exploitation marginal and returns to the government small. Craft timbers include trees for *mokoro* (canoe) construction in the north and wood used for carving, such as *Spirostachys africana* (*Morukuru*). There is some concern about the decrease in the availability of large trees for the former use.

At present, firewood accounts for 48 per cent of total energy used, and almost 100 per cent of domestic energy in rural areas. Significant amounts are also used for fencing and agricultural purposes. Estimates of the amounts of wood used vary between 0.5 and 1.1 tonnes per capita per annum (Arntzen and Veenendaal, 1986). Demand is forecast to increase rapidly over the next two decades.

Approximately 60 per cent of the tree biomass is suitable for firewood. On a national scale, supply exceeds demand but much of the wood is in remote areas, particularly in the north. Consequently concentric zones of woodland depletion are appearing around towns and villages, with towns in south-eastern Botswana (Gaborone, Molepolole, Mochudi and satellites) now harvesting wood at a distance of up to 100 km. The unmet demand for firewood is having a number of environmental and economic consequences, including rising prices, and increased erosion. Some woodlot planting, mostly of eucalyptus species, has been undertaken by brigades and the Forestry Association of Botswana (FAB), but only about 600 ha have been planted to date. A number of possible alternative energy strategies are being explored, but have yet to be implemented on a large scale.

Legal instruments in vegetation use

Traditionally, all citizens are entitled to collect wood and veld products from the tribal lands for subsistence purposes, with controls exerted in the past by chiefs. With the reduction of their influence, protection for vegetation has become less adequate. The following acts provide partial protection:

- The Town and Country Planning Act, together with the Agricultural Resources Act and the Herbage Protection Act, allow for some preservation of trees in planning areas, and for their replanting if removed during development.
- The Forest Act provides for the establishment and control of forest reserves, with a licensing system for exploitation. It also prohibits the cutting of riverine woodland within 10 metres of a channel and provides for the protection of species defined by the Land Board, mostly valuable hardwoods.
- The National Parks Act imposes criminal liability for the damaging or destruction of vegetation and the lighting of fires in parks. Some District authorities (notably Kweneng and Kgatleng) prohibit the export of wood beyond the district by byelaw. This option is being considered by other councils. Despite the government's increased awareness of the impending fuelwood crisis, there is as yet no policy for vegetation control, and present legislation is inadequate.

Wildlife

Botswana has a rich heritage of wildlife, including 164 species of mammals, 540 species of birds, 157 species of reptiles, over 80 fish, 38 amphibians and between five and ten thousand species of insects. The mammals, which traditionally form the most visible of the resources, include most of Africa's major species, with some 10 per cent of the continent's elephants.

National parks and game reserves incorporate 17 per cent of the area of Botswana. The major reserves are the Central Kalahari Game Reserve (52,800 km²), Chobe National Park (9980 km²), Gemsbok National Park (25,000 km²), Nxai Pan National Park (2100 km²), Moremi Game Reserve (3880 km²), Makgadikgadi Pans Game Reserve (3900 km²), Mabuasehube Game Reserve (1800 km²), and the Kutse Game Reserve (2500 km²) (Figure 2.4). In addition, a further 18 per cent of the country has been earmarked for development as Wildlife Management Areas (WMAs). Some significant wildlife habitats, such as the Okavango Delta, lie outside national parks, but are subject to protective measures.

Large concentrations of game animals were present throughout Botswana in the early nineteenth century, but they were subject to habitat destruction, particularly the destruction of wetlands associated with springs and rivers, and to hunting for trophies, meat and animal products. By the beginning of the twentieth century the distribution of game was limited to areas infested by tsetse fly and to remote parts of the sandveld. There has been some expansion of game areas this century, with the demarcation of the game reserves. Most game is now found in, or adjacent to, these parks and reserves.

The actual number of game animals is not known, but data collected in 1980 estimate herd animals such as wildebeest and hartebeest at over 250,000 per species. Some of the ungulates are highly migratory and cover vast distances in search of food and water, with seasonal migration routes through the Kalahari, in the Tuli Block, into and out of the Okavango, and across international boundaries in the north (Figure 2.5). They are also drought prone, with massive losses recorded in the 1960s and 1980s droughts, accentuated by the presence of veterinary fences.

Fish stocks are found in the perennial rivers of the north, and in some of the 250 man-made dams. Commercial fishing is limited to the Okavango with an annual catch of about 1000 tonnes, and aquaculture has yet to be developed.

The exploitation of wildlife is both extractive and non-extractive. Non-extractive uses include tourism which takes place in reserves and areas of outstanding habitat, such as the Okavango and Sua Pan. Northern Botswana is now recognised as one of the finest game-viewing areas in Africa,

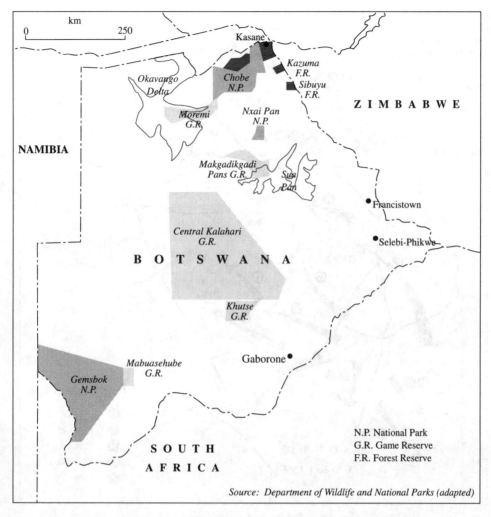

Figure 2.4 *National Parks and Game Reserves*

and the tourist industry has grown rapidly despite a lack of government investment.

Extractive exploitation includes subsistence hunting and recreational hunting. In practice, these two categories incorporate a range of activities from pure subsistence hunting by remote area dwellers in northern and western Botswana, occupying perhaps 10–20,000 people, through a range of recreational types, involving both Batswana and tourists, to obtain meat or trophies. Traditionally game animals have been regarded as a free resource, nominally under the control of chiefs. At present, hunting is controlled by a licensing system for both subsistence and recreational groups. Licences to shoot some 37,000 animals were granted in 1990, with allocation by a raffle system. Subsistence hunters are issued licences free of charge, but are required to hunt by traditional methods, such as the bow and arrow. Recreational hunting is undertaken on an animal-specific licence, with a sliding scale of charges for citizens and foreigners, within a system of 40 delineated Controlled Hunting Areas (CHAs) (Figure 2.6). Control of the licensing system is poor, and there

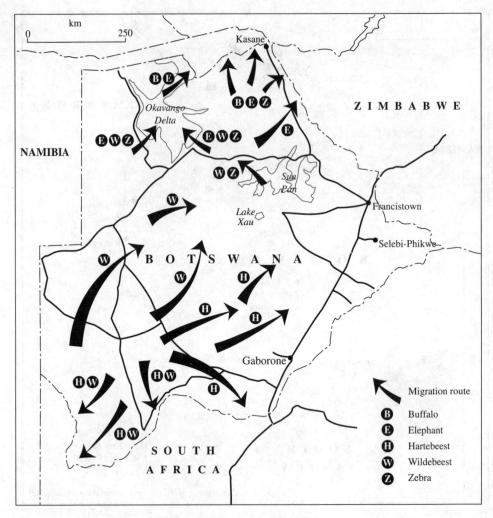

Figure 2.5 *Game migration routes*

is considerable abuse of the system by the transfer of licences, shooting over-quota and by poaching.

Game ranching, a relatively recent innovation in Botswana, forms a third type of utilisation. Crocodile farms operate in Maun and Kasane, and the rearing of ostriches and game animals is being undertaken on some of the freehold farms.

Legal instruments for wildlife utilisation

The National Parks Act (1968) prohibits the hunting of animals within the defined reserves. the Fish Protection Act (1975) controls the seasons and species of fishing, and prohibits fishing by explosives or poison.

The Fauna Conservation Act (1979) defines some 50 protected animals which may only be killed if they endanger life or property, though the animal may not be disposed of for profit. The Act also

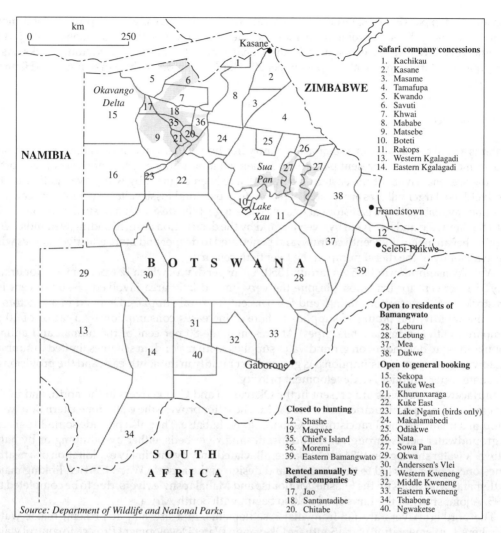

Figure 2.6 *Controlled hunting areas*

controls the issue of licences and the administration of Controlled Hunting Areas, and regulates the trade and export of trophies in accordance with the CITES agreement.

The Fauna Conservation Act also provides for the establishment of Wildlife Management Areas (WMAs) in accordance with the Wildlife Conservation Policy (1986). The WMAs, mostly areas of land adjacent to national reserves, are designed as areas where the wildlife industry can be developed on a sustainable basis by the provision of income under controlled conditions, and as corridors for wildlife migration. Although designated, none of the WMAs has yet been gazetted, partly because of opposition from the cattle lobby at the national level, and from villagers who regard hunting as their right. A pilot wildlife utilisation project began in 1990, and the publication of the National Conservation Strategy should go some way towards the implementation of the wildlife policy.

The government has also recently published a policy paper on tourism, which may curtail the uncontrolled expansion of safari camps in areas such as the Okavango, and provide for a more planned industry. Present problems include the unenforceability of the Fauna Conservation Act, and the very low level of investment in the Department of Wildlife and National Parks. As a consequence, staffing levels, at one person per 2095 km², are amongst the worst in Africa (Hannah *et al.*, 1988).

Water resources

Water is a vital commodity in a semi-arid country like Botswana, as it controls all forms of human and animal activity. The present patterns of settlement around the permanent rivers of the north, and the seasonal rivers of the eastern hardveld, have been dictated by water availability. In the sandveld too, larger villages are located at places, (e.g. pans and fossil valleys) where surfacewater was once available. There is historical evidence to suggest the desiccation of surface resources in both the sandveld and hardveld by over-use and by the destruction of surrounding wetlands. Well digging began in the nineteenth century, and penetrated to deeper and more effective sources with the availability of the diesel pump in the twentieth century.

Water consumption in 1985 was around 350,000 m³ per day, of which 12.6 per cent was for urban use, 35.1 per cent for irrigation (despite the very limited land area involved), 34.6 per cent for livestock, 12.6 per cent for mining, and 5.1 per cent for rural supplies. Demand in all sectors is growing rapidly; the piping of supplies to houses increases consumption by a factor of 10 as compared with communal standpipes. At present some 80 per cent of the human and animal populations are dependent on groundwater supplies, with major dam schemes limited to supplying towns in the east. Consumption has grown most rapidly in the south-east, and the provision of adequate water supplies is a development priority.

Surfacewater supplies are present in the Okavango and Chobe rivers in the north, and in the ephemeral Limpopo tributaries of the hardveld. The latter provide the water for eastern Botswana through dams at Shashe (Francistown), Gaborone and Lobatse. They also provide some 30 per cent of groundwater needs through extraction from sand river beds, either by pumping or by hand lifting. A water shortage in 1984 in Gaborone, alleviated only by the timely exploitation of a nearby limestone aquifer, has led to the planning and design of the Eastern Water Carrier, linking major settlements with dams on the Shashe, Motloutse and Mahalapshwe rivers, due to be completed by 1995. A joint study of the Limpopo has also begun with South Africa.

The northern rivers are far from major settlements, and are not, at present, major water suppliers. Implementation of the Southern Okavango Water Development Project, to control water supplies to Maun, the Boteti corridor and the Orapa diamond mine, and to provide for the conservation of the Okavango Delta, is being implemented. The future transfer of water from the Chobe to the Eastern Water Carrier is being considered. The exploitation of the Zambezi River is subject to international co-operation (ZACPLAN), but no such agreement exists for the Okavango.

Groundwater availability is a function of geological structure and rock type, and available technology for extraction. The latter varies from simple handwells to massive wellfields with extraction depths exceeding 100 m, such as that which supplies the Jwaneng diamond mine. Roughly 30 per cent of extraction comes from sand rivers, 30 per cent from high quality limestone and basalt aquifers, and the remainder from extensive Karoo strata and pockets within the Kalahari Group strata. Water quality varies, with pockets of high salinity encountered in parts of the western Kalahari and the Makgadikgadi basin.

The number of boreholes has increased from 700 at Independence to over 10,000 at the present time, of which 45–50 per cent may be operative at any one time. Borehole location and ownership is a controlling factor in the cattle industry, and is of environmental concern. Contamination of village supplies is also on the increase, particularly in eastern Botswana.

The total groundwater reserve is not known, despite continuing research by the Department of Geological Survey. It is estimated that perhaps 30 per cent of the potential is being utilised, but this may represent the most readily available water. There is also concern that fossil water is being mined in some aquifers.

Legal instruments for water use

Like other natural resources, water is public property whose use and rights are defined and regulated by the Water Act and its subsidiaries, such as the Water Works Act and the Water Apportionment Act. Public waters are not subject to private property rights. All citizens are allowed free access to public water for a number of purposes including watering livestock and domestic use. Owners and occupiers of land are entitled to abstract public water by boreholes, dams, canals and other works for domestic and agricultural use. On tribal land, water use is in accordance with customary rights and agreement with the owners of the water infrastructure. Special provisions apply to forestry and to mineral extraction industries which can use water provided from public supplies, or they can develop their own resources.

The provision of water to urban areas, and by arrangement, to mines, is the responsibility of the Water Utilities Corporation, which controls the major dams in eastern Botswana. Water exploration, planning and infrastructure provision, including the provision of water supplies to large villages, is the responsibility of the Department of Water Affairs. Small villages are provided by the District Councils. The Department of Water Affairs is also responsible for aquatic weed control, a problem which may have serious consequences in the Okavango, where outbreaks of *Salvina molesta* infestation have occurred.

Planning permission for boreholes must be obtained under the Tribal Land Act, with a separation of eight km between water points being regarded as the minimum spacing consistent with sustainable grazing. In practice the spacing is less than this and many unregistered and uncontrolled boreholes exist. Boreholes sunk for non-pastoral use in remote areas, such as wildlife and road construction watering points soon acquire settlements of remote area dwellers, and their livestock, an increasing problem in the Central Kalahari Game Reserve. The Department of Water Affairs also runs a subsidised borehole maintenance service, which is, in effect, a perquisite for large cattle owners.

This fragmentation of the responsibility for water supply is also reflected in pollution control, which is partially and inadequately covered by a variety of acts, including the Water Act, The Fish Protection Act, The Agricultural Resource Act and The Water Works Act. Under the latter, the Department of Water Affairs is also empowered to classify catchments as Water Works Areas for conservation purposes, but to date only large dams have been so delimited.

The government has been preparing a National Water Master Plan since 1987, aimed at centralising all aspects of water control and usage, and providing adequate water supplies into the twenty-first century (National Master Water Plan, 1987).

Mineral resources

Mining has been carried out in Botswana since the Iron Age, and by the end of the nineteenth century production included gold at Francistown, asbestos at Moshaweng, and manganese at Otse. It was not until after Independence, however, that the mineral sector burgeoned to become the driving force of the country's economic growth. Its contribution cannot be underestimated, both in terms of employment and in earnings; the value of mineral production in 1966 was about US$12,000; in 1989, diamonds alone generated US$1.4 billion.

The principal mineral developments include the diamond mines at Jwaneng, Orapa and Lethlakane, the copper-nickel mine at Selebi-Phikwe, coal at Morupule, and the soda ash plant now under construction at Sua Pan. Each of these reserves is large, with the present diamond mines and the copper-nickel plant expected to last well into the twenty-first century. Furthermore, coal and soda ash reserves are virtually unlimited at planned rates of extraction.

Other minerals of commercial interest that are not yet exploited include talc, asbestos, kyanite, manganese, agates, chromite, iron, lead, limestone, uranium and zinc. Exploration is also underway for hydrocarbons in the deeper sedimentary basins of the west. Some small-scale gold mining has been revived in the Francistown area.

Mining activities are large-scale, capital-intensive and export-oriented. They also require a massive investment in infrastructure – in Botswana the towns of Selebi-Phikwe (pop. 30,000), Jwaneng (10,000) and Orapa (6000) are solely dependent on mines. The government is actively involved in the mining sector through partnership (50 per cent in Debswana – diamonds; 15 per cent in BCL Ltd. – copper-nickel matte; and 48 per cent in Soda Ash Botswana Pty), as well as through the control of exploration and mining activities.

One exception to large-scale exploitation is the excavation of sand, clay and rock for building and road metal. These operations range from individual extraction to small quarrying companies. Whilst the latter are subject to permits, extraction in rural areas is often unsupervised.

Legal instruments in mineral development

The Department of Geological Survey, within the Ministry of Mineral Resources and Water, is responsible for the exploration and the monitoring of mineral extraction. They issue licences and leases for prospecting and mining in accordance with the Mining Act. Mining leases give the lessee exclusive surface rights for 25 years (with a renewable option) and allow for mineral exploitation, the building of infrastructure (including boreholes) and the disposal of waste in an approved manner. The prospecting licence is valid for three years and allows for prospecting, the erection of camps and borehole drilling.

Most mining leases are within planning areas under the terms of the Town and Country Planning Act (1977), through which the Town and Country Planning Board can control development by a permit system. Mining leases are also subject to the Atmospheric Pollution (Prevention) Act (1971) which sets standards for air pollution and allows for the monitoring of emissions. Although mining leases have access to groundwater, the Water Act requires that the water should not be polluted to the extent that it causes a danger to public health, animals and crops, and that it should be returned to source if possible. However, no standards have been set for waste water quality and waste discharge permits are not required.

Resource reserves and potential

Resources can be divided into the renewable, which theoretically can be used indefinitely if properly managed, and the non-renewable. The latter includes the mineral resources upon which current national prosperity is based. Fortunately the mineral reserves are large, and permit a breathing space to develop strategies based on renewable resources. Even without further discoveries, the present mining activity will carry the economy for the next thirty or forty years, external factors permitting.

Water is essential for the growth and sustainability of all sectors of the economy. The present water supply is just adequate for today's demand, but future developments will require massive infrastructural development in eastern Botswana in the 1990s, subsequently extending to northern Botswana. Recharge monitoring and pollution control of groundwater will become increasingly necessary, as some of the underground resources are, in the long-term, non- renewable.

Amongst the renewable resources, the land, which supplies the livelihood of the majority of the population, is under increasing pressure from overgrazing and inadequate agricultural practices. Although the current food self-sufficiency strategy calls for increased output, this is more likely to be achieved through improved methods of dryland farming and water harvesting than the proposed irrigation schemes, which place a high demand on water resources and managerial skills. The cattle industry is consistently over-exploiting the available grazing resource, despite strong evidence of land degradation. This is due to a complex mixture of factors, including traditional attitudes to cattle, a powerful cattle lobby within government, and the influence of external agencies. Land degradation becomes a national issue during times of drought, but is unfortunately forgotten during periods of adequate rainfall. This cyclical climatic pattern means that, as in the past, rural impoverishment is going to occur, probably on an increasing scale.

It is probable that the current localised fuelwood shortages are going to increase. Remedial action, through woodlot planting or the development of strategies for alternative energy sources, needs to be developed, but has not yet been initiated.

The grazing and management of cattle is having an increasingly negative impact on wildlife, a major resource which is being utilised by a wide spectrum of the population, but in an uneconomic and wasteful manner. Plans are in hand to implement and adapt methods of wildlife management to provide rural incomes from this sustainable source.

Other resources, such as aquaculture, fishing, tourism and some veld products, are not being utilised to their full potential. Tourism in particular could be expanded beyond national and local plans to the sphere of international co-operation. Recent political changes in the southern African region, together with infrastructural developments such as the building of the international airport at Kasane and the tarring of the Nata-Maun road, will simplify access for overseas tourists to a range of tourist attractions from Victoria Falls and the Hwange National Park in Zimbabwe, through the Botswana reserves and the Okavango, to Etosha National Park in Namibia. It is probable that this corridor will be a regional tourist growth centre in coming years.

Strategies and solutions for environmental sustainability

Botswana has experienced major developments since Independence, from being one of the poorest countries in the world to having one of the highest per capita growth rates. Much of the revenue has been invested wisely in infrastructural developments such as roads, schools, clinics and water, and in the provision of education and health care for the people. The country has evolved as a politically stable democracy in which the free exchange of views and a concerned administration have led to a high level of environmental awareness in government. Most environmental problems, their causes and effects, are well known.

This economic development, however, has been based on a small, capital-intensive sector of the economy. Most of the population remain on the land, and, despite infrastructural development, have not benefited from this growth. Arntzen and Veenendaal (1986) point out that in 1986 some 25 per cent of the population was unemployed, with a further 7 per cent underemployed. Attempts to improve production and sustainability in the arable sector by agricultural schemes and massive investment have failed, whilst the livestock sector has been productive largely at the expense of the environment. In short, attempts to transform the rural economy from subsistence activity to commercial production have not worked. As population increases it is mostly in rural areas that notions of sustainability will be challenged.

The marginal nature of the physical environment, and the demands that are being placed upon it by the expanding population, have been documented in this chapter. However, social forces also play a part in determining the adoption of new ideas. Any attempt to transform the rural economy in the space of one generation will be difficult. It is far easier to introduce new industries such as mining. Underlying this problem is the resistance of the collective consciousness to these changes, a factor which is reflected in the ambivalence of the government to critical issues such as population growth and land use. Many of these arise from the prevailing traditional attitudes of the Batswana, which are framed in an earlier, historical period of territorial expansion and authoritarian rule. Some of these attitudes, such as those pertaining to social and family structures, are of great value in maintaining a stable society during the present stage of transition. Others are no longer appropriate to current conditions. Of these the Botswana Society (1986:17) states:

> Much of the misuse and abuse of national resources of grazing land, soil and water is due to the continued prevalence of out-of-date traditional attitudes to cattle and cattle ownership, and to ignorance of basic causes of overgrazing and land degradation. The dire threat to basic natural resources and to future environmental integrity is thus unappreciated by large sections of the population.

The rapid growth of the human population is bolstered by a belief in large families, and, by extension, the idea, common in many parts of Africa, that a large population can be equated with a great nation. High birth rates were a necessity, in times of physical hardship and high infant mortality, to maintain society. These conditions no longer apply, and population growth rates must be reduced drastically to maintain standards of living, and to offer any hope of achieving sustainable development (Tumkaya, 1987). Although the government is preparing a population policy, limited educational programmes have been introduced and basic contraceptive programmes have been in place since the 1970s, there is a noticeable reluctance on the part of government to tackle this fundamental problem.

Similar attitudes prevail towards resources. Traditional Batswana land use was essentially opportunistic, using resources, such as wildlife or grazing, as and when they occurred in a physically marginal environment. Underlying this system is an assumption that such a resource must be spatially infinite, as indeed it was, for practical purposes, during the expansion phase of the early nineteenth century. Landuse pressure has been steadily increasing since the 1860s, but only recently has there been a growing realisation as to the limits of the land resource. The government is preparing detailed landuse plans at the district and sub-district level but it has difficulty in persuading residents that land for grazing purposes is no longer available. In practice the rural population has a far greater understanding of problems such as overgrazing than planners give them credit for (Fortmann, 1989). However, there is a considerable difference in the solutions to the land shortage and land degradation problems that the two groups propose. Likewise the emphasis on cattle as a form of wealth is less necessary now that alternative sources of wealth are available, yet it is difficult to persuade the people of this. The economic transition of the last quarter of a century has not yet transformed social attitudes.

Possible strategies for environmental sustainability

It is a simple task to outline the priorities for sustainable development; a primary list of these in relation to Botswana has already been indicated earlier in this chapter. It is far more difficult to propose the means by which these strategies may be effectively carried out in a way acceptable to society, and, of course, in carrying through the policies which result. There has been no shortage of suggestions from an environmental viewpoint in Botswana (e.g. Arntzen and Veenendaal, 1986; Botswana Society, 1984, 1986; Bussing, 1989; Kalahari Conservation Society, 1983, 1988), of which some have been incorporated into the National Conservation Strategy.

A reduction in population growth rates is the first priority of the government, and a population policy is in preparation. However, it should be noted that population programmes, whether by education, contraception or sterilisation, have met with limited success in developing countries in Africa, and that in the long run a reduction in the birthrate will accompany rises in the standard of living of the whole population, not just groups within it. This is not to say that attempts to implement education and contraception programmes should not be attempted; the spread of AIDS throughout the sub-continent makes such an approach imperative.

As the total population is relatively small, urban migration has not reached the alarming proportions in Botswana that it has elsewhere. Indeed, it could be argued that such a movement is desirable to provide an industrial labour force, and to relieve the deficiencies of the rural employment sector. However, the drift exceeds the rate of job creation, and migrants are usually young people whose labour is necessary on the land. Present government policy is to legalise squatting rights and to provide, as far as possible, some vocational training. However, an overall lack of employment opportunities in the towns still remains.

Productivity in arable farming is now lower than at Independence, despite massive government support and investment. Given the environmental constraints, improvements in both productivity and the provision of employment will be difficult to achieve. The draft Agricultural Policy paper (Ministry of Agriculture, 1990) proposes that:

- All producer prices be based on import parity;
- Animal draught-power be encouraged both by improved methods and by the withdrawal of grants for tractors;
- Free pest control services be continued;
- Provision be made for further training at the Botswana Agricultural College and by extension schemes;
- Fiscal incentives be made for land improvement via income tax;
- The search for potential land for intensive (usually irrigated) land should continue.

Arntzen and Veenendaal (1986) suggest that more effective use of the land could be made by the adoption of improved practices, including contour ploughing, winter ploughing, bare fallowing, crop rotation and the use of kraal manure. Extension services should also be seen as a crucial factor in communication between farmer and government agencies.

It is unlikely that suitable land for intensive farming will be found, or that irrigation will be feasible on economic or management grounds. However, there is room for the improvement and extension of traditional flood-farming methods in the riverine environments. Other options include the trial of dryland tree crops (such as Morula) and household horticulture in association with water harvesting. Although increasing numbers of buildings in rural areas have galvanised roofs, and a recommendation was put forward by the Botswana Society in 1984 that small-scale water harvesting using roofs to catch rainwater be adopted on a nation-wide scale, it is rarely seen in practice.

Turning to the cattle industry, wide-reaching changes could be made in livestock management, but this is an emotive issue. The principal problems to be addressed are a reduction in stocking to the level of environmental sustainability, an improvement in management and productivity, and the redistribution of the national herd to provide greater rural wealth and employment. Useful suggestions (Arntzen and Veenendaal, 1986; Botswana Society, 1984, 1986) include:

- A restriction on further livestock expansion and an adjustment of stocking rates to the carrying capacity of the land;
- Abolition of dual grazing rights and a review of the Tribal Lands Grazing Policy, (TGLP) including the re-introduction of economic rents for TGLP ranges;
- Withdrawal of all subsidies in the cattle industry, and of loans for breeding stock;
- Restrictions on the numbers of livestock production centres owned by one person, or a taxation system applied to cattle ownership above a certain herd size;
- Discouragement of the practice of absentee landlords and speculative use of grazing land;
- Subsidised herd reduction;
- Increased culling by marketing agencies;
- Enforcement of existing laws and regulations relating to the use of grazing land be enforced, and Land Boards be given greater powers to control land use by amendment of the Agricultural Resources Act;
- Abolition of private borehole water ownership with ownership transferred to the state;
- The setting aside of fallow grazing land for times of grazing stress;
- Improvements in education and extension services and the provision, expansion, and diversification of small stock raising to include pigs and poultry;
- Investment in rangeland monitoring and research.

Government policy continues to accept the existence of the rangeland crisis, but has not developed a specific policy towards it. In addition to the last two recommendations, the specific recommendations of the draft Agricultural Policy paper (Ministry of Agriculture, 1990) include:

- The improvement of management by further fencing, including the fencing of communal lands;
- Improved breeding programmes;
- Encouragement for farmers to grow fodder crops for winter feed;
- Deregulation of the dairy industry.

The provision of rural employment through the utilisation of other resources

Although some 40 per cent of the land area is given over to wildlife in various forms, the resource is ineffectively exploited. The main priorities are the sustainable use of wildlife by all forms of activity, including hunting, game farming and tourism, and the provision of rural incomes from these activities. However, many of the proposals put forward in the last few years for more effective wildlife utilisation are only now being implemented. It remains to be seen how successful they will be, as the long-term viability of the wildlife resource will be dependent on their outcome. These measures include:

- The preparation of a wildlife management policy and a tourism policy by the relevant government departments;
- Strengthening of the Department of Water Affairs;
- Designation of Wildlife Management Areas and the development of a pilot wildlife utilisation policy involving rural people, to be implemented in the near future;
- The development of management plans for the national parks and game reserves. Initial plans for the Central Kalahari, Moremi and Chobe reserves (Anderson 1985), although the latter two are being revised.

In the light of public opinion (Botswana Society, 1986; Kalahari Conservation Society, 1988) future emphasis could be placed on:

- The raising of public awareness of the value of the wildlife resource through education;
- Improved administration and management in both tourist and wildlife industries. This encompasses the suggestion that natural resources such as water, forestry, wildlife and veld products fall under a Ministry of Natural Resources to simplify administration and to provide positive backing when the needs of these industries compete with agriculture;
- The extension of financial assistance to these industries via the Financial Assistance Policy (FAP).

Given increasing demand, vegetation products are another area of potential growth. The harvesting of firewood and veld products provides income for rural dwellers, particularly some of those in remote areas. However, such harvesting must remain within the bounds of sustainability. For veld products, improvements could be made by:

- The extension of financial assistance and technical advice to this industry;
- Control of harvesting of overutilised species by licensing;
- Research into the location, volume and possible utilisation of veld products, together with possible cultivation of the plants, and the improvement of product quality.

Woodland resources require more stringent management. Although the NGO Forestry Association of Botswana (FAB) attempts to raise public awareness over the issue, and Botswana now has a National Tree Planting Day, little is being done to put the forest resource on a sustainable basis. Policies could include:

- Raising levels of awareness in government as to the urgency of a woodland resource and agroforestry policy;
- Improved administration of forest resources, and the provision for Forest Management Areas similar in principle to Water Management Areas;
- The introduction of communal management of woodland resources, and the government sponsorship of multi-species woodlots;
- Development of energy alternatives and energy-reducing strategies;
- Raising of public awareness about the value of indigenous trees, and the concept of trees as an agricultural crop;
- More effective legislation and control of current practices of woodland harvesting.

Expansion of the industrial base and the implementation of pollution control

The creation of employment by government agencies inevitably has limits; already the public service is the second-largest employer in the country after agriculture. Productive labour is the province of the private sector, which has expanded rapidly in recent years, and receives support from the government through Financial Assistance Policy and the involvement of financing organisations such as the National Development Bank and the Botswana Development Corporation. The prospects for a further expansion of industry are good, given the political and economic climate. Plans are being made, for example, for a car assembly plant in the near future. It is unlikely, however, that the private sector can incorporate more than a small fraction of the overall numbers of job seekers.

However, the present economic boom is creating shortages in certain sectors of the labour market, particularly trained artisans. Although the import of labour is controlled via the issue of work permits, there is some concern about the employment of foreigners at all levels, whilst large numbers of Batswana are unemployed. Vocational training at the artisan level is undertaken by the Brigade movement and by trainee release from private companies, in agreement with the Ministry of Labour. Far more could be done in this direction to raise the technical skills of the Batswana. Environmental pollution, as the Botswana Society (1986) notes, is a new problem in Botswana, but is of rapidly-growing significance. A number of solutions are available:

- National standards of air and water quality should be established and enforced by active legislation and by the upgrading of monitoring facilities and staff. This will require a review of existing legislation and perhaps the creation of a single body responsible for pollution control. Some of this legislation (e.g. the Pesticides Act), is now being reviewed;
- The recycling of waste and the production of returnable containers could be encouraged through incentives or legislation. The application of the 'polluter pays' principle should be rigidly enforced;
- The upgrading of existing landfill sites and more careful planning of those designated for future use should be enforced;
- Effective programmes of research into pollution and education at both school and adult level should be encouraged.

It is important that levels of environmental awareness are raised through education. Education takes the major share of the annual recurrent budget, and much has been done to remedy the lack of educational facilities and opportunities available at Independence. The present policy is to provide a 'Nine Year Basic Education for All', no small task given the large size of the school population. There is also considerable investment in education at University and Polytechnic level. The National Curriculum aims to provide basic literacy and numeracy. The science curriculum, at all levels, is being expanded but is hampered by a lack of trained teachers, although agricultural education is being improved at the primary and secondary levels. The Ministry of Education is currently involved in incorporating environmental education into the curriculum and raising the environmental awareness of pupils and teachers up to Junior Certificate level. Environmental education is undertaken by NGOs such as the Forestry Association of Botswana and the Thusano Lefatshang and is aimed at both schools and adults. The mobile section of the National Museum also teaches a unit on the environment when it visits schools and communities around the country. The Department of Wildlife and National Parks has a Wildlife Conservation Education Unit which is understaffed, and the Wildlife Clubs Association of Botswana is involved in environmental education particularly in secondary schools. However, much remains to be done.

At the international scale, the improved political and economic climate in southern Africa allows for greater co-operation in the utilisation of shared resources. Botswana is a member of both SADC and the Southern African Regional Conference for the Conservation and Utilization of Soil (SARCCUS). A number of collaborative resource projects are underway, including ZACPLAN in the Zambezi Basin, a joint South African-Botswana study of the Limpopo, and collaboration with the Namibian authorities on the control of aquatic weeds in the Okavango and Kwando Rivers. Under the auspices of SADC, Botswana participates in the regional network of agricultural expertise, and houses the headquarters of the Southern African Coordinating Conference for

Agricultural Research (SACCAR) at the agricultural college. Long-term development, however, is going to be dependent upon the availability and security of certain resources, of which the most important is water. Present engineering schemes will be sufficient to provide for the nation over the next ten years, but plans are already formulated for the long-distance transfer of water from northern Botswana to the centres of population in the east by a pipeline or canal system similar to the Eastern Carrier in Namibia. This security will require negotiation with the Zambezi states to ensure a share of the waters of that catchment, and with Angola and Namibia to prevent interference with the Okavango.

CONCLUSION

Environmental problems are well known in the country, and attempts are continuously being made to find solutions at different levels and in different regions. However, fundamental problems have yet to be tackled. Botswana has tremendous advantages over many developing countries in the form of a viable economy, a small population and a democratic government. These advantages are being lost by the inability of society to come to terms with the physical and spatial limitations of the natural resources, and to distribute income in an equitable manner. As tremendous wealth is being generated from non-renewable resources, the land on which most of the population relies is being degraded. To this there is no easy technical solution, for the answers lie in fundamental changes in the attitudes and perceptions of those who utilise the resources, from peasant farmers through to the top levels of government. Present patterns of rapid demographic increase will reduce the likelihood of success, and place further pressure on the resource base.

REFERENCES

Anderson, JL (1985) *Chobe National Park and Moremi Wildlife Reserve* Kalahari Conservation Society, Gaborone

Arntzen, JW and Veenendaal EM (1986) *A Profile of Environment and Development in Botswana* NIR/Free University, Amsterdam

Botswana Society (1978) *Symposium on Drought in Botswana* Proceedings of the 1978 Symposium, Gaborone

Botswana Society (1984) *The Management of the Botswana Environment* Proceedings of a Workshop, Gaborone

Botswana Society (1986) *Developing our Environmental Strategy* Proceedings of a Workshop, Gaborone

Bussing, C (1989) *National Conservation Strategy: District Issues and Potential Projects* USAID/MLGL/DTRP, Gaborone

Central Statistical Office (1983) *Statistical Bulletins* 1971–83. Gaborone

Central Statistical Office (1989) *Statistical Bulletins* 1971–89. Gaborone

Fortmann, L (1989) *Peasants' views of rangeland use in Botswana:* Land Use Policy, Ministry of Local Government and Lands, Gaborone

Government of Botswana (1985) White Paper No. 1 *The National Policy on Land Tenure* , Gaborone

Government of Botswana (1986) *Wildlife Conservation Policy,* Gaborone

Hannah, L *et al* . (1988) *Botswana Biological Diversity Assessment* Agency for International Development, Africa Bureau

International Institute for Environment and Development (1989) *World Resources, 1988–89* Basic Books Inc., New York

Kalahari Conservation Society (1983) *Which Way Botswana's Wildlife?* Gaborone

Kalahari Conservation Society (1988) *Sustainable Wildlife Utilization: the Role of Wildlife Management Areas* Gaborone

Larson, M K (1988) *Uses of Population Projections in Health Planning* Workshop on Population Projections, CSO, Gaborone

Letsholo, J (1987) 'The settlement sector' in National Conservation Strategy, unpublished

Manyeneng, W G et al . (1985) *Botswana Family Health Survey 1984*, Ministry of Health, Gaborone

Ministry of Agriculture (1990) *Botswana's Agricultural Policy: Critical Sectoral Issues and Future Strategy for Development*, Draft Policy Paper, Gaborone

Ministry of Local Government and Lands (1989) *Proposed Land Use Plan for the Makgalikgadi region* Central DLUPU/Ngurato Land Board, Serowe

Mpotokwane ,M A (1986) *Changes in settlements and Landuse in southeast Kgatleng district, Botswana, 1952–82*, unpublished MSc thesis, ITC, Enschede, Netherlands

National Master Water Plan (1987) Seminar Proceedings, Government of Botswana

Owens, M and Owens, D (1980) 'The fences of death' *African Wildlife* Vol.34: 25-77

Patterson, L (1987) 'Cordon Fences' *Kalahari Conservation Society Newsletter* No.18, pp 10–11

Schapera, I (1943) *Native Land Tenure in the Bechuanaland Protectorate*, Lovedale Press, Alice, South Africa

Segosebe, E M and Van Der Post, C (1990) *Urban Industrial Solid Waste Pollution in Botswana*, Draft Paper, University of Botswana

Snowy Mountains Engineering Corporation (1987) *Southern Okavango Integrated Water Development Project*, SMEC/Water Affairs, Gaborone

Stocking, M (1987) *A Methodology for Erosion Hazard Mapping in the SADCC Region* SADCC Soil and Water Conservation Programme, No.9, Maseru, Lesotho

Swedeplan (1989) *A Comprehensive Physical Plan for the Greater Gaborone Region* Swedeplan/MTRP, Gaborone

Takirambudde, P (1990) *Resource Distribution: the Legal Implications of settlement, Development and Resource Conservation* National Conservation Strategy Policy Workshop, Gaborone

Tumkaya, N (1987) 'Botswana's population trends: past and future', *Botswana Notes and Records* Vol.19: 113–128

Williamson, D T and Williamson, J E (1981) 'An assessment of the impact of fences on large herbivore mass in the Kalahari' *Botswana Notes and Records* Vol.13: 107–110

Weare, P R and Yalala, A (1971) 'Provisional vegetation maps' *Botswana Notes and Records* No.3: 131–152

Yeager, R (1989) 'Demographic pluralism and ecological crisis in Botswana *Journal of Developing Areas* Vol.23: 385–404

3

LESOTHO

INTRODUCTION

Lesotho, commonly known as the Mountain Kingdom, is 30,335 km² in area. It is completely surrounded by the Republic of South Africa lying between latitudes 28 degrees south and 31 degrees South, and between longitudes 27 degrees east and 30 degrees east. The country is divided into ten administrative districts which fall in one or more of the four ecological zones of lowland, foothills, mountain and Senqu River Valley. Figure 3.1 shows the chief physical features of the country.

In terms of climatic conditions, the average rainfall over the entire country is 730 mm a year, although it is variable regionally, with the highlands receiving the highest amount – 760 mm, followed by the northern part – 750 mm. In the south rainfall levels decline to under 700 mm per annum. Temperatures in the lowlands vary from a maximum of 32°C or higher in summer to a minimum of 2°C in winter. In the highlands, the range is much wider as temperatures below 0°C are common in winter. Frosts occur, even in the lowlands, and snow is common in the Maluti mountains and has been recorded in the capital, Maseru. However, the sun shines on average 300 days a year, with great intensity because of the high altitude (1500–3350 m) and the low levels of atmospheric pollution.

The population of Lesotho is estimated to be over 1.5 million (1986 census), including those working in the Republic of South Africa. The annual growth rate is estimated to have been 3.1 per cent between 1976 and 1986.

Of the total population, an estimated 30 per cent live in the highlands, 20 per cent in the foothills and the rest in the lowlands. About 14 per cent live in the urban areas. Central Maseru (the capital) with a population of 116,000 (1986 census) forms the largest concentration of population, and has an annual growth rate of about 7 per cent, the highest in the country.

Lesotho's economic base is dependent, to a large extent, on remittances from South African mines, which, until recently employed up to 50 per cent of the economically active male population. Their earnings constitute about 42 per cent of the Gross National Product (GNP). Prospects for agricultural production making a major contribution to foreign exchange earnings are limited. The country's agricultural potential is constrained by its small size and the mountainous terrain leaves only about 13 per cent of the country suitable for crop production. In addition, an estimated 0.25 per cent of the arable land is lost by soil erosion each year. The country's key resource apart from its labour is water. The planned Lesotho Highlands Water Project (LHWP), should make a significant contribution to the national economy. The main thrust of the LHWP is to sell water to the industrial centres of the Rand Area of South Africa with the generation of electricity for Lesotho as a secondary objective.

Historically the Basotho nation evolved in the period between the 1820s and the 1840s when Moshoeshoe I rose from being a common chief to becoming a highly respected and widely recognised leader. Prior to the establishment of the Basotho nation, the chieftainship of the Sotho-Tswana tribes was the chief political institution. However, in 1865 war broke out between the Basotho, still under the founder, Moshoeshoe I, and the Orange Free State commandos fighting for

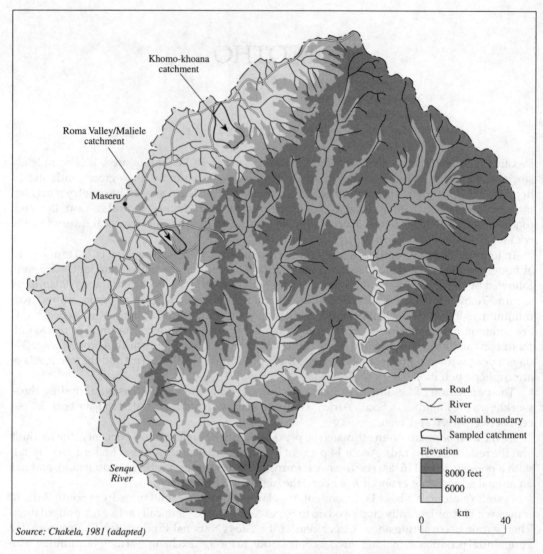

Khomo-khoana
catchment

Roma Valley/Maliele
catchment

Maseru

Senqu
River

Road
River
National boundary
Sampled catchment

Elevation

8000 feet
6000

km
0   40

Source: Chakela, 1981 (adapted)

Figure 3.1 *Relief, drainage and sampled catchments*

control of disputed villages and crops. The latter managed to persuade some Basotho chiefs to sign treaties that in effect resulted in the loss of nearly all the Basotho's arable land. Moshoeshoe was compelled to seek British protection which was granted to Lesotho in 1868. Basutoland, as it was called, became, and remained, a British colony until its independence in 1966. Today, Lesotho is a member of the United Nations (UN), the Commonwealth and the Organisation of African Unity (OAU).

During the 98 years of foreign rule in Lesotho, the vision of nationalism was never extinguished. To the Basotho, the seeking of British protection had been the sensible course during times of threatened Boer conquest. However, during the colonial period, requests for indigenous political autonomy emanated frequently from Lesotho. To that end, political movements were established in Lesotho early in the twentieth century. The Progressive Association was founded in 1907, followed by the Lekhotla La Bafo in 1919. The Basutoland African Congress (BAC) was formed in 1952. In 1958 the BAC changed its name to the Basutoland Congress Party (BCP). In the same year the Basutoland National Party (BNP) was launched and the Marematlou Freedom Party (MFP) was created in 1961.

The first elections of 1965 were won by the BNP and independence was attained on 4 October 1966. After its first term of office in 1970, the BNP declared a state of emergency and the national elections to be null and void. It continued ruling until January 1986 when a military coup toppled the Government. The King (Moshoeshoe II) remains the Head of State, with executive and legislative powers, which he exercises on the advice of the Military Council.

Unlike most former British colonies, the period of colonial rule bequeathed very little by way of development or growth to the tiny mountain kingdom. This was largely because Basutoland was regarded as a labour reserve for South African mines and industries. The little infrastructure that was installed, was essentially to ease and facilitate the flow of labour from Basutoland to South Africa and for the maintenance of law and order. Independence could not by itself change overnight these structures of dependence and underdevelopment, which were the inheritance of the newly-created state in 1966. Lesotho remains a low- income country, highly dependent on South Africa, which totally surrounds it, and with a range of environmental problems which will be examined below.

ENVIRONMENTAL PROBLEMS

Resource-use conflicts

In any discussion of resource-use conflicts it is appropriate to begin with a description of the population dynamics. According to the preliminary results of the 1986 population census Lesotho has 1,577,536 inhabitants. The annual population growth rate between 1976 and 1986 was 3.12 per cent. In 1986 there were 648,021 males and 795,832 females (41.1 per cent and 58.9 per cent respectively). Expressed another way, the sex ratio was 0.81 per cent which means there were 81 males to every 100 females.

The 1985/86 labour force survey for Lesotho included all persons who were 12 years old and above. According to this labour force survey there were 1,123,512 economically active persons, 27 per cent of these were below 20 years old, while 15 per cent were more than 55 years old. Non-economically active persons totalled 629,216.

The distribution of population is strongly affected by migration. In Lesotho, in 1986, 133,633 persons were residing out of the country. Of these, 112,451 (7.1 per cent of the total population) were male and 21,232 female (1.4 per cent).

Internal migration is more dominant among females whilst external migration is dominated by males due to the practice of migrant labour to the Republic of South Africa. Another important feature of internal migration is that it is both rural–rural, particularly from the mountain zone to the lowlands, as well as rural–urban. Internal migration is often caused in Lesotho, by differences in employment possibilities, and the availability of services and facilities. External migration is almost exclusively caused by available employment opportunities in South Africa.

Of the country's population, 1,358,010 persons (86 per cent) live in rural areas and 219,526 (14 per cent) in urban districts (Table 3.1a and b). It can be concluded from Table 3.2 that population densities are high in the lowland districts and lower in the mountain districts. However, analysis of the data under net density per km² of arable land reveals that population pressure on arable land is high in some lowland as well as in the mountain districts. The high population pressure on arable land in some mountain districts could be accounted for by the fact that arable land is very scarce due to the rugged nature of most of the terrain.

Table 3.1a *Urban and rural population distribution by district, 1986*

District	Urban population	%	Rural population	%
Butha-Buthe	8 340	3.8	92 304	6.8
Leribe	24 307	11.1	233 681	17.2
Berea	16 855	7.7	177 776	13.1
Maseru	136 734	62.3	174 425	12.8
Mafeteng	12 171	5.5	183 420	13.5
M.Hoek[1]	7 675	3.5	156717	11.5
Quthing	4 206	2.0	106 070	7.8
Qachas[2]	4 595	2.0	59 389	4.4
Mokhotlong	2 394	1.1	72 282	5.4
T.Tseka[3]	2 149	1.0	101 946	7.5
Total	219 526	100.0	1 358 010	100.0

1 Mohales Hoek

2 Qachas Nek

3 Thaba-Tseka

Source: Lands, Surveys and Physical Planning Department, NSP Working Paper No.4–Population, 1989:16

Population policy

Up to the present, Lesotho does not have a clearly stipulated government policy on population. The lack of policy on population control is caused by the sensitivity of the birth control question, especially in religious and moral terms. It is, however, essential that the government develops population policies because Lesotho's population is increasing rapidly and the availability of land is decreasing. Therefore sustainable development cannot be achieved without a committed national population control policy.

Although urbanisation in Lesotho is very low – only 14 per cent of the population – urban growth rates have been rapid since independence in 1966. This urban growth has been caused by natural increase and by rural–urban migration, especially into Maseru, which now stands out as a primate city. Today Maseru has a 7 per cent annual population growth rate.

Many environmental problems result from Lesotho's high urban growth rate. First, urban areas grow physically. This physical growth is accommodated through encroachment on land formerly used for farming within the rural sector. This land becomes converted into urban settlements either formally, through government housing projects such as low-income housing schemes and settlement upgrading schemes, or informally, as people buy land in the black market and build their own houses. This latter process led to the rapid growth of spontaneous uncontrolled settlements on the margins of most urban areas in Lesotho. At present no effort has been made to quantify land lost to urban settlement use both formally and informally.

Table 3.1b *Total population by district, 1986*

District	Total population
Butha-Buthe	100 644
Leribe	527 988
Berea	194 631
Maseru	311 159
Mafeteng	195 591
Mohales Hoek	164 392
Quthing	110 376
Qachas Nek	63 984
Mokhotlong	74 676
Thaba-Tseka	104 095
Total	1 577 536

Source: Lands, Surveys and Physical Planning Department,
NSP Working Paper No.4–Population, 1989:16

In Lesotho, sustainable development can best be achieved through agriculture. However, it is doubtful whether this objective can be achieved as long as valuable agricultural land is lost to urban settlements. Again an inventory of the scale, the causes, and the implications of formal and informal encroachment by urban settlements into agricultural land must be made to strengthen attempts by the Ministry of the Interior to formulate a national settlement policy for Lesotho.

The second problem caused by rapid urban growth is the fact that expanding populations in urban areas require increased physical and social services. Living conditions in most uncontrolled urban settlements pose a serious environmental threat. There are no access roads, and clean drinking water is lacking. The relatively richer families have made bore-holes, but these have now lowered the water table in areas such as Lithoteng in Maseru. Sewerage and waste disposal are particularly serious problems. Most households in these areas use pit latrines for sewerage. The sewerage from these pit latrines pollutes the underground water used for drinking purposes. The inadequacy of these facilities creates health problems. Competition for capital to be used to provide services is often directed to the middle and upper income groups. In addition, much of the waste in the peri-urban areas is dumped into open pits or into nearby gullies thus making breeding grounds for insects that transmit diseases.

Economic resource conflicts

Lesotho's economy is based mainly on agriculture, migrant labour remittances and foreign aid. Agriculture, in theory, employs about 86 per cent of the total population. Its importance in terms of contribution to the GNP has, however, declined from 22.4 per cent in 1970/71 to only 10.6 per cent in 1984/85 (Ministry of Agriculture, MOA, 1986). There are many reasons for this decline, such as competition for land, labour and capital.

Land

Lesotho has a total area of 3,034,900 hectares. In 1960, 450,800 hectares were arable. This figure decreased to 287,452 hectares in 1985/86 (MOA, 1986). This decline can be attributed in part to the fact that human settlements have been progressively encroaching into arable land as population has increased. Moreover, other arable land has been taken up by industrial uses especially in Maseru and Maputsoe. The opening up of the now defunct De Beers diamond mine at Letseng-la-Drai took away some land that was used as range. Currently, the Highlands Water Project is removing many hectares of land from agriculture through the development of reservoirs in the mountains. Additionally, land has been converted from either crop cultivation and/or livestock grazing into construction camps and resettlement villages. The conversion of some of the best agricultural land in the country into Moshoeshoe I International Airport is yet another example of competition for land amongst the different sectors of the economy.

Table 3.2 *Absolute population densities and population densities per km² of arable land*

District	Total population	Total area (km²)	Arable area (km²)	Gross density per km²
Butha-Buthe	100 644	1 767	105	57
Leribe	257 988	2 828	424	91
Berea	194 631	2 222	326	88
Maseru	311 159	4 279	463	73
Mafeteng	195 591	2 119	531	92
Mohales Hoek	164 392	3 530	396	42
Quthing	110 376	2 916	155	38
Qachas Nek*	63 984	2 349	85	27
Mokhotlong*	74 676	4 075	161	18
Thaba-Tseka*	104 095	4 270	176	24
Lesotho	1 577 536	30 355	2 822	52

District	Net density per km² of arable land	Total population (%)	Total area (%)	Arable area (%)
Butha-Buthe	959	6.4	5.8	3.7
Leribe	608	16.3	9.3	15.0
Berea	597	12.3	7.3	11.6
Maseru	672	19.7	14.1	16.4
Mafeteng	368	12.4	7.0	18.8
Mohales Hoek	415	10.4	11.7	14.0
Quthing	712	7.0	9.6	5.5
Qachas Nek*	752	4.1	7.7	3.1
Mokhotlong*	464	4.7	13.4	5.7
Thaba-Tseka*	591	6.9	14.1	6.2
Lesotho	559	100.0	100.0	100.0

* Denotes mountain districts

Source: LSPP, 1989, No.4, p.13

At present there is very little quantitative data on sectoral use of land, yet this information is crucial for efficient landuse planning and environmental conservation. Even the recently published document by the Department of Lands, Surveys and Physical Planning, *Land Use and Land Tenure* (1989), only shows quantities of land used for crop cultivation and livestock grazing. Other land uses are simply aggregated into an 'others' category. The Resource Survey of Lesotho (1988), completed by the Ministry of Agriculture, gives more quantitative information on land use, particularly for agricultural purposes, first for the entire country (Table 3.3); secondly by district (Table 3.4) and then by agro-ecological zone (Table 3.5). Research that aims to provide Lesotho with information on all land uses by type and quantity is essential as a basis for proper landuse planning and management.

Table 3.3 *Land use in Lesotho, 1988 (ha)*

Land use	Lesotho
Fruit	149 081
Maize	384 650
Sorghum	177 566
Small Grain and Sunflower	65 854
Beans and Peas	39 516
Fallow	63 761
Fodder	10 537
Other Crops	10 537
Cropland total	754 002
Range	1 981 896
Forest	12 118
Rock	103 798
Gullied	59 572
Villages	98 802
Roads	12 118
Water	33 179
Other	1 581
Sub total	2 303 064
Total	3 057 066

Source: MOA Resource Survey of Lesotho, 1988

Labour

The second reason for agriculture's declining contribution to GDP is concerned with competition for labour for other activities. In theory, over 80 per cent of the population is employed in agriculture. Yet in practice, 'over one half of the adult male population of Lesotho aged between 20 and 45 are employed in mining outside the country' (MOA, 1986: 3). Since the 1970s, mining wages have increased markedly compared with earnings in full time farming. This leads to strong competition for labour between agriculture in Lesotho and mining and agriculture in the neighbouring Republic of South Africa. The environmental repercussions of 'absent' labour in Lesotho are that farming is left in the hands of the very young, women and the elderly. These people cannot manage conservation techniques well, both from a biological and physical standpoint, especially in situations where major decisions on land use are still controlled by 'absent' male members of the family. This report proposes that project assistance be given to explore alternative possibilities of off-farm employment within the country so that more labour will be available locally throughout the year to manage the environment. It has also been argued that the migrant labour system divides Basotho families in a socially-degrading way, being associated with problems such as sexual morality, illegitimacy and marital disharmony. However, over the last few years the number of Basotho men employed in the South African mines has declined; migrants are being repatriated in large numbers as the mechanisation of mining and the increased use of indigenous South African workers occurs.

Table 3.4 *Land use by district, 1988 (ha)*

	Crops	*Livestock grazing*	*All other*	*Total*
Butha-Buthe	50 799	110 895	16 265	177 959
Leribe	78 349	177 649	28 816	284 814
Berea	66 680	123 593	33 510	223 683
Maseru	95 347	296 999	38 602	430 948
Maffeteng	111 689	85 323	16 397	213 409
Mohales Hoek	90 078	234 966	30 471	355 515
Quthing	51 866	218 047	23 764	293 677
Qachas Nek	62 651	159 811	14 111	236 573
Mokhotlong	82 228	303 695	24 480	410 403
Thaba Tseka	66 566	337 768	25 651	429 985
Total	75 625	204 874	25 206	305 705

Source: MOA, 1988

Capital

The third area of resource-use conflict amongst various sectors relates to competition for capital resources. Studies on investment distribution in Lesotho show that there is an urban bias in terms of both private and public investment distribution. Maseru, in particular, seems to get a disproportionate share of overall investment. From an economic sectoral viewpoint, agriculture has, in the past, received a relatively higher share of the public budget. An analysis of the latest figures in the national budget, however, indicates that agriculture is receiving a declining proportion. This report urges that priority in terms of budget allocation be given to those sectors that deal with the environment directly if the already-fragile natural resource base is to be enhanced for sustainable development in Lesotho. Empty declarations that agriculture is given top priority without relevant budget allocations and/or visible support to improve the service is deceptive both to the public and to the donor community.

Table 3.5 *Land use by agro-ecological zone (ha)*

	Crops	*Livestock grazing*	*All other*	*Total*
Lowlands	320 064	196 706	88 351	605 121
Foothills	104 768	161 647	30 006	296 421
Mountains	247 669	1 454 140	113 959	1 815 768
Orange River Valley	83 752	236 253	19 751	339 756
Total	756 253	2 048 746	252 067	3 057 066

Source: MOA, 1988

Further issues

It is a measure of Lesotho's extensive environmental problems that within the division of portfolios amongst the SADC Member States, Lesotho has responsibility for soil erosion.

Environmental degradation in Lesotho is to be found in a variety of forms ranging from soil erosion to the pollution resulting from urban waste disposal. But the greatest threat to the ecological stability of the country is soil erosion– sheet, rill and gully erosion. The origins of soil erosion in the country date back to the early nineteenth century. The reason for this is that, unlike other countries to the north, Lesotho was characterised by grasslands even before the missionaries, with timber-based technologies such as ox carts that used highly erodible roads, came and, together with other forces, put pressure on the few trees and fragile soils in the country. Now soil erosion in the country, typified by deep gullies in the lowlands and bare hillsides in the highlands, is very extensive. It has been estimated that some 39 million tonnes of soil are lost every year.

Technical attempts to combat soil erosion were begun in 1936 in the form of contours along the undulating lowlands and tree planting. It has been alleged that these early attempts had limited success because of the forceful methods used by the colonial government. However, prior to independence there do not seem to have been any initiatives to change or modify the prevailing landuse management system that was already acknowledged as being responsible, at least in part, for soil degradation. The first major attempt came at the end of the 1970s when the Land Act of 1979 was put into force.

At the policy level, actions were limited to a series of land acts. The issue of land degradation was not treated as a separate subject in these but was implicit in those acts controlling range management and land utilisation. A major step in dealing with the matter at the policy level was the formulation of the National Environmental Action Plan in 1989. This will be discussed in more detail below.

The main causes of soil erosion remain the continued use of the limited land resources for a multitude of agricultural and other purposes, the harvesting of the scanty vegetative cover and other organic matter for fuel, and most significantly for future policy interventions, the ineffectiveness of the existing landuse management practices.

Agriculture continues to be a major contributor to soil erosion because, firstly, the undulating and mountainous nature of the land is marginal for raising crops. Secondly, the livestock population greatly exceeds the carrying capacity of the grazing lands. Estimates put overstocking between 150 and 300 per cent. Because of the increasing human population, land is also needed for housing and other developments.

As fuelwood is scarce in rural areas, the people also use shrubs, dung and crop residues as fuel. Fuelwood is particularly scarce in the mountains and other less preferred sources of biomass are used for fuel. In the mountains shrubs take a long time to grow. Their removal for fuel (the whole plant is uprooted) leaves bare patches of earth exposed to erosion on the hillsides where the shrubs are mostly found. Furthermore, using dung and crop residues as fuel precludes recycling them as an organic fertiliser.

In recent years, a detailed study of soil erosion and reservoir sedimentation in two catchment areas, the Roma Valley, Maliele area and the Khomo-Khoana district, revealed very disturbing levels of erosion and siltation (Chakela, 1981) (Figure 3.1).

The rates of erosion and sedimentation were investigated to differing degrees in different areas, dependent on the methods employed and the intensity to which the methods could be used. The studies within the Roma Valley and Maliele catchments are relatively quantitative, because of the availability of reservoirs and the intensity of the water and sediment sampling during the field period. Table 3.6 shows the rates of erosion and sedimentation within the Roma Valley and Maliele catchments. The rates of net erosion vary considerably from area to area and cover a range of about 100–2000 t km^{-2} y^{-1}. These values were measured in reservoirs and selected river stations and therefore are only indirect indices of the real rates of erosion in the catchments. This is because large amounts of eroded materials are deposited upstream of the measuring sites.

Table 3.6 *Rates of erosion and sedimentation, Roma Valley, Maliele Catchment and Little Caledon Catchment.*

Catchment	Relief ratio m/km	Catchment area km^2	Sediment yield t km^{-2} y^{-1}	Remarks
Roma Valley area 1	860/7.9	26.0	380	Based on water and sediment discharge measurements, 1976–1977 rainy season
			340	Based on reservoir surveys between 1973 and 1975
Roma Valley area 2	200/0.8	0.5	1700–1870	Based on reservoir surveys between 1973 and 1977
Roma Valley area 3	50/0.9	0.6		Based on reservoir surveys. The reservoir had such a low rate of sedimentation that it could not be used for sediment yield estimate with any certainty
Roma Valley area 4	310/2.6	2.2	825	Based on reservoir surveys between 1973 and 1977
Roma Valley area 5	920/13	57.0	1370	Based on water and sediment discharge in 1976/77 rainy season
Maliele area 1	210/1.4	0.6	220	Based on reservoir surveys between 1974 and 1977
Maliele area 2	325/4.2	6.3	350	Based on reservoir surveys between 1974 and 1977
Maliele catchment	375/6.5	13.5	270	Based on water and sediment discharge during 1976/77 rainy season
Little Caledon Basin	1495/43	945	1979	After Jacobi 1977

Source: Chakela, 1981:143

The catchment surveys and air-photo studies indicated that the severity of erosion in the catchments varied from one landform zone to another. The spurs and pediment slopes, both in the basalt and sandstone terrain, are severely affected by surface wash and rill formation. Gullies are limited to narrow zones in the drainage depressions and to the floodplains of the major streams and their tributaries. The severity of erosion is further aggravated by intensive cultivation of the spurs and pediment slopes in the lowland and by overgrazing on the steep slopes in the mountains and on the scree slopes. Land use, therefore, is also a major factor in the erosion processes in the areas studied. A clear example of the effect of cultivation on erosion and sedimentation is that large areas with fields and villages show higher sediment delivery to the catchment streams than smaller areas with limited cropland. The comparison of sediment concentration at two Roma Valley river stations during the rainy seasons of 1975/76 and 1976/77 showed increased sediment concentration downstream. The intervening area between the two stations is heavily cultivated and under rapid urban development.

The severity of the processes within the Roma Valley and Maliele catchments can be ranked as follows, beginning with the most severe:

1. surface wash and rill formation;
2. gully erosion;
3. local sedimentation at the foot of steep slopes and within gullies;
4. wind erosion on the open spurs and pediments;
5. mass movements on south-facing slopes.

The greatest erosion caused by running water occurs mainly during two periods: after the first heavy rains following the dry season, and during the time of ploughing and weed clearing. In the former there is practically no vegetation to intercept the high-intensity raindrops, as the cultivated areas are bare of crops and the pastures have not yet recovered their grass cover after the dry season. Wind erosion is also very prevalent during the early spring (August and September). The lack, or shortage, of vegetation cover at the beginning of the rainy season and the loosening of the soils on the cultivated lands during the ploughing and weed-clearing periods, combined with the high intensity of the thunderstorm raindrops, all work to aggravate the effect of raindrop erosion and wind erosion during the early, windy part of the spring.

The rates of reservoir sedimentation indicate that most of the reservoirs (exceptions being regulated reservoirs or those with other reservoirs upstream) have a very short useful life. Most of the reservoirs within the study areas are filled within 10 years, and all are filled within 30 years. Reservoir capacity losses are about 4-20 per cent per year. The highest losses occur in the first few years after dam closure.

Within the Khomo-Khoana catchment, ground measurement of freshly eroded gully sites and measured sediment accumulation along gully cross-sections indicate an average of 0.1–1 mm lowering of the ground surface per year in the severely-eroded catchments.

The worst and most widespread erosion in the Khomo-Khoana catchment, though not obvious at first glance, is the loss of the surface layer of soils on spurside slopes and pediment slopes in the lowlands. This leads to bedrock exposure, or to the formation of small rills, descending the side slopes through cultivated lands. Gully erosion is the most obvious and striking erosion feature. Rates of gully growth, however, are variable. Rates as rapid as 100 m in ten years have been observed. The main reason for some gullies growing only slowly seems to be associated with the presence of bedrock or very shallow soil. Another factor may be that all areas liable to gully erosion have already been gullied. This is partly supported by the absence of newly-gullied areas since 1951. The lateral extension of several major gullies is limited to the steep upper reaches of the catchments. The lower reaches seem to have stabilised, with deposition along the gully floors.

The rapid rates of erosion in the investigated areas and those obtained by the Department of Hydrological and Meterological Services of Lesotho correspond to sediment yields of 100–1900 t km^{-2}y^{-1}. These figures, however, are for very short periods, and the range may be lower for long-term rates of denudation. The longest period of observation is 6 years (Little Caledon). The erosion within these areas leads to the rapid sedimentation of:

• sandy, fertile materials at the base of the scree slopes and along gently sloping parts of inter- spur depressions; and
• silty to clayey sediments in the floodplains of major streams and in the reservoirs.

Some arable floodplain land therefore is lost because of such sedimentation. Other results of the erosion and sedimentation are:

- rapid siltation of several of the reservoirs constructed since the late 1950s;
- high sediment loads in the major streams; and
- development of river terraces.

Raindrop erosion, in the form of splash and surface wash (including rill formation), is the most severe erosion process on grazing and cultivated land, both in the basalt and in the sandstone terrain, on spurs and pediment slopes with 3–6° gradients. Observations of splash pillars, buffer strip heights above the field surface, and of pegs along some of the slope transects show that the average annual rates of surface lowering may be as high as 10–15 mm.

Gully erosion is second in importance and is the most spectacular erosion feature in all the areas investigated. Field observations and air-photo comparison revealed no newly-gullied areas since 1951. The largest gullies are found along the major drainage channels and form headward extensions of these. Discontinuous, valley-side gullies are not widespread, but where they occur they are the only gullies that do not follow the general drainage pattern within the catchments.

The third most important erosion feature is the parallel gullies and rills along the livestock tracks. These are formed by livestock and occur between pastures and villages and on large areas of bare ground around homesteads. Channel erosion, mass movements, pipe erosion and regolith stripping form the fourth group of active geomorphic processes. These are, however, very local. Wind erosion may be an important process on the open spur and pediment slopes. Some of the bush pedestals may result from the combined effects of rain splash and wind erosion. The maximum wind activity probably occurs during the dry, windy months of August and September, when the cultivated lands are bare of crops and stubble, and the pastures have not yet regained their grass cover.

The major conclusions that can be drawn are that raindrop erosion and surface wash are more important present-day processes than gully and channel erosion. The period of maximum gully activity is past. However, gullies have created channels for the easy and rapid concentration of runoff and transportation of water and sediment from the catchments.

Rural energy problems

Lesotho, like most African countries, faces the problem of a limited supply of renewable types of energy, caused partly by overgrazing, soil erosion, deficient farming methods and the over-use of animal and plant wastes as well as a lack of indigenous forests. The situation is aggravated by the lack of financial resources necessary for intensive studies into alternative sources of energy, the lack of an energy conservation campaign, the lack of formally-trained manpower in the rural energy sector, and the lack of continuity of foreign technical assistance.

In terms of traditional sources of energy, the rural sector of the country depends largely on firewood and dung for space heating, cooking and heating water. Fires are also used as a source of light at night.

In the modern energy sector, Lesotho relies exclusively on South Africa to meet most of its commercial energy requirements. Imports include refined petroleum products, electric power, coal and firewood imported mainly for the urban areas. Only an insignificant percentage of imported firewood finds its ways to the rural areas. Lesotho meets more than 95 per cent of its electricity needs through imports from the Electricity Supply Commission of South Africa (ESCOM) and electricity is transmitted and distributed locally by the Lesotho Electricity Corporation (LEC). Electricity is supplied via three intake points at Maseru, Maputsoe and Hendrieks Drift. Maseru is estimated to take more than 90 per cent of total imports. Qachas Nek (southeast of the country) works as an isolated system supplied by diesel generators. Only about 2 per cent of the total population uses electricity, a very low electrification rate by SADC standards. The situation is changing gradually following the commissioning of the first two mini-hydro power plants; a 2 MW plant connected to the grid in Montsonyan and a 210 kw isolated plant in Semonkong, both in rural areas. Other mini-hydro power plants in Tlokoeng and Tsoelike are under construction and are due to come on line soon.

In terms of biomass fuel supplies, wood and shrubs form the major energy source still available in the country. Total wood resources including already planted woodlots amount to 6.6 million tonnes of firewood equivalent to 115,500 terajoules (TJ) (1984 figures). Most firewood originates from shrubs grown on 'shrubland' and 'rangeland'. Wood from trees and woodlots contributes only a little to the total supply, as can be seen in Table 3.7.

Table 3.7 *Fuelwood sources in Lesotho*

	Stock (tonnes)	MAI (tonnes/year)
Natural forests	2 170 080	108 504
Shrubland[1]	1 269 615	126 962
Shrubland[2]	5 832 945	583 295
Rangeland[1]	219 790	21 979
Rangeland[2]	2 306 164	230 616
Fruit Trees	520	36
Other areas	34 560	3 456
Woodlot	315 432	28 924
Total woody biomass	12 149 106	1 103 772
Total firewood	6 658 630	607 075

MAI=Mean Annual Increment
1 Near densely populated areas, mostly lowlands
2 Near sparsely populated areas, mostly mountain

Dung is the second largest source of biomass. An annual amount of 510,000 tonnes of dry dung, equivalent to 6423 TJ is available at present.

Crop residues are another source of biomass. The potential of this energy source depends on the production of the five major agricultural products namely, maize, wheat, sorghum, peas and beans. The potential amounted to an estimated 229,200 tonnes, equivalent to 3761 TJ in 1984. Since the Ministry of Agriculture has assumed that agricultural production will increase by 1 per cent per annum the potential of agricultural residues should grow at the same rate. This should mean that the potential available in the year 2010 would be about 300,000 tonnes.

Turning to new and renewable energy sources the total potential of solar energy in 1984 amounted to 579 TJ. Solar energy in Lesotho can be used to satisfy the demand for heating water and for space heating. The wind energy potential of 2 TJ is negligible and it is therefore not considered in the supply forecasts.

The situation in other fuel sub-sectors is as follows:

Petroleum
Demand for petroleum and its products was estimated at 90 million litres in 1984, an annual growth rate of 9 per cent since 1980. Petrol accounted for about 40 per cent of total demand whilst paraffin and diesel had a share of below 30 per cent each. Prices are uniform throughout the country except for the mountain areas.

Coal and firewood

Demand for coal and firewood has grown moderately at 3.1 and 1.9 per cent per annum since 1980 and amount to 80,000 tonnes and 35,000 tonnes respectively. Retail prices in Maseru amount to Maluti 8.50 per 80 kg bag for coal and to Maluti 5.50 per 40 kg bag for imported firewood (1987 figures).

Electricity

Electricity consumption was estimated at about 105 gWh in 1984 and has doubled during the last five years. High growth rates of nearly 20 per cent occurred in the domestic and commercial sectors. Growth slowed down to 7.5 per cent per annum from 1984/85 to 1985/86 mainly due to economic recession. Total peak demand increased at an annual rate of 14.4 per cent to 31.7 MW in 1986/87, the load factor was 43 per cent and transmission and distribution losses are estimated at 10 per cent.

Hydropower

This is Lesotho's most promising energy source. The commercial energy demand could be met by transforming water power into electricity. The total electricity energy potential of Lesotho is estimated to be 1300 gWh per annum.
    The potential energy and power supplies at generation level are given in Table 3.8 below.

Table 3.8 *Potential supplies from hydropower stations*

Project	Projected first year of commissioning	Installed capacity (MW)	Energy generation (gWh/year)
Lesotho Highland Water Project	1995	73.5	225.0
	2000	110.0	346.0
Oxbow	2005	54.0	154.0
Mantsonyane	1988	2.0	6.6
Semonkong	1988	0.34	1.3
Tlokoeng	1990	0.67	3.3
Qachas Nek	1992	0.4	2.1
Total		167.41	513.3

Overstocking and range management

Estimates of the overstocking of rangeland vary from 150 to 300 per cent. Continuous and uncontrolled grazing has resulted in progressive deterioration in the condition of the rangeland, which is manifest in the increasing loss of vegetative cover, depletion of some of the more palatable species of grasses and their replacement by woody shrubs (such as the Karoo shrub, *sehalahala*). The *National Resource Inventory of Lesotho* (1988) produced by the Conservation Division of the Ministry of Agriculture found the condition of only 12 per cent of the rangeland to be 'good' or 'excellent', the remainder being 'fair' (73 per cent) or 'poor' (12 per cent). Unless, stocking rates can be dramatically reduced and range management policies made effective, deterioration will continue at an increasing rate.

Analysis of the underlying causes of environmental problems such as overgrazing is complicated by the fact that causes, and consequences, of the different environmental problems are closely interrelated. For example, crop residues are consumed by animals, due to the traditional right that stockholders have of grazing their animals on stubble after harvest. Overstocking results in the increased use of crop residue that is essential for the improvement of soil fertility and soil structure, thereby contributing to further erosion. At base, this factor arises because of the system of land tenure, which is not only contributing to environmental degradation, but is no longer even fulfilling the equitable social function for which it was intended. As the proportion of the people holding cattle has declined, a situation has arisen where stockholders have increased their individual wealth by increasing stocking rates, transhumance and overgrazing, this being at the expense of society as a whole, which has to bear the substantial cost of soil erosion and land degradation. The net result is that although livestock populations are high, their productivity is very low. As a result of this low productivity, households are not self-sufficient in earnings from livestock production and have to supplement their income by labour migration. The country as a whole is not self-sufficient in livestock products and still has to import most of these from South Africa.

Urban pollution

The widespread encroachment of unplanned human settlements onto agricultural land has been another contributory factor to declining agricultural production.

More generally, urban development without proper planning has introduced a new set of environmental problems, including the careless disposal of waste products such as motor-car wreckage and beer cans, and water pollution from the disposal of wastes into rivers used as sources of drinking water. Inadequate pit-toilet systems in urban areas have become a health hazard leading to the spread of diseases. In general, throughout both urban and rural areas, public health and nutrition levels are low and there is an urgent need for improvement.

Other problems which have arisen in the agricultural sector include the improper use of chemicals, in particular hazardous pesticides. There is a lack of information and of legislative powers in this area, as a result of which harmful substances, banned in other countries, have been finding their way into Lesotho. Industrial forms of chemical pollution, however, have not yet posed much of a problem in the country due to the absence of major industries. Despite this, air pollution is already evident especially in Maseru during winter mornings and evenings due to the burning of coal.

From a broader environmental perspective, the preservation of genetic diversity is recognised as necessary for carrying out breeding programmes to protect and improve cultivated plants and domesticated animals, as well as to assist scientific research, technical innovation and the security of industries that use live resources. Much of Lesotho's flora and fauna has become extinct or rare due to habitat destruction. For example, the spiral aloe is seriously threatened with extinction.

THE NATURAL RESOURCE BASE AND LEGAL UNDERPINNINGS

The country lacks commercially exploitable minerals and the most important natural resource is land. Yet this is very limited in a country with an area of only 30,355 km^2 and a total population of 1.5 million. The overall population density is 53 persons per km^2, but most of the country – two-thirds – is covered by mountains and they are sparsely populated. Hence the population density in the lowlands and foothills where most people live, and where most of the arable land is found, is almost ten times higher than the average figure, standing at 494 persons per km^2. The term 'lowlands' is rather deceptive, as these are not flat, being interrupted with low, rocky hills. As a result of these landforms most of the country is difficult to cultivate.

The land under cultivation has been estimated at 754,000 hectares or 2.5 per cent of the land area. This small area poses a severe constraint on agricultural development, the alternative occupation to employment in the mines of South Africa. In 1986 25.4 per cent of the rural households were already landless.

The only other natural resource in Lesotho is water. At the forefront of the debate over this resource is the Lesotho Highland Water Development project and secondly, the Oxbow project. These two big hydro projects have been much discussed, especially the former. Lesotho contributes about 115 cubic metres per second to one of the most important rivers of Southern Africa, the Senqu-Orange river (half its total flow), whose source springs from the Maluti mountains. This so-called 'white gold' runs 1500 km before discharging into the Atlantic Ocean. The river's length inside Lesotho has yet to be exploited. Controversy about the Highland Water scheme centres on the fact that it will transfer water to the Republic of South Africa and put an onerous debt burden on Lesotho. South Africa, the scheme's main backer, has long coveted a cheaper alternative for satisfying the need for water in some of its drier zones. Lesotho officials emphasise that, although criticism has centred on the reinforcement of dependency on South Africa, the large hydropower capacity, planned for installation in three stages and extending to the year 2018, is an equal component of the project. All told, the Highland Water project is expected to provide Lesotho with some 164 MW of electricity. But the first 73 MW would not come onstream until 1995, at which time the scheme would be expected to cover the peak load.

Although the Oxbow project was originally a part of the Highland Water project, when it was dropped from the overall plan in 1984, the Lesotho government turned to outside consultants to assess its possible development as a solo scheme for taking advantage of the upper catchment of the Malibamatso river. The resultant studies show that if optimised for power generation, Oxbow could generate about 154 gWh/per annum for an installed capacity of 54 MW. It is possible that negotiations on the Oxbow scheme may culminate in its being developed long before the Lesotho Highland Water Project.

Resource markets and the process of social differentiation

In Lesotho the process of social differentiation is largely brought about by differences in access to both the land and livestock resources.

Land resources and rural differentiation

Until the Land Act of 1979, land in Lesotho was, in theory, communally owned. However, even today, in practice, land for agricultural use in Lesotho is still communally owned.

Communal land tenure and use have statutorily been embodied in the laws of Lerotholi which set out all conditions under which land can be owned, used and revoked. The basis of communal land law has been the fact that land in Lesotho belongs to the Basotho and hence each Mosotho is entitled to an allocation of land for farming (three fields) and for building a homestead (one site for each wife). Secondly, land cannot be transferred or used in monetary exchanges, i.e. it cannot be sold, so people have usufruct rights only.

These two bases of land ownership and use have prohibited the formation of social differentiation based on land ownership that results from the commodification of farming land. It has therefore not been possible to have a landed class in the country. Indeed, a lot of the accusations of the so-called 'inefficiency' of communal land tenure in Lesotho are based on the fact that it does not allow for a process of rural differentiation whereby those who have capital can accumulate land and use it to increase output (see LASA, 1978). It is important to realise, however, that not everybody has agricultural land in Lesotho. In fact the degree of landlessness has been increasing over the years from 13 per cent in 1970 to 25 per cent in 1986.

At present 70,593 rural households have no land. This is not because they do not have money with which to buy the land but because land for agriculture has not yet, in practice, been commodified. People have no land because there are too many of them and there is no more land to allocate. The re-distribution of available land by reducing the number of fields already owned is not done because it is not in the laws of Lerotholi, which were made first in 1903 when people were few and land 'plentiful'. Unfortunately, subsequent revisions of the land laws, the latest of which was as recent as 1973 never addressed the issue of re-distribution of land. One can speculate that this was against the interests of decision-makers especially chiefs, who invariably have the biggest fields.

In essence, therefore, rural differentiation in the country is tied first to the household life cycle. Households with more children that are still under its control have more labour at their disposal for farming. This helps to increase output which in turn raises their income levels compared with other households. On the contrary, young households and old households with less labour often fail to raise farm output, and hence remain relatively poor.

Secondly, rural differentiation is tied to differential access to migrant remittances from South Africa. In practice, those households with access to such money can utilise this capital on their land resources and thereby achieve better output levels and standards of living compared to those without such access. Moreover, the former can also use the capital so gained to augment their land assets by engaging in sharecropping with those who may have land but no means of cultivating it. Households with access to remittances from other off-farm activities in Lesotho, such as urban employment, also stand to gain and become better off in the same way (Spiegel, 1980).

The process of differentiation in rural Lesotho has, however, been also largely stifled by other factors beyond the boundaries of Lesotho. When the mining industry was beginning in the late 1800s–early 1900s, there was a sub-regional demand for food in the mines and urban agglomerations. The Basotho responded so well to the penetration of a money economy that they became suppliers of cereals to South Africa– an epoch often referred to as the time when Lesotho was the granary of South Africa (Murray, 1981). Deliberate legislative machinations by South Africa to stifle development in Lesotho and convert it into a labour reserve resulted in the prohibition of the export of grain from Lesotho to South Africa. This move inhibited the process of differentiation that had just begun (Palmer and Parsons, 1977).

Since 1979 new legislation has been introduced which will speed up the process of rural differentiation in Lesotho. This initiative is contained in the Land Act 1979, the main motive of which is supposed to be the reorganisation of the agricultural sector by ensuring that land has a market value and that conversion of land into a marketable commodity will allow the emergence of a class of so-called 'enterprising farmers' who it is hoped will control and use the land to increase output.

The instrument that is to be used to achieve this objective is the lease, which is a saleable legal right to land. In essence, all people who own land at present can apply for a lease for each plot, after which they can sell or mortgage the land. Land that is under leasehold, however, has rent charged on it. This means that those who fail to pay the ground rent will be bought off the land by those who have money. This process is expected to occur 'naturally' as market forces of demand and supply of the land resource 'balance' each other for 'efficiency' of production. It is very clear, however that this so- called efficiency will occur at the expense of the equitable distribution of land resources in society.

The Land Act 1979 also has an in-built mechanism for the promotion of differentiation by the government through earmarking some areas as Selected Development Areas (SDA). These are areas where the government hopes to take landowners' land, give leases for the plots and re-allocate the land with the first preference being given to the original owners. However, specific farming practices seen to be 'modern' will be stipulated by the government and groundrent charged. Farmers here will all be expected to follow these 'modern' farming methods, failing which they will be forced either to sub-lease their land or to sell it completely. It is hoped that this will promote agricultural efficiency. Again, it is clear that this 'efficiency' will occur, if at all, at a high cost to the equitable distribution of land resources. The net effect is likely to be that those with capital will accumulate land resources at the expense of the rest of the community (Mashinini, 1986).

There have been arguments that communal land tenure in Lesotho discourages the conservation of land resources because the users do not see the land as theirs. Therefore, the allegation goes, land users have a 'short-term environmental planning horizon' that shows itself in soil mining, a lack of anti- erosion structures and poor or absent measures to combat erosion by land users. Often, those who argue this way recommend that environmental conservation, especially that of the land in Lesotho, can only be achieved through the privatisation, and, by definition, the commodification, of land because this will bestow land users with so-called security of tenure which will provide an incentive for sound land-management practices.

However, in the case of Lesotho, doubts can be expressed as to whether the privatization of land as envisaged for instance under the 1979 Land Act can actually improve conservation. A recent study in Mohales Hoek by Mashinini (1989) which examined peoples' attitudes to this issue suggests that communal land tenure is not perceived as an impediment to conservation by farmers. Rather, farmers see other factors as impediments. Moreover, the study warns that the conservation of land can only be achieved by farmers when they are convinced that doing so will benefit them.

Livestock ownership and rural differentiation

Livestock ownership is the second largest factor that contributes to the process of rural differentiation in Lesotho. Access to livestock resources is very unequal. The 1986 Agricultural Situation Report stated that there are 47,760 households without both land and livestock resources.

Access to livestock resources is determined by the financial position of households, and also in some cases by inheritance. As a result, households with access to migrant labour remittances, either from within, or outside Lesotho, are often in a better position, other factors permitting, to accumulate livestock wealth. Again, increased access to livestock is tied up with the household life cycle. It needs to be remembered, however, that younger Basotho households are now more likely to spend the money accumulated from migrant labour on the purchase of old cars and/or the construction of brick houses as a status symbol rather than on livestock purchases. An important environmental factor with regard to unequal access to livestock resources in the country is that it determines the *de facto* access by households to use of the rangeland. Those who have livestock use it and those without it do not, unless they have livestock on loan (the *mafisa* system). In view of the fact that the rangeland is communally owned as well, it has been argued by some people, including the government, that those who have livestock misuse the range and also overstock it without care because they incur no maintenance/conservation costs. The costs of conservation become the responsibility of society as a whole, because nobody wants to accept responsibility for conservation. This so-called 'tragedy of the commons' problem is said to be responsible for overgrazing, erosion and the poor productivity of the rangeland in the country.

Policy recommendations that follow from this analysis are that land must be privatised, thereby creating rural differentiation among livestock owners as those who have capital buy more land and those with less become marginalised and eventually proletarianised. However, unlike Botswana, in Lesotho, suggestions made earlier in some policy-making quarters about this 'Western cowboy system' of livestock and range management were refuted by the people. However, a new government policy has just been passed, that levies grazing fees for every livestock unit owned. Again, this policy is intended to commodify rangeland indirectly, in the sense that *de facto* access to its use will be determined by a household's financial position. It is clear that households without financial resources will be marginalised and eventually have no access at all to use of the range. Therefore, this policy will also, when fully in operation, promote and speed up the process of rural differentiation. A crucial question is whether this whole process will lead to better range conservation in Lesotho. Botswana's tribal grazing land policy seems to suggest otherwise, if we are to go by their experience.

Gender issues in land use and resources management

In Lesotho there is a clear division of labour according to sex with respect to land use and management. Customarily, ploughing, seeding and looking after livestock are done by men. Weeding, harvesting, the collection of firewood, vegetables, grasses, water and the general routine of bringing up children are done by women.

In practice, however, this division of labour is not so clear-cut due to the fact that many men are absent from home working in South Africa. As a result, all activities are commonly done by women in the absence of men. From the point of view of land resources management, women are very important as land users and managers. It is they who can effect the structural and biological conservation of land resources to ensure sustainable development. An added advantage is that since they bring up children, they are also important potential vehicles of cognitive environmental education. Again, project interventions that aim to explore ways in which the potential contribution of women to environmental management and sustainable development would be most welcome. This point cannot be emphasised too strongly.

The legislative underpinnings of environmental management in Lesotho are listed below:

Land and landuse legislation

The following are laws that have been passed to regulate access to land, land use and conservation.

- The Laws of Lerotholi 1959: These laws were made as a code that regulates access, use and administration of Land Resources.
- Land (Procedure) Act 1967: This Act provided procedures for applications for land allocation, revocations and appeals on matters pertaining to land.
- Deeds Registry Act 1976: This Act provided for the registration of commercial and/or industrial landuse applications.
- Lesotho Highlands Development Authority Order 1986: This provides laws and regulations intended to regulate the functioning and operation of the LHDA.

- Development Projects Order 1973: This order provided the rules to ensure the smooth functioning and operation of development projects in the country.
  - Thaba-Bosiu Rural Development Project Legal Notice 11/73
  - Training for Self-Reliance Project-Government Notice 109/74
  - Khomokhoana Project - Legal Notice 11/77
  - Phuthiatsana Project - Legal Notice 11/77
  - Southern Perimeter Road Project - Legal Notice 16/81
- Administration of Land Act 1977: The Act introduced special laws governing the rights of urban land allocations and use.
- Husbandry Act 1969: The Act introduced land management and landuse regulations that were considered to be essential for good husbandry of the land.
- Land Act 1979: The Act aimed to introduce efficiency of land use through leases, Selected Development Areas and Selected Agricultural Areas.
- Town and Country Planning Act No. 11 of 1980: This was meant to ensure orderly development of towns and the rural areas.
- Range Management and Grazing Control Regulation (amended 1986): This law introduced regulations on grazing rights.
- National Parks Act No. 11 of 1975: This Act provides laws that allow for the establishment, use, and maintenance of national parks and other open spaces.
- Land Act 1973: This Act was intended to strengthen procedures for land allocations and revocations and to reduce the role of chiefs in land administration on Development Committees.

Wildlife legislation

The harvesting and protection of flora and fauna is covered by the following laws:

- Historical Monuments, Relics, Flora and Fauna Act No. 41 of 1967.
- Game Protection Proclamation No. 33 of 1951.
- Locust Destruction Proclamation of 1925.
- Wild Birds Proclamation of 1914.
- Bees Production Act No. 9 of 1969.

Mineral resources regulation

Access to, and use of, mineral resources is regulated by the following laws:

- Uranium and Thorium Control Proclamation No. 6 of 1946: This laid down conditions regulating the prospecting for, and mining of, these minerals.
- Mining Rights Act No. 43 of 1967: The Act provides conditions for the right to mine, and also for the protection of mineral resources in the country.

Water resources legislation

Access to, and use of, water resources is legislated through:

- Water Resources Act No. 22 of 1978: The Act provides regulations for the allocation of access to, use, protection and conservation of water.

Forest resources legislation

The exploitation and protection of forestry if covered by:

- Liremo Control No. 23 of 1970: This law introduced controls on the cutting of forests.
- Forestry Act No. 11 of 1978: This Act made provision for afforestation, control and management of forest in the country.

Summary

Access, use and conservation of natural resources is permitted through the application of the legislation listed above. It is important to realise, however, that Lesotho's natural resource potential for development is limited. Only two resources, water and scenery, can be identified.

The current investment in the Highlands Water Project is aimed to tap this water potential. Unfortunately, the structure of the project is such that outright sale of the water to South Africa is over-emphasised at the expense of irrigation and the provision of energy for Lesotho.

As for the present emphasis on the sale of water, the South African perception of development prospects for the ordinary Mosotho, are likely to be negative. The project will very likely increase Lesotho's dependence on South Africa rather than help to make the country economically more independent.

Moreover the small income generated by the sale of water is more likely to be squandered on urban developments rather than on much needed rural projects.

In terms of scenery, Lesotho has beautiful mountains that are ideal for tourism, hence the name 'Switzerland of Africa'. However, unlike Switzerland, Lesotho has not yet been able to develop its scenery to attract tourists. Earlier efforts to promote tourism were frustrated by the fact that most tourists were from South Africa and when gambling and other forms of entertainment were introduced in Bantustans, Lesotho was unable to compete.

STRATEGIES FOR SUSTAINABLE DEVELOPMENT

Until recently, environmental policies have been formulated and implemented independently by the various sectors or Ministries concerned.

However, the resulting duplication of effort by different ministries and the total neglect of some aspects of the environment, have recently prompted the government to work towards a comprehensive Environmental Plan that can act as a guide for each ministry in its efforts to enhance sustainable development in the country.

At present, all environmental policies are supposed to be guided by the recently adopted *Environmental Action Plan for Lesotho* (June 1989). This plan is the result of a long process of experiment in bottom-up planning. The idea was actually started by the Head of State, King Moshoeshoe II. The people at grassroots level were asked to submit their views on the plan by identifying key environmental problems and by proposing actions to solve the problems. The peoples' submissions were articulated through their Principal Chiefs, two members of each district's development council and the district co-ordinators to the International Conference on Environment and Development in Lesotho, held on the 11–15 April 1988 in Maseru. The various ministers, institutions of higher education, parastatals, non-government organisations and any other interest groups were invited to submit written and limited verbal contributions to this conference.

After the conference all the material was synthesised by a team of planners to produce the Environmental Action Plan. The first draft was circulated to the invited participants and to the people at grassroots level.

The comments received were used to make a second draft of the plan. This second draft was discussed by a selected national team of technical experts in the various fields involved with Environmental Planning and Management. This discussion took place at a 'High Technical Workshop on Environment and Development in Lesotho' held in Maseru.

The comments from this last Workshop were used to produce the final draft that has become the present *National Environmental Action Plan for Lesotho* (1989) (NEAP). It is too early to assess the actual impact of the Environmental Action Plan on improving sustainable development in the country. In fact the Plan has not yet been implemented.

Proper environmental planning and management can only be achieved when there is adequate quantitative and qualitative data on the present state of the environment. In Lesotho, data on the environment are very poor both in quantity and quality. Therefore, the following surveys and actions are recommended:

- There must be an in-depth study of environmental legislation in Lesotho. Part of this study must also find out why legislation that is already available is being so poorly implemented, and recommend remedial actions.
- Efficient environmental-planning projections can be achieved only when detailed population projections are available. The issue of population size and growth depends heavily on short- and long-term government population policies. It is stressed in this report that the government of Lesotho must devise a clear population policy both for the short and long terms. This will enhance environmental planning projections.
- There is need to strengthen efforts by the Ministry of Health and non-governmental organisations that provide health services, especially in the rural areas.
- Efforts must be made to assist and strengthen actions by the Ministry of Water, Energy and Mining to find and suggest alternative viable sources of energy, especially for the rural population, so as to relieve the pressure on the use of trees, other vegetation and dung as fuel.
- It is recommended that higher-density settlements in the rural areas be identified as rural service centres and that they be up-graded so that they can provide the small villages with basic services.
- A national inventory must be made as to the extent and forms of encroachment on land used for agriculture by other competing uses.
- Most peri-urban areas in the country are very poorly provided for with basic facilities such as sewerage, waste disposal, clean drinking water, and housing. It is recommended that inventories be made as to the level of provision of these basic services in the peri-urban areas of all towns. Secondly, financial assistance should be made available for providing these services through settlement up-grading programmes.
- Studies and financial assistance need to be targeted on off-farm activities in the rural areas to encourage the retention of able-bodied labour within the rural sector, so that more effective management of the environment as a whole can be achieved.
- It is recommended that ways by which women can be encouraged to participate more fully in environmental management and education, be devised. This recommendation is made in view of the fact that in Lesotho it is the women who rear the children and manage the households because of male labour migration to South Africa.

In the following pages a series of more detailed strategies for sustainable development are analysed. In terms of landuse management practices many studies agree on the need for radical improvements.

Landuse management issues

In a recent study, on which the next section draws heavily, Kantesi (1991) observed that Gay *et al.* (1990) recommend the fencing of fields for increased productivity, whilst Low (1986), citing examples from Kenya and Uganda, argues that introducing private land ownership would discourage cattle ownership above subsistence level. The study by the ILO also reached the same conclusions when exploring economic options for Lesotho in 1979. The study observed that communal grazing is inconsistent with improved land and pasture management and improved livestock nutrition. Its recommendation was as follows:

> The land tenure issue is so crucial to changes in the productivity of land and livestock in Lesotho that we recommend an urgent and fundamental review. This should be undertaken with a view to providing smallholders with secure and negotiable titles to land.

The response of the Lesotho government to this recommendation and earlier ones was the proclamation of the Land Act 1979 which has had a negative impact on the intended beneficiaries. The Act has been described by many studies as liable to increase landlessness amongst the poor instead of enhancing security of tenure, as was the intention.

The latest policy response to this issue has been elaborated in the National Environmental Action Plan (NEAP) and the documents that followed upon it, such as the NEAP-Implementation Programme and Policy Framework Paper (PFP) – 1990/91 to 1992/93. The main areas of action outlined in these documents are the introduction of grazing fees and the formalization of share-cropping practices.

The introduction of range user or grazing fees is one of the measures aimed at curbing animal stocking rates in the country. The fees are to be collected at the village level by the village development councils (VDCs) on an annual basis. The revenue is to be used to improve the rangelands controlled by each village. Thus this particular measure will be a decentralized activity. Other measures for rationalizing the livestock population of the country are a culling programme, the objective of which is to control the breed quality of sheep and goats; the National Range Adjudication Programme designed to make an inventory and to recommend changes that should enhance the management of grazing areas, and the establishment of additional grazing associations through the National Range Adjudication Areas Programme.

The formalisation of share-cropping practices is meant to encourage land cultivation by those with the greatest farming skills, rather than just the farmers with user rights. Under the system, the holder of user rights rents or sub-leases his land to another farmer and gets paid (usually a percentage of the quantity of the crop produced) by the lessee. Formalising the system means that such arrangements will now be sanctioned by a regulatory authority, instead of being concluded between two parties, as has usually been the case. As with the livestock measures, this regulation is to be implemented at the village level by the VDCs.

The government envisages implementing all landuse regulations through the VDCs – in line with its policy of decentralisation and peoples' participation in the development process.

The principle of development councils was introduced in 1986 after the change of government. They are considered to be the principal organs of development initiatives in their respective areas of operation. Consequently they have a very broad mandate that includes overseeing the implementation of technical projects such as village water supplies and clinics, as well as being directly responsible for administering land utilisation regulations.

However, one deduction that arises from an analysis of the policy documents is that most of the planned interventions, especially the land regulations, have either not been discussed fully with the councils or are not understood by them. The interventions do not originate in the villages but are the ideas of policy-makers in Maseru and the district headquarters. In other words, policy tends to be externally determined. For instance, in connection with the formalising of the subleases and grazing fees, the Policy Framework Paper states that 'there is currently a lack of awareness on the part of village development councils as to the purpose behind these measures, and a lack of local capacity to implement them'. Elsewhere in the document it is mentioned that the introduction of these measures has in fact been delayed, presumably whilst the report of a Land Policy Review Commission is being reviewed at the village level. Also, in spite of the prominent emphasis on horticulture, there are no specific plans or regulations to promote or facilitate it.

Whilst on paper considerable effort has gone into the formulation of actions required to combat environmental degradation, the organisational and administrative structures required to implement the changes are either non-existent or are only embryonic. Because villagers have not been consulted and because traditional power structures have been maintained, it is not known whether the proposals will be acceptable to them. Yet it appears that the proposals have already been made into enforceable laws. The purpose of the current efforts to publicise the measures in the rural areas is to inform the VDCs how to implement the measures. It is not clear whether their opinions will be accommodated. Above all, the new proposals do not originate from the villages as they need to in order to ensure their sustainability. The policy-makers are aware of this fundamental problem and all the documents reviewed emphasise the need to clarify the role of the VDCs as well as to train them. The remedial actions envisaged remain, however, top-down. It is development from the centre to the periphery, as before. This state of affairs has to be revised if sustainable landuse practices are to be adopted. The first step must be the inclusion of people at the village level in the decision-making process, especially those decisions that affect their means of livelihood.

Another problem that affects the successful implementation of environmental programmes is a lack of co-ordination. There are various organisations or projects related to environmental issues in the country. The Policy Framework Paper cites a Land Management and Conservation Project that is helping local communities to formulate their own landuse plans for sustainable agricultural development. There are also other donors involved in similar activities. The links between these activities and the two most crucial measures, grazing fees and formalising sub-leases is, however, not clarified. Growing trees, which should be integral with other environmental activities, is treated separately. The Policy Framework Paper incidentally, discusses these projects under a section with the heading 'Environmental Action' which is dedicated to activities emanating from the National Environmental Action Plan. This is despite the fact that the recommendations of the National Environmental Action Plan are embodied in the other sections of the Policy Framework Paper, especially agriculture. Hence the National Environment Action Plan is apparently treated as a separate programme that is not necessarily part of other development activities.

This anomaly has apparently not escaped the attention of some of the key ministries, as illustrated by a statement made in a Ministry of Agriculture Paper for the October 1990 Conference. The statement reads:

In its paper the MOA calls attention to the large allocation of monetary and manpower resources that will be required to implement the National Environmental Action Plan (NEAP) especially if, as suggested, it is permitted to stand apart as a non-integrated investment. [Ministry of Agriculture, Co-operatives and Marketing] (MOACM) believes that environmental issues should be part and parcel of overall policies dealing explicitly with production and be programmed within project cycles as described by the Ministry of Planning. Costs should then be controlled.

Thus there is a lack of co-ordination and integration in the approach to the implementation of the National Environmental Action Plan. Hence environmental policies and programmes are in danger of suffering the same fate that has affected previous development programmes. This is a mistake that the country cannot afford. There is a need, therefore, to educate policy-makers on the principles of sustainable development. Training is required, not only at village level, but also at the highest level in government. This is the essential first step for a sustainable development future in Lesotho.

Turning to the energy sector, although the commercial sector is adequately managed, the non-commercial rural sector suffers from a lack of planning. The following proposals have been made recently by Makhera (1988):

- Energy projects would be better co-ordinated under the Department of Energy (DOE).
- Formal training of local personnel involved in the energy sector is a prerequisite and should form an integral part of all projects and programmes.
- Good planning and the prioritization of projects by planners and institutions cannot be over- emphasised. It would alleviate the problem of overlap and duplication in the implementation of projects.
- The Forestry Division should be incorporated into the co-ordination committee. The Division should focus attention upon fast-growing trees in order to meet the demand and also study and recommend to the government ways of discouraging fuelwood imports. The terms of reference of the co-ordinating committee should also be revised.
- Energy technology should be included in the syllabi of vocational Farmer Training Schools.
- Infrastructure, particularly roads should be improved in order to make rural areas more accessible.
- Where possible grants, donations and loans should be channelled though organisations such as the Lesotho Agricultural Development Bank (LADB), so that farmers and other rural dwellers could secure loans easily.

Finally, the following four major conservation measures to combat soil erosion are advocated by Chakela (1981). These are mechanically-constructed contour furrows (terraces); grass strips at 2 m intervals (buffer strips); tree plantation; and dam construction across some gullies. In addition, rock-walls and rock-fills constructed in some areas to check the advance of head-scarps and to encourage deposition within the gullies are necessary.

The effect of these measures seems to have been minimal in all the areas investigated in Chakela's study. A very noticeable problem is the lack of maintenance of the structures. Some of the contour furrows empty directly into active gullies, with the result that such furrows form loci of initiation of side gullies. The spacing of the buffer strips has not been strictly followed, and some strips have been removed. As a result, erosion from the water which accumulated on the upstream parts of the strips intensified. Rills and gullies then formed where the water broke through. Most of the rock-walls and rock-fills were constructed without considering the morphological properties of the soil profiles and the flow conditions in them. Consequently, such rock-walls and rock-fills have been left standing as walls as the gully-head scarp advances by piping or sapping.

It is evident that the need for soil and water conservation measures is urgent and vast in Lesotho. One question which is still unanswered is why the maintenance of the present conservation measures is so bad. Is the problem of erosion understood by the authorities? If so, how is this understanding disseminated to the farmers? A related question is whether the farmer realises that soil erosion is a problem that can be controlled through the measures that have been implemented. Fundamental to the solution of any problem is the understanding that the problem exists and that something can be done about it.

On the whole, the same recommendations that have been made in other areas severely affected by erosion can be recommended for Lesotho:

- Soil and water management in the catchments should be improved. Measures to be used include: controlled stock numbers and grazing; re-seeding of grass to cover eroded lands; and within gullies, increased planting of grasses and herbs instead of the trees presently being planted.
- More moisture should be conserved on cultivated lands. This can be done by mulch cover and by ridging and tie-ridging. On maize and sorghum fields inter-row cultivation can be used. This would minimise the channelling of storm waters along the inter-row spaces after heavy thunderstorms.
- Planning and construction of new reservoirs should include estimates of rates of sediment delivery to the reservoirs. Also detailed maps and capacity curves of the reservoirs should be made immediately after completion of the reservoirs. This will facilitate future studies of reservoir sedimentation. In this way the reservoirs will help estimate rates of erosion in the catchment and thus supply information for checking the effectiveness of the anti-erosion measures used within the catchment.
- A permanent erosion and sedimentation monitoring system should be established. This should supply information on the rates of erosion and sedimentation in different areas of the country and should encourage research on erosion and sedimentation control.

For soil and water management improvement in Lesotho, there is therefore an urgent need for continued research into climatic and hydrological patterns. Within Lesotho, only very limited knowledge and useful data are available at present. Such a research programme should also investigate land use, soil loss and sedimentation of different scales within selected catchment areas, ranging from plot studies to studies at catchment scale.

In areas without reservoirs, gauging stations should be installed in well-situated areas where the gauge readings and protection of the instruments can be assured. The best possible results would come from establishing several instrumented catchments in the vicinity of agricultural extension stations, agricultural colleges, the National University of Lesotho and within each of the rural development project areas. At the catchment scale the methods used in Chakela's study could be used with improved density of slope surveys, instrumentation of the river stations and the introduction of a dense network of rainfall stations, including measurements of evaporation and temperature. The implementation of such a programme could be taken as a joint venture by the hydrological survey section of the Ministry of Water, Energy and Mining, the Soil Conservation Division of the Ministry of Agriculture, the Agricultural College, and the National University of Lesotho Departments of Geography and Biology. Such a programme would not only supply urgently needed information but would also help in training the even more urgently needed personnel in studies of the problems of erosion and sedimentation. This in turn would strengthen the almost non-existent research and know-how which presently characterises these institutions. It is only through such rigorous, scientific studies that appropriate conservation policies can be implemented. Without such programmes Lesotho will be unlikely to achieve the goal of sustainable development.

REFERENCES

Chakela, G K (1981) *Lesotho: Soil Erosion and Reservoir Sedimentation*, Scandinavian Institute of African Studies, Uppsala, Report No.54

Department of Lands, Surveys and Physical Planning (LSPP) (1989) *NSP Working Paper No. 4, Population*, Maseru

Department of Lands, Surveys and Physical Planning (LSPP) (1989) *Land Use and Land Tenure*, Maseru

Gay, J *et al.* (1990) *Poverty in Lesotho: A Mapping Exercise*, Food Management Unit, EEC

International Labour Office, (ILO) (1979) *Options for a Dependent Economy, Development, Employment and Equity Problems in Lesotho* , Geneva

Kantesi, B (1991) *Energy and Sustainable Development in Lesotho*, unpublished M.Phil thesis, University of Liverpool

LASA (1978) *Lesotho's Agriculture: A Review of Existing Information* ,Maseru

Low, A (1986) *Agricultural Development in Southern Africa: Farm Household Economies and the Food Crisis*, James Currey, London

Mashinini, I V (1986) 'La difficile reforme fonciere au Lesotho *Politique Africaine*, March 21

Mashinini, I V (1989) *Land Tenure, Land Use and Conservation*, Roma

Makhera, N M (1988) *Energy for the Rural Sector and Related Institutions in Lesotho*, Maseru

Ministry of Agriculture (MOA) (1986) *Lesotho's Agricultural Situation Report*, Maseru

Ministry of Agriculture (1988) *Resource Survey of Lesotho*, Maseru

Ministry of Agriculture (1988) *Lesotho National Rangeland Inventory, Methodology, Results and History 1981-88*, Maseru

Murray, C (1981) *Families Divided*, Cambridge University Press, Cambridge

NEAP (1989) *National Environmental Action Plan for Lesotho*, Maseru

NEAP (1990/91–1992/93) *NEAP Implementation Programme: Policy Framework Paper*, Maseru

Palmer, R and Parsons, N (1977) *The Roots of Rural Poverty in Central and Southern Africa*, Heinemann, London

Spiegel, A (1980) 'Rural differentiation remittances in Lesotho' in P Mayer (ed) *Black Villagers in Industrial Society*, Oxford University Press, (South Africa), Cape Town

4

MALAWI

INTRODUCTION

Malawi occupies the southern part of the East African Rift Valley. It stretches along the narrow western slope of the East African tectonic trench in which Lake Malawi, at an altitude of 475 metres above sea level, is located. It lies between latitudes 9 degrees and 17 degrees south, and longitudes 33 degrees and 36 degrees East. Malawi is about 725 km west of the Indian Ocean. The country is landlocked and is bordered by Mozambique to the south and east, Tanzania to the east and north, and Zambia to the west. It has a total area of 119,140 km^2 of which 20 per cent is accounted for by water bodies.

In terms of topography, Malawi may be divided into three main regions. First is the Rift Valley floor, which is occupied by Lake Malawi in the north and centre of the country, and by the Shire Valley in the south. This represents the structural continuation of the tectonic depression and it joins the Zambezi river in Mozambique. Second is the plateaux region, between 760 and 1400 metres above sea level. It is characterised by gentle slopes, and is interspersed by broad valleys. The plateaux region encompasses the main agricultural production areas. The last topographic feature is the mountains, with rugged steep areas of granite and other crystalline rocks (Figure 4.1).

These great variations in altitude and latitudinal extent are responsible for a wide range of climatic, soil and vegetational conditions. In terms of soils, Malawi possesses some of the most fertile soils in south–central Africa. Of particular importance are those derived from recent sediments – alluvial, lacustrine and aeolian – in the lakeshore plains, the Lake Chiwa–Phalombe plain, and the upper and lower Shire Valley. Good plateau soils occur in the Lilongwe–Kasungu plains and in the tea-producing areas of Thyolo, Mulanje and Nkhata Bay districts.

Climate varies from tropical to sub-tropical, ameliorated by influxes of maritime air. The Chiperoni wind blows cool and wet on occasions throughout the year in the tea-growing areas in the south. Lake Malawi, the plateaux and the mountains moderate both temperature and rainfall. The country has, in general, three seasons: the cool, dry season which lasts from May to August; the hot season with thunderstorms in late October and November which herald the rains; and the wet season which is fully developed by December continuing to the end of March except in the south of Malawi, where the rains end in April or May. Mean rainfall varies between less than 750 mm per annum in the Shire Valley to 1600 mm in the mountain regions. The mean annual temperature is about 24°C.

Within this broad climatic regime, it is important to mention the various micro-climates experienced in different areas. Some areas like the Shire Highlands, Nkhata Bay and Karonga North experience high rainfall levels of up to 2500 mm per annum. Others in the Shire Valley have as little as 375 mm of rainfall. Some experience extended periods of rainfall, which is fairly predictable, while others have intermittent rainfall interspersed by prolonged drought spells. In some years flash floods may be experienced (UNICEF/Malawi Government, 1991).

In demographic terms, Malawi has a rapidly growing population, with an annual growth rate of 3.7 per cent. The total population is approximately 8 million. The great majority of this population lives in rural areas and the major economic activity of the country is agriculture. The Southern

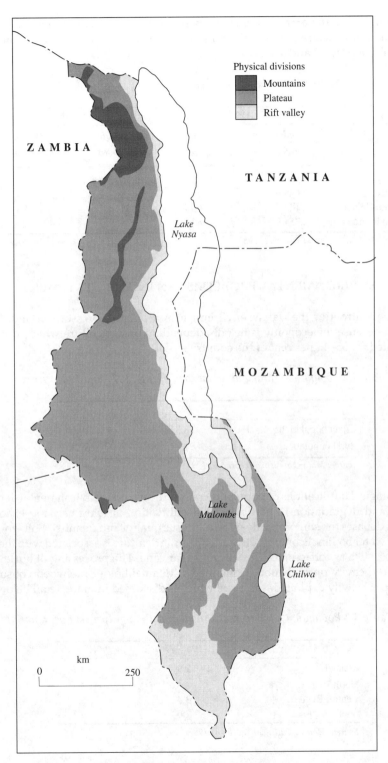

Figure 4.1 *Physical divisions*

Region continues to be the area most affected by population pressure, followed by the Central Region. Population pressure is less serious in the Northern Region. Basic population data are presented in Tables 4.1, 4.2 and 4.3.

Table 4.1 *Population numbers and density, 1967 and 1987*

	1967		1987	
	Population (000)	*Population density per km²*	*Population (000)*	*Population density per km²*
Malawi	5547.5	59	7982.6	85
North Region	648.9	24	·907.1	34
Central Region	2143.7	60	3116.0	88
South Region	2754.9	87	3959.5	125

Source: Malawi Statistical Yearbook, 1987

ENVIRONMENTAL PROBLEMS : AN INITIAL STATEMENT

The major issue confronting the Malawi environment is population pressure on land. The problem is exacerbated because the economy is heavily dependent on agriculture which, throughout the 1980s, accounted for 35–40 per cent of the country's GDP.

Table 4.2 *Population: rural and urban components, 1977 and 1987 (per cent)*

	1977	1987
Urban population	8.3	10.6
Rural population	91.7	89.4

Source: Malawi Statistical Yearbook, 1987

One of the ecological implications of population pressure on land is environmental degradation in general, and land degradation in particular. The cultivation of marginal land exacerbates soil erosion which debases the soil primarily by reducing its quality and quantity. Soil erosion leads to the siltation of water bodies. Economic dependence on agriculture is associated with the cultivation of export crops, such as tobacco, tea, coffee and sugar cane. The processing of burley tobacco in particular relies heavily on fuelwood. Combined with smallholder fuelwood consumption the forest resource is heavily exploited – an issue which is discussed in more detail below.

Table 4.3 *Population – intercensal annual growth rates (per cent per annum)*

	1966–77	1977–87
Malawi	2.9	3.7
North Region	2.4	3.4
Central Region	3.4	3.8
South Region	2.6	3.7

Source: Malawi Statistical Yearbook, 1987

To address the problem of environmental degradation, Malawi faces the following challenges: controlling population growth in order to reduce the level of population pressure on land; avoiding further alienation of land from customary land to estate land; encouraging the adoption of agroforestry in the smallholder subsector; encouraging efficient fuelwood-use technologies both at household and commercial sector level, particularly in the tobacco (burley) industry; effectively promoting non-farm economic activities; and continued efforts in the afforestation programme to offset the imbalance between the supply and demand of the forest resource, wood in particular.

During the colonial period the Malawi economy was neglected because of the perceived absence of exploitable minerals, unlike its neighbours, Zambia and Zimbabwe, whose economies attracted settler interest in mining and commercial agriculture. The Malawi economy was nevertheless exploited by the rest of its neighbours as a supplier of cheap migrant labour which had a good reputation among employers from South Africa to Tanzania.

On independence, the only resources available for domestic exploitation were its labour force and its undeveloped agricultural potential. In the post-independence period the Malawi Government committed itself to making agriculture the mainstay of its economy. The government relied on the promotion of a regulated market capitalism, based on price controls on agricultural inputs and exports, and state participation in distribution and marketing to transform agrarian relations and agricultural production. The strategy chosen was export-led with the maximisation of foreign exchange as a primary goal, followed by the production of primary inputs for the emerging manufacturing sectors and food security for the rural population.

The first five years of independence saw the pursuit of the export-led strategy in agriculture without any attempt to reform agrarian relations which predominantly consisted of a dynamic estate sector and a static subsistence sector with marginal market participation. The period after 1970 experienced a marked transformation in both agricultural production and agrarian relations toward a tripartite pattern of agriculture. During this period, land use was systematically altered at the expense of that available to the subsistence sector by increasing the proportion devoted to estate farming and the 'Achikumbe' scheme consisting of freehold small-scale capitalist farmers.

At independence, Malawi's per capita income was about US$60. Between 1960 and 1979 per capita Gross Domestic Profit grew at a rate of 2.9 per cent per annum so that by 1979 it was around US$200. This rate of growth in per capita income was unparalleled in sub-Saharan Africa for a country without a resource windfall such as oil, diamonds or copper. Between 1960 and 1970 GDP grew at a rate of 4.9 per cent per annum, and at 6.3 per cent per annum between 1970 and 1979, while the population grew at 2.8 per cent per annum. Further, gross domestic investment increased from 10 per cent of GDP in 1960 to 29 per cent of GDP in 1979 and domestic savings increased from 4 per cent in 1960 to 13 per cent of GDP in 1979.

The engine of growth in the Malawi economy has been an export-orientated agricultural sector based on tobacco, tea, coffee, cotton and groundnuts as the main export crops, and maize as the domestic food crop. In the 1970s, total agricultural output grew at an average annual rate of 4 per cent with non-food output growing at 8.6 per cent per annum and food output growing at 3.1 per cent per annum. As a result, food aid imports were negligible.

Between 1969 and 1980 tobacco auction sales increased whilst tea production increased by 38 per cent and that of sugar production by 32 per cent. These rates of growth in agricultural output were almost unparalleled among low-income countries (only Swaziland performed better).

Malawi even managed to launch a fairly successful import-substitution campaign of the type normally recommended by multilateral donors. Between 1970 and 1980 the production of food and beverages for the domestic market increased by 200 per cent, whilst textiles and footwear production increased by 70 per cent and total manufacturing increased by 147 per cent, although there was minimal direct control of the import of inputs, and cheap labour was exploited.

The boom years also brought about a structural change in the economy. Between 1960 and 1979 agriculture decreased from 48 per cent to 43 per cent of GDP. This structural change actually continued into the 1980s, primarily as a result of the decline in agriculture relative to other sectors, so that by 1985 agriculture, industry and services were respectively 38 per cent, 19 per cent and 44 per cent of GDP, (figures rounded).

Finally, one of the most remarkable aspects of Malawi's first decade and a half of development was the growth in formal employment which increased from about 133,000 in 1968 to about 387,000 in 1980, an increase of almost 300 per cent. Agricultural employment increased by about 320 per cent and non-agricultural employment by about 226 per cent during the same period.

However, despite this evidence of growth, Malawi's economy is still characterised by dependency and underdevelopment, as events during the 1980s have demonstrated. In the period 1979 to 1982, Malawi was plunged into an economic crisis as a result of the coincidence of three external factors which underline the vulnerability of the economy: the deterioration in terms of trade, transportation bottlenecks for its exports and imports, and adverse weather conditions that affected the leading sector, agriculture. Thus from an annual GDP growth rate of 5.9 per cent between 1973 and 1979 the economy ground almost to a halt between 1979 and 1982 (0.1 per cent), picking up to 3.8 per cent annual growth due to good weather in 1982 to 1985, but declining at -0.3 per cent in 1986. Taking into consideration a 3.1 per cent annual rate of population growth, the performance of the economy resulted in a 15 per cent decline in per capita GDP from 1979 (US$200) to 1985 (US$170). While total formal employment continued to increase from 359,825 employees in 1980, to 380,853 employees in 1984, its percentage share in the total potential labour force was declining. This share had been 12 per cent in 1966, rising to 30 per cent in 1977 but is estimated to have declined back to 12 per cent in 1987. In general, the 1980s saw a decline in agricultural employment whilst that in manufacturing and in subsistence farming were increasing.

In spite of the admirable achievements of the early years, the agricultural sector was, as in so many African countries, still heavily dependent on the capriciousness of the weather, which in the 1980s was more frequently adverse. The resulting erratic production levels in agriculture had destabilising and negative multiplier consequences for the economy.

During the 1980s the agricultural sector, which is essentially export oriented, was subject to erratic terms of trade as well. The index of commodity terms of trade increased from 100 in 1980 to 123.4 in 1982, falling to 117.5 in 1984, and was estimated to have decreased to 93.56 in 1986. Income terms of trade fell from an index of 100 in 1980 to 96.49 in 1981, increasing to 123.7 in 1983 and is estimated to have fallen to 74.3 in 1986. It should be noted that the terms of trade since the 1960s have not generally been in favour of Malawi since they had declined 28 per cent between 1960 and 1979. The instability in terms of trade has been accentuated by the disruption of Malawi's traditional transport routes to the sea through Beira and Nacala in Mozambique. The consequent re-orientation of export and import routes through other neighbouring countries has drastically increased the cost of transporting imports and exports, let alone the enormous costs incurred in new transportation infrastructure.

The recent depression in the economy has been accentuated by two other factors. First, Malawi with its small open economy and low income levels seems to have exhausted the possibilities of further import substitution for the domestic market, given low levels of protection. Second, the enormous public investment expenditures foisted on the economy in the 1970s, such as the building of a new capital and airport, have come to an end thus depressing aggregate demand in the economy. However, the need to invest in new infrastructure for alternative transportation routes may counter this decline in public investment. The problem nevertheless is that the government has increasingly been compelled to reduce its expenditures as a way of containing the persistent budget deficit, which was reduced from about 12 per cent of GDP in 1981/82 to 6 per cent of GDP in 1985/6.

ENVIRONMENTAL ISSUES

Resource-use conflicts

The major conflicts over resource use in Malawi are associated almost exclusively with land. This dates back to the colonial era. During that period, large-scale land alienation in the Southern Region, together with substantial immigration of the Lomwe people from Mozambique in the early 1900s, resulted in a scarcity of land within the African trust areas and in major conflicts over land between the European estate owners and smallholder encroachers. A 'solution' to this conflict emerged with the development of a tenancy agreement whereby peasants had to supply labour to the estates in exchange for a small plot of land – the system was known as *Thangata*. The social repercussions of this system included the alienation of most families working on estates from their kinship groups and communities. Such conflicts did not occur in the Central and Northern Regions. Despite European settlement in these areas, land shortages were virtually unknown, as hundreds of thousands of hectares of fertile land were retained for peasant use under Trust Land Status (Mkandawire, 1991).

More recently, conflicts over land sparked off by the World Bank experiment of land reorganisation in the Lilongwe Rural Development Programme have arisen. The most common disputes arose with the process of demarcating family plot boundaries. Traditionally, boundaries had to have permanent features. Land consolidation also brought about disputes because of differences in soil quality. The process of land registration and consolidation also created conflicts within the traditional social structure. For instance, the idea of registering land as family land under the head of a family brought some tensions in extended families due to mutual distrust. For the settling of disputes, there was a provision that if a dispute was unresolved the Lands Board, headed by a district commissioner would take up the matter. The presence of government or outside institutional representatives, however, evokes mistrust.

Currently, the interface between the estate and smallholder sectors is plagued by various forms of encroachment. Such encroachment takes many forms. These include smallholders collecting poles, firewood, thatch, or small animals as well as grazing animals and cultivating plots on estate land. Conversely, estates frequently obtain firewood, thatch and other materials from the neighbouring customary areas or government forest reserves. The frequency with which smallholder encroachment occurs suggest that the development of estates has restricted smallholders' access to arable land. These encroachment problems may also be considered as evidence of both the tension points and the interdependencies between the smallholder and estate subsectors.

In Malawi, resource-use conflicts are increasingly caused by population pressure. Population surveys suggest that there are likely to be about 500,000 new entrants into the labour force in the subsistence sector during the next seven years. This growth would require a 12 per cent increase in the area of subsistence land given a modest assumption of 1 hectare per family. By the 1980s Malawi already had begun to approach a critical limit to the privatisation of land and the proletarianization of subsistence farmers. In 1985 Malawi's population density was 85 per km^2. This high population density has been exacerbated by the influx of at least one million Mozambican refugees in recent years. Thus, increasing population density has resulted in a reduction in the size of subsistence holdings and the influx of refugees poses the gravest danger to the use of natural resources particularly in the communal sector near the Mozambican border.

Land pressure in communal areas has resulted in the increasing use of marginal land without necessary investments in restoring soil productivity and in protecting the environment. The increasing use of indigenous wood for curing tobacco among small-scale farmers, coupled with its use as domestic fuel, has also resulted in extensive deforestation in communal areas. The persistence of droughts has further reinforced environmental pressures on land resources.

Malawi's developmental paradigm has so far hinged on a complementary balance between export promotion through land privatisation, and the assurance of cheap labour by impoverishing the subsistence sector. While historically this policy has mainly concentrated on arable agriculture, in recent years it has been extended to fishing, where commercial fishing for export is expanding at a rapid rate at the expense of subsistence and small-scale fishing, and in such a manner that fish resources in lake Malawi are being depleted (see below).

Environmental problems

Land and vegetation degradation

Population pressure on land, exacerbated by the influx of Mozambican refugees, produces a number of environmental problems. The dwindling size of landholdings compels people, especially in heavily affected areas, to cultivate marginal land – defined in terms of soil quality, gradient and rainfall adequacy. For instance, the recommended maximum gradient for cultivation is 12 per cent, but people cultivate slopes as steep as 50 per cent without protective measures; gullies remain unprotected and gully erosion unchecked; bush fires are wantonly lit – destroying soil humus and killing young trees. These processes create soil erosion.

The trends in smallholder landholding sizes are shown below:

Table 4.4 *Trends in landholding sizes*

Land size group (ha)	Mean holding (ha)		Per cent of households	
	1980/81	*1990*	*1980/81*	*1991*
<0.5	0.30	0.25	23.5	26.0
0.5–<1.0	0.73	0.75	31.4	29.9
1.0–<1.5	1.23	1.25	19.0	20.4
1.5–<2.0	1.73	1.75	10.7	11.0
2.0–<3.0	2.40	2.42	10.4	7.8
>3.0	4.14	3.50	5.0	4.8

Source: World Bank, 1990

Furthermore, over 90 per cent of Malawi's energy requirements are provided by fuelwood. The increased demand for land along with the increased demand for fuelwood results in the depletion of natural forest land; less and less land is available for grazing. The dwindling area of uncultivated and forest land threatens the smallholder livestock industry and it leads to overgrazing which, coupled with animal-hoof trampling of the soil, results in further soil erosion. The expansion of estates, particularly those growing flue-cured tobacco, is perhaps the most serious threat to the depletion of forest resources. Overall, there continues to be a growing gap between the demand and supply of poles and fuelwood.

In an attempt to address population pressure the government has recently introduced a family-planning programme with the emphasis on the spacing of births. Land-specific policy options which the government intends to introduce in order to try to alleviate land resource problems are:

- prohibiting further transfer of customary land to leasehold or freehold status and proceeding with studies which will provide the data necessary to evaluate the usefulness of instituting a system of securing land rights in customary areas;
- encouraging the estate sub-sector to allocate some estate land for food-crop production, both for feeding its labour force and for contributing to national food security;
- enforcement of the regulation that requires tobacco estates to allocate a proportion of their land for tree growing in order to reverse the rapid rate of deforestation;
- to increase land utilisation on estates through periodic reviews of land rent; firstly, to increase the productivity of estates as well as to increase employment opportunities, and, secondly, to mobilise resources to fund development activities which can be targeted at the poorest section of the population (Government of Malawi, 1990).

As for the forest resource, the government has identified a series of actions including: undertaking a nationwide programme to identify those water catchments, hillslopes, and other environmentally-sensitive areas suitable for permanent forest cover which require rehabilitation, better protection, and improved management; improving the protection, management and control of woodland; encouraging local communities to afforest sensitive or bare areas; encouraging multiple landuse systems including agroforestry, expanding the future availability of fuelwood by consolidating urban plantation and village woodlot programmes; maintaining, protecting and encouraging the efficient industrial exploitation of hardwoods in forest reserves and softwoods in plantations; and undertaking a timber plantation programme of a size to meet future effective domestic industrial demand (Government of Malawi, 1988).

Water and atmospheric pollution

Because of the narrow industrial base in Malawi, atmospheric pollution is not a major problem – at least for the present. Water pollution, caused by industrial effluent, is equally not a serious issue. However, water pollution as a result of sedimentation has to be considered. Unfortunately, very little quantitative information exists on the sediment load of the streams and rivers of Malawi. Furthermore, the general quality of water in the rivers and streams is not, as yet, monitored. The sediment load of rivers is directly related to the extent of soil erosion. The upgrading of water quality is therefore dependent upon efforts to control soil erosion. Unfortunately, there is no system to monitor, or to determine the extent to which areas are affected by erosion. Nonetheless, it is known that soil erosion is occurring widely and that slopes which are too steep are frequently being cultivated, but no work has been done to define quantitatively where soil erosion rates are unacceptable.

Mineral and energy resource depletion

Malawi's most important energy source is fuelwood. Rapid population growth combined with the rapid expansion of estates continues to threaten the supply of fuelwood from forests. Coal is another energy source. Apart from lime, coal is one of the country's more widely exploited minerals, to the extent that one of the coalfields – Kaziwiziwi in the Northern Region – has been depleted and was closed down in 1990. To supplement the present coal mining at Mchenga (in the north), future plans are to develop the Longwe-Mwabri fields in the Lower Shire valley.

Wildlife resource depletion

Malawi contains a wide diversity of biotic communities ranging from low-lying Rift Valley woodlands to mountain forest and grassland. This is associated with an unusually wide diversity of animals. In addition, Lake Malawi has the most diverse fish fauna of any lake in the world.

It is clear that wildlife resources are under pressure – apart from fish which are exploited less intensively, i.e., the potential supply is still very great. The Government emphasises the economic utilisation of wildlife, and a prerequisite to this is the calculation of what resources are available for harvesting. It is crucial to devise and operate systems for regulating and controlling such harvesting.

The conservation of wildlife resources is expected to be fostered through education via the existing Environmental Unit. This will be supported by law enforcement – especially to contain poaching levels, where particular species such as the rhinoceros are under serious threat. Other measures include selective pest control, electric fencing of national parks and game reserves (to be extended), limiting hunting, and continuing wildlife research and monitoring.

Regarding aquatic resources, Malawi has both traditional and commercial fishing, supplemented by fish farming at both smallholder and estate level. Current information would suggest that there is limited scope for increasing production from traditional demersal stocks in lakes Malawi and Malombe. There seem to be some pockets of under-exploited fish stocks in Domwa Bay, for example, and there could be a large potential in the virtually untouched off-shore pelagic stocks of Lake Malawi.

Future government plans include research into fish processing and marketing; increasing fish exploitation via commissioning a study aimed at the exploitation of fish stocks which are currently under-utilised; the promotion of small-scale and commercial fishing operations; improving the off-shore landing facilities; and expanding the Fish Farming Programme. In the Lower Shire River, fish stocks face a particular threat from the spread of the weed water hyacinth. Its rapid spread threatens not just fish stocks but also fish farming and irrigation schemes in the area.

THE NATURAL RESOURCE BASE AND LEGAL UNDERPINNINGS

Land resources

This section draws heavily on the relevant sections in Agnew and Stubbs, *Malawi in Maps* (1971). Much of Malawi is made up of igneous and metamorphic rocks of the Basement Complex of Precambrian to early Palaeozoic age. These rocks make up a large part of the Malawi Province which is considered a convenient descriptive unit based on some related geological events within the Basement Complex of Africa. This province is bounded by the Zambezi valley on the south, Lake Malawi on the east and the Luangwa valley in Zambia on the north-west. The Malawi Province is part of three large orogenic belts which occur in and surrounding Malawi and which have differing structural and metamorphic characteristics. However, the province derives its name and configuration from the largest and youngest of these belts, the Mozambiquian. The Malawi Province may also be subdivided into northern and southern sub-provinces because of lithological, structural and metamorphic differences.

Mineral resources

Patterns of use, depletion and renewal

A number of mineral deposits have recently been discovered in Malawi. These include coal, phosphates, sulphur, gypsum, glass, high-quality ceramic clay and iron sulphides. Quantitative data for all the known mineral resources are presented below (Table 4.5).

Table 4.5 *Known mineral resources*

Mineral deposit	Proven reserves (million tonnes)	Resources not fully assessed (million tonnes)
Coal	16	>800
Glass Sands	25	5
Limestones	20	600
Ceramic Clays	15	5
Vermiculite	1.6	10
Bauxite	28	NA
Strontianite Monazite	>11	2
Corundum		1.6
Graphite	0.035	0.2
Phosphates	0.985	2
Pyrite/Pyrrhotite	40	10
Kyanite	0.014	0.030

NA: Not Available

Source: Government of Malawi, 1988

Small-scale coal mining began in 1985 through the Mining and Investment Development Corporation with open-cast mining of the high-quality Kaziwiziwi deposits in the Northern Region. In 1988, Kaziwiziwi alone met over 60 per cent of domestic coal consumption. However, the Kaziwiziwi mine was closed in 1990 owing to the depletion of economic reserves and production is now concentrated solely at Mchenga, again in the Northern Region. In the longer term it is hoped to develop the Longwe-Mwabvi fields in the Lower Shire valley, closer to the main centres of demand. Recent coal production trends are shown in Table 4.6.

Table 4.6 *Coal production (000 tonnes)*

1985	1986	1987	1988	1989
1.8	10.7	16.5	NA	41.2

NA: Not Available

Source: Economist Intelligence Unit, 1991

Apart from coal, lime is the principal mineral exploited in Malawi, with an output of 3100 tonnes in 1987. There is also a small-scale production of rubies and sapphires by the Gem company of Malawi. Trial mining of gypsum began in 1990. In 1989, 9855 million tons of phosphate reserves were proved at Tundulu in Mulanje District. This could provide the basis for a future fertiliser industry. It is considered that the reserves are the largest and of the best quality in the SADC region (Economist Intelligence Unit, 1991).

Legal underpinnings

In 1981, a comprehensive Mines and Minerals Act superseded a variety of previous pieces of legislation. It set out the basis of licensing prospecting and mining, and the rights and responsibilities of the Government and investors. Under this Act, small-scale and hand-digging operations are issued simple Mineral Permits by the District Administration. Simple medium-cost operations are regulated by non-exclusive prospecting licenses and mining claims issued by the Commissioner for Mines and Minerals. More sophisticated medium- and large-scale exploration and mining operators are issued with Mineral rights – comprising reconnaissance and mining licenses – by the Minister (Malawi Government, 1988).

Soil resources

The following section is based on Agnew and Stubbs, (1971).

There are four main soil groups, differing markedly from each other in the environmental conditions under which they have been developed, in processes of soil formation, and in profile characteristics and analytical properties. The *latosols* are red to yellow, leached, acid soils in which water movement within the profile is predominantly downwards; they occupy freely-drained sites, mainly on the gently-sloping plains but also in some more steeply dissected areas. The *calcimorphic* soils are grey to greyish brown with a weakly acid to weakly alkaline reaction in which water movement is upward during at least part of the year; they occur on nearly-level depositional plains with imperfect site drainage. The *hydromorphic* soils are black, grey or mottled and are waterlogged for all or part of the year. The fourth group comprises *lithosols* which are shallow or stony soils and *regosols* which are immature soils developed from sands (Figure 4.2).

Latosols

- The ferruginous soils are dark red to reddish brown, mainly clays or sandy clays with a strongly-developed blocky structure and visible clay skins on structural surfaces. They are moderately weathered with clay minerals mainly but not entirely kaolinitic. Typical values are pH 5.0 to 6.0, with an exchangeable cation saturation of 50 to 80 per cent. Development is mainly from rocks of basic to intermediate composition.
- The ferrisols are red clays with a deep, uniform profile. There is a strong structural aggregation, giving a crumbly consistency and free-profile drainage despite the high clay content. The values are pH 4.0 to 5.0, saturation 15 to 40 per cent, and topsoil organic matter content 2 to 4 per cent. This class is developed in areas with a mean annual rainfall exceeding 1270 mm.
- The humic ferrisols are similar to the ferrisols but with a humic topsoil containing 5 to 10 per cent organic matter.
- The ferrallitic soils are yellowish red to red with a moderately sandy topsoil overlying a compact, heavier textured subsoil. The subsoil structure is weakly developed, blocky or structureless with clay skins absent or weakly developed. Highly weathered with clay minerals predominantly kaolinitic, the values register pH 4 to 4.5, saturation 30 to 70 per cent. This soil class is developed mainly from rocks of acid composition

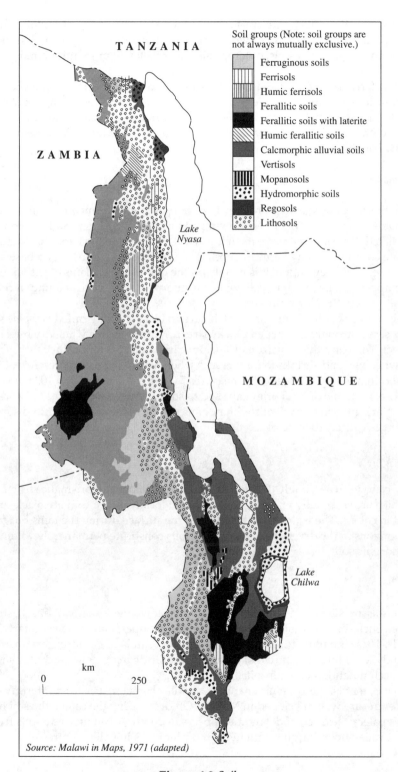

Figure 4.2 *Soils*

- The ferrallitic soils with laterite are similar to the preceding class but contain a horizon of hard iron concretions, partially or wholly cemented together. Laterite, besides occurring widely with this group of soils, outcrops also near valley floor margins amid other latosols.
- The humic ferrallitic soils are reddish to yellowish soils of moderate depth characterised by a humic topsoil with 5 to 10 per cent organic matter in contrast to the 1 to 2 per cent of other latosol classes, pH is 4.0 to 5.0 and cation saturation 5 to 20 per cent. These are developed on high altitude plateaux about 1524 m and on Mulanje Mountain they occur as yellow bauxitic soils.

Calcimorphic soils

- The calcimorphic alluvial soils are grey to dark brown soils formed from alluvium. They are variable in texture, sometimes showing depositional bedding, and have commonly a higher silt content than the very much lower values found in the latosols. Calcium carbonate concretions may occur in depth. The pH registers 6.0 to 8.0 and base saturation 80 to 100 per cent. Development is mainly on the depositional plains of the lake shore and the upper and lower Shire valley but calcimorphic soils are also found in certain river valleys, e.g. the North Rukuru.
- Vertisols or 'Black cotton' soils are dark brown to black. Locally called *makande* soils, they possess a strongly developed blocky structure, very friable when dry but sticky when wet. There is a thick horizon of calcium carbonate concretions in depth. The soil swells when wet and shrinks to form cracks when dry owing to the presence of montmorillonitic clay minerals. PH measures 7.0 to 8.5 and saturation 100 per cent.
- Mopanosols, a name of local origin applied to soils occupied by the tree *Colophospermum mopane*. Dark greyish brown soils with poor structure, alkaline reaction, and sometimes abundant calcium carbonate concretions.

Hydromorphic soils

- Usually clays with a strongly developed, very coarse blocky to prismatic structure; these soils which are seasonally waterlogged are called locally *dambo*, and are black-grey or mottled in colour. The water-table lies close to the surface during the rains but falls to lower horizons in the dry season. The marsh soils constitute permanently waterlogged hydromorphic soils.

Skeletal soils

- The lithosols are stony and often shallow soils. A stone line, usually of quartz stones, is common. Such soils are developed mainly on steep slopes, and also over quartzites.
- Regosols. These are immature soils developed from sands of lacustrine origin and are very sandy, therefore structureless, with little profile development except for slight humus accumulation in the topsoils.
- Soil catenas, that is, the systemic change in profile characteristics from interfluve crest to valley centre, are well developed in Malawi. On descending the catena the soil normally becomes paler or less red and a mottle appears in depth. A belt of sandy soils frequently occurs at valley floor margins with hydromorphic clays in valley centres.

Vegetation resources

The following section is drawn from Agnew and Stubbs (1971).

The principal categories of Malawi's varied vegetative resources are identified below (Figure 4.3):

Montane forests, scrubs and grasslands – The montane communities are those which occur above the low-montane belts of *Brachystegia spiciformis* woodland, at levels of between 1524 to 1828 m above sea level. These highland areas usually present a picture of forest relics in valleys and in isolated stands, with rolling grasslands and scrublands between. The pattern appears to be controlled by annual grass fires and by the moisture of the lower-lying areas maintaining a greener and more fire-resistant margin to the forest relics. The forests vary in composition and include communities dominated by *Widdringtonia whytei* (mulanje cedar) and *Juniperus procera* (African juniper).

Moist semi-deciduous forest – A forest type with evergreen and semi-deciduous elements, found in the high rainfall enclave of the Nsanje Hills. The species include the unique *Burttdavya nyasica*.

Brachystegia woodlands – This woodland category covers those communities referred to as *miombo*, or savanna woodland, in which one or more species of *Brachystegia* is characteristic and *Jubernalia globiflora* is almost ubiquitous. There are many associations involved which have features in common, justifying their grouping into one category. The grass layer is depressed by the relatively light-crowned trees, which have the ability to coppice freely after cutting. The various species of *Brachystegia* are dispersed by the explosive mechanism of the seed pod and often have a distinct distribution of species associated with habitat factors. In the high rainfall areas of Nkhata Bay and Mulanje are tall semi-evergreen forests dominated by *Brachystegia spiciformis* associated with other genera.

Combretum-Acacia-Piliostigma broad-leaved, deciduous woodlands – These are the tall-grass-woodlands referred to as *chipeta* which are subject to fierce annual burns. Fire tolerance and features associated with this character are typical of the species involved. Unlike most trees of the *Brachystegia* woodlands, many of the broad-leaved woodland species are dispersed by animals. Selective felling has given rise to various communities with single species dominance, and cultivation and grazing have produced numerous scrub and thicket communities. Edaphic grasslands are similar in species composition to those of the *Brachystegia* group.

Woodlands scrubs and thickets of the rift escarpment and its foothills — The communities of the escarpments and foothills could be defined according to floristics as *Brachystegia* woodlands or *lowland* woodlands. The terrain, especially of the escarpment, is sufficiently well defined to make it a valid category based upon physiography. Also, floristically the understorey species are often characteristic, particularly the grasses. The escarpments also display clear-cut sequences in the distribution of *Brachystegia* spp. from the higher to the lower levels. On the low foothills standards such as *Adansonia digitata* (baobab) are characteristic, with an understorey of thicket growth. *Oxytenanthera abyssinica* (bamboo) thickets are frequent. The various vegetation types appear to be correlated with the water relations of the sites.

Woodlands, thickets, scrubs and parklands of low altitude – This physiographic division includes the flatter lands below about 500 m. Soils and rainfall vary widely according to location, hence a wide floristic range is encountered. Soils are influenced by drift and colluviation and are often rich in

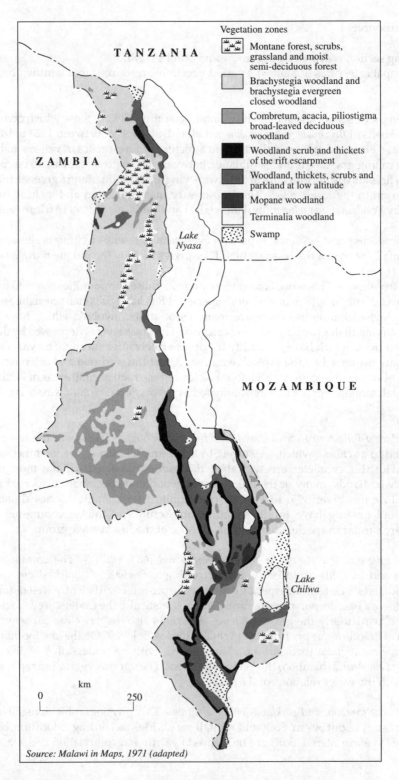

Figure 4.3 *Vegetation resources*

calcium. The most striking feature of the vegetation is the regular occurrence of standard and thicket types, a physiognomic type where tall mature trees such as *Adansonia, Pseudocadia*, and *Sterculia* spp. stand within a dense thicket understorey which includes *Commiphora* spp., *Bauhinia tomentosa* and *Popowia obovata*. These communities are likely to be man-induced since the standards are elsewhere found standing in cultivation parklands. Woodlands and induced thicket are formed by many of the *Mimosacea* such as *Acacia polyacantha* var. *camplyacantha, A. spirocarpa, A. nigrescens, Albiza harveyi* and *Dichrostachys conerea* with *Acacia seyal* and *A. xanthoplea* in wet places. *Ricinodendron rautanenii* and *Terminalia sericea* from woodlands on sandy soils and in the Lower River *Pterocarpus antonseii, Fagara* spp., and *Grewia* spp. with *Acacia pennata* and the *Acanthaceae* form thickets and standards. Base-rich soils support *Euphorbia ingens* and *Commiphora* thicket whilst *Hyphaene ventricosa crinita* and *borassus aethiopum* palms give rise to characteristic communities where the water table is high.

Terminalia woodlands – These are a further floristic division found on semi-swamps, sandy soils and sandbars. The species usually involved is *Terminalia sericea*. Near Lake Chilwa, on soils known as Kawinga grey sands, it forms open woodland with *Brachystegia boehmii*.

Swamp and swamp grasslands – These are edaphic communities under the control of a high water table which may give rise to permanent swamps or seasonally-inundated grasslands. They are complex in species but well zoned according to the depth of the water and the seasonal fluctuations. Typical swamp species include *Typha australis, Vossia cuspidata, Pennisetum purpureum, Echinochloa pyramidalis* and *Cyperus papyrus*. The seasonal swamp areas are typified by *Hyparrhenia rufa, Setaria palustris, Panicum repens, Bothriochloa* spp., and *Cynodon* spp. and by chloris gayana on the base-rich swamps.

Water resources

Lake Malawi

The total area of the Lake Malawi catchment is 96,918 km². of which about 29,604 km² are occupied by the waters of Lake Malawi, making it the third largest of the Central African lakes (Figure 4.4), (Agnew and Stubbs, 1971).

South of latitude 11°S on the eastern side of Lake Malawi the catchment is narrow, not more than 40 km wide, and consists of short impermanent rivers which contribute little to the inflow into the lake. North of this line the catchment widens to include the Ruhuhu River which drains 15,540 km² of Karoo sediments contained within the Livingstone Mountains. From the north-western corner of the Ruhuhu basin the watershed follows the Kipengere Range and then turns westward along the 2134 m summit ridge of the Poroto Mountains. Thereafter the divide crosses the Bundali Range to the Mbozi plateau. From the headwaters of the Songwe River, which separates Malawi from Tanzania, the watershed follows the Malawi-Zambia border to a point near Fort Jameson. Then the divide swings south-east and then eastwards along the Dzalanyama Range to the Kirk Range in the neighbourhood of Dedza and thence to the southern limit of the lake near Mangoche. Between Dedza and Mangoche the divide separates the short parallel rivers draining towards the lake from those flowing southwards into the Shire River rift.

The mean annual rainfall over the Lake Malawi catchment, excluding the lake, is 1179 mm with a recorded maximum of 2946 mm at Kyela and minimum of 686 mm at Rumphi. Less than 5 per cent of the total catchment area receives less than 762 mm of rainfall in an average year.

The Lake Malawi basin is asymmetrical. The eastern side has been downthrown by one main fault or series of faults whereas the western part of the downthrown block has been dropped in a series of western sloping steps by parallel faults. This tilt from west to east is reversed between Nkata Bay and Deep Bay and on the west shore the lake attains its greatest depth of 706 m. On its long axis the average depth of the lake is some 366 m in the north, deepening to over 610 m towards the centre and then becoming shallower in the southern section.

The seasonal variation in the level of Lake Malawi averages just over a metre but has been as much as 2 m. Over long periods the cumulative rise or fall may be much greater and since 1896, when the lake levels began to be recorded, the level has fluctuated from 468 m to over 474 m, a range of more than 6 m.

The long-term changes in the level of Lake Malawi are related to annual rainfall, run-off, evaporation and outflow from the lake. If the amount of water contributed by run-off from the land is greater than the amount of water lost by evaporation over the lake, then this surplus quantity can be stored in the lake or drawn off by the Shire River.

Each year the lake level falls during the dry season and rises again during the rainy season, reaching its highest level about March when the rains are ending. This is the annual fluctuation. Over a period of years with good rainfall and run-off into the lake, the lake level may rise steadily from year to year until a maximum level is reached. Then, if the rainfall and run-off decrease over a number of years, the lake level will fall each year until the trend is again reversed by a new cycle of high annual rainfall.

Water balance of Lake Malawi:

Lake area	28,678 km²
Catchment area	96,918 km²
Ratio Catchment:Lake	3.38
Rainfall, land	1179 mm
Rainfall, lake	1359 mm
Mean air temperature	25.7°C
Evaporation	1945 mm
Outflow	343 mm
Run-off	259 mm
Run-off, per cent rain	22%
Mean free water	+ 295 mm

The Shire River

The outlet of Lake Malawi to the Shire River is across a submerged sand bar 4 km north of Mangoche. Eight km south of Mangoche the Shire River enters the shallow waters of Lake Malombe which is 29 km long and 14.5 km wide.

The Shire River has three main sections. The upper section extends for 132 km from the outlet to Matope and has an average gradient of 5.29 m per km. In the middle section the river plunges through cataracts of a total fall of 384 m in 80 km and the lower section comprises a wide alluvial valley stretching from the foot of the cataracts to the Zambezi River over a distance of 281 km at an average gradient of 0.2 m per km.

A few tributaries of the Shire River are perennial and 80 per cent of their annual flow occurs between November and April. The Ruo is the largest tributary draining a catchment area of 4921 km² which includes most of the heavy rainfall area of Mulanje Mountain and the eastern Shire Highlands. Floods in the lower Shire valley are usually due to the River Ruo.

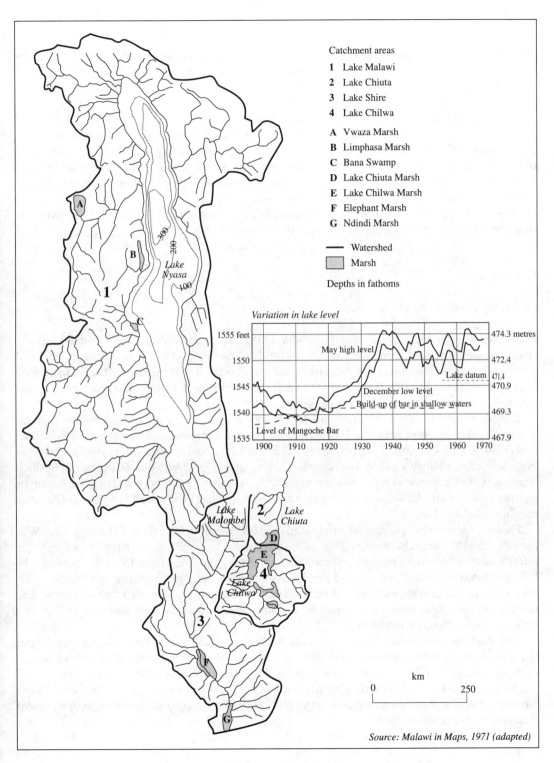

Figure 4.4 *Hydrology*

Lake Chilwa

This lake is saline, occupying a shallow basin of inland drainage of about 2590 km². Margined by swamp, Lake Chilwa periodically dries up but in normal years of rainfall the open water varies in depth between 1.2 m and 4.28 m with a seasonal fluctuation in level from 0.6 to 2.19 m. Raised beaches are evidence of its progressive recession.

Lake Chiuta is separated from Lake Chilwa by a 15.24 m sandbar and is fed by small seasonal streams. The waters remain relatively fresh by reason of their effluence into Lake Amaramba during the dry season. Since Lake Amaramba has a wider drainage net than Lake Chiuta, it rises faster than the latter and when the water level overtops that of Lake Chiuta reversal of flow takes place southwards to the upper lake. Back flow persists until March, then the process is reversed and water drains again from Lake Chiuta into Lake Amaramba.

Seasonal and periodic fluctuations in levels of lakes and seasonal and erratic flow in rivers are characteristic of the hydrology and drainage in Malawi.

Fish resources

Patterns of use, depletion and renewal

Fish resources from Malawi's lakes and rivers have been exploited by traditional methods for many centuries. Commercial fishing started in 1935 (with purse seining) but it was only in 1968 that commercial exploitation became a significant industry. Today 20,000 full-time artisanal fishermen exist and produce about 85 per cent of the total fish landings. A further 1000 employed in the commercial sector account for the remainder of the total catch.

Despite some 35 years of research into fish stocks, actual fish output in Malawi has been far below the potential output of about 150,000 tonnes. The total surface area of water bodies in Malawi is over 29,000 km². This is made up of four main lakes and a number of rivers, and extensive marshes in the lower Shire Valley. Lake Malawi is by far the largest and contributes 40–60 per cent of the total landings; Lake Chilwa, which periodically dries up, contributes 10–30 per cent of the total landings; and the Lower Shire Valley accounts for about 10 per cent. Fish production trends over the years are shown below (Table 4.7).

Fish production rose dramatically from under 20,000 tonnes in 1965 to 84,000 in the early 1970s but has since fluctuated between 60,000 to 70,000 tonnes. The rapid rise after 1965 was due to the introduction of new fishing technologies such as changing from fibre to nylon netting, the introduction of outboard engines and the development of commercial fishing operations. However, commercial operations have not been effective in exploiting identified fish resources. The firms concerned tend to have suffered from rising overheads, low capitalization and certain technical and material limitations.

The most heavily-exploited areas are those of the south-east arm of Lake Malawi, the Upper Shire River and Lake Malombe. In addition to fish exploitation from natural waterbodies, fish farming also occurs. This is undertaken both by smallholders and by estates with a total annual production of 1000 tonnes. The smallholder farmers use local species (talapia, catfish, etc.). Estate farmers in the Lower Shire and Mulanje valleys rear both local and exotic species including prawns (Government of Malawi, 1988).

Legal underpinnings

The Fisheries Department is concerned with all aspects of fisheries. All fishing activity in Malawi is regulated in order to guard against over-exploitation. In this respect, all commercial fisheries are licensed and their catches are monitored at a number of specified central landing points. There are specific restrictions on where, and when, fishing can take place, net mesh sizes, engine power and minimum size of fish that can be landed. Artisanal fishermen are required to license their nets. The Lake Malawi National Park was established by the Government to conserve a representative sample of the wide diversity of the fish fauna found in the lake with special emphasis on species of interest to the aquarium trade – e.g. the 'Mbuna' (rock fish) (Malawi Government, 1988). Within the SADC framework, Malawi has been given the responsibility of co-ordinating all SADC fishery developments. There is tripartite co-operation with Mozambique and Tanzania, exemplified by developments such as the planned Pelagic Resources Research Project.

Table 4.7 *Fish production, 1965–85 (000 tonnes)*

Year	Traditional fishery	Commercial fishery	Total
1965	17.0	1.9	18.9
1966	15.2	2.3	17.5
1967	12.9	1.5	14.4
1968	16.8	2.0	18.8
1969	36.1	5.6	41.7
1970	59.1	7.2	66.3
1971	65.7	7.5	73.2
1972	78.3	5.8	84.1
1973	61.1	9.3	69.4
1974	56.5	13.6	70.1
1975	62.0	8.9	70.9
1976	67.4	7.5	74.0
1977	61.5	6.7	68.2
1978	57.6	7.2	64.8
1979	52.7	7.1	59.8
1980	53.6	7.2	60.8
1981	32.4	7.6	40.0
1982	55.7	6.4	62.1
1983	59.0	7.8	66.8
1984	57.5	7.6	65.1
1985	54.1	8.0	62.1

Source: Government of Malawi, 1988

Landuse patterns and legal underpinnings

Historical overview

Malawi became a British Protectorate in 1891. It was colonised because of its potentially rich agricultural resources which could serve as a source of raw materials for expanding British industries in the nineteenth century. At that time the colony's mineral base was not of any significance. The colonial authorities consequently encouraged British and other European nationals to settle in the country for farming and commerce. The first area to be settled was the Shire Highlands in the early 1900s. Tea, tobacco, coffee and cotton were the main crops grown. Between 1891 and 1894 these settlers had alienated about 15 per cent of land.

In the initial stages, most settlers acquired land through treaties with local chiefs, but by the 1920s the government assumed responsibility for the acquisition of land by issuing certificates of claim to landowners. By this process, the colonial administration conferred private ownership of land on individuals and organisations – mostly as freehold. Subsequently, long-term leases of 21– 99 years were also granted. By 1930, about 78,329 hectares of land had been appropriated as freehold and a further 47,977 hectares as leasehold.

Land not privately owned by individuals or companies was declared to be Crown or African Trust Land. Crown Lands were defined as 'all public lands in the protectorate which are subject to the control of His Majesty by virtue of any Treaty, Convention, or Agreement, and all lands which shall have been acquired by His Majesty for the public service' (Mkandawire et al., 1990). African Trust Land was designated as all other land that was under customary occupation and controlled by a village headman or the chief of a given area.

Post-independence land tenure systems

In post-independence Malawi peasant farming predominates with only a limited number of settler farms. Agriculture was, and continues to be, the dominant sector of the economy. The agricultural sector is divided into two types; the smallholder and estate subsectors, distinguished by legal and institutional rules pertaining to crop production, marketing managements, pricing and land tenure.

In the post-independence period, land tenure has been embodied in the 1965 Malawi Land Bill, which classified land as either public, private or customary. Public land is land which is occupied, used or acquired by the Government and any other land which is not customary or private land. This land consists mainly of forest reserves and game parks. Smallholder farmers or any other individuals are not allowed access to this land without government consent. Any freehold or leasehold land which is surrendered reverts to the government as public land. In contrast, private land refers to land which is owned, held or occupied under private ownership. There are three classes of private land: freehold, leasehold and customary land – converted to private lands under the Customary (Land Development) Act of 1967. Leasehold estate land is granted by the Government in response to applications made by private individuals. Estates have been steadily growing at the expense of customary lands (Mkandawire, et al. 1990). The process of converting customary land to private land has only occurred in the Lilongwe Agricultural Development Division.

Lastly, there is the customary land. This is land which is held, used, or occupied under customary law. Under customary law, all village land is under the custodianship of the village headman. The right to occupy a piece of land depends on being an accepted member of a community. Approval is needed from the village headman before virgin land is utilised and before a household can dispose of its land to someone from outside the community. Thus it embodies usufruct rights – though inherited, these rights are not transferable. They do not constitute the right of ownership.

Prior to 1970, there were relatively few leasehold estates – but they were generally large. In the 1970s, 876 leasehold estates were established, mostly by large private and parastatal corporations such as Press Farming, General Farming, Spearhead Limited and Malawi Dairy Industries. Malawian businessmen, politicians, as well as serving and retired civil servants, also acquired leaseholds during this period. The 1980s witnessed an acceleration in the rate of establishment of estates and in their overall land area. Unlike in the earlier period, however, these new estates are relatively small in size (Table 4.8).

The explanation of the small size of the recently formed estates is threefold:

- the conversion of customary land into leasehold estates by individual smallholders or smallholder extended families;
- the development of new estates by former managers, tenants, clerks or other employees of the large-scale corporations; and
- the investment in estates by medium-level civil servants and small businessmen.

Table 4.8 *Leasehold estate expansion, 1970–89*

Year(s) leased	Number of estates	Area leased (000 ha)	Mean area (ha)
To 1979	229	79.0	345
1970–1979	876	176.8	202
1980	216	17.3	80
1981	765	46.9	61
1982	1914	72.7	38
1983	1006	49.2	49
1984	486	24.9	51
1985	363	31.4	87
1986	592	26.4	45
1987	1867	70.9	38
1988	3839	107.5	28
1989	2402	62.5	26

Source: Mkandawire, et al., 1990

Factors enhancing leasehold estate expansion

In the late 1960s, the government viewed the expansion of the estate sub-sector as a potentially more reliable source of output and revenue growth than the peasant sector. Civil servants and leading political officials were strongly encouraged to establish estates which it was felt would not only expand agricultural output but provide the training ground for the country's future commercial farmers. This policy was subsequently strengthened by other measures. Firstly, given government backing, individuals and co-operatives were allowed to lease large tracts of land at very little cost. Secondly, market opportunities were made available to estate leaseholders with the imposition of sanctions on Southern Rhodesia following the unilateral declaration of independence in 1965. Major international buyers encouraged Malawi to expand production to compensate for the reduction of output and sales in Rhodesia. The Lomé Convention in 1973 was another market opportunity as it provided Malawi tobacco with duty-free access into the EEC. The imposition of the Special Crops Act in 1972 was yet another contributory factor – a licensing system which eliminated competition from smallholders by restricting the production of burley and flue-cured tobacco to the estate sector alone.

Favourable access to low-cost finance also encouraged the expansion of the estate sub-sector in the 1970s. Two major financial sources were commercial banks and smallholder agriculture. Commercial banks were placed under heavy government pressure to extend loans to estates. In the smallholder agricultural sector, the parastatal ADMARC was granted monopoly rights over the purchase and sale of smallholder crops. Largely through the taxation of peasant farmers, ADMARC amassed profits between 1971 and 1980; a large proportion of these profits were invested in the estate sub-sector.

The availability of large and cheap sources of labour was another explanation for the rapid expansion of estates. This inexpensive labour reserve was created because of the heavy taxation of peasant agriculture, the rapid growth of the labour force due to the reduction in international migration, increasing land pressures in certain parts of the country and restrictions on smallholders producing burley tobacco. Added to the supply of cheap labour was the availability of high-quality management in the 1970s. As a result of the intensification of hostilities in Rhodesia, large-scale tobacco producing companies in Malawi recruited many expatriate managers during the independence struggle. (Mkandawire, *et al.*, 1990).

Estate landuse patterns

Tobacco estates: Empirical studies of the estate sub-sector produce evidence that only a small proportion of estate land is used for cultivation – in the range of 8–14 per cent (Kydd, 1988), (World Bank, 1987 and 1990). However, Mkandawire *et al.* (1990) have recently contested this view. They point out that the low figures in these estimates could be due to the omission of the cultivation of maize and other food crops on estates whether by the estates themselves using direct labour, or by their tenants. Furthermore, estate land that is under woodlots and natural woodlands, about 18.5 per cent of the total area, has been disregarded in the compilation of estate-land utilisation statistics. Other excluded categories of estate-land utilisation include areas allocated for grazing and for fallow, representing 14 per cent of the total estate land area. Buildings and roads also account for a considerable use of land – about 7.5 per cent of the total leasehold area (see Table 4.9)

Table 4.9 *Estate landuse patterns*

Description	Area (ha)	Per cent of total
Area planted to crops (tobacco, maize, etc.)	2 763.02	26.6
Area cultivated by encroaching smallholders or estates	131.92	1.3
Area under woodlot or natural woodland	1 918.32	18.5
Grazing area	267.12	2.6
Fallow area	1 227.87	11.8
Area for buildings, roads	779.35	7.5
Other	3 303.73	31.8

Source: Mkandawire, et al., 1990

The same field survey (Mkandawire *et al.* 1990) produced the following conclusions: cropping intensity in leasehold estates correlates negatively with size. In those estates with a cropping ratio of over 50 per cent, smaller estates (0–30 ha) were in the majority (69 per cent). In contrast, only 8 per cent of the larger estates, (<100 ha), recorded a cropping ratio of more than 50 per cent.

A number of factors lead to the under-utilisation of estate land including mountainous terrain, large-scale waterlogging, or the absence of nearby sources of water. Other factors include the lack of sufficient capital, the repayment terms for loans, the small size or absence of a tobacco quota, labour shortages, especially in the northern region, and the desire of estate owners to preserve natural woodland for future use. Finally, poor transport infrastructure is a constraint on the further development of newly-established estates, especially in Salima and Rumphi Districts.

Landuse patterns on tea estates

Since the 1950s the tea estates have encountered strong pressures to utilise their arable land in the face of high population densities and related land shortages. At present about 43 per cent of the total area of Malawi's tea estates is under cultivation – planted to tea or other permanent crops. A further 21 per cent is woodland or woodlot. About 36 per cent was either left undeveloped or put to other uses such as buildings, roads, houses and factories (see Table 4.10).

Table 4.10 *Landuse patterns on tea estates*

Description	Area (ha)	Per cent of total
Total tea estate area	43.903	100
Planted with tea	15.846	36.1
Planted with other permanent crop	2.854	6.5
Fuelwood plantations	7.318	16.7
Other Forest Development	1.823	4.2
Tea seedlings	80.0	0.2
Other uses or undeveloped	15.987	36.3

Source: Mkandawire et al., 1990

Forestry resources

Patterns of use, depletion and renewal

Malawi's economy benefits both directly and indirectly from its forest reserves. Directly, forests provide 90 per cent of the country's fuel requirements, a substantial volume of timber for the timber industry, places for recreation, and also provide areas of botanical importance. Indirectly, forest cover protects steep slopes and upper river catchments from soil erosion, river siltation, flash flooding and low rainfall infiltration.

About 38 per cent of Malawi's forest area is under some form of protection, some of which is permanent forest reserve (Government of Malawi, 1988). The breakdown is as follows: 11 per cent is accounted for by parks and game reserves, 10 per cent by forest reserves and protected hill slopes and 17 per cent by natural woodland on customary land. However, the total forest cover is declining by 3.5 per cent a year due to land clearance for agriculture, and direct wood consumption. The estimated wood production and consumption levels are presented in Table 4.11.

In 1986, total wood demand was estimated at 9.4 million cubic metres, of which rural households accounted for 54 per cent, urban users 11 per cent, the tobacco industry 23 per cent and other industry 5 per cent. Exploitation at this rate poses serious dangers of deforestation, prompting the government to plan measures to improve planting rates and to encourage the increased efficiency of fuelwood use in tobacco barns, charcoal kilns, stoves and braziers (Economist Intelligence Unit, 1991).

A shortage of firewood and building poles has caused considerable deforestation in the country. A survey conducted in 1982 indicated that smallholders were aware of the process of deforestation and that they were planting trees in response. The survey also indicated that farmers' knowledge of silviculture was sufficient to keep most trees alive and that sufficient land was available (Energy Unit, 1982 quoted by SADC, 1986). Extension advice, however, on how to deal with the problems posed by soil erosion is generally reaching only larger-scale male farmers who are credit club members. Extension advice tends to be very general and is not focused on the needs and requirements of women. This is indicated by the relatively low adoption rates of soil conservation measures by female, as opposed to male, farmers in the Ntcheu Rural Development Project, (Barbier 1990).

In view of the problems associated with deforestation, the Government, through the National Forestry Programme, has outlined a general afforestation programme whose main purpose is to meet industrial wood demand and to overcome the problem of deforestation. One part of this programme is the Conservation Forestry Programme, which is carried out on denuded hill slopes and hilltops. The law prohibits the cutting of trees close to river banks, and in general these are well protected from erosion.

Table 4.11 *Estimated accessible wood production and consumption, 1984 and 1985 (million cubic metres)*

	Production	
	Estimated 1984	*Projected 1995*
Forest reserves	0.8	0.8
Estates (natural forests)	0.5	0.3
Cultivated areas	1.4	1.4
Non-cultivated areas	0.6	0.6
Plantation	0.2	1.4
Other	0.8	0.8
Total	4.3	5.3
	Consumption	
	Estimated 1984	*Projected 1995*
Fuelwood:		
urban	1.0	0.9
rural	5.1	7.5
estate	2.0	0.6
rural industry	0.4	0.5
urban industry	0.1	0.1
Poles	0.7	0.9
Wood processing	0.1	0.2
Total consumption	9.4	11.7
Total deficit	5.1	6.4

Source: Government of Malawi, 1988 Development Policies 1987–1996

However, there is no comprehensive database of vegetation types in Malawi. For example, currently there is no programme to map semi-natural and natural vegetation. Information about vegetation was collected during the surveys for the natural regions map and this was compiled into a national vegetation map using an *ad hoc* classification of 'biotic communities'. But this is basically a physiographic classification. The geographical distribution of various pasture types has not been studied at all despite the fact that individual grass species occurring in Malawi are known and listed (SADCC, 1986).

Forest Legislation Policy and Institutional Framework

The following section is based on the paper by Kawerawera (1988). Forest management is governed by the Forest Act of 1984 and the Forest Rules under that Act. The Forest Act covers four major areas. They are:

- the establishment of forest reserves and the use of forest products from reserves;
- responsibility for managing and controlling forest and forest produce on customary lands;
- village forest areas designated to be on customary lands by a village headman, with the approval of the Ministry of Forestry; and
- police powers granted to forest officers and other officers concerning the control of forest produce.

However, for several reasons a comprehensive revision of the Forest Act is necessary. They are:

- The Act is ineffective in dealing with major offences in forest reserves and in dealing with pressure on reserve land to be released for agricultural estates;
- The Act is weak in areas where it overlaps with other Acts. For example, the Road, Telephone and Telecommunications Acts. This undermines efforts to manage forested areas properly;
- The Act is, in several respects, obsolete. For example,
    - whereas in the pre-independence era the approach of government in enforcing the Forest Laws was through the use of force, the present government has insisted on persuasion to instil understanding and co-operation in the general public;
    - The Forestry Department (FD) has an added responsibility of forest extension;
    - The schedule of forest reserves has obsolete boundary descriptions which are not consistent with the present boundaries.
- The Act does not adequately provide for:
    - afforestation and reforestation, and the role of the Forestry Department and its relationship with the other-tree planting agencies;
    - the export of forest produce;
    - the safety of forest patrol staff;
    - the control of vermin in forest reserves;
    - the security of endangered tree species.

In the light of this, there is an urgent need for the Forestry Department, in consultation with the Ministry of Justice, to co-ordinate the revision of the Forest Act in order to accommodate the concerns listed above.

Forests and forest produce on customary land

Two categories of trees are recognised on customary lands. They are: indigenous non-planted trees and indigenous and exotic planted trees. The Act does not regulate the planting or harvesting of planted trees. In effect what this means is that the Forestry Department which administers the Forest Act has no control over planted trees on customary land other than those planted by the Forestry Department itself. The Act, however, provides for regulatory powers over natural trees on customary land. The Act provides that:

...no person shall, provided for regulatory powers over natural trees rules, do any of the following acts on customary land:

- fell, cut, take, burn, injure or remove any tree;
- take any forest produce which is designated as Protected Trees;
- squat, reside, camp, build huts or cattle enclosures or clear, cultivate or break up land within a protected strip or on a protected hill slope, provided that collecting and using dead firewood without causing damage to forest produce, by travellers or workers on public roads, as they require fuel in the course of their journey to work, shall not constitute a breach of this rule;
- keep bees or collect honey or beeswax or any other forest produce for commercial purposes.

The above rules notwithstanding, Malawians are provided with exceptions where they are allowed to do certain things without contravening the Act. Thus, a Malawian may, without licence or repayment of fees or royalties, but not within a protected strip or on a protected hill slope, fell, cut, burn or remove trees or any forest, except protected trees:

- for agricultural purposes;
- for use by himself in erecting his own house, livestock enclosure, granary or food store;
- for making domestic furniture and fittings and agricultural implements;
- for his own domestic use provided that if a Malawian citizen sells any of the forest produce or any charcoal or bricks made therefrom or uses any forest produce or bricks for construction of any building for commercial purposes, the above rules shall apply.

Forests and forest produce on public and protected forest reserves

The Forest Act, for purposes of controlling and managing protected forest reserves, does not make distinctions between planted and natural trees. It makes outright prohibitions to persons without licences and without exception for Malawian citizens for all the acts listed above.

Forest and forest produce on leasehold land

The management, control and protection of forests and forest produce on leasehold land rests with the leaseholder. His actions are governed with respect to the same regulations governing the use of protected trees which cannot be felled without licence from the Forestry Department. With the foregoing we can conclude that while each one of the fuelwood sub- sector implementing agencies contribute to the general supply of woodfuels in Malawi, each one of them takes care of its own production line without recourse from the Forestry Department, particularly with regard to planted wood.

The role of the forestry department

The Forestry Department is part of the Ministry of Forestry and Natural Resources and it manages all public forest resources and administers the Forest Act (Cap.63, Laws of Malawi). The department underwent major re-organisation in 1986. It now has five principal divisions. These are the Viphya Plantations, the Forestry Extension Services, Forest Support Services, the Forest Development Division, and the SADC Forestry and Technical Coordination Unit. A few of these are discussed below.

Viphya Plantations Division – This is responsible for the planning and management of plantations with the primary purpose of growing pulpwood used for the production of pulp and paper at the Viphya Plateau in Chikangawa, northern Malawi. Owing to changes in the economic climate for pulp and paper, both in the domestic and international markets, this project has been subjected to delays. While its primary objective has hitherto been maintained, it has become apparent that alternative uses of ageing timber have to be found. Consequently, charcoal production and timber production plants have recently been launched as supplementary activities. The division also provides ancillary services, including health, education and clean water to local inhabitants and forest workers. It should be understood that while the production of timber is the responsibility of the Viphya Plantations Division, the use of that timber is controlled by the Viphya Pulp and Paper Corporation (VIPCOR), a parastatal organisation enacted through parliament.

Forestry extension services division

This is responsible for the provision of extension services and the implementation of wood energy projects. Specifically, the Forestry Extension Services Division:

- encourages people to protect, control and manage existing indigenous trees and forests on customary lands;
- plants, establishes, and manages fuelwood and poles plantations in selected areas, particularly urban and rural growth centres;
- provides general forest extension farmer training and publicity services which are targeted at individuals, estates and NGOs;
- carries out operational activities which are developmental in nature, e.g. charcoal production, technology transfer and improved stove dissemination.

Forestry support services division

Its divisions are as follows:

- Forestry Research Institute of Malawi,
- Energy Studies Unit,
- Planning Unit,
- Monitoring and Evaluation Unit,
- Malawi College of Forestry.

The Forestry Research Institute of Malawi prepares silvicultural and conducts other forestry-related activities. It is also responsible for the collection, treatment and marketing of forest seeds. The Malawi College of Forestry is the Forestry Department's training arm. It offers forest training at Diploma and Certificate levels. The lines dividing the functions of the Energy Studies Unit,

Planning Unit and Monitoring and Evaluation Unit are thin and not quite clear. Their activities do overlap and, in some instances, duplicate one another. This institutional ambiguity is historic in origin. When the Energy Studies Unit was established in 1980, within the Wood Energy Project I of the Forestry Department, it was clear that its responsibility was to collect tree planting and wood energy related data for the planning of present and future wood energy projects in the country. To carry out this function the Energy Studies Unit had a mobile survey team that conducted surveys which are both monitoring and evaluatory in nature and scope. Additionally the Energy Studies Unit did some work in the development of wood conservation technologies (studies such as the economics and social dimensions of afforestation, energy system development and dissemination, etc.). The Energy Studies Unit work programme brought under one roof economists, sociologists and engineers in the Forestry Department putting together and strengthening forestry activities in the country.

At the inception of Wood Energy Project II, however, the Energy Studies Unit's work programme was disaggregated. Monitoring and evaluation aspects were taken away and given to the newly created Monitoring and Evaluation Unit; charcoal activities were wholly given to an independent consulting firm from West Germany which took the unit's only systems engineer. This left the Energy Studies Unit with a stoves programme without the necessary manpower back-up, and a surveys programme identical to the one mandated to the Monitoring and Evaluation Unit. Both units visit tree planters, administer surveys, compile data and report to Wood Energy Project II management for advice and/or policy direction guidance. Central to this institutional mix-up is the intuitive understanding within the Forestry Department that since the Energy Studies Unit is a non-foresters' niche it is difficult for them to fully comprehend forestry issues and problems and hence the need for another institution run by the foresters' Monitoring and Evaluation Unit. To clear up this misunderstanding, it is recommended that the Monitoring and Evaluation Unit and the Energy Studies Unit merge to form a strong Monitoring, Evaluation and Studies Unit. This would reinforce the view that the social forestry and wood energy problems facing Malawi today are not the sole monopoly of foresters. It is a field encompassing anthropology, economics, engineering etc., and all these need to co-operate in order to bring about the desired results.

Local government and the local authorities

The Ministry of Local Government is responsible for the establishment and management of local institutions, including the installation and legitimising of chieftainships. Since the Land Act empowers local authorities (village headmen, chiefs etc.) to administer certain provisions of that Act, particularly as it affects customary lands, the Forestry Department, in its endeavours to administer the Forest Act in these affected areas, liaises with local authorities to gain access to land to implement their programmes, be it forest reserve delineation or the erection of public amenities. In this capacity chiefs have a functional linkage with the Forestry Department.

Apart from authorising the Forestry Department's activities in customary land areas, chiefs, under the Forest Act (Cap.63:01 Part V – Village Forest Areas), are empowered to 'demarcate any portions of land to be designated as Village Forest Areas for the purpose of environmental protection, preservation of endangered species, exclusive source of wood and other forest produce or any other function the chiefs may decide. These may include natural forest areas, village forest plantations, communal woodlots, and any other area the chief may wish to include'. Once portions of land have been demarcated as provided for in the Act, the chiefs are further empowered to regulate and control:

- squatting, residing or erection of buildings, huts or livestock enclosures;
- grazing or depasturing of livestock or trespassing by livestock;
- clearing, cultivating or breaking up land for cultivation or any other purpose;
- demarcating, marking and maintenance of the boundaries;
- felling, cutting, burning, injuring or removal of any tree or forest produce;
- utilisation and disposal of forest produce;
- burning of grass or undergrowth;
- keeping of bees or the collection of honey; and
- seed collection, the raising of tree seedlings and the planting of village or communal woodlots.

Development committees

Parallel to the Malawi Congress Party political structure there are area development committees which oversee and supervise the planning and implementation of various development projects. They are organised according to the political administrative division of nation, region, district, areas and village. These include:

- The National Development Committee (NDC) which is chaired by the President or his representative. It is mainly involved in reviewing national development programmes.
- Regional Development Committees (RDCs) are three in total, one in each region. They are chaired by the Regional Administrators and are engaged in the preparation and review of development programmes which have a regional impact.
- District Development Committees (DDCs) are 24 in number, one for each of the districts. They are chaired by the District Commissioners. Representatives on these committees are drawn from economic sectors represented in that particular district to discuss development issues affecting their district.
- Area Action Groups (AAGs) represent traditional authorities (TAs) and are 192 in total. The Traditional Authorities chair these meetings and also supervise any projects arising from them.
- Village Action Groups (VAGs) are found in each village in the country. Village headmen chair their meetings and supervise any developmental activity arising from the same.

Apart from discussing and supervising development proposals, District Development Committees, Area Action Groups and Village Action Groups are directly involved in tree- planting efforts through the establishment of woodlots for demonstration purposes and/or the provision of wood products, particularly woodfuel and construction poles. They also help the Forestry Department in arranging and organising the implementation of National Tree Planting Activities. In this way Development Committees act as extension agents and facilitators for afforestation programmes.

Energy policy and strategies

The recently published Statement of Development Policy (SDP), 1987–1996, published in 1988, identifies three central energy issues that the Government of Malawi intends to address over the next ten years. These are:

- the high cost and instability of imported oil and coal supplies;
- the rapid deforestation of the central and southern regions of the country; and

- the design of a least-cost power-system expansion plan.

To address these issues, the government will attempt to minimise the constraints that high energy costs, energy shortages and instability in energy supply have placed on Malawi's economic development. Specific objectives in support of this goal include the following:

- to minimise dependence on imported oil and coal;
- to reduce the unit cost and improve the dependability of the supply of imported oil and coal;
- to achieve an electricity supply system that optimises cost and reliability;
- to attempt to meet future fuelwood demand; and
- to improve the co-ordination of energy sector developments.

The Statement of Development Policy further identifies 12 strategies which will be employed in support of the above policies and these are:

- To develop an indigenous coal resource where this is economically viable and implement an oil exploration programme to be undertaken and financed by competent private companies;
- To set petroleum products prices at levels that, at a minimum, fully recover costs, minimise cross-subsidies between fuels and encourage conservation without causing economic dislocation;
- To minimise oil import costs within an acceptable level of oil supply reliability, by utilising the least-costly supply sources and procurement arrangements available to Malawi;
- To improve the reliability of oil supplies by using a range of supply routes, creating a strategic fuel reserve and designing an emergency fuel allocation plan;
- To support private industry's efforts to expand the production and consumption of ethanol fuel;
- To improve the utilisation of the existing electrical power system, and, to the extent that this will not meet demand growth, expand the system capacity through least-cost investment in the new plant;
- To invest in the expansion of the electricity network where it is economically viable;
- To adjust the level and structure of electricity tariffs to reflect economic costs;
- To electrify the flue-cured tobacco growing areas, if economically viable, as a means of allowing the more efficient use of solid fuels and permitting pumped irrigation;
- To undertake or support state, private and community reforestation efforts as a means of maintaining supplies of fuelwood and limiting rates of wood harvesting from customary lands;
- To introduce improved wood-burning devices, improved charcoal production, solar energy technologies for private, institutional and industrial use, and, if economically viable, utilise thinnings from the Viphya Plantations and other forests in the production of charcoal; and,
- To improve the energy planning capabilities of those state agencies involved in energy matters and strengthen the co-ordination role of the Energy Planning Unit (EPU) of the Department of Economic Planning and Development.

Institutions involved in rural energy

Functionally, public and semi-public departments and organisations and private sector agencies involved in rural energy issues can be grouped into five categories, consisting of planning, co-ordinating, regulating, implementing and financing agencies.

The Energy Planning Unit in the Department of Economic Planning and Development (DEP&D) of the President and Cabinet is the planning agency. This agency has the constitutional mandate to formulate and define national energy policies to be executed by implementing agencies and to ensure that the policies are consistent with overall national development objectives and aspirations.

The co-ordinating agencies are divided into three categories, namely private, public and international. These agencies initiate special studies and activities, organise working groups to discuss energy problems and issues, facilitate the flow of information, identify operational and technical deficiencies in all energy agencies and provide technical and analytical expertise.

The regulating agencies hold and provide critical inputs to the general operations and successes of implementing agencies. The linkages that exist between the implementing and the regulating agencies vary in accordance with the nature and magnitude of resources and authority that the regulatory agency can offer and exert over the implementing agency.

Those agencies which have the technical capabilities, human and financial resources and the prerequisite organisational framework and machinery for specific energy delivery services are the implementing agencies.

Financing agencies include international donor organisations, Malawian-based financial institutions and banks, bilateral organisations and world bodies that extend financial assistance through government channels or otherwise to implementing agencies for the final aim of producing and supplying fuel and/or bringing about improvements in the energy sector.

Conclusion

Over the past decade the Malawi government has been assiduously implementing structural adjustment policies on the advice of the World Bank. Therefore, the nature of environmental exploitation and resource-use conflicts will, in the near future, largely depend on the impact of structural adjustment policies. In theory, structural adjustment policies are anticipated to enhance efficiency in resource use by allowing price flexibility to eliminate market distortions and rigidities. In particular, economic prices for resource-based products are expected to allow for economies in the consumption of such products whilst also ensuring cost recovery to accommodate sustainable use of natural resources.

The current situation in Malawi, suggests that the environmental impact of structural adjustment policies may be restricted to estate and freehold/leasehold viable small-scale farmers only. Indeed, for the majority of the population, concentrated on communally-owned land, which still accounts for the largest proportion of cultivatable land, structural adjustment policies are likely to worsen their plight. Not only will market incentives associated with the implementation of structural adjustment policies increase the pressure to convert customary land to freehold and leasehold tenure, to the advantage of richer individuals and households, but it will also result in increased costs of managing customary land by households that only peripherally participate in the market.

Thus, the pressure on the use of the remaining customary land might actually result in increased land degradation as a consequence of structural adjustment policies. From an environmental perspective the anomaly of the coexistence of customary land use with freehold/leasehold land use might increasingly become untenable and might represent a fundamental conflict in environmental and resource use. The government may eventually be faced with the option of either totally transforming agrarian relations on the basis of freehold tenure, with landless labour absorbed into wage labour in agriculture and industry as has been happening, or increasing its investment in customary land-tenure areas to ensure the long-term sustainability of resource use. Equivocation on this option will merely spell environmental disaster for a greater proportion of the customary land in Malawi.

More generally, the question arises as to whether the present course of resource utilisation and economic development in Malawi is sustainable in the long run. So far, Malawi's development strategy has been based primarily on an agricultural-led strategy and secondarily on an import-substitution industrialisation strategy of processing primary products and the production of mass consumption final goods with low value added. The strategy, given the low starting base of the economy, showed some early successes until the 1980s, when the economy ran into structural constraints and recession. The collapse of the boom of the 1970s revealed the weaknesses of the economy and in particular, the unsustainability of the present pattern of growth. The present pattern of development in Malawi is unsustainable. With reference to immediate factors, the high rates of population growth and labour force participation, coupled with internal migration, resulting from land alienation and the influx of refugees, particularly from Mozambique, have been such that the formal sector has been unable to absorb the majority of the entrants into the labour force, thereby putting substantial pressure on land resources. Additionally, long-term structural problems relate to the inability of the formal sector to develop in a manner that would ensure the efficient use of both natural and human resources. Indeed, the outcome of the enclave-dependent growth of the formal economy has been the proletarianisation and impoverishment of the majority as is shown by an expanding wage labour workforce experiencing declining real wages. As a consequence the majority of the population has had to seek survival in the subsistence sector where increased population pressure has reduced the availability of land.

The unsustainability of Malawi's present strategy for development can be explained as follows:

- The inability of the economy to provide productive employment for the majority;
- The inability to sustain even minimal standards of welfare for the majority given the high incidence of infant mortality, the persistence of malnutrition and very low life expectancy rates;
- The increasing inequities in the economy as declining real wages have occurred at a time of overall economic growth;
- The depletion of the quality of natural resources, particularly on land left for the ever-expanding subsistence population.

In short, the present development strategy, whatever its short-lived benefits, has not resolved, and perhaps has exacerbated, the following:

- The vulnerability of the economy to external shocks;
- The vulnerability of the majority of the population to poverty and disease; and
- The vulnerability of the land as a fragile resource base.

Thus the benefits of the recent development strategy have accrued to a minority whilst its costs have continued to be borne by the majority. Sustainable development for Malawi will therefore require a development strategy that:

- Ensures the increased diversification and interlinkage of the economy to encompass primary, secondary and tertiary sectors;
- Ensures the enhancement of the wage and cash crop income entitlements of the majority through increased formal wage employment with increasing real wages and a more equitable redistribution of access to arable land; and
- Increasing efforts to curb population increases.

REFERENCES

Agnew, S and Stubbs, M (1971) *Malawi in Maps* University of London Press

Barbier, E (1990) *Environmental Degradation in the Third World: Greening the World Economy* Earthscan, London

Economist Intelligence Unit (1991) *Malawi Country Profile* 1991–92, E.I.U. Business International, London

Government of Malawi (1984) *National Sample Survey of Agriculture 1980/81* Vol. 1, National Statistics Office, Zomba, April 1984

Government of Malawi (1988) *Statement of Development Policies 1987–1996* Office of the President and Cabinet, Department of Economic Planning and Development

Government of Malawi (1990) *Food Security Nutrition Policy* Statement Office of the President and Cabinet, Department of Economic Planning and Development

Kawerawera, C (1988) *SADC Rural Energy Institutions Study, Malawi* ZERO, Harare

Kydd, J (1988) 'Policy reform and adjustment in an economy under seige, Malawi 1980–87', *IDS Bulletin*, Vol.19, No.1. Institute of Development Studies, University of Sussex

Malawi Statistical Yearbook 1987 (1989) National Statistical Office, Zomba

Mkandawire, R M *et al.* (1990) *Beyond 'Dualism': the Changing Face of the Leasehold Estate Subsector of Malawi*, Lilongwe

Mkandawire, R M (1991) 'Agrarian change and food security among smallholder farmers in Malawi', a paper presented at a SADC Conference on Food Policy and Agriculture, Mbabane, Swaziland, August 1991

SADC (1986) *Land Degradation and Desertification Control in the SADC Region* SADC Soil and Water Conservation and Land Utilization Programme, Report No.5, Maseru, 1986

UNICEF/Malawi Government (1991) *Malawi: Poverty Situation Analysis*

World Bank (1987) *Malawi: Land Policy Study* Washington DC

World Bank (1990) *Malawi: Growth through Poverty Reduction* Southern Africa Department, Africa Regional Office, March 1990

5

MOZAMBIQUE

INTRODUCTION

Normal discussions of environmental sustainability in the African context have inevitably to be modified in the case of Mozambique which has endured 27 years of war. The Brundtland Report's definition of sustainable development is:

.... development that meets the needs of the present generation without compromising the ability of future generations to meet their own needs.

This has to be seen in a context of the current incapacity to sustain the livelihoods of the present generation of Mozambicans, let alone to make provision to guarantee this for future generations. The country's pressing environmental problems are essentially the product of the war. Half the population is affected with over one million Mozambican refugees currently in neighbouring countries and many of the rest fleeing to the relative safety of the cities, the coastal strip and the transport corridors. The high concentration of people living within 50 kilometres of the coast (an estimated 50 per cent) increases the real population density: the national figures suggest some 18 persons per square kilometre but the reality is some 75 persons per square kilometre in the coastal strip, rising, in Maputo city, to some 2000 persons per square kilometre.

Hence environmental problems in Mozambique must be discussed in the context of the war and policies for sustainable development need to be developed in a specific war context. This means recognising that the war has removed the potential population stress on the environment in large areas but magnified it in the sites of population concentration. A further problem is how to proceed with a sustainable development strategy for a predominantly peasant economy, where wage-earning opportunities for the adult male members of the household, in much of the country, have historically been essential to guarantee the cash to purchase the inputs to sustain the peasant production base. The post-independence context has seen not only the removal of the wage-earning opportunities in the key neighbouring states of South Africa and Zimbabwe, but the physical displacement of a sizeable proportion of the peasantry to the peri-urban zones and the transport and littoral corridors.

The key environmental problem that has to be tackled is the displacement of the rural population to zones where the essential resource, secure land, is in scarce supply and where a reduction in wage-earning opportunity has reduced the capacity to purchase farming inputs. Sustainable landuse strategies have to be devised in a context of intense population concentration and resource scarcity. The other side of the equation is that many of the remaining peasant producers living in the interior and outside the corridors are cut off from resources, the state and even donors by the insecurity of travel because of the intensity of the war.

Sustainable development in Mozambique in the context of war means ensuring the survival of

---

This chapter draws heavily on two sources: Cherrett, I *et al.* (1990) *Norwegian Aid and the Environment in Mozambique* , ETC (UK), It was written before the ceasefire between the government's force and Renamo was announced in the Autumn of 1992; and Chonguica, E M W *et al.* (1990) *Mozambique: the present environmental situation.*

the population concentrations by enabling an intensification of production with a minimum of environmental deterioration. Intensification of production within a sustainable development approach means improving resource management. This effectively means a strategy for the urban, peri-urban zones, corridors and coastline only.

The fundamental need in the context of war and economic collapse will always be, however, that production for immediate survival will remain the priority and a certain environmental cost will have to be accepted until the country returns to normal.

Other environmental problems faced by Mozambique, the indiscriminate slaughter of wildlife, trafficking in ivory and the exploitation of other high market-value primary commodities outside the stated zones above, can only be tackled after the ending of hostilities. The exception remains discussions with neighbouring countries over the use of common river basins.

In terms of the management of natural resources we confront the true limitations and test of implementing a sustainable development strategy in a war context. Quite simply, in most of the country, the lack of access for integrating production into a wider national and global economy is severely limited by the conflict. An enforced fallow period for the land will ensure the natural regeneration of biomass and soil fertility. The 'who manages what' issue, therefore, becomes confined to the zones of population concentration and 'relative' security.

The whole thrust of the government's rethink over development strategy is that the state should withdraw from assuming the production function and, supported by the recommendations of the multilateral agencies (see World Bank, 1988), should move towards facilitating and supporting peasant and commercial farming production. A key component should be support for the development of an extension service with agents trained in the techniques of improved landuse management for low-input intensification of production.

The recommendations to improve family production contained in the World Bank *Mozambique Agricultural Sector Survey* (1988) show that measures to improve family production should:

- require simple management;
- have high benefit/cost ratios not needing intensive extension;
- not be sensitive to timing of inputs;
- make no heavy demands on transport;
- require little foreign exchange.

These could be compatible with a sustainable development approach both in an ecological and economic sense. Technical assistance would also be an important component of such an approach but needs to be considerably reinforced if the objective of a sustained improvement in family production is to be achieved. For this to succeed, however, it will be necessary to carry out a more thorough analysis of the 'family' sector in present-day Mozambique.

Under conditions of peace, or even more modestly with an expanding zone of security around the peri-urban zones, corridors and littoral, it is to be hoped that some of the peasant farmers will move out to newly-available lands under the dual impetus of land scarcity and the absence of alternative urban wage employment. In Maputo alone, it is estimated that there are 100,000 heads of households without employment. The reduction of urban employment opportunities in both industry and the bureaucracy implies that economic logic will lead some to leave the high population concentrations when circumstances allow. Administrative compulsion should be avoided at all costs as this is counter-productive.

Is it possible to develop an environmental policy under the war conditions that Mozambique has faced? The answer to this is yes, in the ways outlined above. Apart from the development of legislation on the environment, institution building and training, actual programmes and projects can occur in the zones specified. In terms of income generation, prawns and cashews currently are the principal exports: they are produced in the coastal area which can generally be defended. Environmental stress is experienced in this area, in particular with the cutting of the mangroves which has a negative environmental effect and can reduce fishing potential. Dune fixation and encouraging the growth of trees for whatever uses people themselves decide can make a significant contribution to sustainable development. These and other options will be explored further in this chapter. It must be remembered, however, that, drought is adding to the problems of Mozambique in the early 1990s.

ECONOMIC STRUCTURE

The influence of the main economic sectors (agriculture, industry and services) on the formation of the Gross Domestic Product (GDP) has fluctuated over the years.

Table 5.1 *Distribution of the GDP by sectors (constant 1980 prices in US$)*

Year	GDP total billion US$	Population (000)	GDP per capita (US$)	EAP total (000)	Mean GDP per EAP (US$)
1970	2 617	9 408	278	2 930	893
1980	2 617	12 130	179	2 573	389
1983	1 720	13 110	131	5 820	296
1985	1 659	13 810	120	5 980	277
Difference	-959	4 402	-158	3 050	-616
Growth rate (%) per annum	-3	2.6	-5.45	4.87	-7.5

EAP – Economically active population
Source: Lisker 1987, Project FAO MOZ/81/051

According to Table 5.1, it can be noted that while the population increased at an annual rate of 2.6 per cent in that period (1970 to 1985), the GDP fell by 3 per cent. As a result the GDP per head fell dramatically from US$278 in 1970 to US$120 in 1985. By 1991 the figure had declined even further to US$80.

The specific share of the agricultural sector in the GDP rose from 19 per cent in 1970 to 39 per cent in 1985, with an annual average rate of increase of 1.8 per cent, even with the fluctuations in the absolute values in each five-year period. The industrial sector has fallen most in importance in the formation of the GDP, with an average annual decrease of about 5.3 per cent. The service sector likewise saw its role decreasing in this period, falling from 63 per cent to 48 per cent of GDP.

Turning to the employment structure, the distribution of the population by sector of activity is characterised by a high concentration in agriculture, with some 86 per cent of the total workforce, followed by the service sector with 8 per cent and lastly by industry with 6 per cent (Table 5.2).

The country's current financial limitations do not facilitate the application of the economic axiom of differentiating employment through investments which permit the absorption of the labour force in sectors other than agriculture. Thus a situation is created where there is a heavy concentration of the workforce in this sector (agriculture), without a corresponding real increase in the sector's productivity. Many people in the rural areas possess inadequate equipment. Agriculture is therefore labour intensive with low productivity. Production levels are low, but at least employment is provided.

Table 5.2 *Economically active population (EAP) by sector*

Year	EAP (10^6)			EAP by sector (10^6)		
	Male	*Female*	*Total*	*Agriculture*	*Industry*	*Service*
1960	1.97	2.21	4.18	2.98	0.36	0.84
1980	2.62	2.95	5.50	4.75	0.39	0.43
1985	–	–	5.98	5.14	0.385	0.455
Growth rate % per annum	–	–	1.44	2.20	0.27	-2.40

Source: Lisker, 1987, Project FAO/MOZ/81/051

ENVIRONMENTAL PROBLEMS

Although the environmental context of development in Mozambique is in some ways similar to that of other sub-Saharan African countries, there are significant differences. Exceptional aspects of Mozambique include:

- a relatively rich, but only partly explored and developed resource base;
- an overall lack of population pressure on resources with some estimated 18 inhabitants per square kilometre in 1987.

However, clouding the aggregate picture is evidence at the local level of severe environmental deterioration. This occurs particularly near urban areas, on the drought-prone soils of the south, in the easily disrupted near-coast ecosystems, and in areas of refugee settlement. In the short term, this local environmental degradation is likely to increase in intensity and spread.

Putting Mozambique within the context of environmental stress in Africa, Table 5.3 is an attempt to summarise the issues that Timberlake (1985) argues are significant in the continent. It is notable that many of these issues are either not significant in the case of Mozambique, or are of local relevance only (Table 5.3). Desertification, soil erosion and deforestation, generally regarded as central problems in the environmental challenge in Africa, are discussed below. Table 5.4 summarises two recent analyses of environmental problems in Mozambique. They may be compared with a recent ETC review of outstanding environmental issues (Table 5.5). Though all three agree that the present emergency is the major cause of environmental problems, there are significant differences elsewhere, for example, in relation to deforestation, health and the marine/coastal environments.

Turning firstly to desertification – severe environmental degradation relating principally to misuse or over-use of the environment – it has been widely perceived as a destructive tendency in sub-Saharan Africa. Over-grazing, the extension of agriculture into non-resilient environments, and the removal of trees for a variety of purposes have been identified as major components of the phenomenon, exacerbated by drought. Famine, malnutrition and population movements have been cited as outcomes of desertification. In Mozambique there is little evidence of severe natural degradation, rather it occurs in locally-specific sites. Famine, malnutrition and population movements are, however, directly related to the impact of war, not to nature.

Table 5.3 *Environmental problems and issues characteristic of many sub-Saharan countries and their relevance to Mozambique*

Problem/issue	Significant nationally in Mozambique	Locally relevant in Mozambique
Population pressure on resources	No	Yes
Resource overuse	No	Yes
Overcultivation	No	Yes
Overgrazing	No	Yes
Overfishing	No	Yes
Conflict between pastoralists and cultivators	No	No
Agriculture and pastoral extension to erosion-prone environments	No	Yes
Perennial drought lasting many years	No	Yes
'Drought' caused by massive soil degradation	No	No
Deforestation	No	Yes
Excessive commercial logging	No	No
Extreme fuelwood scarcity	No	Yes
Limited water availability, poor water quality	No	Yes
International conflict over water use	No	No
Transfrontier pollution	No	Yes
Industrial pollution	No	Yes
Use of Third World countries as dumps for industrial waste	No	No

Source: Derived from Timberlake, 1985

With reference to soil erosion, a complex interaction between land management systems, erosion by rainfall and waterflow and protection offered by plants determines the rate at which soil is eroded from Mozambican watersheds. Such factors as steepness of landscape, frequency and intensity of rainfall, and the thickness, degree of cohesion and openness of soil to percolating water are all important environmental variables, but the intensity of land use and the management strategies of land users are crucial.

Though peasant farmers are aware of the risk and costs associated with soil erosion, in their battle for survival soil erosion is merely one consideration, and rarely the most pressing one. Whilst erosion is not a widespread problem, there are a number of sites where erosion is a serious issue. In the Angonia region of Tete, with more than 1000 mm of precipitation per annum on average, steep slopes and a large number of cattle, erosion has been severe. On the steep slopes of the lavas of western Maputo and Gaza, erosion risk is high, as it is also in the interior highlands of the Beira Corridor, an area of intense refugee settlement.

In 1988, the UNEP report identified as likely to suffer erosion areas of monoculture on commercial farms where land would be exposed after harvesting, and areas where fallow periods had been severely reduced. Given the current collapse of commercial farming, the threat of erosion is temporarily reduced.

Coastal sand dunes, where trees have been removed, are suffering wind erosion and, at a local scale, lines of communication such as roads are prone to erosion, particularly if ditches are not carefully managed to control run-off. Flooding rivers may also cause erosion and large amounts of deposition on flood plains.

Salinisation and alkalinisation of soils in irrigated areas are possibly more significant than erosion of soils in Mozambique (World Bank, 1988). If irrigated land is insufficiently drained, if too much irrigation water is added or if the substrata contain large amounts of alkali or salt, a toxic surface layer may build up relatively quickly. Irrigation can provide the security of stable, high levels of production, even in drought conditions, but it is expensive to achieve and the salt build-up is particularly undesirable.

Table 5.4 *Two recent analyses of environmental problems*

Issue	World Bank 1988 Country Environmental Issue Paper	UNEP 1988 Report on a programming mission to Mozambique
Natural resource richness	++	++
Level of regional differentiation	*	**
Population pressure on resources:		
local	*	**
national	+	
Emergency, problem	***	***
Refugees	*	**
Health		*
Marine environment	(*)	**
Deforestation	***	
Wood energy	**	**
Energy policy	*	
Urbanisation	*	*
Overgrazing	*	*
Land tenure	*	
Soil deterioration	**	*
Large dams	*	**
'Natural' disasters	*	**
Drought	*	*
Floods	*	*
Lack of environmental management organisation		**
Sustainability		**
Integrated water management		**

Key

***	critical problem
**	major problem
*	significant
(*)	mentioned
+	favourable
++	very favourable

This summary by ETC is based on a careful consideration of the wording of the two documents taking into account explicit statements and implicit judgements.

During the war, soil conditions are likely to regenerate in areas where populations have fled but deteriorate in areas of population concentration. It would be prudent to monitor erosion rates, not least because they influence the viability of irrigation schemes through silting of storage reservoirs and irrigation channels. When conditions permit, it would be desirable also to undertake a survey of erosion hazard in critical areas.

Deforestation has been identified as the main environmental issue, with logging, fuelwood collection and clearance for agriculture identified as the major causes (World Bank, 1988). The World Bank also argued that 40 per cent of the wooded area has been degraded towards scrub.

Around some villages, women need to travel six to eight kilometres in a search for fuelwood, whilst inland of Maputo, fuelwood is transported 50-60 kilometres. More particularly, mangroves, particularly *Rhizophora*, have been severely depleted and 70 per cent have been removed in the last 20 years. Removal of trees continues to threaten the stability of coastal dunes. This World Bank review presents a gloomy picture of the state of Mozambican forests, yet it would be a great exaggeration to interpret this as a generalised catastrophe.

Table 5.5 *Outstanding environmental issues*

War as cause of problem	***
Malnutrition	***
Refugee settlements	**
Land tenure	**
Health	**
Urbanization	**
Institutional management capacity	**
Coastal littoral	**
Mangrove	**
Lack of Environment Impact Analysis	**
Population pressure on resources	*
Water availability and quality	*
Deforestation	*
'Natural' disasters	*
Drought	*
Floods	*
Soil deterioration	*
Wood for energy use	*
Marine environment	*
Fisheries	*
Industrial pollution	*
Reallocation of population	+
Energy balance	+
Natural resource richness	+
River basin management	+
Dams and irrigation systems	0
Overgrazing	0

Key:
***	Critical problem
**	Serious problem
*	Local Problem
0	Lack information
+	Has a positive potential

This is a tabular resumé of ETC's perspective on the Mozambican environment.

There are several indicators that suggest deforestation is not as severe as elsewhere in the SADC countries. In the Nampula reforestation scheme, only 7 per cent of the charcoal produced in 1988 could be sold. In fact, charcoal plays only a small part in fuel supplies in the Mozambique fuel market. Urban and peri-urban areas are, however, suffering woodfuel shortages as a result of population concentration. SADC predicts shortages in Maputo, Gaza, Inhambane, Manica and Nampula provinces by 2000, and already there are some indicators of fuelwood problems. In

Chokwe region, for example, maize husks, a low-quality fuel, are used for cooking. In projections for rural consumption, at present almost entirely wood, it is expected that the use of dung, again an indicator of fuel scarcity, will rise. At the national scale however, SADC computes that sustainable yield is almost twice the demand.

The fuelwood problem, therefore, is generally site specific and there are at present shortfalls in Maputo and Nampula provinces. Since 1981 prices of fuelwood have increased by a factor of 10 in real terms, reflecting a growing demand, difficulty of access and because wood became one of the first commodities to be freed from price intervention by the state. Attempts to develop fuelwood production have achieved little success, essentially as the plantation model was adopted. In the Nampula plantation only one-third of intended planting was achieved in 1988 and only 20 per cent of intended planting by the Forestry Experimentation Centre. There is more reason for optimism in the case of smallholder production of farm trees.

The World Bank is probably unduly optimistic in expecting to achieve much substantial conservation through improved stove design quite simply because with a plentiful wood resource in the country as a whole there is little pressure to conserve wood except in areas of scarcity. However, an emphasis on fuel switching offers possibilities in the urban areas.

With all three environmental problems, desertification, soil erosion and deforestation, Mozambique faces problems in areas of high population density with a vulnerable resource base, but land in the interior will naturally regenerate as human stress is reduced. Degradation and resource shortages are most severe in peri-urban areas and monitoring of the urban and peri-urban environment can provide a surrogate for an exhaustive national study. Other special environments, such as coastal mangroves and dunes, also justify monitoring.

Water resources

Turning to environmental problems associated with surfacewater, not enough attention has been paid to the quality of water in Mozambique. One of the many reasons for this is the belief that water in Mozambique is not polluted and it is true that most of the water in the country does not yet suffer from alarming levels of pollution.

In the context of industry and water consumption in Mozambique, manufacturing industry and urban domestic consumption have, or will have, the greatest negative impact on the environment, both in terms of both water pollution and the production of solid waste.

Waste water from industry and from the urban domestic sector, although not yet produced in very large quantities, has considerable potential for pollution, especially when concentrated in small areas.

In terms of environmental hygiene, the city of Maputo stands out. Many parts of the city have drain water leaking on the surface. A new higher-capacity drainage system is under construction. The system could discharge 50,000 m^3 of wastewater a day into the Maputo estuary. This would not protect the estuary from pollution, especially when this water is not treated before it is discharged.

The consequences for the environment arising from the expanding use of fertilisers and pesticides in mechanised agriculture should be stressed. This use is projected to expand even further in the coming decades, particularly on the extensive floodplains of the major river basins. There has in fact been no evaluation of the impact of these accumulating pollutants in the soil and the rivers, nor of their effects on the fishery resources of reservoirs and river estuaries.

Coastal ecosystems

Major environmental problems have been identified on the fragile coastal ecosystems of Mozambique. The mangrove and coral ecosystems are already in a such a state of degradation that measures for their immediate conservation must not be ignored.

The mangroves are being, or may be, totally destroyed through their use for agriculture, fish-farming tanks, salt pans and through excessive traditional uses which exceed sustainable production and do not permit regeneration.

Over-exploitation of the mangroves by their users is very much linked to the general problem of the rapid increase of population at the coast. Besides their importance in providing poles and timber for building, boats, firewood and charcoal and a variety of other products, which include resin, dyes etc., the space occupied by the mangroves provides nourishment and protection for the immature stages of many species of fish, crustaceans and molluscs.

Furthermore, the role of the mangroves in catching and stabilising silt, as well as in protecting the coast from erosion, makes it obvious where they have been damaged or have disappeared completely through the resultant coastal erosion. Evidence of this has appeared at Inhaca and Beira.

Besides their function as a nursery for some species of commercially-caught shrimps, the mangrove forests, through bacterial action, produce a type of detritus which is rich in proteins. The removal of the mangroves from a given area could cause a decline in offshore fishing through the loss of the source of feeding and protection for the immature shrimps and fish.

If the mangroves are intensely affected by development, there is a serious probability that the commercial shrimp catch would fall drastically. In Mozambique's situation, it is safe to say: no mangroves, no shrimps.

At the same time, the increase in the population at the coast in recent years has brought considerably greater pressure on the coral reefs. The traditional strategy for conservation has been abandoned. The result is that large areas of coral along the coast have been seriously harmed. This process will continue until a new way of protecting and managing the coral reefs is found.

The coral reefs serve as a natural barrier against the action of the waves along the coast, protecting it from erosion and other damaging effects of the sea. One of the main reasons for the degradation of the coral reefs is silting as a result of human activity on land. This includes incorrect agricultural and forestry practices, and the over-exploitation of the mangroves. The construction of commercial and recreational facilities on, or close to, the coral reefs also has an immediate physical impact.

There are four sources of pollution in the coastal areas which, one way or another, affect the mangrove and coral ecosystems: domestic waste, industrial waste – toxic and non-toxic solids deposited in the sea close to the coast – port activities and petroleum spillage.

For economic reasons, the coastal cities often discharge domestic sewage directly into the sea. In the case of moderately-large towns, this sewage may not be of great consequence for the marine environment. However, cities with a million or more inhabitants should at least partially treat the sewage before discharging it into the sea. If the beaches of coastal cities such as Maputo, Beira, Quelimane, Pemba and even Nacala want to continue attracting bathers and to safeguard marine life, detailed studies of the subject should be carried out.

Industrial waste from factories is more dangerous for marine ecology. The marine environment can still be affected by industrial waste which is not necessarily chemical or toxic, but which has an unacceptably high temperature for local marine life. Although industrial pollution along Mozambique's coast is still modest and is not projected to reach alarming levels in the near future, it is an issue that should not be neglected.

While pollution from port activity has not yet reached serious proportions, or rather has not come to the attention of the responsible authorities, there are cases which merit due attention, such as the spillage of dangerous cargo from ships in the port area, dredging operations and dumping of the dredged materials.

Despite the fact that fishing authorities throughout the world are making great efforts to persuade ship owners and manufacturers to package cargo more securely, there are still major losses in the ports during loading and unloading operations. The estimates vary, but the losses could reach 40 per cent in some ports. All these losses end up in the water of the port.

There is no accurate information in Mozambique from which to calculate exactly the level of port pollution caused by discharge from ships. Some toxic materials handled both in bags and in bulk, such as fertiliser, could be harmful, making careful assessment necessary.

A serious risk associated with fuel complexes near the coast is pollution of the beaches from oil utilisation, especially in the case of spills. Despite the care that is taken during these operations, some unscrupulous captains sometimes clean their tanks in, or near, ports. The legal instruments necessary to penalise such actions must be created.

Little is known of the toxicity of petroleum and its derivatives. It is known, for example, that the mangroves possess a remarkable capacity for rapid regeneration when they are cut for timber. When they are damaged by pollutants such as herbicides or petroleum, recovery may take much longer. Although there is no evidence of this in Mozambique, it has been observed in other places that petroleum kills the fish in the coral reefs and has detrimental effects on the reproduction, growth rates, colonisation and nutrition of the corals.

Industry

In terms of the environmental impact of industrial production as a whole, Mozambique may be regarded as a country without major problems because the degree of industrialisation is small and the levels of production are low.

However, industry is situated in the urban centres such as Maputo, Matola and Beira in the midst of large concentrations of population which are growing rapidly, given the urban influx from the countryside. The bulk of the plant is old, with obsolete equipment and systems of technology. Production takes place without the minimum of regulations to protect the population against environmentally-dangerous waste, such as the emission of solid, liquid or gaseous effluents. Under these circumstances, certain specific industries could have a strong impact on the state of health of the population living in the urban areas.

For example, the textile and paper industries should warrant careful study with regard to the treatment of their specific waste products (caustic soda in the former and cellulose in the latter), since instances are already known of the dumping of these substances in rivers and streams with a deleterious impact on the ecosystem.

As for the cement industry in Mozambique, it is known that it has problems with the filtration systems, although no study of its environmental impact has ever been carried out. It should be pointed out that a rehabilitation programme for this industrial sub-sector will probably include treatment of its by-products.

The chemical industry, located mainly in Maputo, produces industrial chemicals, as well as explosives, fertiliser and paint. The manufacture of these finished or intermediate products without any form of supervision over the effluent or production regulations could directly or indirectly affect the health of the population.

Mining

Despite its enormous mineral resources, for historical reasons Mozambique has little mining. The principal mines and quarries in the country are listed below (Figure 5.1):

- the Moatize coal mines in Tete;
- the copper mine at Mundonguara in Manica;
- the bentonite mine at Boane in Maputo;
- the marble quarry at Montepuez in Cabo Delgado;
- the garnet mine at Cuamba in Niassa;
- the bauxite mine at Penhalonga in Manica;
- the gold mines at Penhalonga in Manica.

The main local effects on the environment resulting from the exploitation of mineral resources and other related activities are: atmospheric and water pollution, infertility and subsidence of the land, devastation of forests, air pollution of populated areas and changes in the equilibrium of different animal/plant ecosystems. These effects are caused both by the movement of the land involved in mining, by the emission of toxic gases from some minerals and by other factors.

During mineral exploitation, especially in the case of open-cast mining, major works of mining engineering are undertaken. Thus, rivers are diverted from their normal courses, people are moved and farming is affected. The water table is disturbed during and after operations and vast areas of forest are destroyed when the land is cleared.

For example, the development of the coal mines at Moatize will involve opening new mines, including two open-cast ones. To extract the six million tonnes of coal planned each year, some 15 million cubic metres of earth and coal will have to be moved annually, which will cause pollution problems in the town of Moatize and possibly in Tete City, depending on wind direction and strength.

The exploitation of gold in Manica could cause serious problems in the Revue river valley, an excellent farming area, which could be destroyed by alluvial dredging upsetting the hydrological balance.

Mining operations for heavy minerals in Mozambique's coastal sands (Angoche, Pebane, Xai Xai etc.), which are concentrated in dunes and beach sand, will need protection measures for the local ecology. If not, the dunes, the mangroves and the beaches will be destroyed should the process of reclamation be inadequate. With the destruction of the dunes, the effects of coastal erosion would increase, and the chances of the salinisation of the land and inland water would increase.

The exploitation of graphite at Ancuabe (Cabo Delgado) will require large amounts of water for processing the graphite, which could affect the level of the aquifers and the supply of water for the population.

In Mozambique, the greatest problems of atmospheric pollution as a result of mining could occur at the coal mines in Moatize. Many atmospheric pollutants, notably oxides of nitrogen, sulphur dioxide, and carbon monoxide are a danger to people who suffer from respiratory and cardio-vascular diseases. These gases are also emitted by some manufacturing industries.

Urban environmental problems

Turning to urban environmental problems, these result from the incompatibility created between the rapidly-growing population and the continuous reduction in the capacity of the infrastructure in the urban areas.

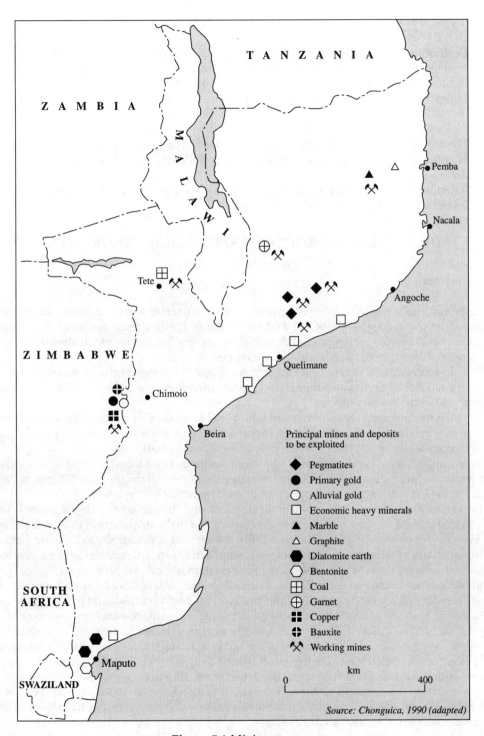

Figure 5.1 *Mining resources*

In the case of Maputo City the following problems have been identified:

- Deterioration of buildings caused by heavy population pressure and poor or non-existent maintenance services; studies carried out by the Ministry of Commerce in 1988 recorded an average of 6.8 persons per room in the city;
- Deterioration of the plumbing systems given the continual interruptions to, or total lack of, water supply, with a consequent impact on public health;
- Lack of a regular urban garbage collection and disposal system;
- The release of domestic and industrial effluent into Maputo Bay without prior treatment;
- Significant reduction in the areas of forest around the city as a result of the heavy demand for firewood;
- Rapid increase in the built-up area with housing made of non-durable materials in insanitary and overcrowded shanty towns.

THE NATURAL RESOURCE BASE AND LEGAL UNDERPINNINGS

Land resources

The shape and location of Mozambique, crossed by such major rivers as the Zambezi, the Save, the Limpopo, the Incomati, the Umbeluzi and the Maputo, implies great diversity in ecological conditions, ranging from semi-arid to high rainfall, from very hot and humid to almost temperate conditions and from plains to uplands and mountains.

The agro-ecological characteristics of the country (Figure 5.2) are determined essentially by such environmental factors as climate, topography, the soil, the vegetation and by the different farming systems used in the various regions.

Climate is the environmental component which wields most influence over the distribution of land use over relatively large areas. Large variations in production from year to year in a given region indicate a lack of adaptation to the prevailing climatic conditions.

In general the average annual rainfall pattern shows an increase from the coast to inland, with major variations according to altitude. The average annual rainfall ranges from 350 mm at Pafuri in Gaza to 2348 mm at Tacuane in Upper Zambezia (Figure 5.3).

The variation coefficient lies between 20 per cent and 40 per cent with the highest rates concentrated in the drought-prone south of the country and in the strip south of the Zambezi river. This variable is of outstanding importance within the context of agricultural production reliability.

The variability of soil types in Mozambique is shown in Figure 5.4. Among the immature soils, the alluvial soils are those which possess the greatest agricultural potential, as well as covering considerable areas in the extensive Zambezi delta and along the banks of numerous rivers. The areas covered by alluvial soils include significant layers of hydromorphic and halomorphic soils.

Other immature soils include the well-drained soils near or on the coast in the provinces of Cabo Delgado, Nampula, Zambezia, Sofala and Maputo and also in the interior of Gaza and Inhambane provinces. They constitute the largest part of the sandy coastal strip, which includes a broad strip inland from the coast stretching from the mouth of the Rovuma river to Ponta do Ouro, interspersed in places with alluvial and other soils from the depressions. They are soils normally of low fertility, with poor water retention and texture. However, it is along the coastal strip that the greatest production potential for tree crops is found, notably cashew and coconut, since it is along the coast that the growth period normally lasts 240 days.

Lithoidal soils cover large areas of Tete, Sofala, Manica, Gaza, Zambezia and Maputo provinces.

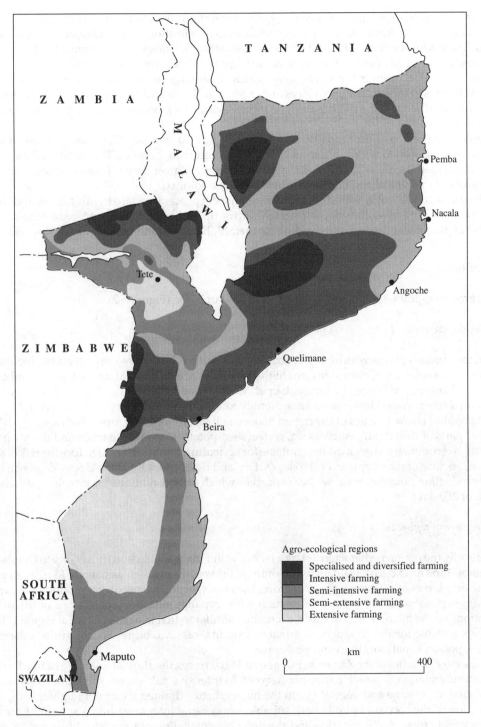

Figure 5.2 *Agro-ecological regions*

They are poorly-developed soils, coarse-grained and stony, with frequent occurrences of gravel, stones and outcrops on the surface. They occur in areas of transition between humid and semi-arid zones. These soils are normally used for extensive natural pastures, but care must be taken with their capacity so as to avoid degradation of the vegetation and erosion of the soil.

Another major group is the sandy soils, which cover large areas with semi-arid or dry sub-humid climates in the southern provinces and in Manica, Sofala and Tete provinces. The richest of these soils are the greyish-red soils derived from volcanic rock occurring in Maputo, Sofala and Manica provinces.

Laterite soils are medium- and fine-textured, well-drained and deep. They are the most widely represented, associated with sub-humid climates and occurring in series. The colour of these soils depends on their depth, with red near the surface and grey lower down. These soils are found in large areas of the central and northern provinces of the country.

The red ferralitic soils, well-drained, clayey and deep, are associated with humid and sub-humid climates and cover considerable stretches in the upland, rainy regions of Niassa, Manica and Zambezia provinces. They are outstanding for their high fertility and great agricultural potential.

Agriculture

Five agro-ecological regions can be identified in Mozambique (Figure 5.2).

Agro-ecological region I

This region includes areas with highly-specialised agriculture. It contains the plateau and highland areas of Mossourize and Chimanimni, the high plateaux of Angonia and Maravia, Upper Zambezia (Gurue, Namarroi, Milange, Tacuance, Upper Molocue) and Maniamba. This region is one of accidented relief. Water deficiencies are generally low, while surpluses reach high levels.

The natural characteristics of the region make it suitable for certain crops which are not viable in other parts of the country, such as tea, coffee, seed potatoes, temperate fruits and dairy cattle. Forestry is recommended even in areas suitable for agricultural production, to reduce the risk of soil erosion, because of the steepness of the slopes. Dryland rice, especially in the Upper Zambezi, has great production potential because there are areas which offer conditions for growing periods in excess of 280 days.

Agro-ecological region II

Climatically the region is characterised by a lack of water in the dry season (June/July to October/November) and an excess of water in four months of the year (December/January to March/April).

The development of various types of crops, many of which have useful by-products for cattle farming, is possible in this region. Infestation with trypanosomiasis (tsetse) is one of the main limitations on the introduction of cattle, a situation similar to that in agro-ecological region I. The region is suitable for the production of maize, peanuts, cassava, beans, cotton, fruits, oilseeds, tobacco, potato, kenaf, sorghum and pineapple.

In the lower reaches of the Zambezi, Pungue and Buzi rivers, the alluvial soils are as a rule fertile, and where irrigation is possible they are devoted to intensive cultivation, the main crops being maize, rice, sugar cane and vegetables. In the higher, better-drained zones with lighter soils, the production of the coconut palm is very suitable, often being integrated into a system of mixed livestock and crops. Reafforestation and the orderly exploitation of the natural forest is recommended for the sub- and middle-plateau regions.

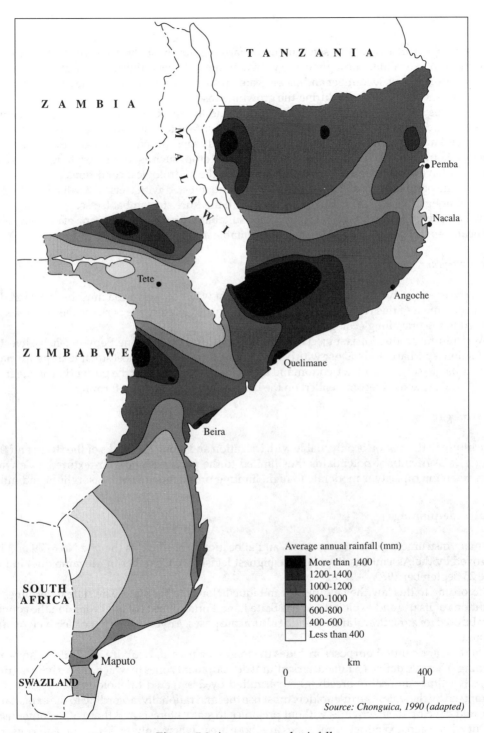

Figure 5.3 *Average annual rainfall*

Agro-ecological region III

This is a region of essentially semi-intensive farming south of the Save river. The irregular distribution of the rainfall throughout the year, together with very high temperatures, cause water shortages from May to December and excess water in the remaining months. The irregularity of the rainfall causes short dry spells during the growing season.

The ecological conditions favour mixed arable and livestock farming. The region is also well suited to the cultivation of tropical fruits relatively resistant to water scarcity, as is the case with cashew and mango in the coastal strip. In terms of food crops, the cultivation of drought-resistant varieties should be considered. More drought-resistant crops such as cotton, sorghum, cassava and sunflower have demonstrated the best adaptation to the hydrological conditions.

From the point of view of livestock, some areas are infested with tsetse fly, which is a limiting factor, although this limitation can be reduced with measures to combat tsetse.

In the sandy coastal strip, dry farming is most suitable, with the intercropping of maize, peanuts and beans, as well as cashew. Forestry is also suitable in this zone.

Agro-ecological region IV

Given the irregularity of the rainfall, various forms of water conservation must be considered for the development of this region. Livestock production and forestry are perhaps the land uses best adapted to the prevailing ecological conditions.

Agricultural production is subject to the risk of crop losses in this zone. Semi-extensive livestock production is perhaps the land use with best potential. In general, the most suitable crops are maize, cassava, beans, sorghum, millet, cotton, and leguminous fodder. Thus, the promotion of integrated agricultural systems is recommended on the basis of livestock and dry farming.

Agro-ecological region V

Agriculture in this region is only viable with irrigation and along the banks of the rivers and their tributaries. Agricultural potential is thus limited to the parts with heavier-textured soils where water retention capacity is moderate to high, limiting production to cotton, sorghum and millet.

Legal underpinnings

The main instrument determining access and allocation of the land is the law No.6/79 of 3 July approved by the Assembleia Popular (the highest legislative Chamber in Mozambique) in force since 25 September 1979.

According to this law the land in Mozambique belongs to the state. The state determines the conditions of its use and exploitation. The State Land Fund consists of all the land in the country. It can be used for agricultural and non-agricultural purposes. Anyone, singly or collectively, can use the land.

Land for agricultural purposes includes the following uses: agriculture, silviculture and cattle breeding. The state defines planned agricultural development zones in which any activity (agriculture, silviculture and cattle breeding) is permitted by designated titleholders whose rights are guaranteed by the state. The titleholders must use the land rationally, according to the exploitation plan, and develop their activities without prejudice to state interests and those of the other users.

Outside designated agricultural zones are those areas where only preservation and conservation activities promoted by the state are allowed. This includes the protection of the soil, forest and

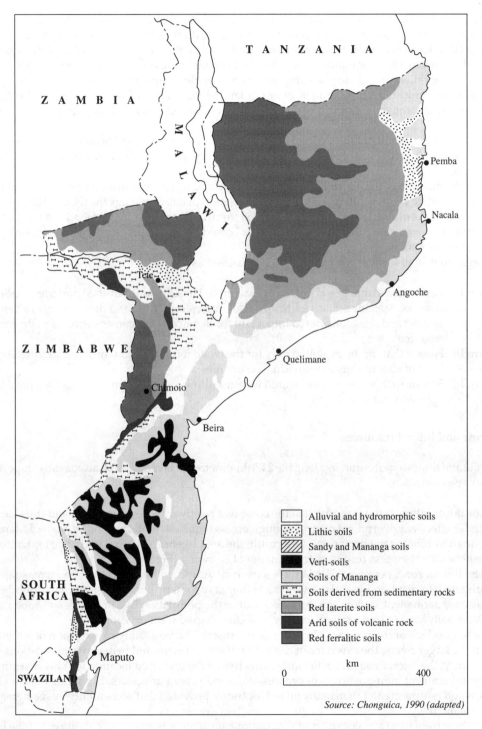

Figure 5.4 *Soils*

Alluvial and hydromorphic soils
Lithic soils
Sandy and Mananga soils
Verti-soils
Soils of Mananga
Soils derived from sedimentary rocks
Red laterite soils
Arid soils of volcanic rock
Red ferralitic soils

km
0   400

Source: Chonguica, 1990 (adapted)

wildlife, historical sites and monuments, and others of national importance, as well as areas for defence and security zones. There are also partial protected zones. Partial protected zones comprise territorial waters, streams and the continental shelf, the sea coast, land surrounding water sources, the beds of any artificial or natural water courses, islands, zones of land along the frontier; zones of land along railways and surrounding railway installations, airports, harbours, meteorological and telecommunications installations; zones of land along roads, railways, bridges and tunnels. Zones of partial protection can also be designated for military defence and for public infrastructure purposes.

It is the responsibility of the Council of Ministers to manage the Land State Fund and to define the powers of the provincial governors, to create, modify or extinguish zones of total and partial protection.

It is the function of the Town Hall in the areas covered by the urbanisation plans to permit the use of the land, to propose alterations to the urbanisation plans, to manage the registration services and to control the utilisation of, and profit derived from, the land. In a recent amendment to the state constitution, it was stated that in future state land could be sold to private owners, so opening up a private land market.

Legal control of forests in Mozambique is classified as follows:

Group I: Forests that cannot be allocated or exploited. These include national parks and national reserves. Specific sensitive sites are also protected such as sand dunes, sites of scientific interest and sites considered important for defence or the conservation of hydrological resources.

Group II: Forests that can be exploited only for the wood industry and which are allocated in the form of concessions to individual companies.

Group III: Forests in this class can be cleared for agriculture and other purposes as they have little economic value.

Marine and littoral resources

Marine and littoral environments along the 2470 kilometres of the Mozambican coast are important for six reasons:

1. For the duration of the war, much of the coast was relatively accessible by sea and thus largely under effective government control, though access required military escort in parts of Maputo, Gaza and Inhambane provinces. As a result, the area has been able to contribute agriculture, fisheries and biomass resources to the national economy (Figure 5.5).
2. The littoral zone, because it is relatively safe, is now, and will in the future, be increasingly attractive to displaced populations, who, if they stay for a prolonged period, will doubtless become permanent settlers. Already over half of the population live in the coastal zone. Potentially, and to some extent actually, resource degradation may follow.
3. Given the lack of steep slopes, the low risk of erosion, the possibility of extension of irrigation on the larger rivers, the existence of a number of larger towns and better communications and security, the littoral zone is particularly attractive as the preferred location for new investment by government, non-government organisations and private investors. Economic risks will be less and returns greater than many inland locations, provided that accessibility by sea transport is maintained.
4. Cashew trees form a major cover of the coastal zone having been an important part of the local agricultural economy as well as a major national export for many years. More recently the

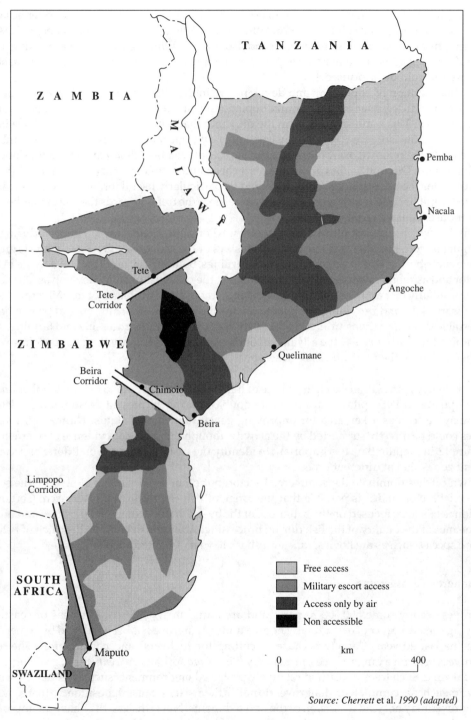

Figure 5.5 *Accessibility under conditions of war, 1989*

management of the industry has been in crisis. For example, in 1983, 18 thousand tonnes was harvested, a fifth of the volume of 1976, although by 1986 it had recovered to 50 per cent. As a peasant tree crop stabilising the fragile sandy soils of the littoral zone as well as making a significant contribution to national exports, the recuperation and maintenance of the cashew industry should be prioritised.

5. The concentration of population and development in the littoral zones entails the risks of environmental degradation and resource depletion, even in a generally productive and resilient environment. This is already shown in the difficulty that self-employed fishermen have in finding suitable large trees for the construction of dug-out canoes, since demands on timber have led to the removal of whole trees near the coast (even the *Casuarina* planted for dune stabilisation). Dug-out canoes are valued as a cheap and accessible entry point to the fishing industry for the poorest in society, and would be particularly useful for displaced people with limited capital. Lack of trunks will certainly accelerate the trend towards the use of plank-built, but more expensive boats.

6. Fisheries, which were not allowed to compete with Portuguese and Angolan imports during the colonial period, have become one of the mainstays of the economy since 1986, with shrimps alone contributing 42 per cent of total export earnings. Some 55,000 families earn a living in this sector and as refugees have moved to the safety of the coast fishing may develop as a basis for their self-sufficient and non-dependent existence, though the problems of teaching the necessary skills and providing equipment are formidable. Traditionally, coastal people have been able to secure a living from a mixture of fishing, fish sale and processing and farming. This combined resource use has the advantage of risk-spreading and providing support from fisheries during the agricultural slack season.

Marine resources provide an excellent source of high-value protein both to fishing families and to urban populations. Per capita consumption has doubled during the present decade, and the fishing sector may be seen as a key area for improving general nutritional status. Ultimately, 100,000 families could be directly supported by the activity, though there is clear evidence of overfishing, for example, in Maputo Bay. It is important to identify the sustainable catch of different species in different zones, and at different times.

Prawn catches dominate the commercial sector, but other species are exploited by the semi-commercial sector, and it is possible that the range of fish caught may be increased. Certainly, attention needs to be focused on the better use of the by-catch from commercial fishing and on the maintenance of the quality of the fish during processing. Attempts to broaden the catch of fish for offshore species such as anchovies, tuna and shark have had limited success to date.

The mangrove ecosystem

Mangroves occupy some 500,000 hectares and are found in 17 different stretches of coastline, occupying some 15 per cent of the total. The area under mangrove has been reduced by 70 per cent during the last 20 years, largely because of cutting for fuelwood and construction. The term mangrove is used for a range of trees, principally *Rhizophora* spp. and *Avicennia* spp. growing in the intertidal zone. Such trees flourish in relatively protected environments such as estuaries, where fine sediment has accumulated. Mangroves do not, in themselves, cause deposition, so that removal of mangroves may not lead to erosion of the fine sediments. Nevertheless, they have an important function in coastal protection since they reduce considerably the effect of occasional storms and surges which would otherwise cause erosion of the backshore (Figure 5.6).

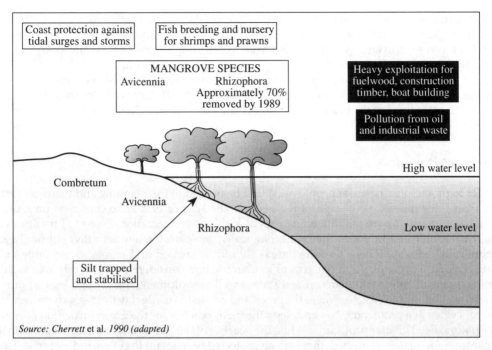

Source: Cherrett et al. 1990 (adapted)

Figure 5.6 *The mangrove ecosystem*

Under natural conditions, mangroves are a self-sustaining and very productive ecosystem, giving a high input of nutrients to the aquatic food chain. They act as fish and crustacean breeding grounds, nurseries and feeding grounds, and support a large and varied bird population, which may be a food supply for people, or the basis of a tourist industry. Overcutting of mangroves threatens their other functions. On the other hand, mangroves act as traps for floating oil which, while it may not destroy the trees themselves, may lead to the death of fish. Near industrial sites, they function as traps for micro-pollutants so that bio-accumulation of toxins is a serious possibility.

The long-term health of the open system of mangroves depends to an unknown extent on the nature of sediment inputs from the coast and rivers. A sediment budget analysis could be attempted, but monitoring of micro-pollutants in sand/silt or organisms is more urgent. And, of course, the re-establishment of mangroves entails protection against woodfuel collection.

Corals form offshore reefs along about 30 per cent of this coast, particularly north of 16°N but with scattered occurrences further south. The taxonomic diversity and aesthetic interest of coral reefs is without parallel in ecosystems. Intact coral reefs form a valuable resource for elite high-value tourism, provided that the system is in pristine condition. For the present, such use must be very limited, but as a future resource, maintenance of the quality of reefs is to be desired. The limited collection of shells and coral and some fishing is possible, but heavy fishing and shell collection are incompatible with maintenance for tourism, though tourism is compatible with balanced resource use.

The identification of particularly valuable areas for conservation as marine nature reserves may be desirable. Pollution by sediment, for instance, caused by the dredging of harbours, or from rivers, increased inputs of freshwater to shallow coastal waters; industrial pollution and sewage pollution are all threats to the quality of reefs which depend for their conservation interest on the maintenance of the micro-scale environment. Oil pollution, unless severe, is unlikely to impair the coral reef itself but will have more severe effects on fish. Recovery rates of the ecosystem after disturbance are slow. At the larger scale, though, coral reefs are very resilient structures and form a powerful protection against coast erosion. In fact, material eroded from reefs during storms forms white sandy beaches, an additional resource for tourism.

Coastal dunes and their associated beaches may in future form a tourist resource, but are also valuable as coastal protectors against storms and tidal surges. If they are to be protected against erosion, it is essential that the vegetation cover of dunes is maintained, since dunes will otherwise be eroded by wind action.

Marine protection areas

In order to protect marine areas people must first be trained in the planning and management of such areas. This raises a very important question. The science of marine conservation must be studied as seriously as are wildlife management and land conservation. Protected marine areas should be established in zones that are ecologically, biologically, aesthetically, culturally and economically valuable. These protected areas should be created and managed as viable units, taking ecological principles and patterns of human use into consideration. This requires suitable training for the planning and management staff as well as equipment, finance and legal approval.

In Mozambique, the beaches where the green and hawksbill turtles lay their eggs have received relatively extensive protection. Nevertheless, the main beaches for the green turtle (*Ilhas Segunda* and *Primeira*) need greater protection. While the beaches of the leatherback and loggerhead turtles appear to be adequately protected, there are no protected beaches for the Olive Ridley turtle. These places should be identified and established as reserves. The feeding areas for the turtles should also be protected. Future conservation work on turtles should place more emphasis on the protection of the whole of their habitat, particularly where co-operation between neighbouring states is required. An example is the protection of the feeding grounds of the loggerhead turtle in the north of Mozambique and in Tanzania to help safeguard the laying stocks on the beaches of the Maputo reserve in the south of Mozambique.

Water

The seasonal nature of the rainfall regime, with a dry season up to five months long, and aperiodic and unpredictable droughts (as in 1988 in the southern coastal zone and in 1991–92) are limitations on water use. Nevertheless, rainfall totals of up to 2200 mm in hilly areas and an average of more than 600 mm over large areas of the country implies great development potential. If the resource is to be fully used, however, storage of wet season water is desirable, both in normal years and for use during droughts. Furthermore, the storage of water would reduce the flood-risk in the lower courses of rivers where valuable agricultural land is threatened.

Water management is desirable for hydropower production, irrigation, flood control, the provision of safe drinking water, stock watering and fish farming. Clearly, improved water management could be a key to development in several sectors of the economy and could make a positive impact on economic activity, quality of life and sustainability. There are possibilities for such development throughout the country. The Zambezi system could be particularly valuable and northern and central Mozambique has a greater potential than the more developed South. A major issue is that of scale: whether to concentrate on capital-intensive large-scale developments or more numerous small-scale schemes. Recent thinking tends to favour the latter, partly on grounds of equity and partly because negative externalities have been identified in large schemes – which in any case provide attractive targets for guerrilla activity.

Approximately one fifth of potential hydro-electric power (HEP) – about 2500 of 11,000 MW – has been developed, overwhelmingly, in the Cabora Bassa Scheme of which Stage 1 has been completed. At present only about 1 per cent of Cabora Bassa's existing production can be used, due to insurgency action. This is a major loss to export earnings. Potential HEP production is predominantly on the Zambezi, but only southern Mozambique, south of the Save River, is without large undeveloped potential. At present there are five schemes in operation: Cabora Bassa, 2075 MW, Chicamba 38 MW and Mavuzi 52 MW, Lichinga and Cuamba. Technically, large and medium schemes are favoured, though in the Pequenos Libombos scheme, 4 MW is projected for near Maputo (Figure 5.7).

In contrast to the fifth of HEP potential actually developed, irrigation has scarcely been started. Though 5 per cent of the country is technically irrigable with supplementary irrigation, and 3 per cent would be very suitable, no more than 1.5 per cent of the potential has been developed. Of the 84,000 hectares developed, only one half is at present in use, due to technical reasons, guerrilla action and soil deterioration (salinization and alkalization). A further problem is the pollution of water by imported pesticides and herbicides.

At present, a high government priority is the rehabilitation of the unused areas of irrigation schemes. Chokwe is one of the more successful of the existing schemes, with 18,000 hectares out of 25,000 being used for paddy rice production. Yields on the scheme are low – two tonnes per hectare for the 14,000 family sector farms and three tonnes per hectare for state and private sector farms. High-yielding varieties and fertilizers may be used to raise productivity but that would involve imported inputs and would tend to put family-sector farms at a disadvantage.

Future developments of irrigation are partly linked to future HEP developments, if multi-purpose schemes are attempted, but there are strong reasons for considering small-scale schemes. The World Bank (1988) emphasises the advantage of small schemes which would favour the family sector and argues that a higher emphasis should be given to rainfed agriculture.

The provision of safe drinking water is a priority for rural areas generally, and particularly for refugee settlements, whether rural or peri-urban. To an extent, this is compatible with irrigation and HEP, though large reservoirs would be less efficient than smaller ones and tube wells would probably be preferable to both. The linked issue of sewage disposal is particularly pressing in urban areas such as Maputo, but also in refugee settlements. With economic restructuring, there is a crisis of maintenance of water systems already installed. This suggests low capital cost schemes are likely to be more sustainable than high cost ones although high cost schemes are usually gravitational ones with low running costs.

Fish farming is still a minor activity in rural areas, but may help to produce more balanced diets. Some progress has been recorded in four small schemes, which produced a total of 14 tonnes for consumption, with tilapia and carp as the main product, and the production of fingerlings as well as full-sized consumable fish.

Legal underpinnings for the use of water resources

The regulations concerning the exploitation of water resources in Mozambique date back to ministerial degrees issued in 1946. According to them, water is considered to be either private or public. The former includes rainwater falling on private land as well as water from private wells. Public water includes the sea bays, lakes and large ponds, rivers, rainfall on state land and groundwater. All these waters are under the administration of the state and the right to use them can be acquired by permit. Anyone is allowed to use water for household purposes and for livestock from fountains, wells and public reservoirs, as well as from streams and ponds in the

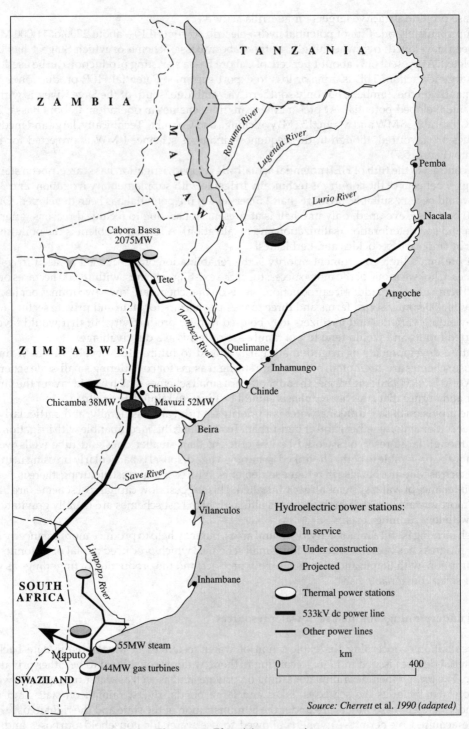

Figure 5.7 *Electricity generation*

public domain.

In order to pump water from public water sources permits must be obtained from the local administrative office. Used water, on return to its source, should not be contaminated with substances harmful to agriculture, livestock, fish or human beings.

Wildlife

In Mozambique, because of war conditions, there is little reliable information about wildlife. Some authorities have concluded that, with the abandonment of much land by the human population, animal populations may have increased. However, there is evidence of much clandestine activity directed towards trafficking in ivory and in the hides of animals such as leopards, lions and crocodiles. As a result, it is likely that populations of such prized animals have fallen.

National Parks and Reserves

Having recognised the need to protect, conserve and utilise the animal communities, the country has developed various types of protected area, namely national parks, total, special and partial reserves and zones of special vigilance (Figure 5.8).

Almost 13 per cent of the country's total surface area is occupied by areas of protection and conservation, including:

- National parks with an area of 15,850 km^2 (1.6 per cent)
- Reserves with an area of 18,800 km^2 (2.4 per cent) and
- Game reserves with an area of 56,700 km^2 (7 per cent)

There are four national parks:

- Gorongosa National Park, 3770 km^2, Sofala province
- Zinave National Park, 5000 km^2, Inhambane province
- Banhine National Park, 7000 km^2, Gaza province
- Bazaruto National Park, 80 km^2, Inhambane province

Besides these national parks, there are also four reserves:

- Niassa Reserve, 15,000 km^2, Niassa province
- Gile Reserve, 2100 km^2, Zambezia province
- Pomene Reserve, 200 km^2, Inhambane province
- Maputo Reserve, 1500 km^2, Maputo province

In relation to the game reserves, most of these are situated in Sofala province, including the former buffalo reserve at Marromeu which is today a wildlife production unit in the Zambezi valley. Apart from those in Sofala province, there is a large area in Gaza province which has game reserve status, called the Upper Limpopo Production Unit.

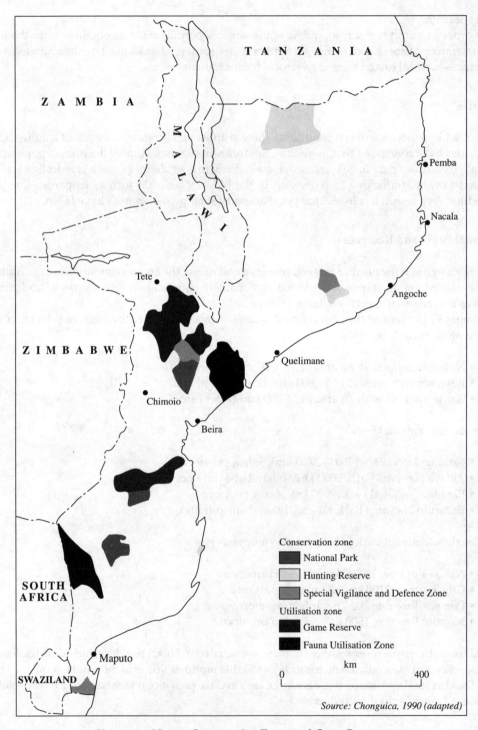

Figure 5.8 *Nature Conservation Zones and Game Reserves*

STRATEGIES AND SOLUTIONS FOR SUSTAINABLE DEVELOPMENT

Any attempt to present a description of the current state of the environment in Mozambique in the light of economic development plans and programmes, and of the population growth trends, is extremely limited by virtue of the destabilisation in the country, which creates enormous difficulties in obtaining the relevant data. The problem is compounded by the scarcity of qualified personnel and financial and technical limitations.

Thus, the analyses offered in earlier sections and the conclusions presented below can in no way be regarded as definitive. They constitute the *beginnings* of a process that must be continued and developed. They should be considered as points for discussion, leading to greater awareness of the urgent need to integrate environmental indicators into the planning mechanisms and systems aimed at achieving sustainable economic development.

Population/economic development/environment issues

- Given the country's socio-economic profile and its demographic and population context, a thorough understanding of the relationships between the components of population-economic development-environment issues is important as to their implications for the preparation of overall plans for national economic development.
- The problems related to the high rate of increase of the urban population because of the influx from the countryside, without a corresponding expansion of basic social and service infrastructure, deserve special attention in the formulation of strategies for the territorial reorganisation of the economy in terms of the spatial orientation of investments and the definition of urban management policies.
- Because of the pressure on woodfuel supplies and the environmental impact of this, the energy question in the urban centres, as well as in densely populated rural areas, requires vigorous and controlled action, not only to augment the availability of alternative sources, but also to improve conditions for the consumers.
- Strengthening the institutional base for research and planning, as well as for the drafting of legal instruments to regulate environmental questions in the context of economic development (exploitation and use of natural resources) are fundamental conditions for establishing a sustainable level of development.
- Taking war devastation into consideration, all these efforts should be concentrated geographically in the areas of greatest security, the transport corridors, the coastal areas and the around the major cities.

The impact of industrial activity on the environment

- Industrial activity is very limited in Mozambique for historical reasons. Except for mining, all industry is located in the urban centres, most notably Maputo and Beira. Thus, in general terms, the environmental problems resulting from industrial production in Mozambique can still be regarded as minor.
- Nevertheless, the high density of the population in urban centres with industrial activities, which, for reasons of technological limitations, do not properly treat liquid, solid and gaseous wastes, constitutes a health hazard for the surrounding population and for river and estuary ecosystems, which are the primary recipients of industrial and domestic sewage.

- In the case of the mining sub-sector, the local impact on human living conditions and agricultural resources can be significant. The scarcity of basic data requires that research be carried out in this sphere, at least in the areas of major mining activities.
- Industrial fishing, developed in the context of international agreements, should be monitored for its effect on marine ecosystems.

Agricultural production and its impact on land resources

- With regard to environmental degradation, it can be stated that the low overall population density and the forced abandonment of large areas because of the war have resulted in the regeneration of the vegetation and the fertility of the soil in large parts of the country. In the densely-populated areas around the cities, along the transport corridors and near the coast the opposite is happening. Here the difficulty of access to land and other resources for the majority of the population and the use of agricultural techniques which are not suited to local conditions, make the problem of degeneration of resources even more acute.
- Family farming, representing 90 per cent of the cultivated area in Mozambique, is the sector which has always benefited least from inputs. Rapid and co-ordinated action is required to minimise its negative environmental effects which cause an accentuated decline in soil productivity and consequently in the levels of food production.

The use of water resources

- Mozambique is a country with significant economic potential in which the economic resources of agriculture and fisheries are largely determined by the hydrological situation. Over 100 river basins covering areas larger than 50 km² can be identified. The country also has some 1300 lakes and ten reservoirs. Wetlands situated near the coastal strip represent very important ecosystems. Thus, a clear policy on the management of water resources is important.
- The existing water-monitoring system is not extensive enough to allow satisfactory coverage in terms of the systematic collection of hydrological data. The flood prevention system in place before 1975 became inoperative during the period of destabilisation which continues to the present. For example, there are no barriers at the mouths of rivers to prevent saline infiltration. Before the construction of the major dams no studies were carried out on the environmental impact of the construction work or on the subsequent operation of the dams. The National Water Board recently began to measure the transport of solids and the quality of water, although this monitoring is only conducted on a small scale.

  Given the importance of these aspects of the rational exploitation of water resources, studies should be encouraged with the aim of finding solutions to these problems by the development of appropriate management strategies.
- The use of surfacewater is basically carried out without treatment in most of the non-urban and suburban areas. There are currently 122 urban water supply systems, one-third of which use ground water. A monitoring system of the use of this water must be established, at least in the densely populated and industrialised areas. This should take account of all aspects such as the systems of latrines, the treatment of industrial waste and the storage of agro- chemicals which can filter through and contaminate the water table.

- There have been major changes in the quantity and quality of water resources. The alteration of the natural surfacewater systems through the use of water in the hydro-electric industry, and in agriculture, implies a steady lowering of the water table, growing marine intrusion and salinization of the low-lying soils near the coast.
- Industrial and urban domestic sewage, although on a smaller scale than in industrialised countries, already has considerable potential for pollution, especially when concentrated in small areas. A minimum monitoring system must be established to evaluate the possible impact of these pollutants on the population and on the water resources.

The use of resources in the coastal strip

- The coastal zone of Mozambique is characterised by the presence of several ecosystems, such as estuaries, mangroves, lagoons and coral reefs. All of these ecosystems are known to be biologically productive and vulnerable to the effects of human activity and its by-products. The abundance and distribution of fishery resources are largely determined by the ecological diversity along the coast. This is why a system of control and monitoring of this class of resources is crucial for the maintenance of the country's future productive capacity in fisheries.
- Besides direct use, the main causes of the degradation of the coastal and marine ecosystems consist of pollution from domestic sewage and industrial waste, including port activity and petroleum residue. Measuring should be started in critical areas to quantify the environmental impact of this pollution.
- Major construction works which affect the level of the water table and cause changes in the corresponding marine ecosystems require a network for the collection of data on the possible impact on these systems. For example, account must be taken of the fact that an excessive decline in the flow from the Cabora Bassa dam in the rainy season could have a disastrous effect on the prawn fishing on the Sofala Bank.

The institutional context for resource management

Environmental issues and concern about the management of Mozambique's natural resources have again become the concern of central institutions because of the prominence given to it during the Frelimo Fifth Party Congress (July 1989). The Report of the Party's Central Committee focused primarily on the effect of the war and of destabilisation on the management of natural resources, although it acknowledged the necessity of seeing natural resource management as a part of socio-economic development.

The issues raised by the Central Committee for immediate action were the following:

- Include environmental issues in the educational curricula;
- Stimulate the organisation of local environmental associations and start awareness campaigns;
- Ensure that environmental issues are considered in socio-economic development plans and stimulate the involvement of all institutions in environmental management and research;
- Make it obligatory to consider the environmental impact of the major economic development projects;
- Prohibit the dumping of toxic waste on Mozambican territory.

Co-ordinating bodies

The National Planning Commission (CNP) was established in 1978 to ensure the correct utilisation of available human, financial and national resources in Mozambique. Subordinate to the CNP, the National Institute of Physical Planning (INPF) was established in 1983 to ensure the correct distribution and utilisation of the country's resources. The INPF has a direct task to study and evaluate existing ecosystems, to ensure the co-ordination between the various institutions involved in environmental planning and management, to evaluate the impact of development on the environment, and to prepare the necessary educational materials that would assist the raising of awareness of the Mozambican public.

Aided by the intake of a large number of foreign professionals, the INPF did make its impact felt in the field of housing, physical planning and environment through its co-operation with individuals in other ministries responsible for economic development. Its role remained that of an *advisory body* to the other institutions and its impact depended very much on individual contacts and collaboration. Its impact on decision making always was, and remains, now more than ever, very limited. It is essential that policy-making occurs with a clear understanding of the limitations imposed by scarce resources at all levels. The institutional and professional capacity of the INPF has been reduced drastically over recent years to such an extent that the existence of the Grupo de Trabalho do Meio Ambiente (GTA) depends entirely on the contacts and the standing of one person within the INPF.

Little is known in Maputo about the situation in the rest of the country and, following in the footsteps of the UNEP report (UNEP, 1988), emphasis is placed on the strengthening of central institutions and monitoring without reference to the environmental problems faced in the development process. In particular, there are few environmental standards for pollution-discharge monitoring. This has to be understood, however, within the institutional power framework within which the INPF wants to become operational again. It is indeed necessary that some strengthening of the co-ordinating capacity at the central level takes place, although this in itself will not result in improved resource management nor resolve the problem of the institutional capacity at the provincial and local level.

The capacity of central and local government is likely to remain limited in the face of the scarcity of available financial and technical resources. Sustainable development can only be effectively tackled through institutions already active at the local level and in particular with the collaboration and co-operation of the local producers.

The institutional challenge

The INPF should be evaluated on a regular basis in relation to operational practice. Training and institution building should be considered in the new socio-economic context in which Mozambique has been placed by adopting its new economic policy, the PRE, through which the majority of its inhabitants are likely to become increasingly divorced from the resources necessary for their survival.

The call of the party's Central Committee to stimulate local environmental associations needs to be linked not only to raising the level of consciousness of the population to environmental issues but also to their capacity to exploit and manage those resources.

The low levels of literacy and education in general in Mozambique are a serious obstacle to institution building and resource management nationally. Although this cannot be resolved except by a high level of investment in education over time, it does mean that donors need to be particularly sensitive to the existing situation. Knowledge and skill transfer needs to be an integral part of all assistance activities as sustainability carries with it the capacity of the local population to manage, if not reproduce, the technologies at their disposal.

CONCLUSION

Legislation and the regulations in relation to environment and resource use have two principal aims: firstly, to determine the access to these resources for potential users and therefore define accessibility, and, secondly, to define the conditions under which these resources can be utilised. The drive for the privatisation of existing enterprises, the emergence of the private sector in agriculture and the new conditions for capital investment will make it necessary for the government to overhaul present legislation concerning accessibility, resource use and the environmental impact of productive activities. Legislation relating to the environment and land use includes laws on national investments, the land, and the utilisation of maritime, mineral resources and forest resources.

The orientation of the party's Central Committee to make improvements to existing laws and regulations should be seen in this context. A more fundamental analysis of present usage and practices of the existing legislation and the capacity of the statutory bodies to implement these effectively needs to be undertaken.

REFERENCES

Cherrett, I et al. (1990) *Norwegian Aid and the Environment in Mozambique* Working Paper D 199016 ETC(UK) for Chr. Michelson Institute, Bergen

Chonguica, E M W et al. (1990) *Mozambique: the present environmental situation* Grupo de Trabalho do Meio Ambiental (GTA), Maputo

Lisker, P (1987) *Project FAO Moz/81 051*, FAO, Rome

Timberlake, L (1985) *Africa in Crisis. The Causes, the Cures for Environmental Bankruptcy* Earthscan, IIED, London

United Nations Environment Programme (1988) *Report on a Programming Mission to Mozambique* Nairobi

World Bank (1988) *Mozambique Agricultural Sector Survey* Washington DC

World Bank (1988) *Mozambique, Country Environment Issues Paper* Washington DC

6

NAMIBIA

INTRODUCTION

Namibia is located in the south-western part of Africa. It is bounded to the north by Angola, Zambia to the east, by Botswana and Zimbabwe to the south, and south-east by the Republic of South Africa. The territory of Namibia covers an area of 824,269 km^2 including Walvis Bay (112,400 ha), which is still administered as a part of the Republic of South Africa. Namibia covers nearly 3 per cent of the total land area of Africa and contains about 0.2 per cent of the total population of the continent.

The country can be divided into three distinct regions: the Namib Desert, the Central Highland and the Kalahari. The two last mentioned regions are part of the Central Plateau (Figure 6.1). The Namib Desert comprises the western marginal area between the escarpment and the coast, stretching along the entire coastline and rising rapidly eastwards. It is 80 to 120 km wide and covers about 15 per cent of the total area of Namibia.

The Central Highland lies east of the Namib Desert. Its altitude varies between 1000 and 2000 metres. The highest mountain in Namibia is the Brandberg (2579 m) in Damaraland. The lower lying extension of the semi-arid Kalahari occupies the eastern and north-eastern parts of the country. The Kalahari, an area of 250,000 km^2 in central-southern Africa, is covered by unconsolidated Kalahari sand. The origin of the Kalahari sand is unclear, but it is widely agreed that aeolian processes have dominated the environmental history of the region. During the Quaternary period, in the area of fixed dunes, the climate must have been drier than today, allowing aeolian processes to operate. In addition, winds may have differed from those of today in terms of prevailing direction and strength.

There are only a few rivers in Namibia. Most of them are periodic, flowing sporadically after intensive rains. Namibia's perennial rivers lie on the southern and northern borders: the Orange River in the south and the Kunene, Kavango, Kwando-Linyanti-Chobe and Zambezi Rivers in the north (Figure 6.1).

Climate

Namibia has a dry climate with extremely variable and unpredictable rainfall. The average annual rainfall increases from less than 20 mm on the coast towards the north-east where Katima Mulilo receives more than 700 mm (Figure 6.2). The potential average annual evaporation varies between 3780 mm in the central-southern area to 2600 mm in the north. It is estimated that about 80 per cent of the total rainfall evaporates shortly after precipitation.

The first rains can be expected in the northern parts of the country in October or November and in the drier southern areas two months later. The rainfall peaks in January–February in the northern areas and in March in the southern regions. In the coastal desert morning fog supports various desert-adapted plants and animals.

Temperatures are influenced by the cold Benguela Current and the altitude of the Central Plateau. The warmest and coldest months differ in different regions. In the north, October and November are the hottest months, with an average daily maximum temperature of 34-36°C. In the

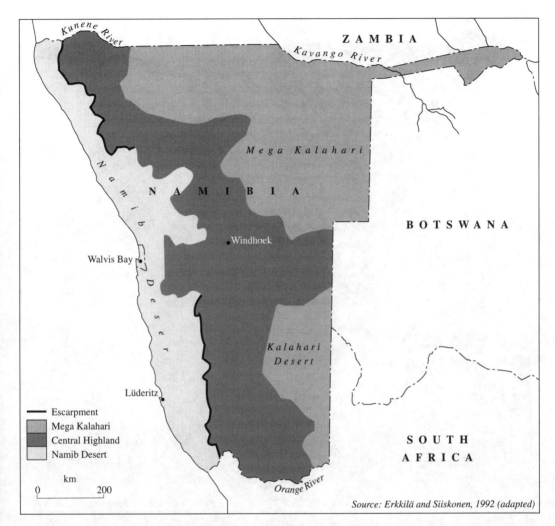

Figure 6.1 *Physical divisions*

central region the warmest month is December, and in the south, January. The coldest month is July in most parts of the country, except on the coast where the lowest temperatures can be expected in August. The average daily minimum for the coldest month varies from less than 2°C to more than 10°C. The absolute maximum and minimum temperatures recorded in Namibia are 48°C and -10°C.

The occurrence of frost increases towards the Central Plateau, from north to south and, of course, everywhere at high altitudes. The probability of a temperature below freezing is highest in the Auas Mountains northwest of Windhoek.

Soils

The pedology of Namibia is characterised by lithosolic (Central Highland), arenosolic (Kalahari) and weakly-developed soil types (Namib Desert). Weakly-developed soils are brown to greyish

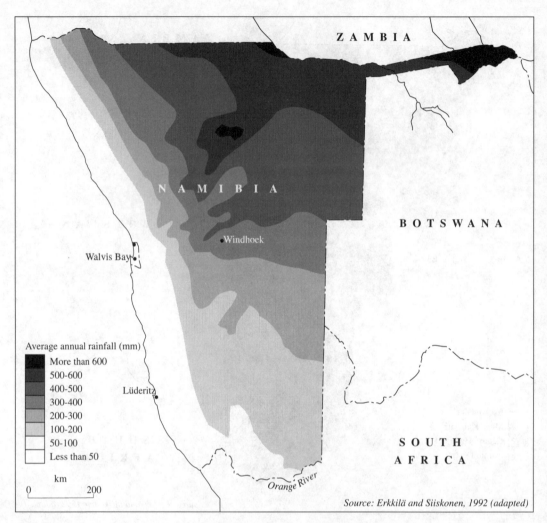

Figure 6.2 *Mean annual rainfall*

and may or may not contain a B-horizon. These soils often contain free lime, and gypsum may occur in areas where the rainfall is less than 300 mm. Lithosols are shallow soils with weak profile differentiation, which contain coarse fragments and solid rock at depths of 30 cm and less; topography is the dominant soil-forming factor. Arenosols have low water-retention capacity and low reserves of weatherable minerals. Their colour is red on upland sites and dune ridges, yellow on level areas and grey on bottomland sites. The parent material is aeolian sand or sands derived from aeolian deposits, which make these soils very sensitive to wind erosion.

Vegetation

Giess (1971) subdivided the vegetation of Namibia, primarily on the basis of rainfall, into three regions: deserts, savannas and woodlands. He distinguished 15 vegetation types, of which two are classified as woodlands, eight as savannas and five as deserts (Figure 6.3).

The deserts in Namibia are the Namib Desert and the Etosha Pan. Woody vegetation – small trees and shrubs (e.g. *Welwitschia mirabilis, Acacia reficiens*) – occurs in the Namib Desert only along the river beds. The Etosha Pan in the northern part of the country is barren, but some *Acacia nebrownii* are found on its less brackish fringes. Deserts cover 16 per cent of Namibia.

Savannas cover 64 per cent of Namibia. One particular vegetation type, Mopane Savanna, is widespread in northwestern Namibia. The dominant tree species is *Colophospermum mopane* (mopane, family Caesalpiniaceae), a 7–10 m tall deciduous tree with a stunted shape. In many areas mopane makes up a sparse woodland with a shrubby understorey. Its southern boundary follows the 5°C isotherm of the mean daily minimum temperature for the coldest month, July. This explains why mopane does not exist either in the eastern part of Ovambo or in Kavango. Close to its southern limit, frost damage is frequent. Towards the western limits of its distribution, scattered shrubby

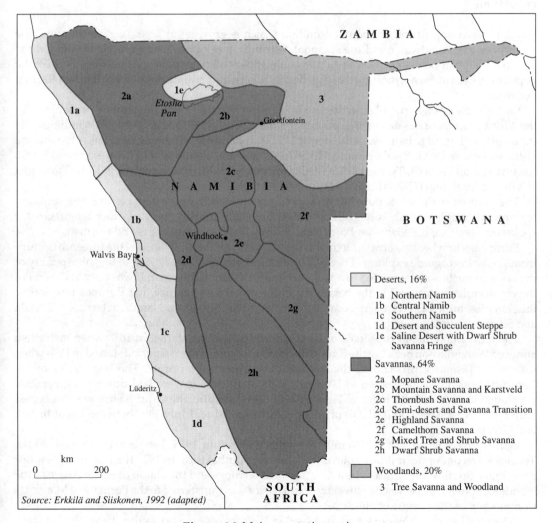

Figure 6.3 *Major vegetation regions*

individual mopane trees occur associated with *Welwitschia mirabilis* in the predominantly dry river beds of the Namib Desert.

Woodlands cover one fifth of the territory of Namibia. One of the dominant species in this region is *Baikiaea plurijuga* (Zambezi teak or mukusi, family Caesalpiniaceae). Zambezi teak is extremely resistant to termites and decay. This semi-evergreen, thornless, 8–18 m tall tree is entirely confined to areas of deep Kalahari sand.

The most important commercial tree species in Namibia, however, is *Pterocarpus angolensis* (wild teak, Transvaal teak, mukwa, dolf or kiaat, family Fabaceae). It grows on Kalahari sand in the northern part of the country. *P. angolensis* can be worked easily and is therefore also preferred among curio makers. Even though it is not as sensitive to fire as *Baikiaea plurijuga*, periodic fires keep it in the sapling stage for several years.

Population

Namibia has a population of about 1.4 million which is growing at 3 per cent per annum. The occurrence of groundwater and the seasonal distribution of rainfall have greatly influenced the pattern of population distribution as did the homelands settlement policy. About 60 per cent of the population lives in the northern part of the country where the annual rainfall is higher than 400 mm per annum.

Overall, the average population density in Namibia is only 1.5–1.6 inhabitants per km^2 whilst the African continent has an average population density of 18 inhabitants per km^2. Windhoek, the capital, is the largest urban area, with about 115,000 inhabitants. The nine next-largest towns are (estimates from 1988): Swakopmund (15,500 inhabitants), Rehoboth (15,000), Rundu (15,000), Keetmanshoop (14,000), Tsumeb (13,500), Otjiwarongo (11,000), Grootfontein (9000), Okahandja (8000) and Mariental (6500) (Figure 6.4).

The majority of the white population, approximately 80,000, reside in the central and southern regions. Although English is the official language of the country, several other languages are spoken in Namibia, e.g. Oshiwambo, Herero, Nama, Bushman, Afrikaans and German.

Europeans first became acquainted with the coast of Namibia at the end of the fifteenth century through the Portuguese explorers Diego Cao and Bartholomeu Dias. Owing to the inhospitality of the land, contacts were restricted to a few anchorage places on the coast. It was only at the end of the eighteenth century and in the beginning of the nineteenth century that European explorers, missionaries, hunters and traders became interested in the interior of Namibian territory (Erkkilä and Siiskonen, 1992).

The intrusion of the European colonial powers into Namibia started in 1878 when the British annexed Walvis Bay on behalf of the Cape Colony. The German colonial period started in 1884 when Chancellor Bismarck proclaimed the Territory a German protectorate. The boundaries of the Territory, which became known as German South West Africa, were laid down in agreements concluded in 1886 with Portugal and in 1890 with Great Britain. The Caprivi Strip was connected with South West Africa on the basis of an agreement signed on 1 July 1890 between Great Britain and Germany.

German colonial rule in the Namibian territory ended in 1915. Between 1915 and 1920 the Territory was under the military rule of the Union of South Africa. In 1920 the League of Nations proclaimed South West Africa to be a 'C'-mandated territory and the Union of South Africa as the mandatory power. Supervisory power by South Africa was transferred to the Permanent Mandates Commission of the League of Nations.

When the League of Nations was dissolved in 1946, its supervisory authority for the Territory was inherited by the United Nations. In 1946 the South African Government requested the UN

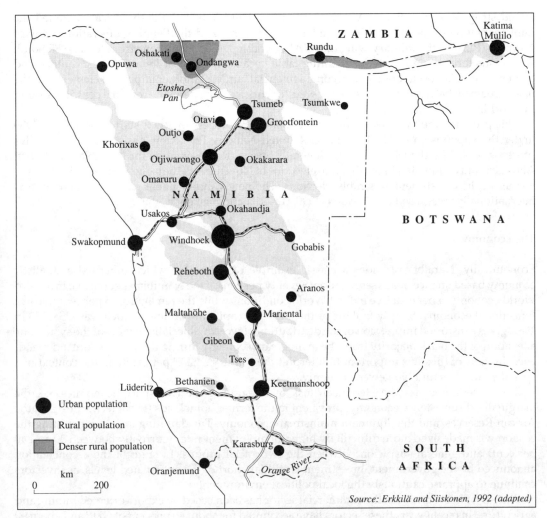

Figure 6.4 *Population distribution*

General Assembly's permission to incorporate South West Africa into the Union of South Africa. South Africa's request was rejected. Accordingly, South Africa refused UN requests to place South West Africa under a trusteeship agreement, arguing that the United Nations was not the automatic successor to the responsibilities of the League of Nations.

In the late 1950s, African nationalist movements such as SWAPO (South West Africa People's Organisation) and SWANU (South West Africa National Union) were formed to resist South African domination. The decision of the International Court of Justice of 1966, when it refused to consider the question of South West Africa's legal status, had important political consequences. African nations immediately put the question before the UN General Assembly. In October 1966, the UN terminated South Africa's mandate and established a Council for Namibia to govern the country. In 1971, after the Security Council had asked the International Court for an opinion, the court reversed the 1966 decision, ruling that South Africa's occupation of Namibia was illegal.

When the International Court failed to rule against South Africa in 1966, SWAPO began its armed struggle against South African occupation. Until late 1987 South Africa continued the implementation of its 'internal independence settlement'; and the People's Liberation Army of Namibia (PLAN), the military wing of SWAPO, continued its liberation struggle. In 1988 South Africa was forced to go to the negotiating table because it had lost its military advantage and because Namibia's occupation had become a financial burden. Another important element was the new agreement between the two superpowers to work towards defusing regional conflicts around the world.

This provided the framework for the independence process that was started on 1 April 1989 under the supervision of UNTAG forces (United Nations Transition Assistance Group). This process was led by the UN Secretary-General's Special Representative for Namibia, Mr. Martti Ahtisaari, and culminated in the first free elections in November of the same year. SWAPO was the winner of the Constituent Assembly elections. The newly-independent nation of Namibia was internationally recognised on 21 March 1990, (Erkkilä and Siiskonen, 1992).

The economy

Economically, Namibia provides a classic example of a country which inherited a dualistic economy based on race-space segregation. Seventy per cent of the Namibian people live in a Third World economy, 5 per cent live in First World conditions while the remaining 25 per cent live in a transitional economy. Simply looking at the GDP per capita in Namibia, which was US$1273 in 1989, gives a distorted impression of the distribution of wealth especially in view of the systematic alienation of the black majority from the mainstream economy during the years before independence. In view of this, it is important to interpret the country's GDP per capita in the context of a spatially and structurally-skewed economy.

The government has the Herculean task of integrating the two space economies, i.e. the marginalised subsistence economy, prevalent in the former homelands (tribal territories) and the African Reserves, and the dominant mainstream economy. The daunting task of integrating the economy is made even more difficult by high unemployment rates (currently between 30 and 40 per cent) and general suspicion between the two racial groups. In spite of the reconciliation announced by the government, investment is still far short of the anticipated levels, as investors continue to appraise cautiously the local political environment.

Since the First World War the commercial sector has been based on export-oriented mining and agriculture. In recent years these sectors have accounted for about 40 per cent of GDP and about 90 per cent of total exports. The subsistence sector, on which about half of the population is dependent, produces only about 3 per cent of GDP.

Namibia's economy has always been very open, the emphasis being on primary production for export, while the bulk of processed goods required for the domestic market has been imported. Under South Africa's administration, Namibia remained, in economic terms, virtually a fifth province with only limited development of manufacturing activities. In this connection only the two most important productive sectors of the economy, mining and agriculture, are considered.

Namibia is one of Africa's major mining countries, especially with regard to uranium, diamonds, refined lead and zinc concentrates. In the 1980s the mining industry provided over 75 per cent of total exports by value. The mining industry is almost totally export-oriented, which has made it particularly dependent on world market prices. In 1988 the industry employed 13,100 workers, including about 3000 South Africans and other expatriates. Most of Namibia's mines are operated by the subsidiaries of overseas-based multinational mining groups, or South African companies and parastatals (Figure 6.5).

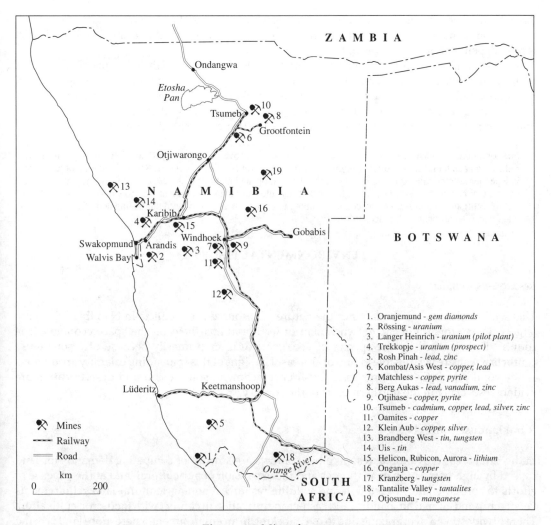

Figure 6.5 *Mineral resources*

1. Oranjemund - *gem diamonds*
2. Rössing - *uranium*
3. Langer Heinrich - *uranium (pilot plant)*
4. Trekkopje - *uranium (prospect)*
5. Rosh Pinah - *lead, zinc*
6. Kombat/Asis West - *copper, lead*
7. Matchless - *copper, pyrite*
8. Berg Aukas - *lead, vanadium, zinc*
9. Otjihase - *copper, pyrite*
10. Tsumeb - *cadmium, copper, lead, silver, zinc*
11. Oamites - *copper*
12. Klein Aub - *copper, silver*
13. Brandberg West - *tin, tungsten*
14. Uis - *tin*
15. Helicon, Rubicon, Aurora - *lithium*
16. Onganja - *copper*
17. Kranzberg - *tungsten*
18. Tantalite Valley - *tantalites*
19. Otjosundu - *manganese*

Agriculture consists of two sectors: the market-oriented European sector and the African subsistence sector. Although agriculture makes up only about 10 per cent of GDP, some 70 per cent of the total population is directly or indirectly dependent on farming.

The commercial sector produces about 80 per cent of the total agricultural yield, but this was severely affected by the drought of 1978–1985. This sector is concentrated firmly on livestock farming, which contributes more than 80 per cent to the gross value of agricultural production. The most important products have been pelts of karakul sheep (Swakara), meat, wool and dairy products. The commercially-oriented crop farming is concentrated in the Grootfontein-Otavi-Tsumeb triangle. The main product has been maize, which is produced for the local market.

During the South African administration, African agriculture and animal husbandry were undermined by the expropriation of land and by the channelling of funds and expertise to the white farmers. Marketing of meat and animals outside the African 'homelands' in the North was prevented by the Red Line cordon fence between the white farmland and the former African 'homelands'. For example, in the Ovambo district, which until the 1960s was self-sufficient in food, production of the staple crop, mahangu millet (*Pennisetum glaucum*), has declined and the district is now dependent on the import of food.

In 1989 Namibia imported 80 per cent of its vegetables, 73 per cent of the white maize, 47 per cent of the yellow maize and 85 per cent of the wheat needed to feed the population. All agricultural machinery and production inputs are imported, mainly from the Republic of South Africa.

According to the Ministry of Finance, independence has brought forward various new and interesting prospects to Namibia's economy. In a 1990 report the Ministry stated:

> First of all the fact [that] the country was now recognised as a sovereign entity, has increased the hopes for material foreign capital inflows and for opening up new markets for Namibia's exports. Secondly, the fact that the pre-independence trade sanctions had now been lifted has re-opened markets that were closed for some time in sectors that had been affected by this. Thirdly, because the Namibian government was now in command and control of its offshore fishing zone, the country is about to expand its economy with the fishing activities foreseen in that zone. (Department of Finance, 1990)

ENVIRONMENTAL ISSUES

Resource-use conflicts

This section identifies and examines the nature of resource-use conflicts in Namibia which are largely a consequence of the entrenchment of territorial apartheid on the space economy. The country is threatened by the spectre of ecological disaster primarily because of resource-use conflicts which are very visible in the rural areas. The signs of this impending calamity are obvious in the rural areas where overgrazing, bush encroachment, soil erosion and desertification are evident, especially in the northern parts of the country.

Rural landuse conflicts

In the rural areas of Namibia, resource-use conflicts are a result of competing demands for land caused by high population growth rates and the expansion of agricultural land at the expense of efforts to conserve land, vegetation and wildlife resources: non-agricultural land requirements versus crop and animal husbandry, and cash-crop cultivation in conflict with food-crop cultivation. There is widespread overgrazing due to overstocking in an environment where more land is being taken up for cultivation to supplement falling yields and to cater for an increasing population.

At the core of landuse conflicts in Namibia lies a land tenure system that was based on an inequitable distribution of land along racial lines. This land tenure system mirrors land tenure systems which prevailed in pre-independence Zimbabwe, Kenya and Zambia. Prior to independence in Namibia the white settlers, who constituted just 8 per cent of the population, owned and had freehold title to 60 per cent of the agricultural land. The land tenure system gave whites freedom to purchase or sell land and to borrow money from lending institutions using their farms as collateral. In sharp contrast, the 33.6 million hectares (40 per cent of the national land) held by blacks in the 'homelands' could not be sold or purchased freely because it belonged to the community.

Differential access to productive resources in Namibia has resulted in patterns of inequality closely related to race. Whilst the average size of farms under freehold tenure is estimated to be 7200 hectares, black Namibian family farms are no more than 17 hectares. Apart from the small size of these holdings, homelands and reserves tend to be found in areas with poor climate and soils, and inadequate water resources. Herero homeland and Damaraland illustrate the point. Over 30 per cent of the Herero homeland's 5,899,680 hectares is unsuitable for any agricultural activity owing to the presence of gilblaar and the shortage of water. About 40 per cent of the entire area in Damaraland (4,656,000 hectares) lies in the barren Namib desert, where there are no prospects for dryland cropping, and livestock farming is of negligible potential.

It is this unequal access to resources that has profoundly influenced the life chances and quality of life of the vast majority of Namibians. The predicament faced by the blacks is further compounded by the highly-differentiated access to markets, agricultural services and other socio-economic infrastructures.

The monetisation of the rural economy has meant that cash crops are now displacing food crops. Consequently, the rural population is now devoting some of its 'best' land to cash-crop production and cultivating food-crops on the more marginal land. At the same time the tradition of determining the status of a family on the basis of the size of the livestock herd owned has led to overstocking and this in turn has resulted in the exceeding of the carrying capacity of rangelands and ultimately to environmental degradation.

Landuse conflicts are likely to persist in the foreseeable future in Namibia because of the high rate of population growth through natural increase (which is about 3.4 per cent per annum for blacks). The return of thousands of political refugees, who had fled mainly to the SADC countries, has intensified the crisis created by a rapidly-growing population. However, if the population continues to grow there will be a greater demand for agricultural land and fuelwood. This is likely to precipitate conflicts between the needs of the poor to meet basic needs, such as land and energy, and environmentalists' concerns about the conservation of forest and wildlife resources.

The indiscriminate clearing of forest reserves in the homelands in the north for domestic use without any allowance for regeneration or reafforestation clearly highlights this resource-use conflict. The northern region is inhabited by ethnic groups such as the Ovambo, Kavango, Lohsi, Subia and Himba. It is here that water resources, pasture, wildlife and other resources face the pressures of a fast-growing human and livestock population. Some people have already predicted that an ecological disaster is in the making in the region. In Ovamboland, the formerly-forested plains inhabited by a rich variety of game and wildlife have already been reduced to lifeless dustbowls. In some of these areas, illegal fencing of communal land is undertaken by unscrupulous farmers who often graze their animals on the open rangelands in the rainy season, thereby reserving their own grazing land for the dry season. However, for the majority of rural Namibians, it is need and not greed which is the root cause of the various resource-use conflicts. In the homelands a combination of poverty, limited resources and a fragile ecosystem has led to the pauperization of the peasants and this has left them with little choice about the degradation of the environment. Thus, there is no ecological zone in Namibia that can be healthy and sustainable when the majority of its inhabitants survive in abject poverty and extreme need.

Urban landuse conflicts

Urban landuse conflicts are also found within the country's towns which together account for about 30 per cent of the total population. One of the most obvious problems in Namibia's major urban centres is that of litter, mainly of aluminium cans and glass. The absence of metal and glass recycling companies partly explains why unsightly litter in the form of glass and tin cans has continued to be an eyesore. The uncontrolled dumping of household refuse and garbage also poses numerous health and environmental problems. This problem is likely to multiply during the next few years because most urban centres, especially Windhoek, are experiencing unprecedented population growth. The massive influx of rural migrants, plus the return of refugees from abroad, will stretch the country's urban facilities further.

The removal of restrictions on the free movement of the population has increased the rate of urbanisation and the demand for urban housing and services. In the past, pre-independence governments used to control the squatter problem through influx control regulations and the pass law system. Squatter camps are now a common sight in most of the townships. The Namibian government is, therefore, faced with a serious housing crisis which, in order to be addressed, needs large-scale financial resources as well as firm political commitment.

ENVIRONMENTAL PROBLEMS

Namibia has a very fragile ecology and most of this can only support livestock. Unfortunately the colonial legacy left a very skewed land distribution pattern which is the main cause of environmental degradation today. With about 5000 huge commercial farms owned by 5 per cent of the population and 120,000 families packed in the former homelands, one is faced with the ingredients for a land shortage induced environmental disaster. Green (1991) has identified the key ecological factors involved in the Namibian environmental problem as land, water, air, vegetation, marine and wildlife resources. Threats to these ecological factors are real and parts of Namibia are indeed overgrazed, overstocked, eroded and silted. In addition, salinization is a serious problem well exemplified at the Hardap irrigation scheme where part of the land has now been rendered unproductive. The processes of desertification are intensifying as people attempt to satisfy basic needs for survival from land which has little agricultural potential. The problem has been intensified by the persistent droughts experienced in several parts of the country, particularly during the 1980s, and again in the early 1990s.

Land degradation in the communal areas

Much has been written about land in the communal areas of Namibia. Generally, the writers fall into two broad ideological camps – the conservatives and the radicals. There is a tendency within the ideologically-conservative camp to exaggerate the severity of the problem and to view the peasants as the main agents of land degradation in rural areas. Typically, the predominant concern amongst this group is the conservation of the aesthetic appeal of the environment regardless of the constraints. Any change in the environment is viewed as the result of misuse or abuse by humans. On the other hand, the radicals accuse the conservatives of failing to realise that poor people can no longer live for the environment. They argue that it is important to consider both the proximate and ultimate causal factors in order to come up with conclusions within the context of which appropriate solutions can be identified.

Baseline studies completed to date in Namibia indicate that owing to the concentration of settlements along rivers and around watering points, environmental degradation has been extensive as land clearing for cultivation, firewood, fencing and building construction has transformed large tracts of savanna woodland into barren plains. This is especially the case in Oshakati, and Ondangwa in Ovamboland. A similar situation has been noted in the Okamtapati region where a lack of water in Hereroland has forced the population to concentrate along the southern and western borders, thereby causing overgrazing around watering places. Localised areas of overgrazing are common along access routes to Katim, Linyati and Ngoma in Kavangoland. The result has been soil erosion from aeolian processes. In the north the situation is worsened by the fact that soils are sandy and hence susceptible to degradation. Elsewhere, the depletion of soil fertility has resulted in falling production per hectare especially in the former homelands where the population is increasing at the rate of up to 3 per cent per annum. Consequently, more and more of the land previously set aside for grazing is now being taken up for cultivation even though it is already overstocked and overgrazed.

However, contrary to widely-held views, the rate of soil loss in Namibia is minimised by the gentle nature of the slopes. Admittedly, in the absence of detailed studies it is difficult to estimate the rate of soil loss in the communal lands, but whatever the rate of soil loss may be, proposed solutions must be formulated within the context of human needs satisfaction since soil erosion is essentially need-driven ecological damage.

Deforestation

Deforestation is a serious problem in Namibia especially in the dry savanna region where large plains occupy what was once savanna woodland. This is particularly true for the Kavango district where land clearing for millet cultivation in an area stretching 300 km along the Kavango river has left nothing but exposed surfaces. This occurrence, especially along the river bank, has implications for the long-term productivity of the river as higher silt loads transported downstream have started destroying fish habitats. Siltation resulting from increased runoff yields due to deforestation is also threatening the wetland ecology in the vleis or oshanas and could have long-term effects on the ecosystem of the Okavango swamps in Botswana. Forest inventories from the 1970s also indicate that much of the vegetation in the national parks is under threat from deforestation.

In the Ovambo region deforestation can be traced back to the nineteenth century. According to Erkkilä and Siiskonen (1992), in the 1850s the Ovambo population in the Cuvelai floodplain (including the Angolan side) was probably 100,000. The following section, and subsequent sections on forestry, draw heavily on Erkkilä and Siiskonen (1992). The area was divided into several communities governed by hereditary rulers, i.e. kings. The size of the communities varied, but the largest had approximately 10,000–15,000 members. The area within the community was cleared for fields. Fuelwood was collected mainly from the surrounding shrubland zone, which was eight to ten km wide; and building poles were taken from the mopane forest lying behind the shrubland.

The communities were clearly separated from one another by forested areas. For example, the missionary Hugo Hahn reported in 1866 that between the communities of Ondonga and Uukwanyama existed a forest area about 60 km wide. Half a century later the width of the forest area was only 40 km. The Finnish missionary Olle Eriksson recalled that in the 1950s the wooded area was still about 10 km wide. Today there is no forest left between Ondonga and Uukwanyama.

The first European to pay attention to deforestation was the botanist Hans Schinz, who visited Ovambo in 1885–86 and warned that deforestation would be a problem in Ovambo in 50 years if population growth continued to follow the same trend and the patterns of wood consumption remained unchanged.

Schinz's prediction came true in the beginning of the twentieth century. The Finnish missionary Martti Rautanen wrote in 1907 that, because of deforestation, households in the southern parts of Ovambo were compelled to use millet stalks as a substitute for poles in building.

The mandate administration also became concerned about deforestation in the beginning of the 1930s as the following words in a letter of the Officer in Charge at Oshikango (near the Angolan border) demonstrates.

> The destruction of forest trees has been carried on in this tribal area during the past 10 years at an alarming rate... In the course of 50 years or so the country will be practically denuded of forest and there is of course no need to dwell on the disastrous effect of such denudation. It is thought that the time has arrived to take active steps to preserve the forests and to reduce lumbering to the barest minimum (Erkkilä and Siiskonen, 1992: 175)

With regard to the future economic development in Ovambo, the Odendaal Commission, appointed by the South African government in 1962, considered deforestation to be one of the greatest economic and environmental problems.

> An alarming phenomenon is the large-scale deforestation which is taking place in the central areas of Ovamboland. The erection of intricate palisades around kraals is an Ovambo tradition, and it frequently happens that in the laying out of a large kraal literally thousands of trees are destroyed. This is an unfortunate national custom which, unless some solution can be found to the problem, will undoubtedly lead to a chronic shortage of firewood in the near future. (Erkkilä and Siiskonen, 1992: 176)

Today Ovambo communities have almost grown into each other. In the most populated areas, mopane woodlands have been transformed into low shrubland with only a few fruit trees growing in the fields. In the western part of Ovambo, mopane woodland has been transformed widely into grazing land. There are still a few mopane woodlots left, but in many cases the trees have been cut one to five metres above the ground.

The less populated eastern part of Ovambo still has a fairly large forest area. The deforestation process is, however, accelerating, especially near the population centres. Due to selective cutting for construction purposes, degradation of the forest is common (Erkkilä and Siiskonen, 1992).

Water and fish resources

Surface-water shortage in Namibia has also been blamed for the degradation taking place at water points, for example around boreholes. Where good groundwater resources exist and are being exploited there is widespread over-pumping, as is happening in the Rossing-Swakopmund-Walvis Bay region which gets its water from the Kuiseb and Omararu rivers.

Several problems have also affected the fisheries sector. Both marine and freshwater fisheries have been subjected to over-exploitation in the past before the exclusive fishing rights zone was demarcated. Riverbank and terrace erosion caused by stream-bank cultivation is thought to be responsible for the decreasing yields of freshwater fish from the Kavango and Kunene rivers. Also, concern has been raised about the culling of seals off the Namibian coast without a clear perception of what the likely impacts are. In addition, the exploitation of seaweed has also been questioned, especially the fact that it is being commercialised even before an environmental impact assessment has been carried out.

The cool Benguela current provides Namibia with fishing grounds rich in deep-water and pelagic fish. In the past, over 50 companies were involved in commercial fishing, with Walvis Bay the leading centre especially for pilchards and anchovies, and Luderitz for shell fish. Between 1960 and 1976 nine large fish factories were operating in Walvis Bay: six were for pilchard canning and meal/oil production; one for meal and white-fish processing; one was a reduction-only plant; and one was a pilchard freezing plant. Since the mid 1970s, however, there has been a marked decline in catches: by 1981 the pilchard had almost disappeared from coastal waters and all the pilchard processing plants (Figure 6.6) had closed down. Over-exploitation and the consequent disruption of the general equilibrium in the sea are responsible for the collapse of the previously lucrative fishing industry. Kaakunga (1990: 116) describes the link between the drastic decline of the hake fish and the other fish like pilchard and anchovy as follows:

> Hake feeds on lantern fish and light fish, which in turn feed on zooplankton. Since the hake and other predatory species such as mackerels are reduced to levels of extinction through excess plundering of the lantern fish and other light fish, biomass has increased and the consumption of zooplankton has therefore increased. Abnormally large species thus compete increasingly with weak, immature ones such as pilchard and anchovy for a dwindling food source. The result could be detrimental for adequate recoupment of pilchard and anchovy.

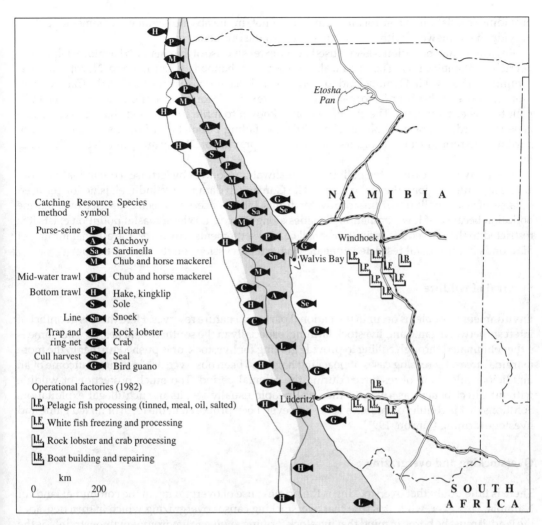

Figure 6.6 *Resources of the Namibian fishing industry*

Pollution

In Namibia air pollution is still limited to urban areas such as Windhoek, where the use of fuelwood in the high density suburbs of Katatura often results in smog. Location in a low-lying bowl, where free air circulation is restricted, has contributed to the pollution problem in Windhoek. In addition to pollution from woodfuel, air pollution is also reported from open-cast uranium oxide mining in Rossing. Ecologists fear that since the dust particles produced contain traces of radiation, they may have harmful long-term effects on the local ecosystem. Smelter plumes at Tsumeb also contain elements of sulphur which can form acid precipitation if released in increasing quantities. What is apparent in these two cases is that, despite the high profit margins, the mining companies are not keen on investing in environmental protection from pollution. The Atmosphere Pollution Prevention Act 45 of 1965 and its appendage, the Prevention of Air Pollution Ordinance 11 of 1976, whilst providing legislation to control air pollution, do not, in the absence of an environmental policy, provide the framework within which to deal with the problems.

Environmental pollution is also caused by the extensive use of the chemical Dichloro- Diphenyl-Tetrachlorethane (DDT). The chemical, whose use is banned in Europe and North America, continues to be used in Ovamboland to eradicate malaria. It is also being used in the Caprivi Strip to eradicate tsetse flies in order to make the area more suitable for livestock farming. However, DDT pollutes the environment. The chemical is also known to infiltrate the food chain causing some genetic disorders. For example, in Zimbabwe the falling population of the fish eagle has been attributed to reproduction disorders caused by the spraying of DDT in areas infested by the tsetse fly.

There have been cases of the pollution of freshwater resources by fertiliser contamination from arable agriculture along the major rivers. The Goreangab dam near Windhoek is no longer used because of heavy pollution from stormwater drains. Little concern has been expressed over marine pollution because of low population densities along the coast. Where coastal pollution exists it is restricted to the immediate vicinity of small coastal settlements. However, the alluvial mining of diamonds in the coastal restricted zone may have repercussions on the marine ecology.

Survival of wildlife

Environmental problems occur in the national parks and nature reserves. Here there is a conflict of interests between game and livestock farming, especially in the southern ranches, as wild game is either eliminated through culling to provide grazing for livestock, or is pushed further to the more marginal areas. Increasing cases of poaching have also been observed as the logical outcome of an injudicious allocation of resources during the colonial period. Too much protection of wildlife without direct benefit accruing to the local people usually results in such illegal exploitation. Solutions to this conflict of interests have, however, been proposed in the form of mixed game and livestock farming (Janson, 1991).

Overstocking and overgrazing

There is little doubt that overstocking is the prime cause of overgrazing in the communal lands of Namibia. However, while it is true that overstocking causes overgrazing which in turn degrades the land, it must be borne in mind that livestock farming, owing to environmental constraints, is the major activity in Namibia. Stocking levels are usually exceeded in the northern communal lands because this is necessary for the peasant farmer's survival. The logic is that in the event of a drought some livestock will survive. It is every extension worker's nightmare to convince a peasant farmer to destock when the farmer feels he still needs more cattle for his security. This partly explains why stocking rates are often dangerously exceeded.

In Okamtapti, for example, the recommended stock rate has been exceeded by 40 per cent. Persistent droughts in many parts of the country and especially in areas such as Okahandja, Otjiwarango, Grootfontein, Tsumeb and Outjo have resulted in the permanent loss of palatable grasses for livestock. As a result, the realistic optimum stocking levels have fallen from 1:10 ha to 1:15 ha in those parts of the country. Land degradation is not limited to the north of Namibia. In the large cattle ranches in the south, however, overgrazing tends to be confined to waterholes, especially on the marginal ranching zones furthest south.

An additional factor that explains overgrazing and general land degradation is communal ownership of land and the much discussed 'tragedy of the commons'. This problem has been aggravated because the Soil Conservation Act has been unenforced despite the fact that it contains provisions for punitive measures against those who engage in environmentally-destructive farming practices. Non-enforcement of this Act may be a result of the realisation that coercion rather than persuasion breeds resistance and non-cooperation. Hence, it has not been politically expedient, nor administratively feasible, to enforce the Act. Drought, which is a perennial spectre haunting Namibia, acts as the only natural check on livestock population in the absence of enforceable legislative measures.

Bush encroachment

A related problem is that of bush encroachment. Bush encroachment is an imbalance in the vegetation between extensive and deep-rooting woody vegetation and shallow-rooting grasses. In most cases it is caused by overgrazing. Overgrazing allows more water to penetrate deep into the soil, thus favouring the woody species. Cattle also eat the pods of thorny acacias eagerly, and seeds passed through the gastro-intestinal tract germinate easily. If overgrazing is repeated for several years, the result could be a dense thorn thicket, or depending on ecological conditions and other human activities, even a man-made desert, (Erkkilä and Siiskonen, 1992).

Near Tsumeb, bush encroachment has occurred partly as the consequence of overcutting for mine props. The removal of trees reduced the moisture content of the soil and thus hindered the regeneration of tamboto (*Spirostachys african*). As a result, more drought-tolerant invader species, such as *Acacia mellifera* ssp. *detinens* (black thorn), *Combretum apiculatum* var *leutweinii* (hairy red bushwillow) and *Dichrostachys cinerea* ssp. *africana* (sickle bush or Kalahari Christmas tree) became dominant. The cut tamboti trees produced waist-high thickets of stump shoots and root suckers. Grass production was thus reduced by extensive shading and root competition. The bush encroachment was aggravated by overgrazing and widespread burning.

The problem of bush encroachment was recognised as long ago as the 1920s. Large areas in the districts of Gobabis, Otjiwarongo and Grootfontein were reverting to desert grass with short bush. Twenty years later bush encroachment had become a serious problem in central Namibia. The long drought and the outbreak of foot and mouth disease in the 1960s led to serious overstocking and worsened the situation by leaving the ground bare for encroaching bush species.

Bush encroachment is more common in areas with low annual rainfall (600 mm or less), which thus have a low carrying capacity. In Namibia this had become a serious problem in the cattle farming areas, mainly in the districts of Tsumeb, Grootfontein, Otjiwarongo, Okahandja and Omaruru. The affected area is 8–10 million ha. It has been estimated that due to bush encroachment the agricultural sector loses an income of R100 million annually, through an estimated loss of between 30–50 per cent in grazing potential.

The Tsumeb Biomass Project has attempted to find solutions to this problem. It was quickly realised that to clear the bush using mechanical eradication or herbicides was out of the question because it was too costly. However, one possibility for tackling the problem is the commercial utilisation of the biomass. In the 1980s the First National Development Corporation (FNDC), the Tsumeb Corporation Ltd (TCL) and the Council for Scientific and Industrial Research (CSIR) started to test existing bush-harvesting methods and to develop new ones. These organisations also tried to develop commercial products from the harvested biomass. FNDC is a parastatal organisation for business development. TCL is a mining company in Tsumeb, which is looking for alternative sources of energy for imported coal. CSIR is the major South African research institute.

In the mid-1980s CSIR tested the low-cost mobile drum chipper and made studies on gasification of whole tree chips from invader bush as well as on the market potential for wood chips. Studies were also made on the utilisation of invader bush in the wood industry. *Acacia mellifera* ssp. *detinens* (black thorn, swarthaak) and *Dichrostachys cinerea* ssp. *africana* (sickle bush) were shown to produce suitable raw material for manufacturing chipboard and wood-cement bricks. Wood-cement panels produced from sickle bush were as good as those made from pine, while black thorn panels were unacceptably weak. The pulp of the sickle bush and the puzzle bush (*Ehretia rigida*) was not suitable for high-quality paper (Erkkilä and Siiskonen 1992: 140–2).

The first attempt to establish a wood industry based on shrub wood biomass was the Tsumeb Bush Project, which was started in 1987. The First National Development Corporation (FNDC) was responsible for project management and co-ordination. The Tsumeb Corporation Ltd (TCL) provided the experimental base and engineering services. Work on technical development was the responsibility of the Council for Scientific and Industrial Research (CSIR).

The major component in the project was biomass production for energy. During the first two years the project produced for TCL about 1300 tonnes of wood chips per month; later, wood-chip production was changed to wood briquette production. The total biomass production from the area of 11,000 ha was 34,200 tonnes or 3.1 tonnes/ha. The preliminary results of the project have been very promising.

THE PRESENT RESOURCE BASE AND LEGAL UNDERPINNINGS

Land resources

It was during the early colonial days that nearly all the best arable and grazing lands on the southern plateau were alienated to the white settlers. The system dates back to 1898 when Governor Leutwien introduced a law creating 'native reserves' for the indigenous black population. After World War II, the South African government consolidated and entrenched this land tenure system.

Act No.49/1919 turned all lands in the Southern Zone, except that which was held privately by settler farmers and/or concession companies, into crown land. The Africans living in the Southern Zone were thus made landless. Specially-demarcated areas, known as reserves, located in desert areas, were set aside for Africans. The land which was expropriated from the Africans was distributed to settlers by a land board which was created for that purpose. A Land Bank was established for the purpose of giving prospective financial assistance in the form of loans with low interest rates (Mbuende, 1986). According to Mbuende (1986) white commercial agriculture was also promoted by the state in other ways such as:

- by giving farms on leasehold, with the option of purchase within 15 years, to white males who were interested in farming;
- by giving 20-year mortgages to farmers wishing to purchase farms; and
- by providing white farmers with breeding stock and technical assistance such as drilling wells and constructing dams.

Because of such measures land was a major object of contention between the colonial state in Namibia and the indigenous people. The policy of race-space segregation effectively divided the country into black homelands, areas for whites and government areas and game reserves (Figure 6.7).

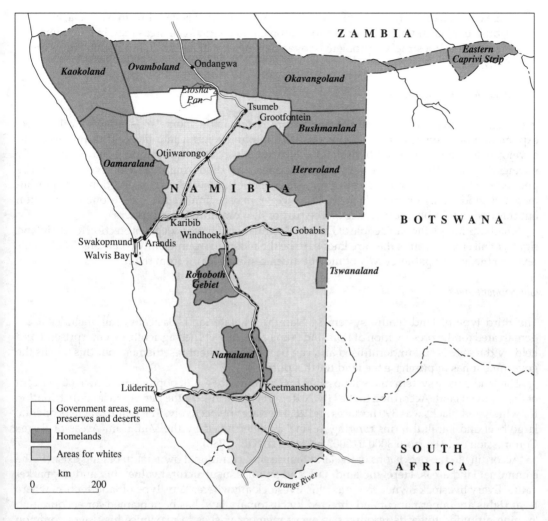

Figure 6.7 *Land tenure systems*

White areas

Land in the former 'white' areas is held under freehold tenure and this makes the land a marketable commodity that can be bought or sold as well as be used as collateral against loans. Freehold tenure is usually preferred since it gives security for long-term investment in the land. The land tenure system in the white areas encourages investment in soil and water conservation by the land-user and this system guards against the exploitation of a resource for exclusive use with minimum input into the resource. However, a number of qualifying statements need to be made at this point:

- Commercial farmers have only been able to make the investment which they have because of enormous government subsidies and loans on very favourable interest terms;
- They have maintained low interest loans either by having large numbers of farms, and/ or hectarage of land – which has allowed them to rotate grazing areas. Some have even

taken stock to wetter areas of South Africa when rainfall is very low in Namibia; and
- Bush encroachment is a more serious problem in commercial areas than in communal lands. It is not simply a problem of overstocking or management, but both features are involved.

African homelands and reserves

In contrast, the customary communal land tenure system in the 'homelands' allows for the direct exploitation of a common resource for use with minimum input into the land to preserve and develop it. In addition, the traditional land tenure rights have little legal standing and are invariably infringed upon by the rural élite or by pastoralists from neighbouring areas. However, it should be pointed out that rural farmers do have some idea about issues such as conservation and environmental degradation. Commitment to these principles may be limited due to the economic situation but this does not imply indifference on the part of the communal land farmers.

Finally, although the San people of Eastern Bushmanland have no legal protection for their land rights, of all ethnic groups they are known to be the most environmentally conscious. Their skills relate to the hunter-gatherer way of life but much could be learnt from them.

Government areas

The third type of land tenure system in Namibia is state land. Basically, this includes areas demarcated for the preservation of flora and fauna and state-owned agricultural enterprises. Land held by the state is still underutilised and can be used for urgent resettlement but this means the government has to purchase the land for this purpose.

The land tenure system made it possible for the minority white population to own 60 per cent of the national land. According to the UNIN Report (1986), in 1977 the per capita land distribution for whites and blacks was 390 hectares and 28.4 hectares respectively. The white ranchers operate large beef and karakul farms ranging in size, as determined by the Minimum Areas of Farms Commission of 1948, from 3000 to 8000 hectares (UNIN, 1986).

According to the provisions of the land tenure acts, communal ownership of land exists in the communal land areas. Here, the land had, and still has, usufructural value only and no market value. Every livestock owner can graze his livestock anywhere. Thus type of land tenure, where legal rights are impermanent and directed by customary law, has been blamed for encouraging 'mining attitudes' towards resources as every member wishes to maximise his use of common resources. Because of this, it is almost impossible for development under communal tenure to be sustainable as the peasants relegated to marginal areas are much more concerned with their present basic needs for survival than with the welfare of future generations. Since there is very little incentive and little ability to invest in the land, annual yields have declined rapidly and in some cases the peasant farmers have responded by extending the area under cultivation to maintain previous subsistence output levels.

The bantustans or homelands strategy

The Report of the Odendaal Commission (1963) recommended the Balkanization of the country into eleven mini-states (ten black and one white) to be known as Homelands or Bantustans. Under the Odendaal Plan, 40 per cent of the total land area of the territory would be allocated to the white homeland, and the remainder, consisting of the diamond areas and game reserves, would be unallocated government lands (D'amato, 1966). It was recommended that the African homelands, most of which were located in the Kalahari Desert, would become self-governing while the white homeland, which occupied the mineral-rich central plateau, would be incorporated into South Africa (Mbuende, 1986).

As early as 1968 the South African government took initial steps to implement the Odendaal Plan when it passed the Development of Self-Government for Native Nations in South West Africa Act. The Act provided for the formation of the following 'Native nations': Ovamboland, Damaraland, Kaokoland, Okavangoland, Bushmanland, Hereroland, Rehoboth Gebiet and Namaland (Figure 6.7). In theory the homelands were to be outside the jurisdiction of South Africa and were to be governed by legislative and executive councils based in these homelands.

The 1968 Act was followed by the South West Africa Affairs Act, No.25/1969 whose goal was to incorporate the 'white-homeland' into South Africa. However, the South African government's plans were aborted when the International Court of Justice intensified its lobby of the United Nations member states to condemn South Africa's presence in Namibia.

The institutionalisation of race-space segregation and ultimately land alienation under the Development of Self-Government for Native Nations in South West Africa Act 54 of 1968 (amended as Act Number 23 of 1973) is largely responsible for the present agricultural pattern. Commercial agriculture, which is concentrated in the south, produces about 80 per cent of all marketed output (Green, 1991). About 90 per cent of sheep and 70 per cent of cattle are owned by white commercial farmers who comprise a tiny portion of the population. The peasant farmers remain relegated to the communal lands where they continue to produce staple crops such as millet, sorghum and maize for consumption by the household. Most of the communal areas, however, cannot feed themselves. For example, Ovamboland which in the past used to export now has to import 25 per cent of its food requirements.

Peasant agriculture

Mbuende (1986) argues that the root cause of low peasant agricultural output, the decline in productivity of peasant agriculture and the low standard of living of the peasants is 'the result of the place of peasant agriculture or the reserve/homelands system within the strategy of imperialism in Namibia'.

Lack of surfacewater due to high evaporation rates and drought is a problem. The quality of soil is another problem. Only 24 per cent of the total land area of Ovamboland, 7 per cent of Ovavango, 52 per cent of the Caprivi and 20 per cent of Okaolo is suitable for crop cultivation. Only 26 per cent of the total land area of the Northern Zone is viable land for cultivation. According to Mbuende (1986), by 1977 there was only 7 ha per capita of productive land in the Northern Zone and this figure is estimated to have declined rather sharply by 1991 due to population growth.

The ecological conditions in the homelands make the development of a viable peasant agriculture difficult, if not impossible, to sustain. The post-independence government has the difficult task of providing both technical and financial assistance to peasant farmers for agriculture to be successful under the existing ecological conditions.

The reserves of the Southern Zone were a creation of the colonial administration. Virtually all the reserves of the Southern Zone lie in desert areas where conditions are unfavourable for crop cultivation and livestock raising. However, stock raising has been predominant where rainfall is scanty while crop cultivation is the major agricultural activity in the wetter Northern Zone. The annual rainfall in the Southern Zone is low and it varies between 85 and 450 mm per annum in normal years. In addition, soils are of poor quality in this zone. Only 17 per cent, 18 per cent and 21 per cent of the total land area of Hereroland, Namaland and Damaraland, respectively, is productive farmland.

Commercial agriculture

Livestock farming is the mainstay of agricultural activities in Namibia. The production and processing of meat and other livestock products comprises 90 per cent of commercial agricultural output. The South African state played a key role in the development of commercial agriculture in Namibia by ensuring that the sector produced commodities in which South Africa was not self-sufficient (Mbuende, 1986). Because of this South African interest, Namibian agriculture has historically specialised in livestock rearing, mainly cattle and sheep, for which demand has always been high in South Africa. Mbuende (1986) argues that crop production and horticulture were underdeveloped largely because there never was a demand for these in the South African market. The other factor is that most of the Namibian territory can only support livestock farming- this being the only commercially-viable agricultural activity.

The commercial cattle industry mainly produces for the external market, especially the South African market. Cattle are exported to South Africa either as live beasts on the hoof (where, in the past, they were sold at below market value prices) or as processed meat. Sheep farmers mainly raise the karakul sheep which are famous for their pelts from which fur coats are made. Table 6.1 shows the gross output from commercial farming from 1976–1981.

Table 6.1 *Gross output from commercial farming, 1976–1981 (R million), R=South African rand*

Year	Karakul	Sheep	Wool	Other	Total
1976	50.2	86.3	2.6	13.3	152.4
1977	36.2	78.0	2.9	14.9	132.0
1978	34.3	79.3	3.2	16.1	132.9
1979	49.7	82.7	2.3	17.1	151.8
1980	42.8	107.8	2.8	30.6	184.0
1981	20.1	130.5	2.5	35.2	188.3

Source: Kaakunga, 1990: 228

Water resources

Surfacewater is a scarce resource in Namibia and it is also one of the major determinants of development potential in the country. Many areas of land with good grazing potential such as Ovamboland are reported to be underutilised due to lack of water. As a result of this dearth in inland perennial waters Namibia finds itself having to rely on border rivers. Most irrigation schemes are limited to the lower Orange River, the Hardap Dam, East Caprivi and Kavango. In Rehoboth, up to 90 per cent of the water used for agriculture is from boreholes. While groundwater seems to be the logical solution to surfacewater deficits, its use is curtailed because it is not found in abundance where it is required and it is expensive to develop. This helps to explain why, although the Kaarsveldt and the Otavi Highlands show great potential for groundwater resources, there has been limited exploitation because of the prohibitive cost. The idea of establishing a desalinisation plant at the coast faces similar problems of high cost. The cost problem is further compounded by the fact that the only deep-water port at Walvis Bay is still an enclave of South Africa.

The exploitation of border rivers has its own problems. Firstly, the settled areas, where there is demand for water, are located away from the borders which means a high delivery and distribution cost for water to reach these centres. Instituting cost-recovery mechanisms might not be feasible since the majority of people most in need of water are the least able to pay. Secondly, for Namibia to divert water from border rivers requires it to negotiate agreements with several countries. In the case of rivers like the Kunene, Orange and Okavango, negotiations have to be with South Africa, Botswana and Angola. Use of the mid-Caprivi Swamps as water sources has been suggested. However, ecologists are opposed to that because they argue that the exploitation may have repercussions on the fragile swamp ecology. Since the swamps are situated far away from the areas of human settlement there are also cost considerations to be considered.

To summarize the problem of water resources, in terms of hydrogeological problems the absolute availability of water is very limited, groundwater is scarce and difficult to locate and high salinity in many areas makes water unsuitable for drinking.

Service provision was very limited during the colonial period. Seventy per cent of the rural population had no secure access to clean water. The best water sources were put in by the South African regime to provide for stock water facilities: this was associated with economic need not with human consumption. In Herero region, for example, relatively sophisticated systems typically consist of a fenced area with motorised borehole, a large storage tank and a cattle trough.

All water points were put in without community participation, and are still maintained by mobile service teams, or by resident caretakers. Communities thus have little sense of ownership, and no control over maintenance issues. This has led to high levels of environmental pollution at most water sources, including:

- much spillage and leakage, leading to standing water which encourages cattle to encroach;
- faecal pollution;
- malaria breeding points (especially in the north).

Vegetation

According to Giess and Tinley (1968) the 8 vegetation types found in Namibia are as follows (Figure 6.3):

- Dry Deciduous Forest with many *Baikiaea plurijuga*
  - this mixed deciduous forest type is very rich in species.
- Undifferentiated: Relatively Dry Types
  - this vegetation type is often a dense woodland very mixed in species with *Burkea africana*, *Combretum mechowianum* and *Lonchocarpus nelsii* as important constituents.
- Woodland Savanna with *Colophospermum* mopane
- Wooded Steppe with Acacia (and *Commiphora*)
  - this vegetation type includes several variations in its extensive range.
- Karoo Succulent Steppe
  - in the Namib Desert succulents are found belonging to the following families: *Mesembryaceae*, *Crassulaceae* and *Geraniaceae*. Lichens tend to be plentiful along the coastal areas.
- Karoo Shrub and Grass
- Subdesert Steppe (Tropical Types)
  - this is transitional vegetation between the desert and the moister inland types. This vegetation type is characterised by endemic species of *Commiphora* such as *C. claciicola* in the drier parts and *C. glaucescens* and *C. multijuga* in the moister inland areas. Grasses are common after rains and are mainly annual and perennial species of *Stipagrostis*.

• Desert

 – this region covers most of the Namib Desert and it is virtually devoid of vegetation, except for widely scattered plants occurring mainly along the water courses. To the north of Walvis Bay, *Arthraeura leubnitziae, Zygophyllum stapfii, Salsola* spp. and *Welwitschia bainesii* are the most common species and are found primarily on the gravel flats. The grasses which grow only appear after rains and are mainly annual species of *Stipagrostis*. Between Walvis Bay and Luderitzbucht is an area of shifting dunes of up to 300 m high.

The only conservation of vegetation in Namibia takes place in the game parks, where it is protected as part of the whole ecosystem. In the north is the Etosha Game Park which mainly contains the *Colophospermum mopane* Savanna, Combretaceous Savanna on sand and halophytic shrub savanna around the Etosha Depression. The Namib Desert Park occupies the desert-arid savanna region of the west coast. Twenty-three kilometres west of Windhoek is the Daan Viljoen Game Park (3944 ha) which contains a variety of highland savanna dominated by Acacia hereroensis-Combretum apiculatum tree savanna. In south-central Namibia is the Hardap Game Park which includes Karoo shrub and grass. In the extreme south near the Fish River canyon is the Ai-ais Park which contains Karoo succulent steppe.

Outside these game-park areas no vegetation conservation exists. Recently, part of the Caprivi Strip between the Okovango and Mashi Rivers has been proclaimed as a game park. This happens to be the only part of the country where the *Baikiaea plurijuga* woodlands on the Kalahari Sand which only occur in the extreme north-east of Namibia can be conserved and protected. There are no vegetation conservation areas in any of the communal lands. However, at present the Forestry Department has a controlled fire-break system in the Okovango tribal territory to guard the woodlands from fire devastation.

In Namibia, three main acts provide scope for the legal control of forest resource exploitation. These are the Flora Protection Ordinance 19 of 1937, the Preservation of Trees Ordinance 37 of 1952, and the Environmental Conservation Act 73 of 1989. However, the implementation of these Acts has, to a large extent, been ineffective since large tracts of formerly wooded land now lie bare.

Much of the commercially exploitable forests concentrated in the north of the Ovambo-Kavango-Mid Caprivi area have been greatly reduced through commercial exploitation and also through deliberate destruction during the war of Independence as occupying armies sought to frustrate the liberation war effort. In the south, deforestation has mainly been concentrated around urban centres, especially Windhoek's townships of Katatura and Khomasdal.

Some commercial eucalyptus plantations do however exist in Eastern Ovamboland, Kavango, Western and Central Caprivi, Tsumeb, Otavi and Grootfontein. Table 6.2 below shows production figures for 1983 forestry products:

Table 6.2 *Commercial forestry output, 1983*

Forest	Volume m³	Tonnage
Ovambo	6 000	4 290
Kavango	8 500	6 070
Caprivi	4 500	3 200
Tsumukwe	750	540
Tsumeb/Otavi	2 000	1 430
Total	21 750	15 530

Source: After UNIN, 1986

In terms of overall biomass resources, the World Bank has funded a biomass assessment project, which covers all of Africa south of the Sahara. The analysis is based on AVHRR data acquired by NOAA satellite in 1986. In Namibia, according to preliminary estimations, the standing stock of woody biomass is estimated to be 670 million tonnes and the mean annual increment 34 million tonnes. Table 6.3 gives details of the different biomass classes.

Table 6.3 *Woody biomass resources, preliminary estimates*

Biomass classes	Area %	Growing stock total 10^6 tonne	per ha tonne	MAI per ha tonne
0 Desert	27.2	–	–	–
11 Veld grassland	1.9	–	–	–
24 Transitional wooded grassland	19.7	34	2	0.1
33 Bushy shrubland	0.9	4	6	0.1
34 Kalahari shrubland	7.8	39	6	1.3
35 Wooded shrubland	6.2	30	6	0.1
41 Dry *Acacia-Commiphora* bushland and thicket	0.3	3	12	0.2
42 Fynbos thicket	0.3	3	14	2.5
43 Dry *Acacia-Commiphora* bushland and thicket	1.7	31	22	0.6
51 *Acacia* woodland mosaic	20.4	311	19	0.6
61 Open woodland	12.2	149	15	1.2
66 Seasonal miombo	0.2	4	27	0.5
72 Cultivation and forest/woodland mosaic	1.2	64	65	0.7
Total/Mean	100.0	672	8	0.4

(MAI = Mean Annual Increment)

Source: Erkkilä and Siiskonen, 1992:143

Mining and mineral resources

Namibia is endowed with substantial mineral resources and its economy has been inextricably linked with mining which provides about two-thirds of the country's total foreign currency earnings. The Namibian mining industry can be divided into the following major sectors: diamonds, uranium, metals, and industrial minerals. Each of the sectors is dominated by one large company with the exception of industrial minerals. For example, diamond mining is dominated by Consolidated Diamond Mines (CDM), uranium by Rossing Uranium which is part of the Rio Tinto-Zinc group (RTZ), and metals by Tsumeb Corporation. The three companies are South African-controlled and two of these are controlled by the Anglo-De Beers group and one by the South African state (Figure 6.5).

Table 6.4 shows the percentages of the world reserve that the country has in diamonds, uranium and other minerals.

According to UNIN (1986), copper, lead, and zinc had expected mining lives of 16.9, 14.3 and 37.6 years respectively. Rich deposits of alluvial diamonds are found in the area between Oranjemund and Luderitz while uranium ore is mined at Rossing. Several other minerals are produced or are awaiting exploitation. The list includes copper, lead, zinc, vanadium, iron, manganese, gold, silver, platinum, tungsten, tin, cadium, limestone, rock salt, silica, sulphur, borghium, rubium, belemium, bismuth, gallium, molybdenum, niobium, tellerium, phospher, soda and mica.

Table 6.5 shows that the contribution of mining to Gross Domestic Product between 1974 and 1983 has ranged from about 27 to 33 per cent. In Namibia mining is a leading contributor to exports and between 1960 and 1980 it accounted for over 60 per cent of the value of exports. Despite its unrivalled contribution to the GDP, mining in Namibia is a relatively small generator of employment, accounting for only 6 per cent of total wage employment.

Table 6.4 *Major mineral resources*

Major minerals	% of world resources
Diamonds	5
Uranium	10
Zinc	1
Cadmium	1
Silver	2
Arsenic	.5
Copper	1
Lead	1

Source: Green et al., 1981

An examination of the various mining acts and fiscal jurisdiction indicates that the present Namibian legislation is based on regalian jurisdiction. The essence of the regalian concept of tenure is state ownership or control of mineral resources, whereby the state in the past meant the government of South Africa (UNIN, 1986). Fiscal provisions in respect of the mining sector of Namibia include licence fees, state lease or royalties and taxes. The basic tax rates on the mining industry are determined by the Income Tax Ordinance of 1968.

Table 6.5 *Contribution of mining to GDP, 1974–1983*

	1974	1977	1980	1983
Mining % contribution	27	33	32	28

Source: Kaakunga, 1990: 233

The high degree of foreign ownership in the mining sector has led to a substantial siphoning of wealth from the Namibian economy in the form of profits, dividends, interest payments, capital transfers and remittances abroad. Furthermore, the mineral wealth of the country has, so far, not benefited the majority of the black population who are either peasants or part of the urban working class. Rather, it has resulted in exploitation through the migrant labour system. Since most of the strategic minerals are in foreign hands, the mining sector in Namibia has failed to be the leading sector with the capacity to foster development throughout the space economy. Meaningful structural changes within the mining industry need to be instituted if this strategic sector is to become an engine of socio-economic transformation.

Mining has influenced the development of Namibia's physical infrastructure. The railway system, for example, links the various mines and the harbours from where the minerals are exported. Similarly, water and electricity supplies have developed largely in relation to the demands of mining (Figure 6.5).

Energy

Unlike most countries in Southern Africa, in Namibia the indigenous production of electricity and coal does not satisfy domestic demand.

In 1980 the country imported 98 per cent of all its commercial energy requirements from, or through, South Africa. Although hydro-electrical power and non-commercial energy sources are available locally, the energy needs of Namibia will not be satisfied unless the new government launches an energy policy that is aimed at utilising the proven reserves of coal at Aranos, Arandis and Hochfeld. In addition, other forms of hydrocarbon resources such as oil and gas, which are believed to exist in the Etosha Basin, will have to be developed (UNIN, 1986).

An analysis of Namibia's energy comsumption patterns shows that the energy sector can conveniently be divided into two, the modern-commercial sector and the traditional sector. Thirty-five per cent of the country's total commercial energy demand is for oil, 38 per cent for coal, 20 per cent for charcoal and wood and only 7 per cent is from hydro-electric power. On the other hand, woodfuel is the main source of energy in the rural-based traditional sector.

Table 6.6 *Estimated Namibian energy demand, 1980*

Energy use by sector	Barrels of oil equivalent/day	Per cent
Transport	6 860	21
Mining industry	17 966	55
Agriculture, fishing/ marine and domestic use	7 840	24
Total	32 666	100

Source: UNIN, 1986

Table 6.6 shows the estimated Namibian energy demand in 1980 by sector. The mining sector consumed more than half of the total barrels of oil equivalent per day. On the other hand, the energy balance sheet for 1980 shows that electricity is the most important source of energy, accounting for 37 per cent of national fuel demand (Table 6.7). Liquid fuels accounted for 31 per cent, while charcoal/wood accounted for only 20 per cent. However, these figures are at best rough estimates, especially for charcoal/wood since most of its use is unrecorded. Annual consumption of fuelwood in Namibia is estimated to be between 1.0 and 1.25 cubic metres per capita for black rural dwellers and about 0.6 cubic metres per capita for black urban residents. In 1980 it was estimated that total fuelwood consumption was about 890,000 tonnes. This shows that in Namibia there is an overwhelming dependence by the rural population and the urban poor on woodfuel. This heavy reliance on woodfuel has serious environmental implications. An analysis of population densities and of likely woodfuel replenishment rates for different parts of the country indicates that annual yields cannot supply the woodfuel needs of the coastal districts or the main peri-urban districts, especially around high density townships and around the densely-populated former homeland areas.

In order to avert the imminent 'rural energy crisis' the government of Namibia might want to consider introducing other forms of fuel in the rural areas and some forms of intermediate technology like Zimbabwe's Tso-Tso stove, which is very energy efficient.

Turning to the Ovambo region, as a regional case study, no marked changes have occurred in the priority of different energy sources. Fuelwood is the most important source of energy for cooking, lighting and heating as 95 per cent of the households in Ovambo have no electricity.

Table 6.7 *Energy balance of Namibia, 1980*

Use by type of energy	Barrels of oil equivalent/day	Per cent
Liquid fuels	10 127	31
Coal	3 920	12
Electricity	12 086	37
Charcoal/Wood	6 533	20
Total	32 666	100

Source: UNIN, 1986

The most marked long-term change in the energy-supply situation has been the increase in the distance fuelwood has to be carried. At the beginning of this century fuelwood was fetched mainly from the adjacent forested areas lying between population clusters or communities, but today these forested areas have almost totally disappeared from densely-populated central Ovambo.

A considerable amount of fuelwood in Ovambo is now brought from forests and woodlands located outside the settled areas. The average hauling distance is 33 km and the wood is transported in pickup vans. The lengthening of this distance has meant that responsibility for the energy supply has been transferred from women to men. Deforestation has also generated the creation of fuelwood markets in the most densely populated areas. However, there is no indication that fuelwood will be replaced by any other source of energy in the foreseeable future.

Wildlife

Namibia has a rich heritage of wildlife and most of the fauna found in Southern Africa is represented in Namibia's national parks and game reserves. Their numbers, however, tend to fluctuate as a result of periodic droughts, habitat destruction, disturbed migration and poaching. It is these factors which largely account for the generally diminishing wildlife populations in the country. However, the government is aware of the booming tourism and commercial hunting industries in Southern Africa and some of its policy statements indicate that necessary precautions will be taken to preserve and halt the indiscriminate exploitation of wildlife resources. The wildlife resources of the northern parks are major tourist attractions and they hold the key to Namibia's future tourism industry. It is sad to note that species like the tsessebe, buffalo, southern white rhino and spotted hyena are near or below sustainable population sizes and are in danger of becoming extinct. Good wildlife management is required to ensure that sustainable herds of these animals remain.

The first game reserves in Namibia were established in 1907. These included the Etosha National Park, areas to the north of Grootfontein, Kaokoland and the Namib desert. About 8.7 per cent of Namibia's land area has been set aside for nature conservation and this area consists of 68,200 km² of State land and 3035 km² of private nature reserves.

The major protected areas are the Etosha National Park (22,270 km²), Namib-Naukluft National Park (23,402 km²), Skeleton Coast National Park (16,000 km²), and West Caprivi Game Park (5300 km²). Together, these four parks account for 98 per cent of the state-owned national parks and nature reserves. Etosha Park is the only park in Namibia which has enjoyed the benefits of skilled management and budgetry allocations. This is because the park has one of the richest ecosystems in Southern Africa and is acclaimed for its biological and economic importance, already having a high international tourist profile. In addition, Namibia has several smaller national parks and nature conservation reserves which often shelter rare ecosystems and also harbour a variety of unique species. For example, the Cape Cross Seal Reserve is the home of approximately 150,000 Cape fur seals, while the 461 km^2 Fish River Canyon National Park is famous for its mountain zebra, klipspringers and a unique vegetation habitat. The Water Plateau National Park (406 km^2) is famous for its unique vegetation, game and rock paintings. Other smaller parks include the Hardap Recreation Resort (251km^2), the Khomas Hochland National Park (39 km^2), and the Tsaobis Game Park.

The exploitation of wildlife resources in Namibia is both extractive and non-extractive. Non-extractive exploitation basically refers to tourism which is largely confined to the national parks and game reserves. Extractive exploitation involves subsistence hunting and commercial exploitation and has been going on in Namibia for centuries. Commercial exploitation includes sport and trophy hunting, game culling and shooting. Since, understandably, there are no conservation measures taken by the indigenous local populations all species of game are exposed to subsistence hunting. The worst type of extractive exploitation experienced in Namibia is game poaching which, during the liberation war, was rife in the Caprivi and Kaokoland regions where South African troops were the main perpetrators.

All wildlife resources in Namibia are managed by the Department of Nature Conservation and Tourism whose main aims are:

- to take care of animal populations and the administration of licenced hunting;
- to combat epidemics carried by wildlife;
- to ensure clean water supplies in protected areas;
- to study the habitat of animals;
- to ensure the efficient operation of the country's recreation facilities.

Hunting regulations are based on the Native Conservation Ordinance of 1967, supplemented by annual notices in the Gazette according to game populations and conditions of the year. Only nine species may be hunted. These are eland, kudu, gemsbok, warthog, duiker, bushpig, blue wilde-beest, springbok and buffalo. Local magistrates are empowered to issue weapons and hunting licences for specified species and quantities. However, since game cropping or farming is still an exclusively white privilege, the government might want to consider giving blacks a share in the game ownership business.

Fishing

Fish processing has for long been the backbone of Namibian manufacturing industry. The fishing industry became an important component of the economy during the 1950s. Before then, the industry had been confined to whale and seal catches. Between 1948 and 1962 the value of fish exports increased from R800,000 to R24 million. In the past over 50 companies were involved in commercial fishing, with Walvis Bay the leading centre especially for pilchards and anchovies, and Luderitz for shell fish (Figure 6.6).

Table 6.8 shows the catches in tonnes of the principal species for the period between 1966 and 1983. Before its decline, the industry provided numerous jobs for the local population. In 1978, for example, the industry provided seasonal jobs for 5000 labourers and 800 fishermen. By 1981, only three of the canneries were operational, namely Wesco, Newesk Fishery and Tune Corporation.

As Kaakunga (1990) observed, the rich fishing fields off the coast of Namibia have been depleted with little benefit to the country, apart from employment, because the immense profits generated in the industry were siphoned away to South Africa by the companies involved in the fishing industry.

The Namibian fishing industry has been, and still remains, more South African than Namibian. The marketing of fresh and frozen fish for local consumption has been by South African companies and trawlers, and the supply has come through South Africa and not directly from Walvis Bay and Luderitz. It is ironic that the Namibian fishing industry, even at its peak, was not able to satisfy the local market. Instead, local demand for fish has been satisfied through the re-importation of Namibian fish from South Africa where 75 per cent of all fish output is exported at prices fixed below the world market. Clearly the Namibian fishing industry illustrates the character of resource imperialism through profit maximisation without due consideration for the future of the industry.

Table 6.8 *Catches of the six principal species of fish, 1966–83*

		1966	1967	1968	1969	1970	1971	1972	1973	1974
Pelegic fish land										
canned	million cartons	4.24	4.65	4.46	4.50	5.01	3.17	6.14	7.50	10.4
Pilchards	000 tonnes	65	74	54	52	51	34	69	106	139
meal	000 tonnes	163	172	238	203	156	135	112	143	161
oil	000 tonnes	35	39	68	45	44	27	28	47	28
Factory ships										
meal	000 tonnes	12	57	143	127	–	(20)	–	–	–
oil	000 tonnes	3	9	40	37	–	(6)	–	–	–
Rock lobster										
canned	tonnes	101	65	25	61	81	4	–	8	–
frozen tails	tonnes	2 633	15 84	2 767	2 093	1 059	674	738	891	–
whole	tonnes	–	–	–	–	–	–	–	–	(55)
total	tonnes	2 734	1 649	2 792	1 541	140	678	746	946	(930)
Meal	000 tonnes	1.8	0.9	1.5	1.3	0.5	0.4	0.3	0.3	–

		1975	1976	1977	1978	1979	1980	1981	1982	1983
Pelegic fish land										
canned	million cartons	10.8	9.70	4.02	1.16	0.86	0.04	–	1.59	1.20
Pilchards	000 tonnes	143	(136)	(56)	(16)	(12)	(1)	–	(22)	20
meal	000 tonnes	147	107	83	89	79	56	61	46	78
oil	000 tonnes	28	19	13	22	22	19	22	9	25
Factory ships										
meal	000 tonnes	–	–	–	–	–	–	–	–	–
oil	000 tonnes	–	–	–	–	–	–	–	–	–
Rock lobster										
canned	tonnes	–	–	–	–	–	–	–	–	–
frozen tails	tonnes	–	–	512	172	329	210	200	(90)	100
whole	tonnes	–	–	37	187	206	232	(219)	(340)	(440)
total	tonnes	(520)	(480)	560	359	535	442	(419)	(430)	(540)
Meal	000 tonnes	–	–	–	–	–	–	–	–	–

Source: Kaakunga, 1990

STRATEGIES AND SOLUTIONS FOR ENVIRONMENTAL SUSTAINABILITY

The term environmental sustainability is now the catch phrase of most development programmes throughout the world.

In Namibia the need to formulate strategies and solutions for environmental sustainability cannot be over-emphasised. The Namibian environment does not have the capacity and resilience to regenerate itself once a certain optimum landuse capability is exceeded. The areas which need urgent attention currently are the 'homeland' areas. In the present quest for economic growth, land distribution and the redistribution of national wealth, there is need to guard against achieving short-term economic gains at the expense of the environment. It is this observation that calls for the formulation and establishment of sound policy and planning instruments which will define, among other things, scales of authority, the importance of local participation or grassroots support and the involvement of women's groups in the development process.

As a fledgling democracy Namibia would do well to develop grassroots involvement in the national planning systems. Instead of the top-down approach to the development process common elsewhere in Africa, a sustainable development process would be well served by a bottom-up approach which takes into account the priorities of the local community directly targeted for development. This, therefore, entails the devolution and decentralisation of planning power and hierarchies. Also urgently required is the integration of the two space-economies, the former homelands and the former white areas. While grassroots participation is advocated, it must be pointed out, however, that the contribution of the local community risks being an empty ritual if there is no system to co-ordinate and collate local plans into national plans. Furthermore, if the local planning authorities are to sustain the devolved and decentralised planning powers they ought to be given strong financial backing. Learning from Zimbabwean experiences, if the planning process is decentralised to the regions whilst finance is dispensed through line ministries, it is likely that local-level planning will be reduced to a shopping list ritual. Hence, little change will occur to the existing regional inequalities created by race-space segregation and institutionalised in the doctrine of separate development.

Namibia should also realise that it is the women, especially in the northern part of the country, who are the direct agents of development since their husbands, in many cases, are migrant labourers. For development efforts to be sustainable, it is vital to appreciate the pivotal role played by women in local-level planning. Recognition must also be made of the fact that imported technology might not be appropriate for their needs, hence planning that ignores women may result in project targets not being met. Whilst a lot of financial and other forms of assistance were pledged when the country attained independence, it must, however, be pointed out that a policy of self-reliance is the linchpin of sustainable development.

Within the context of African development it has been observed that as soon as donors withdraw their support, development projects collapse. To avert this, the community must be motivated to be self-reliant. Instead of applying the doctrine of handouts to local-level planning units, it would be prudent for Namibia to institute some cost-recovery mechanisms in the development process. For example, while free education and health have their own benefits, it must be borne in mind that some cost-recovery mechanisms might actually provide more funds for either expanding existing facilities, building new ones or better still improving the quality of existing ones. Although few people in the former homelands and the reserves are able to pay for these social needs, there is need to introduce nominal charges so that the recipients attach some value to the services provided. Furthermore, instituting nominal charges allows for partial cost recovery of the services provided.

Land

With these thoughts in mind, it is to the credit of the newly established independent government of Namibia that soon after taking office the following steps were taken:

1. It was actually written into the constitution that development must be environmentally sustainable (Article 95L).
2. During the transitional period after Independence the government focused on four major priority sectors:
   - agriculture, rural development and conservation;
   - the involvement of women in rural development;
   - the decentralization of administration to allow the environmental diversity of the country to be taken into account;
   - the importance of household food security to many rural development programmes.
3. A National Planning Agency has been established.

The whole question of land reform is central to the formulation of strategies and solutions for sutainable development. A number of recommendations were made at the 1991 Land Conference which are summarized below. A Commission was established after the conference to examine how these recommendations could be implemented in practice. The following consensus emerged during the conference on land reform.

Firstly, with reference to commercial land:

- *Injustice.* During the colonial period, much of Namibia's farming area was expropriated by the German and South African colonial regimes. It was allocated exclusively to white settlers while black Namibian farmers were confined to reserves mainly. Today, a small minority owns nearly all the freehold farms.

  Conference concluded that there was injustice concerning the acquisition of land in the past and something must be done about it as swiftly as practically possible.
- *Ancestral rights.* Before Namibia was colonised at the end of the nineteenth century, the land boundaries between Namibian communities were not precisely demarcated and shifted frequently. The claims of different communities will inevitably overlap. During the colonial period, there were large population movements with a mixing of previously distinct communities.

  The Conference concluded that given the complexities in redressing ancestral land claims, restitution of such claims in full is impossible.
- *Foreign-owned land.* There is nationwide land hunger and a severe shortage of available farmland. During the colonial period, Namibians were excluded in favour of settlers from abroad, especially South Africa. The constitutional principle of affirmative action is best served by giving priority to Namibians who need to own farmland.

  The Conference resolved that foreigners should not be allowed to own farmland, but should be given the right to use and develop it on a leasehold basis, in accordance with Namibia's open-door policy towards foreign investors.
- *Underutilised land.* There is land hunger and severe pressure on farmland in the communal areas, while land in the commercial zone remains abandoned or not fully utilised.

  The Conference resolved that some abandoned and underutilised commercial land should be reallocated and brought into productive use.

- *Absentee landlords.* Many absentee landlords have alternative sources of income, while many Namibian farmers lack sufficient land to make an adequate living. Some Namibian farm enterprises are split between different locations and others are part-time or weekend farmers. Absentee foreign owners, on the other hand, mostly live abroad.

  The Conference resolved that land owned by absentees should be expropriated. However, there should be a distinction in respect of owners who do not live on their farms, between foreign and citizen owners.

- *Farm size and numbers.* Some commercial farmers own more than one farm or large tracts of land while many Namibians are short of land. In the spirit of national reconciliation, a redistribution of such farms would open up access to a greater number of Namibian farmers.

  The Conference resolved that very large farms and ownership of several farms by one owner should not be permitted and such land should be expropriated.

- *Land tax.* A land tax on commercial farmland will generate revenue for the state from the wealthier section of the farming community. A land tax may serve to promote the productive use of land and penalise those who leave the land idle.

  The Conference resolved that there should be a land tax on commercial farmland.

- *Technical committee on commercial farmland.* In view of the need to establish authoritative data and arrive at sound policy recommendations, conference proposed that a technical committee should be established to evaluate the facts regarding underutilised land, absentee ownership, viable farm sizes in different regions, multiple ownership of farms and possible tax structures, and to make appropriate recommendations for the acquisitions and reallocation of such land identified.

- *Farmworkers.* Many farmworkers suffer degrading conditions of poverty and repression. They have contributed greatly to the prosperity of the commercial farming sector, but have obtained little benefit from that prosperity. Their circumstances demand special attention and protection by law.

  The Conference condemned the injustices perpetrated on farmworkers by some farmers in both the commercial and the communal areas.

  The Conference resolved that:
  - farmerworkers should be afforded rights and protection under the labour code;
  - the government should enact legislation providing for a charter of rights for farmworkers. The charter should be monitored and enforced by a government agency;
  - the charter of rights should include provision for a minimum wage, fixed working hours, sick leave, annual leave, schooling for children, medical care for workers and their families, adequate housing on the farm, pensions, the right to reside on the farm after retirement, and grazing rights for farmworkers' livestock free of charge;
  - the workers' compensation act should cover farmworkers.

- *Assistance to commercial farmers.* In the past, commercial farmers enjoyed disproportionate state support. Such support may be best directed to sustain beginner farmers. All Namibian farmers are vulnerable to adverse conditions, such as low commodity prices and drought. State support may be needed to assist commercial farmers to implement social programmes.

  The Conference resolved that:
  - established commercial farmers should only receive financial assistance from the Government in exceptional circumstances, which include natural disasters such as drought;
  - the government should consider providing assistance to commercial farmers for

programmes of affirmative action, such as improving the conditions of farmworkers.

Turning to the Communal Areas:

- *The future role of communal areas.* The communal areas sustain the great majority of Namibian farmers, especially poor farmers.

  The Conference concluded that the present communal areas should be retained, developed and commercialised where possible, and expanded where necessary.
- *Access to communal land.* Farming households in the communal areas depend on the land for much of their subsistence. A guaranteed right of access is essential for their survival. The former homeland policy which restricted access to communal land on a tribal or ethnic basis is contrary to the Constitution. Namibians have the right to live where they choose. However, in a particular communal area the rights of intending farmers from outside the area need to be reconciled with the rights of the local community having access to the land.

  The Conference resolved that:
  - as provided by the Constitution, all Namibian citizens have the right to live where they choose within the national territory;
  - in seeking access to communal land, applicants should take account of the rights and customs of the local communities living there;
  - priority should be given to the landless and those without adequate land for subsistence.
- *Disadvantaged communities.* Ever-increasing land pressures in the communal areas pose a threat to the subsistence resources of disadvantaged communities and groups.

  The Conference resolved that disadvantaged communities and groups, in particular the San and the disabled, should receive special protection of their land rights.
- *Game conservation and farmers' rights.* In some communal areas there is a conflict of interests between the need for wildlife conservation and the need of farmers to protect their livestock from losses and their crops from damage.

  The Conference resolved that farmers in the communal areas should be allowed to give their crops and livestock effective protection from wild animals.
- *Payment for land.* In certain communal areas, farmers must pay for land allocated to them. Many are small subsistence farmers and cannot easily afford to pay. They also receive no services for their payments.

  The Conference resolved that:
  - communal area households should not be required to pay for obtaining farmland under communal tenure for their own subsistance;
  - those obtaining land for business purposes should be required to pay for it each year;
  - all payments for land should be made to the government rather than to traditional leaders.
- *Rights of women.* Women form the majority of agricultural producers in the communal areas, but suffer discrimination under both customary and statutory law. They have historically been marginalised.

  The Conference resolved that:
  - women should have the right to own the land they cultivate and to inherit and bequeath land and fixed property;
  - a programme of affirmative action be instituted to assist women in training, i.e. low-interest loans and other mechanisms so that they can compete with men on equal terms;

- all customary and statutory laws which discriminate against women be abolished or amended with immediate effect;
- women be granted equal representation on all land boards, district councils or other bodies concerned with the allocation or use of land.
- *Land allocation and administration.* The Constitution envisages that both the traditional leaders and the Government have a role to play in the allocation and administration of land. The precise nature of their respective roles has to be clearly defined in law and in terms of the democratic principles of the Constitution.

    The Conference resolved that:
    - the role of the traditional leaders in allocating communal land should be recognised, but properly defined under law;
    - the establishment of regional and local government institutions is provided for under the Constitution. Their powers should include land administration;
    - land boards should be introduced at an early date to administer the allocation of communal land. They should be accountable to the Government and their local communities.
- *The stock control barrier.* The majority of small farmers who live in the northern communal areas are prevented from selling their livestock in the commercial zone and to foreign markets on account of veterinary restrictions (the 'red line'). This restriction has excluded them from substantial economic benefits.

    The Conference resolved that:
    - the stock control fence – the so-called red line – must be removed as soon as possible, but has to be kept in place for a period in order to preserve Namibia's access to cattle export markets;
    - during this period, the Government should set up quarantine camps to allow farmers in the northern communal areas to market their livestock south of the fence.
- *Illegal fencing.* The uncontrolled fencing of communal land poses a serious threat to the future subsistence of small farmers in the communal areas.

    The Conference resolved that illegal fencing of land must be stopped and all illegal fences be removed.
- *Dual grazing rights.* Some large farmers from the communal areas who have bought commercial farms or acquired fenced communal land continue to graze their livestock on communal pasture. This practice increases the pressure on the already overstretched grazing land in the communal areas at the expense of small farmers.

    The Conference resolved that:
    - commercial farmers should not be allowed to have access to communal grazing land;
    - communal farmers who acquire commercial farms should not be allowed to keep their rights to communal land.
- *Transfer of commercial land to large communal farmers.* Given the existing pressures on communal land, communal farmers with the potential to become commercial farmers can be encouraged, if necessary through government schemes, to acquire land in the commercial sector. Such a transfer would relieve pressure on land in the communal areas and would give small farmers an opportunity to improve their viability and standard of living.

    The Conference resolved that:
    - under the Constitution, no-one may be forced to leave communal land. But large communal farmers having a certain minimum number of livestock should be encouraged to acquire commercial land outside the communal areas;

- communal farmers acquiring commercial land should be assisted through schemes providing support, such as low-interest loans and technical advice. Financial assistance should be strictly limited to those who can prove their need for it;
- the criteria for identifying large farmers should be established for each communal area by further study;
- farmland now used by large farmers in the communal areas should not be expanded and in future should be reduced to make space for small farmers.
- *Access for small farmers to commercial land.* In order to relieve the pressure on communal land, small farmers can be relocated to farmland in the commercial zone through state support schemes.
  The Conference recommended that:
- small farmers in the communal areas should be assisted to obtain access to land in the present commercial zone;
- co-operative ownership and provision of state land for grazing schemes should be considered;
- small farmers moving to commercial land should be given training, technical advice and assistance to buy and improve their livestock.

Vegetation

Policies are required to curb deforestation in Namibia. There are several options available. The first, and most conventional option, is to try to expand plantation activities at state level, primarily for the purpose of supplying the urban market with firewood. The second option is for the government to launch more communal woodlots at the village level in the communal land areas. The idea here would be to try to ensure that the peasantry also participates in the provision of its wood and wood product requirements. At the individual level, farm forestry would provide the most realistic option, since the communal woodlot is usually a victim of the 'tragedy of the commons' if improperly designed. A further advantage of the farm forestry approach is that it assumes that land is scarce since it utilises plot boundaries. Furthermore, farm forestry presents no logistical problems since each family is responsible for its own plot. It must be mentioned here that farm forestry is not a panacea for Namibia's forest problem. Success in reducing deforestation will depend on the way in which an awareness of the need for conservation is inculcated in the peasants in order to enlist their support and participation. More important is the need for an environmental policy which would embody all land, water, air and vegetation protection stratagems.

In a recent survey of forestry in Namibia (Erkkilä and Siiskonen 1992:183–4), the following policy recommendations were made:

- There is a need for a comprehensive national forest inventory and management plan, which should include the assessment of total woody biomass, timber resources, non-timber forest products and conservation aspects.
- The management of indigenous forests should be improved.
- In order to recover the destroyed mopane stands in Ovambo, coppice forestry is recommended. Because of the immense coppicing vigour of mopane, this should not be a technical problem.
- Alternative building materials and solutions for saving wood should be sought for rural homesteads. If the present pattern continues, ecological conditions in many areas will deteriorate severely and living conditions will get worse.

- In order to improve grazing capacity, the problem of bush encroachment in the central part of the county should be tackled.
- Environmental education and awareness should be intensified.
- The utilisation of forests should be diversified. This includes, in addition to timber species, non-timber forest products such as fruits and nuts.
- The local population should be discouraged from clearing forests. More jobs should be created in the forestry sector and the number of beneficiaries increased.
- Forest research should have a high priority. The important research topics are: the natural regeneration of commercial timber species, artificial regeneration (both indigenous and exotic species), agroforestry systems, management of indigenous forests, patterns of wood consumption at both national and local levels, long-term analysis of the deforestation process, previous logging activities and utilisation of woody biomass.
- A management and research programme should be prepared for all plantations. Data collection should begin without delay.
- The national herbarium should be given adequate facilities.
- Useful documents dealing with forestry matters in Namibia might be found at the Central Archives Depot, Pretoria and at the Cape Archives Depot, Cape Town. Nor should documents owned by individual companies, e.g. the Tsumeb Corporation Ltd and Loxton, Venn & Associates, be neglected in this context. Oral sources are necessary when forestry is studied from the point of view of the African population.

The biological and silvicultural prospects for the sustainable development of Namibian forestry are good; the most difficult issues are socio-economic. The status of sustained forestry will be achieved by planned and monitored research and development. Namibia has now taken the challenge and started to build up a new forestry administration with the aim of implementing a successful national forest policy.

In order to conserve vegetation and protect wildlife, areas should be set aside as protected parks in each of the former homeland territories of Ovamboland and the Okovango in northern Namibia. These parks could become communal conservation areas where research could be done on the natural ecosystem to benefit the peasants in each of the communal/tribal areas in the most efficient methods of land husbandry. A small area in the Okovango territory would be the most ideal location because it is away from the heavily-populated Okovango River flood plain and would not interfere with any form of human occupation. Similarly, parks could also be established in the Karst mountain area, in the north-west, and in the western Caprivi Strip.

CONCLUSION

The Namibian ecological environment is not resilient to abuse and care is needed when interacting with it if development practices are to be sustainable. In looking at the sustainability of development efforts it is necessary to realise that we are looking at several aspects of sustainability. The first aspect is ecological sustainability which dictates that Namibian development be compatible with the maintenance of ecological processes, natural resources as well as biodiversity. The second aspect is economic sustainability which infers that Namibian development provides sufficient and consistent returns to investment to meet basic human needs and improve the quality of life. Other important dimensions of sustainable development which are often ignored relate to socio-cultural and political sustainability.

The rationale for insistence on sustainability rests on the principle of intergenerational equity. Within the Namibian context this infers that environmentally-injurious policies and actions consequent upon those policies, whether based on greed or need, will have a bearing on future generations. Namibia's population of 1.4 million people is still too small to be a major threat to the environment; however, equity needs to be the guiding principle in the allocation of resources such as land. Namibia requires an environmental policy that also addresses the unfair land distribution inherited at the time of independence. Reducing human population pressure through resettlement might provide some temporary relief to the overused land but this is not a long-term solution.

Perhaps what is most urgently needed is the development of institutions to support both development and environmental projects in these areas. More extension work and inputs assistance is also vital. As has been stated earlier, environmental conservation in the former homelands and African Reserves should come within the context of rural development so that the local people are led to believe that conservation is not an end in itself but a means to better living conditions. Instead of allowing emotions to guide resettlement efforts it is important to carry out environmental impact assessment studies before people are resettled on fragile land. Furthermore, careful selection is needed in order to ensure that those who are competent are selected and given the land. In the allocation process it must be borne in mind that there are many people who tacitly hope to acquire considerable areas of land through any resettlement programme.

A dimension of sustainable development in Namibia which needs serious consideration concerns women. It is an established fact that owing to the migrant labour system which will continue to exist for the foreseeable future, the women of Namibia remain the major agents of rural development. In view of this, in designing development programmes, due consideration should be taken to ensure that what is designed is compatible with their values.

Finally, as a newly-independent country Namibia faces numerous problems, some of which are beyond its control. These problems should not be allowed to marginalise the very important issue of environmental sustainability.

REFERENCES

Conference on land reform (1991) *Summary of recommendations*, Windhoek

D'amato, A (1966) 'The Bantustan proposals for South West Africa', *Journal of Modern African Studies*, Vol. 4 (2)

Erkkilä, A and Siiskonen, H (1992) *Forestry in Namibia 1850–1990*, University of Joensuu, Faculty of Forestry, Joensuu, Finland

Giess, W (1971) *A Preliminary Vegetation Map of South West Africa*, Dinteria 4:1–114, SWA Scientific Society, Windhoek

Giess, W and Tinley, K L (1968) 'South West Africa', in (eds) I and O Hedberg, *Conservation of Vegetation in Africa South of the Sahara*, University of Uppsala

Government of Namibia, (1990) *Report on Namibia's economy after independence* Department of Finance, Windhoek

Green, R H et al. (1981) *Namibia: The Last Colony*, Longman, London

Green, R H (1991) 'Structural adjustment and national environmental strategies: what interactions?' *Notes from Namibia*, IDS Bulletin, 22:4

Janson, S D (1991) *Environmental Profile of Namibia* , Report for the Swedish International Development Authority, Windhoek

Kaakunga, E (1990) *Problems of Capitalist Development in Namibia: The Dialectics of Progress and Destruction*, Abo Academy Press, Abo

Mbuende, K (1986) *Namibia: the Broken Shield.: Anatomy of Imperialism*, Liber, Malmo

United Nations Institute for Namibia (UNIN) (1986) *Perspectives for National Reconstruction and Development*, Lusaka

7

SWAZILAND

INTRODUCTION

Area and climate

Swaziland lies between latitudes 31° and 32° south and longitudes 25.5° and 27.5° east. It is bordered on its northern, western and southern sides by the Republic of South Africa and in the east by Mozambique. The total area is 17,364 km² which is divided into four physiographic, climatic and ecological zones (Figure 7.1).

The mountainous Highveld, 1000–1200 metres covering 29 per cent of the country, has high rainfall, with an annual average of 1250 mm. Due to the steep slopes, leaching and thin soils, however, only a very small part is regarded as potentially good arable land.

The hilly Middleveld, between 600 and 1000 metres altitude, covers 26 per cent of the land, with a rainfall on average of 900 mm. Unlike the heavily-forested Highveld, this region is primarily used for agriculture.

The Lowveld, 300–600 metres high occupies 36 per cent of the country, the largest region, with a substantially lower rainfall average of 700 mm. Until recently, it was relatively sparsely populated, but the expansion of plantations and of Individual Tenure Farms in this region, has increased its importance and the environmental pressure on it.

The Lubombo Plateau in the eastern edge of the country rises again to the altitude of the Middleveld and has a similar climate. It is by far the smallest region, accounting for only 8 per cent of the area, and is dominated by small-scale farming.

Swaziland is subdivided into four administrative districts which are not the same as the four ecological zones, as each encompasses more than one of the geographic regions. They are Hhohho in the west with the capital Mbabane, Manzini, Shiselweni in the southern part and Lubombo on the eastern plateau (Figure 7.2).

The climatic region to which Swaziland belongs is made up of the southern part of the African continent together with the adjacent Indian Ocean. Climate is closely related to the relief. Differences in temperature between the Lowveld and the Highveld in summer and winter are considerable, ranging from an average maximum of 30°C or higher to a minimum of well below 2°C in winter in the Lowveld. In the Highveld the range is normally 27°C to -5°C for maximum and minimum in summer and winter, respectively.

Temperatures in the West and in the Highveld Region are almost temperate. In the lower East, temperatures rise and most of the Lowveld is very hot in summer. Almost all parts experience cold nights during winter, with the incidence of frosts.

The normal average rainfall over the entire country is 1000 mm per year although it varies regionally according to the ecological zone. Most rain falls between October and April (Figure 7.3). Swaziland suffered severely from drought in 1981/82 and 1982/83, followed by an extremely destructive cyclone in 1984. All of southern Africa received less rainfall than usual due to the drought which persisted until 1986. The actual rainfall was not adequate enough to sustain pastures, crops or even to satisfy basic household needs. However, 1988 brought a return to normal rainfall levels with above average precipitation.

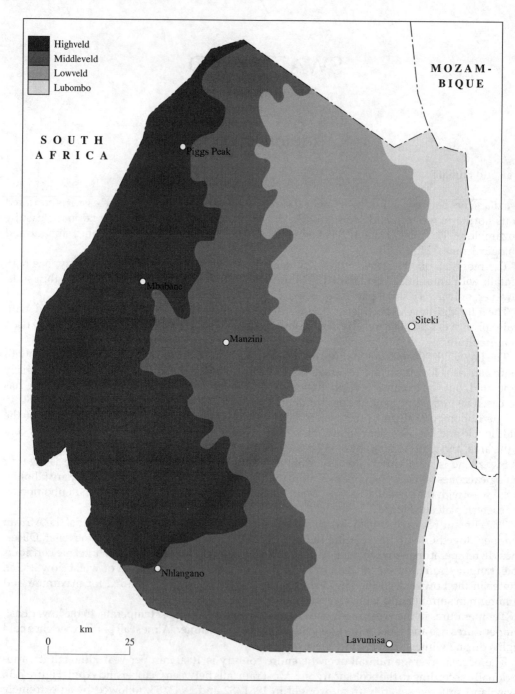

Figure 7.1 *Physical divisions*

Land tenure system

There are basically two forms of land tenure in Swaziland:

- the traditional system of communal property rights; and
- the modern system of private property rights.

Under the traditional system, ownership of land is vested in the king who holds it in trust for the Swazi Nation (Ngwenyama) – this is called Swazi Nation Land (SNL). Private ownership is not recognised. The land is divided into chiefdoms, and the king delegates authority to the chiefs to allocate an arable plot and homestead site to each family in their respective domains. With the introduction of the Rural Development Areas Programme (RDAP), Swazi National Land (SNL), which covers 965,080 hectares, has been divided into rural development areas (RDAs) covering around 50 per cent, with non-RDAs covering 30 per cent, of the Swazi Nation Land. The remaining Swazi Nation Land includes land in trust and other government controlled land.

With Individual Tenure Land (ITL), the freehold system allows absolute rights of ownership to the holder of the land. This land can be bought or sold as the owner sees fit. It is divided into large farms and estates which produce mainly for export. Of the land held under freehold, in 1986 around 40 per cent was held by individual Swazis, another 40 per cent was held by non-Swazis and the remaining 20 per cent was held by major companies, either foreign or Swazi. Table 7.1 shows the principal forms of land use in the two types of land tenure.

Table 7.1 *Land use by land tenure type, 1986 (hectares)*

Landuse category	Whole[1] country	Swazi Nation Land	Individual[2] Tenure Farms
Crop land	164 030	95 518	68 512
Crops	151 307	90 328	60 979
Fallow	12 723	5 190	7 533
Grazing Land[3]	1 165 305	852 750	312 555
Natural veld	1 313 581	852 750	278 831
Improved	33 724	–	33 724
Commercial forests	106 339	–	106 339
Pines	82 805	–	82 805
Others	23 534	–	32 805
Other farm land	49 225	16 812	32 413
All other land	240 161	–	248 916
Total land	1 725 060	965 080	759 980

1 Excludes urban areas of approximately 11,360 hectares
2 Including Sihoya Swazi Nation Land Sugar Project
3 Includes all unallocated communal grazing land and mountains and hills on Swazi Nation Land.

Source: Central Statistical Office, 1986

ECONOMIC STRUCTURE

The labour market of Swaziland is characterised by a workforce which is substantially larger than existing employment opportunities, despite the apparent improvements in the domestic labour market – especially in the private sector – during the last few years.

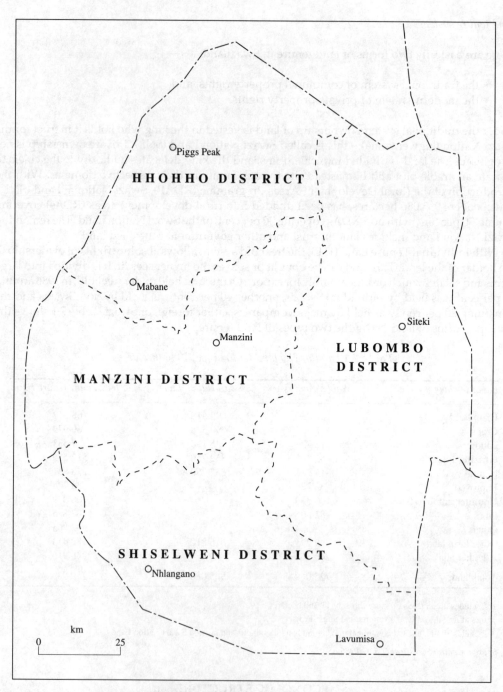

Figure 7.2 *The administrative divisions*

The population of working age, (i.e. those between the ages of 15 and 64) is around 375,000 or about 49 per cent of the total population. About 53 per cent of this group is economically active. The labour force is growing even more rapidly than the population as a whole, largely as a result of the relatively youthful age structure of the population (ILO, 1986).

The number of paid employees was estimated at almost 95,000 in 1987, representing an increase of only 5 per cent since 1981 (see Table 7.2).

Table 7.2 *Estimated paid employment, 1981–1987 (number of employees)*

Sector	1981	1982	1983	1984	1985	1986	1987
Formal employment							
–Private sector	57 243	54 775	54 327	53 605	50 533	53 486	56 629
–Public sector	22 496	22 582	24 246	23 792	22 351	25 635	25 608
Sub total	79 739	77 357	78 573	77 397	72 884	79 121	82 237
Informal employment	10 452	10 873	11 542	11 807	12 341	12 500	12 500
Total	90 191	88 230	90 115	89 204	85 225	91 621	94 737
Growth rate (%)	5.8	-2.2	2.1	-1.0	-4.5	7.5	3.4

Source: Department of Economic Planning and Statistics, 1988

Between 1985 and 1986 paid employment increased by 7.5 per cent, with the largest increase, 43.5 per cent, in the construction sector (see Table 7.3).

Table 7.3 *Employment by sector, 1985–1986*

Sector	% Distribution	% Increase
Agriculture	30.2	0.16
Mining and Quarrying	3.2	1.66
Manufacture	14.3	3.25
Electricity	1.9	7.71
Construction	6.8	43.45
Distribution	9.8	6.07
Transport and Communication	7.4	4.25
Finance	4.5	6.28
Social Services	21.9	3.44

Source: Central Statistical Office of Swaziland, Employment and Wages, 1986

A considerable part of the surplus labour is absorbed by work opportunities in the gold and coal mines of the Republic of South Africa. The number of Swazis recruited for work in South African mines has risen from 11,043 in 1981 to 18,138 in 1986 (Table 7.4). This represents around 15 per cent of Swaziland's male labour force (ILO, 1986). While *de jure* temporary employees, workers in these mines in fact find permanent positions as they are presented with 12-month contracts. The miners are in Swaziland for less than two months between follow-up contracts.

These miners' remittances constitute around 11 per cent of Swaziland's Gross National Product and, with that, Swaziland's ability to maintain the current level of imports is considerably assisted.

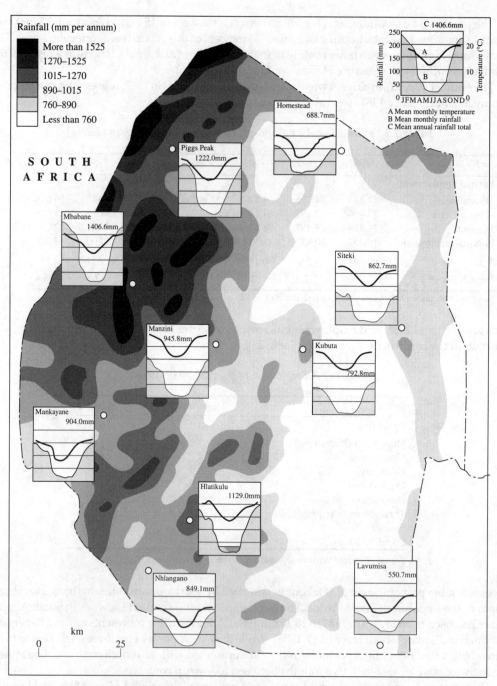

Figure 7.3 *Rainfall patterns*

Table 7.4 *Swazis recruited for South African mines (number of employees)*

Year	Gold mines	Coal mines	Other	Total
1981	10 076	764	203	11 043
1982	12 081	1 406	203	13 690
1983	12 108	1 401	225	13 734
1984	13 693	1 710	260	15 663
1985	14 293	1 523	372	16 188
1986	15 963	1 461	714	18 138

Source: Central Statistical Office of Swaziland, Employment and Wages, 1986

Employment in traditional sectors, predominantly farming, is shown in the table below. The total active farm population grew from 46.3 per cent to 56.3 per cent of the paid workforce between 1982 and 1985. During this period, the rate of increase was fastest in the Highveld Region (36.8 per cent) compared with the other areas.

Table 7.5 *Employment in the traditional sector by region, 1985 (Percentages shown in brackets)*

Region	Unpaid family workers (%)	Paid workers (%)	Total active farm population (%)	Total farm population (%)
Highveld	84 513	1 723	86 236	123 197
	(68.6)	(1.4)	(70.0)	(100)
Middleveld	98 835	1 396	100 231	190 838
	(51.8)	(0.7)	(52.5)	(100)
Lowveld	49 760	1 751	51 511	103 022
	(48.3)	(1.7)	(50.0)	(100)
Lubombo	14 823	521	15 344	32 650
	(45.4)	(1.6)	(47.0)	(100)
Total	247 931	5 391	253 322	449 707
	(55.1)	(1.2)	(56.3)	(100)

Source: Central Statistical Office of Swaziland, Employment and Wages, 1986

One outcome of the Household Energy Survey (GTZ, 1989) which studied the socio-economic background of a range of households, was evidence that a substantial number of people in rural areas frequently seek part-time job opportunities in sectors other than agriculture, especially in the rural informal sector. People are forced to take on additional work to augment the low income earned through the traditional activities in agriculture. This part-time work often involves the processing of natural resources, such as brewing, woodwork, rural construction and services, pottery and weaving.

Macroeconomic parameters

Swaziland's geopolitical position seriously affects its macroeconomy, which is overwhelmingly dominated by the economy of South Africa. Swaziland's dependence on South Africa is indicated, in part, by its membership in the South African Customs Union (SACU) – together with Botswana and Lesotho – which ensures that goods and capital can be freely exchanged between the member countries.

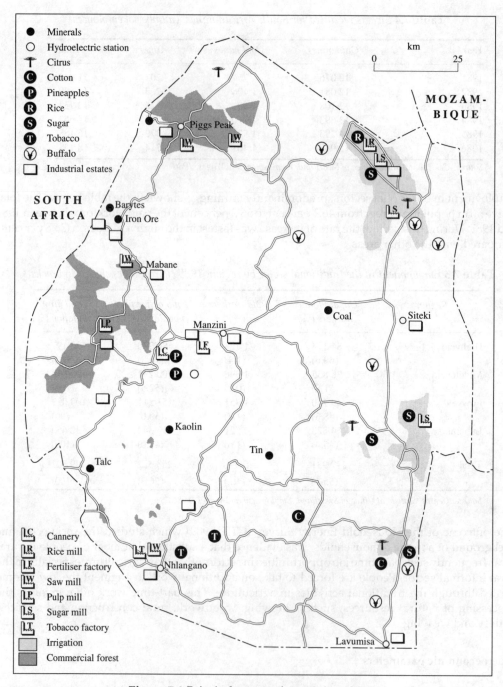

Figure 7.4 *Principal centres of economic activity*

Table 7.6 gives a statistical summary of Swaziland's economic performance for the period 1981–1985. The variations in overall annual growth rates of GDP are largely due to rainfall conditions and the success or failure of the harvests. It should also be noted that, although total GDP increased by an annual average of 3.5 per cent because of an annual rate of population increase of 3.2 per cent, the per capita GDP growth rate was no more than 0.3 per cent over the period. As a summary, Figure 7.4 shows the distribution of the principal centres of economic activity in the country.

Table 7.6 *Gross Domestic Product at factor cost by sector of origin 1981–1985*
at constant 1980 prices (E 000)

Sector	1981	1982	1983	1984	1985	Share of GDP 1981–85 (%)	Annual growth rate 1981–85 (%)
Agriculture	95 709	90 614	90 303	90 358	102 321	23.1	3.8
– Crop production on SNL	16 774	9 331	6 849	16 600	20 100	3.4	4.3
– Crop production in ITF	57 777	59 628	60 106	62 007	59 745	14.6	3.6
– Other agriculture	21 158	21 655	23 348	16 751	22 476	5.1	3.8
Forestry	5 844	5 849	4 859	4 816	4 800	1.3	-2.1
Mining (ex. Iron ore)	14 636	12 763	10 719	11 248	11 697	3.0	-3.6
Manufacturing	88 378	92 996	93 952	93 474	94 031	22.6	3.4
Construction	18 702	18 851	16 905	16 419	17 929	4.3	2.0
Wholesale, retail, hotels and restaurants	35 366	41 931	45 510	45 785	43 824	10.4	4.2
Transport and communication	21 420	41 446	22 163	23 212	24 721	5.5	3.8
Banking, insurance, real Estate etc.	26 155	26 432	26 930	27 342	26 648	6.5	2.5
Owner-occupied dwellings	15 750	15 969	16 047	16 140	16 249	3.9	0.8
Government services	66 081	71 522	69 810	78 735	79 041	17.8	5.3
Other	5 583	5 768	5 725	7 094	8 875	1.6	8.4
Total GDP at factor cost	393 624	404 141	402 923	419 605	430 136	100.0	3.5
Annual GDP growth rate (%)	8.6	2.7	-0.3	4.1	2.5	–	–

NB: Totals may not add due to rounding.

Currency E = 1 Emalangeni=1 South African rand

Source: Annual Statistical Bulletin, (1986)

ENVIRONMENTAL ISSUES

Rapid population growth

In any discussion of environmental problems, rapid population growth must be taken into consideration. Swaziland, like other developing countries, is currently experiencing a high rate of population growth. Over the period 1976–86 an average annual growth rate of 3.2 per cent was recorded, an increase from an annual average of 2.8 per cent over the period 1966–76. Thus the population has almost doubled in 22 years. The determinants of the rising population growth lie primarily in the relationship between the birth and death rates. The birth rate in this country has, for several reasons, increased while the death rate has declined. Life expectancy has correspondingly increased from an average of 44 years in 1966 to 46.5 years in 1976 and to 53 years for males and 60 years for females in 1986.

Table 7.7 *Population growth ,1976–1989*

| Area | Population (000) | | | | Annual growth |
	1976	Per cent	1986	Per cent	Per cent
Swaziland	520	100.0	712	100.0	3.2
Resident population	495	95.1	681	95.6	3.2
Temporary absentees	25	4.9	31	4.4	2.0
Rural population	414	79.9	557	78.2	3.0
Total urban	106	20.4	155	21.8	3.9
Greater Manzini	29	5.6	46	6.5	4.7
Mbabane	23	4.4	38	5.4	5.0
Other urban areas	54	10.4	71	9.9	2.7

Source: *Government of Swaziland, Annual Statistical Bulletin, 1991*

Tables 7.7 and 7.8 illustrate past trends and project future population growth. Table 7.7 shows population growth in rural and urban areas, and Table 7.8 shows population projections to the year 2006.

Table 7.8 *Population projections, 1986–2006 (000)*

Area	1986	1991	1996	2001	2006	1986–2001(%)	2001–2006(%)
Swaziland	712	837	985	1158	1310	3.2	3.1
Rural population	557	649	756	879	971	3.1	2.0
Total	155	188	229	279	339	4.0	4.0
Urban population							
Greater Manzini	46	60	79	102	129	5.2	4.8
Mbabane	38	51	67	88	113	5.5	5.1
Other urban areas	71	82	95	110	127	3.0	3.0
towns <5000	40	49	60	73	89	4.0	4.0
towns >5000	31	33	35	37	38	1.1	0.5

When the population grows in developing countries, the livestock population almost always increases commensurately in order to expand food supplies, family wealth and security. As the number of cattle multiplies, grass cover deteriorates. Overgrazing by goats causes even more damage as it affects trees and shrubs as well. Figures presented elsewhere in this report are indicative of the fact that Swaziland's livestock population is unacceptably high. Overgrazing, combined with deforestation, produces land degradation in rural areas, thus exacerbating soil erosion.

As the human population has grown over the past century, the indigenous forests have receded. The two principal causes of deforestation are directly linked to population growth, land clearing for agriculture and wood gathering for fuel. The cutting of trees for building purposes is a third, but less significant, source of deforestation.

The rapid population growth rate becomes an environmental issue when we consider that the country's population will probably double by the year 2006, yet the country's total land area will remain the same. This means that the population will put tremendous pressure on the country's environmental resources and further exacerbate current environmental problems.

Sex ratio

One of the peculiarities of the population composition is the low sex ratio, i.e. the number of males per 100 females. Swaziland had a sex ratio of 90 male residents per 100 females in 1986 compared to 88 males at the time of the previous census.

On average between 83 and 85 men per 100 women live on Swazi Nation Land in Rural Development Areas and Non-Rural Development Areas respectively, compared with 95 men in towns and 101 men on Individual Tenure Farms. The highest average sex ratio was recorded in company towns with 137 males per 100 females, due to the fact that most workers staying in company towns leave their families in rural areas.

Regional distribution

Swaziland's population is increasingly concentrated in towns and in urban peripheries especially in the areas of Mbabane and Manzini. Population pressure is mounting in the peri-urban areas around the district capitals. The population distribution by district and land tenure type is presented in Table 7.9. The Manzini District continues to be the most populated region with over 28 per cent of the total population, followed by Hhohho (26.5 per cent), Shiselweni (22.8 per cent) and Lubombo (22.5 per cent). Almost 70 per cent of the total population lived on Swazi Nation Land in 1986, of which over 40 per cent resided in Rural Development Areas. Eight per cent of Swaziland's population lives on Individual Tenure Farms and 22 per cent are urban.

A more meaningful variable than the total population is the population density per km^2 and – because the majority of the people subsist on agriculture – probably the most significant indicator would be the population per km^2 in rural and urban areas. This information is given in Table 7.10 and Figure 7.5.

The average population density of Swaziland is 35 persons per km^2 which represents a 22 per cent increase over the 1976 figure of 28.5 persons per km^2. The density per km^2 in rural areas is 52 persons per km^2 while in urban centres and outskirts it is some 784 persons per km^2. For the whole of Swaziland, population density is highest in the Middleveld areas of the Shiselweni and Hhohho Districts. The highest pressure in urban areas is within the municipal boundary of the capital Mbabane and in the Middleveld in the Greater Manzini area.

Soil erosion

The main causes of Swaziland's soil erosion problem are the overutilisation and misuse of land, and the poor application of conservation practices. The effects of population growth are particularly pronounced on Swazi Nation Land where the land resource is communally used, resulting in a 'tragedy of the commons' situation. The difficulty of this is that community members are more concerned about what would benefit them individually than communally, therefore measures against soil erosion tend to lose their sense of urgency and priority.

Figure 7.5 *Population density , 1986*

Table 7.9 *Population distribution by district and land tenure type 1986*

District and tenure	Number of homesteads	Number of households	1986 Resident population		Average number of people per homestead
			Number	Share (per cent)	
Hhohho					
SNL –RDA	8 869	10 434	61 671	9.1	7.0
–Non RDA	7 842	9 184	56 993	8.4	7.3
ITF	1 731	2 190	10 947	1.6	6.3
Towns, company towns and outskirts	10 164	12 904	49 583	7.3	4.9
Sub-total	28 606	34 712	179 194	26.5	6.3
Manzini					
SNL –RDA	8 170	9 442	60 233	8.9	7.4
–Non RDA	7 720	8 814	57 368	8.5	7.4
ITF	2 175	2 775	16 262	2.4	7.5
Towns, company towns and outskirts	9 597	12 444	56 749	8.4	5.9
Sub-total	27 662	33 475	190 612	28.2	6.9
Shiselweni					
SNL –RDA	12 055	13 917	89 930	13.3	7.5
–Non RDA	5 921	6 732	43 608	6.5	7.4
ITF	1 890	2 228	14 506	2.1	7.7
Towns, company towns and outskirts	1 114	1 594	5 829	0.9	5.2
Sub-total	20 980	24 471	153 873	22.8	7.3
Lubombo					
SNL –RDA	10 979	12 607	76 197	11.3	6.9
–Non RDA	3 431	4 030	24 688	3.7	7.2
ITF	2 666	3 124	14 885	2.2	5.6
Towns, company towns and outskirts	7 991	11 417	36 640	5.4	4.6
Sub-total	25 067	31 178	152 410	22.5	6.1
Swaziland					
SNL –RDA	40 073	46 400	288 031	42.6	7.2
–Non RDA	20 914	28 760	182 657	27.0	7.3
ITF	8 462	10 317	56 600	8.4	6.7
Towns, company towns and outskirts	28 866	38 359	148 801	22.0	5.2
Sub-total	102 315	123 836	676 089	100.0	6.6

Source: Department of Economic Planning and Statistics, 1988

Table 7.10 *Population density by land tenure and district (1986)*

District and tenure	Area (km²)	Population	Density (pop/km²)
Rural: Swazi Nation Land			
Hhohho	1 836.1	118 664	64.6
Manzini	1 987.0	117 601	59.2
Shiselweni	1 966.8	133 538	67.9
Lubombo	3 256.7	100 885	31.0
Total	9 046.7	470 688	52.0
Individual Tenure Farms			
Hhohho	1 671.1	10 947	6.6
Manzini	1 987.6	16 262	8.2
Shiselweni	1 794.0	14 506	8.1
Lubombo	2 675.0	14 885	5.6
Total	8 127.8	56 600	7.0
Urban Areas			
Hhohho	62.2	49 583	797.2
Manzini	93.8	56 749	605.0
Shiselweni	18.6	5 829	313.4
Lubombo	15.3	36 640	2 394.8*
Total	189.9	148 801	783.6
Swaziland	17 364.3	676 089	35.0

* This figure represents the company towns in the sugar belt of Lubombo (Big Ben, Mhlume, Simunye etc.).
The high growth rate of company towns in Lubombo is suspected to be due to an under-recording in 1976 (Swaziland, *Economic Review*, 1988).

Source: Central Statistical Office, Annual Statistical Bulletin, 1986, and author's calculations.

Another reason for the poor application of effective conservation measures on communal land is that conservation has long-term benefits while land users need immediate returns. Land degradation is more pronounced on rangelands as a result of overgrazing. The increase in population results in more land being put to residential use thus reducing available grazing land, whilst at the same time the number of livestock increases. Both these factors work together to cause land degradation and result in vegetation being depleted and the top soil being susceptible to soil erosion. The growing of food required to feed the people on limited arable land results in over-exploitation of the arable land and thus requires careful management practices if it is to remain productive. In short, land degradation of Swazi Nation Land is the result of vegetation depletion on rangelands and the growth of settlement areas. On arable land soil erosion is due to monocropping and poor land management.

The average cropland area per homestead is declining due to pressure from over-population. In some areas of the Highveld, population pressure has led to the cultivation of marginal land on steeper slopes, resulting in serious soil erosion and the siltation of reservoirs.

The principle of not cultivating steep slopes has been well established and this practice has helped the problem. However, recently conservation measures seem to be receiving less attention, and this is manifested by increasing erosion problems on arable land. Therefore, a soil conservation earthworks project is in operation to protect arable land.

Grasslands

Swaziland's grasslands are still abundant and varied although they are increasingly being threatened. The major problem facing the grasslands is that of range degradation. Range degradation is a term that encompasses all the symptoms of the deteriorating state of the grasslands in terms of providing forage for livestock, mainly cattle, sheep and goats.

The most readily detectable symptoms of degradation are the adverse changes in species diversity and an increase in bare ground. Adverse changes in species diversity may involve an increase in less palatable grasses and the encroachment of wood species which cannot be utilised by livestock.

The main cause of degradation in Swaziland's rangelands is the high stock density. The available grazing land averages 1.6 ha per livestock unit with the range varying between 0.9 ha in the Middleveld to 2.8 ha in the Lowveld.

Available grazing land to support the increasing livestock population has been decreasing since the early 1940s. Also the increase in human population has resulted in a large number of settlements encroaching into the rangelands which were previously used for grazing. These lands are quickly being turned into crop fields. The Middleveld has been the most severely affected area and in some places has reached a stocking level of 0.9 ha per livestock unit. Coupled with the high rainfall levels in the area, the resulting levels of soil erosion have been severe.

Plantation agriculture is another cause of shrinking rangeland resources. Pineapple and citrus plantations have occupied most of the Middleveld. In the Lowveld, high-income crops such as sugar cane and cotton are taking over grazing lands. In the Highveld, forestry, which is a leading foreign exchange earner, has been taking up more and more of the open grassland.

Bush encroachment is another phenomenon reducing the productivity of the country's grasslands. Large tracts in the Middleveld and Lowveld are being encroached upon by impenetrable thickets of bush, mainly acacias and *Dycrostachys* spp. These thickets completely overshadow the herbaceous layer, making it inaccessible to animals, and thus further reducing the stocking capacity. This problem has been evident since the early 1960s and attempts have been made to eradicate the bush. It is regrettable, however, to note that in some of these areas the problem is still increasing.

Forests

In certain parts of the country Swaziland is fortunate in possessing a physical environment which is well suited to the cultivation of forests. The deep fertile soils and the near-temperate climate of the Highveld and parts of the Middleveld provide ideal conditions for the growing of trees such as gums and conifers. Pulp-wood is harvested on average after 16 years of growth in comparison with 40 years in Northern Europe.

The total woodland area covers about 365,416 ha or 32 per cent of the land area of Swaziland. A little over 100,000 ha are under man-made forests. The indigenous forest cover has been steadily diminishing as a result of overstocking, perennial burning of the veld, the establishment of large-scale agricultural schemes, an increase in the demand for firewood, building poles, wood carvings, traditional uses, prospecting for minerals, and urban and other physical infrastructural development. The steady decline of indigenous forests has resulted in socio-economic problems ranging from acute firewood shortages to serious environmental degradation. This is of particular concern since Swaziland's rural population depends on firewood as a main source of energy.

Factors contributing to the decline of biological diversity

Factors which one can identify as being responsible for the decline of biodiversity in Swaziland are common to most countries in the world. The widest impacts are due to agro-industry such as sugar cane and timber plantations and intense subsistence farming and settlement. The former result in cultural 'green deserts', unfavourable to most local species of fauna, and usually annihilating indigenous flora. The latter results in the destruction of most larger mammals, either for human consumption or due to competition, and the eradication of the more specialised or sensitive species of animal due to habitat destruction. Threats to flora occur through the clearing of fields, the cutting of constructional timber, and the selective pressures on species used in traditional medicines. The persistent use of chemicals such as Lindane, Dieldrin, DDT, Gramoxane, Parathion and Malathion has been evident throughout much of the country. The adverse long-term effects of most of these have been demonstrated elsewhere, but there is little information on the environmental outcome of their continued use in Swaziland.

The main area of pollution which can be identified in Swaziland, other than that caused by pesticides, is water pollution. As a consequence of major industrial expansion, rivers in Swaziland are increasingly susceptible to occasional accidental releases of chemical pollutants. Nutrient enrichment, with accompanying eutrophication, is liable to occur as a consequence of run-off effluent from agro-industrial fields, from factories, and from inadequate sewage facilities in human settlements. Furthermore, since not all of Swaziland's main river systems originate in the country, pollution may originate outside the country's borders.

One of the prime problems affecting the country's rivers is an increased sediment load resulting from soil erosion. This has the dual effect of smothering plants and invertebrates, and markedly changing the nature of the fish species to those species adapted to sediment feeding. Certain rare fish species occurring in Swaziland such as *Opsaridium zambezense* and various *Chiloglanis* species are likely to be eliminated by increased sediment loading.

Local usage of biological resources has increased with population growth threatening certain species. For example, *Breonadia microcephala* and *Bolusanthus specious*, two species of indigenous trees, are threatened due to their use for building in rural areas. Most species of indigenous trees are at risk due to the heavy utilisation of living trees for firewood in the absence of suitable alternative biomass fuels.

The commercialisation of traditional medicine has resulted in the over-utilisation of a variety of plants, for example, *Eucomis autumnalis* and *Kniphofia tysonii lebomboensis* which occurs in just one highly restricted locality in Swaziland. In addition, the commercial exploitation of plants and animals for export is a problem; examples include birds, reptiles and amphibians for the pet trade, rhino horn for traditional medicine in Asia, and cycads as garden plants. The last may have resulted in the extinction of *Encephalartos heenanii* in Swaziland.

The limitations of National Parks in conserving biodiversity

The limitations of natural reserves as agents of conservation of biodiversity in Swaziland are mainly due to their small area, making them inadequate for the maintenance of minimum viable populations of many species. Certain organisms, particularly large bird species, cannot be confined to such small areas and are therefore unlikely to survive in Swaziland. Furthermore, due to their non-contiguous distribution, the present natural reserves in Swaziland are in danger of becoming islands of biodiversity, making them highly susceptible to negative influences.

For the National Trust Commission to oversee the reserves in Swaziland, additional provision for research is needed. Currently there is only one research officer employed within the commission which limits its ability to carry out necessary research. In addition, increased staffing would allow for better management of the reserves.

Pollution of water resources

The agricultural sector

Agricultural inputs such as fertilisers, herbicides and insecticides are the main sources of the contamination of water resources. Amongst the array of pesticides used Endosulphan, Dieldrin, DDT organophosphates such as Aldicarb, Parathion and Monocrotophos which have restricted use or have been banned in their countries of origin. The indiscriminate dumping of highly-dangerous sodium arsenite as a means of disposing of it in some remote rural locations also gives cause for concern.

In 1987 an ecotoxicity survey was conducted on the Mlumati river, which flows through agricultural estates. Widespread toxicity was noted downstream of the estates. In December 1990 there was also a report of fish kills accompanied by reports of gastro-intestinal tract disorders in settlements downstream. This implies that further studies are needed to assess the true impacts of such chemicals on the environment and on human health. The benefits derived from using these chemicals, such as the reduction of malaria, must also be considered when assessing the need for their continued use. Perhaps the laws governing the importation, handling and disposal of these dangerous pesticides need strengthening and stronger enforcement by the relevant authorities.

The industrial sector

The major industries that produce potentially hazardous wastes are the textile, craft and paper mills. Swaziland's pulp mill, which has been in existence since 1961, needs careful monitoring. Several incidents of fish kills downstream from the mill have been reported. In one incident, the causative agent was conclusively identified as tail oil which had escaped from a burst storage dam and infiltrated the nearby river. Recently reported fish kills were considered to have arisen as a result of infiltration into the aquatic ecosystem of escaped phenolic products, a major by-product in water gas production. The fish kills were localised in the sense that they affected only a small portion of the stream. The consequence of this disaster was an increase in the penalty for pollution offences and the intensification of the water pollution inspectorate coverage.

Commercial sector

The main sources of hazardous materials in the commercial sector are photographic and dry-cleaning establishments and automobile garages. The effluents from these are poured down the drains and make their way into the public sewerage system where they disrupt the biological treatment process by killing the bacteria. In other instances, the effluent is disposed of in the municipal solid waste dump where it leaches and subsequently pollutes the groundwater. An additional concern is that of people scavenging in waste dumps thereby exposing themselves to serious health hazards.

Inadequate sanitation and access to safe drinking water and solid waste disposal

Responsibility for water and sanitation is shared between the Water and Sewerage Board, the Ministry of Health, and Town Councils. The promotion of clean water supplies and basic sanitation constitute one of the principal elements of the National Health Policy. National policies and strategies for water supply and sanitation have been prepared. A technical sub-group has been formed consisting of officers from various ministries which meets regularly to co-ordinate activities in the field of water and sanitation.

The rural community suffers from a high prevalence of water-borne and water-related diseases, such as typhoid, cholera, malaria and bilharzia. The cholera outbreak of 1981/82 further emphasised the dangerous nature of water contact diseases. A total of 767 cases and 31 deaths were confirmed during this crisis. Another water-related disease affecting a large portion of the rural population, about 30 per cent of children of school age, is bilharzia. These diseases are most severe in the Lowveld and parts of the Middleveld, where water, even from natural sources such as springs and rivers, is scarce and often contaminated by human and animal wastes. This has resulted in high mortality rates, especially amongst children, and therefore a low life expectancy at birth.

Poor maintenance of water and sanitation facilities has led to the user not gaining maximum benefit. The use of different standards of construction has again led to problems in the operation and maintenance of facilities. As more community members are trained in maintenance and operation, some of these problems are being alleviated. Inadequate funding continues to be a major constraint in the fulfilment of the goal of providing adequate water and sanitation by the year 2000.

Water supply and sanitation

The provision of safe water for rural communities has risen from 20 per cent in 1976 to approximately 50 per cent of households in 1989. Access to sanitation facilities has risen from 15 per cent in 1976 to 40 per cent in 1989. This illustrates that many people still use contaminated sources of water and do not have access to sanitary excreta-disposal facilities. The prevalence of diarrhoeal and other water-related diseases is not surprisingly highest in the Lowveld region where access to water and sanitation is poorest.

Solid waste disposal

In some cases solid waste from hotels and private houses is dumped in deeply-eroded dongas draining into major streams. There is no clear mechanism to control such practices. In the case of industry, uncontrolled dumping takes place in municipal landfill sites. Uncontrolled dumping in urban areas is especially problematic as scavengers commonly comb these sites looking for food and other items.

Urban water supply and sanitation

The Water and Sewerage Board supplies water to urban areas, some of which have water-borne sewerage systems. At present, 63 per cent of urban households have a mains water supply and 12 per cent are converted to a water-borne sewerage system. The main sanitary disposal system is septic tanks, whilst pit latrines are concentrated mostly in the peri-urban areas.

Mineral resources and the environment

The environmental consequences of mining are firstly those related to the day to day operations of the mines, and secondly those that bring about an irreversible change in the long term. The immediate environmental impacts generated by mining projects include air pollution, the degrading of surface water and groundwater resources, the alteration of the landscape, ground subsidence, damage to other minerals, and pollution from dumps and tailings ponds, whose composition and stability is often unknown.

The long-term impacts are mainly the visual impacts of landscape alteration. Examples of these are old workings which constitute sink shafts, pits, holes and other excavations. The old gold mines in the north- west of the country present a serious problem because their exact locations and mine history are not documented. Producing mines have excavation faces, discard dumps, slime dams, and stockpiles. It is worth noting that mines closed in the last two decades had restoration plans but none of them have been put into effect. The main mining activities are for the extraction of asbestos, coal and diamonds.

Asbestos

Asbestos fibre pollutes the air and risks the lives of both the miners and the people in the immediate neighbourhood. For the latter, risks can be reduced by geographically removing the residential area from the mining sites. In addition, rehabilitation of the dump sites is necessary. Dust control is practised in the mines and all the occupational exposures are routinely measured. Low exposure levels are observed in most of the working environments. Occupational exposures for the mine employees are reduced by the use of protective measures such as respirators and appropriate clothing. However, this leaves the non-occupational majority unprotected. Non-occupational exposure is more hazardous as the short fibres are blown from the dry, uncovered waste dumps into the residential areas near the mine.

Fibre blown away from the waste dumps on dry windy days is deposited in water catchment areas and runs off into streams during the rainy season. It has been reported that fibre concentrates and a lack of aquatic organisms are found in the areas around the mines. Acid mine water is not a cause for concern since there is a high water table which causes the dilution of the very minute quantities of minerals.

Asbestos mining and milling procedures cause some release of fibres into the air. Exposure to these fibres leads to the progressive formation of fibrous tissue which causes severe breathing difficulties or cardiac failure, although a detailed breakdown of related health statistics is not available.

Coal

The general population is exposed to pollution from coal mining at two stages: at the mine, and along the haulage roads. Coal miners face occupational hazards due to cave-ins, explosions and incurable lung diseases such as black lung. Although water micro-sprays and mine ventilation are used at the faces to reduce the dust levels, respiratory problems can be experienced at the end of a mine visit. Water pollution from the process chemicals (mostly magnetite) is suspected when process water is discarded into the nearby streams. On the haulage roads particulate matter from coal gets dispersed into the air which is deleterious to the health of the general public.

Diamonds

Diamond mining causes an environmental threat through landscape degradation and through the processing of the clays. The fines are water-retaining, thereby making it difficult for the slime dams to dry. Therefore, additional land is required, causing vegetation to be cleared, and deforestation to occur.

Industrial minerals

Only a few of Swaziland's industrial minerals have been mined. These include ball clays, kaolin, talc, pyrophilite, diaspore, barytes, silica, sillimanite, and building and ornamental stone. Landscape degradation is the major environmental problem, although dust levels are also a concern. Mining generated about 5 per cent by value of Swaziland's export revenues by the late 1980s. Weak environmental controls probably encourage inward investment in this sector of the economy. However, the cost in terms of human life, health and environmental damage must not be ignored and stronger environmental protection must be sought.

Transboundary air pollution

The Eastern Transvaal region of South Africa has diverse industries, some of which emit gases which are harmful to human health and vegetation, pollute water sources and affect soils adversely, resulting in lower crop production. The main polluting industries are power stations, brick works, ferro-alloy works, steel works foundries, sawmills, paper and pulp mills and petrochemical plants.

Inventories of atmospheric sources of pollution made during 1983 and updated during 1984 show the following overall emissions (tonnes per annum) in the Eastern Transvaal for 1984.

Table 7.11 *Industrial emissions in the eastern Transvaal (tonnes per annum)*

Particulates	374 692
Sulphur Dioxide	1 038 556
Nitrogen Dioxide	355 246
Carbon Monoxide	339 574
Hydrocarbons	276 503
Carbon Dioxide	123 605 162

The issue to address is: of the emissions that are dangerous to the environment, at what levels, or in what quantities do they reach Swaziland? Up to the present there has been a lack of national research undertaken to establish the presence, amounts and types of transboundary air pollution. If, however, research on this problem revealed a threat to both human and plant life it could be found that in economic terms transboundary pollution is costly. The challenge to Swaziland is to evolve strategies urgently to tackle this problem with a view of determining to what extent transboundary pollution is taking place and how it affects Swaziland.

If transboundary air pollutants have a marked effect on health, the occurrence of diseases associated with their presence such as lung diseases (bronchitis, emphysema and asthma) would be noted by the health service. Government statistics currently show that these diseases do not occur in sufficiently alarming proportions to cause concern as yet. However, more definitive research is needed. Co-operation with transboundary research teams is necessary to evolve strategies to determine the extent of foreign emissions affecting Swaziland's environment and inhabitants.

Acid deposition

Studies undertaken by several agencies on different types of soils have revealed that acidity of soils has a very important economic bearing on crop production, particularly maize which is the staple food of Swazi people.

Soil acidity as shown in Table 7.12 is not only of concern for crop production but it is also of increasing concern as a factor in environmental pollution. Acid deposition is a problem through its effect on the stability of minerals. Most minerals in soil become increasingly unstable with a decrease in soil pH resulting in dissolution and thus the release of a variety of ions into the solution, some of which are toxic.

Causes of soil acidity

The causes of soil acidity are numerous, but of particular concern is the anthropogenic disruption of the environment through actions such as the combustion of certain fossil fuels and the disposal of municipal sewage. The burning of fossil fuel releases sulphur dioxide into the atmosphere which gives rise to acid rain. Oxides of nitrogen also contribute to acid rain when the oxides react with hydroxyl radicals in the atmosphere to form nitric acid. These reactions contribute to the acidification of soils.

It has been observed that farmers who use lime in correct quantities reap better harvests than those who use inadequate amounts or no lime at all. Research shows that the level of improvement in yields when lime is applied can be up to 30–35 per cent. However, the costs and transport of lime are constraints which particularly affect the small poorer farmer. Acid deposition may therefore be of economic significance in the context of self-sufficiency in staple foods.

Briefly, it could be stated that acid deposition in the soil is counter-productive to crop and food production. Unless acid deposition can be controlled in the future, Swaziland will have to import larger quantities of foodstuffs including maize. Unfortunately, the costs of control are too high for the average Swazi farmer to meet. It is important to conduct further research on the sources giving rise to soil acidity and on more cost-efficient means of controlling it.

Table 7.12 *Acidity of soils in Swaziland (pH)*

Physiographic regions	Number of samples	Minimum	Maximum	Mean	Standard dry
Highveld	490	3.0	7.4	4.5	0.5
Moist Middleveld	389	3.0	6.3	4.7	0.5
Dry Middleveld	153	4.0	6.1	4.9	0.5
Lubombo	14	4.0	5.9	5.2	0.6
Lowveld	47	3.0	6.0	4.9	0.7
Country	1093	3.0	7.4	4.6	0.6

Source: Government of Swaziland, Annual Statistical Bulletin, 1990

Urban air pollution

Comprehensive research on urban air pollution in Swaziland has not yet been undertaken. As such no actual figures exist to quantify the volumes of pollution. However, fossil fuels used both in industry and domestically, together with the increased use of petrol and diesel combustion engines, indicate that urban air pollution occurs and is a growing health hazard.

Chemical pollutants from local industries affect the cleanliness of urban air in different ways depending on the toxic materials and gases produced. In addition, the gases that are emitted in the Eastern Transvaal Highveld in South Africa most likely contribute to some extent to levels of urban air pollution in Swaziland. Larger towns such as Manzini and Mbabane have dry cleaners that use coal which produces particulates and emit gases which pollute the air. The chemical solvents contain chloro-compounds and emit chlorofluorocarbons which threaten the ozone layer. Sawdust from several furniture factories, spray paint gases and fumigas also contribute to air pollution.

As Swaziland develops, the presence of pollutants could increase to the level of being a health hazard. This should be of great concern to the country in that it will affect the people as well as the economy of the country, in the form, for example, of reduced productivity and the need for a larger medical budget. Swaziland clearly requires measuring and monitoring facilities to register and record the levels of pollutants in urban air.

THE PRESENT RESOURCE BASE AND LEGAL INSTITUTIONS

The natural resource base

The Highveld is the wettest of the four physiographic regions occupying almost 20 per cent of the total land area and receiving an average annual rainfall of 1200 mm. The rainy season lasts from October to March and the temperature is modified by altitude. It is very mountainous with steep slopes and an average gradient exceeding 18 per cent. It is underlain by granite gneiss and other ancient igneous and metamorphic rocks. The soils have multiple deficiencies of phosphorous, calcium, magnesium and trace elements. Only 3 per cent has good soil suitable for intensive agriculture on gentle to moderate slopes. Another 7 per cent has fair soil for arable farming. Almost all the man-made forests in the country are in the Highveld.

The Middleveld is a hilly region and occupies 25 per cent of the total area. It lies at an average of 700 m above mean sea level with a mean slope of 12 per cent. The hilly landscape contains three symmetrically-located areas of lower relief, namely the Lomati valley in the north, the Geodgegun-Civide upland in the south and the Ezulwini-Malkerns-Mtilane 'horseshoe' of undulating land in the centre, which is the largest of the three. The lower elevations of the Middleveld have a much greater proportion of quartzose, resistant rocks than the upper elevations, where rock formations weather more easily and develop into commonly-found deep soils. Most of the soils are Kaolisols inherently not very productive. Exposed rock covers about 21 per cent of the upper Middleveld and 34 per cent of the lower Middleveld. Lithosols, which are very shallow and predominantly from quartzose rocks, occupy about 25 per cent of both the upper and lower Middleveld. The upper Middleveld has approximately 15 per cent of good and 4 per cent of fair arable land while the lower Middleveld has about 7 per cent and 3 per cent respectively. The climate is warm and sub-humid. The average annual rainfall is about 940 mm. The Middleveld is the main rain-fed cropping belt of the Kingdom. The major crops include maize, mostly grown for home consumption, and cotton, pineapples and tobacco as cash crops. Irrigation supplements rain- fed crop production.

The Lowveld is a relatively flat region that covers about 37 per cent of the total land area. The average altitude is 200 m and with a mean slope of 3 per cent has the most gentle relief of all the regions. Only isolated hills rise above 400 m and the region is gently undulating. The stratigraphic sequence divides the Lowveld into a western portion founded on Ecca sandstones and shales resting on the archean undermass, with numerous dolerite intrusions and the eastern strip floored by basalt. The climate is hot and dry. The mean annual rainfall is about 700 mm but its effectiveness is reduced by higher evapotranspiration rates than other regions.

The soils are reasonably fertile, especially in the basalt country, but are generally shallow. Clay pans beneath a sandy top soil are found over almost 38 per cent of the western Lowveld, while heavy black or brown vertisols formed from basalt cover 27 per cent of the eastern Lowveld. Nine per cent of the Western Lowveld makes good arable soil and only a further 3 per cent is fair soil. In the Eastern Lowland 18 per cent of the area is covered by good soil and 16 per cent of the soil is fair. Although nearly a third of the Lowveld has lithosols, only 9 per cent is formed of rocky outcrops.

The Lubombo Plateau occupies 8 per cent of the total area and has a mean annual rainfall of 800 mm with an average altitude of 600 m. The Lubombo mountains rise abruptly. The west-facing scarp of the range is unbroken except for the Usutu, Mbuluzi and Ingwavuma gorges. The dipslope has suffered deep dissection. Fifty-nine per cent of the area comprises outcrops, screes or stony land. Rhyolite forms escarpments whilst andesite and tuff underlies the dipslope. Only 9 per cent of the Lubombo range is classed as good arable land, with a further 3 per cent of fair arable quality.

Vegetation

The vegetation types of Swaziland are closely associated with the four main physiographic regions being influenced by variations in soils, climate and topography. The Highveld is occupied by extensive forest plantations of exotic trees, 70 per cent of which are pines. The natural vegetation is dominated by mountain sourveld and highland sourveld. The mountain sourveld, a dense short very sour grassland is found in the north-east escarpment and mountain ranges of the Highveld where it is more moist and subject to less frost than in the plateaux areas. The common grasses include *Themeda triandra, Rendria altera, Ludetia simplex, Monocymbium ceresiliforme* and *Paspalum scrobiculatum. Eragrostis* and *Sprooblus* spp. are common in overgrazed areas. The common trees and shrubs include *Cephalanthus natalensis, Burchellia bubalina* and *Rapanea melanophloeos.*

The Highveld sourveld, a fairly short, sour grassland, slightly less dense than the mountain sourveld, is found in the Highveld plateaux and their rims. The common grasses are *Themeda triandra, Monocymbium ceresiforme, Rendria altera, Loudetia simplex, Hyparrhenia hirta* and *Tristachya leucothrix*. The common trees and shrubs include *Burchellia bubalina, Faurea speciosa, Ekerbergia Pterophylla, Cephalanthus natalensis* and *Cussonia spicata.*

In the Middleveld the predominant natural vegetation is tall grassveld with associated trees and shrubs. Much of the vegetation is disturbed or destroyed by cultivation and overgrazing, causing a sparser grass cover that is more easily eroded than that of the Highveld. The moist tall grassveld is fairly open and moderately sour. Apart from the *Eragrostis* spp., *Sporobolus* spp. and *Cynodon dactylon* common in overgrazed areas, the common grasses include *Hyparrhenia flilipendua, Rendlia altera, Loudetia simplex, Paspalum scrobiculatum, Alloteropsis semialata* and *Eragrostis racemosa*. The most common trees and shrubs include *Acacia karroo, Syzygium cordatum, A. ataxacantha, Measa lancelolata, Vernonia stipulacea* and *Pterocarpus angolensis* found mainly in warm river valleys.

The dry tall grassveld is fairly open grassland dotted with large trees. Tall grasses are dominant in lightly grazed areas with shorter species invading overgrazed areas. Shrubby savanna with dense bush can be noticed in some places. The most dominant common grasses (*Hyparrhenia filipendula* and *H. dissoluta*) are replaced by *Aristida congesta* ssp. *barbicollis, Heteropogon contortus, Pogonarthria squarrosa, Cynodon dactylon* and *Perotis patens*. The common trees and shrubs include *Dichrostachys cinerea, Acacia nilotica, Ficus* spp. *Sclerocarya birrea, Maytenus sengalensis* and *Euclea* spp.

The upland tall grassveld is a sour, open grassland, which in some cases is transitional to Highland sourveld. It is mainly found in the upper Ngwempisi Valley in south-western Swaziland. The common grasses here include *Tristachy leucothrik, Hyparrhenia filipendula, Trachypogon spicatus, Eragrostis racemosa* and *Setaria nigrirostis.*

In the Lowveld the natural vegetation is savanna comprising acacias, broad-leaved trees and tall grasses. The different components of the plant community compete for moisture, nutrients and light. Any destruction of the grasses upsets the natural balance between them and the trees, hence causing bush encroachment.

The lower broad-leaved tree savanna with tall grasses is slightly sour. The common grasses are

Panicum maximum, Themeda trianda, Aristida congesta ssp., *Barbicollis* and *Poganarthria squarrosa.* Common trees and shrubs include *Combretum molle, C. zeyheri, C. apicaluatum, C. transvaalense, C. Suluence, Sclerocarya birrea,* ssp. *caffra, Dichrostachys cinerea, Ficus sycomorus, Pterocarpus rotundifolius, P. angolensis* and *Terminalia sericea.*

The acacia savanna is a tree and shrub savanna varying from open parkland to dense bush. The grasses are sweet and this is good cattle ranching country. However, overgrazing damages the rather sparse sward rapidly and causes bush encroachment. *Themeda triandra* and *Panicum maximum* are the most dominant grasses. In heavily grazed areas *Aristida bipartita, Urochloa mosambicensis,* and *Eragrostis superba* are very common. *Acacia nigrescens, Sclerocarya birrea* ssp. *caffra* and *Dichrostachs cinera* comprise the common trees and shrubs.

The dry acacia savanna is similar to the acacia savanna except that it is slightly warmer and drier. It is found mainly in the south-eastern Lowveld where dense *Acacia gillettiae* thickets occur along dry water courses. The common trees are *Acacia nigrescens, A. rortilis, Sclerocarya birrea* ssp *caffra* and *Acacia wederttzii. Themeda triandra, Panicum maximum, Cenchrus citianz, Alve parvibracteata* and *Sehima galpinii* are the common grasses and succulents.

In the Lubombo Plateau the vegetation is mainly mixed bush and savanna which is extremely variable. Part of the western region is characterised by semi-open grassland interspersed with patches of dense bush and pockets of high forest in the deep ravines. The eastern region is characterised by tree savanna.

In the western part of the Lubombo region *Digitaria didactyla, Themeda triandra* and *Hyparrhenia filipendula* are the common grasses. The common trees and shrubs comprise *Diospyros dichrophll, D. lycioides, Scolopia mundii, nuxia oppositifolia Erythrina lysistemoy, Cussionia spicata, Schlerocarya birrea* ssp. *caffra* and *Acacia davyi.*

In the eastern part of the Lubombo region the main grasses include *Themeda trianda Hyparrhenia* spp., *Bothriocloa insculpta, Cymbopogon excavatus, Tristachya leurothrothrix* and *Cynodon dactylon. Combretum zeyheri, C. molle, Maytenus heterophylla, senegalensis, Acacia nilotica, A. karoo,* and *Gardenia volkensii* ssp. *volker* comprise the common trees and shrubs.

Land use

In the late nineteenth century virtually all of the land in Swaziland was held under land concessions and the indigenous people were technically squatters in their own country. Since then, however, the Swazi Nation has managed to re-possess over 55 per cent of its land. This has been accomplished through laws passed during the colonial period and by land purchase schemes. Under the terms of the Concessions Partition Act 1907, one-third of the country was set aside for the sole and exclusive use and occupation of the Swazi people. Through the Swazi Land Settlement Act 1946, a further 160,642 ha was added to Swazi Nation Land so increasing its proportion to 43 per cent of the land area.

Between 1946 and 1986 approximately 216,200 ha of Individual Tenure Farms were bought through land purchase schemes. This was through the Lifa Fund land purchase programme which was initiated by His Majesty King Sobhuza II in 1946, and the Hobbs land purchase programme which was initiated in 1970 and is financed by the British Government. The farms purchased through these programmes, which cover approximately 12 per cent of the country, have been registered in the name of Ingwenyama, in trust for the Swazi Nation. In effect these farms represent a new type of Swazi Nation Land, i.e. former Individual Tenure Farms that have been brought for the benefit of the Swazi Nation but are not yet administered by the chiefs under Swazi law and custom.

For the purposes of this report, the term Swazi Nation Land refers to both categories of Swazi

Nation Land which now accounts for approximately 60 per cent of the country. The remaining 40 per cent is classified as Individual Tenure Farms. This land category includes land held by freehold title, by concession, and as Crown Land. The third type, Crown Land, is simply land owned and used by the Government.

Crop production

The most important crops in the country include sugar, fruit, cotton and maize which is the staple crop of the nation. Maize production was about 130,000 metric tonnes in the 1989/90 season, a 3.7 per cent decrease over the previous year. The fall in production was due to late planting because of delayed rains.

Total sales of fresh fruit in 1990 increased by about 16.4 per cent to just over 4 million cartons. The increase is attributed to the recovery of orchards which had been hit by severe hailstorms in 1989. Total exports increased by 20 per cent because of increased production and the reopening of the Japanese market. For the current season production is expected to stay at the previous year's level, increasing gradually over the coming years.

Cotton production declined between 1989 and 1990 from 32,538 tonnes to 26,000 tonnes as a result of unfavourable rainfall, especially the drought that lasted from January to the end of the growing season. Adverse weather conditions are likely to have a negative impact on cotton production during the 1990/91 season. Sugar production for the period 1990/91 is estimated at about 497,000 tonnes, an increase of 4.6 per cent.

Livestock

Cattle continue to be dominant in the country's livestock sector. As shown in Table 7.13 the cattle population experienced a significant increase of nearly 5 per cent to some 679,000 between 1985 and 1989. This increase can be attributed to the favourable rainfall pattern which resulted in good grazing, thus increasing the fertility level of the cattle as evidenced by an increase in the calving rate from 35 per cent to 38 per cent. In 1989, 82 per cent of the cattle population was on Swazi Nation Land while the remainder grazed on Individual Tenure Farms.

Table 7.13 *National livestock population, 1985–1988*

	1985	1986	1987	1988	1989	1985–89 Average annual growth (%)
Cattle	648 332	653 222	640 901	639 943	679 188	1.2
Goats	268 422	306 454	311 738	279 516	294 428	2.3
Sheep	29 585	28 034	27 777	19 982	24 803	-4.3
Poultry	665 239	834 115	844 327	869 901	1 200 474	15.9
Pigs	16 333	18 235	21 317	18 039	18 708	3.5
Equines	14 208	15 164	14 384	13 358	13 223	-1.8

Source: Government of Swaziland, Annual Statistical Bulletin, 1991

There was a decline in the mortality rate of cattle from 5 per cent in 1988 to 4.4 per cent in 1989. This can be attributed to the continued dipping programme for cattle and the improved level of awareness of cattle diseases. However, as the drought conditions worsened in many parts of the country during the second half of 1990, there were frequent reports of a considerable increase in the mortality rates of cattle. The cattle offtake rate fell from 15.6 per cent in 1988 to 13.9 per cent the following year, but this rate is likely to have increased in 1990 as a result of increased production by the export abattoir which re-opened in late 1989.

According to the annual livestock census of the Ministry of Agriculture and Co-operatives, the poultry population increased by over 80 per cent during the period 1985–1989. A major expansion of some poultry producers was reported in 1990 which is likely to result in a greater degree of self-sufficiency in poultry, meat and eggs.

Forestry

According to an inventory undertaken in 1990, the total area covered by indigenous forests amounted to 463,500 ha which represent almost 27 per cent of the total land area. Approximately 152,000 ha of this area is classified as bushveld. The total volume of wood in indigenous forests was estimated at 8.6m³.

Man-made forests covered over 100,000 ha (5.8 per cent of the total land area) in 1988 (Table 7.14). Almost 80 per cent of that area was covered by coniferous species which are largely used for the production of wood pulp.

Table 7.14 *Man-made forests in Swaziland, 1988 (ha)*

Species	1982	1988
Coniferous	75 737	79 717
Saligna/Grandis	19 856	16 600
Other gums	2 469	2 209
Wattle	2 657	2 689
Other non-coniferous	197	184
Total	100 916	101 399

Source: Government of Swaziland, Annual Statistical Bulletin, 1991

Water resources

Swaziland has four major river basins, namely the Lusutfu, the Komati, the Mbuluzi and the Ngwavuma. All the rivers originate in South Africa except the Mbuluzi and Ngwavuma. Each river basin is shared either with Mozambique or South Africa or both. Therefore international negotiations are necessary before any water resource development can be undertaken by the country. The three countries have formed a Tripartite Permanent Technical Committee to advise the respective governments on technical matters of common interest relating to water use and availability in any of the basins. Negotiations for the sharing of water resources are based on the Helsinki rules.

Fisheries

Swaziland has a variety of fish species in its ponds, rivers and dams. There is a very high potential for fish farming but to date, exploitation of the resource is very limited. The Ministry of Agriculture and Cooperatives is to establish some aquaculture centres in order to demonstrate the possibilities of fish farming to rural communities as a source of additional income and as an important source of nutrition for the population.

Flora and fauna

Swaziland is not 'big game' country, although some of the larger mammals do exist in small numbers in a few small reserves. Swaziland's major wildlife contribution is a superb variety of flora and habitats. Swaziland's large number of bird species testify to the degree of diversity of habitat found within its borders; over 500 bird species have been identified in the country, as many as in Botswana, which is 40 times larger.

The four physiographic regions of Swaziland enable it to support this wide diversity of flora and fauna. Of those groups well-studied, approximately 50 species of large mammals have been recorded in Swaziland and an equivalent number of small mammal species (although data is scanty for the latter group). The large mammals include such important endangered species as the black rhino *Diceros bicornis*, and the white rhino *Certotherium simum*, both of which have been reintroduced to parts of Swaziland. Other reintroductions of large mammals such as the elephant *Loxodon africana* have occurred in small numbers and current plans are in existence to reintroduce the lion *Panthera leo* to Hlane. Of the indigenous large mammals a number of rare species occur in Swaziland but detailed information is lacking as to their numbers. These include the samongo monkey *Cercopithecus mitis*, Meller's mongoose *Rhychogale melleri* and the hippopotamus *Hippopotamus amphibius*. Species are found in Swaziland which are listed as vulnerable in the South African Red Data Book – terrestrial mammals are the honey badger, the pangolin, the ant bear, the hook lipped rhinoceros, the oribi, Meller's mongoose, the ardwolf, the leopard, the hippopotamus, the red duiker and Sharple's grybok. The square-lipped rhinoceros is not listed as a threatened species.

More than 500 species of bird have been recorded in Swaziland including many rare species. Two examples both found in Malolotja are the blue swallow *Hirundo atrocaerula* and the bald ibis *Geronticus calvus*.

Over 40 species of amphibians, three species of reptiles, and 50 species of freshwater fish, many of which are endangered, have already been identified. Research is continuing in this field. Very little research has been carried out on invertebrates and knowledge of these species is lacking.

The Flora Checklist for Swaziland which updated the annotated checklist of the Flora of Swaziland lists 2715 indigenous plant species (including *Pteridophytes*) and 110 naturalised exotics. Since the publication of the 1983 checklist further species have been recorded in Swaziland, and the total number of indigenous and exotic plant species in the country is estimated to be over 3000. There are a number of species which have restricted distributions, covering small areas within Swaziland and in neighbouring countries. Examples include endangered cycads, *Encephalartos paucidentatus*, *E. laevifolius* and *E. heenanii*, found only in the north-western Swaziland and in adjacent South Africa, and *E. umbeluziensis*, found only in the Lubombo area in northern-eastern Swaziland and in adjacent Mozambique.

The current status of most plant species is unknown but it is recognised that changes in land use (e.g. agriculture) and collection for traditional medicine and other commercial purposes pose a serious threat to a range of species. For example, wild ginger *Siphonochilus aethipicus* and the pepper-bark tree *Warburgia salutaris*, both of which are used for medicinal purposes, may be on the verge of extinction in Swaziland, and kiaat *Pterocarpus angolensis* populations may be being seriously depleted due to use of the timber for carvings. Based on current knowledge of the country's flora, more than 50 per cent of the species listed for Swaziland have been recorded from within either Malolotja or Mlawula, but, in general, little is known of their status even within these reserves.

Minerals

Mining is one of the 12 main sectors that contribute to the economic development of the country. The most important minerals include asbestos, coal, diamonds and quarry stone. In 1990, total ex-mine revenue from the sale of minerals increased by over 10 per cent. Asbestos production increased by 32 per cent. Coal production decreased by 8.6 per cent but sales revenue increased by 39 per cent as a result of an upswing in world market prices for coal.

ENVIRONMENTAL POLICIES AND LEGISLATION

Existing legislation

The coverage of environmentally-related laws in the country is neither complete nor up to date, but even so, it is fairly extensive. The current legislative structure includes a wide range of laws affecting the environment which in turn empower various sectors of Government to implement and enforce them. The results of efforts to protect Swaziland's natural environment have not been particularly impressive. Much of this is due to the lack of co-ordination and enforcement between the different sectors.

A summary of various environmentally-concerned legislative instruments is presented below. The authority responsible for their implementation is listed in parentheses after each piece of legislation.

Land-use planning

- Town Planning Act 1961 for urban planning and zoning controls (Ministry of Natural Resources and Energy, MNRE).
- Human Settlements Authority Act 1989 establishes the Human Settlements Authority which shall ensure the orderly development of existing and future urban and rural human settlements and formulate policy on such matters (MNRE).
- Swazi Nation Land Act 1961 controls land use in rural areas under local law and customs (Swaziland National Council).

Forest and flora conservation

- Forest Preservation Act 1910 protects forests on Government and Swazi Nation Land (Ministry of Agriculture and Conservation, MOAC).
- Flora Protection Act 1952 for the protection of rare and endangered species (MOAC).
- Control of Tree-Planting Act 1972 empowers the Ministry of Agriculture and the Natural Resources Board to designate tree control areas in agricultural land (MOAC).
- Natural Resources Act 1951 gives the Natural Resources Board limited Authority to exercise supervision over the country's natural resources (MNRE).

National Parks and wildlife

- The (revised) Game Act of 1990 increased penalties for poaching protected game (MNRE).
- National Trust Commission Act 1972 calls for the establishment and management of

national parks and nature reserves (MNRE).

- Wild Birds Protection Act 1914 prohibits, with certain exceptions, the sale and export of the plumage and skins of wild birds and provides for the general protection of such birds (MOAC).
- Protection of Fresh Water Fish Act 1937 protects against the exploitation of freshwater fish (MOAC).
- Natural Resources Act 1951 gives the Natural Resources Board limited Authority to exercise supervision over the country's natural resources, including wildlife (MNRE).

Mineral resources development

- Water Act 1967 controls the purification and discharge of waste water from mining activities (MNRE).
- Mines, Works and Factories Act 1958 and Mining Regulations 1958, control licensing for mining and site rehabilitation after mining has ceased (MNRE).
- Natural Resources Act 1951 gives the Natural Resources Board limited authority to exercise supervision over the country's natural resources, including its minerals (MNRE).
- Mines and Quarries, Machinery and Safety Regulations, 1969 (MNRE).
- Mining Act, 1989 (MNRE).

Water quality

- Water Act 1967 covers the abstraction from, and discharge of, water into natural waterways, pollution control, purification of industrial water, and effluent regulations for water quality control (MNRE).
- Natural Resources Act 1951 gives the Natural Resources Board limited authority to exercise supervision over the country's natural resources including water (MNRE).

Air quality control

- Factories, Machinery and Construction Works Act 1972 deals with nuisances to workers' health from dust, fumes and other impurities in factory emissions.

Food and drug quality control

- Nutrition Council Act 1945 empowers the Council to advise the Minister of malnutrition levels and to make recommendations for the improvement of dietary standards (Ministry of Health, MOH).
- Public Health Act 1969 deals with hygiene rather than with quality control of food and drugs; for quality control, the South African Bureau of Standards is used (MOH).

Solid wastes and specific chemical disposal

- Urban Areas Regulations 1962 takes care of the disposal of municipal solid wastes by local authorities, but not in rural areas nor for industrial wastes (Prime Minister's Office).
- Pharmacy Act 1929 controls the use of poison drugs and includes some controls on pesticide use and other toxic substances for industry and agriculture (MOH).

- Control of Radioactive Substances Act 1964 deals with dangers of ionising radiation to health (MOH).

Cultural environment and noise control

- Factories, Machinery and Construction Works Regulations 1972 enforces an 85-decibel noise limit in factories but not control for motor vehicle noise.
- Natural Trust Commission Act 1972 provides for the preservation of national monuments, relics and antiquities (MNRE).
- Natural Resources Act 1951 gives the Natural Resources Board limited authority to exercise supervision over the country's natural resources including royal graves or grave sites (MNRE).

Environmental education and training

- National Trust Commission Act 1972 establishes the Swaziland National Trust Commission which has the responsibility to develop an environmental education programme (MNRE).

It is obvious from this review that much of the country's environmental legislation is out of date and in need of revision in the light of changing needs and technical developments. Swaziland has retained a large number of laws from its colonial days. Immediately after independence the Kingdom was active in preparing and updating several pieces of environmental legislation, particularly in 1969 and 1972. In 1989 and 1990 the Mining Act and Game Act respectively were updated indicating a growing commitment to the pressing needs of environmental protection.

It is important to note that Swaziland's needs lie not only in developing a sound comprehensive legislative base, but also in the firm enforcement of its laws. With the necessary updating, environmental conservation could be successful, given Swaziland's existing legislative base. Unfortunately there seems to be a lack of enforcement and implementation of existing laws from many sectoral agencies. This in turn has led to many pieces of legislation being virtually ignored. In addition, it is crucial that Swaziland adopts and co-ordinates cross-sectoral conservation practices and policies in order to ensure a sustained natural resource base.

Proposed policy and legislation

The Government is currently in the process of drafting and approving several pieces of environmental legislation. Among these is the Swaziland Environmental Authority Bill which is awaiting final review and is expected to be considered by Parliament in 1991. Through this piece of legislation the Swaziland Environmental Authority will be established.

In 1990 the Government responded to another gap in Swaziland's environmentally related legislative base. Following a motion in Parliament, the Ministry of Natural Resources and Energy is currently drafting an anti-litter law. The Anti-Litter Bill was presented back to Parliament in late 1991.

A piece of environmental legislation that has already been drafted is the Disaster Preparedness and Relief Bill of 1987. The object of the Bill is to empower the Prime Minister to declare a state of disaster and to provide for relief in the event of a natural disaster. The need for disaster planning legislation was emphasised in 1984 when cyclone Domoina hit Swaziland causing tremendous damage to rural and urban settlements, crops and infrastructure in many parts of the Kingdom.

The practice of certain countries in the highly-industrialised North of dumping their unwanted waste in developing countries has made Swaziland vigilant and live to issues involving the handling, use and disposal of hazardous and toxic substances. The continued dumping of banned dieldrin in the country by a transnational company and the careless handling of previously inadvertently stock-piled sodium arsenite is a case in point.

As a reaction to this the Interministerial Environmental Health Planning and Coordinating Group drafted the National Health Policy Guidelines on Toxic and Hazardous materials. The Policy Guidelines are directed at those businesses that rate profits above environmental considerations. It is true that the profit motive will always be the driving factor, but this should be seriously reconciled with good environmental conservation practices.

Included in the National Health Policy Guidelines are the following:

- protection of public health, resources and environment should have the highest priority;
- licensing of the import, processing, production, transport, storage, treatment and disposal of toxic and hazardous materials;
- licensing and approval should be subject to review and to the concurrence of an approval body;
- maintenance of a register of all processing operators, disposal sites and materials used, processed, handled or disposed of in the country;
- importers, transporters, processors , or disposers of toxic or hazardous materials should bear full responsibility for the costs of cleaning up any hazardous materials resulting from their actions;
- in so far as possible, the use, production, or disposal of toxic and hazardous materials should be reduced or eliminated;
- establishing institutions for carrying out these policy guidelines, enact required legislation, establish required rules and regulations and establish required institutional bodies and procedures.

STRATEGIES AND SOLUTIONS FOR ENVIRONMENTAL SUSTAINABILITY

Constraints on the sustainable use of resources and the environment

The basic constraint on the use of resources is their availability (in the case of non-renewable resources) and the extent to which they can be regenerated (in the case of renewable resources). The rate of usage may be affected by other constraints. These may either be exogenous (i.e. not amenable to alteration through the agency of authorities within the country) or endogenous (i.e. subject to alteration primarily through the actions of domestic authorities).

Exogenous constraints are those resources which are shared by sovereign states, such as rivers, air etc. On the other hand, endogenous constraints are to be found within the country, and include problems such as institutional inadequacies and market failure.

Endogenous constraints

Population growth

Swaziland's high rate of population growth will worsen existing resource use problems. Each additional person will consume additional energy, require additional food, shelter, water and land.

The outcome (clearly unsustainable), may be obviated by altering the attitudes of the generation which will attain maturity in the 1990s, so as to reduce the rate of population growth.

Land tenure

The traditional system of communal property rights operates on Swazi Nation Land. Under the traditional system, land ownership is vested in the Ngwenyama who holds it in trust for the Swazi nation. As described earlier, the majority of Swazi Nation Land is divided into chiefdoms where the Ngwenyama delegates authority to the chiefs to administer the land according to Swazi law and custom. The chief allocates an arable plot and homestead site to each household in their respective domains. The remaining part of the land is owned on a communal basis and is mostly used for grazing livestock.

Range lands on Swazi Nation Land are a good example of a common property resource. Common property resources are difficult to manage and problems often abound. Overuse of these resources by individuals as they seek to maximise benefits without incurring costs of resource exploitation occurs because individuals reap best returns by equating average revenue product to marginal cost, while optimum economic sustainable yield requires equating marginal revenue product to marginal cost. As a result, excessive, unsustainable use is an inherent tendency with such resources. This tendency is found on Swazi Nation Land grazing lands, and the result is inevitable long-term degradation of the range caused by overstocking and overgrazing; this in turn leads to soil erosion.

At the same time, considerable amounts of farm and range land held under Title Deed tenure remain unused or underutilised. Such land is apparently prized more for the capital gains which accrue to land owners as property prices increase, than for its value in immediate use. Moreover, it is rarely made available to prospective users on the basis of leases.

Given this structure of tenurial relations, optimising behaviour by similarly motivated producers leads to different outcomes: unsustainable range degradation on communal land; and sustainable but socially undesirable accumulation of underutilised, individual tenure farms.

Gender relations

The authority over resources is vested predominantly in men in Swaziland as the society is patrilineal. Resource use is, however, mediated primarily through women. Thus, land on Swazi Nation Land is allocated to married men who are heads of homesteads *de jure*, whilst usage of land for crops depends predominantly on female labour. Similarly, it is women who fetch water and gather firewood, yet it is the councils of men that decide issues pertaining to the usage of water and wood resources.

A divergence arises therefore, between resource use planning and actual utilisation which aggravates the tendency for non-optimal resource usage. If firewood becomes scarce as the trees are felled, it is the women who will know first as they have to walk further to obtain wood, but they will not be in a position to intervene. If water becomes polluted and unsafe for human consumption, again it will be women who will know first, but they will be in no position to act as decisions on these matters are the prerogative of men.

This divergence between policy-making and execution exacerbates the pressure on resource usage and is compounded by the tendency for policy interventions to be directed primarily to men rather than to women who will most likely be the ones to implement them.

Inadequate information and analysis

Swaziland is aware of the possible presence of environmental pollutants but extensive analysis is difficult until such time as relevant equipment and monitoring facilities become available.

There is little data on resource conservation as well as resource use because of lack of equipment and well-executed research. The government is encouraging individuals and environmental groups to focus attention on the many environmental issues. However, up to now, except for meterological tables, the government produces few statistics on environmental resources and problems.

Lack of environmental awareness

Environmental awareness in Swaziland, as in many parts of the world, is limited. The problem is inherent in that there are still many people who do not understand the importance of conserving their environment.

Organisations, such as the 'Clean and beautiful Swaziland' campaign, and Yonge Nawe Conservation Clubs have taken a leading role in raising public awareness and in motivating and assisting other agencies, such as schools and community groups to participate in environmental protection.

Evidence of constraints

Market failures

This implies that markets exist but operate in such a way that prices fail to reflect accurately the true opportunity cost of the resources which are utilised. It may be interpreted alternately to imply that markets do not exist where they should.

In the case of communal grazing land, as indicated, the absence of private title renders this a free resource from the perspective of the individual user. Consequently, as the true opportunity cost is not made manifest, the land is utilised until marginal private benefit approaches zero. At that level of usage, though, social benefits become negative as private optimising behaviour in the absence of a land market has negative social consequences. Nor does the alternative to the market, i.e. regulation by some local authority, improve performance, because the latter also fails to impress upon the large herd owners who are benefiting from the present situation, the true opportunity cost of the grazing land which their herds exploit.

In the case of title deed land, for which a regulated market does exist, prices reflect anticipated capital gains. Thus some of the land is used, but vast tracts remain unused. Whilst this preserves the land, the outcome is socially undesirable in the long run.

Institutional inadequacies

These indicate that there are deficiencies in the organisation, interrelationships and modes of operation of those institutions which deal with the environment. Such inadequacies include the following:

- overlapping jurisdiction, whereby various agencies in national government concerned with, for example, land and land use, are controlled or influenced by the Ministries of Agriculture and Cooperatives, the Ministry of Natural Resources and Energy, and by the

Central Rural Development Board which reports directly to the King. A major consequence of overlapping jurisdictions is that no clear national policy on land and land use can be enunciated. Nor is it then possible to devise a coherent series of interventions designed to protect land from damage or abuse;

- an absence of reliable data, especially on the extent of environmental degradation, be it pollutants in the air or water, rates of deforestation, rates of loss of indigenous fauna and flora or on other aspects of environmental damage. As yet there are few agencies specially devoted to the compilation, organisation and interpretation of such basic data;
- the lack of a regulatory framework: a comprehensive framework for environmental protection does not exist in the country. The absence of such a framework may make Swaziland seem a more attractive place for foreign and domestic investment, which is seeking fewer restrictions. However, this type of development will not be sustainable in the long run; and
- insufficient popular participation. As has been indicated, popular participation in the conceptualisation of national problems and the determination of solutions is limited. Not only is there imperfect mediation between the modern and the traditional systems of government, but there is also discrimination based on gender, competing value systems and a general lack of knowledge about the social consequences of private actions.

Opportunities for sustainable development

Establishing more resource-efficient economic policies

In order for projects to become more resource efficient, they should be fully evaluated before implementation. Such evaluation should be based on both private and social criteria. In the case of private evaluation, the usual criteria (such as the internal rate of return, net present value of cash flows and projected commercial profitability) will be used. In the case of social evaluation, all those factors affecting social welfare (such as changes in the environment, poverty, income distribution and employment) should be considered. If the net impact on the basis of the social evaluation is negative, then the project could either be refused, or allowed on condition that it pay a penalty. If the net impact is positive, then an appropriate subsidy could be given, e.g. in the form of tax credits.

In the case of non-renewable resources, a suitable rent or royalty must be collected by government and invested on social service projects. The latter should be designed to benefit the whole society either directly or indirectly. It should be guided by the desire to compensate society not only for the loss of the resource but also for the environmental damage.

Fiscal and non-fiscal incentives extended by government to industry must explicitly incorporate environmental concerns. Those business enterprises whose operations are environment-friendly could be subsidised, and those that are not should be penalised accordingly.

When pollution standards exist, they must be monitored closely and enforced. Where these are absent, studies should be commissioned.

Environmental issues in Swaziland are presently handled on a sectoral basis by a number of government ministries, departments, NGOs and other bodies that are officially entrusted with specific functions of an environmental nature or whose work relates to certain aspects of the environment.

A specific example of sectoral environmental policy is the water and sanitation policy which includes amongst others, the following policy goals:

- that planning sectoral development in water supply and sanitation be an ongoing

activity;
- that the implementation of sectoral development in water supply and sanitation take high priority;
- that programme implementation be strengthened;
- that human resources development play a major role in sectoral development;
- that benefits from available resources be optimised; and
- that funds be not only committed but attached as well.

It is clear that the broad policy statements laid out for the water and sanitation sector can, and should, be considered and possibly embodied in any environmental policy framework.

The most important and effective method for strengthening sectoral policy is the passing of legislation that makes provision for its effective enforcement. Existing legislation, such as the 1967 Water Act, for example, has been criticised for not being sufficiently explicit in its control of water apportionment and pollution. This created loopholes that could easily be circumvented by land owners and industrial establishments.

Broadening the participation of NGOs

The participation of NGOs in environmental concerns could be broadened by strengthening the existing assembly of NGOs. This organisation could be more effective if its networking links were extended and membership increased to include all grassroots organisations and NGOs. In addition, an effort to foster closer collaboration between government and NGOs should be pursued.

There are several women's organisations in existence which are pertinent here, such as the Lutsango Lwabomake with a large membership in the rural areas. The main aim of this organisation is to develop and improve the status and conditions of women and girls in the country in order to fight ignorance, disease and poverty.

More of these women's groups could be educated and motivated to improve the sanitation in their homes. This in turn would improve the health of children and adults. Women's groups could also be organised to engage in agricultural projects such as setting up vegetable gardens, small-scale egg production and bee-keeping. These activities would enable women to earn money and improve the nutrition of their children.

Another women's organisation, The Swaziland Secretaries' Association, has been involved in environmental conservation projects, particularly 'clean up' campaigns. The members of this association could be even more involved in raising the level of awareness of the importance of environmental issues in their respective places of work through direct interaction with their employers.

There are several youth organisations in the country which are currently involved in environmental activities. If their membership were spread throughout the country and these young people were encouraged and motivated to execute projects that address environmental problems, NGO participation would be greatly improved.

Expanding the role of women in managing natural resources

Because of their special relationship with the natural environment, women have a crucial role to play in sustainable development. Their role is just beginning to be recognised and urgent action is needed to enable more women to participate effectively in development activities that both sustain the environment and benefit them directly.

Women are the major victims of environmental degradation and mismanagement and they are likely to be the hardest hit in future environmental disasters. Women also have the knowledge and experience, both technical and organisational, to be effective resource protectors and managers. It has been shown that project efficiency is improved by their participation, although this can lead to increased work loads on them. For women to play their full part in sustainable development, a variety of supports are needed, including access to, and control over, land and other financial resources, training and appropriate technologies. In many developing countries, including Swaziland, women's potential to contribute towards sustainable development is undermined by their lower socio-economic and political status, lack of education and poorer access to productive resources than men.

Most of the environmental conservation work of Swazi women is to a great extent spearheaded by NGOs and therefore, broadening their participation will in turn expand the role of women.

CONCLUSION

National strategies

Environmental education in Swaziland is pursued at two levels, formally through the Ministry of Education and informally through the National Environmental Education Programme. The motivation for educating the public in environmental issues is to make people aware of the environment so they will appreciate and respect its value and learn to protect it. The following recommendations outline the specific strategies Swaziland plans to pursue in order to achieve these goals.

- Encourage study tours that will enable policy-makers, community leaders and NGOs to exchange ideas on environmental education with people in other countries.
- Train environmental specialists for both the private and public sectors in order to strengthen the country's capability to manage its own environment.
- Hold seminars and workshops throughout Swaziland to educate the general public about the environment and the existing and proposed legislative instruments for its protection.
- Expand the integration of environmental education into curricula at primary, secondary and tertiary levels.
- The National Environmental Education Programme (NEEP) should be improved by the following measures:
  - the provision of adequate training for local conservation personnel;
  - extending the current education programme operating at Malolotja Nature Reserve to the other districts;
  - giving greater priority for environmental education in-service training for teachers, by holding national seminars and workshops;
  - making available environmental education materials at all national, university, college and school libraries;
  - promoting the level of awareness about the environment through giving greater support, both financially and morally, to the radio and television stations. Encouragement should also be given to local newspapers to increase their coverage of environmental matters;
  - increasing the financial and manpower support to the National Environmental

Education Programme and Yonge Nawe in order to expand ongoing training programmes; and
– integrating selected environmental programmes at the University of Swaziland and the Swaziland Institute of Health Sciences.

Public participation

The role and responsibility of the people of Swaziland in combating environmental degradation goes beyond education and awareness. The government realises that it cannot achieve the goal of environmental preservation on its own and acknowledges that the involvement of the people in programmes and projects is a very important, necessary and vital means of preserving the natural environment. Through the strategies outlined below, it is hoped that public participation, in defining and overcoming national environmental problems, will be enhanced.

- Give women a greater role in decision-making about environmental issues at local, national and international levels. In particular, women's organisations should be consulted on questions of local environmental planning as well as being involved in the development and implementation of national conservation and sustainable development strategies.
- Improve the capacity of women to be effective natural resource managers through the provision of credit, training and extension services.
- Identify target groups for afforestation programmes and formulate appropriate strategies to enhance public awareness and involvements in such projects. The Government should also encourage and support NGOs financially, technically and otherwise to become actively involved in the planting of woodlots for firewood and in creating income-generating activities through integrated agricultural development.
- Utilise these environmental education strategies to encourage wide participation of all people in environmental education.
- Maintain a component of public participation in environmental conservation projects.

Legislation and enforcement

The strategies listed below will be pursued in order to achieve the goal of attaining a comprehensive legislative base for environmental matters. The enforcement of environmentally-related laws in Swaziland is weak. Therefore, it is also a goal of the country to develop and maintain a better mechanism for enforcing its legislation.

- Review laws and practices which militate against women's participation in national resource management and amend and remove all the obstacles to their crucial contribution.
- Update and adopt the National Physical Development Plan in order to facilitate its implementation.
- Acquire monitoring facilities to register and record amounts of different types of pollutants.
- Regularly monitor the import and use of toxic substances.
- Expand and improve the current climatic monitoring systems by increasing trained human resources and acquiring additional monitoring equipment.

Research

Swaziland has many areas of environmental concern that need future study. Outlined below are specific research activities which need to be carried out before actual programmes, projects and policies can be defined and implemented.

- Investigate fully occupational health hazards involved in industry, mining and agriculture.
- Improve the system of national income accounts to ensure that the data will reflect the 'depreciation' of the environment caused by modern economic growth.
- Carry out a survey of natural resource utilisation for the whole of Swaziland to ascertain the economic potential of the country.
- Carry out indigenous forestry inventories to assess the annual volume of firewood collected from the indigenous forests and the wood demand for various end users.
- Enact the proposed Disaster Preparedness and Relief Bill.
- Hold a seminar to determine the factors responsible for poor enforcement of existing legislation and to develop more effective enforcement mechanisms.
- Once the Environmental Authority is established it shall:
  - review and revise all existing environmental legislation in order to harmonize their goals and objectives;
  - recommend additional legislation that is required to deal with environmental issues that are not covered by the existing legislative base such as hazardous waste management and various pollution standards.

Monitoring

Swaziland has a limited capacity to monitor the rate and extent of environmental degradation. This is due to a limited institutional framework and an inadequate infrastructure to comprehensively and accurately monitor the state of the environment. Through the strategies listed below the government aims to overcome these weaknesses, as an appropriate monitoring system is essential for the effective implementation and enforcement of environmental legislation.

- Create a mechanism for the systematic collection, organisation and interpretation of data pertaining to the environment.
- Enlist assistance from the international community to carry out research on how transboundary air pollution directly affects Swaziland.
- Participate actively in negotiations with neighbouring countries, namely the Republic of South Africa and Mozambique, in the sustainable use and management of transboundary ecological zones and natural resources.
- Support the development and implementation of regional and sub-regional co-operative arrangements for combating common environmental problems.
- Undertake studies with the assistance of bilateral and multilateral agencies to:
  - assess the scope for limiting emissions of ozone depleting and other greenhouse gases;
  - assess the possible impacts of global warming;
  - identify the technologies needed to minimise the impacts of global warming and for reducing CFCs and greenhouse gas emissions.

REFERENCES

GTZ (1989) *Energy Consumption and Demand in the Domestic Sector of Swaziland* Report to government of
  Swaziland
ILO (1986) *Manpower, Education and Training in Swaziland*
Swaziland, Central Statistical Office, (1986) *Annual Statistical Bulletin*
Swaziland, *Employment Statistics,* (1988) Department of Economic Planning and Statistics
Swaziland, *Economic Review,* (1988) Department of Economic Planning and Statistics
Swaziland, *Economic Review,* (1990) Department of Economic Planning and Statistics
Swaziland, Central Statistical Office, (1990) *Annual Statistical Bulletin*
Swaziland, Central Statistical Office, (1991) *Annual Statistical Bulletin*

8

TANZANIA

INTRODUCTION

Tanzania has a total surface area, including lakes, of some 945,000 km^2 and a land area of some 886,000 km^2. The present overall population density is relatively low, 25 persons per km^2, but it varies in rural districts from under two in Mpanda (Rukwa) to over 200 in some highland districts and around Mwanza. Tanzania exhibits large variations in environmental and climatic conditions which are some of the main factors influencing crop and livestock production and population distribution (Havnevik *et al.*, 1988).

If Figure 8.1 – population density in districts from the 1988 census – is compared with Figure 8.2 – average annual rainfall – a complex and scattered population pattern emerges. Admittedly, both maps give only crude general indications of population density and rainfall. But one noticeable pattern is that the districts with above-average density – with over 30 persons per km^2, – are located along the fringes of the country, around Lake Victoria in the north-west, and in the south-western, south-eastern and north-eastern corners of the country, including the coastal fringe.

Both the well-watered high-potential highlands and the areas of higher rainfall around Lake Victoria along the fringes of the country account for a high share of the total population and production of marketed food and export crops. Large parts of western and southern Tanzania are very sparsely populated, some of them being virtually uninhabited. This has serious implications in terms of extremely high costs of transport and communication to Dar es Salaam, the main consumption and export centre, and in terms of maintaining the infrastructure and input to such rural areas.

The Southern Highlands in Iringa and Mbeya form the largest block of well-watered highlands. Together with the Ufipa Plateau in Rukwa and the western part of Ruvuma Region these regions now account for the highest marketed output of maize based on relatively intensive use of fertiliser. Tea, tobacco, coffee and rice are also important crops in this area. Deforestation, with reduced water-flow, is a problem due to agricultural expansion, commercial exploitation of fuelwood for tobacco curing, brick and charcoal making and bush fires (Figure 8.3).

The most intensive agricultural systems based on critically high population densities are found in Bukoba, on the slopes of Mt. Meru and Kilimanjaro, in the Pare and Usambara Range, in the Uluguru Mountains and in Rungwe District. These highland systems, which have not been affected by villagisation, are characterised by coffee/banana cultivation systems, traditional forms of agroforestry, mixed farming, tea etc., and often depend on manure, mulch or other forms of organic fertility maintenance. Nevertheless, there is generally little room for further intensification. Land degradation with the cultivation of steep slopes and forest encroachment is a problem in the Usambara and Ulguru Mountains. Out-migration from high density areas into lower potential or marginal lands is a common feature.

Along Lake Victoria and Lake Tanganyika the rainfall increases, and the southern and eastern Victoria Lake Zone is characterised by relatively high population densities and fairly intensive cultivation of maize, cassava, sorghum, rice and cotton. The area has been seriously affected by villagisation. Livestock densities are high, and overgrazing, deforestation and fertility maintenance of the poor soils constitute serious problems. Mwanza and Shinyanga have experienced a series of food deficit years over the past decade.

Large parts of western Tanzania receive 800–1000 mm of rainfall. Tsetse-infested miombo woodland is the predominant form of vegetation in large parts of west-central Tanzania, and this precludes livestock husbandry. Since the 1950s significant areas have been cleared for tobacco and maize cultivation in Tabora, but overall population densities are generally low, and the soils are generally of poor quality.

Apart from Mtwara Region and Lindi District where the main crops are cassava, sorghum, maize and cashew nuts, most of southern Tanzania is thinly populated despite reasonable rainfall, partly because of poor soils, tsetse infestation and poor infrastructure, and partly because of the

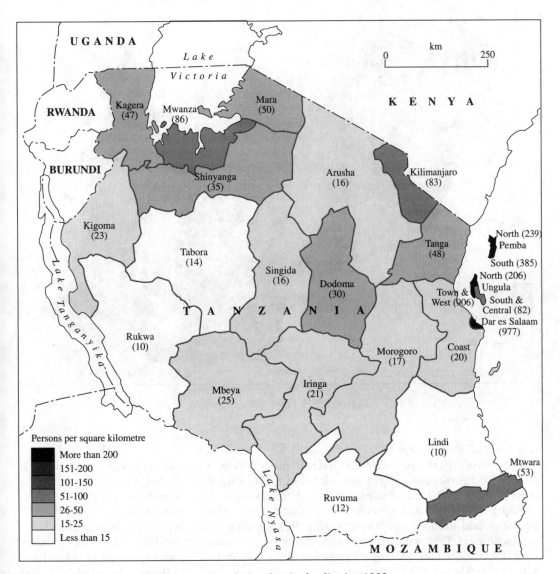

Figure 8.1 *Population density by district, 1988*

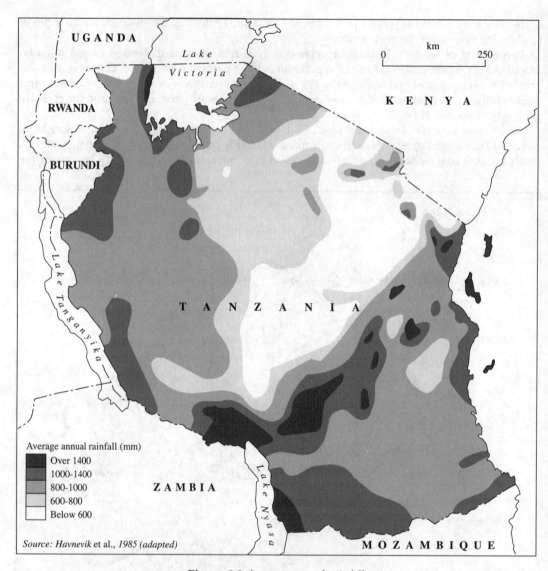

Figure 8.2 *Average annual rainfall*

large Selous Game Reserve.

The final broad category of climate and land use is the vast north-central plateau, most of which is below 1500 metres, receiving on average below 800 mm of annual rainfall. A large part of this area receives less than 750 mm of rainfall, a level defined as critical for rainfed crop production due to the high probability of drought. The production of grains, oil seeds and legumes does take place in these semi-arid areas but agriculture is generally associated with livestock keeping as an insurance against drought. This predominantly agro-pastoral system tends to involve contradictory patterns of land use. Ploughing by oxen is common and tends to involve an expansion of extensively cultivated fields, but this occurs at the expense of grazing land and the well-being of cattle and draught oxen.

Despite the high risks of crop failure, the zone with below 800 mm of rainfall carries about 20 per cent of the human population and well over half of the national herd of 12.5 million head of cattle, 6.4 million goats and 3.1 million sheep (Ministry of Agriculture and Livestock Development, 1984). The heaviest concentration of cattle is found in central and eastern Shinyanga Region, which together with Mwanza Region accounts for the major share of cotton production as well (Figure 8.4). A considerable part of this zone is relatively over-populated and over-stocked and is characterised by overgrazing, deforestation and land degradation. Villagisation has aggravated this problem. The creation of nucleated settlements has more than doubled human and stock densities, and has reduced the mobility of people and herds which allowed for the regeneration of soils and

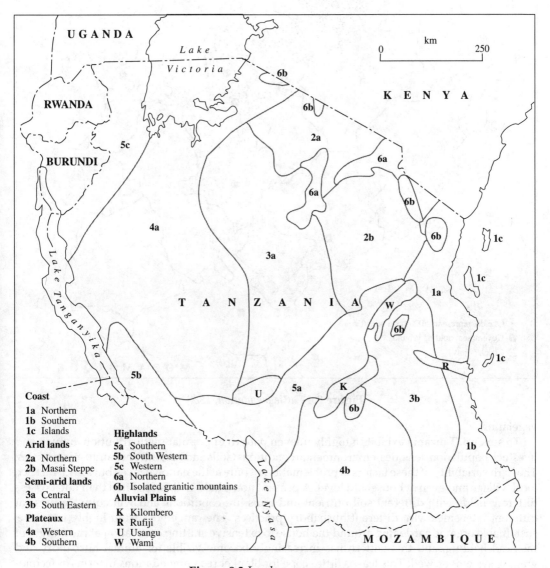

Figure 8.3 *Landuse resource zones*

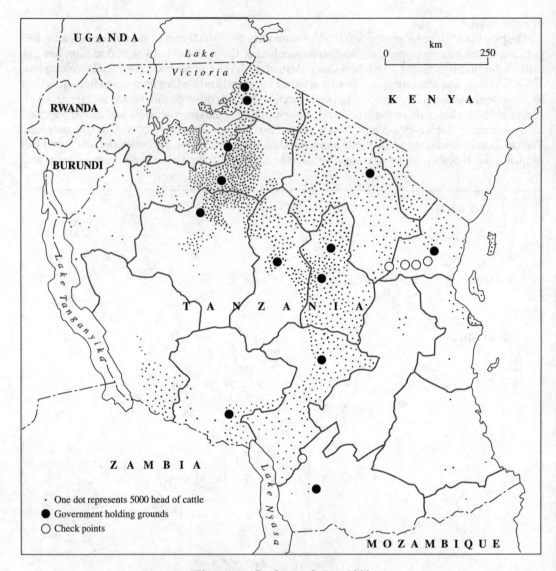

Figure 8.4 *Cattle population, 1989*

vegetation.

To sum up, Tanzania exhibits a highly uneven pattern of population distribution, human and livestock population densities, environmental conditions (soils and rainfall) and landuse intensities. The high variability of these factors is problematic, not only at the national level, but also at district, local, village and even at household level. A peasant household will, more often than not, possess different fields with different soil nutrient and moisture conditions and will cultivate these at different intensities with different husbandry practices. The range goes from highly intensive, sustainable organic gardening around the house to extensive shifting cultivation at the margin of the land holding, and this pattern has increasingly become visible for animal husbandry and grazing systems as well. This leaves little scope for blanket recommendations in terms of technological development.

Overall, given the size of the country and the unequal distribution of the population, only around 10 per cent is cultivated while some 40 per cent consists of rough grazing and fallow land. Roughly half is covered by various types of bush, woodland and forests. This should provide considerable space for expansion of crop land and future population growth. However, estimates of the potential arable land and the future carrying capacity differ considerably.

What is known is that most of the fertile, well-watered highland areas, as well as a considerable proportion of the semi-arid areas, are under relative pressure with existing techniques, and the latter marginal areas have experienced further in-migration and land degradation.

A final important point however, is that the problem of land degradation, whether in the form of deforestation, overgrazing, soil erosion or soil nutrient depletion, is not simply related to population growth. It results from a complex interplay of environmental, historical, social, economic and political factors. Nevertheless, it is worthwhile to keep in mind that over the 1970s and early 1980s the productive peasant sector has been squeezed and has received low development priority relative to most other sectors and social strata.

ENVIRONMENTAL ISSUES

Resource-use conflicts

Landuse patterns are the key to understanding resource use conflicts and they can be summarized as follows (also see Figure 8.3):

Rough grazing lands	44,245,000 ha (50 per cent)
Forest and woodlands	38,500,000 ha (43.1 per cent)
Cultivated lands	4,465,000 ha (5 per cent)
Urban, rocky and swamps	1,160,000 ha (1.8 per cent)

Grazing land is a residual category, and is mainly dry and wooded grassland, suitable to some extent for arable purposes. Intensely-used land is used for cultivation. There are large areas which are not properly managed and these threaten the ecological balance. In some cases, the ecological balance has already been disturbed to the extent that they have been declared disaster areas and steps to address the problem have been taken, e.g. in Dodoma and Shinyanga regions.

Land tenure

Though land tenure laws have been written, in practice not all of these are recognised. Some were passed during the colonial period; they are out of date, and need amendment. The general principle is that all the land belongs to the public through their legally-elected government and all hold it under leasehold. In 1983 it was clearly stated that four types of tenure systems were recognised:

- Government leaseholds;
- Rights of occupancies;
- Customary land tenure laws;
- The collective tenure systems.

The government literally controls the land and has the final say in declaring any land for public use whether for conservation (forest or wildlife) or for public buildings or certain types of developments. This makes it possible for the government to override all other tenure systems, e.g. even to withdraw leases before their expiry if it is considered in the public interest to do so.

The most common system is for the government to give rights of occupancy (title deeds) to individuals, groups, or organisations after mapping and landuse plans have been agreed upon by the relevant authorities at district, regional and national levels. Having paid prescribed fees the right of occupancy will be given with leases either short (1–5 years), medium (up to 33 years) or long term (up to 99 years).

Customary land tenure laws have prevailed longer than any other and vary from place to place (from tribe to tribe). Past colonial governments left the 'native lands' which were not taken by colonial settlers under their own local jurisdiction. It was only in these lands that customary land laws were allowed to prevail. In some tribal areas where land is scarce and perennial commercial crops are dominant (banana/coffee growing areas in Magera, Kilimanjaro, higher lands of Arusha, Mbeya, and parts of Sonhgea, Iringa, Morogoro and Tanga and coastal regions), private ownership is recognised more prominently than in areas where annual crops and pastoralism prevail (e.g. in Shinyanga, Mwanza, Dodoma, and lower lands of Arusha). In the latter areas there is a tendency to have communal or collective tenure systems in grazing areas and on the arable land after the crops have been harvested.

The collective tenure system was legalised by the Ujamaa Village Act of 1975. The Act stipulated that all registered villages own the land. All villagers registered within the village have the right to own certain amounts of land in person and the right to own pieces in the block farm and to graze cattle in the communally-owned grazing land.

Among the problems which have arisen out of collective tenure systems are the following constraints:

- A reluctance to invest in the cultivated areas for the long-term improvement of land;
- An unwillingness to expand crop acreage for fear of being identified as individualistic and hence opposed to collective farming;
- The issuing of short-term leases discourages long-term investment leading to the exploitation of the land for short-term benefit (land mining);
- Discouraging potential investors in agriculture due to the uncertainty of ownership of land.

Land tenure systems in pastoral areas can be treated as a special case. Most of the pastoralists use communal grazing areas and cattle are shifted to other areas with more pasture if drought occurs in the more arid regions. Usually these pastoralists return when vegetation recovers. This migratory type of grazing enables pastoralists to use their land more sustainably. However, arable land has gradually expanded in response to demand due to population growth, thus leaving less and less land for grazing, at least when crops are growing. As a result, overstocking is a problem in Mara, Mwanza, Shinyanga, Arusha, Dodoma, Singida and Tabora (Figure 8.4). The result has been not only seasonal, but permanent migration of pastoralists to other regions such as Iringa, Rukwa, Mbeya, Morogoro and the Coast Regions where pasture is available for most of the year. The latter regions did not have suitable infrastructure for large-scale livestock keeping. This resulted in problems of water shortage for livestock, unplanned grazing and disease outbreaks. The local people in these regions, mainly sedentary peasants, have conflicting relationships with migrant pastoralists especially when cattle accidentally stray and graze on growing crops. This is one area when landuse planning has to be introduced before the over-exploitation of these medium and high potential areas occurs.

Access to arable land

The total area of cultivated land is 4,465,000 ha. If divided among the 19 million rural population, it gives an average of 0.24 ha per person, or about 1.2 ha per average family of 5. In certain areas, due to population pressure, the figure is much lower. In addition, access to land in terms of ownership is limited to men in some areas, e.g. Kilimanjaro (according to customary land tenure); in contrast, in Dodoma, men and women can have plots of their own plus a family plot. This is also typical of other areas, i.e. where land is scarce, land is owned by males, while in other areas it is not a gender issue. Recently, women in these areas have started to question the validity of this biased customary land-tenure system.

Access to pasture land

Tanzania has 44,245,000 ha (50.1 per cent) of the land in the rough grazing lands category. This is residual land and ecologically it is very sensitive. In grazing lands, fires are frequent before the rainy season in December. A good part of this land cannot be inhabited as it is designated as national parks. As a result, there is only about 2.9 ha per livestock unit. Unfortunately, where wood coverage is higher, there is tsetse fly infestation, which makes available even less land per livestock unit.

Further, the uneven distribution of this land does not correspond to the spatial pattern of the cattle population. The livestock-keeping population, especially in Arusha, Mwanza, Shinyanga, Mara, Dodoma and Singida, are short of suitable grazing land. Population pressure has necessitated the utilisation of even marginal grazing land for foodcrops (maize, sorghum, millet) and cash crops (cotton, groundnuts). The result has been over-grazing. Rather than reduce the highly-valued cattle population, most of the pastoralists have migrated to adjacent regions which had no tradition of cattle keeping, e.g. Masai have moved into the Morogoro region. This has created a new problem in these areas, which are forced to accommodate a higher population density.

Access to biomass

The total area of forest cover in Tanzania is 44,371,000 hectares of which 34,626,000 is considered productive. Estimates of the extent of forest in Tanzania vary and definitions of the various categories of forest are not standardised. Every year between 300,000 ha and 400,000 ha of forest are consumed, yielding wood biomass totalling about 49.9 million tonnes per annum. Furthermore, in 1988 about 8 million tonnes of agricultural waste was generated. These included 150,000 tonnes of coconut residue, 8400 tonnes of coffee husks, 150,000 tonnes of sugar residues (bagasse and molasses) and 900,000 tonnes of cotton residues. In terms of energy use, biomass conversion has been traditionally through direct combustion. Since wood biomass consumption is most important, it is worthwhile to look at its supply and consumption patterns. Of the total 25 million cubic metres of solid wood, 97 per cent is consumed as firewood, mainly in rural areas. Nationally, 92 per cent of total energy consumption is in the form of fuelwood.

In rural areas firewood is used for cooking and house-warming and in many cases it is freely gathered from nearby natural forest and woodland. Usually dry branches and twigs are gathered in headloads of about 30 kg, this being sufficient for two days for an average family of five people. However, due to population pressure the natural forests have dwindled around villages and distances of 5–10 km to collect firewood are increasingly common. This has necessitated the commodification of firewood. The use of ox-carts for collecting and selling firewood is now more common. Also, in rural areas agro-processing and other industries are increasingly consuming more and more firewood. Major uses are tobacco curing, fish smoking, bakeries, tea-drying, pottery, brick and tile making and lime production.

Urban landuse conflicts

Urban population growth rates are rapid in Tanzania, with the urban component of 20 per cent in 1988 expected to rise to 30 per cent by the year 2000. This puts great pressure on the urban infrastructure. Land allocation in urban areas has recently reverted to the Ministry of Land Housing and Urban Development though the urban authorities (City Councils, Municipal Councils and Town Councils) participate in overall planning. With the current urban population in Tanzania approaching 5 million and projected to increase to 9 million by 2000, the increase in urban housing problems will be even more critical. The Ministry of Land, Housing and Urban Development gave guidelines in 1988 on:

- the proper use of land;
- the drawing of relevant landuse plans relating to such development;
- the measuring and allocation of plots.

These were intended to overcome previous problems which were created by urban authorities, especially the City and Municipal Councils such as:

- the double or triple allocation of plots resulting in perpetual conflict between applicants;
- delays in the issue of title deeds for the plots.

The main reasons for these problems are:

- a shortage of surveying and mapping in urban areas due to shortages of manpower and equipment;
- a very high demand for houses by the increased urban population;
- corruption on the part of those allocating available plots.

As a result of the shortage of surveyed plots the tendency has been for illegal squatting to occur. In the 1991/92 budget speech the Minister explained the problem of settlements in unsurveyed areas, lacking in appropriate social services and infrastructure. Areas which are occupied by squatters include:

- children's playgrounds;
- land set aside for school expansion;
- graveyards;
- sewage disposal channel routes.

Most of the houses in urban areas do not have adequate sanitation. Waste disposal is a problem, especially for those built in valley areas which are usually condemned by urban land planners as unsuitable. The houses in such areas are more prone to flooding during the rainy season which makes the surrounding area a breeding ground for mosquitoes.

   On the national scale, housing quality is poor. For example, in 1989 at least 50 per cent of houses were without toilets. When one considers that 34 per cent of households obtain water from rivers/lakes and 9 per cent from dams, such water supplies may not be safe, thus constituting a further health hazard. It is assumed that those houses receiving shared pipe water, 18 per cent, and shallow well water, 34 per cent, may have relatively cleaner water as it is normally treated before piping.

In urban areas not all sewer systems are connected. Even in Dar es Salaam many toilets are still pit latrines and many individual houses have isolated septic tanks which require emptying especially when it rains, as the sewage system soak-pits do not work effectively then. Unfortunately no municipal council or city council has an adequate number of cesspit-emptying trucks. It takes weeks before overflowing septic tanks are emptied, in spite of advance payments. The foul smell in many residential areas attests to this.

Waste disposal is one of the problems which faces large cities like Dar es Salaam. Recently there has been a controversy over the site where refuse should be dumped. A court order had to be made to prohibit the city using the old overflowing dump at Tabata where, because of burning refuse, smoke was reducing visibility on the expressway to the harbour, thus endangering traffic. Residents across the road were experiencing foul-smelling smoke which was polluting the air. The dump was closed and a new one opened at a closed quarry site near the sea-shore. Residents of Kunduchi-Mtongani near the new dump also contested the choice in court. A court injunction to prevent the city council using the dump caused an accumulation of refuse in the city which has never been fully cleared – the reason being the shortage of refuse collection trucks. The available trucks require a full day to clear about half of the city's refuse. A delay of 2–3 days is too much for the city refuse collection team to cope with.

What happens in Dar es Salaam is also happening in other towns albeit to a lesser extent. Many town residents with empty areas in their plots have learned to burn or bury their refuse whichever seems to be convenient. Therefore along with housing problems in general, waste disposal is a problem though it is normally only accorded secondary importance. People in need of houses are measured in tens of thousands while those facing waste disposal problems are less numerous.

ENVIRONMENTAL PROBLEMS

Soil erosion

Soil erosion has become a serious problem and has turned many areas of fragile land into near desert in Tanzania.

The over-exploitation of natural resources and poor land management practices have been the main causes of soil erosion. While over-exploitation has been a result of the introduction of a money economy, a lack of appropriate land management techniques and erratic landuse policies have also contributed to soil erosion.

Over-exploitation of marginal lands started during the colonial period. The government showed ignorance of land management when the Overseas Food Corporation in 1946 initiated mechanised agriculture for groundnut schemes in the wooded grasslands, which are marginal areas. Although the project was abandoned in all three areas (Kongwa in Dodoma, Urambo in Tabora and Nachingwea in Lindi) the areas cleared never recovered fully as they were turned into official ranches (for Kongwa and Nachingwea), and for intensive uses such as tobacco growing (for Urambo).

Therefore, over-cultivation, over-grazing and deforestation have been the major causes of erosion. Efforts to manage the erosion through various projects have been made, but these have been inconsistent, over-emphasised at one time and forgotten at other times. Where the situation was becoming critical, the government, through local and international efforts, had to do something to avoid outright disaster. In these situations efforts have included land reclamation through reafforestation, soil conservation policy such as the one in Dodoma region (HADO) involving two districts (Kondoa and Dodoma) which started in 1973, and the one in Shinyanga (HASHI) which started in 1982.

Burning, especially during the dry season, of the grass woodlands and grazing land has been one of the major causes of soil erosion. Although stiff sentences are enacted against anyone responsible for causing fires, culprits are rarely caught.

While rain and wind are blamed for erosion, it is after disturbance of the ecosystem by human beings and livestock that rain and wind carry the top soil away, thus completing the erosion process. The highly erodible soils of Kondoa in Dodoma region are examples where the loosening of soil from the roots of bushland and grass by cultivation and grazing made the soil prone to erosion.

It is encouraging that the better management practices of the HADO Project over 15 years have reversed this trend and people who had to be moved from their areas for over 10 years have gone back to land which has been restored.

River siltation

River siltation was not a common phenomenon in Tanzania until recently when population pressure increased. In the lower areas of the Rufiji, annual floods were recurrent and in many cases were desirable for rice growing, and the deposited alluvial soils maintained soil fertility. But silt quantities increased in the upper parts of the river basin as people cultivated increasingly steep slopes, resulting in more soil being washed into the rivers. A related problem is the silting of dams, e.g. at Mtera and Kidatu in the Rufiji basin.

Pilot studies of four reservoirs in Dodoma recorded annual sediment yields sufficient to reduce their life span to no more than 30 years with an even shorter economic life. Aerial photographs of the catchment area show intense rill and gully erosion. The chief contributory factor explaining the sedimentation of the reservoirs was found to be sheet erosion over large areas of the lower pediments.

Deforestation and its environmental consequences

Tanzania has a total of 44 million ha of forest which has been divided into the four following types:

• Forest reserves	13,024,000
• Forest woodlands inside National Parks and public forest lands	2,000,000
• Miombo Woodlands	29,347,000
	44,371,000

Most of the forest reserves and 60,000 ha of mangroves have been gazetted for production purposes. Only 1.6 million ha are reserves for the protection of catchments. Of the productive forest reserves, around 80,000 ha are plantations producing both soft and hardwood timber as well as poles.

Productive forest is about 34,626 million ha in extent while 9745 million ha is unproductive. The deforestation rate is estimated to be between 300,000 and 400,000 ha per annum. Unfortunately the planting rate is only about 20,000 ha per year. This means it will take more than 10 years to replace one year's deforestation. This constitutes a major problem. Unless the planting rate is increased 10-fold, there will be continuous shrinkage of forest cover. The main reasons for deforestation include clearing for agricultural expansion (shifting cultivation and population increase) and grazing, in particular in Shinyanga, Mwanza, Mara, Singida, Dodoma and Arusha regions. Frequent annual bush fires and uncontrolled harvesting for wood fuels, industrial wood and construction purposes also account for forest loss. Agriculture and livestock activities together with charcoal making are the chief causes of forest clearance. Increasingly, rapid deforestation is the main cause of floods and prolonged drought periods. Survival under these two extreme conditions of floods or drought is difficult.

One major problem of deforestation is that villagers are obliged to travel greater distances for woodfuel of up to 5–10 km round trips. Usually a head load of about 30 kg cannot last the family for more than two days. In some cases, wood scarcity has led to the increasing use of dry dung, crop residues (e.g. cotton) or unsuitable species, the burning of which produces respiratory and eye problems, particularly for women who do the cooking.

Apart from the heavy deforestation of areas with high population densities around villages, deforestation close to urban areas is also a growing problem. This can occur through charcoal making, the sale of firewood for industrial purposes, e.g. brick making and lime burning, and the use of wood for construction. The result has been to increase the distance of areas from where forest products can be obtained. This has pushed costs higher, putting further pressure on low-income urban people who have to use up to half of their incomes on the purchase of firewood/charcoal.

Large-scale deforestation has also occurred in parts of Tanzania for a different reason. In order to ensure the survival of livestock and human beings the tsetse fly had to be eliminated through clearing natural forests. This is what turned the Shinyanga disctrict into an arid area with the subsequent need for the re-afforestation programme now being undertaken through the Shinyanga Soil Conservation Programme (HASHI).

There are still many tsetse fly infested areas with low population densities into which surplus population can move. The only practical solution for getting rid of tsetse fly still seems to be the clear-felling of forests. Unfortunately there is still no other method of eradicating the tsetse fly, though research is still going on.

Deforestation along the coast of trees such as mangroves could result in serious consequences. Sea banks could be eroded and this could mean losing land to the sea with serious consequences for urban areas, where many highly-priced residential areas and hotels are located. There is already severe deforestation in Dar es Salaam, the Coast region and Tanga region. Only Lindi and Mtwara regions have a moderate deforestation problem. This means at least two-thirds of the coast has a deforestation problem which needs to be addressed as a matter of some urgency.

Diseases and pollution

Diseases and pollution are environmental problems which are found in the humid coastal areas, in the more arid areas inland and in woodlands.

Whilst the humid coastal areas are notorious for diseases such as malaria, the drier areas, e.g. Dodoma and Singida, are known for the frequent occurrence of eye diseases. In areas of standing water bilharzia is common. In the drier woodlands one finds the tsetse fly which transmits sleeping sickness to humans and trypanosomiasis in livestock. To control these diseases effectively large-scale public investment is required.

In the urban areas, where large populations exist, there are many environmental problems which make the people prone to exposure to disease and pollution. The following are typical hazards:

- Many factories emit gases which pollute the air. The regulations are not strict enough to force them to improve. Others pour polluting liquids into rivers. Industrial plants such

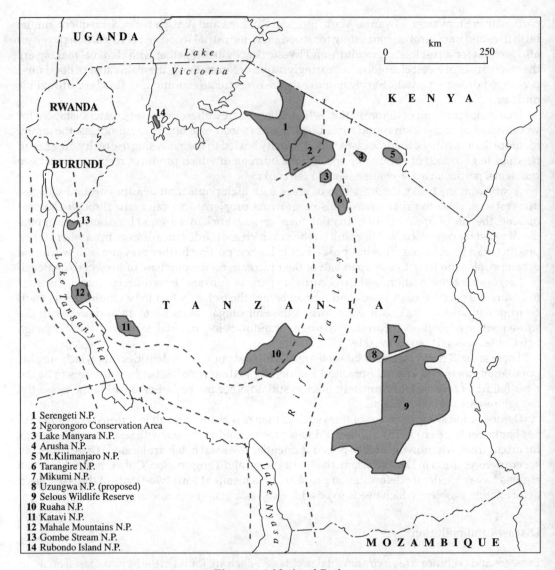

1 Serengeti N.P.
2 Ngorongoro Conservation Area
3 Lake Manyara N.P.
4 Arusha N.P.
5 Mt.Kilimanjaro N.P.
6 Tarangire N.P.
7 Mikumi N.P.
8 Uzungwa N.P. (proposed)
9 Selous Wildlife Reserve
10 Ruaha N.P.
11 Katavi N.P.
12 Mahale Mountains N.P.
13 Gombe Stream N.P.
14 Rubondo Island N.P.

Figure 8.5 *National Parks*

as textile factories, chemical factories, breweries, and asbestos plants have all been identified as polluters of the environment.

- Inefficient and unserviced sewage systems are responsible for flooding which, apart from emitting foul smells, creates breeding grounds for mosquitoes and flies. The result is gross pollution and diseases such as diarrhoea, malaria and bilharzia.
- Burning refuse in cities in dumps located near residential areas.

In rural areas pollution due to the increased use of agricultural chemicals to increase production has been identified. This includes the use of pesticides, fungicides and herbicides, many of which, when left undecomposed in the soil, are carried by surface run-off into streams where fish and people can be adversely affected. In addition the following problems have been observed:

- The importing of agricultural chemicals which have expired has resulted in a dumping problem as such chemicals can pollute surrounding areas.
- In the coffee-growing areas for example, it is not uncommon to see people cleaning their sprayers immediately after work in water which then enters watercourses. These watercourses join bigger rivers or sometimes may feed small lakes or dams supplying drinking water to livestock and humans as well as being used for fishing. Toxic poisoning of fauna can result from such careless practices.

The survival of wildlife

There are 50–60 game controlled areas in Tanzania occupying 121,655 km^2 spread throughout the country (Figure 8.5). The Game Department administers these through Regional Directorates. Licensed hunting of all game species is approved except for specially designated animals (e.g. giraffe, rhinoceros, elephant). The exception is when game is being hunted to control damage to crops, property or human life. In all such cases the matter should be reported to the game officials as soon as possible.

The major problems facing parks include poaching and fire. Poaching varies from one park to another, and from one part of the same park to another. The commonest types of poaching are as follows:

- Elephant for ivory;
- Rhinoceros for horn;
- Leopard and crocodile for skins;
- Wildebeest, eland, zebra, buffalo and hartebeest for meat and trophies.

Fires are caused by poachers, honey gatherers and pastoralists. Sometimes visitors to the parks cause fires. Fires can last for days or even weeks. Fires burn the vegetation on which so many animals depend. Also they can directly kill animals which are slow in movement such as the tortoise, the chameleon, insects and other organisms in and on the ground.

THE PRESENT RESOURCE BASE AND LEGAL INSTITUTIONS

Land

Agriculture is the backbone of the Tanzanian economy; its contribution to the GDP was 62.1 per cent in 1989. Issues related to land tenure and access to land resources have been discussed above under Resource-use conflicts.

Water resources

In Tanzania 60,000 km^2 is under water including the following:

- Lake Victoria (over half in Tanzania);
- Lake Tanganyika (half within Tanzania);

- About a third of Lake Nyasa (though contested by Malawi);
- Other relatively small lakes are Lake Rukwa in South West Tanzania and Lakes Eyasi, Manyara and Natron along the Rift Valley.

The river network is also substantial. The biggest river draining into the Indian Ocean is the Rufiji River. This river has the highest potential (2100 MW) for hydroelectricity. The current (1990) installed capacity is 333 megawatts.

The river Pangani receives tributaries from Kilimanjaro and the Meru and Pare Mountains. The river also drains into the Indian Ocean and is used for electricity at Nyumba ya Mungu (8 MW), Hale (21 MW), and Pangani falls (17.5 MW).

The river Ruvu, the water of which supplies Dar es Salaam, originates in Morogoro and drains into the Indian Ocean just north of Bagamoyo. So does the river Wami which flows north of the river Ruvu and its tributaries are from the Morogoro-Dodoma area.

Water utilisation

Tanzania's water resources have not been fully utilised due to low technological levels and partly due to a lack of economic and manpower capability. Irrigation and the generation of hydroelectricity are cases in point. For example, when there are droughts in the country, many places in Mwanza and Mara suffer as much as people in Singida and Dodoma regions, though the former live around Lake Victoria which could be used for irrigation. The same can be said of many places along the rivers where there are frequent crop failures in farm plots within the flood areas. Small-scale irrigation has not been developed to the extent of being accepted as an alternative to rain and floods.

In contrast, useful schemes are in hand using tributaries around Mt Meru and Mt Kilimajaro for irrigation purposes. Traditional gravity irrigation has been practised since before the colonial period and its use has continued. With reference to hydroelectricity, at least 14 regions out of 20 are connected to the hydroelectricity national grid. Six more need to be connected but the ability to extend and develop the existing potential depends on external financial injections which are not always available.

Large-scale irrigation projects

So far the irrigation projects which are of national economic importance include the following:

- The Mbarali complex in Mbeya involving rice production by harnessing tributaries of the Great Ruaha river by the National Agricultural and Food Corporation (NAFCO);
- The Dakawa rice farm complex drained by the river Wami in Morogoro by the Korea Tanzania Company (KOTACO);
- Sugar cane for sugar production at Mtibwa Sugar Estates and Kilombero Sugar Estates Companies along the rivers Wami and Great Ruaha respectively;
- Ruvu rice production fed by the Ruvu River along the coast by NAFCO;
- The Tanganyika Planting Company (sugar estate) at Moshi, fed by smaller rivers from Kilimanjaro. Rice production under a smallholder scheme by the Kilimanjaro Agricultural Development Corporation which is called the lower Moshi Irrigation Scheme also uses these rivers; and
- The Kagera Sugar Estate in Kagera Region which uses irrigation water from the Kagera river.

It is likely that the dams constructed for hydroelectricity generation will change the adjacent environment. In the areas below the dam, fauna and flora dependent on water are reduced, migrate or become extinct. People who depended on flood irrigation are deprived, unless new irrigation systems are planned for them. Above the dam flora and fauna are drowned and micro-climatic changes call for new landuse patterns. People displaced include those who, for many decades had cultivated the land along the river.

Those who live above dams are usually forced to move and to adhere to strict regulations requiring them not to cultivate the slopes covering watersheds leading into the dam. On the positive side, however, fishermen migrate to harvest freshwater fish which find a new habitat in the dam, e.g. in the Mtera dam where the local people were mostly pastoralists, and fishing was new. In this instance, the majority of fishermen are migrants from Lake Nyasa. Thus, fishermen's villages were developed in the place of pastoralists and crop cultivators.

Legal control

There are more legal controls on water rights than there are land-tenure controls. They are either customary controls, government decrees or local by-laws.

Water control by-laws exist in areas where irrigation has been practised for a long time, e.g. Mt Kilimanjaro and Mt Meru. Whenever water is required it is distributed according to a set rotation allocated by a local committee. This is important when water is required to meet deficits during dry spells when annual or perennial crops (like coffee) are threatened by drought.

Along with traditional water distribution systems there are legal water rights stipulated by the Act 10 of 1981, which is an amendment to basic water rights which has to be conformed with before one can dam a water source and direct the water elsewhere through piping or channels. With the villagisation policy, village government has to be consulted wherever a source of water from the village is needed. The Central Water Board is, however, in overall charge supported by the Regional Water Boards.

Vegetation

The vegetation of Tanzania varies with the climate, the topography and soil conditions. It is generally easier to describe the vegetation according to topographic zone.

The Northern coastal plains (north of the Rufiji River) have mangroves, areas of rainforest and pine plantation. Low-intensity small-holder cultivation dominates with permanent holdings of cashew and coconut as cash crops. Foodcrops include cassava, rice, sorghum and maize. In many areas, citrus, pineapple, fruit and vegetables are grown. Sisal estates around Tanga and Korogwe have taken over the natural vegetation in the area.

The Southern coastal area, apart from domination by cashew plants and coconut, has valuable indigenous timber and pine plantations. A lack of surface water and tsetse fly infestation has limited the settlement of people to certain areas such as the Makonde plains

The extensive interior plateau enclosed by branches of the Great Rift Valley consists of savanna woodlands (miombo). These provide a sparse cover and are small, slow-growing trees often not of good quality timber. Below the trees the understorey of grasses is mixed with herbs and shrubs. The tree cover is dominated by species of the leguminous family which include *Brachystegia*. Other trees in the savanna woodlands are *Brachylaena butchinsii*, *Pterocarpus angolensis*, *Chororophora excels Dalbergia melanoxylon* and *Afzelia quazensis*.

In the arid areas of north-east Tanzania (Northern arid lands and Masai steppe), the vegetation is open grassland and acacia scrub. The Masai steppe occupies rolling plains suitable only for grazing or for national parks (Serengeti, Tarangire and Mkomazi).

Other areas are the central semi-arid lands which are occupied by grassland for grazing. Vast wooded areas are tsetse infested. The south-eastern semi-arid lands (200–600 m) includes low-lying areas around Morogoro the Selous Game Reserve and the Masasi District. Woodlands are the main type of vegetation. Tsetse infestation is high thus leaving fewer tsetse fly-free areas where limited livestock can be grazed and crops raised.

The plateau includes the western plateau of land about 800 m high around Lakes Rukwa and Tanganyika to over 1500 m between Mbeya and Tabora. Most of the zone is covered by 'miombo' (*Brachystegia Julbernadia*) woodlands and all but 10 per cent is tsetse infested. More than half is designated as forest reserve where natural miombo woodland is logged under licence. The Ugalla Game Reserve, Katavi National Park and part of Rungwa Game Reserve are within this zone. Bee-keeping is an important minor industry in the miombo woodlands.

The southern plateau consists of uplands with significant areas of rocky hills, separated by dissected slopes from lower land to the east and north. The Selous Game Reserve occupies most of the northern-third of the zone. The zone is productive with cashew, tobacco, sesame, groundnuts and surplus maize as cash crops. The western quarter of the zone is tsetse-infested due to the forest which is the main type of vegetation.

The Highland areas include the Southern Highlands which include a broad ridge from north of Morogoro to the northern shores of Lake Nyasa. Altitudes range from 1200 to 2500 m. Forestry plantations include pine for pulpwood and together with natural forests they constitute the main type of vegetation.

The South-Western Highlands at 1400–2300 m are adjacent to the Rift Valley. The natural vegetation is forest but mixed farming is increasingly taking place with crops and some livestock.

The Western Highlands include ranges of north to south-trending ridges starting from north of Lake Tanganyika to the Uganda border which are separated by broad, swampy valleys. Altitude ranges from 100 to 1800 m and rainfall from 800 mm to over 2000 mm. The soils are loams and clays of low fertility on the hills and alluvium and ponded clays in the valleys. Due to great population pressure, woodland is restricted to game reserves and to where tsetse infestation occurs. The rest of the Western Highlands is covered by robusta coffee and bananas or by cassava, maize and sorghum where organic fertilisers are less easily available.

The Northern Highlands include volcanic uplands associated with the Rift Valley including the isolated mountains of Kilimanjaro and Meru, with high lava plateaux around them. Another block of land extends from Ngorongoro south-westwards between the Eastern Rift Valley and the Lake Eyasi rift. The Highlands are between 1000 and 2500 m though individual peaks arise over 4000 m. Soils are deep, fertile loams and clays. The rains are bimodal and vary widely – with south and eastern slopes having a long growing season compared to the north and western slopes. Soils in drier areas are highly erodible. The upper slopes of Kilimanjaro and Meru mountains are closed forest towards the top, and lower down commercial production of softwoods and hardwood plantations predominate. Drier slopes have more grass than trees and here semi-nomadic herdsmen and cultivators grow maize and beans.

Isolated granitic mountains include steep-sided mountains (Ulugurus near Morogoro) and extensive highlands separated by steep scarps from surrounding plains such as the Pare and Usambara ranges in the north-east. In the north, bordering Kenya, are the Tarime Highlands. Their altitude is between 1000 and 2000 m and rainfall up to 2000 mm or more is recorded. Soils vary according to terrain, being deep, friable, moderately fertile clay on upper slopes and plateaux, with shallow, stony soils and rock outcrops on steep slopes.

Upper slopes are under-productive forests, with areas like the Usambaras being important sources of indigenous hardwoods and also softwood plantations. There are important remnants of mountain evergreen forest, especially in the Usambaras, containing many indigenous plant species.

Legal controls over vegetation

Most of the grassland in the savanna areas is considered range land and is used by pastoralists as communal grazing land except where legally-established village governments have demarcated their own areas. In other areas the National Ranching Company (NARCO) has established ranches and the government has established state-owned farms, national parks or game reserves. In such areas, too, the grazing land has been taken out of communal control.

Forests have more legal control than pasture land, though most of the forests are public land open for use by the people. The functions of managing, protecting and regulating the utilisation of forest resources in the country are carried out under the guidance of the 1957 Forest Ordinance Cap.389, which is currently under review. Taking a total area of 44.37 million ha of forests, 13.02 million ha are gazetted as forest reserves. Gazetted forest has existed since colonial times (during both the German and British administrations).

Forest reserves include large areas in Tabora, Rukwa and Morogoro. Also along the coast 60,000 ha of mangrove forests are reserved. The reserved areas vary in size with areas as small as 3 ha up to 680,000 ha. The average size is about 25,000 ha. The reserved forests are designated for the production of poles, timber, firewood etc. The Forestry and Bee-keeping Division of the Ministry of Resources and Tourism is entrusted with undertaking forest functions as stated above and with supervising and assisting parastatals under its jurisdiction.

Among the reserved forests, 1.6 million ha are for protection purposes and 80,000 ha are man-made forest (19 plantations) for producing soft and hardwood timber. The catchment forests consist of 577,600 ha distributed as follows:

- Catchment Forest Project, Arusha Region–156,980 ha;
- Catchment Forest Project, Kilimanjaro Region–137,862 ha;
- Catchment Forest Project, Tanga Region–27,740 ha;
- Catchment Forest Project, Morogoro Regions–255,032 ha.
  Total =577,614 hectares.

Others are:

- Usa River Forest Project (Arusha)–6508 ha
- Magamba/Kwamtoro Forest Project –10,193 ha

The main criticism of the legislation is that it is concerned solely with forest reserves and does not protect forests outside the reserves. Provisions referring to gazetting and protecting forest reserves and the removal of products therefrom are given as regulations. For example, the 1985 forest rules concern the removal of products and royalty rates charged but only from the forest reserves.

Significant policy changes have included the nationalisation of all major forest industries in the country, and the establishment of state saw-mills within the old plantations and valuable indigenous forests. Rural afforestation programmes were intensified in areas with high population densities. Town and village afforestation schemes were carried out in places where serious soil deterioration had been observed.

The current forestry policy, proposed in 1988, includes further substantial changes such as centralised forest administration, the emphasis on village forestry programmes, rehabilitating eroded areas, destocking and education to prevent fires. Furthermore, the policy emphasises research to improve the production of forest products and educating the public through the media.

In order to achieve these policy objectives several parastatals have been established to assist in the appropriate exploitation of pasture and forestry resources. For example, the Ministry of Agriculture and Livestock Production controls the National Ranching Company (NARCO) which runs a chain of ranches in the North-West (Kilimajaro) Centre (Kongwa), East (Mkata, Dakawa Ruvu Ranches), in Tanga (Azimio), in the South (Usangu and Sumbawanga) and in the North-East (Kitengule and Kikurura). These ranches exploit the pasture resources to produce quality beef, both for the local market, and for export. Similarly for the dairy industry the Dairy Farm Company (DAFCO) has farms which promote the production of milk which is sold directly or sent to processing plants. In addition to the government-owned livestock breeding farms, no other legal institutions are officially allowed to exploit pasture/forage resources apart from using communal pasture, which is not fenced off and which is thus free for anyone to use as grazing land.

The Forest Department allows many groups and individuals to exploit forestry products following set conditions. Most of these are included in various by-laws and there are workers at local level to advise people as necessary.

The Tanzania Wood Industries Corporation (TWICO) with its subsidiary wood sawmills enjoys the monopoly of exploiting the forestry products. As a by-product of the forest, bee-keeping is assisted by the Ministry's Bee-Keeping Institute in Tabora.

Mining and mineral resources

Tanzania is endowed with mineral resources which have never been fully exploited. The currently known coal and gas resources in the country are shown in Figure 8.6.

The State Mining Corporation (STAMICO) was created in 1972 and was supposed to take over mining companies which had recently been nationalised. It has the responsibility for the exploration and the development of the country's mineral resources including coal. It oversees mineral markets on behalf of its six subsidiaries.

Other important minerals exploited by subsidiary companies include:

- Williamson Diamond Mines Limited in the Shinyanga area exploits the diamonds at Mwadui. Previously a private company, the government has a major shareholding since its partial nationalisation. The output of diamonds is dwindling and mining is becoming more and more costly.
- Uvinza Salt Works Limited exploits natural salt from Uvinza in Kigoma, but several other salt works along the coast near Pangani, Bagamoyo, Dar es Salaam, Lindi and Mtwara are worked by small groups or individuals. These exploit sea water to produce common salt by solar evaporation.
- Gold has been mined by various companies and by individuals in Geita (Mwanza), Sekenke (Singida) and Lupa (Rukwa, Mpanda and Musoma). The hunt for gold has attracted many individual miners to places where large commercial exporters could not make a profit. The small producers, exploiting cheap labour, have flocked to the gold mines to reap the profits from gold sold through the black market for export. The Government had to enact a by-law which makes it legal to sell gold to the Bank of Tanzania without being questioned about the source. This has enabled the government to tap a substantial amount of gold which had previously not been included in official statistics. It is, therefore, not easy to estimate the actual production of gold, as registered production had ceased until the private producers took over production.

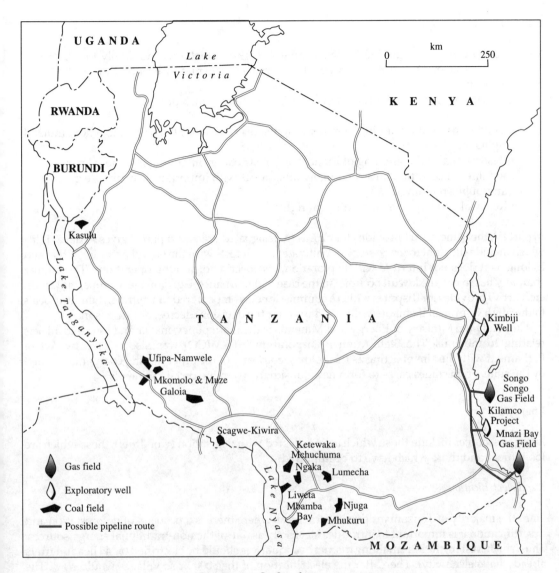

Figure 8.6 *Coal and gas resources*

- The Minjingu Phosphate Company is the sole company which exploits phosphate minerals found some 150 km south-west of Arusha. The rock phosphate was exploited mainly for the fertiliser factory at Tanga. Recently, demand has declined as the import of fertiliser, sometimes in the form of overseas aid, has reduced demand for the local product.
- Mica is another mineral which has been exploited by various companies and individuals. The mineral is chiefly found in the Morogoro region. Other minerals currently being exploited are tanzanite in Arusha (Arumeru/Kiteto districts) and other associated minerals, tin in the Kagera region and limestone associated with the making of Portland Cement at Dar es Salaam, Tanga and Mbeya.

Legal control of mining

Mining in Tanzania is controlled by the Mining Act, 1979 which does not apply to mineral oil (Cap.339). This means that all other prospecting for minerals and mining licences can only be issued by the government.

Further, the act provides for the following mineral rights which prescribe:

- Conditions for the granting of mineral rights; restrictions on the person to whom mineral rights may be granted;
- Restrictions on the granting of licences, e.g. restrictions on mining in national parks, wildlife conservation areas and many other areas with important structures, e.g. roads and public buildings;
- Renewal and amendment of mineral rights.

In part IV, the Mineral Act provides for claims in designated areas and part V gives surface rights which include the right to graze stock or cultivate, which rests with the lawful occupier of the land as long as it does not interfere with exploration, prospecting or mining operations. The mining company has to pay the lawful occupier in the case of disturbance, e.g. damage to crops, buildings, etc. Part VI provides for disputes which a commissioner is empowered to arbitrate, though appeals to the High Court can be made within 30 days after the decision, decree, or order is made.

Currently the Ministry of Energy and Minerals is the main policy-maker and oversees all acts relating to minerals. The State Mining Corporation (STAMICO) was also created by Act of Parliament with the aim of acting as the holding company of the other mining companies owned by the state, or, in somes cases to form new subsidiaries to mine certain minerals.

Energy

Energy resources include those which are associated with vegetation (woodfuel), those which are fossil fuels, and those which have to be imported.

Rural electrification

Since the majority of Tanzanians live in rural areas where there is a problem of deforestation and desertification it is important to introduce electricity as one of the non-traditional energy sources. Thus, as a first step, the 34 remaining district headquarters should be electrified (as 45 headquarters already have electricity). Thereafter the electrification of the 8000 or so villages would start. The limiting factor will be the economics of the supply of electricity to the rural areas with sparse populations (16 persons/km²) It is worthwhile to note here that the work of supplying electricity for the whole country is vested with the Tanzania Electricity Supply Company (TANESCO). It is through this legally-established company that all aspects of electricity development are vested.

Electricity

Tanzania has a total installed capacity of 480 MW consisting of 333 MW of hydro and the balance diesel power. The national grid is connected to 14 of the 20 regions on the mainland and Zanzibar is connected with a submarine cable. Only 6 per cent of households have electricity and per capita consumption is 60 kWh (compared with European countries 3000 kWh per capita or other countries like Malawi, Zambia and Mozambique whose per capita consumption is 67, and 988 and 943 kWh respectively). In 1989 total generation was 1503 GWh of which 1443 GWh (96 per cent) was generated by hydroelectric generation. The hydroelectric generating stations are shown in Table 8.1.

Table 8.1 *Hydro electricity stations*

Station	Installed (MW)	Year in Service
Kidatu	204.00	1975/1980
Mtera	80.00	1988
Hale	21.00	1964
Pangani Falls	17.50	1934
Nyumba ya Mungu	8.00	1968
Tosamaganga	1.22	1951
Kikuletwa	1.16	1935
Mbalizi	0.34	1958

Table 8.2 shows an estimate of future demands up to the year 2000.

Table 8.2 *National demand forecast for electricity*

Year	Sales (GWh)	Growth rate (%)
1990	1315.01	–
1991	1457.01	10.90
1992	1536.14	5.43
1993	1642.78	6.94
1994	1750.23	6.54
1995	1867.01	6.67
1996	1989.90	6.58
1997	2107.30	5.90
1998	2231.61	5.90
1999	2363.30	5.90
2000	2549.59	7.88

Petroleum

Tanzania is a net importer of petroleum products. The market structures emerging include spot trading, the futures market and contract sales. Therefore quick responses to changing situations call for increasing the storage capacity of 30 days supply to 60–90 days supply. With the current loss of 20 per cent due to poor handling and road transport (60 per cent by road), only 70 per cent of demand for petroleum products is being met.

In terms of the use of petroleum, transport was highest (50.9 per cent) followed by manufacturing (26.3 per cent), household (8.3 per cent), agriculture and fisheries (7.1 per cent) and other services (6.4 per cent).

The consumption of petroleum products grew at an annual rate of 7.3 per cent between 1960–1973. Subsequently, the rate dropped to 1.4 per cent per annum in the period 1974–1985 mainly due to purchasing problems rather than to a drop in demand. In the 1990s it is expected to grow at an average rate of 3.5 per cent per annum.

The petroleum sector, like the other energy sectors, is controlled by the Ministry of Energy and Minerals and the Department of Energy and Petroleum Affairs. The Tanzania Petroleum Development Corporation is the focal point of all activities (the TPDC, marketing companies BP(T), AGIP(T) and TAZAMA (Tanzania Zambia Pipeline), TOTAL(T), ESSO(T), CALTEX(TA), SHELL(T), BULK OIL(T), MOBIL(T) and TIPER (the refining company) are the implementing agencies of policy guidelines, projects and trading activities in the oil industry).

Future petroleum policy can be identified as follows:

- The efficient and economic procuring and distribution of the product;
- Improving the security of crude oil and refined product supplies;
- Optimising refining processes so as to meet the demand; the reduction of dependence on imported petroleum through conservation, substitution and the development of indigenous resources;
- Reducing the overall contribution of petroleum to energy requirements by developing alternative energy sources;
- The appropriate pricing of petroleum products;
- Conducting R & D for technologies which will optimise energy use.

Gas

Tanzania has proven gas reserves at Songosongo of about 20 million tonnes of oil equivalent (toe). The following table gives an idea of the reserves (see also Figure 8.6).

Table 8.3 *Natural gas reserves (billion cubic feet)*

	Songosongo	Mnazi Bay	Total
Proved	726	23	749
Probable	157	586	743
Possible	223	–	223
Total	1106	609	1715

Plans for the economic utilisation of the gas are underway. Studies have shown the desirability of utilising gas in industry and for power generation in Dar es Salaam. The construction of a pipeline from Songosongo to Dar es Salaam, the development of a distribution network and a gas-powered station are earmarked for implementation. Further, the utilisation of Mnazi Bay gas for on-site electricity generation for south-east Tanzania is being looked into.

Coal

The existence of coal in Tanzania is well known and reserves are shown in Table 8.4 and Figure 8.5.

Mining has been focused on Songwe-Kiwira, the output of which represents most of the locally-produced coal in Tanzania. The exploitation of this coal (5500 kcal/kg) which was found to be inferior to the Ketwewake-Mchuchuma coal (7000 kcal/kg) was because of the proximity of the former to transport infrastructure. The possibility of using coal as a substitute for petroleum products and biomass is being actively considered.

Proven coal reserves are about 320 million tonnes and estimated reserves are at about 1500 million tonnes. Coal consumption in power generation, households, and agriculture could be increased through:

- investment to provide an efficient coal transport and distribution system;
- investment in expanding coal mining;
- investment in industrial and agricultural coal-using facilities;
- the acquisition of skills in coal usage, including development and popularisation of suitable coal stoves; and
- investment in pit-head power plants.

Table 8.4 *Coal resources (million tonnes)*

Field	Proven	Estimated	Total
Ketewaka-Mchuchuma	186.6	495	681.6
Songwe-Kiwira	35.0	595	630.0
Galula	–	53	53.0
Njunga	–	126	126.0
Liweta	–	34	34.0
Ngaka	97.7	152	249.7
Mbamba Bay	–	29	29.0
Mhukuku	–	19	19.0
Ufipa	–	17–57	17.0–57.0
Lumecha	–	–	–
Total	319.3	1520–1560	1839.3–1879.3

Biomass

This has been defined in the broader sense to include woodfuel, charcoal, and crop and livestock waste.

Fuelwood

The consumption of woodfuel was 25 million cubic metres (m³) of solid wood of which 97 per cent is used as firewood in rural areas and the balance in urban centres and in agro-processing plants. This excludes the amount that is converted to charcoal. Since the yield of fuelwood is far below consumption levels (i.e. 300,000 ha–400,000 ha cleared against a planting rate of 14,000–20,000 ha), woodfuel development programmes have been advocated. The woodfuel development programme would involve the Tanzania Forestry Action Plan (TFAP) in efforts to enhance both woodfuel supply and demand management as follows:

- woodfuel supply development would be carried out through community and farm forestry and woodland management;
- community and farm forestry would involve the development of sustained tree growing and management campaigns in villages and urban areas so that people can meet their needs for woodfuel, poles and fodder.

The objective of woodland management will be to bring public woodlands under proper management and control for future production and a sustainable supply of woodfuel through:

- giving authority to villages to control and manage the forests and woodlands falling within their boundaries under the guidance of forestry experts;
- introducing proper harvesting systems and streamlining licensing procedures. Demand management will be through promoting the use of efficient cooking stoves in both rural and urban areas as well as by improving technologies used in making charcoal. These issues will require liaison and co-ordination with appropriate ministries and institutions in mobilising resources and efforts to popularise the use of energy- saving devices such as improved stoves and kilns, as well as the promotion of alternative source of energy.

Charcoal

This is produced by converting fuelwood into a fuel of higher calorific value per unit weight incurring energy loss in so doing. It is estimated that the efficiency of the earth mound kiln is poor, only about 10 per cent. This inefficiency is attributed to a lack of know-how, i.e. through the use of moist and oversized wood and mounds which do not allow the proper control of combustion. Oxygen gains entry and enables wood to burn to ashes instead of being carbonized. Moisture reduction from around 45 per cent to 15 per cent would go a long way towards improving kiln efficiency. The 'cassamance' kiln currently being tried by the Ministry of Energy and Minerals proved to be more efficient as it shortened the carbonization process to two to three days instead of one to two weeks using the traditional kiln.

In Tanzania 70 per cent of the urban population uses charcoal; this has been a stimulus to charcoal makers in the periphery of these urban areas. Areas between Dar es Salaam and Morogoro as well as between Tanga and Dar es Salaam are heavily deforested because of charcoal making. An estimated 392,000 tonnes of charcoal were consumed in 1988, at an average of 2 kg of charcoal per family per day. There is a clear need to introduce improved charcoal kilns more widely in Tanzania in order to conserve wood resources.

Crop and livestock wastes are another energy source in Tanzania. Estimates of their potential are given below (Sawe, 1990).

Table 8.5 *Crop and livestock wastes*

	Annual potential (tonnes)	Assumed utilisation factor (%)	Availability (tonnes)
Maize	5 000 000	20	1 000 000
Animal wastes (cattle)	50 000	5 for biogas	2500
Coconut waste (shell/husks)	150 000	100	150 000
Cashew-nut waste	12 500	100	14 500
Cotton waste	900 000	90	810 000
Mollases/ baggasse	150 000	100	150 000
Coffee husks	81 400	100	8400

It has been calculated that agricultural wastes to the value of 4.5 million tonnes of oil equivalent are available in addition to 46,000 toe from animal wastes. About 400 biogas plants have recently been constructed. In all, the energy derived from crop and animal wastes represents about 15 per cent of total woodfuel consumption. This is the equivalent of saving about 50,000 ha of woodland.

Legal control of energy

The Ministry for Energy and Minerals is responsible for energy policy. Some of the relevant laws are:

- Electricity Ordinance, Cap.131 of 1957 plus subsequent amendment;
- The Companies Ordinance, Cap.212 of the laws of Tanzania;
- The Companies (Regulation of Dividends and Miscellaneous Provisions) Act No. 22 of 1972;
- The Petroleum (Conservation) Act 1981;
- Other Acts of Parliament establishing parastatals related to energy and environment are:
  - Rufiji Basin Development Authority (RUBADA);
  - The National Environment Management Council;
  - The Tanzania National Commission for Science and Technology.

In some cases the laws may be inconsistent, e.g. in the Rufiji Basin, both RUBADA and TANESCO can establish electricity according to the electricity ordinance Cap.131.

- The Ministry of Natural Resources and Tourism oversees all laws pertaining to Forestry and National Parks. It is the Ministry responsible for the National Environment Council and the Natural Landuse Commission which are concerned with the wood supply, directly or indirectly.
- The Ministry of Agriculture and Livestock is involved with energy supplies through the extension of agro-forestry and village woodlots.
- The Ministry of Community Development, Women and Children has a role in the energy field through the development of tree nurseries and tree-planting campaigns by community groups and women's organisations.

Wildlife

In Tanzania there are 13 national parks including the Ngorongoro Conservation Area and Selous. Together they cover 102,658 km² (about 11 per cent) of the total area of the country. In addition, 39,750km² is occupied by 16 game reserves, (i.e. 4 per cent of Tanzania). Details of the parks are given in Table 8.6 and are shown in Figure 8.5.

In addition, about 50–60 game reserves are listed in Tanzania covering 121,655 km².These areas are administered by the Game Department through Regional Directorates and some are detailed in Table 8.7.

Utilisation

The objectives of the National Parks are:

- To provide places for recreation for people wanting to view wild animals in their natural habitat;
- To preserve the animals and their environment from human interference. This enables research to be conducted in as natural a setting as possible.
- To generate income through tourism. Each tourist spends about US$1000 and this assists in the maintenance of the parks and other government facilities.

Legal control

The law that deals with wildlife is the National Parks Ordinance Cap. 412. Several amendments and Acts of Parliament have been responsible for the introduction of other institutions to the wildlife division of the Ministry of Natural Resources and Tourism.
The following Acts deal with specific aspects of wildlife.

Act 3 of 1974 initiated the Tanzania National Parks (TANAPA) and deals with the implementation of wildlife conservation throughout the country.

Table 8.6 *National Parks*

Name/Area km²	Year established	Location/altitude	Principal features
Serengeti 14 763	1951	1°28'–3°17'S 35°50'–35°20'E 920–1850 m alt.	Central area Acacia savanna. Short and long grass plains south. North hilly more densely wooded in Western Corridor.
Ngorongoro Conservation Area 8288	1959	2°44'–3°26'S 35°00'–35°55'E 1350–3600 m alt.	Scenic craters, good forest, volcanic mountains, extensive plains, highland plateau
Lake Manyara 325	1960	3°20'S 3°40'E 945 m alt.	Lake Manyara, Great Rift Valley and groundwater forest
Tarangire 2600	1970	3°50'S 36°00'E at centre 1110 m alt.	Nine vegetational zones, swamps, rock outcrops and the Tarangire river
Arusha 137	1960	3°15'S 35°55'E 1524–1572 m alt.	Craters, lakes,rugged Mt Meru and forest
Mount Kilimanjaro 756	1973	2°50'–3°10'S 37°20'–37°40'E	Shira Plateau, Mawenzi and Kibo peaks
Mikumi 3230		7°00'–7°50'S 37°00'–37°30'E 549 m alt.	Swamps and miombo woodlands and Mkata river flood plains
Ruaha 12 950	1964	7°45'S 35°40'E at centre 750–1900 m alt.	Rivers, escarpment, springs, hills, Miombo woodland
Katavi 2253	1974	6°40'–7°05'S 35°50'–56°50'E 900 m alt.	River, lakes, swamps and miombo woodland
Mahale Mountain 1577	1985	6°00'–6°28'S 29°43'–30°07'E 2000–2462 m alt.	Mountain range, Rift Valley and forests, Lake Tanganyika
Gombe Stream 52	1968	4°40'S 29°38'E at centre 681–1524 m alt.	Mountains, Rift Valley, Lake Tanganyika, valleys with streams
Rubondo Island 240	1977	2°30'S 31°45'E at centre 1150 m alt.	Lake Victoria, about a dozen small islets belonging to the park and forest
Udzungwa Mountains 1000	1991	7°45'S 36°36'E at centre 300–1200 m alt.	Forest reserve
Selous Wildlife Reserve 55 100	1922	7°15'–10°15'S 36°00'–38°45'E 100–1250 m alt.	Rivers, hills, forest, Tanzania–Zambia railway line, Miombo woodland, Rufiji river

Under section 18 of Cap. 412 (The National Parks Amendment Regulations, 1989), there is a schedule which gives the types of fees to be paid which include:

- Entry permits for each person by age and nationality (resident or non-resident);
- Similar permits for vehicles by weight;
- Permits for camping;
- Permits for landing aircraft and helicopters, whether local or foreign registered.

In the second schedule, fees for cine/video filming for commercial ventures are given.

Act 6 of 1970 relating to fisheries was enacted to develop and control the fishing industry. Various punishments are given for breaking the regulations. Further regulations relating to fish:

- Prohibit fishing by explosives or poison;
- Prevent the sale of fish which was dynamited or poisoned;
- Prevent coral reef destruction by explosives or electrical devices;
- Prevent water pollution by chemical, biological and radiological means.

Table 8.7 *Game Reserves*

Name	Area (km²)	Regions
Selous	55 000	Coast, Morogoro, Lindi
Rungwa	9000	Singida
Moyowosi	6000	Kigoma
Ugalla	5000	Tabora
Uwanda	5000	Rukwa
Kizigo	4000	Singida
Maswa	2200	Sinyange
Burigi	2200	Kagera
Biharamulo	1300	Kagera
Umba	1500	Tanga
Mkomazi	1000	Kilimanjaro
Kilimanjaro	900	Kilimanjaro
Saadani	300	Coast
Orugundu	800	Kagera
Mount Meru	300	Arusha
Ibanda	200	Kagera
Sea Nane Island	0.5	Kwanza

An Act to establish the Tanzania Fisheries Research Institute and to provide for its powers and operation in relation to the promotion and conduct of research into fisheries was passed in 1979.

The fishing potential of Tanzania is indicated in Figure 8.7 which shows that the highest catches are in Lake Tanganyika, 115,000 tonnes, and Lake Victoria, 99,000 tonnes, the coastal shelf, 30,000 tonnes, Lake Nyasa, 20,000 tonnes, Lake Rukwa, 7000 tonnes and Manyara Kitangiri, 4000 tonnes. While there is potential for catching more in Lake Tanganyika and the Shelf (potential 150,000 and 60,000 tonnes respectively), the potential for Lakes Victoria, Nyasa and Rukwa are not known.

Meanwhile the country maintains the 200 km Economic Exploitation Zone for sea fishing along

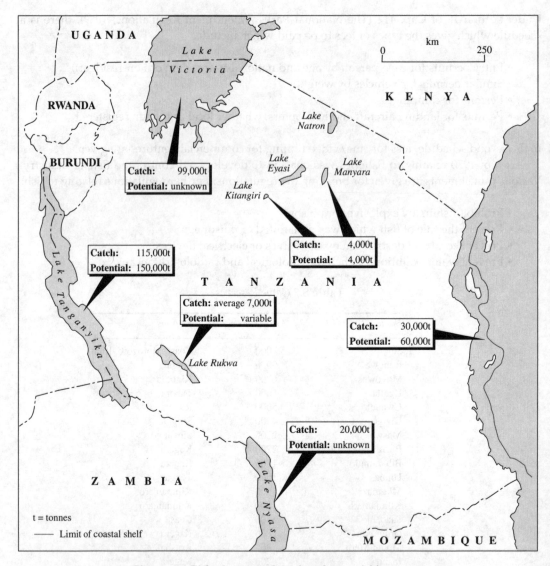

UGANDA

Lake
Victoria

RWANDA

KENYA

Lake
Natron

BURUNDI

Lake
Eyasi

Lake
Manyara

Lake
Kitangiri

Catch:	99,000t
Potential:	unknown

Catch:	4,000t
Potential:	4,000t

Catch:	115,000t
Potential:	150,000t

T A N Z A N I A

Lake Tanganyika

Catch:	average 7,000t
Potential:	variable

Catch:	30,000t
Potential:	60,000t

Lake Rukwa

Catch:	20,000t
Potential:	unknown

ZAMBIA

Lake Nyasa

t = tonnes

—— Limit of coastal shelf

M O Z A M B I Q U E

0   km   250

Figure 8.7 *Fisheries: annual catch and potential by source*

the Indian Ocean. This means that international fishing agents or companies will have to seek permits to fish either by paying fees or by co-operating with the local fishing agency the Tanzania Fishing Corporation (TAFICO), the parastatal created to promote fishing in Tanzania.

The Wildlife Amendment Act of 1978 enables the Minister to establish the Wildlife Protection Unit, the main functions of which will be the protection of wildlife against unlawful hunters and the general enforcement of the provisions of this Act relating to 'hunting'.

STRATEGIES AND SOLUTIONS FOR ENVIRONMENTAL SUSTAINABILITY

Government policies and programmes

Government policies on land, water, vegetation and wildlife are currently being implemented under different Ministries and in some cases these resources are managed by more than one ministry.

Land

All land is owned by the public (Government) but it can be leased under various regulations and laws. Within this main framework the government recognises four main types of system:

- Government Leaseholds
- Right of Occupancies
- Customary Land Tenure
- Collective Tenure Systems

Over the last few years the following programmes, related to land, have been developed by the Ministry of Land (which up to 1990/91 included Natural Resources and Tourism, Housing and Urban Development):

- Planning, surveying, mapping and the allocation of land for various uses.
- Preparation of masterplans for villages and towns.

Registration Offices are organised by zones as follows:

Coastal   For the regions of Dar es Salaam, Coast, Morogoro, Lindi, Ruvuma and Mtwara.
Moshi   For the regions of Mwanza, Tabora, Shiyanga, Mara, Kagera and Kigoma.
Dodoma   For the regions of Dodoma, Iringa, Mbeya, Singida and Rukwa.

The Zonal Registration Offices perform the following functions:

- The preparation of Certificates of Occupancy;
- Mortgages;
- Sales of houses;
- Revocations and surrender of chattels transfer;
- Deeds of acquisitions etc.

Through the use of the National Landuse Commission the Ministry continues to prepare landuse plans and has completed such plans for Arusha, Kilimanjaro and Tanga.

Agro-ecological zone mapping has been completed and includes residential, agricultural, livestock and conservation areas. Policies include:

- Encouraging people to save money and build houses using their savings;
- Giving advice on various sources for obtaining housing finance;
- Building houses under co-operative systems;

- Strengthening the capacity of the National Housing Corporation (NHC) to build houses and preparing the NHC to enter into partnership with other parties;
- Re-examining existing laws concerning urban housing in order to adjust them so as to encourage the building of urban housing;
- Co-operating with all institutions concerned with the supply of building materials;
- Establishing a National Housing Advisory Council so as to attract new ideas and recommendations which will assist in building residential houses;
- Analysing and preparing a strategy for cooperation with the National Provident fund (NPF), the National Insurance Corporation (NIC), a Parastatal Pension Fund (PPF) and the Local Authority Fund in contributing to residential and other houses;
- Establishing a Plots Development Revolving Fund which will be paid into by those obtaining plots so as to create a capital source for further work in developing high, medium and low density plots, industrial plots, business institutions and farms;
- Allocating prime land by tender for hotel, industrial and business uses;
- Reviewing land rent levels from time to time so as to have more land revenue to allow for inflation.

Soil erosion policies

Soil erosion is of concern to the government and many laws and by-laws have been passed to prevent soil erosion and to conserve soil. As with land policies, there is no single Ministry which is responsible for soil erosion. Therefore several policies exist which leads to duplication and overlap of ministerial responsibilities.

Current preventative measures against soil erosion are identified as follows:

- the prevention of erosion along the coast by preventing deforestation and by improving beach erosion defence structures;
- Starting the HASHI project in Shinyanga region which has so far enabled the planting of 4082 ha of trees; bunds have been constructed, and 25,000 ha of further land has been earmarked for conservation purposes.

In this project the grassroots involvement of the people and their training have been mentioned as one of the main keys to success.

The establishment of the Landuse Planning Commission was a policy decision which gives several functions to the Commission related to soil conservation directly or indirectly. In any landuse activity the issue of soil conservation must be taken into consideration.

The establishment of the National Environmental Management Council is also a policy landmark which has strengthened the implementation of policies relating to the environment.

Mining regulations state that the methods used should involve soil conservation as much as possible and provision for the revegetation of areas mined at the conclusion of the mining operation should be made.

The afforestation programmes being undertaken by the Ministry of Natural Resources and Tourism at national level are aimed at assisting soil conservation. Other programmes include the Division of Forestry with 19 national plantations; the conservation of mangrove forests along the coast; catchment forests in four areas totalling 577,617 ha, and the village afforestation programme of between 12,000 and 14,000 ha each year.

Water resource policies

The water resources of Tanzania are exploited under various regulations. Water from rivers which have dams for electricity is governed by TANESCO rules, e.g. water may not be drawn from the dam, though fishing may be allowed. In areas where irrigation is practised, water rights have to be obtained from the local District or Regional or Central Water Boards. All applicants must comply with the basic Water Utilisation (Control and Regulation Act No.42 of 1974 and subsequent amendments).

The government has a stated policy of supplying water to all people, with the support of NGOs and private investment. Those with water rights are always requested to share water for domestic purposes with their neighbours.

In rural areas most of the water supply is developed by the government but thereafter the villagers have to contribute to the maintenance of the service. The Government plans to supply clean water to all by the turn of the century. It is well known that the government cannot achieve this alone as it does not have adequate resources. There are many organisations which assist in water supply provision. Although currently 60 per cent of the urban areas and 40 per cent of rural areas are supposed to have clean piped water, 40 per cent of the pumping facilities are out of order. This confirms the importance of individuals, groups and NGOs contributing more to investment in the water supply sector.

Among the current contributors to the water supply apart from the Government are:

- The Health, Sanitation and Water Project (HESAWA), which among other activities assists in the installation of water around the Lake Zone to four regions (Kagera, Mwanza, Mara and Shinyanga).
- FINWATER is a project which has been installing shallow well pumps in some regions (Lindi, Mtwara and Morogoro) assisted by Finland.
- TIRDEP is a German (GTZ) funded project which has been working in Tanga Region and in one of its schemes the Village Water Supply Project (VWSP) has been assisting through the training of technicians and the installation of shallow well pumps in villages.
- DANIDA has been assisting water supply projects in three regions – Songea, Mbeya and Iringa.

The most comprehensive project is that of the Rufiji River basin, under RUBADA, covering 117,000 km². The main tributary is the Kilombero supplying 62 per cent of the total flow, and the Great Ruaha and Luwegu supplying 15 per cent and 18 per cent respectively. The development of hydroelectricity at Kidatu Dam power station (204 MW) and the regulating reservoir at Mtera (80 MW), has already occurred.

Detailed studies at Stiegler's Gorge dam and the Flood Control Project envisages a final installed capacity of 2100 MW. The other major activity is irrigating the estimated 600,000 ha considered suitable for development. The three potential areas identified for irrigation are the Usangu Plains, the Kilombero Valley and the Lower Rufiji. Of the 200,000 ha of irrigable land, only 3500 ha have been developed so far. Irrigation schemes now under development are at Kapunga (5000 ha) and Madibira (9000 ha). Irrigable land in Kilombero covers 300,000 ha, part of which is under the Kilombero Sugar Cane Plantation. In the lower Rufiji Valley 80,000 ha of irrigable land is envisaged for irrigation after the Stiegler's Gorge dam is built.

Other areas where major irrigation projects exist are the lower Moshi where there is irrigation for smallholder rice farming, in Morogoro, the Mtibwa Sugar Estates, and in Kagera Region the Kagera Sugar Estates.

Vegetation

The Government programmes on vegetation, afforestation and the reforestation of pasture are the responsibility of the Ministry of Agriculture and Livestock Development, the Ministry of Natural Resources and Tourism and their respective parastatals.

Apart from the rehabilitation work being done by the HADO programme in Dodoma and HASHI in Shinyanga, the following programmes were established as long ago as 1980:

- National tree plantation projects in 19 plantations (Figure 8.8)
- The village tree-planting programme (Table 8.8)

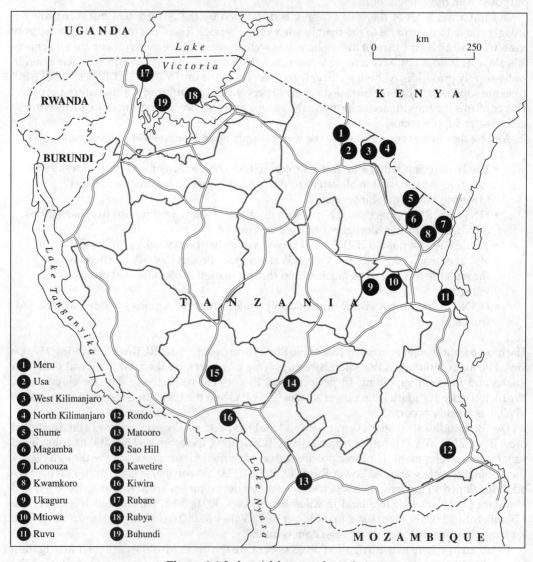

Figure 8.8 *Industrial forestry plantations*

- NGO and donor agencies funded tree-planting programmes found in most rural projects.

Five destocking campaigns of the Ministry of Agriculture and Livestock included the following rangeland measures:

- Improvement of the forage base by systematic bush clearing to destroy the habitats of tsetse flies;
- Propagation of appropriate range grass/legume species over denuded areas;
- Use of fire as a tool for range management;
- Organised destocking, based on proper landuse planning so that areas not suitable for crops and livestock may be utilised; and
- the establishment of water supply points for livestock use in grazing areas.

Table 8.8 *Tree planting in villages 1981/82–1985/86 (ha)*

Region	1981/2		1982/3		1983/4		1984/5		1985/86	
	Target	Actual	Target	Actual	Target	Actual	Target	Actual	Target	Actual
Arusha	662	662	794	811	953	850	1143	490	1373	1129
Dodoma	1 019	1 019	1 223	832	1 467	539	1 761	297	2 135	812
Dar es Salaam	44	44	53	51	63	43	76	85	91	118
Iringa	2 028	2 028	2 434	1 723	2 920	1 582	3 504	1 671	4 205	2 068
Kagera	684	684	820	371	984	430	1 182	289	1 418	426
Kilimanjaro	500	500	908	241	1 090	356	1 308	288	1 569	588
Kigoma	557	557	908	241	1 090	8356	1 308	202	1 569	356
Lindi	28	28	34	100	40	140	48	28	58	134
Mara	600	600	720	340	864	657	1 037	304	1 244	557
Morogoro	414	414	497	498	569	213	715	300	858	398
Mbeya	896	896	1 075	606	1 290	657	1 548	357	1 858	976
Mtwara	90	90	108	146	129	850	155	55	187	587
Mwanza	841	841	1 009	552	1 211	213	1 455	484	1 744	740
Pwani	56	56	67	303	81	151	97	187	116	238
Rukwa	297	297	256	242	428	807	513	267	616	930
Ruvuma	935	935	1 122	1 488	1 346	750	1 615	829	1 936	1 598
Shinyanga	927	927	1 112	425	1 335	434	1 602	452	1 922	314
Singida	851	851	697	422	837	421	1 004	625	1 204	802
Tanga	193	193	232	271	278	301	333	276	400	451
Tabora	498	498	598	288	717	124	860	1 543	1 032	576
Total	12 050	12 050	14 459	10 221	17 379	9 091	20 818	9 016	24 984	13 788

Further, landuse planning has been established under the chairmanship of the Prime Minister's Office and a number of plans have been prepared for the use and management of ecologically important areas including entire watersheds, forest reserves and game reserves. For purposes of planning, Tanzania mainland has been divided into five physical planning zones: the Lake Zone, the Northern Zone, the Central Zone, the Uhuru corridor and the Southern Zone.

Further current major projects include:

- The Afforestation Campaign and the Village Afforestation Programme (1980 to date)

which previously involved eight regions (Mara, Mwanza, Shinyanga, Tabora, Singida, Dodoma, Arusha and Kigoma), but subsequently was extended to all regions. This implementation was by the Ministry of Natural Resources in Cooperation with Adult Education and the Assistance of SIDA and FAO. The programme involves the establishment of nurseries and the distribution of seedlings for:
– communal village woodlots;
– schools;
– government fuelwood demonstration plots;
– individual family plots, farm boundaries and road verges. Success has been achieved mainly in schools, around houses, farm boundaries and along roads.

The Arid Zone Afforestation Project (1979 to 1983) phases I and II involved identifying suitable species for the afforestation of arid areas such as around Dodoma. This multi-purpose project involved research into fuelwood, fodder and construction material provision. There are other projects which combined land reclamation, agriculture and range land developments which include:

• The Makonde Escarpment project which started in 1973 and involved the reclamation of 87,800 ha of degraded land by the Forest Division of the Ministry of Natural Resources. This deterioration was caused by continuous cultivation replacing the 5-year fallow system which used to be practised. The aim of the project was to conserve the soil and to reduce the incidence of soil erosion on the escarpment;
• The Ngorongoro Conservation Area Project which started in 1982 was aimed at restoring land in the Oldean-Karatu region, an area of heavy erosion.

Wildlife

Wildlife management in Tanzania is a large-scale enterprise and involves more than 11 per cent of the land surface. Unfortunately the human resources deployed to conserve wildlife are inadequate.

Unlike the other areas which are open for human activity, wildlife conservation areas and national parks have minimal human activity and the environment is left mainly to nature. Only in a few areas where dams are constructed will wildlife inevitably be interfered with.

Rather than creating more organisations to deal with wildlife and thus straining the already constrained budgets, consolidating what already exists is important. Educating the people, especially starting with young people on the role of national parks and conservation areas in development, might go a long way to help manage the parks. If there is minimum human interference in the parks and conservation areas then minimum management efforts will be required. It is for this reason that the efforts made by NGOs like the 'Malihai clubs' of Tanzania which educate the young on conservation matters require much encouragement.

Turning to fish resources, there is potential for catching more fish, 30,000 tonnes from the coastal shelf, and 35,000 tonnes more from Lake Tanganyika. It is likely that there is greater potential in Lakes Nyasa, Victoria and Rukwa although the sustainable yield is not known. Tanzania has a Fisheries Research Institute of Marine Sciences in Zanzibar. Also there are two Fisheries Training Institutes – one in Mwanza for freshwater fish and another at Bagamoyo for seawater fish. Therefore the institutions for research exist already. In addition the Tanzania Fishing Corporation promotes commercial fishing. The problem lies more with the fishermen themselves who lack the necessary modern fishing gear to fully exploit the known potential. In addition, there are many foreign companies which come to fish within the 200 mile (320 km) fishing zone well beyond the continental shelf. It is not easy to police such an area effectively against illegal fishing from outside the country.

Tanzania has three lakes and a sea at its borders, three lakes within the country and several rivers and tributaries. The fishing potential is well over 340,000 tonnes per year but there is:

- Need to improve the capacity of fishing from the current 275,000 tonnes a year to the known potential of 340,000 tonnes of fish a year;
- Studies of the unknown potential of Lakes Victoria, Nyasa and Rukwa should be carried out;
- More vigorous efforts should be made to educate fishermen as to the disadvantages of using dynamite to catch fish and the policing of fishing should be tightened so as to catch fisherman using dynamite and poison;
- Improve facilities for tourists to view wildlife, and for sport hunting and fishing. More private operators should be brought into the tourist industry to build infrastructure such as lodges and hotels.

REFERENCES

Havnevik, K J *et al.* (1988) *Tanzania: Country Study and Norwegian Aid Review*, University of Bergen, Centre for Development Studies, Bergen

Ministry of Agriculture and Livestock Development (MALD) (1984) *Livestock Census*, Dar es Salaam

Sawe, E W (1990) *Issues in New and Renewable Sources of Energy*, Seminar paper on National Energy Policy for Tanzania, Dar es Salaam

UNDP/World Bank (1984) *Tanzania: Issues and Options in the Energy Sector*, Report No. 4969-TA, Report of Joint UNDP/World Bank Energy Sector Assessment Programme

9

ZAMBIA

INTRODUCTION

Zambia is a land-locked country in central Africa with a total area of 753,000 km². It lies between latitudes 8° and 18° south and longitudes 22° and 33° east. The central part of the country is deeply indented by southern Zaire, this being known as the pedicle. Its other neighbours are Tanzania to the north and east, Malawi to the east, Mozambique and Zimbabwe to the south and Angola to the west. There are short borders with Botswana and Namibia in the south-west.

The majority of the country is on the Central African Plateau, at an altitude of around 1000 m with hills and mountains rising to nearly 2000 m. The plateau is, however, deeply incised by large rivers, three of which (Zambezi, Kafue and Luangwa) belong to the Zambezi catchment area and flow from north to south, while the fourth, the Luapula, is in the Congo catchment and flows from south to north. The alluvial plains of the Kafue and of the Zambezi with an altitude of about 300 m are the lowest-lying parts of the country (Figure 9.1).

Although Zambia is tropical, temperatures are generally modified due to the height of the plateau. There are three distinct seasons: the cold, dry season between April and August, the hot, dry season from August to November, and the rainy season between November and April.

Average temperatures range from a mean monthly minimum of about 10°C in June and July to a mean monthly maximum of about 30°C in October and November. In general, the great majority of the rainfall is concentrated over the period October to March. Rainfall is variable in amount and distribution over time and locality; long-term averages range from about 700 mm in the south-west to about 1400 mm in the north-west.

The natural vegetation is predominantly miombo woodlands covering over 70 per cent of the country, mainly on the plateau and escarpment country. Mopane woodland covers much of the hot, dry southern valleys of the Zambezi and Luangwa. The country has abundant wildlife. There are 19 national parks and 31 game management areas covering about 32 per cent of the land area.

The latest census in Zambia, held in 1990, gave the total population of the country as 7.82 million people. During the period 1980–1990, the population increased at an average annual rate of 3.7 per cent, which is one of the highest growth rates recorded in Africa. On the basis of the 1980 census, the Central Statistical Office (CSO) in Zambia projected the total population to increase to eight million by 1990. The 1990 census figure demonstrates the accuracy of this projection.

Zambia is the most urbanised country in the SADC region, with a little over 50 per cent of its population living in urban areas. The average population density is 14 persons per km².

There are, however, substantial regional variations in the density of population, with densities ranging from as high as 76 persons per km² in the Copperbelt to as low as 4.6 persons per km² in the Northern Province. About 55 per cent of the total population is concentrated in a band about 60 km wide on each side of the railway line from Livingstone to the Copperbelt where the bulk of commercial, industrial, mining, and other ancillary economic activities take place. By 1990, the capital Lusaka recorded a population of 1.2 million, compared with 691,000 only ten years previously (Figure 9.2).

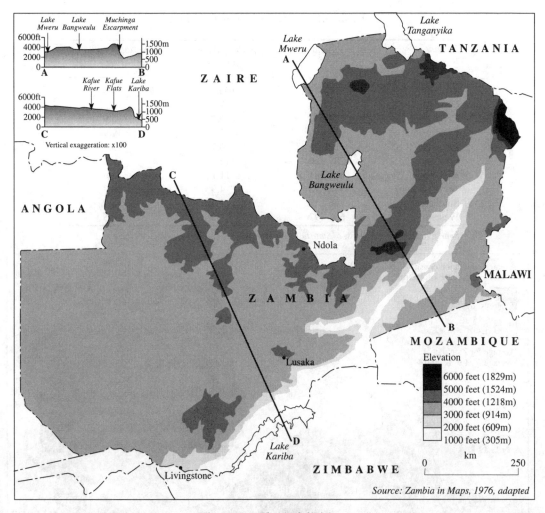

Figure 9.1 *Physical divisions*

About 40 per cent of the land area of Zambia is classified as potentially suitable for cultivation. However, only about 5 per cent is currently cultivated. The current system of land tenure distinguishes three types of land: state land, reserve and trust land. Land ownership on state land is under title deed. On the other hand, land ownership on trust land is communally based and is allocated by the traditional chiefs.

Zambia's economy is highly dependent on the exploitation and export of copper and other base metals such as lead and zinc. Before 1975, huge foreign exchange reserves and high copper and other metal prices assured the country of a sound economic base. Between 1965 and 1976, real GDP increased at an average rate of about 3.1 per cent. Since 1976, the economy has been in a protracted economic depression as a result of a 60 per cent decline in copper prices. GDP per capita fell an average of 3 per cent per annum between 1980 and 1986. The fall in copper prices has had negative repercussions for the Zambian economy.

Table 9.1 *Population by province, 1990*

Province	Population	Percentage of population	Average population density (per km²)
Zambia	7 818 447	100.0	14.0
Central	725 611	9.3	10.2
Copperbelt	1 579 542	20.2	75.9
Eastern	973 818	12.5	17.9
Luapula	528 705	6.7	15.8
Lusaka	1 207 980	15.4	60.4
Northern	867 795	11.1	4.6
North-western	383 146	4.9	8.7
Southern	946 353	12.1	15.0
Western	607 497	7.8	10.5

Source: CSO Monthly Digest of Statistics, Feb/March 1991

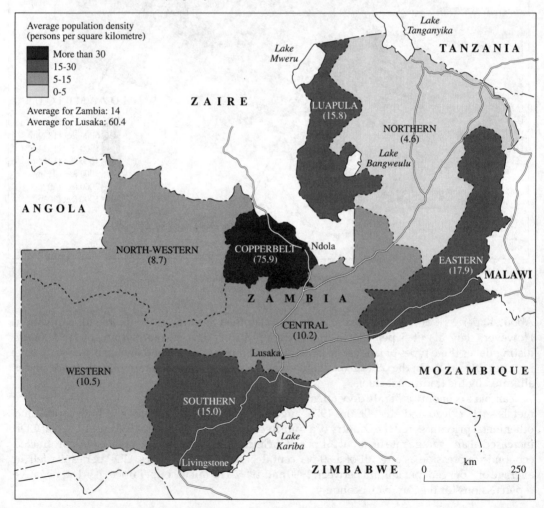

Figure 9.2 *Population distribution , 1990*

Table 9.2 *Land utilisation classification, 1974–75 (million ha)*

Reserve and trust land (available for agriculture)	41.17
State land (available for agriculture)	1.20
Forest estate of which	6.68
National forests	6.27
Protected forests	0.41
Other land	26.52
Total land area	75.57

With almost 90 per cent of its foreign exchange coming from copper, the effects of a drastic decrease in export earnings have resulted in serious balance of payment problems and this, in turn, has forced Zambia to borrow extensively, creating a severe debt-servicing problem. External debt rose from US$1.8 billion in 1980 to US$5.2 billion in 1987. The total external debt as a percentage of GNP stood at 158 per cent in 1989, up from 91 per cent in 1980.

The manufacturing sector in Zambia, with its heavy dependency on imported inputs and spares, has also been adversely affected by the fall in export earnings. Until 1976 the sector had an average annual growth rate of 4.7 per cent, but this dropped to 2.5 per cent during the period 1980 to 1989. Capacity utilisation was low, averaging between 40 to 50 per cent during this period.

The economic crisis in Zambia has forced the government to change its economic policy and restructure the economy away from over-dependency on the copper mining sector. Agriculture and rural development have now been accorded a high priority as being the sectors of greatest potential for replacing the mining sector as the most important parts of the economy. The priority accorded to agriculture and rural development has been reflected, in recent years, in the proportion of the government development budget allocated to agriculture, which rose from 11 per cent in 1974/76 to 30 per cent in the mid and late 1980s.

Although the agricultural sector accounts for only 13 per cent of GDP, it provides a livelihood for about 50 per cent of Zambia's population. The sector is characterised by a relatively small modern sector of about 1000 heavily capitalised farmers on one hand, and about 700,000 farming families using hand hoe/or ox-cultivation on the other hand.

The main food crops are maize, sorghum and cassava. The main cash crops are irrigated wheat, cotton and oilseeds. The development of agricultural exports has historically been very limited. Apart from limited quantities of maize, which were exported to neighbouring countries in the 1970s, tobacco and groundnuts are the only regular exports, accounting for less than 1 per cent of total exports. Agricultural output during the 1980s has grown at an average annual rate less than the rate of population growth. This has resulted in increased agricultural imports during this period. The major commodities imported have been maize, wheat, and vegetable oils and oilseed cakes.

Zambia was first brought into the modern world exchange system in the closing years of the nineteenth century. At this time interest was stimulated in the mineral potential of the territory north of the Zambezi. Prospecting parties located deposits of copper at Kansanshi (1899), at Broken Hill (1902), in the Hook of Kafue and in the area of the present Copperbelt. Largely on the strength of these discoveries, which were mostly on the sites of African workings, the British South Africa Company (BSAC) accepted administrative responsibility for what became called Northern Rhodesia. The BSA's greatest contribution to local economic development in the territory was the construction of the railway, which determined the geographical pattern of development that persists to this day.

The few European farmers who settled in Northern Rhodesia faced tremendous physical and economic hazards. Nevertheless maize and cattle were produced along the railway, which reached the Katanga markets in 1909. Around Fort Jameson in the east, experiments were made with cattle, cotton and, most successfully, with tobacco.

Except for a small-scale trade in cattle and maize in the south-western part of the country, the indigenous people at first took little part in the modern exchange economy. With the introduction of the hut tax, however, young men were forced to migrate for wage labour to the farms, mines and factories of Southern Rhodesia and South Africa, leaving the rural areas to stagnate. Thus the company created a typically colonial dual economy comprising a relatively developed sector under European control, and an underdeveloped rural sector whose role was to provide labour and bear most social costs.

Although Zambia has been independent since 1964, the economic and social patterns established over 60 years of colonial rule have persisted for decades after formal independence was achieved. In order to finance economic and social infrastructure programmes, the newly-independent government increased revenues from mining.

As mining and related activities expanded, the urban population increased rapidly from less than 20 per cent of the total population in 1964 to over 50 per cent today. Demand for food increased commensurately and the government embarked on a series of agricultural programmes to accelerate food production. Recently, structural adjustment policies, some of which aim to reduce levels of government expenditure, have weakened the ability of the government to fund development and environmental programmes.

ENVIRONMENTAL ISSUES

Resource-use conflicts

Although there were some conflicting demands on environmental resources in the pre-colonial period, a series of survival mechanisms ensured sustainable adjustments to the existing order. However, in more recent times the demands of modernisation, especially those that are the product of external influences have adversely affected their operations. Indeed, conflicts in resource use seem to have been reinforced.

In the agricultural sector resource-use conflicts can be seen in a number of areas. For small farmers with limited land there tend to be competing demands for cash crops as against food crops and conflicts between cropping patterns and livestock rearing.

With the progressive monetisation of the economy in the rural areas, most farmers are forced to grow a cash crop so that they can meet their monetary obligations. However they still need to grow food crops. As a result, food-crop growing tends to give way to cash cropping. Since the money realised does not usually meet the household requirements, especially food, participating farming households tend to be severely affected.

In this context it is imperative to find a strategy which would ensure a reasonable income to meet cash obligations, as well as providing enough land for food crops, or for the cash income to meet all obligations including food requirements.

The most common conflict in the smallholder agrarian system is associated with the allocation of land between crop production and livestock rearing. Since in areas where smallholders operate there tends to be no title land, customary practice allows livestock holders to use the same land. Nonetheless, during the time that the fields are under crops, animals are not supposed to graze in the croplands. However, in most cases animals tend to destroy the field crops. To make matters worse, no one individual is given full rights over grazing land as it is all communal. This normally leads to a situation in which the land-carrying capacity tends to be exceeded. The only feasible option in this area is to review the communal grazing system so that individual livestock owners could be allocated individual grazing areas which they could control in order to ensure a sustainable use of the grazing land.

In terms of conflicting landuse problems, the worst examples are found in peri-urban areas. As the metropolitan areas expand they tend to take up space which was previously for agricultural use. The larger towns now face grave squatter problems. Squatters are living in squalor on their fringes where they highlight a fundamental dichotomy in Zambian society between the backward rural poor and the more prosperous sections of urban society. In Lusaka, for example, there is a chronic shortage of housing and jobs for the large influx of rural migrants. Unauthorised shanty towns have mushroomed around the city, where up to half of Lusaka's inhabitants live in conditions of social breakdown and disease. Other Zambian towns repeat the squatter problem.

To exacerbate the problem, industries which produce harmful effluents, tend to be located in these areas as well. A good case in Zambia is the Kafue industrial complex which is 45 km from Lusaka. Apart from dumping industrial waste on the land to the west of the industrial complex, these companies are also dumping industrial waste in the Kafue River. There is very serious concern about the pollution effects on the waters of the Kafue River.

Demographic trends also pose a serious problem for environmental sustainability. The annual population growth rate in Zambia is currently at 3.7 per cent whilst the GDP has a growth rate of 0.2 per cent. This means that there is serious pressure on available resources. Indeed, this is easily seen in the field of social and housing amenities. Due to the Government budget deficit which had reached K3.5 billion in 1989 or 7.8 per cent of GDP and an external debt of close to US$7 billion in 1989, the Government capacity to provide adequate facilities has been severely eroded. This has resulted in councils failing to maintain the housing stock, neglecting sewage systems, and being unable to collect refuse etc. In early 1990, there was a series of cholera outbreaks in most of the major urban areas. The disease was concentrated particularly in the high density areas where most of the underprivileged and the poor live. By the time the outbreak was controlled almost 150 people had died. Again, in 1991 there was another outbreak of the disease. These incidents highlight the seriousness of minimal budgetary allocation for environmental protection and the adverse effects on the poor.

At the heart of resource-use conflicts in Zambia lies the land tenure system. As stated above, there are three categories of land, namely, state, reserve and trust lands. Reserves, which are for the sole use of the indigenous population, are administered under customary or traditional land tenure systems. State land, on the other hand, is used exclusively for commercial farming, townships and the transport and communication infrastructure, and is administered under the statutory leasehold system. The third category, trust land, is reserved for the common benefit (either directly or indirectly) of the population.

Whereas customary systems allow for both individual and communal ownership, the statutory leasehold system is characterised by private ownership. The essence of customary systems appears to be that they are based on clearly-defined user rights with the traditional authorities exercising overall jurisdiction and responsibility. The principle of a commonality of interest in the land, most evident in the use of land for grazing, drawing of water, fire-wood collection, hunting and fruit gathering is balanced by the recognition of the value of individual crop production. Even then, individual rights to land are suspended during the period after harvesting and before the new planting season. Under the statutory leasehold, under which state land in Zambia is administered, private ownership prevails. It is under this system that the highest degree of commercialisation is obtained.

Except for the state land in the Eastern Province, most of the commercial farming activities follow the line of rail, which incidentally was developed to serve the better soil areas of Zambia (Bruce and Domer, 1982). The deliberate policy of the colonial government to serve the interests of settlers meant that most land along the line of rail, which stretches from the Southern Province to the Copperbelt Province, was allocated to white settlers.

The major factor militating against communal land ownership and use relates to the prevailing grazing patterns. This is particularly evident in the cattle-rearing areas of Zambia. According to the Sakala Commission (1982), large tracts of land in the Southern Province are overstocked and consequently overgrazed. The situation is compounded by the reluctance of peasant farmers to sell off their cattle; cattle among peasant farmers are considered to be a measure of wealth.

The depletion of fertile land is further aggravated by the fact that no one is prepared to conserve or improve the pasture in land used communally. Since the land is exploited communally, no one farmer can be held responsible for the overgrazing that occurs. It is argued that overstocking and overgrazing would not occur if peasant farmers were allocated individual grazing units since individuals who abuse their grazing lands would suffer the resultant consequences. It needs to be recognised that a cattle owner's economic freedom to dispose of cattle is constrained to a considerable extent by social obligations and controls. In addition to other sources of income, such as crop production, fishing, and brewing, cattle act as a sort of bank deposit which is drawn upon if money is badly needed.

The bureaucracy and costs involved in the issue of title deeds affords most land held under the customary system very little likelihood of any legal premise of ownership of land. That is, whereas the statutory land system enables the owner to obtain title deeds in respect of allocated land, very few, if any, title deeds have been given under the customary system. However, it needs to be pointed out that a provision exists to obtain title deeds to land acquired under the customary system in the reserves and trust land. An applicant can apply to the Commissioner of Lands for a lease. Before a lease is issued, the land is surveyed by the Surveyor General. In practice most of the land in the reserves and trust land is not surveyed because of the prohibitive cost payable by the person whose land is under review. In cases where the land is not surveyed, the Lands Department can issue rights of occupancy limited to 14 years (Sakala Commission, 1982). The term of the lease can be extended to 99 years once the land in question has been surveyed. The picture that emerges is clear: the 'haves' have secure tenure of the land that they work and live on, whilst the 'have nots' do not.

The reversion of reserves and trust land to state land on the acquisition of title deeds militates against peasants obtaining title deeds. Traditional leaders fear losing tracts of land and the accompanying prestige and power in this manner and are reluctant to give the required consent. Peasant farmers, consequently, are further denied the opportunity of obtaining credit using title deeds as security. The predicament of peasant farmers dafes back as far as 1962, when the colonial government presented proposals to provide for the acquisition of certain rights to land under the customary law and to allow for the registration of title in such land for purposes of obtaining financial assistance. There was, however, strong opposition from African representatives in the legislative council on the grounds that the measures would reduce the powers of the Chiefs and eventually lead to their abolition (Sakala, 1982).

African societies are characterised by a very strong bond of family ties. It is argued that individual ownership of land undermines the extended family system prevalent in African societies. Land is considered to be owned by the community for the benefits of the community. Traditional norms imply that a share in the village lands is viewed as a birthright by the descendants of the land-holding family, regardless of where they live. This practice may be beneficial in that it acts as security in so far as one can easily return to the village and work on family land upon retirement or failure to secure employment in the towns or mines.

On the other hand, however, the birthright notion attached to land can lead to the under-utilisation or the total neglect of land. Clan ownership of land has in some instances resulted in land being idle for up to 15 years (Sakala, 1982). Furthermore, land disputes have arisen; the Sakala Commission (1982) points to cases where peasant farmers long to return to their ancestral land that was taken from them by the colonial authorities. This has led in some instances to peasant farmers resorting to squatting on state land designated for commercial farming or on abandoned commer-cial farms.

There are a number of shortcomings that can be cited in the case of private ownership of land. One major problem is the prevalence of unused or underutilised land. A major contributing factor is the lack of a land-monitoring unit to determine the degree of land utilisation.

Private ownership of land is also said to lead to speculation, prohibitive prices, and conflict over use. There is evidence to suggest that land is being held for speculatory purposes and sold at very high prices. It is the view of this chapter that this problem has arisen due to delays by the Government in opening up new land for development which has contributed to the land shortage currently being experienced in Zambia. Prospective land buyers are therefore left with no option but to bid for land in developed areas. The availability of basic infrastructure and services on land in developed areas raises the price of such land and is available only to those who can afford the prices. The landless who cannot afford the high prices and have settled on underdeveloped land, which is usually owned by an absentee landlord, be it individuals or the state, are labelled squatters.

Secondly, the high price of land can be traced to the overall economic environment, character-ised by high inflation, in which the land market operates. Whilst almost all other economic activities have been liberalised, the land market is bureaucratically administered. The sale of land, a central element under private ownership, contributes to the increasing size of land-holdings and to the emergence of a landless class; in other words, an increasingly polarized society.

On the other hand, certain features of customary land tenure, it is argued, tend to impede the optimum use of land. The inalienability of land, whilst protecting community members' rights to use land by virtue of kinship, inhibits individuals, extended families, and even entire communities from participation in the development process because inalienability constrains individual invest-ment, innovation and entrepreneurial activity in agriculture, and the rationalisation of land use to maximise such activity. With no fully-fledged market in land, there is no guarantee that the potentially best land will be allocated to those who can realise its potential productivity and who would thus be willing to purchase it at market price.

The choice is therefore a trade-off between the reallocation of land from commercial farmers to small farmers with a consequent reduction in the marketed output, the latter a consequence of the small farmers' lack of land-utilisation skills. The extent to which choice will be attained or reached depends on a whole range of issues. The extent to which marketed output will fall will depend, for example, on the measures taken to improve the small farmers productivity; the amount of land that can be reallocated will depend on the relative importance and political influence of the competing parties. With Zambia's drive to diversify the economy and the superior organisational structure of the Commercial Farmers Bureau, the amount of land reallocation to the peasants is likely to be negligible.

A discussion of the land market and conflicts over the use of the land cannot be complete without taking into consideration gender issues. Though women form the backbone of peasant agriculture, their lowly position in society hinders the realisation of their full contribution to development efforts. Women, who undertake about 80 per cent of farm work, are not accorded an equal say in the operations. Not only do the men remain in charge of farm planning and management but the land tenure systems condemns women to membership of a 'landless class'. Even where land is acquired, women are considered as legal minors and therefore not entitled to hold title deeds. This is despite the fact that 35 per cent of rural households in Zambia are headed by females.

ENVIRONMENTAL PROBLEMS

On independence Zambia inherited an unbalanced economy dependent on the mining industry. Post-independence Zambia was therefore faced with the pressing development need of diversifying the economy. Development necessarily entails exploitation of a country's natural resource base. However, development has serious implications for the environment. In the absence of conservation practices, sustained growth risks damaging the environment. This section looks at three development sectors and their implications for the environment. The three sectors, agriculture, mining and industry, have been selected on the basis of their dominant role in Zambia's development strategy and their impact upon the environment.

Agriculture

Because of the impending closure of the copper mines, forecast to occur at the turn of the century, agriculture has been prioritized as the prime development sector. Unfortunately, this prioritization has been merely expressed as policy pronouncement and has not been matched by the provision of adequate resources. Over the Fourth National Development Plan Period, 1986–1990, only 14 per cent of the total funding was targeted for agricultural developments. Although a number of strategies and measures have been designed to facilitate this development approach, the question of sustainability of agricultural resources has not been directly addressed. Agriculture depends upon such ecological processes as soil regeneration and nutrient recycling, which are particularly endangered when efforts are made to increase productivity without conservation as part of management.

The main form of environmental degradation arising from agricultural practices is soil erosion. In Zambia the situation is compounded by the prevalence of infertile soils that are susceptible to erosion. According to Chidumayo (1979), the region most seriously affected by soil erosion is the dry sub-humid zone which incidentally is the main agriculture production belt of Zambia (Figure 9.3). The problem of soil erosion results from the inherent environmental characteristics of the region as well as human and farming practices. Twenty per cent of the region consists of hilly land, while the sandy soils of the Western Province have low resistance to erosion. In some areas, pressure on land, a consequence of the scarcity of land, created conditions causing the cultivation of steeply-sloping land. In the Gwembe district of the Southern Province, the Kariba dam provides an example of the land pressures so created. As Scudder (1985) aptly puts it, while it is true that the Kariba dam catalysed the development of the district between 1955 and 1974, apart from the immediate trauma of removal, Kariba resettlement schemes caused a radical and unfavourable redistribution of population in relation to arable land.

Land management practices

Peasant farmers' agricultural practices do not in most instances entail sound land management principles. Though there are cases of degradation in state land designated for commercial farming, erosion here is not so severe. A national seminar on Environment and Development concluded that while the conservation practices found on state lands were adequate, the more serious problems related to erosion in the reserve areas (Zambia Geographical Association, 1979). A contributing

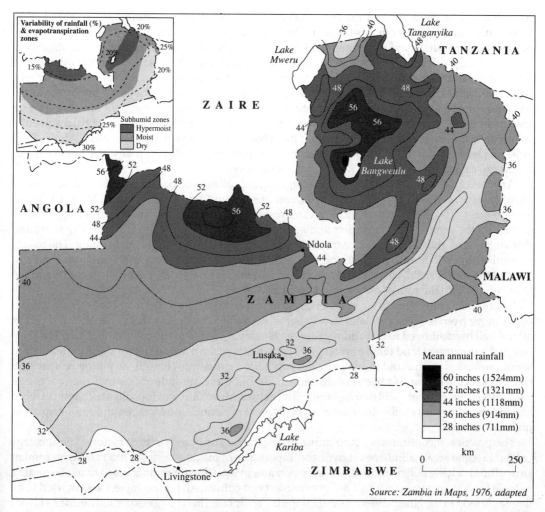

Figure 9.3 *Precipitation, evapotranspiration zones and rainfall variability*

factor to this problem is the practice of bush burning. Fire is used to clear fields during the dry season, before the planting season. With the soil exposed to the baking action of the sun and the impact of raindrops, soil degradation poses a real danger on land (Chidumayo, 1979).

Equally disturbing is the effect of deforestation on the environment. Two practices emerge as causes of deforestation in Zambia, namely the *Chitemene* system of cultivation and woodfuel collecting. The Chitemene system (a form of shifting cultivation) is practised in northern Zambia. The soils in the Chitemene belt are heavily baked and mineral nutrients are absorbed by the vegetation. The trees are cut and burnt as a method of transferring nutrients to the soil (Chidumayo, 1979). However, nutrients are drained out of the soil by leaching and crop removal, resulting in the abandonment of cultivated land after three years. It is estimated that at least 9000 km² of woodland is cultivated using the Chitemene system. In other words, at least 9000 km² of woodland loses fertility over one cycle.

To add to the problem of deforestation, rural societies, and a significant proportion of **urban** households, rely on woodfuel for their energy requirements. It is estimated that 2000 km² of woodland is lost each year in this manner. The importance of woodlands must be seen in the light of the vital function they play in watershed conservation; wholesale destruction of woodlands can cause hydrological disturbances (Chidumayo, 1979). In Zambia, the situation is aggravated by the fact that rapid deforestation occurs in the headwaters of the major rivers. For the urban poor who rely on woodfuel, there is a serious economic consequence. As charcoal-collecting points near the consumption areas are depleted, points further away become new collection points; transport costs rise leading to increases in the price of woodfuel. Furthermore, the wheelruts of trucks used to collect charcoal are known to collect run-off into channels which promotes the initial stages of soil erosion. Deforestation through charcoal production is so large scale that many of Zambia's major towns are ringed by widening areas of land degradation.

Another cause of soil erosion is overgrazing. Critical soil erosion occurs where stocking rates are about two to three animals per hectare. The reserves around Mazabuka, Pemba, Monze, Choma, Mongu and parts of the Central and Eastern Provinces are particularly affected. Erosion which is caused by the removal of vegetation and surface compaction by hooves is more critical around drinking places and along tracks near kraals, and is aggravated by rangeland burning. The Sakala Commission (1982) found overstocking, and accompanying overgrazing, in the Reserve and Trust Land of the Southern Province. The reluctance of the small farmers to dispose of their cattle resulted in an annual off-take rate of only about 4 to 5 per cent.

Continuous cultivation is yet another cause of soil erosion. In pre-colonial times small farmers could move from one piece of land to another when a particular piece was exhausted and return after it had been allowed to rest and regenerate. However, owing to the colonial and later the post-colonial government land tenure systems this practice is seldom now practised. The immobility of small farmers is compounded by growing population pressure. Though very little research on continuous cultivation has been conducted in Zambia there are indications that the practice of continuous monoculture will damage the soil structure. Most Zambian topsoils are coarse textured and are therefore susceptible to erosion and compaction hazards, and yet continuous cropping of maize is common.

The practice of continuously cultivating maize can be attributed to three factors. The shortage of land in some areas (alluded to above), the importance of maize as a staple food and government agricultural pricing policy. Indeed, it is the government's pricing policy that led to maize becoming a staple food in areas where it had not previously been cultivated. For example, cassava used to be the staple food in the North-Western and Luapula Provinces. This change explains Scudder's (1985) observation that farmers in low rainfall areas have suffered from the national emphasis on maize production at the expense of other cereals. First, research has produced more high-yielding varieties of maize with agricultural staff trained to extend its production even to inappropriate areas; second, the price for maize has risen far faster than other cereals. Nyirongo and Shula (1989) make similar observations on the effect of price variations between crops. In a study of contract farming in Zambia, they found that, in terms of land use and crop patterns, maize accounted for the largest share of the planted area, and was both a major cash and food crop. Because of the predominance of rainfed crop cultivation, the relative importance of maize as a cash and food crop and the growing shortage of land in some areas, crop rotation as a means of maintaining soil fertility is not commonly practised. Therefore, the clearing of woodland for monocultural maize cultivation exposes the soil and makes it particularly vulnerable to rainstorm erosion.

Mining

The dominant role of the copper industry in Zambia is well documented. The copper industry earns the country at least 90 per cent of its total export earnings. However, the exploitation of mineral resources raises two conservation concerns: depletion of natural resources and the environmental hazards created by the mining process. Mineral resources are non-renewable and their exploitation requires processes that maximise their market value but which impact adversely on the environment.

Copper production involves a number of processes, which range from mining through concentration to smelting. As a result there is a serious danger posed by the mining industry of land degradation and water pollution. Large tracts of land covered with mine dumps and slag lie barren. The position is aggravated by weak mining (dumps) regulations which should enforce reclamation of land for productive use. The plight of some Copperbelt farmers illustrates the harmful effects of the mining industry. A study by the National Council of Scientific Research and the Department of Veterinary and Tsetse Control found that polluted water was responsible for the deaths of livestock on the Copperbelt. The study found that the copper content in the affected rivers was on average about 80 times higher than the accepted level. The affected farmers consequently sued the mining company and were subsequently compensated by a court ruling.

An associated environmental problem, particularly in the Zambian Copperbelt, is the presence of derelict land associated with mining operations.

On the Copperbelt about three-quarters of the copper produced comes from underground mining. Underground mining is complicated and costly. Shafts are sunk, and from them tunnels are driven towards the ore body. This means that enormous quantities of mineral and spoil are removed. The mined ore is crushed and milled with water to a very fine particle size. Chemicals are then added to the pulp which is agitated with air in tanks.

The mineral particles containing copper cling to the bubbles and float on the surface, and the waste materials sink and are discarded. The spoil is dumped on the surface together with the waste, and with various other forms of industrial debris. This dumping is done in the vicinity of the mines creating a large zone of residues. Such large piles of waste, in the form of crushed rock and sand, are built up on the surface as hills or low ridges. These are commonly left with the material lying at, or close to, its natural angle of repose. Thus, they often drain rapidly, retaining little water close to the surface. This combination of physical and chemical characteristics renders the tips steep, barren and unproductive, resembling a sterile landscape. During the seven-month dry season these residues crumble to dust from which even a wind of moderate force can produce a miniature sand storm. During the rainy season the soaked dumps revert to an amorphous slurry, which spreads to the nearby cultivated land and water supplies. The mines use vast quantities of water, and much of what they discharge contains elements that can be classified as pollutants. One practical means of reducing this form of pollution is to create large dams or lakes in which water improves in time by mere retention before discharge into public streams (Perara, 1979).

Industry

The dumping of waste, especially when not vigorously checked, is responsible for some observed environmental problems. The environmental damage caused by industrial wastes has been and remains a source of concern. Perhaps the most disturbing environmental danger posed by industry is the harm it inflicts on human life. Not only is the air polluted but water is equally affected. A report by the National Council for Scientific Research (NCSR) concludes that hazardous industrial products are capable of causing acute or chronic illness because the substances enter the body by inhalation or through the skin and deactivates enzymes and other sensitive organs of the body (Times of Zambia, 15 December 1988). Water pollution renders domestic water sources highly dangerous. Among the industries established during the post-independence era that have frequently been listed as discharging substances which pollute the environment are Nitrogen Chemicals of Zambia, Kafue Textiles of Zambia and Chilanga Cement Limited. Unfortunately, the NCSR merely monitors the effluent levels but has no jurisdiction to enforce adherence to acceptable standards. The industrial waste of most industrial plants is discharged into the air, water or land. One of the major sources of concern is the problem of soil acidity. A serious effect of soil acidity in Zambia is poor root development particularly as regards depth of roots, thus making a crop on acid soil very sensitive to even a few days of dry weather. The situation is compounded by the heavy application of nitrogen fertilisers which tends to increase soil acidity.

Turning to atmospheric pollution on the Copperbelt, conditions producing temperature inversions are found on 60 per cent of the days. This can lead to the concentration of atmospheric pollutants, particularly sulphur dioxide, which is emitted as a waste product in the copper smelting process. Although opinions differ as to the level of environmental damage caused by emission levels, short-term botanical damage has been noted close to the smelters, and respiratory discomfort in humans has been recorded. The copper mining companies do, however, monitor emission levels and they have introduced alternative production techniques. However, the absence of an independent monitoring body with strong powers of enforcement has left the mining companies as their own regulators. This is not a satisfactory situation.

The environmental effects of industrial development are well illustrated in the Kafue district, about 40 km south of Lusaka. One of the reasons for the establishment of the industrial estate at Kafue was the location of plants there which were considered unsuitable to be sited in Lusaka for environmental reasons. Industries in the Kafue estate include textiles, chemicals, plastics, yeast manufacturing and tanning.

Air pollution is found at Kafue. Surrounding the industrial estate a valley contains domestic dwellings. Thermal inversions occur and the valley and old town area fill with industrial emissions, trapped by the thermal inversion and unable to be displaced horizontally. Workers at the National Irrigation Research Station (some 30 km westward along the Kafue River) have commented that a distinct brown haze could be seen hanging over the Kafue area on a number of occasions. Further, workers of the Kafue Basin Research Committee have also reported the occurrence of early morning smog (05.00–06.00 hrs). It is worth paying some attention to the mechanisms by which such air pollution could arise.

Emissions from the Nitrogen chemicals factory supply a continuous source of nitrogen dioxide. It has been calculated that about 40 tonnes per day of nitric oxide are released into the atmosphere giving 60 tonnes per day of nitrogen dioxide after oxidation in the air.

Any compound reacting with oxygen atoms will disrupt this equilibrium and this occurs in the presence of hydrocarbons. A complex reaction sequence results, with substantial amounts of aldehyde and PANs (peroxyacy nitrates) being formed. Leaf injuries occur at 0.01 mg kg^{-1} PAN concentrations and ozone, aldehydes and nitrogen oxides themselves can have adverse physiological effects on both humans and vegetation at low concentrations. Hydrocarbons are introduced into the Kafue atmosphere from a number of sources – domestic fuels, industrial emissions, automobiles, organic volatiles from plants (terpenes), etc. Photochemical conversion occurs easily in the dry season and it can be seen that all the essential requirements of a photochemical smog are present. Medical health problems can easily arise.

It must be recognised that there is a need for Zambia to become self-sufficient in fertilisers and mine explosives, and that Nitrogen Chemicals plays a crucial role in achieving this. However, one would hope that eventually the monitoring of air around the industrial township will become routine – especially since the environment around the township is already polluted.

In terms of water pollution, an examination of the control and monitoring of effluent into the Kafue River produces a more satisfactory picture. All the indications are that the concentration of pollutants in the industrial effluent is currently well within the accepted international standards. However, in view of some evidence of eutrophication a number of points should be made. The Kafue River fish catch provides 13 per cent of the total national protein requirement. It has also been stated that the Kafue River has a very low oxygen content during two periods of the year, due to the flooding which covers up vegetable matter, which in turn consumes oxygen on decomposition. Hence fish-kills occur naturally throughout these periods. The consequences of eutrophication and of altering the flood pattern to accommodate the requirements of the hydroelectric generating scheme at Kafue Gorge do not augur well for the fish population. Taking into account the increased efficiency of fish catching (one of the consequences of the Kafue Reinforced Plastics boat-building scheme) and the observation that average fish size in the Kafue has increased indicating a decreasing immature fish population, the situation should be carefully monitored.

THE NATURAL RESOURCE BASE AND LEGAL UNDERPINNINGS

Land resources

Soils

The following sections draw heavily on Mackel (1976). In Zambia, soil characteristics are mainly due to climatic factors, parent rock material and topography. The decisive climatic factor in Zambia is rainfall, which has affected the degree of soil weathering and leaching. In southern Zambia, where annual rainfall is under 1000 mm per annum, these processes are slower than in the rainier north, with up to 1250 mm. The effects of increasing rainfall on the extent of leaching are modified by underlying parent rock material, which influences soil texture, colour and structure. Eight generalised soil groups have been identified in Zambia (Figure 9.4).

Fersiallitic soils occur mainly on parent rock materials rich in ferromagnesian minerals (dolomite, calcareous schist, etc.), but may even cover old alluvium – 'Kafue basin alluvium'. They have a moderate base status (pH five to seven). Fersiallitic soils are formed on uplands in Central Province (Lusaka, Mumbwa, Kabwe), in the Monze-Mazabuka Districts, and in Eastern Province (Petauke-Chipata), usually on nearly level to gently undulating topography, with slopes ranging from under one to over 5 per cent. Here average annual rainfall is under 1000 mm. Fersiallitic soils are suitable for cultivation of a wide range of climatically-adapted crops. They include the most fertile Zambian soils, now widely cultivated.

Ferrallitic soils derive from various parent rocks, including granite, gneiss, sandstone and schist. Covering half Zambia, they occur mainly on gently undulating uplands with slopes of up to 3 per cent or more. Usually clay content increases with depth: a sandy surface horizon occurs on loamy sand or sandy loam, underlain by sandy clay loam. These soils, found in Southern, Eastern and Central Provinces are partly suitable for cultivation. However, sandy soils particularly require careful management, while large areas are best suited to permanent vegetative cover utilised through timber production, grazing or wildlife. In contrast, the northern ferrallitic soils are more leached because of higher rainfall with lower base saturation (pH four to five). The clay content is generally higher. They occur in North-Western, Western, Northern and Luapula Provinces, and are widely used for *Chitemene* cultivation. They may be used for local crops under good soil management and for timber production or pasture grasses.

Barotse sands are deep, loose, structureless sands. They comprise wind and water-sorted quartzitic sands with very low clay and silt content throughout the soil profile, usually under 5 per cent clay plus silt. Their origin is controversial. One view is that they were transported by wind from the Kalahari Desert during late Tertiary times: another, that they are developed from underlying Karroo sandstone by a process of water transport and subsequent wind action. Vast areas of western Zambia are covered by Barotse sands, which extend as shallower lobes into Mwinilunga, Kasempa and Namwala Districts. They are best suited to permanent vegetation cover (woodland, grassland), utilisable through grazing, timber production or wildlife habitat.

Vertisols of the Kafue Flats consist of deep, calcareous cracking clays. The surface pH ranges from 5.7 to 7.3, increasing to 8.5 in the subsoil. A characteristic calcium carbonate horizon generally occurs within 120 cm of the surface. The Kafue vertisols are formed on the nearly-level flood plains of the Kafue Flats. Of alluvial (lacustrine) origin, they experience seasonal flooding. An estimated 7000 km^2 is covered by these soils between Iteshi Teshi and the Kafue Gorge, which may also be found as small bodies along other rivers and swamps. They may be utilised for grazing cattle and wildlife and, particularly in border zones, may produce crops adapted to wet habitats after adequate drainage management.

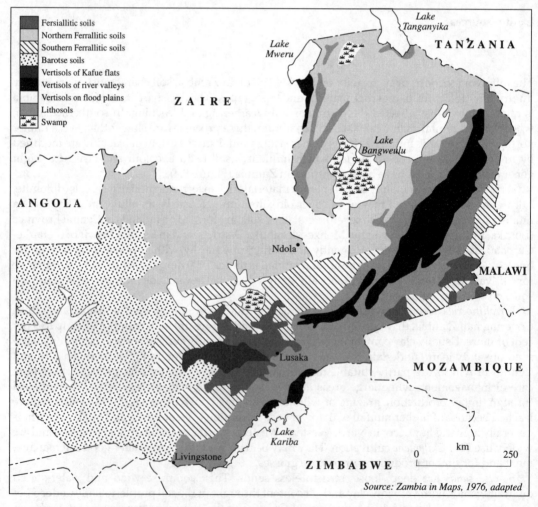

Source: *Zambia in Maps, 1976, adapted*

Figure 9.4 *Soil types*

Vertisols of the river valleys cover the Luangwa and its tributary valleys, the Luapala, and parts of the Zambezi valley. They are believed to derive from Karroo sediments, largely by colluvial and alluvial processes. They comprise a mixed group of soils. The fluvial deposits have been variously sorted during transport. In parts of the Luangwa valley, especially where drainage is poor, soils tend to be holomorphic due to salt accumulation.

Vertisols of flood plains are derived from siliceous parent material. They may have a peaty organic horizon, ranging from under 25 to over 180 cm thickness. The peat horizon usually has a pH of 3.5 to 4.5, if not drained and cultivated. These soils are found in the flooded areas of the Zambezi and tributary rivers in Western Province, around major swamps (Lukanga, Bangweulu, Busanga) and in depressions of dambos. Parts may be used for grasslands or locally adapted crops if protected from flooding and adequately drained.

Lithosols, finally, are shallow to very shallow escarpment soils, often intermixed with outcrops and surface rocks. They are frequently underlain by laterite crusts as well as quartz gravels or weathering rocks. Texture ranges from sand through loamy sand to sandy clay loam, rock material increasing with depth. Lithosols are developed from granite, gneiss, schist or sandstone. They are best suited to a permanent vegetation cover utilisable for wildlife or a few woodland products such as charcoal.

Vegetation

According to Mackel (1976) Zambia's vegetation can broadly be divided into 'forest', 'woodland' and 'grassland' (Figure 9.5). In the forests the upper tree layer is mostly closed and the middle layer often characterised by a dense thicket understorey. There is at best a discontinuous grass cover. Woodlands show a dense tree cover with more or less closed canopy. The middle layer, however, is open and there is only a sparse grass cover. True woodlands often merge into open grassy woodlands, in which the canopy is not closed, and there may be a complete grass cover ('woodland savanna'). Grasslands encompass areas with scattered trees and/or shrubs and treeless plains.

Together with climatic and edaphic factors, man has influenced the natural vegetation and helped to degrade forests and woodlands by burning and cultivation. Fire is undoubtedly the dominant single factor in maintaining a fairly open vegetation.

Of the major forest types, livunda forest covers parts of north-western Zambia. It is a dry evergreen low forest characterised by *Chryptosepalum pseudotaxus* ('Livunda'), with lianes forming a fairly dense understorey. Mutemwa Forest is a dry deciduous forest confined to areas of Kalahari sand, occurring widely in southern Western Province and as relics in Balovale, Kabompo and Sesheke Districts. It is dominated by *Baikiaea plurijuga* ('Zambian Teak') and *Pterocarpus antunesii.*

Woodland of various types covers four-fifths of Zambia. Mushibe Woodland occurs widely on Kalahari sand in Western Province, with evergreen species increasing northward. Typical species are *Guibourtia coleosperma* ('Mushibe'), *Burkea africana* and *Erythrophleum africanum*. Miombo woodland covers over half Zambia, mainly on plateau and escarpment country, and is characterised by *Brachystegia*, *Jubelnardia* and *Isoberlinia* species. Mopane woodland covers much of the hot, dry southern valleys of the Zambezi and Luangwa. Dominated by *Colophospermum mopane*, it may be mixed with *Kirkia accuminatas*, *Sterculia africana* and other species and have significant stands of baobab.

Chipya Woodland occurs particularly around Lake Bangweulu and also around Lake Mweru, in the Luapula valley and north-east of Mwinilunga. It reveals mixed tree growth of *Pterocarpus angolensis*, *Erthrophleum africanum*, *Parinari curatellifolia* and others, with small trees (*Terminalia*, *Combretum*, etc.) standing in very tall grass and herbs. Another open grassy woodland is Lusese woodland in Western Province and Namwala District, dominated by *Burkea africana*, *Dialium*

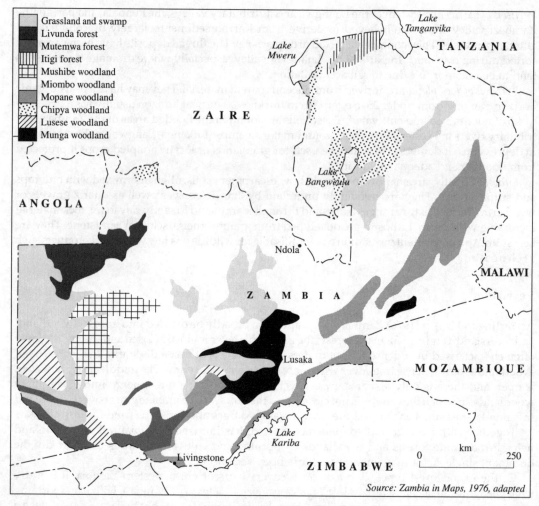

Figure 9.5 *Vegetation types*

engleanum and species of *Baikiaea* and *Colophospermum*.

Larger grasslands occupy seasonally flooded Kalahari sands (*Loudetia grassland*) and great swampy depressions such as Lukanga, Bangweulu and Kafue (*Hyparrhenia grassland*). Smaller grasslands line dambos, streams and rivers. Virtually permanently flooded areas of Hyparrhenia grassland are occupied by swamp and papyrus sudd.

The Forest estate

Some 64,750 km² of Zambia is classed as Forest Reserves, comprising reserved forest areas on state land and protected forest areas elsewhere, as against over 310,800 km² of unreserved forests. Reserves are classed as Protection Reserves (protecting hill ranges, headwaters, etc.) and Production Reserves (to assure future timber supplies), the latter comprising two-thirds of the total area.

The utilisation of indigenous forests is patchily distributed. In the south-west, 'Zambian Teak' and Mukwa are extensively logged along a private railway from Livingstone and used for construction, flooring, railway sleepers, furniture and props in mines, some being exported. A low-quality timber is also produced in the north. Larger quantities of wood, mostly from Copperbelt Province, are used for mining construction and pit props.

Inadequate local production, particularly for the mines during World War II led to extensive development of exotic softwood plantations in reserves in the Copperbelt, especially around Ndola and near Kalulushi. After much experimentation, most planting has been of *Eucalyptus* and of tropical pines. Eucalypts are used for fencing, telephone and other poles and for boxwood and processed boards. Pines are mainly for structural, general purpose and mine timbers. Recent manufacturing developments have led to further planting under the First National Development Plan, especially in North-western Province and along the line of rail.

Charcoal is of greater immediate value to many Zambians than timber. Many urban dwellers cook with charcoal and a few thousand people live by making and selling it, mostly under licence in forest reserves. Because of its bulk, virtually all charcoal making occurs near towns and major roads, being located by markets rather than vegetation types. Beeswax is quite an important forest product and production is expanding, about half coming from Western and North-western Provinces, where it is traded into Angola. The bushland widely permits collection of supplementary food, including edible berries, roots and caterpillars. Medicinal herbs are also gathered for traditional remedies.

LEGAL UNDERPINNINGS

In terms of accessibility to land, the current procedures on land alienation are contained in Land Circular No.1 of 1985 published by the Ministry of Lands and Natural Resources. Regardless of status, all land in Zambia is vested absolutely in the President who holds it in perpetuity, for, and on behalf of, the people of Zambia. These powers are spelt out in the various legislative orders such as:

- The Zambia (State Land and Reserves) Orders, 1928 to 1964;
- The Zambia (Trust Land) Orders, 1947 to 1964;
- The Zambia (Gwembe District) Orders, 1959 to 1964;
- The Land (Convention of Title) Act No. 20 of 1975 as amended.

The actual day-to-day administration of land matters has been delegated to the Commissioner of Lands. The Commissioner is empowered, under Statutory Instrument No.7 of 1964, to make grants or dispositions of land to any person subject to the special or general directions of the Minister responsible for land matters.

With reference to State Land, the method of acquiring land in Zambia depends upon the granting of development permissions and differs according to factors such as the nature of the prospective developer – Government, private or non-Zambian; the location of the land, whether it is subject or not to town planning control, city or town, traditional or state land; the type of proposed development – farming or non-farming; and whether the land is surveyed or not. The authority to be consulted, application forms and submission requirements may vary accordingly.

Before land is recommended to the Commissioner of Lands for allocation, the relevant District Council advertises in the national press inviting prospective developers to make applications. On receipt of the applications the District Council concerned proceeds to select the most suitable applicants for the plots and makes its recommendations to the Commissioner of Lands. The Commissioner of Lands considers such recommendations and may make offers to the successful applicants who are then expected to pay lease fees and development charges.

In the Reserve and Trust Lands, the powers of the President in making grants or dispositions of land are limited by the requirements to consult the local authorities affected by such grants or dispositions. Local authority in this case means the traditional ruler (Chief) and the District Council concerned. This implies that the consent of these authorities is the basis for any approval of applications for land in the Reserves and Trust Lands. To ensure that local consent has been obtained, each recommendation to the Commissioner of Lands is supposed to be accompanied by the following supporting documents:

- the written consent of the Chief;
- extracts of the Minutes of the Committee of the Council responsible for land matters embodying the relevant resolutions;
- extracts of the Minutes of the full Council with the relevant resolution;
- four copies of the approved layout plan showing the site applied for, duly endorsed and authenticated by the District authorities.

Currently the maximum hectarage of land that can be allocated for farming purposes in the Reserves and Trust Land areas is 250 hectares.

Under the Land (Convention of Titles Amendment No.2) Act of 1985, no land can be alienated to a non-Zambian. However, under the same amendment, a non-Zambian can be granted a piece of land if his application has been approved by the President. To obtain this approval an application has to pass through the relevant District Council for scrutiny so that they also can be seen to support the intended purpose for which land is to be used. When recommending the application to the Commissioner of Lands, the District Council is required to give relevant information in support of, or against, the applicant in addition to the documents requested when applying for land under the Reserves and Trust Lands category.

Water resources

This section draws heavily on Archer (1976). Water resources may be derived from either surface or underground sources: Zambia depends fairly equally on each source. The extent and availability of *groundwater* depends on two main factors, the bedrock geology and the depth of weathering, which is related to the age of the plateau surfaces. Limestone and dolomites are generally the best aquifers. Solution along joint planes in these rocks has often produced extensive fissures which hold and permit the extraction of water. Sandstones and conglomerates of the Karroo system are also useful sources but the more widespread shales of the same system yield little water. Yields from boreholes in the Kalahari sands have not yet been extensively investigated but a system of water extraction from shallow depths in unconsolidated rocks, known as 'well points', has proved successful. Schists, gneisses and granite are variable in character as aquifers, the more deeply and irregularly weathered providing the best water sources. Quartzites are usually poor aquifers, being massive and little decomposed. The basalts of the Livingstone area are poor aquifers except in vesicular zones at the top and base of the lava flows, and Luapula porphyry similarly has very low groundwater potential. The greatest groundwater potential in the country is fortuitously located along the line of rail and has been exploited by several urban centres such as Lusaka and Kabwe.

On the Copperbelt, several towns, notably Chiliabombwe, Mufulira, Chingola and Kalulushi, depend at least partly on groundwater pumped from the mines. Away from the line of rail, township water requirements are small and can often be met by less extensive groundwater supplies from decomposition basins in schists and gneisses. In addition to the townships, institutional supplies for rural schools, missions and agricultural stations are most commonly derived from boreholes, while commercial farms frequently use underground sources for household supplies.

Surface water has been the only source for many towns since they were established, but several others, which originally depended on sub-surface sources, have reached the limit of groundwater exploitation and must now either supplement or replace these by surface supplies.

The Kafue River system is the most extensively used, and several Copperbelt and Central Province towns extract water from it. Kitwe's domestic water supply, the largest in the country is taken entirely from the Kafue River. Like many Copperbelt towns, Kitwe has two separate domestic water supply systems, one operated by the city council and the other by the mine at Nkana. The latter authority treats about three-quarters of the total, supplying the mine townships and selling the surplus to the city council. Part of the water supply of Ndola, Luanshya, Chingola, Garneton, Kalulushi and Chililabombwe is derived from the Kafue or its tributaries, so that on some tributaries it has been necessary to build dams to maintain supplies throughout the dry season.

The Zambezi River supplies Livingstone and several smaller townships, while Lake Kariba provides water for adjacent settlements. In Northern and Luapula Provinces, the headwaters of the Chambeshi and Luapula Provinces supply several towns, while Lakes Tanganyika, Mweru and Bangweulu are all used by lakeside settlements.

A perennial water supply is a fundamental factor in the distribution of rural settlement and most of Zambia's rural population depends on surface sources or groundwater sources that can be tapped by wells at shallow depth. Consequently, there is a low density of population in areas where such supplies are severely limited, such as the escarpment zones, the western plateau areas covered by Kalahari sands and on the floor of the rift valley. However, the provision of deep wells and well points, largely through rural councils, has allowed expansion into areas not previously suitable for settlement.

Fishing resources

This section is based on McGlashan (1976). Zambia is a land-locked country, but it is generously endowed with large lakes, swamps and rivers. These provide a wide variety of fish environments and over 300 different species of fish have been identified. Zambians as a people eat considerable quantities of fish; indeed, it is thought that more fish is eaten than meat.

The three major river systems and their associated lakes have differing types of fish. The first, Lake Tanganyika has the unique ndagaa fishery. Here the fish have evolved in a habitat of internal drainage separated from other sources of fish species and in great depth of water in the rift valley lake. The two species of ndagaa (family *Clupeidae*), commonly known as kapenta or freshwater sardine, are up to 10 cm long. They are either sun-dried or packed and frozen commercially for sale. Three species of perch (*Lates*) are also caught. These much larger fish, about 15 to 75 cm long, feed on the kapenta. The most common method of catching the deep-swimming fish is at night with paraffin pressure lamps which attract shoals of kapenta and the predator perch.

The fisheries of the Congo headwaters – Lakes Bangweulu, Mweru and Mweru-Wantipa and the River Luapula – produce over 100 fish species of which some thirty are commercially important and one, *Tilapia* (bream) is outstanding, being highly prized for its flavour. Some of the catch in this region is sold to fish traders from the Copperbelt towns, who transport fresh fish in special boxes on lorries and either bring their own ice or buy it on arrival at Lake Mweru. Much of the rest of the catch is partly sun-dried and then smoked for local consumption or sale.

The main commercial fisheries of the Zambezi system are the Kafue Flats and the Lukanga Swamps. A feature of these fisheries is the annual flooding of the plains from December to April, which causes the waters to be especially rich in alkaline salts and in phyto and zoo-plankton species. The main fish caught are the commercially popular cichlids (*Tilapia* species), the most common method of fishing utilising gill nets.

Every river and stream in Zambia contributes its quota of fish to the subsistence of local people. They use a variety of fishing methods not used by commercial fishermen, including elaborately constructed traps, weirs and scoop baskets and even multi-pronged spears. The use of modern nets and lines, however, has spread among them from contact with commercial fishermen.

Mineral and metal resources

This section is drawn from Hywel Davies (1976). Zambia's principal metal resource is copper. The copper ores, mostly sulphides (pyrites, chalcopyrites and bornite), with important secondary oxide ores, are found in the Katanga system, which overlies schists and old granite of the Basement Complex. Regional foldings of Katanga sediments between massifs formed the Kafue Anticline, the northwest-southeast axis of the region, which controls the Kafue drainage pattern. Subsequent peneplanation removed Katanga sediments, exposing the basement. The Katanga system is preserved in the Mulfulira Syncline to the north-east and in a set of *en echelon* synclines, bordering a major synclinorium, to the south-west. The orebodies are located in the lower Roan group in the Katanga Mines series. The ore formations are mainly argillites and micaceous dolomites, only locally mineralised to ore grade. They are mostly 4.6 to 15.2 m thick with an ore content around 3 or 4 per cent.

Although discovered in 1902, prospecting only began in earnest in 1923, when the mining rights were granted to large mining companies. The oldest mine began production in 1931 and since then a series of mines in the Copperbelt have worked both the superficial oxide ores and the richer sulphide ores.

In addition to copper mining, lead and zinc have been exploited in Zambia since the early part of the century, originally by the Zambia Broken Hill Development Company. Some silver has been produced as a by-product of zinc and lead mining, and cobalt has been produced from copper mines. Further mineral resources include manganese at Mansa in Luapula Province, coal in the Gwembe Valley and high grade iron ore at Sanje, near Mumbwa. Small quantities of precious and semi-precious stones (except diamonds) are obtainable in Southern Province, including amethysts. Small-scale exploitation of mica has occurred sporadically in Eastern Province.

Energy resources

The following section is based upon Suba (1990). As is the case with most African countries, the overall national energy sector in Zambia is sharply divided between the commercial and traditional sectors. The commercial sector relies almost entirely on conventional fuels – electricity, petroleum and coal/coke. Woodfuel is the main source of energy in the traditional sector. Most of the households in Zambia still depend on wood as a primary energy source, either in its raw form or after conversion to charcoal. Rural households depend on wood for cooking and lighting almost exclusively. Charcoal rather than wood is widely used by the low and middle-income urban households. This is because its light weight makes it much more economical to transport from the rural areas.

The most recent energy balance data available is for 1987. Wood is the most important source of energy, accounting for 65 per cent of domestic final demand. The remaining 35 per cent was provided for by electricity (13 per cent), petroleum (13 per cent) and coal/coke (9 per cent). It is important, however, to treat these figures as no more than estimates, especially for the traditional sector, where most transactions are unrecorded.

In terms of the sectoral pattern of energy consumption, mining, which in 1987 consumed 72 per cent of electricity, 37 per cent of coal, 100 per cent of coke and 24 per cent of petroleum products, dominates conventional fuel consumption. The transport sector is the main user of petroleum products and accounted for almost 51 per cent of the total consumption. The household sector is the dominant consumer of woodfuel, accounting for 84 per cent of total woodfuel consumption (Table 9.3).

Table 9.3 *Sectoral pattern of energy consumption, 1987 (%)*

Sector	Electricity	Oil	Coal	Coke	Woodfuel
Agriculture	2	3	–	–	8
Mining	72	24	37	100	–
Industry	12	13	58	–	8
Transport	–	51	–	–	–
Households	8	9	–	–	84
Other Services	6	–	5	–	–
Total	100	100	100	100	100

Source: SADC, 1989

At the national scale the domestic primary production of woodfuel, electricity and coal is more than enough to satisfy demand. On the other hand, all the country's petroleum requirements are imported, mainly in the form of crude oil as are Zambia's coke requirements.

The rural energy situation in Zambia is characterised by the overwhelming dependence of the rural population on woodfuel. Figures on rural energy consumption are notoriously difficult to estimate. However, there is overwhelming evidence that woodfuel contributes over 90 per cent of rural energy consumption. Small amounts of kerosene are used for lighting, and a little charcoal. The most reliable estimates were carried out by the National Resources Department and the detailed figures are given in Tables 9.4 and 9.5.

Table 9.4 *Relative use of different household energy sources, 1980 (%)*

	Rural areas	Small urban areas	Urban areas
Consumption	59 TJ	06 TJ	15 TJ
Electricity	0.25%	4.1%	1.2%
Kerosene	0.9%	4.0%	2.4%
Charcoal	1.4%	63.7%	89.25%
Firewood	97.5%	28.3%	7.2%

TJ=Terajoules

Source: SADC, 1989

Although there are few studies on rural energy consumption and supply problems in Zambia, it is generally agreed that there is little evidence at present of a 'rural energy crisis'. In most of the country the woodfuel supply is still sufficient and accessible. There are specific regions of shortage or impending shortages (mainly in Copperbelt, Lusaka and Central Provinces) but even there the problem is localised.

Table 9.5 *Per capita annual consumption levels in the household sector, 1980*

	Rural areas	Small urban areas	Large urban areas
Electricity (kWh)	13.0	36.0	90.0
Kerosene (litre)	4.1	6.5	8.0
Charcoal (kg)	8.0	68.0	161.0
Firewood (m³)	2.5	1.4	0.3

Source: SADC, 1989

In rural areas, where wood is the most common fuel, the small population and, more importantly, the low population density, combined with reasonably good ecological conditions, mean that wood is accessible and that fuel shortages are rarely felt. The problem in the rural areas is not with wood as a fuel, but with long-term damage that commercial tree removal for the urban market is doing to the potential of the land for sustained agriculture. Even then, according to the surveys carried out by the Natural Resources Department (NRD), deforestation is not primarily caused by energy needs, but by agricultural needs. The conversion of forests to crop land is identified as one of the major causes of deforestation and the environmental problems commonly associated with it. Surveys show that over 20 per cent of forest land in Eastern, Southern, Northern and Luapula Provinces has been cleared for farming. Even then, deforestation and the environmental problems commonly associated with it, such as erosion, gullying and wind-blown soil loss are less serious in Zambia, compared with other countries in the region.

It should be noted that the energy problem appears to be given low priority by the rural people in comparison to activities such as farming. This finding is to be expected since woodfuel supply is generally still sufficient and accessible. However, there is growing circumstantial evidence that the problem is likely to deteriorate in the near/medium term as:

- shifting cultivation systems break down under local population and production pressures;
- high population growth rates continue;
- increasing areas of natural forest land are depleted for urban woodfuel; and
- increasing expansion of cropland for small-scale farmers occurs through woodland clearance.

Energy: legal underpinnings

According to Suba (1990) the government's objectives are articulated in five-year national development plans. The national development plans state sectoral policies and targets, and translate these policies and targets into programmes and activities. In terms of rural energy, very little mention was made of the rural energy problem in national development plans prior to the Fourth National Development Plan (FNDP) 1986–90. Apart from plans for rural electrification and a brief description of the problems of charcoal production, all the objectives of the past plans were aimed at the commercial energy sector. However, the Fourth National Development Plan has incorporated some objectives and strategies aimed at solving the problems of rural and household energy demand and supply. More specifically, the FNDP has set the following objectives for the energy sector:

- to ensure that supplies of energy meet demand;
- to promote efficient use of energy in the economy;
- to conserve energy, particularly oil, wherever practical and economical;
- to substitute imported forms of energy, particularly petroleum products, by hydroelectricity and coal wherever practical and economical;
- to allocate resources within the energy sector to areas yielding the greatest social and economic benefits;
- to exploit opportunities for interchange of energy with neighbouring countries for mutual benefit.
- to improve the supply of energy for household use throughout the country;
- to improve the supply and utilisation of woodfuels, for both industrial and domestic uses;
- to minimise the environmental damage caused by energy production and consumption, particularly woodfuel;
- to promote research and development in new and renewable sources of energy.

It is significant to note that three objectives of the Fourth National Development Plan, to improve the supply of energy for households throughout the country, to improve the supply and utilisation of woodfuels, and to minimise environmental damage of energy products and production, were not part of the objectives of the Third National Development Plan. The inclusion of these new objectives is a reaction by the government to evidence that the problem of deforestation, and subsequent ecological degradation, is likely to deteriorate in the near to medium term if no concerted efforts are made to reverse the trend. The realisation that in the absence of ecologically-enlightened resource management methods the disruption of the ecological processes that maintain the productivity of the natural resource base will have a harmful and irreversible impact on both rural and urban activities is the foundation for government concern about these issues in the Fourth National Development Plan.

Unfortunately, the problem of rural energy does not seem to be well defined and thus there is no comprehensive rural energy development strategy. The government is tackling the problem by a project-by-project approach. This problem, however, is recognised and steps are being taken to address the issue. The Department of Energy, with the assistance of the World Bank Energy Sector Management Assistance Programme (ESMAP), launched a study aimed at, among other things, the formulation of a comprehensive strategy for rural energy.

In terms of policy formulation, the National Commission for Development Planning (NCDP), under the Ministry of Finance and Development Planning, is charged with the overall responsibility of preparing comprehensive policies and plans for all sectors of the economy. In terms of the energy sector, the NCDP relies heavily on the contribution of the Department of Energy. In the preparation of the Fourth National Development Plan, the National Commission for Development Planning set up inter-departmental working groups to assist in preparing the plan. In the energy sector, two relevant subcommittees were set up:

- Household Energy: membership includes the Forest Department, the University of Zambia, the Natural Resources Department, the Department of Energy, the National Council for Scientific Research, the National Energy Council, and representatives from Zambia Electricity Supply Company, the Ministry of Mines, and Lusaka Urban District Council.
- Rural Energy: membership includes the Department of Energy, the National Commission for Development Planning, the University of Zambia, the National Council

for Scientific Research, the Zambia Electricity Supply Company, the Department of Water Affairs and the National Energy Council.

There is no overall legislation covering the whole issue of energy production and use in its various forms in Zambia. The only energy legislation that is in existence is the Electricity Act, Cap. 811, of the Laws of Zambia. The rest of the laws are only concerned with the establishment of power supply undertakings and the exploration, development and production of petroleum in Zambia. Coal use is not covered in any of the existing legislation; neither is the development and use of new and renewable sources of energy. Apart from the Forestry Act, the exploitation and use of forests for energy is also not catered for in the legislation.

Rural energy: institutional framework

The overall responsibility for the development of the energy sector has been vested in the Ministry of Power, Transport and Communications (MPTC). Among other things, the MPTC was established to co-ordinate the many different aspects of energy sector development in the country. In particular, the Ministry provides policy guidance and supervision of the parastatals dealing with electricity, petroleum refining and distribution. It is also, through the Department of Energy, responsible for planning, policy evaluation and co-ordination of all energy projects and programmes.

It is notable that, although the Ministry of Power, Transport and Communications has overall responsibility for national policy on major energy sector issues, a number of activities in rural energy policy-making, planning, implementation and co-ordination lie outside the domain of the Ministry of Power, Transport and Communications. The Ministry of Water, Lands and Natural Resources retains responsibility for forest and woodland resources management. The Ministry of Agriculture and Cooperatives is responsible for agroforestry activities. The Ministry of Higher Education, Science and Technology, through the University of Zambia and the National Council for Scientific Research, have been in the forefront of research and development in rural energy. Apart from these central government ministries there are also a number of non-governmental institutions which play an important role in the development of the rural energy subsector.

It is quite apparent from the above section that the task of co-ordination between, and amongst, the institutions involved in energy development is a critical one. According to its mandate, the Ministry of Power, Transport and Communications is the body charged with this sector-co-ordinating role. However, it is questionable whether the Ministry has effectively performed this function. According to the Fourth National Development Plan,

> lack of effective overall coordination has led to a situation where the above mentioned institutions have not worked closely with each other. The need for an effective institutional set-up for policy harmonisation and coordination of the energy sector institutions is a matter of priority.

The institutions in rural energy are described in detail below.

The National Energy Council (NEC)

The National Energy Council was established in 1980 by an Act of Parliament. According to its charter, the National Energy Council is charged with the responsibility of advising the Minister of Power, Transport and Communications on key issues pertaining to the development of an appropriate energy policy and its implementation.

The National Energy Council comprises 12 part-time members from government, parastatals, the university and private business organisations. They are appointed by the Minister of Power, Transport and Communications. It has a small technical secretariat, which usually meets every three months and reports directly to the Minister. The Council plays no more than a limited, part-time advisory role.

The Department of Energy (DOE)

The Department of Energy, in the Ministry of Power, Transport and Communications, was created in 1982 but only became fully operational towards the end of 1983. The Department of Energy was established with technical assistance from the Danish aid organisation, DANIDA. Up to the end of 1988, there were 12 professional staff members, including five expatriates, mostly recruited under a DANIDA grant. However, most of the expatriates have been phased out and the Department of Energy now has seven local professional staff and one expatriate.

The Department of Energy, which is headed by a director who is responsible to the Permanent Secretary of the Ministry of Power, Transport and Communications, is divided into three sections: Planning and Administration, Industrial Energy Conservation and Management and Rural and Household Energy Development.

The Department of Energy's official functions are:

- to advise on energy policy,
- to develop a comprehensive energy plan to cover short, medium and long-term strategies in energy supply and demand, energy conservation and management, and rural and household energy development. An aspect of this is the establishment of a computerised energy data base,
- to co-ordinate rural electrification by channelling and prioritising projects from different donors,
- to develop energy conservation and management in industry by undertaking industrial energy conservation audits, and
- to formulate a comprehensive strategy for rural and household energy problems.

The problem of rural energy is tackled through the Rural and Household Energy Development Section of the Department of Energy.

The effectiveness of the Department of Energy in carrying out its official functions and duties has been severely constrained by the following factors:

- a small budget, focused on rural electrification projects;
- a confused set of responsibilities vis-a-vis other ministries;
- a lack of adequate manpower to monitor the activities of energy parastatals such as ZESCO (Zambia Electricity Supply Company).

The Forest Department (FD)

The Forest Department, under the Ministry of Water, Lands and Natural Resources (MWLNR), has the overall responsibility for managing Zambia's designated Forest Reserves. It is responsible for the formulation of national forest resources policies and programmes. The Forest Department consists of the following five technical divisions:

- Management and Surveys;
- Forest Research;
- Forest Products Research;
- Training (Zambia Forest College);
- Nine Provincial Forest Offices (PFO) to administer the forest provinces.

The Forest Department is charged with, among its other responsibilities, woodfuel operations, including the allocation and management of supplies for charcoal burners and the licensing of burners. Because of budgetary constraints, no major increases in provincial forest personnel have occurred in recent years and the existing training facilities at the Forest Training College limit the number of guards and rangers that can be trained to less than 40 and 25 per year, respectively. Thus, the Forest Department does not have sufficient staff and resources to control illegal and indiscriminate tree felling for charcoal production effectively. This is reflected in wide differences between recorded firewood harvesting and actual charcoal output from both forest reserves and other woodland areas.

The Forest Department recognises that, in order to curb the indiscriminate felling of natural woodlands effectively, it will have to place more emphasis on social and community participation in forest conservation rather than focusing on strict protection methods. The redirection of Forest Department policy from standard methods of forest conservation towards broader social and economic uses of forest resources is clearly necessary.

The expansion of forest services in the country has been constrained by the inadequate supply of manpower, especially at the professional level. This is shown by the fact that, at present, there is no local institution which can offer university level degree training in forestry. This situation is likely to continue in the long term.

The Natural Resources Department (NRD)

The Natural Resources Department, which is also a department of the Ministry of Water, Lands and Natural Resources, is responsible for all other non-agricultural natural woodland, except for the areas of national parks. The Natural Resources Department is responsible for land conservation, monitoring and conservation of bush burning; and monitoring and control of shifting cultivation.

The Natural Resources Department, although it has a long history like the Forest Department, is small both institutionally and in manpower. Although a relatively small department of the ministry, the Natural Resources Department has undertaken a considerable amount of research into the woodfuel problem. In terms of institutional linkages, the Natural Resources Department seems to have less substantial links with the Forest Department, which, ironically belongs to the same ministry. Its links with the Department of Energy and the National Energy Council also seem rather weak.

In the energy sector, implementing institutions include ZESCO, responsible for all electricity supplied in Zambia, the Forest Extension and Advisory Service (FEAS), responsible for public participation in forest conservation, National Tree Planting Day and extension services to schools and colleges.

Research and development institutions include the Engineering and Technical Development Advisory Unit (TDAU) of the University of Zambia and the National Council for Scientific Research (NCSR). The latter has been involved in feasibility studies for making smokeless coal briquettes out of slurry wastes from the Mamba collieries. The National Council for Scientific Research is also carrying out research on biogas plants: two pilot projects have already been installed.

STRATEGIES AND SOLUTIONS FOR SUSTAINABLE DEVELOPMENT

The fundamental necessity for sustained development cannot be over-emphasised. Equally, what cannot be denied is the need to devise strategies and solutions that not only ensure environmental sustainability but also rural transformation. The natural environment has a capacity to regenerate itself, to replenish its resources so as to be utilised again. However, if a certain optimum landuse capability is exceeded, the environment's capacity to generate itself diminishes.

In the current quest for economic growth there does not seem to be any serious effort to conserve environmental resources. In agriculture, for example, a comparison with pre-independence times illustrates this dilemma. In pre-independence times not only was conservation practised on arable land in both reserves and state land but also good land management advice was given to the farmers. This no longer applies.

There are a number of issues that need to be addressed in the debate on environmental protection and rural transformation. The major weakness in Zambia's efforts to promote conservation and control environmental degradation is the lack of appropriate legislation. It must be mentioned, however, that an Environmental Protection and Pollution Control Bill was passed on 8 June 1990. The bill establishes an Environmental Council which, among other functions, is empowered to carry out all necessary activities to protect the environment and control pollution. In addition, the council is required to advise government on the formulation of environment management policies. In more detail, the act empowers the Council to:

- advise the Government on the formulation of policies relating to good management of natural resources;
- recommend measures aimed at controlling pollution resulting from industrial processes or otherwise;
- advise on any aspect of conservation;
- advise on the need to conduct and promote research analysis, surveys, studies, investigations and training, of personnel in the field of environmental conservation protection and pollution control;
- receive and review reports and make recommendations on standards relating to the improvement of the environment and the maintenance of a sound ecological system;
- conduct studies and make recommendations on standards relating to the improvement of the environment and the maintenance of a sound ecological system;
- co-ordinate the activities of all ministries and other bodies concerned with the protection of the environment and the control of pollution;
- advise on co-operation between national and international organisations on environmental matters;
- advise on the need for, and embark upon, general educational programmes for the purpose of creating an enlightened public opinion regarding the environment;
- identify projects or types of projects, plans and policies for which environmental impact assessment is necessary and undertake or request others to undertake such assessments for consideration by the Council;
- consider and advise, on all major development projects at an initial stage and for this purpose the Council may request information on the major development projects;
- monitor trends in the use of natural resources and their impact on the environment.

Previously, industries responsible for high levels of pollution, such as the mining industry, carried out their own studies on pollution. It is not surprising, therefore, that efforts by the National Council for Scientific Research, who through their numerous studies reported high levels of pollution, were rendered ineffective. It is not realistic to expect a major polluting industry to monitor itself impartially. Before 1990, legislation under which pollution control was undertaken consisted of the Mines and Mineral Act, the Fish and Natural Resources Act, the Town and Country Planning Act and the Factories Act. According to environmental experts, these Acts were mainly concerned with the ownership, control and use of a given resource, with their development and with co-ordination, construction, operation and maintenance. The Acts did not define, in detail, the quantity and nature of pollution (Times of Zambia, 10 November 1985). The seriousness which the Government attaches to environmental control can be measured by the fact that the Environmental Protection and Pollution Control Bill was drafted as far back as 1982. The capacity of the Government to adequately fund the Environment Council given the Government's huge budget deficit may militate, however, against the sound intentions laid out in the Bill.

In order to ensure a more integrated legislative framework for environmental protection, existing legislation needs to be amended. A land tenure system that provided security to the users, for example, would encourage them to manage land with due consideration to conservation issues and discourage the wanton destruction of land resources. Not only should title deeds be extended to reserve land, but the state's power to repossess land must be checked by the judiciary.

There are numerous other measures that a national conservation strategy should consider. With particular reference to the need for rural transformation whilst safeguarding environmental protection, the amendment of the Land Tenure Act outlined above must be accompanied by the guidelines outlined below.

Land management practices

There is an urgent need to introduce conservation-based farming practices, particularly among the peasant farmers. Chiti et al. (1989) reason that the major constraint in trying to diversify the economy, especially agriculture, is the disparity between commercialised and traditional farming systems, in particular their different input demands. Diversification leads to the allocation of more land and transforms farming intensity, resulting in increased exploitation of the country's resources. With more farmers taking up cash crops, the use of chemical fertilisers and improved varieties of seeds, the pressure on the environment is alarming.

In these circumstances, better land, animal and crop husbandry and management systems need to be put in place. The training of extension workers needs to focus not just on increased yields and improved varieties of seeds, but on the environmental impact of more intensive farming methods. It is only when the extension worker understands environmental conservation that the farmers can be expected to respond as well. Nevertheless it must be pointed out that a rural development programme which incorporates environmental conservation must be based on an approach that emphasises the benefits to the farmer that accrue from conservation practices rather than the conservation benefits per se (Kalapula and Roder, 1979).

The use of agricultural chemicals for increased productivity also poses a danger to the soil. Though the use of fertiliser, pesticides and herbicides benefits farmers through increased yields and a reduction of crop loss, the effects on the environment must be monitored. Excess phosphate fertilisers have drained from agricultural land into water courses causing eutrophication. The use of unsuitable pesticides is another problem. DDT, for example, which is banned in many developed countries, but not in Zambia, is an organochlorine which takes a long time to decompose; it remains in the soil and as well as killing soil organisms is also likely to be washed into rivers. It is imperative that the use of organic fertilisers is encouraged.

Overgrazing is another source of environmental degradation. Adequate land management skills necessary to increase the carrying capacity of land do not exist in the Reserves and Trust Land areas (Sakala, 1982). The tendency to overstock cattle, compounded by the reluctance to sell livestock, aggravates the situation. The alarming overgrazing in cattle areas is further increased by the reluctance of farmers, who strongly adhere to entrenched customs and practices, to move elsewhere. There is an acute need to take corrective measures to prevent uncontrolled exploitation of the environment in Reserves and Trust Land, where customary land tenure prevails. Customary land tenure allows for communal rights to cattle grazing areas and to individual fields during the post-harvest period. Communal rights to land entails that no person is accountable for the overgrazing that occurs. It seems logical, therefore, that individual units of grazing land should be allocated to individual farmers. Though such measures would draw widespread protest, relaxing the rules for obtaining title deeds would certainly mollify public opinion, provided that the title deeds were accompanied by material and financial benefits.

Taxation policies

Although taxes are best known as a source of government revenue, they can also be used to implement the attainment of public policy initiatives. In relation to the degradation of land resources taxation can be used to address environmental and conservation issues. Two forms of taxes are of special concern to land resources, namely property taxes and severance taxes. Property tax involves a yearly charge on the assessed value of the taxable properties located within the taxing authority's jurisdiction. Severance taxes on the other hand, relate to charges for the privilege of activities such as harvesting or mineral extraction.

In Zambia there is a charge on property but no tax is imposed to ensure that those utilising land resources institute conservation measures. It is crucial therefore that those responsible for environmental degradation meet the costs of environmental reclamation. However, caution must be exercised to ensure that the institution of severance taxes does not produce negative effects. For example, severance taxes may cause an increase in production costs which in monopolistic economies like Zambia is likely to be passed on to the consumer. In the case of imposing severance taxes on copper mining, whose price is determined at the London Metal Exchange, the profitability and viability of the sector would be compromised, an event that would not be in the interests of the country. Even so, it is doubtful whether the tax authorities are currently capable of calculating the costs and benefits of such 'polluter pays' principles. Nevertheless, there is a need to devise effective tax measures for environmental protection.

Popular participation

It is now clear that two issues emerge as pre-conditions for sustainable growth, namely the need for sound policy and effective machinery to implement the policies. However, these conditions are necessary but not sufficient to ensure environmental protection and rural transformation. There is one condition that is often ignored and yet is necessary to ensure the effectiveness of any development policy. This condition is the participation of the population in the development process, particularly the peasantry who constitute the majority of the population in most developing countries. The agrarian crisis is not only the most visible aspect of the development crisis but also the deepest. The inequitable distribution of land, the deteriorating food supply situation, the shortage of raw materials, the negligible agricultural foreign exchange earnings are merely a few examples that illustrate the depth of the crisis. The crisis is compounded by the mistaken belief that the solution to the problem lies in physical and technical 'fixes'. This belief has led to the neglect of the basic human context. Onimonde (1988) rightly concludes that the agrarian materialism which focuses on the physical and technical aspects is illustrated by green revolution policies. However, in Zambia rural transformation policies for sustainable development must incorporate reforms of the political economy.

Any serious and lasting strategy to counter the agrarian crisis must therefore incorporate both the material and human dimensions of the crisis. Such a transformation strategy must address five basic issues (Onimonde, 1988):

- peasant power
- state structure
- agricultural reorganisation
- land relations
- technical change.

Participation in this context refers to the active and willing participation of the farmers in the development process. Such participation requires that the rural poor not only share in the distribution of the benefits of development, be they material benefits of increased output or other benefits enhancing the quality of life, but they should share also the task of creating these benefits. In short, the peasant majority must exercise political and economic power. The role of the state and its organs is therefore one of ensuring that the development process creates opportunities for all members of the population to participate in the process. The state that must evolve is one that guarantees the power and interests of the farmer. However, the reorientation of the state to meet this challenge is bound to be resisted by those élites whose interests the present structure guarantees.

Table 9.6 *Acceptability to local and other élites of rural development approaches*

Dimensions of rural deprivation	Examples of direct approaches	Acceptability to local and other élites
Physical weaknesses	Eye camps	High level of acceptability
	Feeding programmes	
	Family planning	
	Curative health services	
Isolation	Roads	
	Education	
	Extension	
Vulnerability	Seasonal public works	
	Seasonal credit	
	Crop insurance	
	Preventive health	
Poverty	Distribution of resources	
	Redistribution of assets	
Powerlessness	Legal aid	
	Enforcement of liberal laws	
	Trade unions	
	Political mobilisation	
	Non-violent political change	
	Violent political change	Low level of acceptability

Source: Chambers, 1983

Chambers (1983) shows that most rural development support programmes concentrate on policies which have the support of the élite groups. As Table 9.6 shows, the degree to which these élite groups accept direct approaches to the five categories of rural deprivation varies with the extent to which such intervention threatens their entrenched privileges.

It is not surprising therefore that in Zambia the urban workers have powerful unions that have applied pressure for cheap food which, in collusion with Government policy, has led to a deterioration of the terms of trade of farmers compared with urban workers. The rural poor, characterised by a lack of organisation, illiteracy and poverty, are preoccupied with survival. Under such circumstances, rural transformation is inherently a struggle for political empowerment.

CONCLUSION

Sustainable development guarantees future generations a sound resource base for economic activities. Environmental control and protection is one important element that ensures sustainable development. Whereas the pre-colonial agrarian systems had, to some extent, in-built adjustment mechanisms for environmental control, the coming of colonial rule distorted these relationships. The way in which land and water resources came to be utilised and allocated demonstrates this process. The advent of political independence has not brought about any significant changes in landuse patterns. The current concern about environmental sustainability is mainly due to the fact that in spite of the attainment of political independence, the inherited pattern of natural and physical resource exploitation does not seem to have altered significantly. The pursuit of rapid modernisation has led to the import and transplantation of inappropriate development models. In consequence, the brunt of environmental degradation normally falls on vulnerable groups.

Resource-use conflicts arise from the manner in which resources are used, in turn a reflection of the general economic framework. In the predominantly-peasant agricultural sector there tend to be competing demands on land for cash crops against food crops, cropping land against livestock rearing. Rapid population growth compounds the demand on land even further. The land tenure system in Zambia allows for both individual and communal ownership under the Reserves and State Land. The principle of communality of interest in the land is most evident in the use of grazing land. Even though crop production is undertaken on individually-owned land, communal grazing rights extend to individual lands during the period after harvesting and before the new planting season. Communal grazing poses environmental hazards due to the lack of accountability of any cattle owner for the overgrazing that occurs.

Provisions for the acquisition of title deeds exist for both the Reserve and Trust Land and State Land. However, on account of the costs involved in surveying the land for the purpose of acquiring title deeds, title deeds are seldom sought by those that own land under customary law. Security of land is therefore more tenable under the State Land provisions, most of which is accessible to the élites and to commercial farmers. Cases of repossessing land from peasant farmers and reallocating it to large-scale farmers are common.

The situation of women vis-a-vis the land market is precarious. Women, who undertake about 80 per cent of farm work, are not accorded equal say in the operations. Not only do the men remain in charge of farm planning and management, but the land tenure systems condemn women to the status of a landless class.

The unbalanced economy inherited at Independence necessitated urgent developmental programmes. Occurring alongside these changes has been the development of environmental problems. The need to increase the economic returns from agriculture without due regard to environmental protection has resulted in serious environmental problems. The main form of environmental degradation arising from agriculture is soil erosion, which in Zambia is worsened by the prevalence of low fertility soils with structures susceptible to erosion. Additionally, waste from industries established after Independence such as Nitrogen Chemicals and Kafue Textiles, is discharged into the air, water and land. Studies have shown that industrial wastes are capable of causing acute or chronic illnesses to humans because the substances enter the body by inhalation or through the skin.

The major weakness in Zambia's efforts to promote conservation and to control environmental degradation has been the lack of appropriate legislation. Though an Environmental Protection and Pollution Control Bill has been passed, it is doubtful whether the Government's financial position will enable it to fund the Environmental Council adequately.

Finally, ensuring environmental protection and rural transformation demands the participation of all levels of rural society. The continued emphasis on the physical and technical aspects of development has underplayed the importance of the human factor. As a result, programmes are designed for the rural population without due regard to their participation. A long-lasting solution that ensures sustainable development can only be guaranteed with the willing and active participation of the people, not only in the sharing of the benefits of development, but also by participating in the task of creating these benefits.

REFERENCES

Archer, D R (1976) 'Water supply' in (ed.) D Hywel Davies, *Zambia in Maps*: 96–97

Bruce, J and Domer, P (1982) *Agricultural Land Tenure in Zambia: Perspectives, Problems and Opportunities*, mimeo

Chambers, R (1983) *Rural Development: Putting the Last First*, Longman, London

Chidumayo, E (1979) 'Environment and Development in Zambia: an overview' in *Proceedings of the National Seminar on Environment and Development*, Geographical Association, Lusaka: 9–18

Chiti, R.M et al., (1989) *National Soil Conservation and Agroforestry Needs Assessment*, Department of Agriculture, Lusaka

Hywel Davies, D (1976) 'The copperbelt mining region', *Zambia in Maps*: 92–93

Hywel Davies, D (1976) *Zambia in Maps*, Hodder and Stoughton, London

Kalapula, E and Roder, W (1979) 'Environmental problems: the villagers views' in *Zambia Geographical Association*, Lusaka: 253–266

Mackel, R (1976) 'Soils' in *Zambia in Maps*: 26–27

Mackel, R (1976) 'Vegetation' in *Zambia in Maps*: 24–25

McGlashan, N.D (1976) 'Fisheries', in *Zambia in Maps*: 78–79

Nyirongo, G and Shula, E (1989) 'Contract farming and smallholder outgrowth schemes in Zambia', *East African Economic Review*, Kenya Economics Association, Nairobi

Onimonde, B (1988) *A Political Economy of the African Crisis*, Institute for African Alternatives, Zed Press, London

Perara, N P (1979) 'Derelict Land in Zambia', in Zambia Geographical Association: 217–234

SADC (1989) SADC Energy Statistics, 1987, *An Annual Review of Energy Production and Consumption in the SADC Region*, Vol. 1, Beijer Institute, Stockholm

Sakala Commission (1982) *A Report of the Commission of Inquiry into Land Matters in the Southern Province*, Government Printer, Lusaka

Scudder, T (1985) *A History of Development in the Twentieth Century: The Zambian Portion of the Middle Zambezi Valley and the Kariba Basin*, Clark University, Institute for Development and Anthropology, USA

Suba, M R (1990) *Zambia: Rural Energy Institutions Study*, Draft Report for ZERO, Harare, Zimbabwe

Zambia Government (1989) *The Fourth National Development Plan*, Lusaka

Zambia (1991) Central Statistical Office, Monthly Digest of Statistics, February/March 1991

Zambia Geographical Association (1979) *Proceedings of the National Seminar on Environment and Development*, Lusaka

10

ZIMBABWE

INTRODUCTION

Zimbabwe is a tropical land-locked country situated in south-central Africa. It is 389,000 km² in area, 715 km north-south and 830 km east-west. Zimbabwe is in the same latitude as Paraguay in South America and Queensland in Australia and lies between 15° 35' and 22° 30'S.

The altitudinal range of Zimbabwe is 2395 metres between the lowest point, 197 metres where the Save and Runde rivers enter Mozambique and 2592 metres at the summit of Mount Nyanga in the Eastern Highlands. The straight-line distance to the sea is only 170 km but the shortest route from Mutare to Beira by road and rail is 287 km. Harare is 439 km by road from the second largest city, Bulawayo, and only 500 km by road from Lusaka, capital of neighbouring Zambia. Harare is 1093 km from Gaborone in Botswana.

The eastern border intersects open flat country in the Zambezi and Save lowlands, but its central part is in rugged country. Road and rail communications eastward from Harare use the Christmas Pass at Mutare into Mozambique to Chimoio and Beira. A road north-eastward from Harare links Zimbabwe to Malawi through the Tete province of Mozambique, a route kept open by Zimbabwean and Mozambican military co-operation. Driving north to Zimbabwe from South Africa, the Limpopo river is crossed by a major road and railway at Beitbridge, from which a substantial amount of freight passes to and from the South African ports of Durban (1700 km from Harare), East London (2125 km) and Cape Town (2600 km). There are no major physical barriers to movement between Zimbabwe and Botswana, to the west, but the overwhelming bulk of traffic crosses at Plumtree on the road and railway from Bulawayo to Francistown and thence to Gaborone.

Zimbabwe's high ground tends to be undulating or hilly rather than mountainous. Even the most rugged area, the Eastern Highlands, has rounded hilltops rather than peaks. Steep slopes do however, occur here and there along the Zambezi escarpment. Steep slopes are a developmental constraint in those areas but, in general, only affect about 5 per cent of the land surface of the country.

The landforms of the country are broadly determined by the central watershed, dividing the Zambezi and Limpopo/Save river basins and the Eastern Highlands along the border with Mozambique (together sometimes termed the 'highveld'). The central watershed lies across the country on a NE–SW alignment and the Zambezi, like the Shangani, Sanyati, Manyame and Mazowe rivers, divides the northern part of the country into clearly distinguishable river basins. South of the central watershed the basins of the Save and Limpopo form one large lowland (often termed the lowveld) (Figure 10.1).

Although most of Zimbabwe is a plateau at 600–2300 metres, the gently undulating land surface is often broken by bornhardts (enormous upstanding, usually bare, rocks sometimes known as inselbergs) and kopjes (prominent isolated granitic hills). They occupy a high proportion of the communal land in Masvingo and parts of Manicaland Province and are of little value to farmers.

Conversely, the extreme flatness of the lower Zambezi valley and the Limpopo-Save lowlands in the south-east somewhat inhibits drainage. The Zambezi valley is demarcated as a distinct physiographic and geomorphological zone by the escarpment, to the east of Kariba, an abrupt

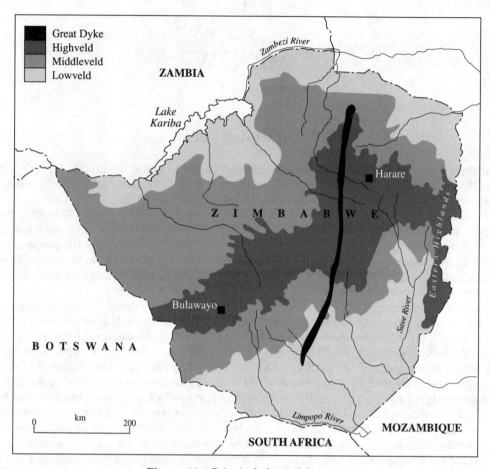

Figure 10.1 *Principal physical features*

descent over a short distance from the plateau to the valley floor. West of Kariba, where the escarpment is less marked, the main feature is the inundation of the valley floor by Lake Kariba itself, behind the Kariba dam.

The spectacular Victoria Falls, shared with Zambia in the north-west, form the world's largest sheet of falling water. The falls drop some 90 metres, across a width of 1.7 km. Together with the adjoining national parks, the Victoria Falls have been nominated jointly by Zambia and Zimbabwe as a World Heritage Site. Zimbabwe lacks large natural lakes, but small wetlands known as vleis or dambos are common, often having formed at the headwaters of streams by the local decomposition of schists. Their spongy vegetation retains moisture and releases it gradually into streams after the rains have stopped.

Physiographically, the country is divided into four zones based on altitude:

- Lowveld, below 600 metres;
- Middleveld, 600–1200 metres;
- Highveld, 1200–1500 metres, constituting the high central plateau;
- Eastern highlands, above 1500 metres on the edge of the Central African Plateau.

The climate and weather of Zimbabwe are moderated by altitude, aspect and proximity to maritime influence from the Mozambique Channel. The influence of the mid-continental high pressure (the 'Botswana upper high') induces calm sunny days from May to September and the passage of the Inter-Tropical Convergence Zone brings stormy unsettled weather, especially in January. There are three seasons:

- the hot dry season, from mid-August to the onset of the rains, which may begin as early as October or as late as January. Cloudiness builds up towards the end of the season;
- the warm to hot wet season characterised by thunderstorms from the onset of the rains until March or April; rains are often interrupted by a mid-season dry spell in February;
- cool to warm dry season, with cool nights and generally warm sunny days, from April to August; high evapotranspiration rates are typical in this season.

The national mean annual rainfall of 685 mm yields an average annual increment of 266,666 million cubic metres (m m³) of water to the whole country. Of that total, approximately 7.5 per cent (20,000 m m³) reaches the rivers whilst the remainder is accounted for by evaporation, transpiration, infiltration and percolation. The average of 685 mm encompasses regional variations from over 2000 mm in the Eastern Highlands to less than 600 mm over a quarter of the land area in the south and south-west, as well as seasonal variations. In consequence, only the Zambezi (Africa's fourth largest river) retains a significant dry-weather flow during the most acute conditions of drought. Normally however, all the major rivers flow perennially.

In terms of the soils of Zimbabwe, Whitlow (1980) has identified eight soil groups which are rated against four crucial development factors in Table 10.1.

In addition to those types, there are localised patches of alluvial and colluvial soils, mainly in the Zambezi Valley. The distribution and agricultural potential of these soil types is discussed below.

Except in dambos, the climax vegetation throughout Zimbabwe would be forest but the natural vegetation has been much modified by fire and by the displacement of indigenous woodland by crops, pasture and exotic trees. Less than a tenth of the land area remains under closed canopy forest or plantations while about half retains patchy tree cover on grazing land. Vegetative variety is primarily determined by differences of altitude, rainfall and soil fertility. Miombo, an open canopy woodland, and mopane, thorny woodland associated with the fat-trunked baobab tree, are the two most extensive woodland types.

Table 10.1 *Characteristics of eight main soil groups*

Group	Depth	Texture	Nutrients	Structure
Regosols	very deep	very low	very low	very poor
Lithosols	very shallow	very low	low	poor
Vertisols	moderate/deep	moderate/high	very high	poor
Siallitic	shallow/moderate	moderate	moderate/high	good
Fersiallitic	moderate/deep	low/moderate	low	good
Paraferrallitic	deep	low/moderate	low	good
Orthoferrallitic	deep	low/moderate	low	good
Sodic	shallow	low	low	extremely poor

Source: Whitlow, 1980

In terms of wildlife Zimbabwe has a diverse tropical fauna with 122 species of fish, 153 species of reptiles, 640 species of birds and an unknown but enormous number of insect species. Greater concentrations of eagles occur in Zimbabwe than anywhere else in Africa. Of the 17 species, the best known are the fish eagle, the black eagle of the Matopos, the very large martial eagle and the brightly-coloured bateleur. The country is also richly endowed with at least 250 mammals, including the large carnivores, monkeys, elephants and the rhinoceros. They represent a major tourist resource.

To summarise this introductory section use can be made of the Zimbabwe Natural Regions and Farming Areas map. It derives agro-ecological potential from a sophisticated combination of rainfall total and incidence, by assessment of the occurrence of 'rainy pentads' – defined as the 'centre of one of three five-day periods which together receive more than 40 mm of rainfall and two of which receive at least eight mm of rainfall'. In so doing, it lays great emphasis upon rainfall which, although most important, is not the only factor that should be considered. It is, however, useful to outline the map's five broad categories of 'natural region' (i.e. 'agro-ecological zones') as they are frequently termed (Figure 10.2).

- Natural Region 1: 5835 km².
  This consists of the Eastern Highland slopes of Manica Province, along the border with Mozambique. It is characterised by high altitude, cool temperatures and high, reliable rainfall of over 1000 mm. The highland slopes are very susceptible to erosion when devegetated. It is intensively used for dairying, forestry, tea, coffee, tree-fruits, vegetables and, in the valleys, maize.
- Natural Region 2: 72,745 km².
  This intensively-cropped (mainly commercial) farmland of northern Mashonaland occupies much of the north-east quadrant of the country, receiving on average 700–1000 mm of rainfall annually. The main area of rainfed maize and tobacco cultivation, it is also important for winter wheat, cotton and vegetables. It is made up predominantly of large-scale commercial farms.
- Natural Region 3: 67,690 km².
  Composed of semi-intensively cultivated land, this region occupies much of Mashonaland and Midlands Province, and receives 650–800 mm rainfall, mostly during infrequent heavy storms. There is rainfed cultivation of drought-resistant cotton, soya beans and sorghum, but water storage and irrigation are needed for other crops. There is a high proportion of communal land.
- Natural Region 4: 128,370 km².
  This hot, lower-lying land, situated north and south of the semi-intensively cultivated area, is subject to seasonal drought and has a mean annual rainfall of 450–650 mm. Suited to semi-intensive animal husbandry, it is marginal for rainfed maize cultivation (yields are often only 0.5 tonnes per ha). There is a high proportion of communal land. It was particularly hard-hit by the 1982–84 drought, and by drought in the early 1990s.
- Natural Region 5: 112,810 km².
  Without irrigation, this very hot low-lying zone, with less than 450 mm annual rainfall, is suitable only for extensive animal husbandry. However, the impounding of Lake Kyle facilitates extensive irrigated cultivation of sugar-cane in the south-eastern lowveld and intensive wheat production at Chisumbanje. Again, the drought of 1991–92, which lowered the level of Lake Kyle dramatically, has threatened these irrigation projects. A smaller similar region in the north, below the Zambezi escarpment, is also drought-prone.

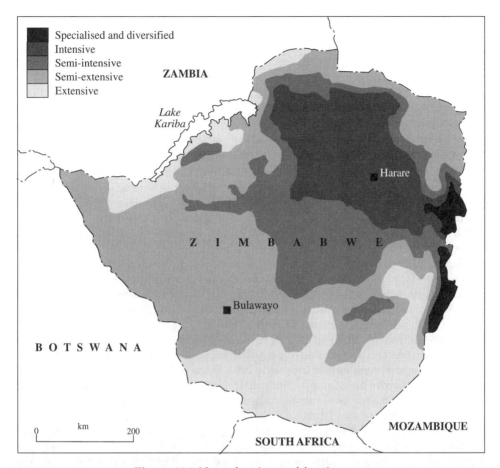

Figure 10.2 *Natural regions and farming areas*

Turning to the evolution of man-environment relationships in Zimbabwe, land was not a scarce resource for the population of the nineteenth century and earlier. Traditional methods of resource utilisation were well adapted to conservation. The limited scale of subsistence agriculture, trade, mining and quarrying imposed little stress upon the environment, except on the fertile well-watered but steep slopes of the Eastern Highlands. Elsewhere, rotational methods of resource utilisation enabled recovery of the natural resource base. Periodic drought was the principal natural constraint on production, ameliorated by recourse to a wide variety of food sources, not all of which would succumb to drought. Additionally, wild animals and plants were important elements of food security during periodic droughts.

The arrival of the first European settlers in the late nineteenth century heralded competition for land and natural resources. Lobengula, the King of the Ndebele, issued hunting regulations, restricting white hunters to particular routes, and charged licence fees in an attempt to protect Ndebele hunting rights, but his efforts were overwhelmed by the development of the Victoria hunting ethos and concomitant restrictions imposed on African access to game.

Indirect rule was followed by direct rule and then by the exercise of self-rule by the minority white settler population. Land and mining rights were appropriated. A land market developed as much of the fertile land was allocated to large-scale commercial farmers, the peasant population was displaced onto less fertile marginal lands with a greater propensity for environmental degradation. For the communal peasantry directly dependent on local natural resources for food, fuel, fodder, shelter and water, the increasing land pressure had serious economic, environmental and demographic implications.

European principles of resource management were introduced by the settlers. For 40 years settlers took for granted the 'inexhaustible' fertility of the rich red soils until the evidence of severe soil erosion had become so great that a conservation unit was formed in the Division of Agriculture and Lands in 1929. However, surveys conducted in the 1930s indicated that soil loss from commercial farms had continued unabated.

After a thorough investigation (MacIlwaine, 1939), the Natural Resources Act was passed in 1941 to 'make provision for the conservation and improvement of natural resources'. It did so, in respect of large-scale commercial farms only, by identifying 70 Intensive Conservation Areas within which farmers had to take responsibility and appropriate measures for conservation, particularly of soil. The Department of Conservation and Extension (CONEX) was established in 1946 to research and teach (and in some cases implement) conservation measures.

Indigenous traditions of resource management were overwhelmed by the consequences of land apportionment and the application of restrictive measures. Alienation of land was institutionalised by the Land Apportionment Act of 1930. Increasing population pressure also resulted in landlessness among the African population of the communal areas. Half of the African population was landless in 1978, up from 30 per cent in the late 1950s (Figure 10.3).

In addition to land alienated for large-scale commercial farms, additional land allocations were made for national parks and demarcated forest, urban expansion, mining, dumping of mine wastes and the flooding of reservoirs – most especially Lake Kariba, which displaced large numbers of valley Tonga in Zimbabwe and Zambia. The penetration of the communal areas by an economy based on wages, taxation and consumer expenditure, changed the relationship of families to their land. Peasant populations became labour pools and the communal areas themselves became labour reserves and dormitories for dependent children, old people, wives and unemployed men.

In contrast, commercial farmers enjoyed massive state support in terms of credit, agricultural training and extension, infrastructural development and market facilities. Peasant farmers lacked access to such facilities. Commercial farmers were able to implement the prescribed conservation measures, particularly contour ploughing and tie-ridging, to combat soil erosion. Peasants were less able to afford the land and labour, while traditional conservation measures (mainly the use of fallow) became less practicable with increasing population density.

The Native Land Husbandry Act (1951) was intended to improve conservation and agricultural productivity in communal areas but attempted to enforce conservation of natural resources by further restricting access to them. Not surprisingly, conservation measures were perceived as a tool of oppression when their effects were to deny access to land, wildlife and trees and to restrict the movement of cattle. To this day, in the minds of many African farmers, conservation has not shed unpopular associations with coercion and restriction.

Community development measures were introduced, among other things, to encourage acceptance of the conservation legislation and its implementation. Traditional leaders were given a supervisory role under the Tribal Trust Lands Act (1967) and the Land Husbandry Act (1970), but the measures themselves remained broadly unacceptable, more especially as they were administered by officials of the ministry variously known as Native Affairs or Home Affairs, which had political as well as technical functions. The formation in 1978 of a Department of Agricultural Development (DEVAG), charged with conservation and extension in the communal areas, came too late to have much effect.

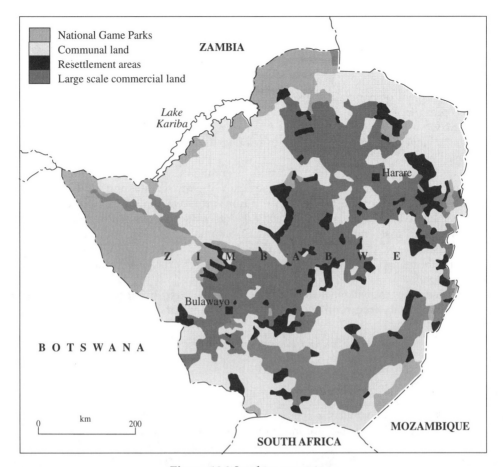

Figure 10.3 *Land tenure systems*

By then, the nationalist movement, previously urban, had spread widely into rural areas, largely in response to the unpopularity of the restrictive measures, on top of the inequitable land apportionment. The liberation struggle was inevitably accompanied by further negative impacts on the environment, as population was compressed into restricted areas. As access to land and natural resources was a rallying factor in mobilising the people for the struggle, inevitably it was a major topic for negotiation at the Lancaster House Conference. The pledge of British aid for resettlement was conditional upon the guaranteed tenure of large-scale commercial farms, with resettlement to be conducted only upon a willing-buyer, willing-seller basis.

The newly-elected government sought to abolish dualism in the treatment of commercial and communal farmlands; thus the Department of Agricultural Development (DEVAG) and the Department of Conservation and Extension (CONEX) were merged to form the Department of Agricultural, Technical and Extension Services, (AGRITEX) in 1981, which aimed to redress resource conflicts inherited from the colonial period. The first National Development Plan emphasised agrarian reform, human resource development, extension of social services and the increased participation of blacks in the economy.

Since it did not command the resources necessary to alleviate all the socio-economic disadvan-

private resources be devoted to the needs of the young. A significant reduction in the child dependency ratio might release resources for investment in other sectors.

Table 10.2 *Age structure in rural and urban areas (%)*

Area	Children under 15 years	Adult males	Adult females	Totals
Rural	53	20	27	100
Urban	34	45	21	100

Source: Moyo et al., 1991

The average annual population growth rate from 1969 (a census year) to 1985 was 3 per cent. Sustained growth at that rate would produce a 1990 population of 9.5 million, with 10 million in 1992, 15 million in 2006 and 20 million in 2016. Such population growth would exert a profound effect on resource demand and allocation, and would maintain the present extreme youthfulness of the population. Even if the fertility rate continues to decline, as it is now apparently doing, the effect would be no more than to defer the attainment of a population of 10 million to 1995 and 20 million to 2030.

In 1982 the population density was 19.3 people per km², a 48 per cent rise from 13 per km² in 1969. The highest density at provincial level was recorded in Mashonaland East (60 people per km²), a rise of 70 per cent from 35.2 people per km² in 1969. The lowest density was in Matebeland North (7.8 people per km²) which registered a rise of 28 per cent from 6.1 people per sq km over the same period (Figure 10.4).

With reference to rural areas, in the communal lands, where 57 per cent of the population lives, the average density was 25.2 people per km² in 1982, with densities as high as 59.8 people per km² in some areas. Almost all communal-land dwellers derive their livelihood from agriculture. So, in the short to medium term, any improvements of living standards would have to be based on agricultural development. The high population densities in these areas have already led to extreme land fragmentation, deforestation and soil erosion, factors that have contributed to labour migration to the urban areas. By way of contrast, in commercial farming areas the recorded population density was only 9.4 people per km², an increase of 28.7 per cent from 7.3 in 1969 (Figure 10.4).

Between 1969 and 1982 the urban population growth rate averaged 5.4 per cent per year, and by 1982 urban areas (centres with 2500 or more inhabitants) held 25 per cent of the total population. This trend can be attributed to the influx of Africans both to the towns and mines after the repeal of restrictive laws such as the African (Urban Areas) Accommodation and Registration Act and the Vagrancy Act, coupled with the worsening environmental conditions in communal areas. Unfortunately municipal housing programmes fell far short of meeting the accelerating demand.

Since their designation, the communal areas have served as a labour reserve for mines, large farms and industries, turning able-bodied men into migrants. Half of the households in the communal areas remain, for a good part of the year, under female headship, while the men work or seek work in the urban centres. In Marondera District, for example, as many as 49.5 per cent of able-bodied adult males were recorded as absent from their district of origin in 1982, whilst 47 per cent and 39 per cent respectively were recorded absent in some districts of Mashonaland Central and Manicaland.

Owing to a general lack of security (no pension and no unions) and over-crowding in towns, most migrants opt to run two homes, one in the communal areas and the other in the workplace.

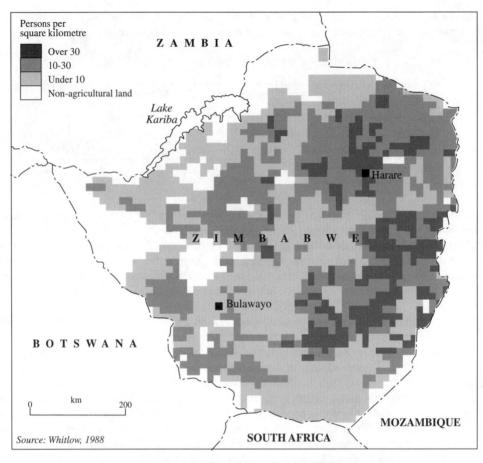

Figure 10.4 *Population density, 1982*

The prevalence of split families maintaining two homes has retarded the rationalisation of land redistribution in the communal areas, but on the other hand migrant workers remit funds to communal areas and do invest in peasant agriculture.

Landuse practices

Turning to access to land, the areas of the main types of land tenure in Zimbabwe are shown in Table 10.3. State lands, comprising 15 per cent of the total land area, are held in trust by the government for the preservation and development of their resources but do not have any market value. Commercial land, 36 per cent of the country, is freehold and a clearly-defined land market exists. Communal land, 42 per cent of the country, is communally managed. Increasing population densities and landlessness led the government at independence to introduce a fourth category, resettlement areas, to accommodate some of the population in the communal areas. They occupy almost 7 per cent of the total land area.

Table 10.3 *Land tenure types*

	Total area (million ha)	Proportion of total area (%)	Proportion of arable land (%)
Non-agricultural			
National parks	4.70	12.1	–
State forests	0.92	2.3	–
Urban and other	0.22	0.6	–
Sub total	5.84	15.0	
Agricultural			
Large-scale commercial farms (LSCF)	12.65	32.5	38.3
Small-scale commercial farms (SSCF)	1.42	3.7	4.3
Communal areas	16.35	42.0	49.5
Resettlement areas	2.64	6.8	8.0
Sub total	33.06	85.0	100.0
Total	38.90	100.0	100.0

Source: Whitlow, 1988

Farms reallocated under the resettlement programme have had their titles revoked and thus belong to the state. Reasonable, but not total, security of tenure rests with the resettlers. A majority of resettlement has been of the 'Model A' type where individual peasant holdings are created by sub-division. 'Model B' schemes involve the allocation of whole farms (usually around 800 to 1600 hectares) to communal farming co-operative societies.

Table 10.4 *Distribution of land categories by natural region (%)*

Natural region	State	Communal	Commercial		Ressetlement model	
			LSCF	SSCF	A	B
1	8.2	0.7	3.0	0.5	0.4	21.7
2	1.3	8.7	28.6	17.8	18.5	48.9
3	18.6	17.1	17.5	37.9	46.9	29.4
4	28.7	47.6	25.2	36.9	30.9	–
5	43.7	25.9	25.7	6.4	3.8	–
Total (some rounded)	100.0	100.0	100.0	100.0	100.0	100.0

Source: Moyo et al., 1991

The distribution of land-tenure categories amongst Zimbabwe's natural regions is given in Table 10.4. Almost a third of large-scale commercial farm land, but less than a tenth of communal area land, falls into natural regions one and two. Just over a half of large-scale commercial farm land, but more than three-quarters of communal area land, is in the poorest zones, four and five. The resettlement programme has enabled a small proportion of blacks to move into natural regions one and two but, as may be seen from Table 10.5, the amount of land in those areas used for resettlement remains small.

Within Zimbabwe's towns urban authorities control the nature and form of exploitation of resources giving rise to constant conflict with cultivators of urban streambanks. Most urban authority areas are so large that they include substantial tracts of rural land which is used for the usual mix of peri-urban uses, including agriculture, horticulture, 'horsey-culture' (riding schools), quarrying, waste disposal, cemeteries and extensive institutional land, plus squatter areas and neglected land.

Table 10.5 *Distribution of natural regions by land category (%)*

Land category	Natural 1 Region	Natural 2 Region	Natural 3 Region	Natural 4 Region	Natural 5 Region
State	1.1	0.0	0.2	0.2	0.4
Communal	20.2	23.7	42.4	63.0	52.9
Large-scale communal farms	73.7	66.4	37.0	28.4	44.8
Small-scale communal farms	1.2	4.2	8.2	4.2	1.1
Model A resettlement	1.2	5.2	11.9	4.2	0.8
Model B resettlement	2.6	0.5	0.3	0.0	0.0
Total	100.0	100.0	100.0	100.0	100.0

Source: Hoiser, 1988

State land consists chiefly of five and a half million ha of protected areas designated as forests, national parks, safari areas, recreational parks, botanical reserves and bird sanctuaries, holding one of the world's largest remaining concentrations of wildlife. The 72.4 per cent of state lands situated in natural regions four and five is mainly national parks and the 8.2 per cent in natural region one is mainly softwood plantation managed by the Forestry Commission in Manicaland. The Forestry Commission controls 0.92 million ha of land through its State Forestry Enterprise and the State Forestry Authority.

Forms of wildlife utilisation such as commercial hunting are permitted in safari areas but national parks are primarily for the conservation of biological diversity. Zimbabwe has 11 natural parks of which Hwange, at 1,465,100 ha, is by far the largest. Most are in areas of the lowest class of agro-ecological potential. Four-fifths of state land is managed by the Department of National Parks and Wildlife Management (Figure 10.3).

The high and increasing value of wildlife as a resource will benefit local residents in areas with considerable wildlife populations, as projects for the local ownership and management of wildlife develop. The CAMPFIRE initiative, for example, is being tried out in several areas and such schemes have the potential for the provision of a level of income generation that could never be derived from subsistence agriculture in marginal areas.

Commercial farmers are already responsible for the wildlife on their properties. Besides the exploitation of free-ranging wildlife on their properties, farmers have introduced game ranching, which integrates livestock and wildlife. The extension of this into marginal areas offers some hope for the promotion of sustainable development in these areas.

Communal and commercial land are differentiated not only by the land tenure and density of population, but also by land use and environmental conditions. Whilst there are exceptions, it is broadly true that communal land includes the most densely-settled rural areas, has a peasant farming economy and exhibits the most serious environmental degradation in terms of loss of tree cover and soil erosion. Commercial areas, including towns, generally occupy the plateau on either side of the watershed, plus the intensively-farmed areas of the north-east, Eastern Highlands and the irrigated lowveld.

There is considerable underutilisation of land on commercial farms. In the 1981–82 season in Mashonaland, only 10 per cent of the land that is potentially arable was actually cropped by the commercial sector (Moyo, 1986). In the main cropping provinces, the typical cropped area is in the order of 100–125 ha per farm, with maize farmers averaging around 250 ha per farm. Overall, 34 per cent of the large-scale commercial farm land is cultivated and 66 per cent fallow.

In marked contrast, communal area farms, based on family arable holdings, are generally cultivated by ox-plough drawn by the family's livestock, which are grazed on common land. Peasants gain right of use of land but never get legal title to it. Because of rapid population growth the average communal farm size has been progressively reduced. Holdings of less than three ha are now common. Under such conditions, intensive utilisation of available resources is inevitable, but it may also be compounded by the 'tragedy of the commons', whereby over-utilisation of communal grazing rights rewards the user regardless of the cost to the community. Such a situation never arose when sufficient land and resources were available and traditional communal husbandry was prevalent.

In Malthusian terms, the problems and constraints on agricultural production stem from the rapidly-growing population and the finite boundaries of the communal areas. For example, demand for household arable plots leads to encroachment into grazing areas, while cattle numbers continue to rise. Over-stocking is most frequently cited as an indicator of imbalance between resources and people, and a symptom of non-sustainable land use.

The Riddell Commission (1981) considered that 'peasant land in 1977 had exceeded its ecologically-safe carrying capacity by some 2.5 times', and that 'in numbers, this amounted to an excess of 2.5 million people'. The Whitsun Foundation (1978, 1983), attempting to identify communal areas with desperate land pressure, related population density to the capacity of the land (agro-ecological potential), the cropping rate, and the cattle stocking rate in relation to carrying capacity. All were deemed to be at unsafe levels in many areas.

There is indeed very real land pressure facing people in many communal areas and, for planning and policy purposes, it is important to identify the options appropriate to different areas. Analysis of land pressure is not, however, entirely straightforward and, a different perspective from that in most standard discussions should be considered. The methods used in conceptualising and measuring the problem need careful scrutiny.

For example, not all areas are currently facing over-population. In many that do, land pressure takes different forms: predominantly a shortage of grazing, or arable land, or of draught animals, or all of those. There can be a balance between population and resource base that meets conservation requirements but not the subsistence needs of the people. That contradiction has to be explored: too many people and cattle on the land in agro-ecological terms, while there is a shortage of male labour and a lack of adequate draught power.

In spite of the constraints, production has been increasing in communal areas. Since the mid-1980s, communal farmers have produced more maize than commercial farmers which is, however, partly due to commercial farmers switching to higher-value crops. In 1984, communal areas in natural regions one and two marketed 63.1 per cent of the maize delivered to the Government Marketing Board and intermediate buyers (Moyo, 1986).

For the poorer communal area farmers, however, the situation has not improved. They remain purely subsistence farmers with low yields and infertile soils. This, coupled with the continued degradation of the land and increasing population, is the socio-economic basis for the soil erosion that is identified as the greatest physical threat to the attainment of sustainable development in Zimbabwe.

Most of the land acquired for resettlement was of poor quality in natural regions three and four, largely in consequence of the Lancaster House stipulation that land should be acquired only from willing sellers. Unsurprisingly, then, average yields of arable produce have been low. Many collective co-operatives have been too under-capitalised to utilise their land allocations fully. The lobby against land reform remains influential, and has argued that resettlement replicates the environmental conditions of the communal areas.

ENVIRONMENTAL PROBLEMS

Environmental constraints cause most of Zimbabwe's environmental problems. Development may be in the wrong place, such as cultivation on steep slopes or streambanks; by inappropriate techniques, such as deep ploughing of fragile soils, or may be simply insensitive to environmental factors. Environmentally insensitive development pollutes the air, water and soil, reduces biodiversity in favour of exotic crops and livestock, and disregards the holistic nature of the environment.

The neglect of natural opportunities may also be an environmental problem. Natural resources may be underutilised if extensive land use is practised where an intensive one would be feasible and sustainable, or if resources are wasted or opportunities are simply not recognised, as may result from the under-valuation of indigenous biota. The now famous silk-producing moth, for example, that breeds plentifully on mopane trees, has been a commercial success in Botswana but not in Zimbabwe, where mopane trees continue to be cleared for agriculture in areas of low agro-ecological potential.

The removal of vegetative cover reduces nutrient cycling in the ecosystem, causes the decline of soil fertility, exposes soil to heavy rain and direct solar radiation, generates soil erosion, reduces soil moisture and damages soil structure. The loss of vegetative cover also reduces the infiltration of rainwater, accelerating surface run-off that carries away fine soil particles. These particles cause sedimentation of rivers and dams, further reducing water quality and availability. In the relatively dry savanna zone that covers most of Zimbabwe, the end result of these processes is, at worst, desertification, or, at best, stabilisation of the ecosystem at a lower level of productivity. This is by no means a hypothetical prognosis: parts of the Upper Save catchment that have endured several years of soil erosion at 50 tonnes per ha per annum now retain very little agro-ecological potential. Desertification, which has more to do with people and trees than with sand-dunes, has been predicted for this area.

While rural communities have deep knowledge of local resources, they cannot be aware of the dangers of ecological collapse because it is unprecedented in Zimbabwe. Furthermore, it is improbable that local communities could be aware of the sudden acceleration that occurs at the later stages of tropical environmental degradation, largely caused by the enormous soil carrying capacity of a single heavy storm prior to ecological collapse (usually heralded by drought, but plant or animal disease, a plague of locusts or a flood could have similar effects).

Soil

With reference to soil characteristics two sets of environmental management problems arise: first, designing landuse systems appropriate to local soil conditions and, second, combating soil loss and degradation.

Natural vulnerability to soil erosion is a complex product of steepness of slope, erosivity of soil, sparsity of vegetation, intensity of rainfall and occurrence of bornhardts. The first four factors combine to produce the high vulnerability in northern and north-western parts of Zimbabwe, with the Zambezi escarpment being especially at risk. Rapid runoff from rock outcrops (bornhardts and kopjes) induces sheetwash and initiates gullying. Unfortunately the distribution of rock outcrops in Masvingo and Manicaland Provinces coincides closely with the area of rural population density greater than 30 people per square kilometre, in consequence of discriminatory land apportionment (Whitlow, 1988).

Table 10.6 *Extent of soil erosion by land tenure class (%)*

Erosion class	Per cent of land in each class			
	Communal	*Commercial*	*Other*	*Zimbabwe*
No erosion	7.2	14.7	55.5	17.2
Very limited	29.7	64.7	40.4	45.7
Limited	20.3	15.9	3.2	16.0
Moderate	19.6	3.4	0.6	10.2
Extensive	11.3	1.2	0.3	5.6
Very extensive	11.9	0.1	0.0	5.3

Source: Whitlow, 1988

The distribution of severe actual (as opposed to potential) soil erosion is more related to human activities than to natural vulnerability. Activities include logging, road construction, deep ploughing of fragile soils, clearance for cultivation or fuelwood, over-grazing, cultivation to the foot of bornhardts, cultivation up and down slopes rather than along contours, and streambank cultivation. The cultivation of steep slopes is an increasingly common reaction to landlessness. Soil loss is then accelerated simply because the surface runoff gains velocity so rapidly that gullies form and grow quickly.

Peasant farmers formerly practising traditional farming methods, particularly the cultivation of small plots integrated with animal husbandry and the rotation of cultivation and fallow, endured no erosion problems in the past, yet do so acutely today. Land degradation in the communal areas is fuelled by population growth, increased livestock numbers and the reduced productivity of already degraded land.

The annual cost of soil erosion in Zimbabwe has been calculated by Z$2.5 billion, this being the cost, at 1985 prices, of substituting artificial fertilisers for the annual loss of 1.6 million tonnes of nitrogen, 0.24 million tonnes of phosphorus and 15.6 million tonnes of organic carbon. Weathering and micro-biological activities generate soil formation in Zimbabwe at rates of 0.15 to 0.5 tonnes per ha per annum. The disparity between the annual national soil formation rate (very approximately in the order of 10 million tonnes per annum) and soil loss through erosion, is Zimbabwe's most serious physical problem and the greatest threat to the realisation of sustainable development. Not all of the soil that is displaced reaches the Indian Ocean, but sites where it accumulates on the way, such as the banks of streams and the bottoms of dams, are not readily accessible for agriculture.

Water resources

Turning to water resources, the annual increment of surface water flow available for utilisation has been estimated at 80,000 m m³ (Grizic, 1980). Fully utilised, it would suffice for a population two to three times greater than that of 1990, even allowing for a doubling in the per capita consumption. Thus, total hypothetical availability will not become a serious constraint for at least 30 years, by which time improved pumping technology should have become available, repurification of urban water more general, and more economic irrigation methods (especially trickle systems) should have become more widely used.

The three critical water-supply constraints are, therefore, likely to be:

- geographical disparities in water availability in relation to population distribution;

- rainfall variability;
- ability and willingness to pay for water.

As would be expected in a country with a seven-month dry season, mechanisms which deal with local and temporary water shortages are well-developed in Zimbabwe. These include the migration of people and stock, the impoundment of water in dams, the raising of groundwater, and conservation in the use of water, including destocking. Water shortage crises occur during abnormal droughts, especially due to the lowering of the water table. This leads to the desiccation of perennial streams. Crises also occur when the human and livestock populations of an area have increased, when restrictions on movement prevent migration or when water-supply infrastructure, such as a pump, breaks down. The 1982–84 drought, in particular, encouraged the construction of numerous small earth dams in communal areas.

Due to accelerated run-off as a consequence of deforestation, rivers dry up sooner than previously. The major rivers of Zimbabwe, such as the Save or Limpopo, become rivers of sand with muddy pools joined by a trickle of brown water by the end of the dry season. Only the Zambezi, with its enormous catchment area, retains significant dry-season flow under drought conditions. Many large dams have still not recovered from the 1982–84 drought. Lake Kyle, for example, upon which the irrigated sugar industry of the lowveld depends, is presently at a dangerously high level of evaporation. As a result of renewed drought conditions in 1991 and 1992 Zimbabwe's water supply has reached crisis levels, particularly, but not exclusively, in the south of the country.

Faced with the problem of reservoir siltation, the National Master Plan for Water and Sanitation included a special study of soil and water conservation, for which a sedimentation survey of 30 dams was undertaken. Sediment yields as widely varied as 10–700 tonnes per km^2 per year were found, largely due to different levels of erosion. In the middleveld, where densely-populated communal areas are situated, the levels of erosion and siltation are very high. Many small dams in those areas, drawing water from large, badly-eroded catchments, have silted rapidly. In contrast, the highveld and lowveld have had low levels of siltation.

Attempts to combat the siltation of dams are meeting limited success, in spite of a standing requirement that before the building of a major dam a report outlining the state of the catchment area has to be produced by the Natural Resources Board. Neither the Board nor its service department, the Department of Natural Resources, has the appropriate methodology, manpower or equipment to execute such studies. Most dams are still constructed without adequate information and without effective conservation of the catchment area. If the catchment basin lies in a communal area, rapid siltation tends to occur.

Although Zimbabwe has considerable groundwater reserves, particularly under the Kalahari sands in the west of the country, the quality of groundwater is extremely variable. In Omay communal area, for example, pumped water is very saline. Elsewhere, fluorides and/or nitrates in quantities far above the World Health Organization's recommended rates have been found.

The siltation of dams and the contamination of watercourses with run-off containing fertiliser and dung encourages the colonisation of water bodies by aquatic weeds. In Zimbabwe, the following aquatic weeds have been declared noxious: water hyacinth, *Eichhornia crassipes*, *Azola* spp., water lettuce, *Pustria stratiopes*, and Kariba weed, *Salvoria molesta*. Water hyacinth and Kariba weed cause the most problems. Control has relied more on the physical removal of mature plants than on tackling the nutrient source. Attempts at chemical control have foundered since the pesticides (such as 2–4D) either have harmful side effects or simply do not work. An adequate biological control method has not yet been found.

Forest products

With reference to access to forest products, at the provincial level, Manicaland, Mashonaland East, Masvingo and Midlands are fuelwood deficit areas, as are more than half of Zimbabwe's 55 districts. Almost 50 districts endure local shortages. That four provinces remain in surplus does not offset the deficit elsewhere. Wood deficiency is essentially a local problem: where it becomes most severe, fruit trees and even sacred trees can be sacrificed. Remedial measures must be implemented at the local level.

Currently Zimbabwe's forest cover is being reduced at a rate of 1.5 per cent per year. Wood stocks in communal areas were halved between 1963–78 and probably have halved again since then. Deforestation has also occurred on large-scale commercial farms, particularly in Matabeleland South and the northern parts of Mashonaland. Trees are cleared from land required for cultivation and, in the absence of alternative energy sources, are used for fuelwood.

It has been estimated that 70,000 to 100,000 ha of woodland is cleared for agriculture annually. Other causes of deforestation are commercial felling, the effects of fire and urban expansion. The removal of trees for building poles and thinning for woodfuel tend to reduce woodland quality and density more than creating complete deforestation.

Table 10.7 *Total wood stocks and supplies by land tenure category*

Land type	Stocks (million tonnes)	Supplies (million tonnes)
Commercial-area exotic forest	0.09	0.07
Commercial-area indigenous forest	251.69	5.68
Resettlement-area indigenous forest/grazing	10.87	0.27
Communal-area exotic forest	0.19	0.02
Communal-area indigenous forest/grazing	103.81	2.04
Parks and reserves	269.40	0.24
Demarcated exotic forest	28.75	0.64
Demarcated indigenous forest	0.70	0.00
Total	665.50	8.96

Source: Beijer Institute, 1985

Whitlow (1980) found that 20 per cent of the communal areas could be described as especially short of forest products. The distribution of critical areas can be related to the varying degrees of population pressure occurring within communal areas in the mid 1970s. Of the nearly 40 per cent of communal areas subjected to extreme population pressure, nearly 75 per cent also exhibited severe land degradation, such that regeneration of the vegetation cover under existing circumstances is unlikely to occur. This is the process of 'desertification', a popular but misleading word that confuses the seasonal and possibly long-term spread of sandy deserts with the devegetation of semi-arid lands that climatically retain the potential to recover from the appearance of desert-like conditions.

To compound the problem of timber resources, there is a mis-match between resource and access. National parks and forest reserves contain 40 per cent of the total woody biomass stocks but supply barely 3 per cent of national wood requirements. Table 10.7 (Beijer, 1985) summarises total wood stocks and supplies by landuse category.

The large reserves on large-scale commercial farms are attractive to residents of adjoining communal areas. Although they have no legal access to these resources, faced with severe wood deficit pressure, they 'poach' from the commercial farms. Resource conflicts of this nature can be expected to increase unless policies that allow a more equitable distribution of resources are developed and implemented.

Pastoral resources

In terms of environmental problems associated with pastoral resources, over-grazing is produced by the cropping of pasture faster than the natural rate of regeneration. This simple definition, however, encompasses a complex situation in which an 'over-grazed' pasture can well recover if rested.

Many peasant farmers challenge the concept of the livestock carrying capacity of a pasture and point to the survival of their herds as evidence that a high stocking rate is not necessarily excessive. Nevertheless, there is ample evidence of over-grazing and the problem is increasing as livestock numbers rise even faster than human populations in the communal areas. The increase of herd sizes ultimately would stop, without official intervention, as a result of the reduced availability of pasture. This has already occurred in Malawi where the same rationale for maximising herd sizes is accepted. To await herd reduction by natural process however, is an intolerably negative attitude that implies acceptance of the ecological consequences of over-grazing, notably soil erosion.

Wildlife

With reference to the wildlife resources of Zimbabwe, many animals such as elephants, hippopotamuses, baboons, duikers, crocodiles and cheetahs have been increasing in number over recent years. There are degraded habitats and endangered species in Zimbabwe but, on the whole, Zimbabwe's wildlife has been well conserved, both before and since independence, to the extent that Zimbabwe finds itself the custodian of a large proportion of southern Africa's wildlife. That, in itself, is a responsibility but not really an environmental problem.

Thus, it appears that the protection afforded to wildlife by the Parks and Wild Life Act, 1975, and by the management activities of the Department of Parks and Wildlife Services, is adequate except for the case of the black rhinoceros. Saving the black rhinoceros has become a test-case of wildlife conservation. Few Zimbabwean issues have received such international attention. In Africa, black rhinoceros numbers have declined from 65,000 in 1970 to less than 4500 today. Zimbabwe holds half of that number and sustains, in the Zambezi valley, the only contiguous population of more than 500.

This situation poses two major problems for Zimbabwe. First, the animal may indeed become extinct, despite the enormous and well-supported efforts of the Zimbabwe Rhino Survival Campaign. Second, the enormous publicity, necessarily given to the campaign for fund-raising purposes, maintains the paramilitary image of wildlife protection and sours relations with neighbouring Zambia, from where most of the poachers come.

Traditional peasant attitudes to plentiful wildlife were, and remain, pragmatic. Crop raiders such as elephants, bushpigs and baboons were killed. Former tsetse fly control campaigns by game slaughter were welcomed both for the supply of meat, and the removal of the threat of trypanosomiasis to cattle. Otherwise, wildlife was unromantically valued for its nutritional value, especially as a means of surviving periods of crop failure and livestock death due to drought.

Zimbabwe is attempting to restore wildlife conservation and utilisation by promotion of the Communal Area Management of Indigenous Resources Programme (CAMPFIRE) that seeks to place the custody of the resources with the resident communities and to produce a framework within which they can manage and benefit from them. Communities join the programme on a voluntary basis after negotiation and a certain amount of self-organisation. That poses an initial but not insurmountable obstacle, given the communal ethic already in existence. Little wildlife remains in communal areas, except those bordering protected areas, but with sufficient funds and man-power, restocking of wildlife is possible.

Conservation of wildlife for aesthetic reasons – that future generations should be able to hear the cry of the fish eagle over the Zambezi or see a cheetah hunting in the wild – appears as an irrelevant luxury to a poor farmer. In a society where the majority lack the means to satisfy their basic needs the responsibility for meeting the cost of aesthetic needs must rest with the wealthy until, preferably in the near future, aesthetic needs can be aligned with the needs of the African farmer. Zimbabwe already has the mechanism for charging the wealthy: tourists and safari hunters pay high prices for visits to parks and safari areas. The central problem is how to involve and remunerate poorer residents of wildlife areas in wildlife management and utilisation. A related problem derives from the perception that wildlife conservation occupies a large area, albeit of poor land. Even poor land however, is attractive to the landless.

The conservation of a biogenetic diversity and plant genetic resources poses a different type of problem, in that the first beneficiaries are likely to be northern shareholders in pharmaceutical and agro-chemical companies. Within that context Zimbabwe has no responsibility, but does bear responsibility as a custodian of endangered plants with knowledge of traditional pharmacy. The University, the National Herbarium, the Zimbabwe National Traditional Healers Association and the Municipality of Harare are collaborating to document, conserve and develop herbs useful for medicinal purposes.

Pollution and waste disposal

Turning finally to pollution, waste disposal, and pest management, air pollution is not a serious problem, but the emission of diesel fumes is increasing as truck operators economise on mainte-nance. Increasing quantities and the changing composition of urban waste impose a burden on urban authorities unable to afford clean disposal technologies. Dumping and burning are cheap but dirty solutions.

Given the long history and wide distribution of mining in Zimbabwe, there has been relatively little disfigurement of the landscape. Dumps of even the most inert inorganic material are eventually revegetated, although it can take half a century if not assisted by reclamation. Copper sulphate and sulphuric effluents sometimes enter surface water from copper mines in the lowveld. Residues of arsenic, cadmium, copper, lead and manganese, presumably originating from mining operations, have been identified in fish.

The eutrophication of reservoirs which has resulted from the discharge of untreated sewage and run-off following careless and excessive application of fertilisers has promoted weed growth in watercourses. Harare's reservoir, Lake Chibero (formerly Lake MacIlwaine) and the Upper Umgusa Dam near Bulawayo have experienced both eutrophication and the growth of aquatic weeds. Several municipalities in Zimbabwe have for many years used irrigation schemes for the tertiary treatment of sewage effluent. However, some disadvantages have become evident. If the soils are acid sands, denitrification is retarded by their low pH, and eutrophication ensues. On the other hand, heavy textured red clays have been utilised successfully at Bulawayo for over 25 years without adverse effects. Clearly the problem relates not to the system itself but to its use under inappropriate soil conditions.

Sewage with a high sodium content, derived from soaps and detergents, has resulted in saline and sodic profiles developing in low-lying parts of some peri-urban irrigation schemes. The discharge of sodium chloride from an abattoir apparently came close to destroying an irrigation scheme near Masvingo in the early 1970s.

Storm water run-off from towns contributes high concentrates of lead (from exhaust fumes), phosphates and nitrogen (from decaying matter). Spillages from sewage works, due to stream water overflow, and fertilisers transported from urban gardens to rivers during flooding also contribute to this kind of pollution.

Pest management

With reference to pest management, pests cause two types of environmental problems: the actions of the pests themselves, and the adverse consequences of some pest control techniques. Pests range in size from elephants that trample crops, to rodents and quelea birds, down to common flies that flourish in insanitary over-crowded conditions, tsetse flies that transmit trypanosomiasis and malarial mosquitoes.

Crop-damaging insects are very numerous, and there is a major industry manufacturing as well as importing pesticides. The quantity of pesticides applied in Zimbabwe constantly increases. Though the agro-chemical industry adheres to a high standard of self-regulation, the fact remains that introducing chemicals to the environment can, and does, cause accidental poisoning when containers are mishandled and recommendations on dosage and use of protective clothing are ignored. In the longer term, excessive reliance on chemical control generates pesticide resistance and kills helpful insects and birds, so reducing the potential for integrated pest management.

Although there are merits to tsetse fly control, it must also be mentioned that many environmentalists are concerned that tsetse control is proceeding faster than effective landuse planning. Uncontrolled settlement, followed by environmental degradation of the cleared areas could result. DDT is still used extensively in Zimbabwe for the control of both mosquitoes and tsetse flies. Applications are made at very low densities and DDT degrades much more rapidly under tropical conditions than in temperate countries, where it has been banned. Nevertheless, it is a cumulative poison that has been detected in human milk as well as in the eggshells of birds of prey.

THE NATURAL RESOURCE BASE AND LEGAL UNDERPINNINGS

In terms of the land, agricultural land resource potential is determined by the interaction of climate, soils, slope and secondary terrain features. Whitlow (1980) rated the importance of the main factors as follows (Table 10.8):

Prior to Whitlow's survey, climatic criteria, principally the amount and reliability of rainfall, were used almost exclusively to determine agricultural potential at the official level, and to demarcate the five natural regions into which Zimbabwe is conventionally divided (Figure 10.2).

Soils in Zimbabwe are divided into eight main groups (Table 10.1). Regosols are sandy soils, mainly found in marginal areas, such as Hwange and Gona-re-Zhou National Parks, which are quite useless for agriculture. Lithosols are shallow stony soils, highly erodible and also almost unusable for agriculture. Sodic (natric) soils occur mainly in the Zambezi Valley and near Gweru, and are initially attractive to cultivators because they are easy to till, but become useless when the sodic B-horizon is exposed. Exposure leads to hard panning and loss of water infiltration.

Table 10.8 *Environmental factors influencing agricultural potential*

Main variable	Significant properties	Relative importance (Scale 1–10)
Climate	Rainfall amount and variability	2–10
Soils	Depth, nutrient status, structure, moisture-holding capacity	3–8
Slope	Degree of slope	1.5–7.5
Secondary terrain factors	Such as waterlogging, occurrence of rock domes	Very important if present

Source: Whitlow, 1980

Vertisols are highly fertile soils that occur in low-rainfall areas; the group includes the 'black cotton soil', found around Chisumbanje, famous for its fertility and notorious, when damp, for immobilising vehicles. The main problem encountered in the cultivation of all vertisols is their extreme intractability. They are almost impossible to build on, due to their expansion and contraction between wet and dry conditions. Vertisols near the Great Dyke contain toxic minerals. Otherwise, they are among the best soils of Zimbabwe but difficult to use.

The siallitic group contains fertile moisture-retaining soils derived from Triassic sandstones and quartzites and ranges from thin sandy soils to thick loams. The sandy nature of most of these soils reduces their available water capacity. Generally occurring in drier areas, they respond well to cultivation.

The fersiallitic group contains a wide variety of soils, of which most types have particular problems such as sandiness, acidity, infertility, hydromorphy (sogginess), sodicity, susceptibility to leaching or a tendency to capping (formation of a surface crust). The fersiallitic red clays, however, that occur on the central watershed (predominantly on large-scale commercial farms) in areas receiving an average rainfall of 700–950 mm are the most productive in the country. They are fertile, tractable and respond well to irrigation. Paraferrallitic and orthoferrallitic soils are less fertile and more prone to leaching but otherwise resemble fersiallitic soils.

Regosols, lithosols and sodic soils mainly occur in the hotter, drier regions of the far north and south. Naturally they have been avoided by farmers until the present. Now, however, land pressure generated by population growth, and the removal of other constraints by tsetse control and the tapping of groundwater, has led to the promotion of resettlement schemes in those areas.

Agriculture is the principal outcome of the utilisation of land and it contributes 20 per cent of the national GDP. A full 75 per cent of the population is directly dependent on the land, though only a minority are formally employed. Agriculture contributes 40 per cent of the inputs to manufacturing and supplies 40–50 per cent of exports by value.

Production is diversified, and, in value, tobacco, maize, cotton and sugar dominate, with wheat, coffee, sorghum, groundnuts, tea, citrus fruit and vegetables making significant smaller contributions.

Cotton and wheat are bulk crops, 0.3 million tonnes each per year, but the weight of the maize crop, 0.5 to 2 million tonnes, depending on the rainfall, can exceed that of all other crops combined, as does the land area under maize cultivation, approximately 1.6 m ha.

Tobacco production has steadily increased since 1980 but is below peak pre-UDI levels*. Most Virginia tobacco is grown on large-scale commercial farms north of Harare, whereas burley tobacco is produced by communal farmers. Tobacco is a demanding crop, for soil nutrients and for fuel. Wood consumption for curing has, however, been reduced by the substitution of coal. The tobacco crop is almost entirely exported.

Cotton, grown in the northern and central parts of the country, supplies the local textile industry, still leaving 70 per cent for export. Cotton seed is a major source for vegetable oil in Zimbabwe. Cotton farmers use large quantities of pesticides. Picking is highly labour-intensive and seasonal labour shortages occur in the commercial sector.

Maize, tobacco and cotton can be produced successfully without irrigation in natural regions one and two, although much higher yields are obtained with irrigation in natural region two. In natural regions three and four, irrigation is essential for reasonable maize yields in three years out of five. Lower value sorghum and millet are much more tolerant of drought.

Maize, sorghum and vegetables are the principal subsistence crops. Production for local consumption remains paramount in the majority of communal areas in natural regions three and four. However, increasing quantities of maize and cotton are being marketed from communal areas in more favourable agro-ecological zones. More than 60 per cent of maize marketed by the communal sector comes from the relatively few communal areas in natural regions one and two. Communal farmers have increased their share of the maize crop from 6 per cent in 1980 to 50 per cent in 1988. As would be expected, most sorghum marketed from communal areas comes from natural region three, mainly in the Midlands and Masvingo Provinces.

Cotton, sunflowers (for expressing edible oil) and groundnuts are major cash crops for communal farmers. Cotton has increased as groundnuts have declined in popularity. Peasant farmers now produce half the total cotton crop, 75 per cent of the sunflower crop and 80 per cent of sorghum. Coffee has been successfully promoted as a peasant crop in Manicaland, although total production remains small.

Peasant farmers in Zimbabwe utilise low levels of energy, and are in fact more energy efficient than commercial farmers. Most use a simple plough drawn by a pair of oxen, the same oxen that provide draught power for the cart used for fetching inputs and delivering produce. Very few peasants own tractors or motorised transport, although they are sometimes expensively hired. Tillage without draught power is laborious and limits the area that can be covered.

At the interface of ranching and arable land, at the edge of natural regions three and four, there is pressure for more intensive land use. In contrast, at the drier edge of natural regions four and five, in the northernmost part of Matebeleland for example, there is a tendency for wildlife utilisation to displace cattle ranching. Cattle ranching is a lucrative but extravagant use of land when there is such land pressure in the country. It is generally accepted to be the agro-ecologically appropriate land use in natural region four, but in the same region, many communal farmers are struggling to survive on land holdings too small to permit the adequate fallowing of land.

In Zimbabwe legislation over land resources has not been designed to promote sustainable development. Notwithstanding the wide scope of the Natural Resources Act (see below), natural resource control is exercised through many different laws, some of which are directed at specific resources whilst others impinge indirectly.

The legislation reflects structural inequity related to land tenure and private property rights. It caters for the creation of a range of institutions and provides for resources which enable sustainable development on state lands (forest, national parks) and private farm land. It does not, however,

---

* UDI means Unilateral Declaration of Independence, proclaimed by the Smith régime in 1966.

make provision for the efficient utilisation of private land. Regulation, or appropriation for the national good, of prime land is circumscribed by the operation of market forces, reinforced by provisions of the Lancaster House agreement.

The Communal Lands Act and its predecessors, e.g. The Land Husbandry Act, theoretically gave sweeping powers to the District Administrators, and more recently to representative District Councils to control both the occupation and the use of communal land. However, acute pressure on land and other natural resources has rendered this legislation largely ineffective.

There is an uneasy compromise between enabling and restrictive legislation on the one hand, and the tradition of common property management on the other. Both the enabling measures, such as those relating to grazing schemes and villagisation, and the restrictive measures, such as those prohibiting stream-bank cultivation, lack popular support, whilst the communal management tradition is now equally inadequate for the task of securing environmental conservation and sustainable development. This is because the problems of the communal areas cannot be resolved solely within the communal areas.

In terms of legislation, the Natural Resources Act (1941) was amended in 1975 and 1981. Its main objective is to control the use of natural resources. It created the Natural Resources Board and makes provision for local conservation committees.

For two reasons, provisions of the Act apply mainly to commercial lands. First, holding legal title to land requires compliance with the act and second, the act provides for the establishment of Intensive Conservation Areas (ICAs). Through conservation committees, commercial farmers undertake soil conservation measures in each of the 150 or so ICAs. Furthermore, enactment of the Farmers' Licensing Act, 1942, led to the formation of the Commercial Farmers' Union (CFU) which both represents commercial farmers' interests and requires compliance with its own regulations.

In communal areas, on the other hand, there are three principal constraints to the application of the law. First, the absence of legal title to land precludes the attachment of legally enforceable conditions of tenure. Second, the tradition of communal husbandry of resources has largely been lost and now is considered by many to be a colonial legacy. Third, the law does not provide for conservation committees as such in communal areas. Provision is made for conservation sub-committees of the District Council, to be set up under the District Councils Act. To date, however, there are only 55 such committees in the communal areas.

Thus, the Natural Resources Act is of limited use as an instrument of natural resource management precisely in the areas where the degradation is most acute. Its provisions for conservation in communal areas refer mainly to taking degraded land out of use and destocking over-grazed pastures. Conservation works may be undertaken by the government and the cost of such works recovered by imposition of a local levy.

Finally, it is a general problem in both commercial and communal areas that while the enforcing institution for the Act is the Department of Natural Resources of the Ministry of Natural Resources and Tourism, the Department of Natural Resources depends on other government institutions such as AGRITEX, the Forestry Commission and the Water Pollution Unit, for implementation of the Act. Those institutions base their activities on their respective acts, and are not assigned responsibilities under the Natural Resources Act.

Water resources

In terms of water resources, the storage of approximately 5000 million cubic metres (m m^3) of water in about 8000 dams (other than Lake Kariba), of which 100 are classified as large dams, having a capacity greater than two m m^3, is the principal means of retaining water for urban and agricultural purposes. Total water consumption, other than from unprotected sources, is approximately 1500 m m^3 per annum, of which almost 90 per cent is used for agriculture. Per capita average daily consumption, for the entire population, is approximately 600 litres, compared with about 1200–1800 litres in industrialised countries.

Because the pumping costs to areas with good agricultural potential would be prohibitive, almost no agricultural use is made of the world's greatest volume of artificially-impounded water, that behind the Kariba Dam. With an area of 5250 km^2, it is Africa's largest reservoir, having a capacity of 180,000 m m^3). Lake Kyle (91 km^2, 1400 m m^3 capacity) near Masvingo, provides water for the irrigation of lowveld sugar estates. Most towns have secure reservoirs, of which nine have capacities of 100–500 m m^3 and other 11 have capacities of 35–99 m m^3 metres. Actual water storage in dams is frequently well below capacity. In 1990, dams in natural regions three and four were holding only 15–25 per cent of capacity, even towards the end of the rainy season. Since then the water supply situation has deteriorated during the 1991/92 drought.

Otherwise, groundwater is the most important source of domestic water. It is drawn up at thousands of boreholes and wells throughout the country, and rapid expansion and improvement of rural water supplies has been undertaken since independence by the District Development Fund, with substantial Norwegian government assistance. The great majority of rural dwellers, however, still depend on water being carried by women and girls from the borehole, well or stream.

Total available groundwater supply amounts to some 2000 m m^3 per annum (Grizic, 1980). The degree to which it can be recovered for use depends on the nature of the underlying geological formation. The granitic and metamorphic rocks that underlie 60 per cent of Zimbabwe have low groundwater potential. Boreholes are extensively used in those areas to provide water for domestic use and for livestock, but yields are low. Such boreholes could, at best, sustain only small irrigation schemes and very small settlements. Groundwater sources in the softer sedimentary rocks, however, have higher and more reliable yields that can suffice for medium-sized irrigation schemes and settlements of up to 2000 people.

In terms of legislation the Water Act controls all water above and below the surface, including the use of, and access to, wetland areas such as dambos, creating conflicts between local cultivation and river catchment protection. It provides for the regulation of dams and requires the pre-study of catchment areas. It controls the discharge of pollutants.

However, there is an institutional overlap between the Water Pollution Control Board of the Ministry of Energy and Water Development and the Natural Resources Board of the Ministry of Natural Resources and Tourism, regarding the application of the act. The act does not address adequately the problem of degradation of water catchments in communal areas, nor does it compensate those residents of communal areas who are displaced by new reservoirs.

Forest resources

With reference to forest resources, forest cover protects water catchments, steep slopes and escarpments from soil loss, and the farmland below from flooding and erosive runoff. However, in Zimbabwe, less than 1 per cent of the land area has forest cover specifically for those purposes. In the semi-arid Kalahari sands areas of Matabeland, forest cover inhibits the creation of dustbowl conditions.

Only 2.4 per cent of the land area is afforded legal protection as demarcated forest. Commercial forestry is based on the sustainable utilisation of some 95,000 hectares of timber plantations, mainly of exotic softwoods such as pines, gums and wattle in the Eastern Highlands, plus a very large area (more than one million ha) of indigenous hardwoods, mainly teak and mukwa, in Matabeleland. Less than half of the consumption of hardwood is derived from the managed forests; the rest comes from rapidly-disappearing unprotected forests. Uses for wood include building, fencing, telegraph poles, furniture and paper manufacture.

The Forestry Commission has a five-year forestry development programme worth Z$60 million which covers a massive rural afforestation-reforestation effort, improvement of the management of indigenous woodlots, a resource inventory, the upgrading of existing operations and staff training. The multiple use of forests is an objective of the Forestry Commission but its implementation is making slow progress. The Commission is investigating ways in which it can respond to the needs of communal families, for example by allowing controlled access for grazing and woodfuel collection. Uses compatible with forestry include safari hunting, recreation, agriculture and controlled gathering of fallen wood. The extension of agro-forestry, on the other hand, holds great promise for environmental rehabilitation. Intercropping with lines, belts and small plots of trees need not diminish food and cash-crop production and may well increase it by binding soil, reducing wind velocity, and retaining soil and air moisture. Leguminous trees fix nitrogen in the soil; fruit and nut trees provide food; fodder trees provide supplementary animal feed and bamboo is usable for small domestic items and furniture. Fuelwood may be obtained from fallen branches and trimmings, and suitable species are regularly coppiced for that purpose.

Given such a range of benefits, it is worth investigating the reasons why such intercropping is not more widely practised in order to overcome the constraints. Possible constraints include the unavailability of seedlings, shortages of water, and damage by goats. Farming families in communal areas not suffering from acute land pressure do enjoy such benefits, as may readily be seen in many areas. Urban families similarly are quick to cultivate fruit trees, especially quick-growing mulberries and highly-productive avocado and mango trees.

In terms of legal underpinnings, the Forest Act established the Forestry Commission and the Forestry Board and deals with commercial plantations on state land. The Forestry Commission is a parastatal organisation which, by the Parastatal Commission Act, is required to attain profitability. Consequently, the Forestry Commission has no legal obligation to address deforestation problems on communal areas. Recognising this shortcoming, the Communal Land Forest Produce Act was enacted, but its powers were limited to the control of the destination of forestry products.

Both the Forest Act and the Natural Resources Act regulate cultivation on riverbanks. Unfortunately, the former sets the limit at 100 metres from the bank whereas the latter sets 30 metres. Such inconsistency compounds the considerable resistance to these measures and brings them into disrepute.

Finally, the Communal Land Forest Produce Act has some potential to bring about improved local management of the timber resources in the communal areas through control of the exploitation, and use of, timber resources. It seeks to prevent outsiders from gaining access to timber and removing it from communal areas.

Wildlife resources

Amongst Zimbabwe's rich wildlife resources, elephants are not only the largest and most conspicuous wild animal but also the most important economically. Greatly attractive to tourists, they also provide the main source of income in wildlife utilisation schemes. In safari ranches in the poorest agro-ecological zone, profits from game are Z$0.63/ha compared with Z$0.18/ha for cattle ranching (Taylor, 1988). The cashflow generated from commercial wildlife utilisation schemes is reported to be Z$23 per ha per year.

Wild buffalo are eradicated from areas where they might transmit foot-and-mouth disease to cattle, in order to maintain Zimbabwe's lucrative status as a beef exporter to the EEC. The omission of buffalo from hunting quotas significantly reduces wildlife utilisation potential from hunting licences. Although commercial wildlife utilisation is a recent development, Zimbabwe has a comparative advantage in its existing game population, the rapid generation of expertise and marketing facilities and a source of capital in well-developed tourism and commercial farming sectors that can afford to invest and take risks.

The legal framework for the protection of wildlife in Zimbabwe is based on the Parks and Wildlife Act. This Act established a Parks and Wildlife Board and the Department of Parks and Wildlife Management (DNPWM). It also made provision for the establishment of national parks, safari areas and recreational parks. On freehold land, the titleholder owns and is responsible for wildlife. This provision has enabled the development of private game ranching, which is developing rapidly on large-scale commercial farms in natural regions three and four.

The legal responsibilities of the Parks and Wildlife Board and the Department are limited to state land, except for the care of protected species such as the pangolin. The Department of Parks and Wildlife Management has no legal obligation to work in communal areas except when stray wild animals represent a threat to human life.

Mineral resources

Zimbabwe is rich in minerals. The same shallowness of soil that constrains agriculture is advantageous for mining. Surface conditions generally give good guidance to mineralisation, except where the Kalahari sands are 100 metres or more thick, or where suspected deposits, such as coal and oil in the Zambezi valley, are deeply buried. The greenstone belts of the central plateau are sources of gold, chrysotile asbestos, chrome, nickel and iron ores. The margins of the Great Dyke are heavily mineralised; chrome and platinum are the main products but mining conditions are made difficult by the fragmentation of the ore bodies. This enables small mining co-operatives to exploit small deposits or difficult seams of gold and chrome that would not interest the large mining companies. Many major mines are, however, controlled by transnational companies such as Rio Tinto Zinc and Lonrho.

Of 40 minerals produced, the seven listed below contribute 90 per cent of the total output.

Table 10.9 *Mineral production 1985*

Mineral	Value (Z$ 000)	Contribution (%)
Gold	241 312	41
Asbestos	84 544	15
Nickel	73 429	9
Coal	66 845	9
Copper	43 339	7
Chromite	33 676	6
Tin	22 592	3
Others	62 860	10
Total	628 597	100

Source: Moyo et al., 1991

Gold occurs in extensive fields in the basement schists throughout the highveld and in bordering middleveld areas. More than 1000 small mines have been worked in Zimbabwe within the last century. Zimbabwe has an estimated 20 million troy ounces of gold reserves and can be a significant player in the world gold market. Known gold and copper ore deposits (600,000 tonnes) would be exhausted, at present rates, in ten years. Copper and silver are mined at the edge of the Archaean basement complex, particularly around Chinhoyi and Mhangura. Nickel production has declined, due to the high cost of processing, but substantial reserves remain.

Asbestos, like gold, is found in the basement schists and is in larger amounts in the Mashava-Zvishavane areas. Zimbabwe has estimated reserves of up to five million tonnes. Asbestos mining is controlled by the Shabani-Mashava Company.

Coal deposits occur in the younger rocks at the northern and southern edges of the basement shield. Around three million tonnes per year of coal are mined at Hwange, mostly of a poor quality, with a high content of ash, sulphur and phosphorus. Enormous reserves remain, particularly in the Sebungwe area. Estimates range from 4000 million tonnes to more than 20,000 million tonnes. Iron ore is mined from banded ironstones at Redcliff, near the ZISCO steelworks, and in the south at Buchwa near Zvishavane. Iron ore reserves should suffice for at least 30 years.

Chromite (the ore of chromium) has been mined in Zimbabwe for more than 80 years, yet it has been estimated that the exploitable reserves of 560 million tonnes (out of a total of 3000 million tonnes remaining in the Great Dyke) are enough to meet world demand for many decades. Chromite is mined by the Anglo-American Corporation and Union Carbide.

In terms of environmental impact the discharge of effluent from mine workings is monitored and controlled, but toxic residues do enter the ecosystem as usually sterile, sometimes toxic, waste. Alluvial gold panning in the Mazowe area destabilises streambanks.

Several acts on the statute book attempt to control the environmental damage associated with mining. The Hazardous Substances and Articles Act and the Atmospheric Pollution Prevention Act are administered by the new Department of Environmental Health in the Ministry of Health. For the implementation of these acts, the main problems are the lack of information from producers on the chemical composition of substances and a lack of equipment for monitoring the emission of air pollutants. Furthermore, both acts suffer from inadequate administrative support for their implementation. The Department of Research and Specialist Services of the Ministry of Lands, Agriculture and Rural Resettlement exerts some, albeit insufficient, control over the application of toxic chemicals by farm workers.

The Mines and Minerals Act overrides most other acts in that very few restrictions are attached to the exploitation of mining rights once a mining permit has been obtained. Regrettably, the act leaves the way open for negative impacts on the environment such as extensive timber felling without reforestation, poaching by mine workers, siltation, dumps and non-compliance with quittance requirements when mines are closed.

Energy resources

Within the commercial energy sector, Zimbabwe has enjoyed cheap electrical power supplies from the Kariba hydroelectric scheme established in the late 1950s. A rapid rise (2.7 per cent per annum) in the consumption of electrical energy led to the opening of the thermal power station at Hwange in 1984. Electricity is supplied almost exclusively to major towns and commercial farming areas, although it is now being extended to designated growth points under the rural electrification scheme. Currently, Kariba supplies 61 per cent of electricity, 4 per cent is generated thermally and 35 per cent imported from Zambia. Imports are rapidly being reduced and will ultimately be terminated.

Ethanol is produced from sugar at a plant established in 1982 at Triangle in the lowveld. It is blended with imported petrol for motor fuel. Alternative energy sources (solar, wind, geothermal, biogas) have been studied but not yet widely adopted in Zimbabwe. Consumers who could afford the appliances are content to rely on electricity, whilst the investment cost is too great for the vast majority of woodfuel consumers.

Wood is by far the most important source of fuel in Zimbabwe, meeting the energy needs of more than six million people. More than four million tonnes of wood is consumed annually. This is equivalent to clear-felling 100,000 ha: it is the sustainable yield from two million ha of reasonable quality woodland, or the yield from more than 10 million ha of sparse cover on rough grazing land. Acute shortages are experienced in areas with a population density greater than 20 persons per km². Demand for woodfuel exceeds supply in four of the eight provinces (Manicaland, Mashonaland East, Masvingo and Midlands). Early in the next century, only Mashonaland West and Matebeleland South, provinces with the lowest densities of population, are likely to retain a wood surplus.

Table 10.10 *National fuelwood supply and demand (million tonnes)*

	1982	1987	1992	1997	2002
Demand	8.33	9.47	10.62	12.14	14.03
Yields	7.13	6.81	5.63	4.92	4.67
Stock depletion	1.20	2.66	3.77	1.57	3.01
Shortfall	0.00	0.00	1.22	5.65	6.35
Total stocks	666.29	654.49	633.32	603.19	605.87

Source: Katerere, 1988

As woodfuel is a bulky low-value commodity it is not generally transported long distances, except to supply the metropolitan market. A national shortfall has developed in the 1990s with a consequent reduction in the remaining stock. The projection to the year 2002 indicates a depletion rate of 0.5 per cent per annum.

Legislation concerning energy is summarised below. The Zambezi River Act, 1986, established the Zambezi River Authority, a jointly Zambian/Zimbabwean institution. The Electricity Act, 1985, established the Zimbabwe Electricity Supply Authority and the NOCZIM Act, 1986, established the National Oil Company of Zimbabwe. Activities of the latter two bodies are co-ordinated by the Department of Energy.

Industrial resources

Turning to industrial resources, Zimbabwe's well-developed and diversified manufacturing sector contributes about 25 per cent to gross domestic product and accounts for about 16 per cent of wage employment. Rapid growth of manufacturing industry occurred in the 1960s due to the policy of intensive import-substitution and diversification to save foreign currency, to increase self-reliance and to circumvent trade sanctions. Restricted access to externally-manufactured goods has continued to stimulate secondary industry in the post-independence period, but the same foreign exchange restrictions impose difficulties in obtaining components and spare parts.

Manufacturing in Zimbabwe is closely tied to farming and mining. For example, 25 per cent of Zimbabwe's manufactured goods fall into the food, drink and tobacco category, 90 per cent of whose inputs come from local agriculture. Products derived from Zimbabwe's mineral base contribute more than 30 per cent of total industrial production. The government is involved in this sector through the Industrial Development Corporation.

The regional context

Within the context of Southern Africa, Zimbabwe and the other SADC countries are in a position to supply virtually all the strategic minerals currently exported to the north by South Africa. Zimbabwe alone has platinum, with small but valuable quantities of palladium, lithium and chromite to meet most of the shortfall that would derive from trade sanctions against South Africa.

The Zambezi and Limpopo rivers are, of course, shared with neighbouring countries but, as has been noted, they are not at present major sources of water due to their low altitude. Zambia and Zimbabwe jointly derive hydroelectric power from the Kariba Dam. Zimbabwe is, however, concerned about the reduction of HEP generation potential on the Zambezi that would result from the proposed diversion of a major proportion of the flow through Botswana to South Africa. The enormous upper catchment of the Zambezi is a relatively sparsely populated area, and therefore the silt burden in the river has remained light.

Significant deforestation upstream would lead to the sedimentation of Lake Kariba with a consequent reduction of HEP potential, and increased wear and tear on the turbines. Zimbabwe's progress to energy self-sufficiency through expansion of the Hwange thermal power station is a source of concern to Zambia and Mozambique as they have actual, and potential, electric power surpluses through HEP generation at Kariba and Cabora Bassa respectively.

Zimbabwe has the responsibility of conserving the upper reaches of the major rivers flowing through central Mozambique. Within this context, deforestation in Manicaland undoubtedly was a contributory cause of the devastating floods in Mozambique in 1990.

Zimbabwe shares wildlife resources with neighbouring countries but large-scale migrations of mammals are less marked than in East Africa. However, Zimbabwe is an important northern winter destination for many migratory birds.

Through the EEC-funded Regional Tsetse and Trypanosomiasis Control Programme (RTTCP), Zimbabwe shares a major tsetse fly and trypanosomiasis control programme with Malawi, Zambia and Mozambique. The fly can easily reinfest cleared areas in Zimbabwe from the neighbouring countries, but it has not yet been determined that tsetse eradication of the Zambia portion of the fly belt would be economically justified, since it largely comprises national parks and game management areas in the Zambezi and Luangwa valleys. Tsetse fly control in this vast infested area requires Zimbabwe to maintain expensive holding operations near its frontiers. Highly successful experiments with odour-baited tsetse targets in Zimbabwe provided a useful local technology that is available for use in neighbouring countries with the same species of tsetse flies.

Through collaboration with the SADC Soil and Water Conservation Unit based in Lesotho, the SADC Natural Resources Unit based in Malawi, and the IUCN Regional Office for Southern Africa based in Harare, Zimbabwe is well placed both to benefit from, and to contribute to, the development and dissemination of environmental expertise within the region. Zimbabwean research methods, such as the tsetse trap, are often more transferrable to neighbouring countries than is technology from the north, and are often produced locally. According to the SADC Soil and Water Conservation Unit, however, the transfer of research findings is inadequate amongst the countries of the region. Results are often published in expensive northern journals rarely seen in the region outside university libraries. Universities and training institutes in the region can, and do, collaborate on programmes that would be wasteful or impossible to maintain in each country, but there is scope for much more co-operation.

Summary

Zimbabwe has a wide range of legal instruments aimed at environmental conservation and natural resource management. However, there are several constraints inherent in these instruments in respect of their ability to implement overall government policies and objectives, as well as solving environmental problems.

First, many acts were inherited from the colonial period. They have not been revised to make them accord more closely to present goals and policies. Second, in colonial times, conservation was perceived by the farmers in the former tribal trust lands as a restrictive activity by the colonial power. This image has remained in the communal areas to the present day. Third, there are conflicts between some of the acts. Fourth, the laws are not equally applicable to different categories of land. Some are, for instance, only applicable to commercial lands and some only to state land. Provisions for conservation are neither applicable to, nor enforceable in, communal areas where environmental problems are most serious.

In recognition of these shortcomings, the National Conservation Strategy prescribes the creation of a Parliamentary Select Committee on the Environment to be charged with:

- reviewing all legislation to ascertain whether it has environmental implications,
- ensuring that all government institutions dealing with natural resources are held accountable.

At a wider scale Zimbabwe is a signatory to the following international conventions:

- World Heritage Convention: Great Zimbabwe and Mana Pools National Parks have been proclaimed World Heritage Sites, and Victoria Falls has been nominated jointly by Zambia and Zimbabwe.
- Convention on International Trade in Endangered Species (CITES) and Migratory Species Convention.

Zimbabwe deeply respects the principles of CITES but feels that there is a conflict between CITES regulations and the promotion of crocodile farming and, more recently, the ivory trade. Properly conducted, they are excellent examples of the sustainable utilisation of wildlife, whereas some signatories to CITES question the effect of such farming on crocodile and elephant populations. The government will seek an amendment of CITES to allow for the international marketing of crocodile products and ivory if administered locally by the Department of Parks and Wildlife Management. The imposition by some countries of restrictions more stringent than those of CITES, requiring bilateral negotiations, is seen as unduly restrictive in Zimbabwe, when it precludes legal and controlled trade in animal products.

STRATEGIES AND SOLUTIONS FOR ENVIRONMENTAL SUSTAINABILITY AND RURAL TRANSFORMATION

In institutional terms, it is generally felt that Zimbabwe's well-developed central government system should be able to address environmental problems. However, there are obvious constraints such as institutional overlapping and a shortage of qualified personnel and operational equipment. There is need to promote further applied research on the most acute problems. A less obvious, but equal need, is to raise environmental consciousness among administrators and councillors involved in rural development and decision-making. It will be important to strengthen both the

Department of Natural Resources and the Ministry of Finance, Economic Planning and Development, with personnel trained in environmental science.

An example of institutional weakness is Zimbabwe's National Conservation Strategy (NCS). Published in 1987, it has two parts; Part One: The Resource Base, in which information on natural resources and environmental problems is presented and discussed, and Part Two: The Strategy, which may be summarised as follows:

- The goal of the NCS is to integrate sustainable resource use with every aspect of the nation's social and economic development and to rehabilitate those resources which are already degraded. The objective is to develop and implement action plans to ensure that the utilisation of Zimbabwe's natural resources is undertaken in an equitable, productive and sustainable manner.
- The plan of action of the NCS is to make an inventory of the state of the various resources available to Zimbabwe and, in consultation with responsible government and non-government agencies, to specify parameters and targets for the sustainable utilisation of these resources.

As a policy document, the National Conservation Strategy has a rather unclear position. It has not been presented to Parliament and it is hardly referred to in the National Development Plan. In many ways it seems to be perceived as a 'sectoral' activity under the Ministry of Natural Resources and Tourism. Among those who do refer to the National Conservation Strategy, there is general agreement about its overall objectives, but there is also a feeling that its shortcomings will have to be overcome before these objectives can be realised.

Since independence, government programmes have addressed environmental problems in two ways, at different levels. These are:

- socio-economic development programmes which also aim at alleviating the pressure on natural resources and the environment;
- physical programmes, primarily aimed at restoring the natural resource balance and preventing further environmental degradation, as well as the conservation and use of specific resources.

With reference to the first category, previous chapters have shown that the present land ownership pattern, and consequent population distribution and human settlement pattern, is widely skewed both in terms of farm size and the quality of land. Fewer than 5000 commercial farmers occupy approximately 39 per cent of the country's agricultural land, whilst human and livestock population pressure in the communal areas has led to landlessness and land degradation on a large scale.

During the period of the National Development Plan, the government will give priority to land reform and proper land utilisation in order to change present ownership relations as well as promote proper land management. The measures will include increasing the number of state farms, the promotion of co-operatives and the intensification of land resettlement schemes. In addition to these measures, the government will continue to provide back-up services such as credit facilities, extension services and training of peasant farmers in proper land management methods. The government will also support the improvement of marketing facilities in these areas. Land reform is felt to be a prerequisite for any meaningful attempt at reversing land degradation and as such should be considered in any strategy for environmental sustainability and rural transformation.

In order to redress the inequitable distribution of land, the government embarked on the resettlement programme. The government planned to resettle 162,000 peasant families over a three-year period (1980–83) at a cost of Z$260 million, at constant 1981 prices. So far 2.5 million ha of land has been purchased for resettlement and by April 1986, 36,000 families had been resettled. The willing-buyer/willing-seller condition constrained the government from acquiring blocks of farms large enough to accommodate 500 or more families. Financial constraints have limited the acquisition of land and, more critically, investment in resettlement schemes.

Resettlement areas were often planned in isolation as discrete self-contained units. Inadequate water supply has been the major on-farm constraint, but settlers on schemes adjoining communal areas have also been surprised to find themselves subjected to wood poaching and fence cutting by their neighbours.

In 1985 the government introduced a Land Acquisition Act which aimed to eliminate some of the legal constraints to the acquisition of land for resettlement purposes and to accelerate land reform. The government will continue to implement resettlement schemes, although with reduced funds. In the Estimates Expenditure 1988–89, the funds allocated for resettlement were reduced to Z$4,000,000 from $11,215,000 in the previous fiscal year. A more recent Land Acquisition Act (1992) aims to transfer large sections of commercial land to African ownership.

However, more equitable access to resources would not automatically lead to resource-use optimisation. On the contrary, without supporting investment in the improved use of resources and without a reduction in the pressure exerted by rapid population growth, the effect might be to extend environmental degradation. However, neglecting such reform would cause current trends in environmental degradation to continue. Thus the choice, in broad terms, is the adoption of a policy that might achieve sustainable development or the continuation of one that certainly would not.

One of the underlying problems associated with planning for sustainable development in Zimbabwe is the emphasis on short-term and highly sectoral development programmes. Holistic planning, utilising long-term cost-benefit analysis, would address the interrelated needs and constraints confronting the peasants and the urban poor. If the government accepts such a planning approach, then it must further accept the necessity of investing heavily in projects such as water development in the communal areas in the intermediate term. This need, if not met today, would resurface in the form of extreme land hunger in the next ten to fifteen years with attendant local conflicts and political agitation.

Planning in Zimbabwe has also been preoccupied with agriculture to the exclusion of the wider set of resources, which themselves also require equitable distribution. Planning which is negatively based on agro-ecological constraints needs to be challenged by imaginative planning based on actual resource potential, including human and technological resources. Agro-ecological constraints cannot be wished away, but there are more constructive approaches to planning than simply listing what cannot be done under certain conditions.

Demographic pressures, with increases in the size and number of households, suggest that the resettlement programme could never satisfy demand. Resettlement cannot seriously reduce land pressure and so the sustainable development strategy also has to include the development of existing resources within the communal areas, as well as investment by the state in communal areas and other sectors to create employment.

The current macro-economic structure in Zimbabwe, with its relative over-reliance on land-based resource development in terms of GNP contribution, formal and self-organised employment, industrial linkages and incomes, suggests that land redistribution and improving natural resource accessibility in communal areas has to be addressed through imaginative and specific investment, resettlement, redevelopment and pioneering programmes, as elaborated below. A greater commitment to investment in communal areas to improve land and labour productivity is an unavoidable medium-term option.

Investment policies must revitalise and broaden the orientation of industry, maximising the benefication of raw materials for local and export markets, harnessing the capacity for small-scale decentralised formal and informal industries, and supporting agro-based industries with incentives, infrastructure, subsidies and legislation. Special employment promotion policies, incentives and programmes need to be developed. Further investment in research and development is needed to introduce new technologies to improve the productivity of labour (particularly rural women) in agriculture, industry and mining, and to introduce new products.

There is a need to redefine the concept and selection of growth-points so that investment in infrastructure, services and technology can help relieve the communal areas employment problems, thus reducing the burden on land-based resources.

At present, the social function of parastatals in the development process is confused with commercial responsibilities. In pursuit of their social roles, parastatals should help implement development models that encourage self-reliance and reduce dependence on the state or other funding agencies. This means that the peoples' participation has to be encouraged in a manner that recognises their needs whilst the parastatals catalyse and provide technical back-up. The full benefits of enabling activities should be incorporated into parastatals' accounts, or their commercial and socio-economic roles should be clearly separated.

The role of institutions in a sustainable development strategy should not be underrated. The fragmentation of structures, interests and responsibilities is a major constraint to realising sustainable development. Perhaps the creation of the Central Planning Agency within the Ministry of Finance, Economic Planning and Development will facilitate closer co-ordination between, and involvement by, other planning agencies.

In order to reduce the centralised and sectoral approach to rural development and to facilitate co-ordinated and comprehensive development at the 'grassroots' level, the government introduced the Provincial Councils and Administration Act (1985). Chairpersons of Ward Development Committees (which comprise approximately six Village Development Committees, the lowest planning committee comprising 100 families) are represented on the District Development Committee which is responsible for preparing a Provincial Development Plan. The whole framework is currently in place, but it is under-resourced and consequently it under-performs. Decentralised networks of information and expertise must function better if policies and interventions are to reach rural people. Stronger institutional resource mobilisation will be required. Present arrangements are not without problems. Extension workers have discovered that the most effective entry point for rural projects is the Village Development Committee. At the village level there is greater participation and involvement of the people than at the Ward Development Committee level.

Existing legislation will require extensive rationalisation, and the attainment of sustainable development needs more appropriate enabling legislation. That would complement research, training, and the dissemination of information, all of which are needed but are currently under-resourced. The reliance on long-standing conventions, questionable scientific truisms, and parochial natural resource interests needs to be reviewed through more open public debate on the sustainable development strategy.

Access to natural resources on state or commercial land is available only from the periphery of communal areas. In communal areas, surrounded by other communal land subject to similar pressures, self-reliance would be necessary. The problems of such communal areas can be partially resolved by resettling people in order to reduce the pressure on the land. However, given the serious level of degradation of most of the communal areas, reducing land pressure will not create a productive base for the remaining population. This means that the most critical intervention strategy to rehabilitate the more remote communal areas is investment. Such an investment strategy will require the involvement of many institutions and the active participation of the local people.

Given that the greatest constraint to economic development in the communal areas is lack of water, investment in this resource must be given a high priority. Investment in water (dams, boreholes) should also be accompanied by investment in small-scale irrigation and livestock schemes and in energy in order to increase levels of production.

The inhabitants of the communal areas are generally dependent on biomass for their livelihood (food, fodder, fuel, shelter) and the provision of adequate supplies of biomass has to be guaranteed. The state will have to support programmes that integrate the three production systems (crops, biomass and animal husbandry) in an integrated approach that will establish a sustainable production base. The Co-ordinated Agricultural and Rural Development (CARD) programme being implemented in Gutu by the Agricultural Research and Development Administration (ARDA) and the German aid agency (GTZ) has the potential to be repeated in other parts of the country.

Integrated rural development strategies as suggested above will involve various tree-planting projects such as agroforestry, woodlots, enrichment planting, cattle schemes and efficient cropping systems. Agro/sylvo/pastoral integration can permit higher biomass yields. The successful implementation of these strategies will require a high level of popular participation, education, and an effective extension service backed by workable technical packages and a sound policy on population.

For the communal areas that are not surrounded by communal land, the resource-sharing model provides for controlled access to resources near, but inaccessible to, the communal areas. This implies that a mechanism must be developed to permit resource sharing between communal areas and large-scale commercial farms and between the communal areas and resources on state land. It does not imply, of course, that investment in these communal areas is unnecessary; but in fairness to the greater needs of the less accessible communal areas, it could be proportionately less in view of their alternative opportunities.

Pending the overdue revision of natural resource legislation, *de facto* resource sharing is already occurring in Zimbabwe in the form of resource 'poaching' where resource-starved communal peasants are venturing onto neighbouring large-scale commercial farms and state lands to harvest trees, water, game and thatching grass. Some private land owners have 'legalised' resource sharing, allowing controlled access by peasants in the interests of peaceful co-existence.

In a similar way, mechanisms for improved access to protected resources (forests, wildlife) have to be refined; the alternative to controlled and planned access is 'poaching', not protection. In western Zimbabwe, where the opportunities for cereal production are minimal, peasants should be directly involved in wildlife management as an economic activity along the CAMPFIRE model which has suffered from a lack of commitment by the state.

The Forestry Commission is planning to implement resource-sharing models involving the state forests and communal areas in Matabeleland North. The proposed programmes will permit managed sustained harvesting of forest resources (grass, wood, honey) by peasants. As resource-sharing relieves pressure on the more degraded communal areas, so rehabilitation schemes should be implemented there.

The option of taxing unutilised or underutilised land presents possibilities for resource sharing. Tax concessions could be made to commercial farmers who agree to resource-sharing schemes. This option may prove difficult to implement, however, since farmers could put land to unsustainable use to appear to be using it in order to avoid the law. Land reforms should encourage more intensive use of land by commercial farmers so that freed land can then be purchased by the state. Farmers with land acquired cheaply before independence have little incentive to farm intensively.

In terms of conservation options, environmental accounting has to be introduced into the national budgets, recognising that environmental degradation has long-term costs. The government must employ environmental economists who can translate environmental programmes into financial terms, and who can reject potentially damaging proposals that omit true environmental costs from their internal rates of return.

Also Zimbabwe should secure its biogenetic resources in both national parks and seed banks. It can sell, lease, share or simply conserve those resources but must retain ownership and control. Multi-national agro-chemical companies, often also petro-chemical giants seeking to extend their control of world food security, must not be allowed to add the control of wild plant stocks to their portfolios of seeds, fertilisers and pesticides, given their record of reducing genetic diversity in favour of a few vulnerable varieties that require massive doses of agro-chemicals to survive.

Certainly there will always be a need for agro-chemicals, particularly in the development of conservation tillage, but Zimbabwe should be extremely cautious not to lock itself into a dependency on chemicals which prejudices integrated pest management by poisoning natural predators.

To combat over-grazing, the government is making several attempts to promote grazing schemes. In one such attempt, the government is experimenting with a pilot grazing scheme in Gwanda District, in Matabeleland South, where a vacant commercial ranch is being used to hold communal cattle under a rotational grazing system in order to allow a group of families from nearby communal areas to rest their land during part of the year and to replan its use.

Where no such resource is available, grazing schemes require groups of villagers to set specific areas aside from communal grazing to be subdivided into blocks (paddocks) for rotational grazing, including certain rest periods.

Participants normally pay an initial fee to cover the costs of the herdsmen and watering facilities, and an annual fee to cover maintenance costs. Some people without cattle take part just to benefit from the use of draught power and manure. By-laws are sometimes drawn up, stipulating the rights and obligations of the members, such as specifying the maximum number of animals allowed in the scheme.

The basic constraint inhibiting the success of such schemes is that they are isolated experiments surrounded by the much larger and universally accepted communal grazing system. In such a situation there seems to be no way to prevent non-members from encroaching on the grazing scheme, and to keep members from reverting to the traditional grazing system outside the scheme.

The government is now beginning to embark on a nationwide programme that could substantially modify the communal grazing system. This programme is linked to self-management at Village Development Committee and Ward Development Committee levels. By promoting the demarcation of boundaries at the village and ward levels, and thereby restricting access to the common grazing resources, the government has adopted a programme to alter the basic practices of the communal grazing system, based on the participation of the population itself.

Several types of action aimed at improved soil conservation are being practised and promoted, although they all meet with specific constraints. They include:

- conservation lay-out and contouring (terracing);
- conservation tillage;
- controlling cattle numbers or controlling grazing;
- stream bank protection;
- improving soil quality;
- afforestation.

Conscious of the need for improved soil conservation, government attempts have included many types of intervention. Landuse planning and the inclusion of conservation measures in new projects are given high priority while more funds have been made available for gully reclamation, Z$896,000 for 1988–89, compared with Z$90,000 for 1987–88.

Regarding preventive measures, various institutions at the central level are involved. In the Ministry of Lands, Agriculture and Rural Resettlement, the Department of Research and Specialist Services and the Agricultural, Technical and Extension Services (especially through its Soil and Water Conservation Unit) are important. The Department of Natural Resources, the Agricultural Research and Development Administration and the Department of Agriculture also participate in different ways. However, institutional fragmentation seems to be an impediment to the formulation and implementation of larger-scale conservation works.

At present, there is no single institution with the capacity to carry out public conservation works, as did the predecessor of Agricultural, Technical and Extension Services for commercial farmland, the Department of Conservation and Extension, which had its own plant and tractor fleet. The Department of Agricultural, Technical and Extension Services may identify conservation problems, but at present the budget for carrying out these works is located in another ministry, the Ministry of Natural Resources and Tourism, which is also charged with responsibility for monitoring the state of natural resources.

The institutional framework and the division of responsibility for the promotion and enforcement of good conservation practices at the local level, on the contrary, are fairly well defined. The Ministry of Natural Resources and Tourism, through its Lands Inspectorate within the Department of Natural Resources, is entrusted with monitoring the state of the country's natural resources and, where violations of prescribed conservation practices occur, enforcing compliance. The Extension Branch of the Department of Natural Resources and Agricultural, Technical and Extension Services is responsible for extending conservation advice and assistance directly to farmers and to conservation committees, which themselves perform an important monitoring function.

In the Forestry Commission, a Rural Afforestation Department has recently been created to promote the planting of trees in communal areas. The government has launched a pilot Rural Afforestation Project aimed at the establishment of woodlots by farmers, councils, schools and various other groups.

Fifty-four nurseries have been established in 24 districts and three in urban areas. Research into multi-purpose species suitable for arid and semi-arid areas will be encouraged and the research infrastructure strengthened. Particular attention will be paid to the climatic and soil conditions in relevant communal areas. So far, these programmes have promoted exotic varieties such as eucalyptus and pine but, more recently, research and the promotion of indigenous varieties have been undertaken.

The government is implementing programmes and projects to protect and preserve the country's wildlife heritage, which is also an important tourist attraction. The government intends to curb poaching and supervise commercial hunters more rigorously but at present there are only 360 wildlife officers to cover the whole country.

Relations with communities that live along the boundaries of national parks will be improved to ensure that these communities benefit financially from wildlife. To this effect the Communal Areas Management Programme for Indigenous Resources (CAMPFIRE) will be further developed.

Game ranching in the commercial lands and in the communal areas, especially in Matabeleland South and in the south-east, lowveld is being encouraged. The farming of suitable animals such as crocodiles, ostrich, buffalo and eland will be increased to maximise returns of foreign currency from the export of meat, hides and curios. The manufacture and marketing of game products will be improved, and an appropriate marketing authority will be set up. During the plan period, agricultural research will be strengthened and fish breeding in reservoirs will be increased.

Adequate water supplies for agricultural, industrial and domestic purposes, with special emphasis on communal areas requirements, is the primary objective for water resources in the National Development Plan. The government is engaged in the construction of water conservation works, major water supply schemes and rural water supply schemes. Studies for the development of surface and underground water are underway. Promotion of the use of the ventilated improved pit latrine, invented at the Blair Research Institute in Harare, will help to reduce contamination of rural water supplies by human waste.

The objectives for the energy sector in the National Development Plan are as follows:

- to achieve, as far as possible, self-sufficiency and security in certain types of energy supplies;
- to increase the amount of electricity produced from coal and hydropower;
- to reduce the rate of deforestation by increasing the use of coal, biogas and solar energy;
- to ensure conservation of oil through research and other measures in order for the country to reduce the amount of imported oil.

The adoption of those objectives has not noticeably reduced dependence on biomass and the rural electrification programme has been suspended for lack of funds. Without donor funding, the programme has to subsidise rural consumers out of revenue from urban sales.

The government is involved in several environmental education campaigns such as:

- an education and extension campaign on resource use in communal areas run by the Department of Natural Resources;
- an Interpretive Unit introduced by the Department of Parks and Wildlife Management whose role is to explain the value of wildlife to communal dwellers;
- a combined literacy and environmental programme run by the Ministry of Community Development and Women's Affairs, a tree planting campaign, run by the Forestry Commission, a co-operative members' education campaign with materials provided by the Ministry of Cooperative Development;
- a farmers' extension service promoted by the Department of Agricultural, Technical and Extension Services.

CONCLUSION

Zimbabwe's environmental legislation is comprehensive but suffers from having been enacted during the colonial period and from being of limited use in the areas where the environmental problems are most severe. There are also contradictions and overlaps between some acts. The recommendation in the National Conservation Strategy that a Parliamentary Select Committee be appointed to review this legislation has not been implemented.

The country has developed an administrative system and a local government system which should be able to address environmental problems. However, this system has limitations due to a lack of adequate funds and qualified personnel. There are also institutional overlaps and conflicts, both at central and local levels.

Zimbabwe has developed a set of policy documents and programmes, aimed at solving environmental problems. These documents all reflect advanced knowledge of the problems and the measures required to address them. However, there are contradictions between long-term policies

---

Details of further government programmes in the fields of population policy, regional (SADC) programmes and resource allocations, can be seen in Moyo et al. 1991: 119-121.

and short-term measures for checking environmental degradation. To make matters worse, the budget allocations for resettlement schemes and preventative environmental measures have been reduced.

REFERENCES

Beijer Institute (1985) *Policy Options for Energy and Development in Zimbabwe*, Energy Accounting Project, Harare

Grizic, P M (1980) 'Water the vital resource', *Zimbabwe Science News*, Vol. 14 (12): 297–298

Hosier, R H (ed) (1988) *Energy for Rural Development in Zimbabwe*, Beijer Institute, Stockholm, SIAS, Uppsala

Katerere, Y (1988) *Fuelwood Consumption and Supply Patterns, Tree-planting and Farm Forestry in Zimbabwe*, in R H Hosier, (ed) (1988)

MacIlwaine, R Sir (1939) *Report of the Commission to Inquire into the Preservation of Natural Resources of the Colony*, Government Printer, Salisbury

Moyo, S (1986) 'The land question', in I Mandoza (ed) *Zimbabwe, the Political Economy of Transition*, 1980–86, CODESARIA Dakar, Senegal

Moyo, S et al. (1991) *Zimbabwe's Environmental Dilemma: Balancing Resource Inequities*, ZERO, Harare

The Riddell Commission (1981), Harare

Taylor, R D (1988) 'The indigenous resources of the Zambezi Valley: an overview', *Zimbabwe Science News*, Vol.22 (1-2): 5–8

Whitlow, J R (1980) 'Environmental constraints and population pressures in the tribal areas of Zimbabwe', *Zimbabwe Agricultural Journal*, Vol. 77 (4): 173–181

Whitlow, J R (1988) *Land Degradation in Zimbabwe: A Geographical Study*, Department of Geography, University of Zimbabwe, Harare

The Whitsun Foundation (1978) *A Strategy for Rural Development: Databank No.2, the Peasant Sector*, Salisbury

The Whitsun Foundation (1983) *Land Reform in Zimbabwe*, Harare

INDEX

absentee landlords 60, 189, 277
accidents 16
acid deposition/rain 214–15
aeolian processes 158, 160
aerosols 43
afforestation 95, 117, 251, 267, 310, 338; aimed at assisting soil conservation 264; arid areas 268; facilitators for programmes 121; general programme 116; target groups for programmes 231
African Reserves 164, 176, 194
agates 56
Agnew, S 100, 102, 105, 107
Agostinho Neto University 24
Agricultural Research Institute 25
agriculture 13–14, 134, 140–2, 165, 211, 278; acute shortage of products 10; arable 33, 46, 98, 172; badly hit 10; clearance for 131, 144; commercial 178; declining contribution to GDP 71; declining production 79; drastic effect upon output capacity in 9; economies based mainly on 69, 94, 112; entrepreneurial activity in 277; export-orientated 95, 164; extension into non-resilient environments 129; high concentration of population in 128; inadequate practices 57; intensive 234; land clearance for 115, 204–5; major products 77; mechanised 133; *mopane* trees cleared for 316; peasant 114, 177; planning preoccupied with 334; plantation 209; rainfed 149; receiving a declining proportion of capital 72; shallowness of soil that constrains 328; sites not readily accessible for 317; small holder 113; soils unusable for 323; subsistence 307, 314; sustainable development best achieved through 69; traditional 40, 46; tripartite pattern 95; white commercial 174
agro-chemicals 154, 322
agroforestry 234
agro-industrial fields 210
Ahtisaari, Martti 164
AIDS 59
air pollution 40, 43, 171, 282, 329; due to the burning of coal 79; legislation to control 172; of populated areas 136; standards of 56; transboundary 214, 232; urban 215–16
air quality 62, 223
aldehyde 282
alkalisation 102, 104, 130, 149
alluvium 283
altitude 32, 92, 105-7, 138, 159, 303; climate tempered by 5, 305; high plateaux 104; modified by 16, 216;

weather moderated by 305
ancestral rights 188
Ancuabe (Cabo Delgado) 136, 138
Anderson, J L 61
andesite 217
Angola 5–31, 63, 158, 169, 179, 287
Angonia 130, 140
animal husbandry 38, 165, 166, 238, 298
animal species: amphibians 50, 221; endangered 24; game 52, 247; hunted 185; mammals 50, 331; primates 14, 20; protected 24, 328; reptiles 50, 221, 305; services which used to monitor and control 20; under serious threat 100; valuable, poaching of 38; wild buffalo 327; *see also* wildlife
Anstey, S G 22
apiculture *see* bee-keeping
aquaculture 24, 50, 57
aquatic resources 100
aquatic weeds 43, 55, 321;
declared noxious 318
aquifers 32, 44, 55, 136; basalt 54; best/poor 288
arable land 37, 44, 68, 69, 324; access to 125, 241; availability of 34; carrying capacity 239; erosion due to monocropping 208; expanded in response to population growth 240; floodplain 76; good 217; lost by soil erosion 65; potentially good 195; pressures on tea estates to utilise 115; relationship to 278; settlements encroaching into 70; unfavourable redistribution of population in relationship to 278
Archer, D R 288
arenosols 32, 159, 160
arid regions 16, 240, 245, 249
Arntzen, J W 34, 35, 36, 39, 41, 42, 49, 57, 59
arsenic 321
artisanal fishermen 110, 111
Arusha 240, 241, 245, 253
asbestos 55, 56, 213, 222; chrysotile 328
Atlantic Ocean 80
Auas Mountains 159
awareness 61, 193; lack of 227

bacteria 134, 211
Bagamoyo 248, 252, 268
balance of payments 11, 273
Balkanisation 176
bamboo 327
bananas 234, 240, 250
Bangweulu, Lake 285, 256, 289
Bantustans 176-7

Barbier, E 116
Barolong Farms 38, 46
basalt 54, 74, 76, 216, 288
Basement Complex of Africa 100
basic facilities 86
Basotho nation 65–6, 72, 81, 82
Basutoland 66–7
Batswana people 33, 38, 44, 58, 62
beaches 134, 135, 136; white sandy 148
beans 77, 140, 142
bedrock exposure 75
bee-keeping 24, 121, 250, 252
Beira 96, 130, 134, 135, 153, 303
belemium 182
Benguela 9, 15; current 5, 16, 170; railway 16
Bié 13, 14
Bikuar 21, 22
bilharzia 43, 212, 245
biodiversity 20, 30, 193, 210–11
biogenetic resources 336
biomass: absence of suitable alternative fuels 210; access to 241–2; affected by seasonal and moisture availability 42; commercial utilisation of 173; concept of 14; crop residues another source of 77; defined in the broader sense 257; dependence on, for livelihood 335; fuel supplies 77; less preferred sources 73; natural regeneration of 127; overall resources 181; production for energy 174; resources 144; second largest source of 77; shrub wood 174; tree 49; vegetation, depletion of 40–1; wood 241; woody 181, 192
biomes 22
biotic communities 100
birth control 36, 68
birth rates 58, 59, 204
birth spacing 98–9
Bismarck, Otto von 162
bismuth 182
black market 68
boats 146; illegal or unregulated movement of 43
Boer conquest 66
boreholes 33, 54–5, 56, 69, 288, 326; abolition of private ownership 60; degradation around 170; irreversible desertification of 42; overstocked 39; planning permission for 55; provision of permanent water from 37
borghium 182
bornhardts 303, 316
Boteti river 44, 46; villages 42
Botswana 32–64, 158, 179, 201, 221, 270, 330; 'upper high' 305; *see also* Francistown; Gaborone

Brandberg 158
Brazil 10
breathing difficulties 213
brick making 234, 245
British Government 218
Bruce, J 276
Brundtland Report (1987) 126
budget deficit 96–7
buffer strips 76, 89
building poles 116, 134, 169, 209
Bulawayo 303, 321
Bundali Range 107
bunds 42, 264
Busanga 285
bush 239; burning 279; dense 217;
  encroachment 41, 166, 173, 176, 193,
  209, 217–18, 287; fires 98, 234, 245;
  invader 173; mixed 218; systematic
  clearing 266
Bushmanland 176, 177
bushmen 44
bushveld 219

Cabinda 14, 16, 20, 23
Cabora Bassa 149, 331
cadmium 182, 321
calcium carbonate concretions 104
CAMPFIRE (Communal Area Management Programme for Indigenous
  Resources) 310, 314, 320, 336, 338
Cao, Diego 162
capacity utilisation 273
Cape Colony 162
Cape Cross Seal Reserve 185
Cape Town 193, 303
capital 34, 72, 81, 83; access to 46;
  transfers 182
Caprivi 43, 162, 172, 177, 185, 193;
  Central 180; East 178; Game Park
  184; Swamps 179; West 180
carbon dioxide 30
carbon monoxide 136
cardiac failure 213
cargo 135
cash crops 167, 216, 241, 249, 250, 274;
  major 280, 324; main 273; *see also*
  cashews; coconut; cotton; groundnuts; maize; sesame; tobacco
cashews 128, 138, 142, 144–6, 235, 249,
  250
cassava 19, 140, 142, 235, 249, 250
Cassinga 10, 15
cataracts 108
cation saturation 104
cattle 19, 37, 47, 57, 59, 60; accidental
  straying on growing crops 240;
  breeding 142; controlling factor in
  industry 54; dairy 140; dominance of
  219, 220; export markets 191; foot-
  and-mouth disease 34, 327; good
  ranching country 218; grazing of 33;
  increased concentrations 13; loans
  38, 46, 82; measure of wealth 46, 58,
  276; numbers of 130, 238;

overgrazing problem 173; ownership and management of 35; ranching lucrative but extravagant use of
  land 324; restricting movement of
  308; small-scale trade in 274; watering 39
caustic soda 135
cellulose 15, 135
Central Kalahari Game Reserve 37,
  55, 61
cereals 46
Certificate of Rights 44
Chakela, G K 73, 74n, 89, 90
Chambers, R 300–1nn
charcoal 132, 183, 245, 257, 287, 290;
  associations of producers 25;
  deforestation through production
  258, 280; improving technologies
  used in making 258; kilns 115; production 14, 119, 122, 234; supplies
  for burners 296
chemicals 79, 135, 210, 213, 215;
  agricultural, importing of 247;
  improper use of 79
Cherrett, I 126n
Chibero, Lake (Lake MacIlwaine) 321
Chidumayo, E 278, 279, 280
Chikwa, Lake 107, 110
children 212, 310
Chiperoni wind 92
chipeta 105
Chitemene cultivation 279, 283
Chiuta, Lake 110
chlorofluorocarbons 215
Chobe District 46; floodplain 48;
  National Park 33, 61; river 32, 43, 54
Chokwe region 133, 149
cholera 212, 275
Chonguica, E M W 126n
chrome 328
chromite 56, 329, 330
church organisations 24
clay pans 216
clays: calcareous cracking 284;
  ceramic, high-quality 101;
  fersiallitic 323; heavy textured 321;
  hydromorphic, in valley centres
  104; montmorillonitic 104; red 321,
  323; sandy 102
climate 46, 65, 90, 92, 138, 195; coastal
  16; cyclical pattern 57; dry 140, 158,
  216; hot 216; humid 140; moderated
  by altitude 5, 305; near-termperate
  209; parameters 42; regional 16;
  semi-arid 32, 140; sub-humid 140;
  tropical 5, 16
coal 33, 56, 215, 256–7, 290, 291; air
  pollution due to burning 79;
  demand for 78, 183; imported 76,
  121, 122, 173; indigenous resource
  122; mines 136, 199; pollution from
  mining 213; reserves 23, 38;
  resources 246; small-scale mining
  101; widely exploited 99

coastal areas 16, 20, 142, 154, 158, 183,
  240, 245, 261; access to, during war
  144; arid or semi-arid 5; sandy 138;
  use of resources in 155; *see also*
  beaches; climate; desert; dunes; eco
  systems; erosion; littoral; marine;
  maritime; pollution; sands
cobalt 290
coconut 138, 140, 241, 249
coffee 9, 19, 94, 95, 112, 140, 250, 323;
  cultivation systems 234; growing
  areas 240, 247; husks 241
commercial banks 113
commercial farms/farmland 46, 289,
  311; land tax on 189; large-scale 308,
  309, 315, 336; squatting on state land
  designated for 277
commercial sector 211
commodification 81, 82, 241
commodities 11; imported 273
Commonwealth 66
communal land 190–2, 314, 315; access
  to 190; future role 190; illegal fencing
  of 167; overgrazing in 38; tenure
  system 80, 176; *see also* grazing;
  pasture; woodlots
Congo 5, 16, 270, 289
conservation 54, 176, 192, 194, 224,
  331; activities 142–4; appropriate
  policies 90; areas 21; biogenetic
  diversity 321; coastal ecosystems
  134; communal areas 193; concerns
  281; costs of 83; efforts to promote
  302; flora 222; forest 167, 222; game
  190; genetic resources 321; land 82,
  148, 296; land earmarked for 264;
  legislation 308; local committees 325;
  marine 148; measures in new
  projects 337; poor application 205,
  208; requirements 315; soil 89, 175,
  244, 264, 318; traditional measures
  307, 308; vegetation 180; water 89,
  142, 175, 318; watershed 280; wild
  life 22, 100, 167, 190, 320, 321; wood
  133
construction poles 121
contamination 44, 54–5, 212; fertiliser
  172
Continental Crust 20
contour furrows (terraces) 89
contraception 36, 59
copper 181, 280–1, 321, 328; fall in
  prices 271; foreign exchange from
  273; impending closure of mines
  278; residues identified in fish 321;
  smelting process 282
copper-nickel 33, 40, 43, 56
copper sulphate 321
coral reefs 134, 135, 147, 148; *see also*
  ecosystems
cotton 140, 142, 216, 219, 241, 323–4;
  experiments with 274; farmers use
  large quantities of pesticides 324; for
  export 95; main crop 112; predomi-

nance of 19
crocodile farms 52, 332
cropping 114; mixed 46; *see also*
  intercropping; monocropping; share-
  cropping
crops: annual/perennial, threatened
  by drought 249; commercially-
  oriented farming 165; damage to 224,
  322; development of various types
  140; drought-resistant 142; dryland
  tree 59; effect of price variations
  between 280; export 94, 95, 234;
  failure 46, 237, 320; important 234;
  locally adapted 285; main 95, 112,
  235; most important 219; need to
  protect 190; percentage of country
  suitable for production 65; residues
  77, 79, 245; rotation 59, 280; smallholder 114; staple 166, 177, 219;
  subsistence 324; tree, production
  potential for 138; tropical oil-seed 19;
  utilisation of different types 40; *see
  also* cash crops; food crops
Cuamba 149
Cuanza-Sul province 7, 13, 15
culling programmes 87, 170, 185
customary lands 112, 115, 119; grants
  47; tenure 241, 277, 299

Daan Viljoen Game Park 180
dairy industry 252
Damaraland 158, 166, 167, 177
D'amato, A 176
dambos 104, 285, 286, 304
dams 20, 54, 89, 248-9, 264, 268; cattle
  42; impoundment of water in 318;
  large/major 55; sedimentation of
  316; slime 213; water storage below
  capacity 325; *see also* Goreangab;
  Hardap; Kariba; Kidatu; Stiegler's
  Gorge; Upper Umgusa
DANIDA (Danish aid organisation)
  295
Dar es Salaam 234, 243, 245, 248, 252,
  253, 256, 258, 290
DDT (dichloro-diphenyl-trichloro-
  ethane) 172, 210, 211, 298, 322
death rate 204
debt 273
decentralisation 187, 188
deforestation 129, 132, 133, 169-70, 239,
  254, 319; causes 204-5, 213, 234, 258,
  279, 280; considerable 116; contributory cause of devastating floods 331;
  dangers of 115; environmental consequences 244-5; experimental work
  to halt 24; extensive 98; policies required to curb 192; rapid 99, 121, 280;
  reducing the rate of 338; serious 14
demand and supply 82
demographic issues 33, 36, 92, 275, 334
de-nationalisation 10
denitrification 321
depositional bedding 104

desalinisation plant 178
desert 174, 180; coastal 158; cultural
  green 210
desertification 14, 129, 133, 166, 254;
  end product of land degradation
  41; experimental work to halt 24;
  intensifying 168; long-term irreversible 42; predicted 316; process
  described 319
detritus 134
devegetation 319
development committees 121
development councils 87
diamonds 10, 54, 56, 70, 164, 176, 222;
  alluvial 181; dramatic slump in
  prices 9; dwindling output 252;
  earnings from 56; exploitation of 20,
  51; extraction of 11, 213; growth of
  output in sector 8; percentage of
  total mineral value 33; pollution
  because of mining 12, 15; reserves
  181, 182
Dias, Bartholomeu 162
Dieldrin 210, 211, 225
diesel 78
diets 149
disadvantaged communities/groups
  190
disaster planning 224
discrimination 228
disease 47, 245-7, 275; animal 34,
  42-3, 316, 327; attendant upon stagnant water 12; breeding grounds
  for insects that transmit 69; eradication of 34; eye 245; lung 213, 214;
  outbreaks 240; plant 316; respiratory and cardio-vascular 136;
  spread of 79; transmittable 12;
  vulnerability of majority to 124;
  water-borne 11, 43, 212; water-
  related 212
ditches 130
diversification 125, 330
dividends 182
Dodoma 240, 241, 243-5 *passim*, 248,
  265, 268
dolerite intrusions 216
dolomites 283, 288
Domer, P 276
drainage 25, 32; collapse of surfacewater systems 11; depressions 74;
  free-profile 102; imperfect 102;
  inland 110; major channels 76
dredging operations 135, 136, 147
drinking water: clean, provision of 12;
  disposal of wastes into rivers used
  as sources of 79; safe, access to 44,
  211-12; stand-pipe 25; underground water used for 69; urban
  and rural supplies 12
droughts 33, 36, 40-2 *passim*, 46-7,
  131, 148, 240, 316; abnormal 318;
  annual or perennial crops
  threatened by 249; crops resistant to

142; endemic 32; insurance against
  236; invader species tolerant to 173;
  major 34; only natural check on live
  stock population 173; periodic 184,
  307; persistent 98, 195; prolonged 13,
  92; soils prone to 129
dug-out canoes 146
dumps/dumping grounds 135, 243,
  281, 321; chemicals in sea and rivers
  30; industrial waste 275; mine
  wastes 308; toxic industrial waste 16;
  uncontrolled 40, 167
dunes 130, 136, 148; devegetated 42;
  fixed 128, 158; stability of 132
dung 73, 77, 245
Durban 303
dust particles 171
dust storms 42
dustbowls 167
Dzalanyama Range 107

earnings: diamonds 56;
export earnings 146, 273, 281; farming
  71; foreign exchange earnings 9, 10,
  65; livestock production 79
East African Rift Valley 92
East London 303
Eastern Transvaal 214, 215
economic growth 124; major factors
  which have adversely affected 7;
  rapid 33
economic structures 5-11, 128-9,
  164-6, 197-203 ecosystems: animal/
  plant 136; aquatic 211; coastal
  13, 134-5, 155; coral 134; damage to
  15; deleterious impact on 135; delta
  43; disturbance by human beings
  and livestock 244; estuary 153;
  fragile 167; impact of hydroelectric
  schemes on 16; mangrove 134, 146;
  marine 154, 155; near-coast, easily
  disrupted 129; nutrient cycling in
  316; river 153; sensitive and unique
  40; toxic residues enter 329; very
  important 154
ecotoxicity 211
education 33, 44, 57, 62, 156; access to
  facilities 310; awareness through 61;
  conservation fostered through 100;
  environmental 83, 193, 224, 339; free
  187; health 12; programmes 59
EEC (European Economic Community) 47, 327; duty-free access into
  113; investment from 34
effluents: commercial sector 211;
  industrial 43, 99, 138; mine discharges 329; monitoring of 282-3;
  run-off 210; solid, liquid or gaseous
  135; sulphuric 321
electricity 76-7, 122, 150, 291, 329, 338;
  percentage of households without
  184; *see also* hydroelectricity
élites 300-1

employment 33, 56, 59, 60–1, 199;
agricultural 96; opportunities 67;
part-time 201; urban 81, 127
encroachment 37, 69, 70, 97; bush 41,
166, 173, 176, 193, 209, 217–18, 287
endogenous constraints 225–7
endosulfan/pyrethroid mixtures 43
energy 25, 254–9, 290–2; alternative
sources 38, 57, 173, 258, 319, 329;
biomass production for 174; depletion of resources 99; domestic 49;
legal control of 258–9; legal under
pinnings 292–4; legislation 294; low
levels of 324; most important sources
38, 99, 290; planning capabilities 122–
3; policy and strategies 121–2;
projects 89; provision of 49; rural
294–6; rural 76–8, 123; sector developments 122; solar technologies 122;
timber exploitation for 19; use of 241;
see also charcoal; coal; electricity;
firewood; fuelwood; gases; oil
environmental degradation 73, 94, 95,
154, 167, 176; absence of reliable data
on extent of 228; combating 88, 231;
concentric zones 42; efforts to control
302; fuelwood production and 14;
greater propensity for 308; local 129;
main cause of 168; main form of 278,
301–2; monitoring rate and extent
232; most serious 314; overgrazing
another source of 298–9; risks of 146;
serious 33; tropical 316; *see also* land
degradation
environmental issues 97–8, 166–8, 203–
16, 239–43, 274–8, 310–15; hygiene
133; management 27–31; programmes 25-6; sustainability 59, 194;
see also environmental degradation;
environmental problems; environmental sustainability; legislation;
policies
environmental problems: Angola 5,
11–16; Botswana 40–4; Lesotho 67–
76; Malawi 94–100; Mozambique
129–38; Namibia 167, 168–74; Tanzania 243–7; Zambia 278–83;
Zimbabwe 316–22
environmental sustainability 57–8,
187–93, 225–30, 262–9, 332–9;
possible strategies for 58–60
Eriksson, Olle 169
Erkkilä, A 159n, 162, 163n, 164, 169,
170, 173, 174, 181n, 192
erosion: 42, 74, 83, 131; backshore 146–
7; channel 76; coastal 26, 134, 136,
148; flooding rivers 130; gully 41, 73,
75, 76, 98, 244; increased 49; low risk
of 144; pipe 76; problem of 89; raindrop 76; rainfall 130; rainstorm 280;
rill 41, 73, 244; river banks well
protected from 116; roads prone to
130; running water 75; severe, on
grazing and cultivated land 76;

sheet 73, 244; trees well protected
from 116; waterflow 130; wind 75,
130, 160; *see also* soil erosion
escarpments 158, 270, 285, 289, 303,
316; rift 105; rare forest 23; rhyolite
forming 217
Estosha National Park 184–5
ethanol 122, 329
ethnic groups 167, 176
Etosha 161, 183; Game Park 180
eutrophication 210, 283, 321
evaporation 90, 108, 158; solar 252
evapotranspiration 32, 216, 279, 305
exhaust fumes 322
exports: agricultural 95, 164; cattle
markets 191; commercial exploitation of animals for 210; commercial
fishing 98; copper and other base
metals 271; crops 94, 234; earnings
from 146, 273, 281; income from 9;
principal 128; regular 273; revenues
214; timber 14, 18; transportation
bottlenecks for 96
external shocks 124
Eyasi, Lake 248, 250
Ezulwini-Malkerns-Mtilane horseshoe 216

families: extended 276, 277; large,
traditional belief in 33, 36, 58
family-planning programmes 98–9
famine 129
farmers: commercial 189–90, 308;
displacement of 10; large communal 191; proletarianisation of 97;
small 192; subsistence 97, 190;
training 119
farms/farming: affected 136; arable
39; dry 142; dryland 36, 57; family
154; flood recession 33, 46; game 60;
large beef and karakul 176; large-
scale commercial 309; mixed 142,
234, 250; percentage of population
dependent on 165; productive 177;
sedentary 13; semi-intensive 142;
settler 112; size and numbers 189;
small-scale 195; subsistence 210;
traditional flood methods 59; *see
also* commercial farms; fish
(farming)
faults 107–8
fences/fencing 60; cordon 38, 165
electric 100; illegal 167, 191
fertilisers 149, 211, 336; basis for a
future industry 101; careless and
excessive application 321; contamination 172; expanding use of 133;
imports of 252; intensive use of 234;
nitrogen 282; organic 250
financial assistance 61
Finland 265; FINNIDA 25
fire-break system 180
fires 244, 247, 279; bush 98, 234, 245;
natural vegetation much modified

by 305; periodic 162 tolerance to 105
firewood 49, 61, 76, 77, 78, 245;
commodification of 241; dead 118;
heavy utilisation of living trees for
210; increase in demand for 209;
major uses 242; planting of woodlots
for 231; shortage of 116; supplying
the urban market with 192; used for
cooking and house-warming 241
first European settlers 307
fish 50, 52, 283, 289, 305: anchovies
146, 170, 185; aquarium 111; bream
289; breeding grounds 147;
'Cachucho' 13; changing the nature
of species 210; deep-water 170;
demersal stocks in lakes 100; economi-
cally-imported 43; freshwater 221,
249, 268, 289; hake 170; immature
134; kills of 135, 211, 283; local and
exotic 110; most caught 290; most
diverse, of any lake 100; offshore
100, 146; pelagic stocks 100, 170;
pilchards 170, 185; principal 185,
186; reserves 289; sardines 289;
seawater 268; shark 146; shell 170,
185; shrimps 134, 146; three species
of perch 289; under-exploited stocks
100; tuna 146; variety of 220; *see also*
fish resources; fisheries; fishing
activities
fish resources 98, 170–1, 268; patterns
of use, depletion and renewal 110
Fish River Canyon National Park 185
fisheries 146, 220, 262: coastal 19; commercial 111; effects on resources of
reservoirs and river; estuaries 133;
marine and freshwater 170; *ndagaa*
289; promotion and conduct of
research into 261
fishing activities 29, 57, 185–6, 261,
289–90; canneries 185; changing
from fibre to nylon netting 110;
commercial 50, 98, 100, 110, 170, 185;
farming/production 100, 110, 111,
134, 149, 220; foreign fleets granted
concessions 10; gill nets 290; illegal
268; industrial 154; key importance
to foreign exchange earnings 10;
mining 19; net mesh sizes 111; no
control over methods in coastal
waters 13; offshore 134; policing of
269; potential for, in natural water
ways 20; promotion of, in inland
waters 24; purse seining 110;
reduced potential 128; second most
important producing nation 19;
small-scale 10, 98; sport 269; traditional 100; unknown potential for 20;
urgent need for tighter controls over
methods 19; use of dynamite 269
flies 246
flood plains 33, 48, 74, 76, 169, 290;
deposition on 130; extensive 133;

heavily populated 193; nearly-level 284; vertisols of 285
floods/flooding 12; annual 244, 290; areas more prone to, during the rainy season 242; causes of 245, 331; reservoirs 308; rivers 130
floristic diversity 47, 48
fluorides 318
fodder 327; leguminous 142
food 114, 249; aquatic chain 147; daily ration 11; demand for 81, 274; dependence on local natural resources for 308; imported 10, 11, 166, 177; quality control 223; supplementary 287
food crops 167, 274; main 273; major 280; *see also* cassava; maize; rice; sorghum
food security 99, 307
foot-and-mouth disease 34, 327
foothills 80, 105
footwear 95
foreign aid 69
foreign exchange: earnings 9, 10, 65; from copper 273; maximisation of 95; reserves 33, 271
foreign investors 188
forest reserves 37, 49, 112, 115, 251, 267, 286–7; control of vermin in 117; establishment of 117; indiscriminate clearing of 167; industrial exploitation of hardwoods in 99; public and protected 118
forestry 140, 142, 219–20; commercial 326; coppice 192; extension services division 119; farm 192; leading foreign exchange earner 209; patterns of use, depletion and renewal 115–17; resources 115–21; support services division 119–20; sustained 193
forests: burning of 23; cleared for agriculture 144; commercially exploitable 180; cover 209, 241; demarcated 308; destroyed 136; devastation of 136; dry deciduous 179, 285; estate 286–7; evergreen 250, 285; hardwood 14; indigenous 76, 119, 192, 204, 209, 219, 251, 287; legislation policy and institutional framework 117; man-made 14, 16, 209, 216, 220; management of 192; mangrove 251; moist semi-deciduous 105; mountain 23, 100, 105; natural 14, 16, 120, 241; overexploited 18; potential yield of 16; productive 244; products 117–18, 193, 318–19; protected areas designated as 314; rare escarpment 23; resources 14, 49, 85, 98, 99, 119, 326–7; semi-evergreen 105; sub-tropical 18; tropical 20, 23; utilisation of 193, 287; village plantations 120; *see also* afforestation; conservation; deforestation; forest reserves;

forestry; plantations; reafforestation; reforestation
formal training 89
Fort Jameson 274
Fortmann, L 58
foul smells 243, 246
Francistown 39, 43, 47, 55, 56, 303; rail line to Gaborone 33
free lime 160
Frelimo 155
frosts 65, 159, 195
fruits 49, 209, 216, 219, 327, 329; citrus 209, 323; temperate 140
fuels: absence of suitable alternative biomass 210; conventional 290; ethanol 122; fossil 215, 254; liquid 183; low-quality 133; solid, more efficient use of 122; sub-sectors 77–8; supplies 132; see also charcoal; coal; electricity; firewood; fuelwood; gases; oil
fuelwood 16, 24, 98, 121, 167, 257–8; collection 131, 147, 169; commercial exploitation for tobacco curing 234; converting into fuel of higher calorific value 258; coppiced 327; discouraging imports 89; efficient use 95; energy requirements 280; future demand 122; increased efficiency of use 115; localised shortages 57; main source of energy in traditional sector 183, 290; most important energy source 99, 184; national supply and demand 330; overwhelming dependence on 291; percentage of total energy consumption 38, 241; pressure on supplies 153; prices of 133; problems 132-3; processing of burley tobacco relies heavily on 94; production and environmental degradation 14; scarce in rural areas 73; smallholder consumption 94; smog a result of 171; sources 77; substitution 38; travel in search for 132; trees cleared for cultivation used for 319; uncontrolled harvesting for 245
fungicides 246

Gabela 9
Gaborone 36, 39, 40, 49, 54, 303; rail line to Francistown 33
gallium 182
game 33, 50, 51, 185; conservation and farmers' rights 190; controlled areas 247; culling 185; farming 60, 172; management areas 270; migration routes 52; parks 112, 180; poaching 185; ranching 52, 314, 338; *see also* game reserves
game reserves 37, 50–1, 60–1, 115, 176, 184, 259, 261, 267; development of management plans 60; electric fencing 100; race-space segregation and

174; tourism largely confined to 185; woodland restricted to 250
gases 14, 183, 245, 246; for on-site electricity generation 256; harmful to human health and vegetation 214; spray paint 216; toxic 136
gastro-intestinal tract disorders 211
gauging stations 90
Gay, J 87
Gaza 130, 132, 138, 144
GDP (gross domestic product) 7–8, 94–7 *passim*, 128, 164, 165, 182, 203, 271, 273, 275, 323
gender: discrimination 228; issues in land use and resources management 83–5; relations 226
genetic diversity 79
geological resources 20
geomorphology 16, 17
Germany 162
Ghanzi and Xanagas farms 37
Giess, W 160, 179
gilblaar 167
glass 101
gneiss 288, 289
GNP (gross national product) 65, 199, 273, 334
goats 33, 46, 87, 204
gold 55, 181, 252, 328; alluvial panning 329; exploitation of 136; mines 199, 213; small-scale mining 56
government 174–5; farming and livestock schemes 34, 47; institutions 24–5; livestock breeding farms 252; policies and programmes 262–9; restrictions on official prices and supplies 11
grain 91, 236
granite 216, 250, 288, 303, 326; old 290; rugged steep areas of 92
grants 44, 47, 89
graphite 136
grass species 49, 249; adverse changes in diversity 209; common 217; less palatable 41, 47; more palatable 79; most dominant 218; palatable, permanent loss of 172; perennial 32, 42; shallow-rooting 173; sweet 42, 47, 218; tall 105; thatching 336
grasslands 16, 32, 100, 209, 250, 251; burning of 121; discontinuous cover 285; edaphic 105, 107; larger 286; open woodland 285-6; replacement by shrub cover 42; sour 217; swamp 107
grassveld 217
gravel 140, 285
grazing/grazing land 13, 19, 33, 36, 44, 73, 121, 167; areas allocated for 114; best 174; capacity 193; communal 37, 47, 240, 251, 275, 315, 337; continuous and uncontrolled 78–9; deforestation and 244; dual rights 191; failure to rotate 47; fallow 60; fees

88; good, inexhaustible reservoir of 34; grassland 250; less land available for 98; marginal 241; mopane wood land transformed into 170; over-stretched 191; potential 178; rough 239, 241; schemes 336, 337; severe erosion process on 76; shortage of 315; speculative use of 60; substitute 38; systems 238; tribal policy 83; two types 46; water resources for 39; un-planned 240; *see also* overgrazing; TGLP

Great Britain 162
Great Dyke 323, 328, 329
Green, R H 168, 177, 182n
greenstone belts 328
Grizic, P M 317, 326
Grootfontein 162, 165, 172, 173, 180, 184
groundnuts 95, 250, 273, 323, 324
groundwater 47, 162; degradation of resources 212; extent 288; less exten-sive supplies 288–9; most important source of domestic water 326; needs 54; pumped from mines 288; raising of 318; reserves 32, 55; scarce 179; tapping of 323; *see also* water pollution
guerrilla activity 149
gullies 42, 98; dam construction across 89; deposition within 89; parallel 76; scarp advances by piping or sapping 89; side 89; *see also* erosion
Gwembe 278, 290
gypsum 101, 160

habitats 20, 33, 221; degraded 320; destruction of 14, 50, 79, 169, 184; fish 169; protection of 5; severe impact upon 14; tsetse fly 266; unique swamp and riverine 48
Hahn, Hugo 169
handwells 54
Hannan, L 54
Harare 303, 321, 323, 338
hard iron concretions 104
hard panning 323
Hardap: Dam irrigation scheme 168, 178; Game Park 180; Recreation Resort 185
hardveld 32, 33, 41, 46, 54
Havnevik, K 234
hazardous substances 225
head-scarps 89
health 129, 135, 167; access to facilities 310; budget as a percentage of GDP 12; care 57; education 12; environ-mental 11; free 187; gases harmful to 214; hazards 79, 153, 211, 215, 216, 232, 243; improved facilities 36; industrial 16; medical problems 282; occupational 232; provision 12; public 138; services 86
herbicides 173, 211, 246

herbs 249
Herero 179: homeland 166–7
Hereroland 168, 177
Hhohho 205, 207
highland areas 65, 130, 140, 234, 250
Highveld 215, 303, 304, 318, 328; average rainfall 195, 216; employ-ment 201; grazing land 209; vegeta-tion 217
hills 80, 105, 216; granitic 303; pro-tected slopes 115, 118; rocky 250
homelands 174–7, 166–7, 187; densely-populated areas 183; former 164, 165–6, 168, 183, 193, 194; settlement policy 162
housing: demand for 168; deteriora-tion of buildings 138; deterioration of existing facilities 11; failing to maintain stock 275; low-cost 39; low-income schemes 68; made of non-durable materials 138; self-build 25
Huambo 7, 9, 13, 14
humus 98, 102, 104
hunter-gatherers 44, 176
hunting 33, 60; commercial 21, 184, 314; controlled areas 51, 53; fauna mainly valued for 21; illegal 31; licensed, all game species 247; limit-ing 100; no control being exercised over 23; recreational 51; regulations 185, 307; safari 321, 326; sport 185, 269; subsistence 51; trophy 185; un-lawful 261; within defined reserves 52
husbandry 38, 165, 166, 238, 298
hut tax 274
Hwange 314, 328; National Park 57; thermal power station 331
hydrocarbons 56, 183, 282
hydroelectricity 20, 23, 78, 155, 183, 330; big projects 80; generating sta-tions 254–5; highest potential for 248; impact of schemes on ecosys-tems 16; potential power 149, 331
hydrogeological problems 179
hydrology 90, 109, 110, 136, 142, 154; disturbances 280
hydroxyl radicals 215
hygiene 16, 133; serious lack of basic knowledge 12

illegitimacy 72
illnesses 302
ILO (International labour Office) 16, 87
immigration 6, 97
import restrictions 9
import substitution 43, 95; intensive 330
Indian Ocean 195, 248, 261
indigenous biota 316
Individual Tenure Farms 195, 205, 218, 219

industrialisation 43, 124
industry 135, 211, 281–3; emissions 282; impact of 14–16, 153–4; orienta-tion of 334; resources 330
infant mortality 12, 58, 124
infiltration 305, 316, 323; saline 154
inflation 277
infrastructure 25, 57, 89, 136, 144, 240, 310; basic 153, 277; considerable strain on 33; damage to 224; eco-nomic and social 5; massive invest-ment in 56; physical 182, 209; poor 235; service 153; social 153, 274, 310; socio-economic 167; such as lodges and hotels 269; transportation 96; urban, great pressure on 242; water 55
Inhambane 132, 138, 144
injustice 188
insecticides 211
insects 50, 69, 305; crop-damaging 322; *see also* mosquitoes; tsetse flies
inselbergs 303
institutions: central level 337–8; chal-lenge for environmental manage-ment 27–31; context for resource management 23–6, 155–6; inadequa-cies 227–8; involved in rural energy 123; legal, present resource base and 216–22, 247–69; role of 335
integrated rural development strate-gies 335; intercropping 142, 326–7
interest payments 182
intergenerational equity 193
international conventions 332
International Court of Justice 163, 177
interventions 87–8, 133
investment 34, 56, 72, 334, 335; lack of 10
Iona 21, 22
Iringa 234, 240, 265
iron 10, 15, 56, 181, 328
iron sulphides 101
irrigation 54, 130-1, 140, 168, 265, 324; agriculture only viable with 142; hardly developed 19; large-scale projects 248-9; lowveld 314, 325; more economic methods 317; natu-ral 33; possibility of extension of 144; proposed schemes 57; pumped 122; scarcely started 149; schemes 100, 178, 321, 326; soils that respond well to 323; supplement to rain-fed crop production 216
ivory trafficking 127, 151, 332

Janson, S D 172
job creation 33, 34, 59
Jwaneng 39, 54, 56

Kaakunga, E 170, 182n, 186
Kabwe 283, 288, 291
Kafue 273, 282, 284, 286, 290; indus-trial complex 275

Kafue river 270, 275, 289; monitoring of effluent into 282–3
Kagera 253, 265
Kalahari Desert 20, 49, 50, 54, 158, 177, 284
Kalahari sand 32, 41, 158, 162, 180, 286, 288, 289, 326, 328
Kalapula, E 298
Kalulushi 287, 288, 289
Kangandala 21, 22
Kantesi, B 87
Kaokoland 177, 184, 185
kaolin 214
kaolisols 216
Kariba dam/hydroelectric scheme 278, 304, 325, 329, 330
Kariba, Lake 289, 304, 308, 331
Karoo: sediments 20, 107; shrub and grass 179, 180; strata 54; succulent steppe 179, 180
Kasai river 13, 15
Kasane 52, 57
Katanga 274, 290
Katatura 171, 180
Katavi National Park 250
Kavango 161, 169, 178, 180
Kavango river 169, 170
Kawerawera, C 117
Kaziwiziwi 99, 101
Kenya 166, 250
Ketwewake-Mchuchuma 256
Kgalagadi 42, 43
Kgatleng 36, 37
Khomas Hochland National Park 185
Khomo-Khuanda district 73, 75
Kidatu 244; Dam power station 265
Kilimanjaro, Mt 234, 240, 241, 248, 249, 250, 252
Kipengere Range 107
Kirk Range 107
Kongwa 243, 252
kopjes 303, 316
kraal manure 59
Kunene river 170, 179
Kweneng 36, 42
kyanite 56
Kydd, J 114
Kyle, Lake 318, 325

labour 67, 71–2, 81, 124, 197; absent 71; cheap 96, 114, 252; direct 114; division of, according to sex 83; landless 124; migration 79; potential, declining 96; rapid growth 114; shortages 115; surplus 199
lakes 247–8; demersal fish stocks in 100; saline 110; small inland 20
Lakes Malawi and Malombe 100
land 69–71, 247, 263–4; alienation of 95, 97, 112, 124, 177, 308; allocated to large-scale commercial farmers 308; allocation and administration 191; carrying capacity 173, 275, 299; clearance for agriculture 115, 204–5;

commercial 188–90, 191, 192; considered to be owned by community 276–7; derelict 281; devegetation of 319; enormous pressure on 13; fallow 239; fertile, depletion of 276; foreign-owned 188; freehold 44; high price of 277; infertility of 136; leasehold estate 112; management practices 87, 278–80, 298–9; marginal 73, 94, 97, 167, 208, 243, 308; most important natural resource 80; natural forest, depletion of 98; overutilisation and misuse 205; pastoral 37; payment for 190; potentially suitable for cultivation 271; privatisation of 97, 98; salinisation of 136; scarcity of 278; semi-arid 250, 319; shortage of 280; state 44, 47, 314; subsidence of 136; tribal 44; under increasing pressure 57; underutilised 188; undulating 303; unlimited availability of 33; *see also* arable land; commercial farms; conservation; communal land; customary lands; grazing; land degradation; land-fill sites; land market; land resources; land tenure; land use
land degradation 13, 38, 40, 42, 57, 58, 79, 94, 98–9, 172, 239; communal areas 168–9; fuelled by population growth 317; large scale 333; mining industry and 281; more pronounced on rangelands 208; overgrazing and 34, 204; reduced productivity 317; widening areas of 280
land-fill sites 40, 62, 212
land market 277, 307–8; clearly-defined 312; women *vis-à-vis* 301
land resources 16–19, 100, 138–40, 174–8, 283–5; agricultural production and its impact on 154; agriculture and 13–14; legal underpinnings 287–96; legislation over 324; and rural differentiation 80–2
land tenure 44, 166, 197, 226, 239–40, 275, 309, 324; customary 241, 277, 299; freehold 124, 175; main types 312–15; post-independence 112–15; regalian concept 182; security of 82, 87, 276; traditional systems 40
land use 45–7, 71, 72, 74, 218–22, 277; classification 273; conflicts 34, 166–8, 242–3, 275; encroachment of 37; essentially opportunistic 58; estate patterns 114–15; legal underpinnings 111–12; legislation 83–4; management issues 73, 87–90; not controlled by the community 13; patterns 236, 239; planning 222, 267, 337; practices 312–15; resource zones 237; zoning 39
landlessness 80, 124, 277, 310, 312, 333; common reaction to 317;

increasing 81, 87
landscape: alteration 212, 213; degradation 214; hilly 216; relatively little disfigurement of 321; steepness of 130; sterile 281
landslides 12
languages 162
Larson, M K 36
laterite crusts 285
latosols 102–4
lava 130, 288
law enforcement 100
Laws of Lerotholi (1959) 80, 81, 83
lead 56, 181, 271, 290, 321, 322; refined 164 leaf injuries 282
League of Nations 162, 163
leasehold estate expansion 113–14
legal controls: energy 258–9; forest resource exploitation 180; forests 144; mining 253–4; vegetation 251–2; water rights 249
legal instruments 135, 331; land control 47; mineral development 56; vegetation use 49–50; water use 55; wildlife utilisation 52–4
legal underpinnings 142–4; land-use patterns and 111–12; natural resource base and 44–63, 80–5, 100–23, 138–52, 174–86, 283–7, 322–32; use of water resources 149–51
legislation 44, 81, 86, 326; air pollution 172; appropriate, lack of 302; enforcement of 231-2; existing 222–4; implementation of 232; land resources 324; natural resource, overdue revision 336; pesticide use 43; proposed 224–5; *see also* legal controls; legal instruments; legal underpinnings
legumes 142, 236, 327
Lesotho 65–91, 201
Letsholo, J 39
Leutwien, Governor 174
liberation struggle/war 164, 185
life expectancy 124, 204; at birth 212
lime burning 245
limestone 56, 182, 253, 288
Limpopo river 32, 62, 138, 303, 318, 330; tributaries 54
Lindi 235, 243, 252
Lisker, P 128n, 129n
lithium 330
lithosols 102, 104, 159, 216, 285, 323
litter 43, 167
Little Caledon Catchment 74, 75
littoral regions 14: corridors 126; resources 19, 144–6
livestock 73, 76, 79, 167, 168, 245; deaths of 281, 320; densities 234, 238; depasturing 121; disturbance of ecosystem by 244; earnings from production 79; forage for 209; government-owned breeding farms 252; grazing for 172, 315; husbandry

methods 38; increased numbers 208, 317, 320; need to protect 190; on loan 38, 46, 82; ownership and rural differentiation 82–3; permanent loss of palatable grasses for 172; pressure 333; reluctance to sell 299; smallholder industry 98; transhumance of 40; trespassing by 121; water shortage for 240; *see also* cattle; goats; sheep

living standards 311
Livingstone 270, 287, 288, 289
Livingstone Mountains 107
loams 250, 283, 323
loans 38, 39, 46, 89, 113
Lobatse 39, 54
Lobengula, king of the Ndebele 307
local government/local authorities 120–1
logging activities 131
Lomé Convention (1973) 113
Lomwe people 97
Low, A 87
Lower Shire river 100; valley 101, 110
lowlands 65, 80, 105
Lowveld 304, 318, 321, 329, 338; diseases 212; grazing land 209; irrigated 314, 325; rainfall average 195; vegetation 217, 218
Luanda 7, 9, 12-14 *passim*, 19, 24–6 *passim*
Luangwa river 270; valleys 100, 285, 331
Luapula 280, 283, 289, 290; porphyry 288; river 270, 289; valley 285
Lubombo 207, 221; Plateau 195, 217, 218
Luderitz 170, 181, 185, 186
Lukanga 285, 286; Swamps 289–90
Lusaka 270, 275, 283, 288, 291, 303

McGlashan, N D 289
MacIlwaine, Sir R 308
Mackel, R 283, 285
macroeconomic parameters 201–3
mafisa system 38, 46, 82
maize 46, 77, 114, 140, 165, 177, 219, 235, 249, 273, 323; acidity of soils and 214; continuous cropping 280; husks used for cooking 133; intercropping 142; produced successfully without irrigation 324; small-scale trade in 274; white/yellow 166
Makgadikgadi 37, 49; basin 38, 48, 54; fossil lake beds 32
Makhera, N M 89
Makonde 249, 268
Malange 7, 9
malaria 43, 172, 211, 212, 322
Malawi 92–125, 248, 270, 303, 320, 331
Malawi, Lake 92, 100, 107–8, 110
Malibamatso river 80
Maliele area 73-4, 75
malnutrition 124, 129

Malombe, Lake 100, 108, 110
Maluti mountains 65, 80
manganese 55, 56, 181, 290, 321
mangoes 142
Mangoche 107, 108
mangroves 128, 132, 135, 136, 244, 249; consequences of deforestation 245; reserved 251; traps for floating oil 147; *see also* ecosystems
Manica 132, 136, 138, 140
Manicaland 303, 311, 314, 318, 324, 329, 331
manufacturing industries 33, 136, 330; decline of 10; increased 95
Manyara Kitangiri 248, 261
Manyeneng, W G 36
Manzini 195, 205, 207, 215
Maputo 126, 130, 132, 140, 156; beaches 134, 148; coastal access during war 144; environmental hygiene 133; heads of households without employment 127; industry 135, 153; problems 138; sewage 149
Maputo river 138
Maputsoe 70, 77
Mara 240, 241, 245, 248, 265
marine environments 129; protection areas 148; resources 13, 19, 31, 144–6; sediment basins 20
marital disharmony 72
maritime air/influence 92, 305
market failures 227
market structures 255
Maseru 68, 69, 70, 77, 78, 79, 88
Mashinini, I V 82
Mashonaland 314, 319; Central 311; East 318, 329; West 329
Masvingo 303, 318, 321, 324, 325, 329
Matabeleland 319, 324, 326; North 336; South 329, 336, 338
Matola 108, 135
Maun 43, 44, 47, 52
Mbabane 195, 205, 215
Mbeya 234, 240, 250, 253, 265
Mbozi plateau 107
Mbuende, K 174, 177, 178
Meru, Mt 234, 248, 249, 250
metals 181, 290
mica 182, 253
micro-pollutants 147
Middleveld 205, 217, 304; average rainfall 195, 216; diseases 212; grazing land 209; vegetation 217
migrations 33, 239, 311–12; disturbed 184; external 67; game routes 52; internal 67, 124; international 114; labour 71–2, 79, 86, 182; mammals, large-scale 331; people and stock 318; population distribution strongly affected by 67; rural-urban 7, 68, 167; urban 59; wildlife corridors 53
millet 33, 46, 142, 169, 177, 241; mahangu 166 mineral resources 15,

55–6, 165, 212–16, 290, 328–9; depletion 99, 101–2; development 223; enormous 136; exploitation of 33; newly-found 34; patterns of use and renewal 101–2 regulation 84
minerals 222, 328; damage to 213; exploration and monitoring of extraction 56; ferromagnesian 283; industrial 181, 214; legal instruments in development 56; montmorillonitic clay 104; phosphate 252; predominantly kaolinitic 102; prospecting for 209; stability of 215; strategic 182, 330; toxic 323; widely exploited 99
mines/mining 15, 55–6, 71, 136, 154, 280–1; centres 39; companies 171; export-oriented 164; impact of 14–16; industry 81; leases 56; legislation 20; licensing prospecting and 102; long history and wide distribution of 321; open-cast 101; percentage of water for 54; producing 213 regulations 264; resources 137, 181–2, 252–4; revenues from 274; stagnant industry 10; see also diamonds; gold; mineral resources; minerals
minority groups 33
miombo (brachystegia) woodland 16, 105, 169, 249, 250, 270, 285, 305; tsetse-infested 235
mixed cropping 46
Mkandawire, R M 97, 112, 114
Mkata 252; Bay 105
Mmusi, P S 34
Mochudi 39, 44, 49
Molepolole 39, 49
molybdenum 182
monitoring 133, 232; air 282; effluent 282–3; emissions 56; erosion and sedimentation 90
monocropping 208
Monze 280, 283
mopane 32, 104, 161–2, 169, 170, 192, 210, 270, 305, 316
Mopane worm (*Goninbrosia melima*) 49
Morogoro 240, 241, 248, 250, 251, 253, 258, 265
mortality rates 36, 46–7, 212; *see also* infant mortality
Morupule 33, 56
Moshoeshoe I, chief of Basotho 65–6
Moshoeshoe II, king of Lesotho 67
mosquitoes 242, 246, 322
Motloutse river 43, 54
mountains 65, 73, 80, 100, 217, 270; development of reservoirs in 70; granitic 250; ideal for tourism 85; population densities lower in 67–8; *see also* slopes
Moyo, S 313n, 314, 315
Mozambique 92, 97, 124, 126–57, 220, 221, 270, 331; tripartite cooperation with Malawi and Tanzania 111; *see also* Beira; Maputo; Nacala

Mozambique Channel 305
Mpanda 234, 252
Mpotokwane, M A 37
Mulanje 92, 101, 105; Mountain 104, 108; valleys 110
Mulfulira Syncline 290
multilateral agencies 127
Mumbwa 283, 290, 291
Munslow, B 6
Mupa 21, 22
Murray, C 81
Mwanza 234, 235, 237, 240, 241, 245, 248, 252, 265 Mweru, Lake 285, 289
Mwinilunga 284, 285

Nacala 96, 134
Namaland 177
Namib Desert 158, 159, 161, 167, 179, 180, 184 Namib-Naukluft National Park 184
Namibe 9, 14, 24, 26
Namibia 5, 29, 57, 63, 158–94, 270
Nampula 133, 138; reforestation scheme 132 National Conservation Strategy (Botswana) 34, 35, 53, 59
National Directorate of New and Renewable Resources (Angola) 24
National Energy Council (Zambia) 294–5
National Institutes (Angola): Geology 25; Hydrometeorology and Geophysics 25; Marine Research 25; Physical Planning 25; Public Health 25
National MAB Committee (Angola) 28
national parks 21–3, 144, 151–2, 260–1, 268, 270, 336; additional land allocations for 308; development of management plans 60; electric fencing 100; environmental problems 172; limitations in conserving biodiversity 210–11; utilisation of 259; wildlife proection 222–3; *see also* Central Kalahari Chobe; Estosha; Fish River Canyon; Hwange; Katavi; Khomas Hochland; Namib-Naukluft; Quicama; Quissama; Skeleton Coast; Water Plateau; *also under* game reserves; nature reserves
'Native nations' *see* Bushmanland; Damaraland; Hereroland; Kaokoland; Namaland; Okovangoland; Ovamboland; Rehoboth Gebiet
native reserves 174
natural resources 27, 61, 216–17; degradation or renovation of 26; dependence on, for food 308; depletion of quality of 124; expanding the role of women in managing 229–30; information and management of 30; legal framework 16–26; most important 80; overdue revision of legislation

336; scarcity of 37–40; *see also* legal underpinnings
Natural Resources Department (Zambia) 296 nature reserves 172
Ndola 287, 289
negative externalities 148
Ngorongoro 250, 268
NGOs (non-governmental organisations) 24–5, 38, 61, 62, 119, 264–8 *passim*; broadening the participation of 229
nickel 328; *see also* copper-nickel
niobium 182
nitrates 318
nitrogen 136, 215, 282, 322, 327
Nkata Bay 92, 108
noise 30, 224
Norwegian government 25, 326
Nsanje Hills 105
nurseries 338
nutrients 147, 210, 238, 239, 279, 316
nutrition 12, 146, 220; *see also* malnutrition
Nyasa, Lake 248, 249, 250, 261, 268
Nyirongo, G 280

OAU (Organisation of African Unity) 66
Odendaal Commission (1963) 176–7
oil 122, 147, 183; exploitation 13; imported 121, 122; international market 8, 11
oilseeds 19, 23, 140
Okahandja 162, 172, 173
Okovango (tribal territory) 38, 180
Okovango river 42–4 *passim*, 54, 55, 63, 179, 180; delta 32, 54, 48, 49, 50; flood plain 193; swamps 169
Okovangoland 177
Onimonde, B 300
Orange Free State 65
Orange river 178, 179
Orapa 39, 56
organophosphates 211
Oshakati 168, 169
Otavi 165, 178, 180
Otjiwarango 162, 172, 173
outcrops 140, 216, 316
output: agricultural 95; industrial 9; petroleum and diamond sectors 8; reliable source of 113
Ovambo 161, 166, 169, 170, 180, 183, 184, 192
Ovamboland 167, 168, 172, 177, 178, 193
overgrazing 49, 74, 76, 79, 98, 129, 166, 172–3, 234, 239, 276; acceptance of ecological consequences 320; cause of soil erosion 280; communal lands 38; goats 204; land degradation the result of 34, 204; range degradation caused by 208, 226; responsibility for 83; source of environmental degradation 298-9;

vegetation destroyed by 217, 218; watering places 168
overstocking 172–3, 226, 276, 280, 315; rangeland 78–9
Owens, D 38
Owens, M 38
oxen 236, 237, 324
ozone 215, 282

palladium 330
Palmer, R 81
Pangani 252; river 248
pans 32, 48, 54
PANs (peroxyacy nitrates) 282
paraffin 78
parastatals 43, 113, 164, 251, 265, 334
Parathion 210, 211
Pare Range 234, 248, 250
parklands 105–7
Parsons, N 81
partial protected zones 144
particulates 215
pastoral resources 320
pastoralism 33, 35
pasture 240; access to 241; communal 191, 252; cropping of 320; improved management 87; natural, extensive 140; over-grazed 320
Patterson, L 38, 47
pauperisation 167
peanuts 140, 142
pediments 74, 75, 76
Pemba 134, 280
Perara, N P 281
percolation 305
peri-urban areas 86, 133, 127
pesticides 43, 210, 246, 322, 336; expanding use of 133; hazardous 79; toxicity of 24
pests 34, 42, 43, 322; selective control 100 petroleum 78, 122, 134, 291, 294; growth of output in sector 9; imports 76, 255; refined 76; residue 155; toxicity of 135
petty crime 39
phenolic products 211
phosphates 15, 101, 252, 322
phospher 182
photochemical conversion 282
photovoltaic waterpumps 24
pineapples 140, 209, 216
pit latrines 69, 212, 243; inadequate systems 79; ventilated improved 338
plains 169, 249, 250; gently-sloping 102; lakeshore 92; suitable only for grazing or for national parks 249; treeless 285; *see also* flood plains
plantations 89, 192; eucalyptus 16; exotic trees 217, 287, 326; expansion of 195; hardwood 244, 250; national projects 266; pine 249; pineapple and citrus 209; softwood 99, 244, 287, 326; sugar cane 210; timber 99, 210, 326; village forest 120

plants 49, 130, 210, 316
plateaux 92, 217, 289, 328; high 104, 140, 250; *see also* Central African Plateau; Lubombo; Mbozi; Ufipa
platinum 182
ploughing 75, 236, 324
poachers/poaching 52, 172, 184, 247, 320; game 37; levels 100; resource 336; valuable species 38
policies 61, 222–5; externally determined 88; intended to commodify rangeland 83; proposed 224–5; required to curb deforestation 192; tourism 53
political ideology 26
political movements 66–7
political stability 33
pollution 11, 15; atmospheric 99, 136, 214, 282; chemical 79; coastal 134, 172; control of 55, 57, 62; diseases and 245–7; domestic sewage 155; dumps and tailings ponds 213; encouraging a reduction in 30; fines for 30; generally low levels 20; implementation of control 61–3; industrial 147, 155; main area of 210; oil 135, 147; port activity 135; sediment 147; urban 79; waste disposal 73, 321; *see also* air pollution; water pollution
popular participation 231, 299–301
population 65, 162–4; concentrations of 13, 132, 146; increases 35–6, 58, 70, 125, 270; issues 153; movements 129; over- 11; policy 68–9; pressure 138, 333; programmes 59; relatively homogeneous 33; relatively small 34; *see also* population density; population distribution; population growth
population density 80, 97, 206, 234, 235, 238, 311; average 162, 270; high 5, 67, 133, 241, 251; highly uneven pattern 238; increasing 312; by land tenure and district 208; low 7, 13, 33, 44, 289, 329; lower in mountain districts 67–8; rural 316
population distribution 128, 207, 272; highly uneven pattern 238; strongly affected by migration 67
population growth 86, 95, 96, 157, 225–6; annual rate 67; arable land expanded in response to 240; high 34, 124, 166; land degradation fuelled by 317; profound effect on resources 311; rapid 92–4, 99, 203–5, 242, 301, 315; unequal 239
Poroto Mountains 107
port activities 134, 155
Portugal 6, 7, 10, 162
Post, C Van der 40
poultry 219
poverty 124, 167, 189
prawns 110, 128
precious hardwoods 31

precipitation 32, 158, 279; above average 195; acid 171; highest level of 16; *see also* rainfall
Pretoria 193
productivity 59; agricultural 177, 308; degraded land, reduced 317; low 37, 128; poor 83; potential 277; river, long-term 169; soil 98, 154
profits 114, 182, 252; from game 327
protein 134, 283
pulses 33, 46

quarry stone 222
quartz 10, 104, 285
quartzites 104, 323
Quicama National Park 16
Quissama 21, 22; National Park 24

race: inequality closely related to 166; race-space segregation 164, 174, 177
radiation 171
raindrops 76, 279; high-intensity 75
rainfall 16, 110, 203, 235, 250, 306; adequate 42, 57, 98; amount and reliability 322–3; annual 19, 32, 102, 107, 108, 138, 141, 160, 173, 216, 217, 236, 305; average 65, 138, 141, 148, 236; bimodal 250; delayed 219; frequency and intensity 130; general indications 234; heavy 5, 25, 75; high 92, 105, 195, 283; irregularity 142; low 14, 173, 176, 237; mean 92, 102, 107, 160, 216, 217, 305; patterns 6, 200; seasonal 5, 162; stations 90; unpredictable 158; variability 9, 40, 41, 270, 279; *see also* erosion
rainforest 249
rainwater: infiltration 305, 316; roofs to catch 59
rainy pentads 306
Ramotswa 39, 44
ranches 47, 172, 218, 252; commercial 38; game 52, 314, 338; leasehold 47; safari 327
rangelands 33, 82–3; burning 280; carrying capacity 167; degradation of 209, 226; overstocking 78–9; policy intended to commodify 83; shrinking resources 209; user or grazing fees 87
Rautanen, Martti 169
reafforestation 19, 140, 167, 244
recycling 44, 62, 167
reforestation 117; community efforts 122
refugees 5, 126, 149; influx of 97, 98, 124; intense settlement 130; political 167; return from abroad 167
regeneration 134, 167, 237–8, 320; artificial 193; low rate of 14; natural 18, 127, 193; rapid 135
regolith stripping 76
regosols 102, 104, 323
Rehoboth 162, 178

Rehoboth Gebiet 177
remittances 65, 69, 81, 82, 182, 312
remote area dwellers 37
Renamo 126n
rent 82, 99
reserves 275; see also African Reserves; forest reserves; game reserves; national parks; native reserves; nature reserves
reservoirs: Africa's largest 325; aquatic weeds problem 43; development of, in the mountains 70; effects on fishery resources 133; eutrophication of 321; flooding 308; new 90, 326; planning and construction 90; sedimentation 73, 74, 75, 90, 244; siltation 76, 208
resettlement 310, 312, 313, 315, 333, 334 British aid for 309; reducing population pressure through 194; schemes 278
residues 281; arsenic 321; cadmium 321; copper 321; crop 73, 77, 241, 245; lead 321; manganese 321; petroleum 155; toxic 14, 321
resource-use conflicts: Botswana 35–40; Lesotho 67–8; Malawi 97–8; Namibia 166; Tanzania 239; Zambia 274–8; Zimbabwe 310–15
respiratory ailments 43, 136, 245
Revue river valley 136
Rhodesia: Northern 273–4; Southern 113, 114, 274 rhyolite 217
rice 234, 265; dryland 140; paddy 149
Riddell Commission (1981) 315
Rift Valley 248, 250; woodlands 100
Rights of the Sea Convention 29
rills 41, 73, 75, 76, 89, 244
riverine environments 48, 59
rivers 20, 158, 212; banks 42, 116, 169, 170, 327; basins 133, 220; beds 15, 54; border 178, 179; diverted from normal courses 136; dry 162; ephemeral 32; large 32, 270; long-term productivity 169; major 138, 172, 305, 318, 331; most important 80; perennial 43, 50; pollution in 12–13; sand 32, 42, 54; seasonal and erratic flow 110; sediment load of 99, 210; short parallel 107; siltation 244; stations 74; substantial network 248; terraces 76, 170
rock salt 182
rocks 75, 89, 250; crystalline 92; exposed 216; granitic 32, 326; metamorphic 326; outcrops 216, 316; rapid runoff from 316; volcanic 140; weathering 285
role of small and medium-scale enterprises 10
Roma Valley 73–4, 75
Rossing 170, 181
rubies 101
rubium 182

Rufiji basin 244, 248, 259, 265
Rukwa 240, 251, 252; Ufipa Plateau 234
Rukwa, Lake 248, 250, 261, 268
Rungwa Game Reserve 250
rural electrification 254, 310

SADC (Southern African Development community) 29, 62, 63, 73, 102, 132, 167, 310; Biomass Assessment exercise 23; FINNIDA-funded project 25; fishery developments 111; Forestry and Technical Coordination Unit 119; most urbanised country in region 270; Soil and Water Conservation Unit (Lesotho) 331; standards 77; sustainable development and 1-4
safaris 54, 321, 326, 327
Sakala Commission (1982) 276, 277, 280, 299 salinity 179
salinisation 130, 136, 149, 154, 155
salt 130; build-up 131; pans 40, 134; works 252; *see also* sodium chloride
Salvina molesta infestations 43, 55
San people 176, 190
sand storms 42
sandbars 107, 110
sands 102; acid 321; Barotse 283–4; beach/coastal 136; Kawinga grey 107; loamy 283; quartzitic, wind and water-sorted 283; *see also* Kalahari sand
sandstones 74, 76, 288; Ecca 216; Karoo 284; triassic 323
sandveld 32, 33, 34, 49, 50, 54
sanitation: adequate facilities 44; inadequate 211–12; lack of 11, 12, 242; programmes 25
sapphires 101
savannas 161, 316; deciduous shrub 32; forest 16; grassland in areas 251; shrub 16, 180, 217, 218; tree 217, 218; tropical 23; *see also* woodlands
Save river 138, 149, 303, 318
sawdust 215
scavengers 212
Schapera, I 37
Schinz, Hans 169
schistosomiasis *see* bilharzia
schists 288; calcareous 283; decomposition of 289, 304
scree slopes 74
scrubs 105–7, 131
Scudder, T 278, 280
seasons: dry 46, 75, 104, 108, 140, 167, 270, 305; hot 92, 305; rainy 75, 108, 216, 242, 270; warm 305; wet 40, 305
seaweed 170
secondary oxide ores 290
sedimentary basins 56
sedimentation 76; dams 316; lakes 331; reservoirs 73, 74, 75, 90, 244; rivers 99, 316, 318; streams 99
sediments 20, 75, 99, 107, 210, 290;

Kalahari Group 32; pollution by 147; water-borne 42
seeds 24, 121, 140, 336
Segosebe, E M 40
Selebi-Phikwe 33, 39, 40, 56
Selected Development Areas 82
Selous Game Reserve 236, 250
semi-swamps 107
Senqu river 65, 80
septic tanks 212, 243
Serengeti 249
sesame 250
settlements 211; coastal 172; damage to 224; European 97; growth of areas 208; high-density 43, 86; in unsurveyed areas 242; lakeside 289; major 54; nucleated 237; permanent 37; population unevenly distributed in 33; refugee 130, 149; small 36, 172, 326; spontaneous uncontrolled 68; squatter 39; unplanned 79; upgrading schemes 68; urban, agricultural land lost to 69, 70; *see also* resettlement
sewage: collapse of systems 11; contamination from 44; disposal of 215; domestic 134, 153, 155; inadequate facilities 210; industrial 153; neglecting systems 275; pollution from 147, 155; soak-pits 243; spillages from works 322; tertiary treatment of effluent 321; untreated 321; with a high sodium content 321
sex ratios 36, 67, 205
sexual morality 72
shales 216, 288
shanty towns 11, 138
sharecropping 81, 87
Shashe (Francistown) 54
sheep 33, 46, 87; karakul 165, 176, 178
sheetwash 41
shell fish 170, 185
shifting cultivation 238, 244
Shinyanga 235, 237, 240, 241, 244, 245, 252, 264, 265
Shire Highlands 112; river 107, 108; valley 92
Shiselweni 195, 205, 207
shooting 185
shrubland zone 169
shrubs 73, 77, 174, 204, 249, 285; common 217, 218; halophytic 180; replacement of grassland by 42; woody 79; *see also* savannas
Shula, E 280
Siiskonen, H 159n, 162, 163n, 164, 169, 170, 173, 174, 181n, 192
silica 182
silk 49, 316
silt 104, 169; catching and stabilising 134
siltation 94; reservoir 7, 76, 208; river 244
silver 181, 328

silviculture 116, 142, 193
Singida 240, 241, 245
sisal 15, 249
Skeleton Coast National Park 184
slag 281
sleeping sickness 42, 245
slopes: gentle 92, 169; pediment 74, 76; scree 74; south-facing, mass movements on 75; *see also* steep slopes
smallholders 94, 97, 98, 112, 113, 114
smog 171
smugglers 9
snow 65
Sobhuza II, king of Swaziland 218
social differentiation 80–3
soda 182
soda ash plant 33, 40, 56
sodium arsenite 211, 225
sodium carbonate 33
sodium chloride 33, 321
Sofala 138, 140
soil erosion 14, 40, 26, 73, 94, 98, 99, 104, 129, 130, 133, 166, 169, 205–11, 239, 243–4, 314; arable land lost by 65; land with arable potential prone to 32; main form of environmental degradation 278, 301–2; overgrazing cause of 226, 280, 320; overstocking contributing to 79, 226; policies 264; severe 317; substantial cost of 79; topsoil susceptible to 208
soil fertility 41, 79, 92, 244, 323; decline 316; depletion 168; high 140; low 138, 302; natural regeneration of 127; reasonable 216; reduction of 40
soils 47, 92, 143, 159–60, 250, 283–5, 316–17; acidity of 102, 214, 215, 282, 321; alluvial 104, 138, 140, 244, 284; animal-hoof trampling of 98; 'Black cotton' 104; calcimorphic 102, 104; catenas 104; clay-rich 32; deep, commonly-found 216; degradation 279; drought-prone 129; fair 216; ferrallitic 102, 104, 140, 283; ferruginous 32, 102; fersiallitic 283; fragile 146; good 216; halomorphic 138; heavier-textured 142; highly porous 41; humic 104; hydromorphic 102, 104, 138; immature 102, 104, 138; influenced by drift and colluviation 105; lacustrine 32, 104, 284; laterite 104, 140; leached 32, 102, 195, 279, 283; lighter 140; lithoidal 138; loosening of 75; low-lying 155; main groups 305; *makande* 104; management of 90; mining 82; moisture-retaining 323; morphological properties of 89; multiple deficiencies 216; nutrients 238, 239, 279; ortho-ferrallitic 323; paraferrallitic 323; poor 44, 235; poorly-developed 140; prone to droughts 129; quality of 97, 177; rate of loss minimised 169; regeneration of 237–8; rich in cal-

cium 105–7; salinisation and alkanisation of 130; sandy 104, 107, 140, 146, 168, 278, 323; serious deterioration 251; shallow 42, 75, 102, 104, 285, 323, 328; skeletal 104; sodic (natric) 323; stony 102, 104, 140, 323; thin 195; unusable for agriculture 323; utilisation of different types 40; very sensitive to wind erosion 160; weakly-developed 159–60; well-drained 138; yellow bauxitic 104; *see also* arenosols; conservation; ferrisols; humus; kaolisols; latosols; lithosols; productivity; soil erosion; soil fertility; topsoil; vertisols
solar energy technologies 122
sorghum 19, 33, 46, 77, 140, 142, 177, 235, 249, 250, 323, 324
Sotho-Tswana tribes 65
sourveld 217
South Africa, Republic of 19, 54, 65, 71, 83, 126, 158, 166, 176–9 *passim*, 188, 195, 220, 221, 303; companies 186; dependence on 201; dependence on 67, 76, 79; employment in mines 36, 72, 80, 199, 201, 274; energy imports from 183; hardwood sales to 14; 'internal independence settlement' 164; labour migration to 36, 86, 95, 274; migrant remittances from 81; sale of water to 85; strategic minerals exports 330; troops 185; *see also* Union of South Africa
South West Africa 163; German 162
species: bird 50, 305, 306; commercially-viable 48; encroaching bush 173; endangered 117, 120; exotic 110, 193; game 247; indigenous 193, 221, 250; insect 50, 305; invader 173; licensed hunting of 247; local 110; natural regeneration of 193; phyto- and zoo-plankton 290; plant 24; 221, 250; poaching of 38; preservation of 120; protected 328; protection of 24; threatened 221; under serious threat 100; unsuitable 245; valuable 38; vegetation 41, 105, 107; *see also* animal species; fish; grass species; trees
speculation 277
Spiegel, A 81
spiral aloe 79
splash pillars 76
springs 212
spurs 74, 75, 76
squatters 37, 121, 168, 218, 275; illegal 242; influx to urban centres 39; on state land designated for commercial farming 277
State Secretariat for Geology and Mines 29
steep slopes 115, 130, 140, 195, 216, 326; cultivation on 98, 208, 316, 317; developmental constraint 303; lack of 144; overgrazing 74; sedimentation

75
steppes 16, 179, 180, 249
sterilisation 59
Stiegler's Gorge dam 265
Stocking, M 41
storm water 172, 322
stoves 115, 258; energy efficient 183; improved 24, 119, 133
streambanks 329; cultivation on 170, 316, 325 streams 20, 99; small seasonal 110
street lighting 25
structural adjustment policies 123
stubble 79
Stubbs, M 100, 102, 105, 107
stumpveld 38
Sua Pan 33, 56
Sua township 40
Suba, M R 290, 292
subleases 88
subsidence 12, 212–13
subsistence sector 97, 98, 164
sugar 219, 241, 323, 329
sugar cane 19, 94, 140, 210
sulphides (pyrites, chalcopyrites, bornite) 290 sulphur 101, 171, 182
sulphur dioxide 43, 136, 215, 282
sun 279
sunflowers 324
supplier of cheap migrant labour 95
surface wash 75
surface water 32, 178, 289; annual increment of flow 317; degradation of resources 212; drainage collapse of systems 11; lack of 177, 249; pollution of supplies 40; shortage 170
sustainable development 1–4, 34, 124, 156, 187; best achieved through agriculture 69; Brundtland Report's definition 126; opportunities for 228–9; planning for 334; solutions 26–31, 153–7, 297–301; strategies 26–31, 85–90, 127, 153–7, 297–301, 335
Swakopmund 162, 170
swamp 48, 107, 110, 169, 179, 286
SWANU (South West Africa National Union) 163
SWAPO (South West Africa People's Organisation) 163–4
Swaziland 95, 195-232
Swedish government 25

Tabora 235, 240, 243, 250, 251, 252
Takirambudde, P 40
talc 56, 214
Tanga 240, 245, 249, 252, 253, 258, 265
Tanganyika, Lake 234, 247, 250, 261, 268, 289
Tanzania 92, 95, 107, 148, 234–69; tripartite cooperation with Malawi and Mozambique 111
tanzanite 253
taxation 299, 336

Taylor, R D 327
tea 94, 95, 112, 140, 234, 323; producing areas 92
technical assistance 127, 295
technology transfer 119
tellerium 182
temperatures 32, 65, 90, 158–9, 161; almost temperate 195; below freezing point at high altitudes 16; generally modified 270; lowest mean and annual 16; modified by altitude 216; monthly variation 9; very high 5
terms of trade 96
territorial apartheid 166
Tete 136, 138, 140, 303; *see also* Angonia textiles 95, 135
TGLP (Tribal Grazing Lands Policy) 34, 37–8, 44, 47, 60
Thangata system 97
thatching materials 49, 336
thermal inversion 282
thickets 105–7; bamboo 105; dense 285; impenetrable 209
thunderstorms 75, 90, 92
timber 14, 99, 192, 326, 210; building 134; commercial 49, 193; craft 49; demands on 146; exploitation for energy purposes 19; large-scale commercial exploitation 20; low quality 287; natural regeneration of 193; not good quality 249; preventing outsiders from gaining access to 327; problem of resources 319; soft and hard wood 244; valuable 20
Timberlake, L 129, 130n
tin 182, 253
Tinley, K L 179
title deeds 240, 276
tobacco 95, 112, 140, 216, 234, 235, 250, 273, 323; burley 94, 113, 114; estates 99; flue-cured 113, 122; fuelwood use in barns 115; growing 243; indigenous wood for curing 98; produced successfully without irrigation 324; quota 114; successful experiments with 274
topsoils 208; coarse textured 280; humic 102, 104
tourism 33, 50–1, 57, 60, 61; additional resource for 148; beautiful mountains ideal for 85; booming 184; charges for 321; confined to national parks and game reserves 185; high-value 147; policy paper on 53; potential resources 30; wildlife 22, 269
towns: largest 162; planning and construction 25 townships 40, 180, 183, 289
toxic materials 24, 134, 135, 225, 323; residues 14, 329
toxins 147
trade surplus 33
traditional beliefs 33, 36, 58
traditional medicine 210, 287

'tragedy of the commons' 83, 172, 192, 205 trained artisans 62
transhumance 40, 79
transpiration 305
trees: baobab 105, 305; cashew 144–6; categories recognised on customary lands 117–18; commercial timber 193; commercially-viable 48; common 217, 218; coniferous 220; damage to 204; deep-rooting 48; dense cover 285; disappearance of some species 42; dominant species 161; drought-tolerant 173; encouraging the growth of 128; endangered, security of 117; eucalyptus 49; exotic 118, 217; fast-growing 89; fodder 327; fruit 327; fruits of 49; gasification of whole tree chips 173; indigenous 118, 119; large 217; leguminous 249, 327; living, heavy utilisation for firewood 210; loss of cover 314; Mokola palm 49; *mopane* 32, 104, 161–2, 169, 170, 192, 210, 270, 305, 316; non-planted 118; pine 249, 250, 326; plantation 89; planted 118; planting 24, 73, 116, 264, 267; protected 118; removal of 129, 130, 132, 173; scattered 32, 285; small, slow-growing 249; tall mature 107; teak 162, 285, 287, 326; well protected from erosion 116; young, killing 98; *see also* forests; plantations; timber; woodlands; woodlots
trophies 51, 53, 185
tropical fruits 142
trypanosomiasis 140, 245, 322, 331
Tsaobis Game Park 185
tsetse flies 34, 42, 50, 142, 172; areas subject to 49; control 323, 331; habitats 266; infestation 235, 241, 249, 250; restriction 43; *see also* trypanosomiasis
Tsumeb 162, 165, 171, 172, 173, 174
tuff 217
Tuli Block 44, 46, 50
Tumkaya, N 36, 58
tungsten 182
typhoid 212

Ugalla Game Reserve 250
Uhuru corridor 267
Ujamaa Village Act (1975) 240
Uluguru Mountains 234, 250
UN (United Nations) 66, 162–3, 177; Children's Fund (Unicef) 26; Conference on Environment and Development (UNCED) 12, 23, 25, 27; Education, Scientific and Cultural Organization (Unesco) 23, 24; Environment Programme (UNEP) 34, 156; Food and Agriculture Organization (FAO) 25, 267; Institute for Namibia (UNIN) 176, 181, 182, 183; Transition Assistance Group) (UNTAG) 164

unemployment 11, 62, 164
ungulates 50
Union of South Africa 162, 163
uplands 216, 217, 283; interior 5; volcanic 250; with significant areas of rocky hills 250
Upper Umgusa Dam 321
uranium 56, 164, 181
urbanisation 12, 68, 144, 168
usufruct rights 36, 38, 81, 112

valleys 285; broad 92; dry 32; fossil 48, 54; wide alluvial 108
vanadium 181
Veenendaal, E M 34, 35, 36, 39, 41, 42, 49, 57, 59
vegetables 140, 166, 323, 324
vegetation 47–9, 160–2, 173, 179–81, 192–3, 217–18, 240, 249–52, 254, 265–8, 285–6; being depleted 208; climate and 92; deep-rooting 173; degradation 98–9; depletion of biomass 40–1; halotrophic 48; information about 116–17; legal controls over 251–2; legal instruments in use of 49–50; long-term decrease in resources 42; natural 270, 305; predominant form 235; products 61; regeneration of 237–8; removal 42; resources 105–7; spongy 304; toxic effect on 43; unique 185; woody 173; zones 18; *see also* bush; conservation; grass; shrubs; trees
veld products 42, 49, 57, 61
vermin 117
vertisols 104, 216, 284, 285, 323 veterinary services 33, 34
Vicente, Paulo 22
Victoria Falls 57, 304
Victoria, Lake 234, 247, 248, 261, 268
Village Action Groups 121
village development councils 87, 88
villagisation 234, 237, 249, 324
Viphya Plantations Division 119, 122
vleis 304
vocational training 62

Walvis Bay 162, 170, 178, 180, 185, 186
war 5, 11, 20, 126, 144, 151; accessibility under conditions of 145; devastation 153; effort 7; impact of 129; implementing sustainable development strategy in context of 127; liberation 185; population concentrations due to conditions 13
waste: agricultural 44, 241, 258; disposal 40, 79, 212, 242, 243; domestic 40, 134; dumping 16, 40, 69, 275, 281, 308; environmentally-dangerous 135; flytipping of 43; gaseous 153; heavy-metal 43; human and animal, water contaminated by 212; industrial 13, 16, 40, 44, 134, 155, 275, 282, 302; liquid 56, 133, 153;

mine 308; potentially hazardous 211; recycling 62; solid 133, 153, 212, 223–4; tannery 43; toxic 14, 16; *see also* pollution
water 1489; absence of nearby sources 114; border river 179; clean 11, 44; consumption of 54; investment in 335; lack of 168; livestock dependent on availability of 46; management of 90; movement of 102; national standards of quality 62; over-exploitation of points 47; percolating 130; quality of 62, 223; retention capacity 142, 160; rich in alkaline salts and phyto and zoo-plankton species 290; sale of 85; satisfying the need for 80; shortages of 167, 240; stagnant, diseases attendant upon 12; supplies of 11, 44, 47, 57, 136, 212, 242; toxic metals in 24; unsuitable for drinking 179; utilisation 248; waste 56, 133; *see also* boreholes; conservation; diseases; drinking water; erosion; groundwater; infrastructure; storm water; surface water; water pollution; water pumps; water resources; water table; watercourses; waterflow control; waterlogging; watersheds
water holes 13; *see also* boreholes
Water Plateau National Park 185
water pollution 99, 133, 136, 210, 211–12, 282–3; freshwater resources 172; groundwater 40, 57; heavy, from stormwater drains 172; responsible for the deaths of livestock 281; rivers 12–13; surface-water supplies 40; tributaries 15; watercourses 24
water pumps 24, 25
water resources 12–13, 54–5, 107–10, 133, 178–9, 220, 247, 288–9, 317–18, 325–6; for grazing 39; inland 20; legal underpinnings for use of 149–51; policies 264-5; regulation 84; use of 154–5
water table 69, 104; disturbed 136; high 107
watercourses 24; weed growth in 321
waterflow control 20
waterlogging 114
watersheds 130, 249, 267, 280, 303
wealth: alternative sources 58; cattle as a measure of 46, 58, 276; redistribution of 187; rural, greater 59; substantial siphoning of 182
Weare, P R 48
weather: adverse 96; moderated by altitude 305 welfare 124
wells 54, 288, 289, 326; deep 289; private 149
Western and Northwestern Provinces 287
Western Province 285, 286
wetlands 32, 154; destruction of 50;

small 304

wheat 19, 77, 166, 323

whites: areas for 174–5; commercial agriculture 174; farmland 165; former areas 187; freedom to purchase or sell land 166; homelands 176, 177; privilege 185; ranchers 176; settlers 188, 307

Whitlow, J R 305, 313n, 316–17, 319, 322

Whitsun Foundation (1978, 1983) 315

wildlife 32–3, 50–2, 62, 151, 184–5, 259–62, 268–9, 305–6, 320–1; abundant 270; and biological diversity 20; corridors for migration 53; effective utilisation 60; game ranching which integrates livestock and 314; heritage 338; improved facilities for tourists to view 269; indiscriminate slaughter 127; industry 61; legal control 259–61; legal instruments for utilisation 52–4; legislation 84; management 57, 148, 310, 336; negative impact on 57; one of the world's largest remaining concentrations 314; ownership of 310; preventing elimination 43; protection 5; survival 172, 247; sustainable utilisation of 332; tourism 22; *see also* conservation; wildlife resources

wildlife resources 34, 327–8; depletion 100; long-term viability 60; value of 61

Wildlife Conservation Policy (Botswana, 1986) 38

Williamson, D T 38

Williamson, J E 38

wind *see* erosion

Windhoek 159, 162, 167, 171, 172, 180

women 132, 226, 245, 277–8; activities commonly done by 83; involvement in rural development 188; participation in environmental management and education 86; percentage of rural population 310; pivotal role in local-level planning 187; rights of 190–1; role in managing natural resources 229–30; *vis-à-vis* the land market 301

wood: biomass 174, 241; chips 173; consumption 115, 183, 323; deficiency 319; improved burning devices 122; most important source of energy/fuel 290, 329; pulp 209, 220; resources 77; sawmills 252; *see also* fuelwood

woodlands 18, 105–7, 162, 239, 241, 245, 279, 319; chipya 285; concentric zones of depletion 49; deciduous 105; indigenous, displacement of 305; lowland 105; management and control of 99; natural 114, 115; open grassy 285–6; resources 49; riparian 32; tall-grass 105; wholesale destruction of 280; *see also miombo* woodland

woodlots 77, 114; communal 120, 121, 192; *mopane* 170, 270; multi-species 61; planting 57, 231

World Bank 97, 114, 123, 127, 130–3, 149, 181, 293 World Heath Organization 318

Yalala, A 48

Yeager, R 35

Zaïre 5, 13, 15, 270

Zambezi river 32, 43, 92, 108, 138, 148–9, 270, 318, 330; alluvial soils in lower reaches 140; basin 62; dry-weather flow 305; escarpment 54, 303, 316; lowlands 303; valley 285, 323, 331; water supplies to townships 289

Zambia 5, 92, 95, 158, 270–302, 304, 308, 330; pre-independence land tenure 166; tsetse fly programme 331; *see also* Luangwa river; Lusaka

Zanzibar 268

Zimbabwe 95, 126, 158, 270, 303–40; falling population of fish eagle 172; pre-independence land tenure 166; Tso-Tso stove 183; *see also* Hwange

zinc 14, 56, 164, 181, 271, 290

Zonal Registration Offices (Tanzania) 263

Index compiled by Frank Pert

THE SOUTHERN AFRICAN ENVIRONMENT